D0917290

Contemporary Philosophic Problems

THE MACMILLAN COMPANY
NEW YORK • CHICAGO
DALLAS • ATLANTA • SAN FRANCISCO
LONDON • MANILA
IN CANADA
BRETT-MACMILLAN LTD.
GALT, ONTARIO

CONTEMPORARY PHILOSOPHIC PROBLEMS

Selected Readings

Edited by

Yervant H. Krikorian

and

Abraham Edel

The City College, New York

The Macmillan Company, New York

First Printing

Library of Congress catalog card number: 59-5047

The Macmillan Company, New York
Brett-Macmillan Ltd., Galt, Ontario

Printed in the United States of America

PREFACE

Our century, with its new knowledge, new techniques, and new problems, is a matrix for altered and deepened philosophical ideas. Whether it will in the long run stand out as an Age of Upheaval, or an Age of Criticism, or an Age of Analysis, or an Age of Anguish; whether it will be seen as the first era after the end of the Great Systems or rather as a lull between the Old Systems and the New Systems; whether it will be looked on chiefly as a time of philosophical dissensions, or as a time in which a basic convergence began to emerge—all these are as yet unanswered questions.

To present the range of contemporary philosophizing, we have gathered substantial philosophical selections, organized around central concepts and problems. The wealth of excellent materials available forced us to omit many other worthwhile selections. But we hope that this collection, organized in this way, will be of helpful interest to the general reader who seeks to set in focus a field so complex and so uneven as the contemporary philosophical world, and that it will provide convenient materials for course work on an upper level, whether in contemporary philosophy or in advanced problem study.

We should like to express our major indebtedness to Professor V. J. McGill for his advice and assistance in planning and carrying out the work of this book. Particularly because of his extensive knowledge of European continental philosophy, many areas of the work gained in scope. We are especially grateful for his valuable suggestions in Parts I and II.

For specific criticisms, suggestions, and advice, we are grateful to Professor Ernest Nagel, Mr. K. D. Irani, Dr. Max Rieser, Professor Maurice Mandelbaum, Mr. Irving Horowitz, Dr. Albert Lataner. Professor Dorion Cairns very kindly allowed us to use a selection from his unpublished translation of Husserl, and we are indebted to the many authors who readily gave permission for the inclusion of their work. We are also appreciative of the patient and friendly assistance given us over a long period by Mr. *J*. G. Case of The Macmillan Company.

Y.H.K.
A.E.

CONTENTS

General Introduction

Philosophy hands on its heritage of problems from generation to generation and century to century. The problems are often called perennial, and one is reminded of the quip about the professor who always asked the same questions on the examination, but justified his procedure by saying that the answers always changed! Philosophical answers, it is true, do appear to change. When one line of replies becomes too assured of its permanence, too established as a philosophical school, there grow up alternatives from quite different sources. Or else the school itself, heavy with confidence, breaks down into opposing camps. And so some have thought that there are perennial differences, or perspectives that must appear and reappear, whether in the same or in opposing camps. On the other hand, through the course of these historical changes, there does appear to be substantial advance in the refinement of methods, the accumulation of specific results, and perhaps most strikingly, the development of the questions themselves. For this is where philosophy differs from the procedure of the professor in our story. Not only do the answers change, but the meaning of the questions undergoes transformation—for it is increasingly deepened, clarified and refined.

What is the source of change in philosophical questions and answers? This is itself a question on which philosophies provide different answers. But some clues seem clear. Because philosophy has the comprehensive aim of providing a general outlook, it is related in some degree to all major branches of human life and activity. It is therefore subject to a multitude of influences. When sharp changes take place in scientific ideas, when men's minds are troubled by the conflicts in their societies, when traditional modes of thought become incongruous with the lives men lead, then philosophic thought becomes pressing and persistent. Not merely the occasions of philosophical intensity, but the contents as well are subject to varied influences. Models and techniques arising in some special field—as far apart as frontiers of physics and linguistic interpretation in classical research—may provide keys to open up new areas of philosophical ideas. These may be generalized, tried out in other domains, or offered as clues to large-scale syntheses. Philosophy, receptive to influence, serves as a kind of market-place in which special ideas brimming with potentially wider significance jostle up against one another in the effort to show what they can do.

Physics has been one of the most fertile sources of philosophical stimulation in the twentieth century. The emergence of Relativity and Quantum Theory involved sharp changes in traditional concepts of space, time, matter, energy. These profoundly affected thinking about the nature of the ultimate categories to be employed in understanding the world. One of the most significant indications of this is the twentieth century metaphysical emphasis on process, events, change, and the partial eclipse of substance concepts. Even more, the changing scientific scene forced greater precision in and deeper re-thinking of concepts of causality, determinism, and traditionally accepted mechanical models. Nor was this all. As a major example of the readjustment of ideas in the advance of knowledge, physics provided a store-house of materials for winning a clearer appreciation of the complex ways in which concepts operate in the development of theory and its relation to observation and experiment. Contemporary philosophy of science is still in the process of absorbing the lessons of this development. Its growing methodological clearness in turn is reacting on the development of the psychological and social sciences. The full force of this understanding, which emerged from the shifts in scientific theory, is probably still to be felt in the long-standing traditional issues about the nature of man, human freedom, and questions of value.

Developments in mathematics and the publication of Whitehead and Russell's PRINCIPIA MATHEMATICA likewise exerted a powerful influence. New problems were formulated and old ones reformulated, with greater rigor in language supplied by symbolic logic. An interest in the structure and function of language—whether scientific, philosophical, or commonsense—became intense and pervasive. The rise of behaviorism and the rapid development of learning theory in psychology fed the same stream of interest. Attempts were made to understand signs and their use in the light of animal learning experiments, clinical interpretations, formal languages, and mythology.

Specific techniques combined with old interests to produce far-reaching effects. For example, a new technique like Russell's theory of descriptions—enabling him to cut down certain types of abstract entities—sharpened Occam's razor for a whole generation to cut away at the body of metaphysics. In general, the revolt against metaphysics—shared by the logical positivists, the pragmatists, operationalists, and many empiricists and naturalists—was one of the major tendencies of the first half of the century. It was launched primarily through a theory of meaning. To be meaningful statements had either to be analytic or verifiable in some sense; or at the very least they had to be in agreement with common usage; or, in a looser framework, they had to have practical consequences. Metaphysical statements had a hard time meeting such requirements, except when, with William James, they were turned into emotional attitudes. But it is interesting to note that in this broad revolt many different methodological interests were involved. British empiricism, on the whole, looked for certainties whether in sensation or in logic. Others, carried along by the growing interest in probability and induction—itself stimulated in part by the wider role of statistical methods—thrust aside the quest for philosophical certainty. By the end of the half-century probabilism held sway.

Intersecting many of the conceptions of knowledge as well as reality were the sharp changes in the understanding of man and his place in the animal world. The Darwinian revolution forced a reassessment of the understanding of human thought that seeped into philosophy and emerged as an outright demand for the naturalization of the human spirit. Thinking, contemplation itself, became understood as an event in the natural world, serving purposes, both expressing and refashioning conditions and forces around it. Values came to be seen as interests on all levels of human development. The belief in moral and practical certitudes that could be read off by men carefully introspecting about their ideas and feelings yielded grudgingly to behavioristic studies of human responses or was occasionally even banished by behavioristic manifestoes. Freud opened the vast domain of what lies behind the narrow circle of consciousness, and of patterns that might be used to explain the irrational elements in consciousness. In a similar vein in social theory, the twentieth century developed Marxian insights concerning the social role of ideas in articulating social interests and purposes into a general theory of ideology in which reason began to mistrust its own foundations. All these influences found expression in activist, irrationalist tendencies. These, however, had a complex character. Sometimes they were obviously in revolt against the extension of a scientific outlook over the whole range of human life. But sometimes their central focus was upon calling men to assume responsibility in vigorous action, rather than to drift with the tide.

Obviously the crucial social issues of this century have had a powerful effect, too, not only in setting the problems of social philosophy, but even in the more theoretical issues. For example, the sharp conflict of ultimate outlooks, as in the battle between Nazism and the liberal-democratic or rationalistic-humanitarian philosophies, posed profound theoretical problems of the nature of basic disagreement, and the possible limits of rationality. These can be traced through a major segment of the problems of methodology as they became central in ethical theory. Again, the widespread insecurities of the era provided ground for the resurgence of religious philosophies, which, interestingly enough, have not always given simple reassurances in older absolutistic terms, but have in many of their forms, especially under existentialist influence, stressed the anguish in the predicament of man.

If this brief review of influences suggests that the picture of contemporary philosophy is extraordinarily complicated, this is intentional and, we think, accurate. There is, for example, no ready simplification possible in terms of schools. These provide important unities and to some extent can be mapped. The empirical movements seem to predominate in English-speaking countries, at least on the academic philosophical scene. But there are also vigorous rationalist, religious, idealist, and outright materialist schools and trends, especially on the Continent. Among these are phenomenology, existentialism, neo-Thomism, and dialectical materialism. Some of these exert strong influence in European countries and Latin America, as well as in the United States. On the whole, one has to be careful in dealing with schools not to reduce them to an oversimplified pattern or platform. In every case there are significant differences within each, and it is not unusual to find representatives who deny that theirs really is a school of thought. Even where there is a standardized tradition the differences may be wide. Thomism, for example, has representatives who look primarily back for inspiration, and those who seek to integrate the full scope of modern knowledge. Materialism must obviously distinguish its mechanical and dialectical branches, and the latter too has disparate trends. These can be seen in the constant controversy over the Marxian corpus in the early part of this century, and in more recent practical divergences. The logical empiricism of today bears but limited resemblance to the sensationalistic positivism of but a short time ago. On the empiricist side there has been a deep absorption of pragmatist elements, and on the logical side many of its adherents have shifted to an analytic trend that stresses the informal rather than the formal. Phenomenology has gone in at least two different directions. Originally united in the view that experience must be described in its purity as it occurs—purely as phenomenon—without behavioristic, physical, or psychological reduction, it has led on the one hand to an enriched empiricism, and on the other to an often idealistic pursuit of essences. Existentialism has turned out to have an extremely tenuous unity—sometimes it seems more a flavor than a "doctrine"—with both religious and atheist branches, and some representatives even think of it as having a largely negative function.

But if there is no simple formula for ordering contemporary philosophy the sense of its riches, its vitality, its diversity, may be grasped by looking at its central concepts and sampling the diversity of their formulation. This principle has guided the preparation and selection of this book. Five central concepts that have loomed large in contemporary philosophy have been taken as the central focus. They are all, of course, familiar in the philosophical tradition—in fact there would be no philosophy without something like them—but the way some of them have been developed in contemporary philosophy has been distinctive in many respects. MEANING has had a central place, perhaps beyond all proportion, for any previous philosophical era. KNOWLEDGE has, perhaps, reigned supreme. It is a commonplace that the ancients gave a central place to ontology and the moderns to epistemology; and the contemporary has not yet outgrown the modern! But in one way or another attention is turning afresh to the problem of BEING, even if in the empirical philosophies it is only in the form of what categories shall be used in describing the world. VALUE is a concept that has taken over a host of fields—moral, aesthetic, and so forth—and although many regard it as an upstart it has slipped into a secure position. It thus provides an advantageous way in which to get an insight into the major movements of contemporary philosophy in dealing with the human spirit. Finally, while philosophy has always had a practical or orientational side, the contemporary world has had to choose more deeply and profoundly among alternatives in ways of looking at and feeling about the world and a man's place in it. In this sense the concept of VISION AND ACTION directs attention to synoptic outlook, not as mere synopsis, but as the deepest readiness for one's mode of life.

I. MEANING

Meaning

I

The concept of meaning has had a central and distinctive place in twentieth century philosophy. This development was fed by major advances in logic and mathematics, in physics, in psychology. It led to extravagant hopes that a theory of meaning would provide a sovereign criterion for what was sense and what was nonsense, and would thus hand over a smooth-working key to authentic, as distinguished from spurious, philosophizing. But at the same time it prompted the most careful researches into the many phases of language—its structure, its various modes of functioning, its behavioral sources and relations, its conscious or subjective aspects, and so on.

Problems and theories of meaning are, of course, not new; they have been very numerous and are found throughout the history of philosophy. In ancient India the Nyaya School concluded that a word has an eternal meaning, even though the letters which compose it are meaningless. When we hear the last of its sounds uttered, the earlier ones are still retained, and the meaning of the word is brought to mind in a flash. In our own time, William James, while discussing the perceptual present in his PRINCIPLES OF PSYCHOLOGY, could make a similar but more plausible analysis for the sentence. The meaning of the sentence is not realized till the last word has been combined instantaneously with the uncompleted meanings of the previous ones, retained in immediate memory. The Nyaya philosophers discovered something else which was to be prophetic, namely, that the meaning of a word can be the same whether it is written large or small. Meaning therefore cannot be identified with any of the sounds or signs which express it. The word as a meaning is something over and above the particular sounds or signs which are its vehicle. It is a word-essence (sabda-dardana).

In both the Indian and the Graeco-Christian traditions we find the belief that the meaningful word is creative. For Plato and Plotinus things *are what they are because they are reflections or embodiments of meaning. Similarly, the Gospel according to St. John begins with "In the beginning was the Word" (Logos), and at least one of the multiple meanings of "Logos" is Reason. The rationale of the doctrine of the meaningful word as creative is that nothing can be said or thought about particular things except as they reflect or embody meanings which are universal. And since particular things are, it might seem, nothing except what can or could be said about them, they are nothing apart from these universal meanings.*

A companion paradox was propounded by Parmenides in the 5th century B.C. Every thought, he said, must have an object; to think about nothing is not to think. It follows that references to non-existent things are meaningless. Yet we know that this is not the case. "The golden mountain exists" or "The sultan of Scotland plays golf" are as meaningful as are "The City of Paris exists" or "The president of the United States plays golf." There have been many attempts to resolve such difficulties. For example, at the beginning of this century, the Austrian philosopher Alexius von Meinong agreed in effect with Parmenides that all thoughts must have an object. But the object need not exist; in the case of fictions such as the golden mountain, the object merely subsists. Quite contrary to Meinong's theory of subsisting objects was Bertrand Russell's theory of "descriptions", for according to this theory statements about the golden mountain or the sultan of Scotland may be meaningful though such entities neither exist nor subsist, nor are, in fact, anything at all. "The golden mountain exists" means, roughly, "There is an object, and only one object, which is golden and is a mountain." A term may have no meaning by itself and yet a statement in which it occurs can be completely meaningful, and be either true or false. Once the nature of such "logical fictions" is realized, we are spared trying to make up entities corresponding to "the round square" just because it is not meaningless to say, "The round square does not exist."

Whitehead and Russell's PRINCIPIA MATHEMATICA, *by its detailed analyses of logical and mathematical concepts, and its general attempt to show that mathematics, or at least a great part of it, could be evolved from the logic of classes and relations, greatly stimulated refined consideration of problems of meaning. For example, a theory of "types" was introduced, systematically excluding certain symbolic expressions as meaningless. Thus the statement, "What I am now saying is false," leads to a contradiction; for, on the assumption that it is true, it is false, and on the assumption that it is false, it is true. The theory of types got rid of contradictions by ruling out as meaningless the expressions which led to them. Others* since then have tried to remove contradictions in different ways. In such technical controversies, the meaning of meaning has itself been etched in sharper outline.

Other influences came from the sciences and their generalized lessons. While the whole empirical tradition had insisted that the test of truth was experience (that is, sensory experience), the reference to experience now moved into the very notion of the meaning of an idea. This happened chiefly along two channels. One was the biological evolutionary background and the way it changed men's outlook on thinking as a human phenomenon. The other stemmed from the revolutionary changes in physics.

The traditional view that thinking was a kind of direct grasping or a lighting up of the eternal structure of things—a view that underlay the Platonic theory of meanings and the Aristotelian mediaeval idea of basic truths—had long been challenged by the empirical attempts to build ideas out of the building-blocks of elementary sensations. But the evolutionary theory of the nineteenth century set going a wholly fresh current of interpretation. Thinking was now seen as a tool developed by man in his evolutionary emergence, and one geared essentially to practical problem solution. Its distinctive character was its fashioning of more generalized, more widely applicable, and thus more effective methods of resolution; and its pure joys were not wholly separated from this enhanced power of prediction and control. That thought has a purposive character became in many views a part of its essence. For example, the idealist tradition during the nineteenth century had a strong voluntaristic representation, and in such a figure as Josiah Royce in the opening of the twentieth century we find meaning analyzed in this vein: an idea is treated as a partial fulfillment of a purpose. But that thought has a purposive practical character is most clearly to be seen in the writings of Charles Sanders Peirce, whose influence was to grow afresh in the second quarter of the twentieth century when his collected works were made widely available. Peirce brought the laboratory attitude into the theory of meaning. Of special significance is his application of this attitude to an intellectual idea, whose meaning is thus seen in terms of the program of research or anticipated sensory results which the use of the idea will bring. An idea is thus a habit of action, or a rule of action. William James, taking this cue, enunciated as the meaning of an idea the effects it would have in practice, giving it a wider scope which could include under practical effects its contribution to human feeling and conduct; this became the central theme in the theory of meaning of pragmatism as a philosophy.

John Dewey, guided by the twin insights that thinking is a natural event and that it therefore has its own distinctive effects in nature, worked out carefully, in one field after another, the theory of an idea as a tool for reconstruction of problem-situations in the natural world and the human milieu.

The influence of changes in physical science tended in a roughly parallel direction. Looking for the lessons of Einstein's work, many philosophers and theorists of science laid stress on what seemed the new way in which he had treated concepts. Thus he had not taken such notions as simultaneity for granted in an intuitive way, but had pressed relentlessly, with startling results, for the modes of actual measurement, the frame of reference within which the data would be gathered to confirm a scientific judgment. The general question raised thereby was the rôle of standards by means of which concepts are applied, and how far they furnish a kind of definition or meaning of the concept. Thus, Hans Reichenbach developed the notion of a coordinating definition as playing a key role in understanding the meaning of terms used in science, and P. W. Bridgman elaborated a theory of operational definitions going so far as to assert that the concept is synonymous with the operations by which it is applied. This generalized approach had considerable vogue in the psychological and social sciences, where it served on the one hand to bring about a more critical attitude to vague concepts, but on the other to disparage at times the use of theoretical constructs.

II

The strength of the theory of meaning which logical positivism forged in the third and fourth decades of this century lay predominantly in the fact that it combined these several strains—the logical-mathematical influence, the scientific influence, and then the pragmatic influence. Dedicated simultaneously to logic and empiricism, and disillusioned by the slender progress and prospects of traditional philosophy, the logical positivists sought to eliminate metaphysical problems—which they regarded as the bottleneck of philosophy—by a definition of meaning in terms of which these problems were meaningless ("pseudo-problems"). Statements were taken to have meaning when they were either purely logical ("tautological", "analytic"), so that their truth or falsity could be certified on purely logical grounds, or else—and there lay the rub—when, and only when, they were in principle confirmable in a scientific way. In the latter case it had to be possible to predict that under certain conceivable circumstances perceptions could be had which would favor one side as against the other. The statement "There are mountains on the other side of the moon" is meaningful, for we can at least conceive of space-ships which would enable us to make the decisive observation—a familiar example in the literature which has since come almost within the range of practicable verification. But in the case of idealism vs. realism no decisive observation is even conceivable. In the same way, or at least by implication, a thousand other metaphysical and epistemological questions were thrown out of court. But philosophers of other persuasions, though there may have been soul-searching and discouragement in their ranks, did not accept this determination of the logical positivists, but continued to ply metaphysics, though perhaps with less rhetoric and more precision of language than before. Nor was it all plain sailing for the logical positivists themselves. The formulation of the verifiability principle was no easy task. Logical difficulties arose from within, and the present status of the principle is a highly controversial one.

To the notions of logical meaning and empirical meaning, logical positivism (or logical empiricism as it came increasingly to be called) found it necessary to add that of emotive meaning. For as assertions from many domains—religion, art, morality—were taken to have no empirical mode of confirmation, they were analyzed as expressive, as giving vent to or conveying some emotion. This category of meaning proved to be a starting point for many inquiries in value theory.

A somewhat different but not wholly contrasting direction of development received a powerful impetus from psychological experimentation. Empirical meaning, defined in terms of confirmability, is sometimes contrasted with causal meaning. "A sudden fall in the temperature means rain," illustrates both these senses of the word "meaning", for the statement itself is confirmable, and the meaning it asserts is causal. Causal meanings are usually considered confirmable, but for almost all philosophers the class of confirmable meanings is much wider than that of causal meanings. The exceptions are the philosophers who give a strictly behaviorist account of meaning.

Although in the main stream of philosophical thought meaning is conceived as a unique relation, not analyzable into simpler relations, it will be remembered that Spinoza defined the leading concepts of his ETHICS in terms of causality. Love, for example, was pleasure accompanied by the idea of the object causing it. The history of philosophy affords many examples of such naturalistic definitions. To explain supposedly unique relations which separate man from the rest of nature in terms of simpler relations is indeed one of the deepest motives of naturalism. To control and predict is another aim which inspires, in particular, the modern behaviorists. The fact that meanings can be learned, manipulated, and controlled in the educative process suggests that their nature is not subjective but behavioral, and that they belong to the subject-matter of the behavioral sciences. In classical conditioning experiments the buzzer comes to mean food for the dog. A new meaning has been produced in the dog and the strength of it can be controlled quantitatively. The situation is different in instrumental conditioning. There you might say that the correct turns in the maze come to mean food at the end of the run. If standard learning experiments are taken as a first model of the meaning situation, it is thus possible to explore the dynamic and functional aspects of the subject.

Such an approach puts meaning out in the open where the public can observe it, and links the subject to the psychology of learning and the biological sciences. Many philosophers object to this determination. The phenomenologists in particular contend that the behaviorists exclude the one area in which meaning itself is to be found, namely consciousness. The meanings which the behaviorists suppose to be passively present in external behavior, they say, are really intentions. They are what you and I mean. Even his objectivity, on which the behaviorist prides himself, is not something observable in the external world; it is a kind of intentionality, a modification of consciousness. The behaviorist is said to be "naive" and unscientific in forgetting that he has a mind in which the categories and distinctions he employs are evolved. Phenomenology is thus the foundation of any behavioral science. This argument, it is to be noted, does not set phenomenological investigation in opposition to science. In fact the usual formulation of the phenomenological approach sees it as a kind of neutral or presuppositionless description of direct conscious experience. It puts aside both the natural world with its causes and the subjective self. Questions of the relations of the given in experience to the physical and the empirical-psychological are taken to concern subsequent explorations of the relations of the initial data; it is simply claimed that the data have to be delineated without initial bias. Nor is the phenomenological approach without its specific scientific impact. In Gestalt psychology, especially in the study of perception, and in its emphasis on insight into the meaningful as against simply repetitive association in exploring phenomena of thinking, there is a strong phenomenological influence, which has been spreading recently also into social psychology and into psychiatry.

In the last decade, even apart from the opposing tendencies we have *indicated, the theory of meaning has become increasingly a matter of controversy. Many questions that had appeared to be settled were reopened. This has been true especially of the contemporary British analytic or, as it has often been called, the ordinary-language school. This movement grew out of the meticulous analysis practised without resort to formalism by G. E. Moore over several decades. It was further inspired by the work of Ludwig Wittgenstein, whose earlier* TRACTATUS LOGICO-PHILOSOPHICUS *had played a large part in the growth of positivism, but who increasingly began to look at concepts not in terms of their definition or their individually ascertainable meaning, but in terms of the way they were used, how for example one might teach them to someone who did not understand them to begin with. To this school the simple division of meaning into logical, empirical, and emotive seemed much too wholesale. Its outcome instead was a multitude of explorations of concrete usage in various parts of each of the fields of logic, ethics, epistemology, even—it would appear at present—metaphysics. In this outlook, there is in the exploration of meaning some of the sensitivity to variety of shades that is found in the phenomenologists, a stress on use and mode of functioning comparable to that of the instrumentalists; it has the concreteness of the positivists and the same ready utilization of logical techniques. But there is, on the whole, a pluralistic conviction that usage involves an unavoidable multiplicity of modes of functioning of language so that no over-all systematic picture is likely to emerge. There is also considerable controversy over whether there are clear criteria of "correct" use. This school is still in the ascendant phase; it has not formulated its underlying theses so much as embodied them in practice, and it is not wholly clear whether we have here a well-articulated theory of meaning or a convergence of reactions against those that had monopolized the field. But the net effect of all their interactions has been to open up traditional philosophical questions on a much more sophisticated level.*

III

The selections that follow certainly cannot encompass or even sample all those for whom meaning is an important philosophical notion. What we have done is to illustrate the variety of approaches and, where possible, try to catch each either at a critical point or in a representative mood.

Peirce's "Practical and Theoretical Beliefs" (1902) gives his mature reflections on the meaning of intellectual ideas just about a quarter of a century after his well-known "How to Make Our Ideas Clear," which was the first statement of his thesis. It is prefaced by a brief selection of his presentation of the laboratory outlook in meaning theory.

The selection from Morris's SIGNS, LANGUAGE, AND BEHAVIOR *shows the broad behaviorist trend in meaning theory. This work is perhaps the most thorough philosophical analysis of this approach.*

The selection to exhibit the phenomenological approach is taken from Husserl's LOGICAL INVESTIGATIONS (LOGISCHE UNTERSUCHUNGEN). *A small part of the first Investigation, "Expression and Signification," which is here reproduced and translated into English for the first time, furnishes an introduction to the phenomenological analysis of meaning and shows by its procedure the phenomenological mode of thought.*

Hempel's article on "Problems and Changes in the Empiricist Criterion of Meaning" reviews the successive efforts to find a satisfactory formulation of the verifiability principle. It is probably the most thorough review in a short space that has yet appeared, but it should not be thought conclusive. The argument still continues.

Waismann's "How I See Philosophy," with its wide scope and its emphasis on fresh vision as the recurrent feature of the philosophical enterprise, shows clearly the hopes that inspire the present analytical school at its best.

Strawson's "Construction and Analysis" is a clear weighing of the different emphases of the "formalists" and "informalists" in contemporary meaning analysis.

Since questions of meaning merge with views of knowledge and of mind, and these in turn with conceptions of being and of man, it is natural that some of the selections in the later parts, on questions of logic and the possibility of metaphysics and the meaning of value expressions, will also be of interest from the point of view of theory of meaning.

Charles S. Peirce

Pragmatism and Meaning *

THE EXPERIMENTALISTS' VIEW OF ASSERTION **

The writer of this article has been led by much experience to believe that every physicist, and every chemist, and, in short, every master in any department of experimental science, has had his mind moulded by his life in the laboratory to a degree that is little suspected. The experimentalist himself can hardly be fully aware of it, for the reason that the men whose intellects he really knows about are much like himself in this respect. With intellects of widely different training from his own, whose education has largely been a thing learned out of books, he will never become inwardly intimate, be he on ever so familiar terms with them; for he and they are as oil and water, and though they be shaken up together, it is remarkable how quickly they will go their several mental ways, without having gained more than a faint flavor from the association. Were those other men only to take skillful soundings of the experimentalist's mind—which is just what they are unqualified to do, for the most part—they would soon discover that, excepting perhaps upon topics where his mind is trammelled by personal feeling or by his bringing up, his disposition is to think of everything just as everything is thought of in the laboratory, that is, as a question of experimentation. Of course, no living man possesses in their fullness all the attributes characteristic of his type: it is not the typical doctor whom you will see every day driven in buggy or coupé, nor is it the typical pedagogue that will be met with in the first schoolroom you enter. But when you have found, or ideally constructed upon a basis of observation, the typical experimentalist, you will find that whatever assertion you may make to him, he will either understand as meaning that if a given

* Reprinted by permission of the publishers from *Collected Papers of Charles Sanders Peirce,* edited by Charles Hartshorne and Paul Weiss. Cambridge, Mass.: Harvard University Press. Copyright 1935 by The President and Fellows of Harvard College.

** Volume V, pp. 272–274. (Originally published in *The Monist,* Volume 15, pp. 161 f., 1905.)

prescription for an experiment ever can be and ever is carried out in act, an experience of a given description will result, or else he will see no sense at all in what you say. If you talk to him as Mr. Balfour talked not long ago to the British Association [1] saying that "the physicist . . . seeks for something deeper than the laws connecting possible objects of experience," that "his object is physical reality" unrevealed in experiments, and that the existence of such non-experiential reality "is the unalterable faith of science," to all such ontological meaning you will find the experimentalist mind to be color-blind. What adds to that confidence in this, which the writer owes to his conversations with experimentalists, is that he himself may almost be said to have inhabited a laboratory from the age of six until long past maturity; and having all his life associated mostly with experimentalists, it has always been with a confident sense of understanding them and of being understood by them.

That laboratory life did not prevent the writer (who here and in what follows simply exemplifies the experimentalist type) from becoming interested in methods of thinking; and when he came to read metaphysics, although much of it seemed to him loosely reasoned and determined by accident prepossessions, yet in the writings of some philosophers, especially Kant, Berkeley, and Spinoza, he sometimes came upon strains of thought that recalled the ways of thinking of the laboratory, so that he felt he might trust to them; all of which has been true of other laboratory-men.

Endeavoring, as a man of that type naturally would, to formulate what he so approved, he framed the theory that a *conception,* that is, the rational purport of a word or other expression, lies exclusively in its conceivable bearing upon the conduct of life; so that, since obviously nothing that might not result from experiment can have any direct bearing upon conduct, if one can define accurately all the conceivable experimental phenomena which the affirmation or denial of a concept could imply, one will have therein a complete definition of the concept, and *there is absolutely nothing more in it.* For this doctrine he invented the name *pragmatism.* Some of his friends wished him to call it *practicism* or *practicalism* (perhaps on the ground that πρακτικός is better Greek than πραγματικός). But for one who had learned philosophy out of Kant, as the writer, along with nineteen out of every twenty experimentalists who have turned to philosophy, had done, and who still thought in Kantian terms most readily, *praktisch* and *pragmatisch* were as far apart as the two poles, the former

[1] *Reflections Suggested by the New Theory of Matter;* Presidential Address, British Association for the Advancement of Science, August 17, 1904.

belonging in a region of thought where no mind of the experimentalist type can ever make sure of solid ground under his feet, the latter expressing relation to some definite human purpose. Now quite the most striking feature of the new theory was its recognition of an inseparable connection between rational cognition and rational purpose; and that consideration it was which determined the preference for the name *pragmatism*.

PRACTICAL AND THEORETICAL BELIEFS *

Let us begin by considering practical belief, such as that anthracite is a convenient fuel, leaving purely theoretical belief, such as that the pole of the earth describes an oval of a few rods' diameter, or that there is an imaginary circle which is twice cut by every real circle, for a supplementary study. Let us use the word "habit," throughout this book, not in its narrower, and more proper sense, in which it is opposed to a natural disposition (for the term *acquired habit* will perfectly express that narrower sense), but in its wider and perhaps still more usual sense, in which it denotes such a specialization, original or acquired, of the nature of a man, or an animal, or a vine, or a crystallizable chemical substance, or anything else, that he or it will behave, or always tend to behave, in a way describable in general terms upon every occasion (or upon a considerable proportion of the occasions) that may present itself of a generally describable character. Now to say that a man believes anthracite to be a convenient fuel is to say no more nor less than that if he needs fuel, and no other seems particularly preferable, then, if he acts deliberately, bearing in mind his experiences, considering what he is doing, and exercizing self-control, he will often use anthracite. A practical belief may, therefore, be described as a habit of deliberate behavior. The word "deliberate" is hardly completely defined by saying that it implies attention to memories of past experience and to one's present purpose, together with self-control. The acquisition of habits of the nervous system and of the mind is governed by the principle that any special character of a reaction to a given kind of stimulus is (unless fatigue intervenes) more likely to belong to a subsequent reaction to a second stimulus of that kind, than it would be if it had not happened to belong to the former reaction. But habits are sometimes acquired without any previous reactions that are externally manifest. A mere imagination of reacting in a particular way seems to be capable after numerous repetitions of causing the imagined kind of reaction really to take place upon subsequent occurrences of the stimulus. In the formation of habits of deliberate action, we may imagine the occurrence of the stimulus, and think out

* Volume V, pp. 376–385 (from "Reason's Rules," c.1902).

what the results of different actions will be. One of these will appear particularly satisfactory; and then an action of the soul takes place which is well described by saying that that mode of reaction "receives a deliberate stamp of approval." The result will be that when a similar occasion actually arises for the first time it will be found that the habit of really reacting in that way is already established. I remember that one day at my father's table, my mother spilled some burning spirits on her skirt. Instantly, before the rest of us had had time to think what to do, my brother, Herbert, who was a small boy, had snatched up the rug and smothered the fire. We were astonished at his promptitude, which, as he grew up, proved to be characteristic. I asked him how he came to think of it so quickly. He said, "I had considered on a previous day what I would do in case such an accident should occur." This act of stamping with approval, "endorsing" as one's own, an imaginary line of conduct so that it shall give a general shape to our actual future conduct is what we call a *resolve*. It is not at all essential to the practical belief, but only a somewhat frequent attachment.

Let us now pass to the consideration of purely theoretical belief. If an opinion can eventually go to the determination of a practical belief, it, in so far, becomes itself a pratical belief; and every proposition that is not pure metaphysical jargon and chatter must have some possible bearing upon practice. The diagonal of a square is incommensurable with its side. It is difficult to see what experiental difference there can be between commensurable and incommensurable magnitudes; but there is this, that it is useless to try to find the exact expression of the diagonal as a rational fraction of the side. Still, it does not follow that because every theoretical belief is, at least indirectly, a practical belief, this is the *whole* meaning of the theoretical belief. Of theoretical beliefs, in so far as they are not practical, we may distinguish between those which are expectations, and those which are not even that. One of the simplest, and for that reason one of the most difficult, of the ideas which it is incumbent upon the author of this book to endeavor to cause the reader to conceive, is that a sense of effort and the experience of any sensation are phenomena of the same kind, equally involving direct experience of the duality of the Without and the Within. The psychology of the sense of effort is not yet satisfactorily made out. It seems to be a sensation which somehow arises when striped muscles are under tension. But though this is the only way of stimulating it, yet an imagination of it is by association called up, upon the occasion of other slight sensations, even when muscles are uncontracted; and this imagination may sometimes be interpreted as a sign of effort. But though the sense of effort is thus merely a sensation, like any other, it is one in which the duality which appears in every sensation is specially prominent. A sense of exertion is at the same time a sense of being resisted. Exertion cannot be experienced without resistance, nor resistance without exertion. It is all one sense, but a sense of duality. Every sensation involves the same sense of duality, though less prominently. This is the direct perception of the external world of Reid and Hamilton.[2] This is the *probatio ambulandi,* which Diogenes Laertius perhaps gets mislocated. An idealist need not deny the reality of the external world, any more than Berkeley did. For the reality of the external world *means* nothing except that real experience of duality. Still, many of them do deny it—or think they do. Very well; an idealist of that stamp is lounging down Regent Street, thinking of the utter nonsense of the opinion of Reid, and especially of the foolish *probatio ambulandi,* when some drunken fellow who is staggering up the street unexpectedly lets fly his fist and knocks him in the eye. What has become of his philosophical reflections now? Will he be so unable to free himself from prepossessions that no experience can show him the force of that argument? There may be some underlying unity beneath the sudden transition from meditation to astonishment. Grant that: does it follow that that transition did not take place? Is not the transition a direct experience of the duality of the inward past and outward present? A poor analyst is he who cannot see that the Unexpected is a direct experience of duality, that just as there can be no effort without resistance, so there can be no subjectivity of the unexpected without the objectivity of the unexpected, that they are merely two aspects of one experience given together and beyond all criticism. If the idealist should pick himself up and proceed to argue to the striker, saying "you could not have struck me, because you have no independent existence, you know," the stricker might answer, "I dare say I have not separate existence enough for that; but I have separate existence enough to make you feel differently from what you were expecting to feel." Whatever strikes the eye or the touch, whatever strikes upon the ear, whatever affects nose or palate, contains something unexpected. Experience of the unexpected forces upon us the idea of duality. Will you say, "Yes, the idea is forced upon us, but it is not directly experienced, because only what is within is directly experienced"? The reply is that *experience* means nothing but just that of a cognitive nature which the history of our lives has forced upon us. It is *indirect,* if the medium of some other experience or thought is required to bring it out. Duality, thought abstractly, no doubt requires the intervention of reflection; but that upon which this reflection is based, the concrete duality, is there in the very experience itself.

[2] *The Works of Thomas Reid,* ed. by Sir W. Hamilton, Note A, §1; Note C.

In the light of these remarks, we perceive that there is just this difference between a practical belief and an expectation so far as it involves no purpose [or] effort; namely that the former is expectant of muscular sensation, the latter of sensation not muscular. The expectancy consists in the stamp of approval, the act of recognition as one's own, being placed by a deed of the soul upon an imaginary anticipation of experience; so that, if it be fulfilled, though the actual experience will, at all events, contain enough of the unexpected to be recognized as external, yet the person who stands in expectancy will almost claim the event as his due, his triumphant "I told you so" implying a right to expect as much from a justly-regulated world. A man who goes among a barbarous tribe and announces a total eclipse of the sun next day, will expect, not only "his" eclipse from Nature, but due credit for it from that People. In all this, I am endeavoring so to shape what I have to say as to exhibit, besides, the close alliance, the family identity, of the ideas of externality and unexpectedness.

As to purely theoretical beliefs not expectacious, if they are to mean anything, they must be somehow expectative. The word "expect" is now and then applied by careless and ignorant speakers, especially the English, to what is surmised in regard to the past. It is not illogical language: it is only elliptical. "I expect that Adam must have felt a little sore over the extraction of his rib," may be interpreted as meaning that the expectation is, that so it will be found when the secrets of all hearts are laid bare. History would not have the character of a true science if it were not permissible to hope that further evidences may be forthcoming in the future by which the hypotheses of the critics may be tested. A theory which should be capable of being absolutely demonstrated in its entirety by future events, would be no scientific theory but a mere piece of fortune telling. On the other hand, a theory, which goes beyond what may be verified to any degree of approximation by future discoveries is, in so far, metaphysical gabble. To say that a quadratic equation which has no real root has two different imaginary roots does not sound as if it could have any relation to experience. Yet it is strictly expectative. It states what would be expectable if we had to deal with quantities expressing the relations between objects, related to one another like the points of the plane of imaginary quantity. So a belief about the incommensurability of the diagonal relates to what is expectable for a person dealing with fractions; although it means nothing at all in regard to what could be expected in physical measurements, which are, of their very nature, approximate only. Let us examine a highly abstract belief; and see whether there is any expectancy in it. Riemann [3] declared that infinity has nothing to do with the absence of a limit but relates solely to measure. This means that if a bounded surface be measured in a suitable way it will be found infinite, and that if an unbounded surface be measured in a suitable way, it will be found finite. It relates to what is expectable for a person dealing with different systems of measurement. The Roman church requires the faithful to *believe* that the elements of the eucharist are really transformed into flesh and blood, although all their "sensible accidents," that is, all that could be expected from physical experience, remain those of bread and wine. The Protestant episcopal church requires its ministers to teach that the elements remain really bread and wine, although they have miraculous spiritual effects different from those of ordinary bread and wine. "No indeed," say the Romanists, "they not only have those spiritual effects but they really are transmuted." But the layman declares that he cannot understand the difference. "That is not necessary," says the priest, "you can believe it implicitly." What does that mean? It means that the layman is to trust that if he could understand the matter and know the truth, he would find that the priest was right. But trust—and the word belief means trust primarily—essentially refers to the future, or to a contingent future. The implication is that the layman may sometime know, presumably will, in another world; and that he may *expect* that if he ever does come to know, he will find the priest to be right. Thus, analysis shows that even in regard to so excessively metaphysical a matter, the belief, if there can be any belief, has to involve expectation as its very essence.

It now begins to look strongly as if perhaps all belief might involve expectation as its essence. That is as much as can justly be said. We have as yet no assurance that this is true of every kind of belief. One class of accepted truths which we have neglected is that of direct perceptual facts. I lay down a wafer, before me. I look at it, and say to myself, "That wafer looks red." What element of expectation is there in the belief that the wafer *looks* red at this moment?

In order to handle this question, it is necessary to draw a distinction. Every belief is belief in a proposition. Now every proposition has its predicate which expresses *what* is believed, and its subjects which express *of what* it is believed. The grammarians of today prefer to say that a sentence has but one subject, which is put in the nominative. But from a logical point of view the terminology of the older grammarians was better, who

[3] Art. II, §2, "Ueber die Hypothesen, welche der Geometrie zu Grunde liegen," *Abh. d. König. G. d. W. zu Göttingen,* 13 Bd. (1866–7).

spoke of the subject nominative and the subject accusative. I do not know that they spoke of the subject dative; but in the proposition, "Anthony gave a ring to Cleopatra," Cleopatra is as much a subject of what is meant and expressed as is the ring or Anthony. A proposition, then, has one predicate and any number of subjects. The subjects are either names of objects well known to the utterer and to the interpreter of the proposition (otherwise he could not interpret it) or they are virtually almost directions how to proceed to gain acquaintance with what is referred to. Thus, in the sentence "Every man dies," "Every man" implies that the interpreter is at liberty to pick out a man and consider the proposition as applying to him. In the proposition "Anthony gave a ring to Cleopatra," if the interpreter asks, What ring? the answer is that the indefinite article shows that it is a ring which might have been pointed out to the interpreter if he had been on the spot; and that the proposition is only asserted of the suitably chosen ring. The predicate on the other hand is a word or phrase which will call up in the memory or imagination of the interpreter images of things such as he has seen or imagined and may see again. Thus, "gave" is the predicate of the last proposition; and it conveys its meaning because the interpreter has had many experiences in which gifts were made; and a sort of composite photograph of them appears in his imagination. I am told that "Saccharin is 500 times as sweet as cane-sugar." But I never heard of saccharin. On inquiry, I find it is the sulphimide of orthosulphobenzoic acid; that is, it is phthalimide in which one CO group is replaced by SO_2. I can see on paper that there might be such a body. That it is "500 times sweeter than sugar" produces a rather confused idea of a very familiar general kind. *What* I am to expect is expressed by the predicate, while the subjects inform me *on what occasion* I am to expect it. Diogenes Laertius, Suidas, Plutarch, and an anonymous biographer tell us that Aristotle was unable to pronounce the letter R.[4] I place Aristotle perfectly, of course. He is the author of works I often read and profoundly admire and whose fame far surpasses that of any other logician—The Prince of Philosophers. I have also met people who could not pronounce R; but in other respects they did not seem to be much like Aristotle—not even Dundreary. Should I meet him in the Elysian Fields, I shall know what to expect. That is an impossible supposition; but should I ever meet a great logician, spindle-shanked and pig-eyed, who cannot pronounce R, I shall be interested to see whether he has other characteristics of Aristotle. This example has been selected as one which should seem to a superficial eye to involve no gleam of expectation; and if this testimony of four respectable witnesses, as in-

[4] See Zeller's *Die Philosophie der Griechen,* II Th., 2 Abt., Anmerkung.

dependent as under the circumstances they could be, is destined never to receive confirmation nor contradiction, nor in any other way to have its probable consequences confronted by future experience, then in truth no expectation does it carry. In that case, it is an idle tale that might, for any practical purpose, have been as well the creation of some ironical poet. In that case, it is, properly speaking, no contribution to knowledge, for at least it is only probability, and probability cannot be reckoned as knowledge, unless it is destined to be indefinitely heightened in the future. Knowledge which should have no possible bearing upon any future experience—bring no expectation whatever—would be information concerning a dream. But in truth no such thing can be presumed of any knowledge. We expect that in time it will produce, or reinforce, or weaken some definite expectation. Give science only a hundred more centuries of increase in geometrical progression, and she may be expected to find that the sound waves of Aristotle's voice have somehow recorded themselves. If not, it were better to hand the reports over to the poets to make something pretty of, and thus turn them to some human use. But the right thing to do is to expect the verification. It is the degenerate pronunciation that is to be expected; the occasion is when Aristotle's voice shall become virtually heard again or when we shall have some other information which shall confirm or refute those reports.

Now if the reader should say, "Talk as you please, the assertion that Aristotle was τραυλός simply brings to the mental ear the voice of a man unable to pronounce the letter R, and labels that image with an indication of Aristotle, a man who lived three hundred years before Christ," the author may surprise him and grieve any whom he may have convinced, by declaring "I agree with you entirely"; only this assertion, which is identical with the previous one, though translated into other language, *means* nothing unless it be that Aristotle having been brought, directly or indirectly, to our experience, *will be* found, if found at all, to be incapable of pronouncing the R. Let us distinguish between the *proposition* and the *assertion* of that proposition. We will grant, if you please, that the proposition itself merely represents an image with a label or pointer attached to it. But to *assert* that proposition is to make oneself responsible for it, without any definite forfeit, it is true, but with a forfeit no smaller for being unnamed. Now an *ex post facto* law is forbidden by the Constitution of the United States of America, but an *ex post facto* contract is forbidden by the constitution of things. A man cannot promise what the past shall have been, if he tries. It is evident that to guarantee that, if a piece of work has not already been done right, one will pay for it, and to guarantee that, *if it shall be found* not to have already been done right, one will pay for it, have one and the same meaning. One or other of them therefore must be an elliptical or otherwise unliteral expression, or else both are so. But nobody will maintain that to promise to pay for the work, if it shall be ascertained not to have been already done right, really means to promise to so pay, if it shall in fact not have been already done right, whether it be ascertained or not. It would be equally absurd to say that there was any third meaning which should have reference to an unascertained past. It follows, then, that to contract to pay money if something in the past has been done or not done *can only* mean that the money shall be paid if it is ascertained that the event has happened or has not happened. But there would be no reason why the literal sense should not be understood if it made any sense. Hence there can be no meaning in making oneself responsible for a past event independent of its future ascertainment. But to assert a proposition is to make oneself responsible for its truth. Consequently, the only meaning which an assertion of a past fact can have is that, if in the future the truth be ascertained, so it shall be ascertained to be. There seems to be no rational escape from this.

Now let us take up the perceptual judgment "This wafer looks red." It takes some time to write this sentence, to utter it, or even to think it. It must refer to the state of the percept at the time that it, the judgment, began to be made. But the judgment does not exist until it is completely made. It thus only refers to a memory of the past; and all memory is possibly fallible and subject to criticism and control. The judgment, then, can only mean that so far as the character of the percept can ever be ascertained, it will be ascertained that the wafer looked red.

Perhaps the matter may be stated less paradoxically. Everybody will agree that it would be perfectly meaningless to say that sulphur had the singular property of turning pink when nobody was looking at it, instantly returning to yellowness before the most rapid glance could catch its pink color, or to say that copper was subject to the law that as long as there was no pressure upon it, it was perfectly yielding, becoming hard in proportion as it was pressed; and generally, a law which never should operate would be an empty formula. Indeed, something not very far from the assertion about copper is contained in all treatises on dynamics, although not limited to any particular substance. Namely, it is set down that no tangential force can be exerted upon a perfect fluid. But no writer puts it forth as a statement of fact; it is given as a definition merely. A law, then, which never will operate has no positive existence. Consequently, a law which has operated for the last time has ceased to exist as a law, except as a mere empty formula which it may be convenient to allow to remain. Hence to assert that a law positively exists is to assert that it will operate, and therefore to refer to the future, even though only conditionally. But to say that a body is hard, or red, or heavy, or of a given weight, or has any other property, is to say that it is subject to law and therefore is a statement referring to the future.

Charles W. Morris

Signs and Behavior Situations *

1. THE PROBLEM OF APPROACH

. . . There is wide disagreement as to when something is a sign. Some persons would unhesitatingly say that blushing is a sign, others would not. There are mechanical dogs which will come out of their kennels if one claps one's hands loudly in their presence. Is such clapping a sign? Are clothes signs of the personality of those who wear them? Is music a sign of anything? Is a word such as 'Go!' a sign in the same sense as is a green light on a street intersection? Are punctuation marks signs? Are dreams signs? Is the Parthenon a sign of Greek culture? Disagreements are widespread; they show that the term 'sign' is both vague and ambiguous.

This disagreement extends to many other terms which are commonly used in describing sign-processes. The terms 'express,' 'understand,' 'refer,' 'meaning' would provide many instances. So would 'communication' and 'language.' Do animals communicate? If so, do they have a language? Or do only men have language? Yes, run some answers; no, run others. We find the same diversity of replies if we ask whether thought or mind or consciousness is involved in a sign-process; whether a poem "refers" to what it "expresses"; whether men can signify what cannot be experienced; whether mathematical terms signify anything; whether language signs are preceded genetically by non-language signs; whether the elements in an undeciphered "dead" language are signs.

In the face of such disagreements, it is not easy to find a starting point. If we are to seek for a formulation of the word 'sign' in biological terms, the task is to isolate some distinctive kind of behavior which agrees fairly well with frequent usages of the term 'sign.' Since usage of the term is, however, not consistent, it cannot be demanded that the chosen behavioral

* Reprinted with permission of Prentice-Hall, Inc., from *Signs, Language and Behavior* by Charles W. Morris, pp. 3–11. Copyright 1946 by Prentice-Hall, Inc.; published by Prentice-Hall, Inc., Englewood Cliffs, New Jersey.

formulation agree with all the various usages which are actually current. At some point the semiotician must say: "Henceforth we will recognize that anything which fulfills certain conditions is a sign. These conditions are selected in the light of current usages of the term 'sign,' but they may not fit in with all such usages. They do not therefore claim to be a statement of the way the term 'sign' is always used, but a statement of the conditions under which we will henceforth admit within semiotic that something is a sign."

Then from such a starting point a behavioral theory of signs will build up step by step a set of terms to talk about signs (taking account of current distinctions but attempting to reduce for scientific purposes their vagueness and ambiguity), and will endeavor to explain and predict sign phenomena on the basis of the general principles of behavior which underlie all behavior, and hence sign-behavior. The aim is to take account of the distinctions and analyses which former investigators have made, but to ground these results whenever possible upon general behavior theory. In the nature of the case such a scientific semiotic will often deviate from current terminology, and can only be developed slowly and laboriously. It will often seem pedantic and less illuminating for many purposes than less scientific approaches—which therefore are to be encouraged in the light of the many problems and purposes which a treatment of signs aims to fulfill. It is not to be expected that all discussions of literary, religious, and logical signs can be translated at once with profit into a behavioral formulation. The present approach does not therefore wish to exclude other approaches to semiotic. But it does proceed upon the belief that basic progress in this complex field rests finally upon the development of a genuine science of signs, and that this development can be most profitably carried on by a biological orientation which places signs within the context of behavior.

2. PRELIMINARY ISOLATION OF SIGN-BEHAVIOR

We shall begin by taking two examples of behavior to which the term 'sign' is often applied both in common usage and in the writings of semioticians. Then a superficial analysis of these examples will disclose the features which a more technical formulation of the nature of a sign must embody. If both situations reveal certain common elements, then both may be called sign-behavior; the differences in the two situations would then suggest differences between kinds of signs. If analysis shows too great differences, then the alternative would be to choose different terms to describe the two situations, and to adopt a narrower definition of 'sign':

in either case we would then be in a position to consider whether any additional phenomena are to be called signs, that is, whether the characterization of signs based upon the two examples in question is to be held as a basis for determining when something is a sign or whether it is to be expanded to include situations of a widely different sort.

The first example is drawn from experiments on dogs. If a hungry dog that goes to a certain place to obtain food when the food is seen or smelled, is trained in a certain way, it will learn to go to this place for food when a buzzer is sounded even though the food is not observed. In this case the dog is attentive to the buzzer but does not normally go to the buzzer itself; and if the food is not made available until some time after the buzzer has sounded, the dog may not go to the place in question until the time interval has elapsed. Many persons would say in such a situation that the buzzer sound is to the dog a sign of food at the given place, and in particular, a non-language sign. If we abstract from the experimenter and his purposes in this example, and consider only the dog, the example approximates what have often been called "natural signs," as when a dark cloud is a sign of rain. It is in this way that we wish the experiment to be considered.

The second example is drawn from human behavior. A person on the way to a certain town is driving along a road; he is stopped by another person who says that the road is blocked some distance away by a landslide. The person who hears the sounds which are uttered does not continue to the point in question, but turns off on a side-road and takes another route to his destination. It would be commonly said that the sounds made by the one person and heard by the other (and indeed by the utterer also) were signs to both of them of the obstacle on the road, and in particular were language signs, even though the actual responses of the two persons are very different.

Common to these two situations is the fact that both the dog and the person addressed behave in a way which satisfies a need—hunger in the one case, arrival at a certain town in the other. In each case the organisms have various ways of attaining their goals: when food is smelled the dog reacts differently than when the buzzer is sounded; when the obstacle is encountered the man reacts differently than when spoken to at a distance from the obstacle. Further, the buzzer is not responded to as food nor the spoken words as an obstacle; the dog may wait awhile before going for food and the man may continue to drive for a time down the blocked road before turning off to another road. And yet in some sense both the buzzer and the words control or direct the course of behavior toward a goal in a way similar to (though not identical with) the control which would be exercised by the food or the obstacle if these were present as stimuli: the buzzer determines the dog's behavior to be that of seeking food in a certain place at a certain time; the words determine the man's behavior to be that of getting to a certain town by avoiding a certain obstacle at a given place on a given road. The buzzer and the words are in some sense "substitutes" in the control of behavior for the control over behavior which would be exercised by what they signify if this was itself observed. The differences between non-language and language signs remain for subsequent discussion.

It is clear at once that the formulation of 'sign' frequent in early behavior theory is too simple: namely, it cannot be simply said that a sign is a substitute stimulus which calls out to itself the same response which would have been called out by something else had it been present. For the response to food is to food itself, while the response to the buzzer is not to it as if it were food; and the actual response to the situation in which the sign appears may be greatly different from the response to a situation where what is signified, and not the sign, is present. The dog, for instance, may salivate when the buzzer is sounded but it cannot actually eat unless food is present; the man may feel anxiety when he is addressed, but his turning off the road before reaching the obstacle is a very different response from that which he would make if he had gone directly to the place of blockage itself (and even more different from the behavior of the person who told him of the obstacle).

Nor can the difficulties in the earlier attempts to identify signs with any and all substitute stimuli be avoided by attempting to say that whatever influences a response with respect to what is not at the moment a stimulus is a sign. For example, a drug will influence the way an organism will respond to stimuli which later affect it, and yet it would be too great a departure from common usage to call such a drug a sign.

The difficulties in these formulations may perhaps be avoided if, as our examples suggest, signs are identified within goal-seeking behavior. So in the light of our analysis of what the two examples chosen as a point of reference have in common (and neglecting for the time being their differences) we arrive at the following preliminary formulation of at least one set of conditions under which something may be called a sign: *If something, A, controls behavior towards a goal in a way similar to (but not necessarily identical with) the way something else, B, would control behavior with respect to that goal in a situation in which it were observed, then A is a sign.*

The buzzer and the spoken sounds are then signs of food and obstacle because they control the course of behavior with respect to the goals of getting food and getting to a certain place in a way similar to the control which food and obstacle would exercise if they were observed. Whatever exercises this type of control in goal-seeking behavior is a sign. And goal-seeking behavior in which signs exercise control may be called *sign-behavior.*

3. TOWARD PRECISION IN THE IDENTIFICATION OF SIGN-BEHAVIOR

For many purposes the preceding account of a sign is adequate; it at least suggests a behavioral way of formulating what is commonly meant in saying that a sign "stands for" or "represents" something other than itself. But for more strictly scientific purposes a more exact formulation is required in order to clarify the notions of similarity of behavior and goal-seeking behavior. We might at this point simply leave it to the scientists in their field to state further refinements, and indeed anything we add is in the nature of the case tentative. But since our concern is to push semiotic as rapidly as possible in the direction of a natural science, the following suggestions are made.

Implicit in the preceding account are four concepts which need further clarification: preparatory-stimulus, disposition to respond, response-sequence, and behavior-family. When these notions are elucidated a more precise statement of a set of conditions sufficient for something to be called a sign can be given.

A *preparatory-stimulus* is any stimulus which influences a response to some other stimulus. Thus it has been found by O. H. Mowrer that the magnitude of the jump of a rat to a shock stimulus is increased if a tone sounds before the shock stimulus is encountered. Such a stimulus differs from other stimuli, say the shock, in that as a preparatory-stimulus it influences a response to something other than itself rather than causing a response to itself (it may of course also cause a response to itself, that is, not be merely or solely a preparatory-stimulus). By a *stimulus* is meant, following Clark L. Hull, any physical energy which acts upon a receptor of a living organism; the source of this energy will be called the *stimulus-object.* By a *response* is meant any action of a muscle or gland; hence there are reactions of an organism which are not necessarily responses. A preparatory-stimulus affects or causes a reaction in an organism, but, as Mowrer makes clear, it need not call out a response to itself, but only to some other stimulus. In the account toward which we are moving it is not held that all preparatory-stimuli are signs, but only that preparatory-stimuli which meet certain additional requirements are signs. That a preparatory-stimulus need not when presented call out a response makes intelligible the fact that a command to turn right at a certain place may produce at the time of utterance no overt, or as far as we know, "implicit" response of turning right, and yet may determine that the person commanded turns right when he reaches the place in question. A preparatory-stimulus does however cause some reaction in an organism, affects it in some way, and this leads to the introduction of the term 'disposition to respond.'

A *disposition to respond* to something in a certain way is a state of an organism at a given time which is such that under certain additional conditions the response in question takes place. These additional conditions may be very complex. An animal disposed to go to a certain place to obtain food may not go there even if food is observed—he may not be willing or able to swim across an intervening water barrier or to move if certain other animals are present as stimulus-objects. The complex of conditions also includes other states of the organism. The person commanded to turn at a certain corner may not turn even when the corner is reached: as he walked to the corner he may have come to believe that his informant was deliberately trying to misdirect him, so that confidence in one's informant may be at times a necessary condition for making a response to which one is disposed because of signs.

There may be dispositions to respond which are not caused by preparatory-stimuli, but every preparatory-stimulus causes a disposition to respond in a certain way to something else. Logically, therefore, 'disposition to respond' is the more basic notion, and a preparatory-stimulus is a stimulus which causes a disposition to respond in a certain way to something else. And since not all preparatory-stimuli would normally be called signs, and not all dispositions to response which are caused by preparatory-stimuli are relevant to the delimitation of sign-processes, additional criteria are involved; and to be in accord with our own preliminary formulation of sign-behavior, these criteria must introduce the notion of behavior toward a goal.

A *response-sequence* is any sequence of consecutive responses whose first member is initiated by a stimulus-object and whose last member is a response to this stimulus-object as a goal-object, that is, to an object which partially or completely removes the state of the organism (the "need") which motivates the sequence of responses. Thus the series of responses of a hungry dog which sees a rabbit, runs after it, kills it, and so obtains food is a response-sequence. For the sight of the rabbit starts a series of responses to the rabbit in terms of which the rabbit is finally obtained as food. The intervening responses in the sequence can occur only if the environment provides the necessary stimuli for their release, and such sources of stimuli may be called *supporting stimulus-objects.* The terrain over which the dog runs in this case provides the support necessary for the responses of following the rabbit and tracking it down, while the rabbit provides the stimuli initiating and terminating the series of responses.

A *behavior-family* is any set of response-sequences which are initiated by similar stimulus-objects and which terminate in these objects as similar goal-objects for similar needs. Hence all the response-sequences which start from rabbits and eventuate in securing rabbits as food would constitute the rabbit-food behavior-family. A behavior-family may in an extreme case have only one member; no limit is set to the number of possible members. Behavior-families have various degrees of inclusiveness. All the objects which a dog eats would, for instance, determine an extensive "object-food" behavior-family which would include the rabbit-food behavior-family as a subordinate behavior-family.

In these terms it is possible to formulate more precisely a set of conditions sufficient for something to be a sign: *If anything, A, is a preparatory-stimulus which in the absence of stimulus-objects initiating response-sequences of a certain behavior-family causes a disposition in some organism to respond under certain conditions by response-sequences of this behavior-family, then A is a sign.*

According to these conditions, the buzzer is a sign to the dog since it disposes the animal to seek food in a certain place in the absence of direct stimulation from food objects at this place, and similarly, the spoken words are signs to the driver since they dispose him to response-sequences of avoiding an obstacle at a certain point on a certain road although the obstacle is not itself at the time of hearing the sounds a stimulus-object.

The merit of this formulation is that it does not require that the dog or the driver respond to the sign itself, the sign serving merely as a preparatory-stimulus for response to something else. Nor does it require that the dog or the driver finally respond overtly as they would if food or an obstacle had been stimulus-objects; it merely requires that if the animal makes the response-sequences which it is disposed to make when certain additional conditions are met (conditions of need and of supporting stimulus-objects) these response-sequences will be of the same behavior-family as those which the food or obstacle would have initiated. In this way the difficulties which earlier behavioral formulations of signs encountered are avoided. And yet objective behavioral criteria are furnished for determining whether something is or is not a sign. It is further believed that these criteria do not deviate from those which underlie certain common usages of the term 'sign.'

Edmund Husserl

Expression and Signification *

[*Introductory note:* ** Husserl's *Logical Investigations* are divided into two parts. The second part, "Investigations Concerning the Phenomenology and the Theory of Knowledge," contains six investigations, the first of them entitled "Expression and Signification." The following excerpt comes from the first chapter of this introductory investigation.

In earlier sections of Chapter I, "The Essential Distinctions," Husserl has distinguished two senses of the word *Zeichen (sign, mark)*. One thing is an *indicative* sign of another, if belief in the existence of the first motivates belief in the existence or likely existence of the second. On the other hand, a thing is an *expressive* sign, or an *expression* (in one sense of this word), if it has what Husserl calls a sense or signification. In communicative speech a declarative sentence is both an indicative sign and an expression. It *indicates* and *makes known* to the hearer certain of the speaker's mental processes. At the same time it *expresses* the sense of one of those processes, namely an act of judging a proposition. This asserted proposition is the signification of the sentence. In solitary or silent thinking the same sentence would not function as an indicative sign, yet it would still express the same signification.

The part of Chapter I that begins with §9 makes distinctions of two kinds: "phenomenological" distinctions among mental processes themselves, and "objective" distinctions among their objects and objective senses. For example, "phenomenologically" the consciousness of the sentence is distinguished from the consciousness of its signification, i.e., the proposition, and from the consciousness of what the proposition is about. "Objectively" the sound of the sentence is distinguished (as something real) from the sentence itself (as something ideal), and the sentence is

* From *Logische Untersuchungen* by Edmund Husserl. Translated by Dorion Cairns. Second edition. Tübingen: Max Niemeyer Verlag. Reprinted by permission of Gerhart Husserl and the translator.

** by the translator.

likewise distinguished from its signification (the ideal proposition) and from its object (the real or ideal affair or situation that the proposition is about).

All too frequently the exposition of these and related distinctions is ambiguous. The author of the first investigation was still far from seeing all the relevant differences, and he lacked terms for stating unequivocally the ones he saw. These defects will be apparent, particularly to readers acquainted with Husserl's later work. The following excerpt is not a final statement of results. It is valuable rather as an early but concrete example of "phenomenological" investigation.]

§9. THE PHENOMENOLOGICAL DISTINCTIONS BETWEEN THE APPEARING OF THE PHYSICAL EXPRESSION [*PHYSISCHER AUSDRUCKSERSCHEINUNG*], THE SENSE-BESTOWING ACT, AND THE SENSE-FULFILLING ACT

If we disregard the subjective processes belonging *specifically* to making known and consider the expression with regard to distinctions pertaining to it whether it is functioning in soliloquy or in colloquy, two things seem to remain: the expression itself and what it expresses as its signification (as its sense). Nevertheless there are various relations interwoven here; and reference to "what is expressed" and to "signification" is correspondingly ambiguous. Turning to the field of pure description [1], we find that the concrete phenomenon pertaining to the expression animated with a sense has as members: on the one hand, the *phenomenon pertaining to something physical* [*das physische Phänomen*], i.e., the phenomenon in which the expression is constituted in respect of its physical side, and, on the other hand, the *acts* that give the expression *signification* and perhaps *intuitional fullness,* acts in which, moreover, relation to an expressed objectivity becomes constituted. By virtue of these acts the expression is more than a mere verbal sound. It *means* something; and, by meaning something, it relates to something objective. By virtue of accompanying intuitions this something objective can be appearing as actually present or at least as made present (in a phantasy-image, for example). Where this is the case, relation to the objectivity is realized. But the case may be otherwise: The expression functions sensefully; it continues to be more than an empty verbal sound, though it lacks the founding intuition that would give it its object. The relation of expression to object is now unrealized, being comprised in the mere significational intention. The *name,* for example, names its object under all circumstances, since it *means* it. Mere meaning, however, is the

[1] First edition: "the field of psychological description".

end of the matter, if the object is not there intuitionally and hence is not there as a named (that is, a meant) object either. When the initially *empty* significational intention becomes fulfilled, the object-relation becomes realized, the naming becomes a relation (between name and named) of which there is actual present awareness.

If we take as a basis this fundamental distinction between significational intentions devoid of intuition and fulfilled significational intentions, then—even after separation of the sensuous acts in which the appearing of the expression as a verbal sound comes to pass—two different acts or act-sequences are to be distinguished: On the one hand, those that are *essential* to the expression if it is to remain an expression at all—that is, a verbal sound animated with a sense. We call those the *signification-conferring acts* [*bedeutungverleihende Akte*] or *significational intentions* [*Bedeutungsintentionen*]. On the other hand, acts that, to be sure, are non-essential to the expression as such but nevertheless relate to it in a manner fundamental for logic, since they fulfil (confirm, corroborate, illustrate) the significational intention of the expression and, precisely thereby, actualize its object-relation. These acts (which become fused with the signification-conferring acts in the unity of a cognition or of a fulfilment) we call *signification-fulfilling acts* [*bedeutungerfüllende Akte*]. The shorter expression, *significational fulfilling* [*Bedeutungserfüllung*], should be used only in contexts that preclude the likely confusion with the *total* subjective process within which a significational intention finds fulfilment in the correlative act. In the realized relation of the expression to its objectivity [2], the expression animated with a sense unites with the acts of significational fulfilling. First of all, the verbal sound is united with the significational intention; and this in turn becomes united with the appropriate significational fulfilling, in the manner in which all intentions become united with their fulfillings. Now by the unqualified word "expression", unless we are talking about the "mere" expression, we mean as a rule the expression *animated with a sense*. Accordingly (though we often speak in this fashion) we cannot properly say *the expression expresses the significational intention* [*seine Bedeutung (die Intention)*]. More fitting here is the other way of talking about expressing, according to which the *fulfilling* act figures as the one *expressed by the full expression*—as, for example, when we say of a statement that it gives expression to a perception or an imagination.

[2] Author's note: I often choose the less definite expression, objectivity, because here it is always a matter, not only of objects in the narrower sense, but also of states-of-affairs, traits, non-selfsufficient real or categorial forms, and the like.

It hardly needs to be pointed out that, in the case of communicative speech, the signification-conferring as well as the signification-fulfilling acts can belong to what is made known. Indeed, the former make up the most essential core of what is made known. To make *them* known to the hearer must be the principal interest of the intention to communicate; only by attributing *them* to the speaker does the hearer understand him.

§10. PHENOMENOLOGICAL UNITY OF THESE ACTS

The acts distinguished above—on the one hand, the appearing of the expression and, on the other, the significational intention, perhaps also the significational fulfilling—do not make up a mere ensemble in consciousness, as if they were given merely simultaneously. They make up on the contrary an intimately fused unity, which has a peculiar character. As everyone knows from internal experience, the components on one side and the other are of unequal value. This reflects the unlikeness of the sides of the relation between the expression and the object expressed (named) by means of the signification. Both the word-objectivation and the sense-bestowing act go on in mental life. But, while the word-objectivation is going on in our life, we are living not at all in objectivating the word, but exclusively in producing its sense, its signifying. And while we are doing this, while we are absorbed in execution of the significational intention and perhaps in execution of its fulfilling, our entire interest belongs to the object intended in it and named by means of it. (Closely examined, both phrases turn out to say the same thing.) The very function of the word (or rather of the intuitive word-objectivation) is to excite in us the sense-conferring act and point to what is intended "in" it and perhaps given by a fulfilling intuition, to urge our interest exclusively in this direction.

This pointing is not perchance to be described as merely the objective fact that interest is diverted regularly from one to the other. The circumstance that, by virtue of a hidden psychological coordination, a pair of intentional objects [*Vorstellungsobjekte*], *A* and *B*, stand in such a relation that, with the objectivating [*Vorstellen*] of *A*, the objectivating of *B* is regularly awakened and interest turns herewith from *A* to *B*—this circumstance is not enough to make *A* an expression of objectivated *B* [*für die Vorstellung des B*]. Rather is expressionhood an observable and describable feature of the *union in mental life* between sign and what is designated.[3]

As for the describable difference between the appearing of the physical sign [*der physischen Zeichenerscheinung*] and the significational intention

[3] In the first edition the sentence continues: "—more precisely, *between the appearing of the sign animated with a sense and the sense-fulfilling act*".

appertaining to it and stamping it as an expression, that difference stands out most clearly if we turn our interest first to the sign all by itself—for example, the printed word, just as something printed. If we do this, we have an external perception (or an external intuitive memory or phantasy [*anschauliche Vorstellung*]) like any other; and its object loses the character of a word. Then, if the mark is again functioning as a word, the character of the objectivation of it [*ihrer Vorstellung*] is entirely altered. The word (as an external individual) is, to be sure, still present to us intuitionally; it is still appearing. But we are not aiming at it; now it is no longer, in the proper sense, the object of our "psychic activity". Our interest, our intention, our meaning [*Vermeinen*]—given suitable breadth, these expressions signify the same thing—aims exclusively at the affair meant in the sense-bestowing act. Stated purely phenomenologically, this signifies precisely that the intuitive objectivation in which the appearing of the physical word [*die physische Worterscheinung*] is constituted undergoes an essential phenomenological modification, if its object assumes the status [*Geltung*] of an *expression.* While that component of the objectivation in which the appearing of the object consists remains unaltered, the intentional character of the mentally lived process is altered. In this manner, without it being necessary that any fulfilling or illustrating intuition occur, an act of signifying becomes constituted, which finds its support in the intuitional content of the word-objectivation but is essentially different from the intuitive intention directed to the word itself. With this act of signifying there are often fused, in a peculiar manner, those acts or act-complexes that we called fulfilling, the ones whose object appears as the object signified in or named by means of the signification.

In the next chapter we shall have to conduct a supplementary investigation to find out whether the "significational intention" (which, according to our exposition, is the phenomenological characteristic of the expression, as opposed to the empty verbal sound) consists in mere annexation of phantasy-images of the intended object to the verbal sound or else can be constituted only on the basis of such phantasy-images, or whether, on the contrary, accompanying phantasy-images are part of the expression's non-essential equipment and rightly pertain to the function of fulfilling, even though fulfilment with them may be characterized as only partial, indirect, or precursory. In the interest of closer connectedness in the principal train of thoughts, we refrain from entering more deeply into phenomenological questions here—as indeed, throughout this whole investigation, we shall go into the phenomenological only far enough to ascertain the first essential distinctions.

From the preliminary descriptions we have presented up to now, it can already be seen that more than a few circumstantialities are required if we want to describe the phenomenological situation correctly. They appear as in fact unavoidable if only one has made it clear to oneself that all objects and object-relations are for us what they are, solely by virtue of acts of meaning (essentially distinct from them) in which they become objective [*vorstellig*] for us, in which they—precisely as *meant* unities—stand over against us. For the purely phenomenological [4] mode of observation there are only tissues of such intentional facts. When it is not the phenomenological but the naïvely objective interest that controls, when we are living in the intentional acts instead of reflecting about them, naturally everything we say becomes uncomplicated and clear, and free from circumlocution. Regarding our present case we then speak simply of expression and expressed, of name and named, of the transfer of interest from one to the other, and so forth. When, on the other hand, the phenomenological interest is decisive, we labor under the difficulty of having to describe phenomenological relationships that, to be sure, occur countless times in mental life but of which, normally, there is no objective awareness; and we must describe them with expressions attuned to the sphere of normal interest, to appearing objectivities.

§11. THE IDEAL DISTINCTIONS

First, between expression and signification as ideal unities.

We have been considering, up to now, intelligent [*den verständnisvollen*] expression as a concrete subjective process. Instead of its factors on one hand and the other, the appearing of the expression and the sense-conferring or else sense-fulfilling subjective processes, we now want to take into consideration what is, in a certain manner, given "in" them: the expression itself, its sense, and the corresponding objectivity. We are turning, therefore, from the real relation of the acts to the ideal relation of their objects or contents. Subjective consideration yields to objective. The ideality of the relationship between expression and signification, in respect of both members, shows itself forthwith in the circumstance that, when asking for the signification of some expression or other ("quadratic remainder", for example), we obviously do not mean as the expression this sound-formation uttered *hic et nunc,* the fleeting noise that never returns identically. We mean *the* expression, *in specie. The* expression "quadratic remainder" is identically the same, regardless of who

[4] First edition: "the descriptive-psychological (purely phenomenological)".

may utter it. And the like is true of our reference to the *signification,* which is obviously not a reference to the sense-conferring subjective process.

That an essential distinction is in fact to be made here is shown by every example.

When I state (in truthful speech, which we will always presuppose), "The three altitudes of a triangle intersect in just one point," naturally the basis for doing this is that I so judge. Someone who hears my statement with understanding knows also that I so judge—that is to say, he apperceives me as so judging. But is my judging, which I have *made known* here, also the signification of the declarative sentence? Is it what the statement *says* and, in this sense, gives expression to? Obviously not. Hardly anyone will normally understand the inquiry for the sense and signification of the statement in such a manner that it might occur to him to turn to the judgment, as a psychic process. On the contrary, everyone will answer to this inquiry: What this statement states is *the same,* whoever may enunciate it assertively and no matter when or under what circumstances he may do so; and this identical something is precisely *that the three altitudes of a triangle intersect in just one point.* It is nothing more or less than that. Essentially, therefore, "the same" statement is repeated; and it is repeated because it is the one particularly fitting form of expression for the identical something called its signification. In this identical signification (of which we can at any time become conscious as evidently the same one, with repetition of the statement) nothing like a judging and a judger is to be discovered. We believed we were assured of the objective obtaining [*Geltung*] of a state-of-affairs and gave that obtaining expression *as* objective, in the form of the declarative sentence. The state-of-affairs itself is what it is, whether we assert its obtaining or not. It is a unity obtaining in itself [*Geltungseinheit an sich*]. But its obtaining appeared to us; and we declared its obtaining as objective, as it appeared to us. We said: This is how things are. Naturally we could not have done this, we could not have made the statement, if the obtaining of the state-of-affairs had not appeared to us—in other words, if we had not judged. Accordingly our judging is involved in the statement as a psychological fact; it belongs to what is made known. But only to what is made known. For, whereas what is made known consists in psychic states and processes, what is stated in the statement is nothing subjective at all. My act of judgment is a fleeting subjective process; it comes into being and ceases. But what the statement states—this content, *that the three altitudes of a triangle intersect in just one point* —is not something that comes into being and ceases. As often as this same statement is uttered in the same sense by me or by anyone, there is a new judging. The acts of judgment are different from case to case. But *what* they judge, *what* the statement says, is the same throughout. It is something identical, in the strict sense of the word; it is one and the same geometrical truth.

So it is with all statements, even if what they say is false, even if what they say is absurd. Likewise in such cases we distinguish, from the fleeting subjective processes of regarding as true and stating, their ideal content: the statement's signification, as the unity in the multiplicity. As something evidently identical pertaining to the intention, it is also recognized by us at different times in acts of reflection: We do not put it into the statements arbitrarily; on the contrary, we find it in them.

If "possibility" or "truth" is lacking, then of course the intention of the statement can be carried out "only symbolically"; it cannot draw from intuition and categorial functions exercisable in the basis of intuition the fullness in which its cognition-value would consist. In that case, as is usually said, it lacks "true" or "proper" signification. Later we shall have to explore with greater precision this difference between intentive and fulfilling signification. To characterize the different acts in which these correlative ideal unities are constituted, and to clarify the essence of their actual "coincidence" in cognition, will require difficult and comprehensive investigations. This however is certain: Whether a given statement functions cognitionally [*in Erkenntnisfunktion steht*] or not (that is to say, whether or not it fulfils or ever can fulfil its intention in corresponding intuitions and categorial acts that give them form), every statement has it meaning [*Meinung*]; and in its meaning, as its unitary specific character, the signification [*Bedeutung*] is constituted.

This ideal unity, furthermore, is what someone has his eye on, when he designates as the signification of "the" declarative sentence "the" judgment; but the fundamental equivocality of this word judgment usually drives him forthwith into confounding the insightfully grasped ideal unity with the real act of judgment—that is to say, into confounding what the statement says with what it makes known.

Our demonstration for the case of complete statements is easily extended to actual or possible parts of statements. In case I judge, "If the sum of the angles in any particular triangle is not equal to two right angles, the parallel postulate is false," the hypothetical antecedent clause is not a statement: after all, I am not asserting that there is any such inequality. Yet it too "says" something; and, once more, what the clause "says" is completely different from what it makes known. What it says is not my psychic act of hypothetical presupposing; though naturally I must have performed this act if I can to speak truthfully, as I do. But while this subjective act is being made known, something objective and ideal is becoming expressed, namely *the* hypothesis with its conceptual constituents—which can present itself as the same intentional unity in many possible subjective thinking processes and which, in the objective-ideal considering that characterizes all thinking, stands before us evidently as one and the same.

The like is true of the other parts of statements, including parts that do not have the form of clauses.

Carl G. Hempel

Problems and Changes in the Empiricist Criterion of Meaning *

1. INTRODUCTION

The fundamental tenet of modern empiricism is the view that all non-analytic knowledge is based on experience. Let us call this thesis the principle of empiricism. Contemporary logical empiricism has added to it the maxim that a sentence makes a cognitively meaningful assertion, and thus can be said to be either true or false, only if it is either (1) analytic or self-contradictory or (2) capable, at least in principle, of experiential test. According to this so-called *empiricist criterion of cognitive meaning, or of cognitive significance,* many of the formulations of traditional metaphysics and large parts of epistemology are devoid of cognitive significance—however rich some of them may be in non-cognitive import by virtue of their emotive appeal or the moral inspiration they offer. Similarly certain doctrines which have been, at one time or another, formulated within empirical science or its border disciplines are so contrived as to be incapable of test by any conceivable evidence; they are therefore qualified as pseudo-hypotheses, which assert nothing, and which therefore have no explanatory or predictive force whatever. This verdict applies, for example, to the neo-vitalist speculations about entelechies or vital forces, and to the "telefinalist hypothesis" propounded by Lecomte du Noüy.

The preceding formulations of the principle of empiricism and of the empiricist meaning criterion provide no more, however, than a general and rather vague characterization of a basic point of view, and they need therefore to be elucidated and amplified. And while in the earlier phases

* From "Problems and Changes in the Empiricist Criterion of Meaning" by Carl G. Hempel, in *Revue Internationale de Philosophie,* 4th Year, January 15, 1950, pp. 41–63. Reprinted by permission of the editor.

Note: Footnotes are here omitted.

of its development, logical empiricism was to a large extent preoccupied with a critique of philosophic and scientific formulations by means of those fundamental principles, there has been in recent years an increasing concern with the positive tasks of analyzing in detail the logic and methodology of empirical science and of clarifying and restating the basic ideas of empiricism in the light of the insights thus obtained. In the present article, I propose to discuss some of the problems this search has raised and some of the results it seems to have established.

2. CHANGES IN THE TESTABILITY CRITERION OF EMPIRICAL MEANING

As our formulation shows, the empiricist meaning criterion lays down the requirement of experiential testability for those among the cognitively meaningful sentences which are neither analytic nor contradictory; let us call them sentences with empirical meaning, or empirical significance. The concept of testability, which is to render precise the vague notion of being based—or rather baseable—on experience, has undergone several modifications which reflect an increasingly refined analysis of the structure of empirical knowledge. In the present section, let us examine the major stages of this development.

For convenience of exposition, we first introduce three auxiliary concepts, namely those of observable characteristic, of observation predicate, and of observation sentence. A property or a relation of physical objects will be called an *observable characteristic* if, under suitable circumstances, its presence or absence in a given instance can be ascertained through direct observation. Thus, the terms "green", "soft", "liquid", "longer than", designate observable characteristics, while "bivalent", "radioactive", "better electric conductor", and "introvert" do not. Terms which designate observable characteristics will be called *observation predicates*. Finally, by an *observation sentence* we shall understand any sentence which—correctly or incorrectly—asserts of one or more specifically named objects that they have, or that they lack, some specified observable characteristic. The following sentences, for example, meet this condition: "The Eiffel Tower is taller than the buildings in its vicinity", "The pointer of this instrument does not cover the point marked '3' on the scale", and even, "The largest dinosaur on exhibit in New York's Museum of Natural History had a blue tongue"; for this last sentence assigns to a specified object a characteristic—having a blue tongue—which is of such a kind that under suitable circumstances (e.g., in the case of my Chow dog) its presence or absence can be ascertained by direct observation. Our concept of observation sentence is intended to provide a precise interpretation of the vague idea of a sentence asserting something that is "in principle" ascertainable by direct observation, even though it may happen to be actually incapable of being observed by myself, perhaps also by my contemporaries, and possibly even by any human being who ever lived or will live. Any evidence that might be adduced in the test of an empirical hypothesis may now be thought of as being expressed in observation sentences of this kind.

We now turn to the changes in the conception of testability, and thus of empirical meaning. In the early days of the Vienna Circle, a sentence was said to have empirical meaning if it was capable, at least in principle, of complete verification by observational evidence; i.e., if observational evidence could be described which, if actually obtained, would conclusively establish the truth of the sentence. With the help of the concept of observation sentence, we can restate this requirement as follows: A sentence S has empirical meaning if and only if it is possible to indicate a finite set of observation sentences, O_1, O_2, . . ., O_n, such that if these are true, then S is necessarily true, too. As stated, however, this condition is satisfied also if S is an analytic sentence or if the given observation sentences are logically incompatible with each other. By the following formulation, we rule these cases out and at the same time express the intended criterion more precisely:

(2.1) *Requirement of complete verifiability in principle:*

A sentence has empirical meaning if and only if it is not analytic and follows logically from some finite and logically consistent class of observation sentences.

This criterion, however, has several serious defects. The first of those here to be mentioned has been pointed out by various writers:

(*a*) The verifiability requirement rules out all sentences of universal form and thus all statements purporting to express general laws; for these cannot be conclusively verified by any finite set of observational data. And since sentences of this type constitute an integral part of scientific theories, the verifiability requirement must be regarded as overly restrictive in this respect. Similarly, the criterion disqualifies all sentences such as "For any substance there exists some solvent", which contain both universal and existential quantifiers (i.e., occurrences of the terms "all" and "some" or their equivalents); for no sentences of this kind can be logically deduced from any finite set of observation sentences.

Two further defects of the verifiability requirement do not seem to have been widely noticed:

(*b*) Suppose that S is a sentence which satisfies the proposed criterion, whereas N is a sentence such as "The absolute is perfect", to which the criterion attributes no empirical meaning. Then the alternation SvN (i.e., the expression obtained by connecting the two sentences by the word "or"), likewise satisfies the criterion; for if S is a consequence of some finite class of observation sentences, then trivially SvN is a consequence of the same class. But clearly, the empiricist criterion of meaning is not intended to countenance sentences of this sort. In this respect, therefore, the requirement of complete verifiability is too inclusive.

(*c*) Let "P" be an observation predicate. Then the purely existential sentence "(E*x*)P(*x*)" ("There exists at least one thing that has the property P") is completely verifiable, for it follows from any observation sentence asserting of some particular object that it has the property P. But its denial, being equivalent to the universal sentence "(*x*) ~ P(*x*)" ("Nothing has the property P") is clearly not completely verifiable, as follows from comment (*a*) above. Hence, under the criterion (2.1), the denials of certain empirically—and thus cognitively—significant sentences are empirically meaningless; and as they are neither analytic nor contradictory, they are cognitively meaningless. But however we may delimit the domain of significant discourse, we shall have to insist that if a sentence falls within that domain, then so must its denial. To put the mattter more explicitly: The sentences to be qualified as cognitively meaningful are precisely those which can be significantly said to be either true or false. But then, adherence to (2.1) would engender a serious dilemma, as is shown by the consequence just mentioned: We would either have to give up the fundamental logical principle that if a sentence is true or false, then its denial is false or true, respectively (and thus cognitively significant); or else, we must deny, in a manner reminiscent of the intuitionistic conception of logic and mathematics, that "(*x*) ~ P(*x*)" is logically equivalent to the negation of "(E*x*) P (*x*)". Clearly, the criterion (2.1), which has disqualified itself on several other counts, does not warrant such drastic measures for its preservation; hence, it has to be abandoned.

Strictly analogous considerations apply to an alternative criterion, which makes complete falsifiability in principle the defining characteristic of empirical significance. Let us formulate this criterion as follows: A sentence has empirical meaning if and only if it is capable, in principle, of complete refutation by a finite number of observational data; or, more precisely:

(2.2) *Requirement of complete falsifiability in principle:*
A sentence has empirical meaning if and only if its denial is not analytic and follows logically from some finite logically consistent class of observation sentences.

This criterion qualifies a sentence as empirically meaningful if its denial satisfies the requirement of complete verifiability; as is to be expected, it is therefore inadequate on similar grounds as the latter:

(*a*) It rules out purely existential hypotheses, such as "There exists at least one unicorn", and all sentences whose formulation calls for mixed —i.e., universal and existential—quantification; for none of these can possibly be conclusively falsified by a finite number of observation sentences.

(*b*) If a sentence S is completely falsifiable whereas N is a sentence which is not, then their conjunction, S.N (i.e., the expression obtained by connecting the two sentences by the word "and") is completely falsifiable; for if the denial of S is entailed by some class of observation sentences, then the denial of S.N is, *a fortiori,* entailed by the same class. Thus, the criterion allows empirical significance to many sentences which an adequate empiricist criterion should rule out, such as, say "All swans are white and the absolute is perfect."

(*c*) If "P" is an observation predicate, then the assertion that all things have the property P is qualified as significant, but its denial, being equivalent to a purely existential hypothesis, is disqualified (cf. (*a*)). Hence, criterion (2.2) gives rise to the same dilemma as (2.1).

In sum, then, interpretations of the testability criterion in terms of complete verifiability or of complete falsifiability are inadequate because they are overly restrictive in one direction and overly inclusive in another, and because both of them require incisive changes in the fundamental principles of logic.

Several attempts have been made to avoid these difficulties by construing the testability criterion as demanding merely a partial and possibly indirect confirmability of empirical hypotheses by observational evidence.

(2.3) A formulation suggested by Ayer is characteristic of these attempts to set up a clear and sufficiently comprehensive criterion of confirmability. It states, in effect, that a sentence S has empirical import if from S in conjunction with suitable subsidiary hypotheses it is possible to derive observation sentences which are not derivable from the subsidiary hypotheses alone.

This condition is suggested by a closer consideration of the logical structure of scientific testing; but it is much too liberal as it stands. Indeed, as Ayer himself has pointed out in the second edition of his book, *Language, Truth, and Logic,* his criterion allows empirical import to any sentence whatever. Thus, e.g., if S is the sentence "The absolute is perfect", it suffices to choose as a subsidiary hypothesis the sentence "If the absolute is perfect then this apple is red" in order to make possible the deduction of the observation sentence "This apple is red," which clearly does not follow from the subsidiary hypothesis alone.

(2.4) To meet this objection, Ayer has recently proposed a modified version of his testability criterion. The modification restricts, in effect, the subsidiary hypotheses mentioned in (2.3) to sentences which are either analytic or can independently be shown to be testable in the sense of the modified criterion.

But it can readily be shown that this new criterion, like the requirement of complete falsifiability, allows empirical significance to any conjunction S.N, where S satisfies Ayer's criterion while N is a sentence such as "The absolute is perfect," which is to be disqualified by that criterion. Indeed: whatever consequences can be deduced from S with the help of permissible subsidiary hypotheses can also be deduced from S.N by means of the same subsidiary hypotheses, and as Ayer's new criterion is formulated essentially in terms of the deducibility of a certain type of consequence from the given sentence, it countenances S.N together with S. Another difficulty has been pointed out by Professor A. Church, who has shown that if there are any three observation sentences none of which alone entails any of the others, then it follows for any sentence S whatsoever that either it or its denial has empirical import according to Ayer's revised criterion.

3. TRANSLATABILITY INTO AN EMPIRICIST LANGUAGE AS A NEW CRITERION OF COGNITIVE MEANING

I think it is useless to continue the search for an adequate criterion of testability in terms of deductive relationships to observation sentences. The past development of this search—of which we have considered the major stages—seems to warrant the expectation that as long as we try to set up a criterion of testability for individual sentences in a natural language, in terms of logical relationship to observation sentences, the result will be either too restrictive or too inclusive, or both. In particular it appears likely that such criteria would allow empirical import, in the manner of (2.1) (*b*) or of (2.2) (*b*), either to any alternation or to any conjunction of two sentences of which at least one is qualified as empirically meaningful; and this peculiarity has undesirable consequences because the liberal grammatical rules of English as of any other natural language countenance as sentences certain expressions ("The absolute is perfect" was our illustration) which even by the most liberal empiricist standards make no assertion whatever; and these would then have to be permitted as components of empirically significant statements.

The predicament would not arise, of course, in an artificial language whose vocabulary and grammar were so chosen as to preclude altogether the possibility of forming sentences of any kind which the empiricist meaning criterion is intended to rule out. Let us call any such language an *empiricist language*. This reflection suggests an entirely different approach to our problem: Give a general characterization of the kind of language that would qualify as empiricist, and then lay down the following:

(3.1) *Translatability criterion of cognitive meaning:*

A sentence has cognitive meaning if and only if it is translatable into an empiricist language.

This conception of cognitive import, while perhaps not explicitly stated, seems to underlie much of the more recent work done by empiricist writers; as far as I can see it has its origin in Carnap's essay, *Testability and Meaning* (especially part IV).

As any language, so also any empiricist language can be characterized by indicating its vocabulary and the rules determining its logic; the latter include the syntactical rules according to which sentences may be formed by means of the given vocabulary. In effect, therefore, the translatability criterion proposes to characterize the cognitively meaningful sentences by the vocabulary out of which they may be constructed, and by the syntactical principles governing their construction. What sentences are singled out as cognitively significant will depend, accordingly, on the choice of the vocabulary and of the construction rules. Let us consider a specific possibility:

(3.2) We might qualify a language L as empiricist if it satisfies the following conditions:

(a) *The vocabulary of L* contains:

(1) The customary locutions of logic which are used in the formulation of sentences; including in particular the expressions "not", "and",

"or", "if . . . then . . .", "all", "some", "the class of all things such that . . .", ". . . is an element of class . . .";

(2) Certain *observation predicates.* These will be said to constitute the basic empirical vocabulary of L;

(3) Any expression definable by means of those referred to under (1) and (2).

(b) *The rules of sentence formation for L* are those laid down in some contemporary logical system such as *Principia Mathematica.*

Since all defined terms can be eliminated in favor of primitives, these rules stipulate in effect that a language L is empiricist if all its sentences are expressible, with the help of the usual logical locutions, in terms of observable characteristics of physical objects. Let us call any language of this sort a thing-language in the narrower sense. Alternatively, the basic empirical vocabulary of an empiricist language might be construed as consisting of phenomenalistic terms, each of them referring to some aspect of the phenomena of perception or sensation. The construction of adequate phenomenalistic languages, however, presents considerable difficulties, and in recent empiricism, attention has been focussed primarily on the potentialities of languages whose basic empirical vocabulary consists of observation predicates; for the latter lend themselves more directly to the description of that type of intersubjective evidence which is invoked in the test of scientific hypotheses.

If we construe empiricist languages in the sense of (3.2), then the translatability criterion (3.1) avoids all of the shortcomings pointed out in our discussion of earlier forms of the testability criterion:

(*a*) Our characterization of empiricist languages makes explicit provision for universal and existential quantification, i.e., for the use of the terms "all" and "some"; hence, no type of quantified statement is generally excluded from the realm of cognitively significant discourse;

(*b*) Sentences such as "The absolute is perfect" cannot be formulated in an empiricist language (cf. (*d*) below); hence there is no danger that a conjunction or alternation containing a sentence of that kind as a component might be qualified as cognitively significant;

(*c*) In a language L with syntactical rules conforming to *Principia Mathematica,* the denial of a sentence is always again a sentence of L. Hence, the translatability criterion does not lead to the consequence, which is entailed by both (2.1) and (2.2), that the denials of certain significant sentences are non-significant;

(*d*) Despite its comprehensiveness, the new criterion does not attribute cognitive meaning to *all* sentences; thus, e.g., the sentences "The absolute is perfect" and "Nothingness nothings" cannot be translated into an empiricist language because their key terms are not definable by means of purely logical expressions and observation terms.

4. THE PROBLEM OF DISPOSITION TERMS AND OF THEORETICAL CONSTRUCTS

Yet, the new criterion is still too restrictive—as are, incidentally, also its predecessors—in an important respect which now calls for consideration. If empiricist languages are defined in accordance with (3.2), then, as was noted above, the translatability criterion (3.1) allows cognitive import to a sentence only if its constitutive empirical terms are explicitly definable by means of observation predicates. But as we shall argue presently, many terms even of the physical sciences are not so definable; hence the criterion would oblige us to reject, as devoid of cognitive import, all scientific hypotheses containing such terms—an altogether intolerable consequence.

The concept of temperature is a case in point. At first glance, it seems as though the phrase "Object x has a temperature of c degrees centigrade", or briefly "$T(x) = c$" could be defined by the following sentence, (D): $T(x) = c$ if and only if the following condition is satisfied: If a thermometer is in contact with x, then it registers c degrees on its scale.

Disregarding niceties, it may be granted that the definiens given here is formulated entirely in reference to observables. However, it has one highly questional aspect: In *Principia Mathematica* and similar systems, the phrase "if p then q" is construed as being synonymous with "not p or q"; and under this so-called material interpretation of the conditional, a statement of the form "if p then q" is obviously true if (though not only if) the sentence standing in the place of "p" is false. If, therefore, the meaning of "if . . . then . . ." in the definiens of (D) is understood in the material sense, then that definiens is true if (though not only if) x is an object not in contact with a thermometer—no matter what numerical value we may give to c. And since the definiendum would be true under the same circumstances, the definition (D) would qualify as true the assignment of any temperature value whatsoever to any object not in contact with a thermometer! Analogous considerations apply to such terms as "electrically charged", "magnetic", "intelligent", "electric resistance", etc., in short to all disposition terms, i.e., terms which express the disposition of one or more objects to react in a determinate way under specified circumstances: A definition of such terms by means of observation predicates cannot be effected in the manner of (D), however natural and obvious a mode of definition this may at first seem to be.

There are two main directions in which a resolution of the difficulty might be sought. On the one hand, it could be argued that the definition of disposition terms in the manner of (D) is perfectly adequate provided that the phrase "if . . . then . . ." in the definiens is construed in the sense it is obviously intended to have, namely as implying, in the case of (D), that even if x is not actually in contact with a thermometer, still if it *were* in such contact, then the thermometer *would* register c degrees. In sentences such as this, the phrase "if . . . then . . ." is said to be used counterfactually; and it is in this "strong" sense, which implies a counterfactual conditional, that the definiens of (D) would have to be construed. This suggestion would provide an answer to the problem of defining disposition terms if it were not for the fact that no entirely satisfactory account of the exact meaning of counterfactual conditionals seems to be available at present. Thus, the first way out of the difficulty has the status of a program rather than that of a solution. The lack of an adequate theory of counterfactual conditionals is all the more deplorable as such a theory is needed also for the analysis of the concept of general law in empirical science and of certain related ideas. A clarification of this cluster of problems constitutes at present one of the urgent desiderata in the logic and methodology of science.

An alternative way of dealing with the definitional problems raised by disposition terms was suggested, and developed in detail, by Carnap. It consists in permitting the introduction of new terms, within an empiricist language, by means of so-called reduction sentences, which have the character of partial or conditional definitions. Thus, e.g., the concept of temperature in our last illustration might be introduced by means of the following reduction sentence, (R): If a thermometer is in contact with an object x, then $T(x) = c$ if and only if the thermometer registers c degrees.

This rule, in which the conditional may be construed in the material sense, specifies the meaning of "temperature", i.e., of statements of the form "$T(x) = c$", only partially, namely in regard to those objects which are in contact with a thermometer; for all other objects, it simply leaves the meaning of "$T(x) = c$" undetermined. The specification of the meaning of "temperature" may then be gradually extended to cases not covered in (R) by laying down further reduction sentences, which reflect the measurement of temperature by devices other than thermometers.

Reduction sentences thus provide a means for the precise formulation of what is commonly referred to as operational definitions. At the same time, they show that the latter are not definitions in the strict sense of the word, but rather partial specifications of meaning.

The preceding considerations suggest that in our characterization (3.2) of empiricist languages we broaden the provision *a* (3) by permitting in the vocabulary of L all those terms whose meaning can be specified in terms of the basic empirical vocabulary by means of definitions or reduction sentences. Languages satisfying this more inclusive criterion will be referred to as thing-languages in the wider sense.

If the concept of empiricist language is broadened in this manner, then the translatability criterion (3.1) covers—as it should—also all those statements whose constituent empirical terms include "empirical constructs", i.e., terms which do not designate observables, but which can be introduced by reduction sentences on the basis of observation predicates.

Even in this generalized version, however, our criterion of cognitive meaning may not do justice to advanced scientific theories, which are formulated in terms of "theoretical constructs", such as the terms "absolute temperature", "gravitational potential", "electric field", "ψ function", etc. There are reasons to think that neither definitions nor reduction sentences are adequate to introduce these terms on the basis of observation predicates. Thus, e.g., if a system of reduction sentences for the concept of electric field were available, then—to oversimplify the point a little—it would be possible to describe, in terms of observable characteristics, some necessary and some sufficient conditions for the presence, in a given region, of an electric field of any mathematical description, however complex. Actually, however, such criteria can best be given only for some sufficiently simple kinds of fields.

Now theories of the advanced type here referred to may be considered as hypothetico-deductive systems in which all statements are logical consequences of a set of fundamental assumptions. Fundamental as well as derived statements in such a system are formulated either in terms of certain theoretical constructs which are not defined within the system and thus play the rôle of primitives, or in terms of expressions defined by means of the latter. Thus, in their logical structure such systems equal the axiomatized uninterpreted systems studied in mathematics and logic. They acquire applicability to empirical subject matter, and thus the status of theories of empirical science, by virtue of an empirical interpretation. The latter is effected by a translation of some of the sentences of the theory—often derived rather than fundamental ones—into an empiricist language, which may contain both observation predicates and empirical constructs.

And since the sentences which are thus given empirical meaning are logical consequences of the fundamental hypotheses of the theory, that translation effects, indirectly, a partial interpretation of the latter and of the constructs in terms of which they are formulated.

In order to make translatability into an empiricist language an adequate criterion of cognitive import, we broaden therefore the concept of empiricist language so as to include thing-languages in the narrower and in the wider sense as well as all interpreted theoretical systems of the kind just referred to. With this understanding, (3.1) may finally serve as a general criterion of cognitive meaning.

5. ON "THE MEANING" OF AN EMPIRICAL STATEMENT

In effect, the criterion thus arrived at qualifies a sentence as cognitively meaningful if its non-logical constituents refer, directly or in certain specified indirect ways, to observables. But it does not make any pronouncement on what "the meaning" of a cognitively significant sentence is, and in particular it neither says nor implies that that meaning can be exhaustively characterized by what the totality of possible tests would reveal in terms of observable phenomena. Indeed, *the content of a statement with empirical import cannot, in general, be exhaustively expressed by means of any class of observation sentences.*

For consider first, among the statements permitted by our criterion, any purely existential hypothesis or any statement involving mixed quantification. As was pointed out earlier, under (2.2) (*a*), statements of these kinds entail no observation sentences whatever; hence their content cannot be expressed by means of a class of observation sentences.

And secondly, even most statements of purely universal form (such as "All flamingoes are pink") entail observation sentences (such as "That thing is pink") only when combined with suitable other observation sentences (such as "That thing is a flamingo").

This last remark can be generalized: The use of empirical hypotheses for the prediction of observable phenomena requires, in practically all cases, the use of subsidiary empirical hypotheses. Thus, e.g., the hypothesis that the agent of tuberculosis is rod-shaped does not by itself entail the consequence that upon looking at a tubercular sputum specimen through a microscope, rod-like shapes will be observed: a large number of subsidiary hypotheses, including the theory of the microscope, have to be used as additional premises in deducing that prediction.

Hence, what is sweepingly referred to as "the (cognitive) meaning" of a given scientific hypothesis cannot be adequately characterized in terms of potential observational evidence alone, nor can it be specified for the hypothesis taken in isolation: In order to understand "the meaning" of a hypothesis within an empiricist language, we have to know not merely what observation sentences it entails alone or in conjunction with subsidiary hypotheses, but also what other, non-observational, empirical sentences are entailed by it, what sentences in the given language would confirm or disconfirm it, and for what other hypotheses the given one would be confirmatory or disconfirmatory. In other words, the cognitive meaning of a statement in an empiricist language is reflected in the totality of its logical relationships to all other statements in that language and not to the observation sentences alone. In this sense, the statements of empirical science have a surplus meaning over and above what can be expressed in terms of relevant observation sentences.

6. THE LOGICAL STATUS OF THE EMPIRICIST CRITERION OF MEANING

What kind of a sentence, it has often been asked, is the empiricist meaning criterion itself? Plainly it is not an empirical hypothesis; but it is not analytic or self-contradictory either; hence, when judged by its own standard, is it not devoid of cognitive meaning? In that case, what claim of soundness or validity could possibly be made for it?

One might think of construing the criterion as a definition which indicates what empiricists propose to understand by a cognitively significant sentence; thus understood, it would not have the character of an assertion and would be neither true nor false. But this conception would attribute to the criterion a measure of arbitrariness which cannot be reconciled with the heated controversies it has engendered and even less with the fact, repeatedly illustrated in the present article, that the changes in its specific content have always been determined by the objective of making the criterion a more adequate index of cognitive import. And this very objective illuminates the character of the empiricist criterion of meaning: It is intended to provide a clarification and *explication* of the idea of a sentence which makes an intelligible assertion. This idea is admittedly vague, and it is the task of philosophic explication to replace it by a more precise concept. In view of this difference of precision we cannot demand, of course, that the "new" concept, the explicatum, be strictly synonymous with the old one, the explicandum. How, then, are we to judge the adequacy of a proposed explication, as expressed in some specific criterion of cognitive meaning?

First of all, there exists a large class of sentences which are rather generally recognized as making intelligible assertions, and another large class of which this is more or less generally denied. We shall have to demand of an adequate explication that it take into account these spheres of common usage; hence an explication which, let us say, denies cognitive import to descriptions of past events or to generalizations expressed in terms of observables has to be rejected as inadequate. As we have seen, this first requirement of adequacy has played an important rôle in the development of the empiricist meaning criterion.

But an adequate explication of the concept of cognitively significant statement must satisfy yet another, even more important, requirement: Together with the explication of certain other concepts, such as those of confirmation and of probability, it has to provide the framework for a general theoretical account of the structure and the foundations of scientific knowledge. Explication, as here understood, is not a mere description of the accepted usages of the terms under consideration: it has to go beyond the limitations, ambiguities, and inconsistencies of common usage and has to show how we had better construe the meanings of those terms if we wish to arrive at a consistent and comprehensive theory of knowledge. This type of consideration, which has been largely influenced by a study of the structure of scientific theories, has prompted the more recent extensions of the empiricist meaning criterion. These extensions are designed to include in the realm of cognitive significance various types of sentences which might occur in advanced scientific theories, or which have to be admitted simply for the sake of systematic simplicity and uniformity, but on whose cognitive significance or non-significance a study of what the term "intelligible assertion" means in everyday discourse could hardly shed any light at all.

As a consequence, the empiricist criterion of meaning, like the result of any other explication, represents a linguistic proposal which itself is neither true nor false, but for which adequacy is claimed in two respects: First in the sense that the explication provides a reasonably close *analysis* of the commonly accepted meaning of the explicandum—and this claim implies an empirical assertion; and secondly in the sense that the explication achieves a *"rational reconstruction"* of the explicandum, i.e., that it provides, together perhaps with other explications, a general conceptual framework which permits a consistent and precise restatement and theoretical systematization of the contexts in which the explicandum is used—and this claim implies at least an assertion of a logical character.

Though a proposal in form, the empiricist criterion of meaning is therefore far from being an arbitrary definition; it is subject to revision if a violation of the requirements of adequacy, or even a way of satisfying those requirements more fully, should be discovered. Indeed, it is to be hoped that before long some of the open problems encountered in the analysis of cognitive significance will be clarified and that then our last version of the empiricist meaning criterion will be replaced by another, more adequate one.

Friedrich Waismann

How I See Philosophy *

I

. . . From Plato to Schopenhauer philosophers are agreed that the source of their philosophizing is wonder. What gives rise to it is nothing recondite and rare but precisely those things which stare us in the face: memory, motion, general ideas. (Plato: What does 'horse' mean? A single particular horse? No, for it may refer to *any* horse; *all* the horses, the total class? No, for we may speak of this or that horse. But if it means neither a single horse nor all horses, what *does* it mean?) The idealist is shaken in just the same way when he comes to reflect that he has, in Schopenhauer's words, 'no knowledge of the sun but only of an eye that sees a sun, and no knowledge of the earth but only of a hand that feels an earth'. Can it be, then, that nothing whatever is known to us except our own consciousness?

In looking at such questions, it seems as if the mind's eye were growing dim and as if everything, even that which ought to be absolutely clear, was becoming oddly puzzling and unlike its usual self. To bring out what seems to be peculiar to these questions one might say that they are not so much questions as tokens of a profound uneasiness of mind. Try for a moment to put yourself into the frame of mind of which Augustine was possessed when he asked: How is it possible to measure time? Time consists of past, present and future. The past can't be measured, it is gone; the future can't be measured, it is not yet here; and the present can't be measured, it has no extension. Augustine knew of course how time is measured and this was not his concern. What puzzled him was how it is *possible* to measure time, seeing that the past hour cannot be lifted out and placed alongside the present hour for comparison. Or look at it this way: what is measured is in the past, the measuring in the present: how can that be?

* From "How I See Philosophy" by Friedrich Waismann, in *Contemporary British Philosophy,* Third Series, edited by H. D. Lewis. New York: The Macmillan Company, 1956, London: George Allen & Unwin, Ltd., pp. 449–458, 461–467. Reprinted by permission of The Macmillan Company and George Allen and Unwin, Ltd.

The philosopher as he ponders over some such problem has the appearance of a man who is deeply disquieted. He seems to be straining to grasp something which is beyond his powers. The words in which such a question presents itself do not quite bring out into the open the real point—which may, perhaps more aptly, be described as the recoil from the incomprehensible. If, on a straight railway journey, you suddenly come in sight of the very station you have just left behind, there will be terror, accompanied perhaps by slight giddiness. That is exactly how the philosopher feels when he says to himself, 'Of course time can be measured; but how *can* it?' It is as though, up to now, he had been passing heedlessly over the difficulties, and now, all of a sudden, he notices them and asks himself in alarm, 'But how can that be?' That is a sort of question which we only ask when it is the very facts themselves which confound us, when something about them strikes us as preposterous.

Kant, I fancy, must have felt something of the sort when he suddenly found the existence of geometry a puzzle. Here we have propositions as clear and transparent as one would wish, prior, it seems, to all experience; at the same time they apply miraculously to the real world. How is that possible? Can the mind, unaided by experience, in some dark manner actually fathom the properties of real things? Looked upon in this way, geometry takes on a disturbing air.

We all have our moments when something quite ordinary suddenly strikes us as queer—for instance, when time appears to us as a curious thing. Not that we are often in this frame of mind; but on some occasions, when we look at things in a certain way, unexpectedly they seem to change as though by magic: they stare at us with a puzzling expression, and we begin to wonder whether they can possibly be the things we have known all our lives.

'Time flows' we say—a natural and innocent expression, and yet one pregnant with danger. It flows 'equably', in Newton's phrase, at an even rate. What can this mean? When something moves, it moves with a definite speed (and speed means: rate of change in time). To ask with what speed time moves, i.e. to ask how quickly time changes in time, is to ask the unaskable. It also flows, again in Newton's phrase, 'without relation to anything external'. How are we to figure that? Does time flow on irrespective of what happens in the world? Would it flow on even if everything in heaven and on earth came to a sudden standstill as Schopenhauer believed? For if this were not so, he said, time would have to stop with the stopping of the clock and move with the clock's movement. How odd: time flows at the same rate and yet without speed; and perhaps even without anything to occur in it? The expression is puzzling in another way. 'I can never catch myself being in the past or in the future', someone might say; 'whenever I think or perceive or breathe the word "now", I am in the present; therefore I am *always* in the present.' In saying this, he may think of the present moment as a bridge as it were from which he is looking down at the 'river of time'. Time is gliding along underneath the bridge, but the 'now' does not take part in the motion. What was future passes into the present (is just below the bridge) and then into the past, while the onlooker, the 'self' or the 'I', is always in the present. 'Time flows *through* the "now" ', he may feel to be a quite expressive metaphor. Yes, it sounds all right—until he suddenly comes to his senses and, with a start, realizes, 'But surely the moment flies?' (Query: How to succeed in wasting time? Answer: In this way, for instance—by trying, with eyes closed or staring vacantly in front of oneself, to catch the present moment as it is flitting by.) He may come now to look at matters in a different way. He sees himself advancing through time towards the future, and with this goes a suggestion of being active, just as at other times he may see himself floating down the stream whether he likes it or not. 'What exactly is it that is moving—the events in time or the present moment?', he may wonder. In the first case, it looks to him as if time were moving while he stands still; in the second case as if he were moving through time. 'How exactly is it', he may say in a dubious voice, 'am I always in the present? Is the present always eluding me?' Both ring true in a way; but they contradict each other? Again, does it make sense to ask, 'At what time is the present moment?' Yes, no doubt; but how *can* it, if the 'now' is but the fixed point from which the dating of any event ultimately receives its sense?

So he is pulled to and fro: 'I am always in the present, yet it slips through my fingers; I am going forward in time—no, I am carried down the stream.' He is using different pictures, each in its way quite appropriate to the occasion; yet when he tries to apply them jointly they clash. 'What a queer thing time must be', he may say to himself with a puzzled look on his face, 'what after all *is* time?'—expecting, half-expecting perhaps, that the answer will reveal to him time's hidden essence. Ranged beyond the intellectual are deeper levels of uneasiness—terror of the inevitability of time's passage, with all the reflections upon life that this forces upon us. Now all these anxious doubts release themselves in the question, 'What is time?' (*En passant* this is a hint that *one* answer will never do—will never remove all these doubts that break out afresh on different levels and yet are expressed in the same form of words.)

As we all know what time is and yet cannot say what it is it feels mystifying; and precisely because of its elusiveness it catches our imagination. The more we look at it the more we are puzzled: it seems charged with paradoxes. 'What is time? What is this being made up of movement only without anything that is moving?' (Schopenhauer). How funny to have it bottled up! 'I've got here in my hand the most potent, the most enigmatic, the most fleeting of all essences—Time.' (Logan Pearsall Smith of an hour-glass.) For Shelley it is an 'unfathomable sea! whose waves are years', a 'shoreless flood', for Proust—well, why not leave something to the reader?

But isn't the answer to this that what mystifies us lies in the *noun* form 'the time'? Having a notion embodied in the form of a noun almost irresistibly makes us turn round to look for what it is 'the name of'. We are trying to catch the shadows cast by the opacities of speech. A wrong analogy absorbed into the forms of our language produces mental discomfort; (and the feeling of discomfort, when it refers to language, is a profound one). 'All sounds, all colours . . . evoke indefinite and yet precise emotions, or, as I prefer to think, call down among us certain disembodied powers whose footsteps over our hearts we call emotions' (W. B. Yeats).

Yet the answer is a prosaic one: don't ask what time is but how the *word* 'time' is being used. Easier said than done; for if the philosopher rectifies the use of language, ordinary language has 'the advantage of being in possession of declensions', to speak with Lichtenberg, and thus renews its spell over him, luring him on into the shadow chase. It is perhaps only when we turn to languages of a widely different grammatical structure that the way towards such possibilities of interpretation is entirely barred. 'It is highly probable that philosophers within the domain of the Ural-Altaic languages (where the subject-concept is least developed) will look differently "into the world" and be found on paths of thought different from those of the Indo-Europeans or Mussulman's (Nietzsche).

II

It may be well at this point to remind ourselves that the words 'question' and 'answer', 'problem' and 'solution' are not always used in their most trite sense. It is quite obvious that we often have to do something very different to find the way out of a difficulty. A problem of politics is solved by adopting a certain line of action, the problems of novelists perhaps by the invention of devices for presenting the inmost thoughts and feelings of their characters; there is the painter's problem of how to suggest depth or movement on the canvas, the stylistic problem of expressing things not yet current, not yet turned into cliché; there are a thousand questions of technology which are answered, not by the discovery of some truth, but by a practical achievement; and there is of course the 'social question'. In philosophy, the real problem is not to find the answer to a given question but to find a sense for it.

To see in what the 'solution' of such a 'problem' consists let us start with Achilles who, according to Zeno, is to this day chasing the tortoise. Suppose that Achilles runs twice as fast as the tortoise. If the tortoise's start is 1, Achilles will have to cover successively 1, ½, ¼, ⅛, . . .; this series is endless: so he can never catch the tortoise. 'Nonsense!' (a mathematician's voice), 'the sum of the infinite series is finite, namely 2, and that settles it.' Though perfectly true, his remark is not to the point. It does not remove the sting from the puzzle, the disconcerting idea, namely, that however far we go in the series there is always a next term, that the lead the tortoise has in the race, though naturally getting smaller and smaller, yet never ceases to be: there *can* be no moment when it is strictly zero. It is *this* feature of the case, I suggest, that we do not understand and which throws us into a state of confusion.

But look at it this way. Suppose that we apply the same sort of argument to a minute, then we shall have to argue in some such way as this. Before the minute can be over the first half of it must elapse, then one-quarter of it, then one-eighth of it, and so on *ad infinitum*. This being an endless process, the minute can never come to an end. Immediately we have the argument in this form, the blunder leaps to the eye: we have been confusing two senses of 'never', a temporal and a non-temporal one. While it is quite correct to say that the sequence 1, ½, ¼, ⅛, . . . never ends, this sense of the word 'never' has nothing whatever to do with time. All it means is that there is no last term in the series, or (what comes to the same) that to any term, no matter how far out in the sequence, a successor can be constructed according to the simple rule 'halve it': that is meant here by 'never'; whereas in saying, for instance, that man will never find out anything to avert death, 'never' is meant in the sense 'at no time'. It is clear that the mathematical assertion concerning the possibility of going on in the sequence by forming new terms according to the rule does not state anything about actual occurrences in time. The mistake should really be obvious: in saying that, since the start is getting progressively smaller and yet can never cease to be, Achilles can never catch the tortoise, we jump from the mathematical, *non*-temporal to the temporal sense. Had there been two different words in our language to mark these senses the confusion could never have arisen, and the world would be poorer for one of its most attractive paradoxes. But the same word is as a matter of course used with different meanings. Result: something like a conjuring trick. While our attention is diverted, while, 'in our mind's eye', we stare fixedly at Achilles as he is speeding along, with each big bound diminishing his distance from the tortoise, the one sense is so innocuously palmed off for the other as to escape notice.

This way of bringing out the fallacy also holds when the other key term is used for presenting the puzzle. As there will 'always' be a next term in the sequence, i.e. a next step in the scheme of subdividing the race-course (the word 'always' looking just as spotless and innocent) we readily fall into the trap of concluding that the tortoise will 'always' be ahead of Achilles, eternally to be chased by his pursuer.

Many are the types of bewilderment: there is the obsessional doubt—can I ever know that other people have experiences, that they see, hear and feel as I do? Can I be sure that memory does not always deceive me? Are there really material objects and not only sense-impressions 'of' them'? There is the doubtlike uneasiness—what sort of being is possessed by numbers? There is the anxiety-doubt—are we really free? This doubt has taken many different forms one of which I shall single out for discussion—the question, namely, whether the law of excluded middle, when it refers to statements in the future tense, forces us into a sort of logical Predestination. A typical argument is this. If it is true now that I shall do a certain thing tomorrow, say, jump into the Thames, then no matter how fiercely I resist, strike out with hands and feet like a madman, when the day comes I cannot help jumping into the water; whereas, if this prediction is false now, then whatever efforts I may make, however many times I may nerve and brace myself, look down at the water and say to myself, 'One, two, three—', it is impossible for me to spring. Yet that the prediction is either true or false is itself a necessary truth, asserted by the law of excluded middle. From this the startling consequence seems to follow that it is already now decided what I shall do tomorrow, that indeed the entire future is somehow fixed, logically preordained. Whatever I do and whichever way I decide, I am merely moving along lines clearly marked in advance which lead me towards my appointed lot. We are all, in fact, marionettes. If we are not prepared to swallow *that,* then—and there is a glimmer of hope in the 'then'—there is an alternative open to us. We need only renounce the law of excluded middle for statements of this kind, and with it the validity of ordinary logic, and all will be well. Descriptions of what will happen are, at present, neither true nor false. (This sort of argument was actually propounded by Łukasiewicz in favour of a three-valued logic with 'possible' as a third truth-value alongside 'true' and 'false'.)

The way out is clear enough. The asker of the question has fallen into the error of so many philosophers: of giving an answer before stopping to consider the question. For is he clear what he is asking? He seems to suppose that a statement referring to an event in the future is at present undecided, neither true nor false, but that when the event happens the proposition enters into a sort of new state, that of being true. But how are we to figure the change from 'undecided' to 'true'? Is it sudden or gradual? At what moment does the statement 'it will rain tomorrow' begin to be true? When the first drop falls to the ground? And supposing that it will not rain, when will the statement begin to be false? Just at the end of the day, at 12 P.M. sharp? Supposing that the event *has* happened, that the statement *is* true, will it remain so for ever? If so, in what way? Does it remain uninterruptedly true, at every moment of day and night? Even if there were no one about to give it any thought? Or is it true only at the moments when it is being thought of? In that case, how long does it remain true? For the duration of the thought? We wouldn't know how to answer these question; this is due not to any particular ignorance or stupidity on our part but to the fact that something has gone wrong with the way the words 'true' and 'false' are applied here.

If I say, 'It is true that I was in America', I am saying that I was in America and no more. That in uttering the words 'It is true that—' I take responsibility upon myself is a different matter that does not concern the present argument. The point is that in making a statement prefaced by the words 'It is true that' I do not *add* anything to the factual information I give you. *Saying* that something is true is not *making* it true: cp. the criminal lying in court, yet every time he is telling a lie protesting, his hand on his heart, that he is telling the truth.

What is characteristic of the use of the words 'true' and 'false' and what the pleader of logical determinism has failed to notice is this. 'It is true' and 'it is false', while they certainly have the force of asserting and denying, are not descriptive. Suppose that someone says, 'It is true that the sun will rise tomorrow' all it means is that the sun will rise tomorrow: he is not regaling us with an extra-description of the trueness of what he says. But supposing that he were to say instead, 'It is true *now* that the sun will rise tomorrow', this would boil down to something like 'The sun will rise tomorrow now'; which is nonsense. To ask, as the puzzle-poser does, 'Is it true or false *now* that such-and-such will happen in the future?' is not the sort of question to which an answer can be given: which *is* the answer.

This sheds light on what has, rather solemnly, been termed the 'timelessness of truth'. It lies in this that the clause 'it is true that—' does not allow of inserting a date. To say of a proposition like 'Diamond is pure carbon' that it is true on Christmas Eve would be just as poor a joke as to say that it is true in Paris and not in Timbuctoo. (This does not mean that we cannot say in certain circumstances, 'Yes, it was true in those days' as this can clearly be paraphrased without using the word 'true'.)

Now it begins to look a bit less paradoxical to say that when a philosopher wants to dispose of a question the one thing he must not do is: to give an answer. A philosophic question is not solved: it *dis*solves. And in what does the 'dissolving' consist? In making the meaning of the words used in putting the question so clear to ourselves that we are released from the spell it casts on us. Confusion was removed by calling to mind the use of language or, so far as the use *can* be distilled into rules, the rules: it therefore *was* a confusion about the use of language, or a confusion about rules. It is here that philosophy and grammar meet. . . .

III

What, only criticism and no meat? The philosopher a fog dispeller? If that were all he was capable of I would be sorry for him and leave him to his devices. Fortunately, this is not so. For one thing, a philosophic question, if pursued far enough, may lead to something positive—for instance, to a more profound understanding of language. Take the sceptical doubts as to material objects, other minds, etc. The first reaction is perhaps to say: these doubts are idle. Ordinarily, when I doubt whether I shall finish this article, after a time my doubt comes to an end. I cannot go on doubting for ever. It's the destiny of doubt to die. But the doubts raised by the sceptic never die. Are they doubts? Are they pseudo-questions? They appear so only when judged by the twin standards of common sense and common speech. The real trouble lies deeper: it arises from the sceptic casting doubt on the very facts which underlie the use of language, those permanent features of experience which make concept formation possible, which in fact are precipitated in the use of our most common words. Suppose that you see an object in front of you quite clearly, say, a pipe, and when you are going to pick it up it melts into thin air, then you may feel, 'Lord, I'm going mad' or something of the sort (unless the whole situation is such that you have reason to suspect that it was some clever trick). But what, the sceptic may press now, if such experiences were quite frequent? Would you be prepared to *dis*solve the connection between different sense experiences which form the hard core of our idea of a solid object, to *un*do what language has done—to part with the category of thing-hood? And would you then be living in a phenomenalist's paradise with colour patches and the other paraphernalia of the sense-datum theory, in a disobjected, desubstantialized world? To say in such circumstances, 'Look, it's just tabling now' would be a joke (for even in the weakened verb forms 'tabling', 'chairing' an element of the thing-category lingers on). That is why the sceptic struggles to express himself in a language which is not fit for this purpose. He expresses himself misleadingly when he says that he doubts such-and-such *facts:* his doubts cut so deep that they affect the fabric of language itself. For what he doubts is already embodied in the very forms of speech, e.g. in what is condensed in the use of thing-words. The moment he tries to penetrate those deep-sunken layers, he undermines the language in which he ventilates his qualms—with the result that he seems to be talking nonsense. He is not. But in order to make his doubts fully expressible, language would first have to go into the melting-pot. (We can get a glimmering of what is needed from modern science where all the long-established categories—thinghood, causality, position—had to be revolutionized. This required nothing less than the construction of some new language, not the expression of new facts with the old one.)

If we look at the matter in this way the attitude of the sceptic is seen in a new light. He considers possibilities which lie far outside the domain of our current experience. If his doubts are taken seriously, they turn into observations which cast a new and searching light on the subsoil of language, showing what posibilities are open to our thought (though not to ordinary language), and what paths might have been pursued if the texture of our experience were different from what it is. These problems are not spurious: they make us aware of the vast background in which any current experiences are embedded, and to which language has adapted itself; thus they bring out the unmeasured sum of experience stored up in the use of our words and syntactical forms.

For another thing, a question may decide to go in for another career than dissolving: it may pass into science. Frege, for instance, was prompted to his inquiries by philosophical motives, namely, to find a definite answer to the question about the nature of arithmetical truths—whether they are analytic or synthetic, *a priori* or *a posteriori.* Starting from this question and pursuing it with all possible rigour, he was led to unearth a whole mine of problems of a scientific nature; and proceeding along these lines, he came to fashion a new instrument, a logic, which in delicacy and range and power far surpassed anything that went by this name before, a subject revealing to this day new and unexpected depths. True, the question from which Frege set out was not too clearly defined owing to the imprecise nature of the Kantian terms in which it was expressed.

A whole chapter might be written on the fate of questions, their curious adventures and transformations—how they change into others and in the process remain, and yet do not remain, the same. The original question may split and multiply almost like a character in a dream play. To mention just a few examples: can logic be characterized completely in a formal way, i.e. without bringing in any extraneous ideas such as the use of language and all that goes with it? Can arithmetic be characterized in any such way, entirely 'from within'? Or will any interpretation include some *Erdenrest* of the empiric? These questions have given rise to extensive research on mathematical interpretation of formal systems. The query how far logical intuition is correct has got ramified into a bunch of questions pertaining to the theory of logical types, the axiom of choice, etc., indeed to a far more fundamental issue, namely, whether ordinary logic itself is 'right' as contrasted with the system of inferences evolved by the intuitionists. Or again, are there undecidable questions in mathematics, not in the restricted sense of Gödel, but undecidable in an absolute sense? Are there natural limits to generalization? It is interesting to watch how from a question of this sort, not too precise, somewhat blurred, new and better defined questions detach themselves, the parent question—in Frege's case philosophic *par excellence* —giving rise to a scientist's progeny.

Now something else must be noted—how these questions become, not only precise, but clear (which is not the same thing). To illustrate, can the infinity represented by all natural numbers be compared with the infinity represented by all points in space? That is, can the one be said to be less than, or equal to, the other? When it was first asked, the question had no clear sense—perhaps no sense at all. Yet it guided G. Cantor in his ingenious search. Before set theory was discovered—or should I rather say 'invented'?—the question acted as a sort of signpost pointing vaguely to some so far uncharted region of thought. It is perhaps best characterized by saying that it guides our imagination in a given direction, stimulates research along new lines. Such questions do not 'dissolve': they are solved, only not in the existing system of thought but rather by constructing a new conceptual system—such as set theory—where the intended and faintly anticipated sense finds its full realization. They are therefore of the nature of incitements to the building of such systems, they point from the not-yet-meaningful to the meaningful.

The question is the first groping step of the mind in its journeyings that lead towards new horizons. The genius of the philosopher shows itself nowhere more strikingly than in the new kind of question he brings into the world. What distinguishes him and gives him his place is the passion of questioning. That his questions are at times not so clear is perhaps of not so much moment as one makes of it. There is nothing like clear thinking to protect one from making discoveries. It is all very well to talk of clarity, but when it becomes an obsession it is liable to nip the living thought in the bud. This, I am afraid, is one of the deplorable results of Logical Positivism, not foreseen by its founders, but only too striking in some of its followers. Look at these people, gripped by a clarity neurosis, haunted by fear, tongue-tied, asking themselves continually, 'Oh dear, now does this make perfectly good sense?' Imagine the pioneers of science, Kepler, Newton, the discoverers of non-Euclidean geometry, of field physics, the unconscious, matter waves or heaven knows what, imagine them asking themselves this question at every step—this would have been the surest means of sapping any creative power. No great discoverer has acted in accordance with the motto, 'Everything that can be said can be said clearly'. And some of the greatest discoveries have even emerged from a sort of primordial fog. (Something to be said for the fog. For my part, I've always suspected that clarity is the last refuge of those who have nothing to say.)

The great mind is the great questioner. An example in point is Kant's problem 'How is geometry possible?' The way to its solution was only opened up through the rise of the 'axiomatic method'. Seeing that the axioms of geometry are capable of an indefinite number of different interpretations and that the particular way they may be interpreted is irrelevant to deductive purposes, Hilbert separated what belongs to the logical form of the axioms from what belongs to their intuitional (or other) content and turned the whole question by saying: a point, a straight line, etc., may be anything that satisfies the axioms. As the business of deduction hinges only on the relations in which the basic terms stand to each other and not on the 'content' we associate with them, and as these relations are fully set out in the axioms, the axioms in their totality determine what a 'point', a 'line', etc., is so far as it is sufficient for deductive needs. Through the rise of this technique it became apparent that the word 'geometry', as understood by Kant, covers, in fact, two totally different sciences, mathematical and physical geometry. It was the failure to distinguish between them that produced

Kant's perplexity. 'So far as the laws of mathematics refer to reality, they are not certain; and so far as they are certain, they do not refer to reality' (Einstein). Kant's credit lies in having *seen* that there is a problem, not in having solved it.

But here a new problem presents itself: How do we know what will satisfy a given question? More generally: How does the answer fit the question? Questions of the current sort ('What is the right time?) show already by their form what sort of answer to expect. They are, so to speak, cheques with a blank to be filled; yet not always so: Augustine's question, 'How is it possible to measure time?' or Kant's question, 'How is geometry possible?' do not trace out the form of the answer. There is no *obvious* link between question and answer, any more than there is in the case of asking 'What is a point?' When Hilbert's idea—that the axioms of geometry jointly provide the 'implicit definition' of the basic terms—was first propounded it came totally unexpected; no one had ever thought of that before; on the contrary, many people had an uneasy feeling as if this were a way of evading the issue rather than an answer, amongst them no less a man than Frege. He thought the problem still unsolved.

Now is there anything one can do to make a man like Frege see that the axiomatic method provides the correct answer? Can it, for example, be *proved* to him? The point to which attention must now be drawn, though it should really be obvious, is that such a proof cannot be given, and it cannot because he, the asker, has first to be turned round to see the matter differently. What is required is a change of the entire way of thinking. Indeed, anyone who is puzzled by this problem and yet refuses to accept Hilbert's solution only betrays that he has got stuck in the groove hollowed out by the form in which the question is put. 'A point is —' he begins and then stops. What is to be done to help him to get out of the groove or, better still, to make him shift for himself when he feels 'cramped' in it, is a *discussion,* not a proof.

Frege behaves not so very unlike a man mystified by the question, 'What is time?' We may suggest converting the latter into the question how the word 'time' is being used (which would bring him down to earth). But aren't we cheating him? We seem to be holding out the answer to *one* question, but not to that one which he was asking. He may suspect that we are trying to fob him off with the second best we have in store, his original question still remaining an enigma. Similarly Frege: he considered it a scandal that the questions 'What is a point?', 'What is a number?' were still unanswered.

In either of these cases, the aim of a discussion, in the absence of a proof, can only be to change the asker's attitude. We may, for instance, scrutinize similar, or partially similar, cases, point out that the form of the answer is not always that of the question; by going patiently over such cases, the vast background of analogies against which the question is seen will slowly change. The turning up of a wide field of language loosens the position of certain standards which are so ingrained that we do not see them for what they are; and if we do this in an effective manner, a mind like Frege's will be released from the obsession of seeking strainingly for an answer to fit the mould. Arguments are used in such a discussion, not as proofs though but rather as means to make him see things he had not noticed before: e.g. to dispel wrong analogies, to stress similarities with other cases and in this way to bring about something like a shift of perspective. However, there is no way of proving him wrong or bullying him into mental acceptance of the proposal: when all is said and done the decision is his.

P. F. Strawson

Construction and Analysis *

In earlier lectures in this series, Mr. Pears has described the metaphysics of Logical Atomism; Professor Ayer has set out the programme of Logical Positivism; and Mr. Paul has spoken of the work of Professor Moore in Cambridge from 1900. You will perhaps have noticed that, in spite of their differences, Atomists, Positivists, and Professor Moore all have something in common, even if it is only a word, to be pronounced with approval. The word is 'analysis'. Certainly they did not all have exactly the same conception of analysis. Wittgenstein, in the *Tractatus,* gave no indication of thinking that analysis into the ultimate elements could actually be carried out; nor did he indicate at all clearly what he thought the ultimate elements were. The Positivists, on the other hand, were less non-committal. They had the ultimate elements clearly identified as 'sense-contents'; and they thought that at least the principles of analysis could be laid down, even if the details could not always be filled in. Atomists and Positivists alike accepted the skeleton language of the new mathematical logic as providing the formal structure of the ultimate and penultimate statements. Professor Moore stands rather apart from the members of both these groups. For he was not committed, as they were, to ultimate elements, nor was he tied so closely to the forms of mathematical logic; he was not bound, as they were, by a foreknowledge of the pattern to be revealed. For him, analysis was not the instrument of a wholesale metaphysics, but the method of a piecemeal elucidation. For him, analysis was not a programme, but a practice.

But what exactly did those who prescribed or practised philosophical analysis, *mean* by this expression? In particular, what were they claiming to analyse? Was it, for example, *sentences,* of the indicative or assertive

* From *The Revolution in Philosophy* by A. J. Ayer and others. London: Macmillan & Co., Ltd.; New York: St. Martin's Press, 1956, pp. 97–110.

kind? Or was it the meanings of those sentences—by some, rather unhappily, called *propositions?* Or was it the *thoughts* or *beliefs* which the sentences expressed? Or the *statements* they were used to make? It does not matter much, now, which we say; though each of these answers may, in its own way, be misleading. Analysis of sentences, for example, suggests the grammarian; analysis of thoughts or beliefs, the psychologist; and analysis of statements, perhaps the policeman or the advocate. Maybe it is best to say, as Moore always said, that the objects of analysis were propositions. This answer, whatever its shortcomings, emphasizes, without over-emphasizing, the linguistic nature of the enterprise, the preoccupation with meaning. For, however we describe the objects of analysis, particular analyses, whether given in detail or sketched in outline, always looked much the same. A sentence, representative of a class of sentences belonging to the same topic, was supposed to be elucidated by the framing of another sentence. This second sentence was to be more or less equivalent in meaning to the first, but was to make explicit at least some of the complexities of meaning concealed by the verbal form of the first. Presumably, for those who held that analysis had a terminus in logical atoms, there would exist, in theory, for every sentence of common speech, a *final* analysis—a sentence in which *all* complexities of meaning would be made *completely* explicit, in terms of the ultimate logical elements. Not that all analyses were thought of as reducing the complex to simpler elements. Some were thought of, rather, as a *recasting* of the verbal form of a sentence in such a way as to reveal the logical affinities of the proposition it expressed, and to dispel the illusion of other logical affinities which it did not really possess. It was as if propositions belonged to logical families, most of the members of each of which wore a certain kind of verbal dress; but some members of some families masqueraded in the verbal clothing characteristic of other families; and had to be re-garbed to prevent confusion. This, too, was the task of analysis.

So, then, the general conception of analysis was that of a kind of translation, or perhaps better, a kind of paraphrase. For it was to be translation within a language, not from one language to another: a translation from a less explicit to a more explicit form, or from a misleading to an unmisleading form. If your problem was, say, the nature of *truth,* or, say, the nature of *existence,* you hoped to solve it by finding a formula for translating sentences in which the adjective 'true' or the verb 'exists' occurred, into sentences in which these expressions did not occur, and in which no straightforward synonyms of them occurred either. Nor was this, after all, so very revolutionary a conception of philosophy. The search for definitions of problematic ideas was almost as old as philosophy itself. What was new was rather the substitution of sentences for words, of propositions for concepts, as the unit upon which analysis was to be practised. And for this change, as earlier lectures have shown, there were very good reasons.

Although, in Cambridge, Wittgenstein was already doing something very different, on the whole the method of analysis dominated English philosophy in the thirties. It brought some advances in some fields. But in the main the results were disappointing. The sentences of common speech seemed somehow to resist the simplifying expansions which theory had prepared for them. Even Russell's earlier brilliant glosses on the structure of ordinary sentences, in terms of the syntax of the new formal logic, began in the end to seem a little queer. And those who went to work with fewer preconceptions about their results were apt to find that if they preserved the sense of the original, they achieved no simplification: and that if they gained a simplification, they did so at the cost of losing the sense.

So what was to be done? Philosophers sought understanding of the concepts which were the apparatus of our thinking. They looked—and this seemed natural enough—to the propositions, the sentences, in which these concepts found their employment, the sentences in which we commonly express our thoughts and beliefs. But if these sentences resisted translation into more perspicuous forms, what was to be done? Well, of course, there were many possibilities. But, among them, two have been of dominant importance in post-war philosophizing. One involves turning away from the forms of common speech, while preserving much of the apparatus of the original programme of analysis. The other involves continued close attention to the forms of common speech, together with a vastly altered and extended conception of the nature and techniques of analysis.

Let me say more about these two contrasting courses. The first method, incidentally, is pursued mainly in America, and is associated especially with the names of Carnap and Quine. The second method is pursued mainly in England, and is associated especially with the names of Austin and Ryle. For the sake of convenience, I may speak of the American School and the English School. But I need hardly say that the titles cover quite wide divergences between individuals. The main inspiration of the American School is still, as it was for the Logical Atomists, the new formal logic, due to Frege and Russell. For this logic provides a skeleton language in which the meaning of every element is absolutely precise, and the articulation of the elements absolutely clear. By using this framework, this basic linguistic apparatus, other systems of concepts can be constructed in which the mutual relationships of the parts will have just the same clarity and precision as in formal logic itself. Of course, systems so constructed, and indeed the logical system itself used in their construction, are not natural growths, like the language of daily life, but artificial creations. But just in this very fact, it is claimed, lies the philosophical superiority of system-construction over the attempt to analyze ordinary language. That attempt, it is suggested, is defeated by the looseness, the untidiness, the shifting complexities of common speech. Instead of pursuing it, then, we are to construct clear models of language in which all the essential logical relations of our concepts can be made plain, while the irrelevant tangles of actual usage are cut away. Of course, some preliminary or incidental remark will have to be made, connecting key expressions of the system with expressions we ordinarily use. Otherwise it would not be clear what the system was about, what concepts it was intended to clarify. But once these points of contact are made, the system stands on its own, a precise and rigid structure to which our ordinary conceptual equipment is a rough and confusing approximation. The system of formal logic is itself the greatest of all achievements of this kind, as well as being the prerequisite of others. For it reveals the underlying structure of all our thinking. From those little logical words which are indispensable to all developed discourse—words such as 'the', 'a', 'all', 'some', 'if', 'not', 'or', 'and', 'is'—it distils what is essential and discards the troublesome remainder. Formal logic is the model for other philosophical models, as well as the framework on which the others are to be built.

Very roughly, that is the case, or an important part of the case, for system-construction as a method in philosophy. Evidently, it has its appeal. It offers something clear and orderly, in the place of something apparently confused and imprecise. It is not only attractive, but plausible. For there are many things which can be better understood as a result of the construction of a simplified model of their working; and why should not the concepts which exercise philosophers be among these things?

But the case for the alternative method can also be made to sound very plausible. After all, we are seeking to gain an understanding of the concepts and categories in terms of which we carry on our thinking; not only, or primarily, our advanced and technical thinking, but our common, daily thinking. For it is the most general, most fundamental and most ordinary ideas which give rise to the major problems of philosophy. Is it, after all, so reasonable to think that our ordinary use of language blurs and distorts these ordinary ideas? For common speech is subjected to the severest of all tests for efficiency, as a medium for the expression and communication of our thoughts—the test of constant use. If we want to understand the habits and way of life of an animal, we must carefully observe his behaviour in his natural surroundings; it is no good turning our backs on his actual behaviour, constructing a clockwork model from an engineer's designs and then studying that. So with our concepts. If we want to know how they work, we must watch them at work. As for the failure of the original programme of analysis, as applied to the sentences of common speech, the fault there lay not in common speech, but in a too rigid and too narrow conception of analysis. Why should it be supposed that the only way to gain understanding of the words which express the philosophically puzzling concepts was to translate sentences in which they occurred into sentences in which they did not occur? The belief in the exclusive efficacy of this method is just the troublesome legacy of discredited theories. It is too rigid a conception of analysis, because it supposes the existence of exact quasi-definitional relations between classes of concepts, which do not in fact obtain. It is too narrow, because it neglects altogether very many quite different features of the functioning of language, which it is of the first importance accurately to note and describe, if our philosophical problems are to be resolved. And the programme of system-construction suffers from just these same limitations. For it, too, confines itself to exhibiting quasi-definitional relations between constructed concepts. Admittedly the relations do really obtain in the constructed system; because they are made to. But even this limited success is purchased at too high a price: the price of divorce from the conceptual realities of common speech. So, for the old, limited and theory-ridden programme of analysis, we are to substitute a different aim: that of coming to understand philosophically puzzling concepts by carefully and accurately noting the ways in which the related linguistic expressions are actually used in discourse. Of course, not all features of the use of these expressions will be relevant to the philosopher's task. It is his special skill to discern *which* are relevant, and *how* they are relevant.

I have presented these two views of philosophical method as if they were in sharp and irreconcilable conflict. And, indeed, the partisans of each frequently enough write and speak as if this were so. But it is in fact not so clear that the philosophical builders of artificial languages, and the philosophical investigators of natural language, must necessarily be each other's enemies. Up to a point, at least, each method may be seen as the complementary of the other. For, on the one hand, the simplicities of a constructed model may cast light, if only by contrast, on the complexities of actual usage; and, on the other hand, some observation of the workings of natural language seems necessary for the successful construction of the simplified model. So it might seem that the situation calls for co-operation rather than competition. And so, up to a point, it does. Yet I am partisan enough to want to upset a little the symmetry of this friendly picture—or perhaps I should say, cautious enough to want to delimit spheres of influence. And, to explain my reasons for this, I shall have to try to fill a notable gap in what I have so far said. I shall have, that is, to say something about the general nature of philosophical problems, and of philosophical understanding. I shall have to say what I think the philosopher's tasks are.

There is one task about which there will be little disagreement. Sometimes, instead of just setting our concepts and speech-forms to work in the ordinary way, we reflect upon them, or with them, at a level of unusual generality; and when we do so, we may find ourselves driven towards conclusions not simply bizarre, not simply shocking to common sense, but somehow intrinsically unacceptable; and intrinsically unacceptable because at variance with the ordinary use, and hence with the ordinary meaning, of the very words in which we are tempted to express them. Yet such conclusions may seem, though unacceptable, inescapable. In this situation, some conceptual distortion has taken place; and, in general, the distortion is the consequence of an undue pressure exercised by *some* only of the features of the language in which we express the concept in question, to the temporary exclusion of others. To correct the distortion, we must clearly expose the full logical workings of the distorted concept, and perhaps of others too; and locate, if we can, the source of the distorting pressure. This is one of the tasks confronting the critical philosopher; and is worthy of a first mention, because so much of philosophy begins with paradox and the resolution of paradox. But it would itself be a paradox to represent the whole task of philosophy as the correction of philosophical mistakes. Even if such mistakes provide the initial impulse to this conceptual anatomy, the enterprise then acquires its own momentum and may be pursued for its own sake. There may be pure research as well as *ad hoc* therapy. So the philosopher may undertake a more detailed examination, a more systematic ordering and description, of speech-forms, of types of discourse, of types of concept, than would be necessary simply to relieve the pressures of paradox.

This is still not all that may be required of the philosopher. So far I have represented him as trying to exhibit the ways in which our concepts and forms of thought actually operate—partly for the sake of doing so, partly for the sake of clearing up conceptual confusions, diagnosing philosophical disorders. But there are other and more imaginative sides to his activity, not strictly separable from these, but distinguishable from them. For fully to understand our conceptual equipment, it is not enough to know, to be able to say, how it works. We want to know also *why* it works as it does. To ask this is to ask to be shown how the nature of our thinking is rooted in the nature of the world and in our own natures. This is not an impossible enquiry; for it is quite possible to imagine our experience being different in fundamental ways, and then to consider how our conceptual apparatus might naturally be adjusted to accommodate these differences. In seeing this, we also see how our concepts, as they are, are rooted in the world, as it is. This kind of thinking might be called the explanatory work of the philosophical imagination. There is another kind of thinking which might be called the creative or constructive work of the philosophical imagination. To engage in this kind of thinking is to consider how, without the nature of the world being fundamentally different, we might nevertheless view it through the medium of a different conceptual apparatus, might conduct our discourse about it in forms different from, though related to, those which we actually see. Evidently, both these kinds of imaginative philosophical thinking are complementary to the analytical kinds I first distinguished. In practice, each kind tends to be so interwoven with the others that there is a certain artificiality in so distinguishing them. But it is not wholly artificial. For one strand or another may be decisively dominant in any one piece of work, or in the work of any one philosopher. Let me, for convenience, give names to these different strands in philosophical thought. In the order in which I first mentioned them, I shall distinguish the analytical strands into the therapeutic and the systematic; and the imaginative strands into the explanatory and the inventive.

And now, I think, we are in a better position to assess the relative claims of the English and American schools in post-war philosophy. For the task of therapeutic analysis, as I have described it, it is obvious that the methods of the English school are of primary importance—while the method of system-construction is, at best, of secondary helpfulness. For the paradoxes and perplexities in question had their root in a vivid, but imperfect, picture of the working concepts concerned—in a kind of caricature of their logical features. The only fully rational method of correction here is to replace the caricature with an accurate delineation of those features, which will show how the caricature distorted, what it exaggerated and what it missed out. And it is in the actual use of the linguistic expressions for the concepts concerned, and nowhere else, that we find the data from which we can draw this accurate picture. A simplified diagram from which the puzzle-generating features are, perhaps, absent, is here no substitute, though it may be a help. What of systematic analysis? This, as I described it, was simply a more generalized and systematic attempt to distinguish and describe the logical features of our concepts and speech-forms. Its data, therefore, and its methods are fundamentally the same as those of therapeutic analysis, though it has not the same anxious concern with possible sources of perplexity and paradox. There may appear to be a slight oddity in speaking of systematic analysis of language and then declaring that the way to pursue it is not by the constructing of linguistic systems. But if this does seem odd, it is only a superficial oddity. For evidently there is a difference between constructing a segment of artificial language and systematically describing the workings of a slice of natural language. One must not exaggerate the difference. The task of tracing patterns in living language is difficult, and would be almost impossible if one were not allowed to do a little regimenting. Still the difference remains a vital one. The living creatures of language, even when mildly regimented, are still seen as performing a range of functions of immense diversity; whereas only a few of these functions can be imitated by the logical machines built by the constructionist.

What of the imaginative side of philosophy? Obviously neither a facility in the techniques of system-construction, nor a keen eye for the linguistic facts is of direct help in the *explanatory* task. But when we turn to the *inventive* or *constructive* side—one might almost say, the metaphysical side—the case is different. The system-builder, guided by certain ideals of quasi-mathematical elegance and exactness, provides us with models of ways in which we might have thought and talked, had we been less complex and many-levelled creatures than we are. In doing so, he may, as I have already said, cast much direct and indirect light on fundamental features of the ways in which we actually do think and talk. And this is not all. A philosopher's systematic reconstruction of concepts and speech-forms may sometimes have an application in other branches of knowledge than philosophy. It may provide useful, and even indispensable, tools for the advance of mathematics and the more mathematical sciences. And here again there is a parallel with the inventive speculations of more traditional metaphysics. What begins as metaphysics may end as science. But this is not its only justification; and it is time to drop the prim pragmatism which pretends that it is.

So, then, the appearance of a deathly struggle between these two methods in contemporary philosophy is, in part at least, a misleading appearance, an illusion. The illusion is not necessarily regrettable: it may act as a spur to effort on both sides. And it is not wholly illusion; for there is here something of a clash, almost of temperament—between the desire to understand what exists, and the desire to make something new and, in some sense, better. Nevertheless, the apparent conflict is largely an illusion, even if a useful one. For the two methods are not rival ways of attaining just the same end—ways of which one must be quite wrong if the other is quite right. They are, partly, complementary methods of achieving one end; and, partly, both of them, appropriate and closely related methods of achieving different, though closely related ends. For me to say which of these different ends I considered the more important would have no more interest than any other expression of personal preference; but it may not be altogether fanciful to find in the *national* preferences which I mentioned earlier, some indication of a characteristic difference between the New World and the Old.

II. KNOWLEDGE

Knowledge

I

All cognitive processes—perception, memory, intuition, inference, and practice—are subject to error, singly and combined. This is why the scope, validity, and nature of knowledge have been problems since the earliest beginnings of philosophy. Many attempts have been made to establish the validity of knowledge in general, usually by reducing its scope. When our claims to know are confined to what we really can know, it is said, then error can be eliminated or reduced to a minimum. Much psychotherapeutic advice for the avoidance of error has been given, and though no infallible rules have been discovered there is no question that a great deal of progress has been made. Each age copes with new experience, and devises its own refinements of method and theory.

Although there are no water-tight compartments, it is still useful to speak of empiricists and rationalists, intuitionists and pragmatists. The empiricist is one who holds that of the various sources of knowledge perception is the most important or decisive in vindicating beliefs about the world. In the same way, the rationalists, intuitionists, and pragmatists put their main reliance on inference, intuition, and practice respectively. None of these philosophers, of course, denies the importance of the other sources of knowledge; they all maintain simply that one source is the most important. There are also philosophers who insist on the reliability of common sense. The language of common sense embodies the long experience of the race and much of its wisdom, and is therefore, if it is properly understood, a most important source of philosophical knowledge. This emphasis can be seen in the current analytic school in Great Britain.

But philosophers cannot always be confined within these compartments. The analytic philosophers who defer to common sense seem to rely equally on a kind of intuition, and at times it is difficult to see any clear distinction between the two methods. Pragmatism furnishes another illustration. Practice should not be taken in a narrow or opportunistic sense. Dewey agrees with the present-day logical empiricists that the warrant for empirical knowledge is to be found in the process of verification. He differs from them, however, when he insists that, except in very simple cases, the critical percepts are not simply given but must be understood, and in his refusal to exempt logical statements from the test of verification. He is an empiricist, but with important differences. It will be noted that the philosophers who appear in the selections below vary according to the weight they give to sense perception, inference, and the other sources of knowledge. They disagree in many other respects too but this difference remains fundamental.

Owing to the fabulous success of the inductive sciences in modern times, more and more attention has been given to the cognitive status of perception and to the nature of verification. Advances in the area of logic, semantics and scientific method have sharpened interest in the inferential process, realism and nominalism have been revived in new forms, and there have been semantic and other fresh approaches to the subject of truth.

II

Since perception is the original source of knowledge on which all the others depend, it is natural to start with the cognitive status of perception. Philosophers have always been concerned with one aspect of perception: the knowing relation between the perceiver and the perceived object. One question has been whether when we perceive things we know them directly or only indirectly. In the latter case the problem arises: How can we ever be sure that the real physical objects we think we are seeing are really there, or are what they seem to be? Common sense takes it for granted that we see physical things directly. A table, a book, a river, or a tree is bodily present in perception, or at least a considerable part of its surface is given or revealed. If there is any doubt about what visual perception discloses, common sense subjects it to the test of touch and manipulation, for the tactual sense is considered more reliable than sight. But the final test for common sense is practical utility or importance. If we eat from the table, lie in the shade of the tree, read the book, or swim in the river, any lingering doubts that our perceptions are authentic disappear.

But the common-sense man is easily jolted out of his epistemological smugness. We have only to remind him that in dreams he is also convinced that he sees, touches, and feels the practical impact of things, though in this case the physical objects he thinks he perceives are entirely lacking. We can also ask him to explain how he can reduce the size of a tree simply by walking away from it. If what he sees is always the tree, whether he is close to it or at a great distance, then the same tree can be sixty feet tall and also a mere speck on the horizon. He can hardly maintain that the tree has been so transformed merely by his walking away from it. He will most likely say that the tree itself has remained the same, but that something else has changed, namely, his percept of the tree. What he has had immediately before him was not an unchanging tree but his changing percept.

The common-sense man starts out with the view that physical objects are directly revealed to him in perception, but he can be easily converted, perhaps too easily, to the contrary view that they are only indirectly perceived, via the percepts we have of them. The first view is called epistemological monism, because it holds that the perceived object and the percepts of it are one and the same; whereas the second view is called epistemological dualism, meaning that the perceived object—the tree or the table—is different from the percepts of it. Dualism had been given its classical statement by John Locke in the seventeenth century, but monism was not explicitly formulated till the twentieth century.

It was this issue which divided the contemporary realists. At the turn of the century William James developed his theory of "neutral stuff." Our percepts are in themselves neither physical nor mental but neutral. They are mental or physical, not according to their nature but depending on how they are related. When related to our biographies they are mental; when related to the objective physical order they are physical. There was no difficulty, James held, in their belonging to both orders simultaneously. Utilizing James's theory of neutral stuff, Ralph Barton Perry argued vigorously against Berkeley's idealism (to be is to be perceived), and also against Locke's dualism. That is to say, he upheld realism, which is the denial of Berkeley's idealism, and defended epistemological monism. In England G. E. Moore published his influential article, "The Refutation of Idealism," in 1903, which was also directed against Locke's dualism as well as Berkeley's idealism. It challenged the basic contention of the dualists that our percepts are mental. Many other authors about this time or a little later embraced the monistic form of realism. In England there were Moore, Bertrand Russell, Samuel Alexander, and G. Dawes Hicks. In the United States a group of monistic realists—Ralph Barton Perry, William P. Montague, E. B. Holt, W. B. Pitkin, Walter T. Marvin, and E. G. Spaulding—brought out in 1912 a cooperative volume called THE NEW REALISM, which argued the claims of epistemological monism against Lockean dualism.

Eight years later another group of American realists published a new cooperative volume, ESSAYS IN CRITICAL REALISM, which vigorously opposed the New Realists, and upheld, if not Lockean dualism, at least modern and more adequate versions of dualism. The Critical Realists represented in this volume were R. W. Sellars, George Santayana, Arthur O. Lovejoy, C. A. Strong, A. K. Rogers, J. B. Pratt, and Durant Drake.

Although this issue which divided the two camps of realists is distinctly modern, the arguments on both sides frequently adverting to recent developments in physics, physiology, and psychology, it was nevertheless pre-figured in many discussions of past eras. Let us consider an example or two.

The nature of true or veridical perception has received some attention throughout the history of philosophy. In ancient India the mistaking of a rope in the road for a snake became a profound symbol of the illusory character of all perception. In Plato's THEAETETUS we find Socrates objecting to Protagoras' doctrines that "man is the measure of all things" and "knowledge is perception." "How can anyone maintain that knowledge is perception," he asks, "or that to every man what appears is?" Against such contentions he cites the objection "about dreams and diseases, in particular about madness, and the various illusions of hearing and sight, or of other senses. For you know that in all these cases the esse-percipi theory appears to be unmistakably refuted, since in dreams and illusions we certainly have false perceptions; and far from saying that everything is which appears, we should rather say that nothing is which appears." [1]

But Socrates now faces about and, as any good philosopher should, tries to see the question from the other side. Protagoras, he points out, would have had an answer to such arguments. He would admit that the wine which tastes sweet to a man in good health will taste bitter to him when he is ill, but would claim that he was right on both occasions. The taste of the wine, after all, is a product of two factors—the wine and the taster. For the man who is ill the wine is bitter, just as it is sweet for him when he is in health. Both perceptions are true and irrefutable. The sweetness and bitterness of the wine, it might be said, belong to the wine only in relation to different chemical states and conditions of the perceivers. In the same way, illusions of all kinds could be conceived as valid perceptions of qualities-from-certain-positions-and-conditions-of-perceivers.

Socrates' objections to Protagoras' theory anticipated the arguments of contemporary epistemological dualists, whereas Protagoras' answer (as construed by Socrates), prefigured Whitehead's ingenious theory, in the twentieth century, of "multiple-inherence." The big problem for epistemo-

[1] 157E–158A (Jowett translation).

logical monism is to account for false perceptions or illusions, and the multiple-inherence and multiple-relation theories are subtle and daring attempts at a solution. They aim to heal the breach made by the dualistic theories between the perceptual world and the physical world, and to restore the unity of nature.

The big problem for epistemological dualism is to account for true or veridical perception. Theories of this kind must explain how, if the physical world is in no sense given in perception, it can be an assured fact of knowledge. If all we are given in perception are private sense-data, experienced by each of us in his own private space, how do we know that these sense-data are not the whole show? How defend realism against the Berkeleyan idealist and phenomenalist? Perhaps the best answer is that the hypothetico-deductive method employed in science must be boldly extended. We are justified in inferring the existence of the physical world because deductions from it square with perceptual experience, and furnish better explanations.

A related problem is faced by epistemological dualism, namely: What do we mean when we point to a given datum, such as a green patch, and say that we are perceiving a tree composed of millions of molecules which are invisible and in no sense given? Dissatisfied with Brentano's formalistic approach to this question, some American epistemological dualists, especially Roy Wood Sellars, have worked out a biological, evolutionary explanation, looking upon the perceiver not only as a knower, but also as a top-rung organism adapting to the environment.

III

Another aspect of knowledge that calls for analysis is the nature of universals. What universals are is an issue of long standing. In contemporary philosophy Bertrand Russell's book THE PROBLEMS OF PHILOSOPHY (1912) furnishes an excellent introduction to the subject of universals. The view upheld is a modern version of Plato's theory of "ideas", or universals, which is usually called Platonic or extreme realism. According to this view a universal such as "blue" is timeless and spaceless. It can characterize particular things such as violets and summer skies, but is never where or when they are, and could never, therefore, be in them. Thus while we say "Violets are blue," what is meant is that violets have blue, or are instances of blue. Russell extended Plato's theory to relations. Betweenness and similarity are also timeless universals which have instances in our concrete world.

A rival view, moderate realism—held by Aristotle, Averroes, Aquinas, and many others—asserts that the universal is located in all particulars, but that the mind can abstract it from every other quality of these things and consider it by itself.

Another theory, especially popular today, is nominalism. It contends that there are no universals, but only particular things. "Blue" must accordingly be a particular word which somehow refers to each and every blue thing. It has been construed as the name of a "general image," and also as the name of a class of things similar to a given percept. Russell himself, after writing THE PROBLEMS OF PHILOSOPHY, turned to nominalism but soon ran into a snag. The attempt to replace the universal by the class of things similar to a given thing appeared to be circular, for similarity is a relation, and relations in Russell's view are not particular things but universals. Whereas other relations might be defined in terms of similarity, similarity itself apparently could not.

On the current scene, nominalism has attracted a number of logicians, such as W. V. Quine, who attempts to solve the baffling technical problems it involves. Nominalism appeals to the "tough-minded" empiricist, who welcomes ontological simplifications and economy, and desires to eliminate if possible a troublesome hierarchy of entities known as "classes."

The pragmatic outlook presents still another approach to the nominalist-realist controversy. In John Dewey's instrumentalism, universals, far from being accepted as indescribable private entities disclosed only in introspection, are interpreted as "ways of behaving." As such they are public, denotable, describable—a phase of the process of inquiry. A subtle behaviorism here, as in other cases, seems to go far toward giving an account of phenomena formerly hidden in the individual mind and exempt from checks and confirmation. For the phenomenologists, however, universals are given in consciousness, whatever else may be said about them; and the only problem which remains is to provide adequate description and interpretation.

IV

Still another aspect of knowledge is inference. When we use such expressions as if—then, since, and because we are usually carrying out an inference explicitly, but inferences are not always expressed in words and are not always conscious. In solving problems a new response to a new situation may be learned without any awareness that an inference is being used. In this sense inference runs through all of our experiences. Inferences also become habits so that in perception, for example, patches of color are immediately perceived as ink-wells, trees and houses. The usual view is that, whether inference is conscious and explicit, or behavioral and non-verbal, it holds by virtue of the universals involved, not by virtue of the particulars. Thus, if I infer from a barometer reading and particular flashes of lightning I see that it will rain today, my prediction presupposes a general rule or law that rain always follows certain significant signs.

The if-then experience is well-known, but not well understood, for it is one thing to use an expression correctly and another to make a correct analysis of what it means. Of course a central feature of the study of inference in contemporary philosophy is the extent to which inference has been formalized, and the logic of inference captured in complex symbolic systems. In their effort to explain the nature of inference, philosophers have turned up a number of puzzles which were not apparent on the ordinary level of discourse. Lewis Carroll, for example, showed that the rule of inference—what follows from a true proposition is true—could not be written down as a premise in any argument, though it seemed to be needed, for when it is written down in this fashion no conclusion can be drawn. More recently, certain perplexities in the use of contrafactual conditionals have engaged attention.

Philosophical controversies about the nature of logical principles in inference have not abated. Out of the nineteenth century there had emerged roughly three major positions. Many formal logicians drew a sharp distinction between formal or analytic truths on the one hand, and empirical synthetic truths on the other; logical principles were taken to be of the first type, requiring no appeal to experience for their certification. An extreme empiricism was represented by John Stuart Mill in his attempt to elaborate a basic logic of induction. The idealist philosophers, in the Hegelian tradition, insisted that inferences cannot be isolated or taken singly, since each involves the whole system of knowledge. The validity of inference in this theory depends on how well it coheres with the total organization of knowledge, and logical principles express partial structural features of this whole system. In the early twentieth century this idealist position was urged by philosophers like Bradley and Bosanquet against Russell and the formal logicians. With the impressive development of logical calculi, formalist positions became dominant. The distinction between analytic and synthetic truths was sharply drawn, and there was a strong tendency to interpret logical principles in positivist vein as rules of discourse or of language. Recently there has been sharper stress on the fact that logical calculi as formal systems do not determine how they shall be interpreted, and there are signs of a new freedom in reconsidering even established interpretations. The sharp distinction between analytic truths and synthetic empirical truths is even questioned by some, and this carries with it the renewed claim for some broad empirical components in the status of logical principles.

Overlapping these controversies is the consideration of the relation between deductive and inductive inference. Some have taken the view that all inference is deductive, with induction being simply a way of speaking about the use of deduction in hypothetico-deductive-verification processes. Others have considered it a major error to assimilate scientific inferences to this "deductive model." Instead, they have urged the development of induction as a distinct logic of inference. One consequence of this widespread tendency has been to focus sharply on the logic of probability, and to explore numerous problems in the analysis of this complex concept. Still others have begun to allow themselves even greater liberties in the elaboration of models of inference, speaking as Ryle does, of "unscheduled logics" in different areas of the use of ordinary language. To the defender of the primacy of the deductive model, such trends seem to be another example of the age-old confusion of the normative logic of inference with the descriptive psychology of particular habits of inference.

V

Finally, the discussion of knowledge naturally involves the nature of truth. Of the many traditional analyses of truth, the correspondence theory recommends itself to most philosophers and to all non-philosophers who give the subject any attention. A proposition is true, it contends, if what it says is the case, if it squares or corresponds with reality. A proposition is false, on the other hand, if what it says is not the case, if it disaccords with the fact with which its contradictory accords. There is considerable variation in the language used to describe the correspondence of a true proposition with the fact that makes it true, and different ways of meeting the difficulties involved. One of the problems faced by correspondence theory is whether one fact can establish the truth of several propositions or only one. How far does the syntax of propositions correspond to the structure of facts, and how could comparisons be made to certify such correspondence?

The problem of making a proposition in the mind correspond with external reality is eliminated in idealistic systems, or at least it takes a very different form. This is because in idealistic systems there is no reality external to the mind. Since reality is considered mental or spiritual, the problem is rather to bring the subjective judgment into accord with the whole closely meshed net of reality. Hence the stress is on coherence rather than correspondence.

Vigorously opposed to both correspondence and coherence is the pragmatic theory of truth advocated by William James. The early version of the pragmatic view has been very influential, but it is important to note that it is very different from that of Dewey and his followers. For the latter, truth seems to be assimilated to verification, though Dewey himself preferred to speak of "warranted assertibility." We are warranted in asserting a proposition, that is, when it has been scientifically verified. Truth itself, for Dewey, is the ideal limit of the process of verification.

Intuitionist theories of truth do not lack representation in the twentieth century. On the whole, they less frequently take intellectualistic forms or make claims for directly intuitable axioms. Occasionally there are assertions of self-evidence in the phenomenological analysis of direct experience. But the most striking type of intuitionism is to be found in Bergson's reaction against the claims of scientific method to provide basic knowledge, and in his affirmation that intuition can give an immediate access to truth without the use of symbols at all.

VI

The selections of this part correspond to the major problems of knowledge already indicated—perception, universals, inference, and truth.

The selections dealing with perception are from the careful discussions of Lovejoy, Broad, and Ayer. Lovejoy presents a dualistic view, Broad a multiple inherence theory, and Ayer a critical analysis of the phenomenalistic position.

The selections dealing with universals are from Russell's well-known early book, THE PROBLEMS OF PHILOSOPHY, where he presents a Platonic or extreme realistic view of universals; from C. I. Lewis's influential book, MIND AND THE WORLD ORDER, where he argues for conceptual pragmatism; and from Quine's development of a nominalist program in his paper, "Speaking of Objects."

In the third group of selections, dealing with inference, Feigl presents a basic survey of the situation from a logical empiricist perspective; Carnap, in a well-known article, systematizes different conceptions of probability; and Ryle attempts to extend the family of logics to include informal logic.

The final group of selections, on truth, are from Bergson's classic defence of intuitionism; James's original presentation of a pragmatist theory of truth; Joachim's careful formulation of the coherence theory of truth; and Ledger Wood's attempt to work out a modern conception of the correspondence theory of truth which will meet the traditional objections that have stood in its way.

Perception

A. O. Lovejoy

Natural Dualism *

The past quarter-century's discussion has shown that it is not easy for the critics of dualism to keep clearly in view its essential outlines in their entirety and in their simplicity, free from extraneous complications and confusions, and to recognize that it, rather than what is called "naïve" or "direct" realism, is the way of thinking natural to man so soon as he becomes even a little reflective about certain facts, of which most are matters of ordinary experience, and all have long been generally accepted. . . .

Specifically, men naturally make at least five assumptions (we need not yet ask whether they are valid assumptions) about the character or status of what may, for short, be called *cognoscenda*—the things-to-be-known-if-possible. (1) Many *cognoscenda,* including most of those to be known, if at all, visually, are assumed to be at places in space external to the body of the percipient. Man may be described biologically as an animal whose habitual and paradoxical employment is the endeavor to reach outside his skin. As a physical organism *homo sapiens,* like other creatures, has a definite spatial boundary of rather irregular outline, formed chiefly of a single material substance. All that, physically or spatially speaking, constitutes the organic functioning of an individual of the species takes place within the narrow room defined by this epidermal surface. What the man as a biological unit is, and what the events that make up his life are, are sought by the biologists wholly within those confines. Yet man is forever attempting, and, as he is wont to believe, with success, to apprehend, to "get at," things which lie beyond this surface. The individual's actual existence as it appears *to him,* can in only very small part be described as a succession of subcuticular events. The stuff of which it *seems* to be mainly composed consists of entities and happenings on the far side of the boundary, some of them so slightly removed from the epidermal surface that they are said to be in con-

* From *The Revolt Against Dualism,* by Arthur O. Lovejoy, Lecture I, "Cartesian Dualism and Natural Dualism," pp. 10–11, 12–24.

Note: Footnotes are here omitted.

tact with it, others incalculably remote. The human animal, in short, does not for the most part live where its body is—if an organism's life is made up of what it really experiences; it lives where the things are of which it is aware, upon which its attention and feeling are directed. (How far this may be true of other creatures we cannot judge.) One of the most curious developments in the entire history of thought is the invention in our day of what may best be named the Hypodermic Philosophy—the doctrine, resulting from the application to a cognitive animal of the biological concepts found sufficient in the study of animals assumed to be non-cognitive, that the organic phenomenon of knowing may be exhaustively described in terms of molecular displacements taking place under the skin.

(2) Equally insistent in man, and yet more paradoxical—had most men but the capacity for philosophic wonder which would enable them to see it so—is the demand that he shall have a real traffic with things that are not, because they are by-gone or have not yet come into being. What time and nature have extinguished he makes the matter of his present contemplation, and gains thereby his power to foresee what is still unborn. In memory and in forecast and anticipation he expressly conceives himself to be apprehending entities or events (even though they may be only other experiences of his own) which are not co-existent with the acts or states through which they are apprehended—to be reaching what is nevertheless at that moment in some sense beyond his temporal reach.

(3) An even more exigent desire for knowledge normally arises in man —though some philosophers who profess to have rid themselves of it would have us believe that it is equally wanting in others. Besides his craving to reach that which is spatially and temporally external to himself at the moment of cognition, there is, plainly, in the natural man a wish to attain an acquaintance with entities as they *would be if unknown,* existences not relative to the cognitive situation—in short, with things as they literally are in themselves. He has a persistent, if not easily gratified, curiosity about what M. Meyerson calls the *être intime,* the private life, of things. Tell him that at every moment of his existence he is contemplating nothing but the ghosly offspring of that moment's contemplation itself—even though they be projected into other places—and you contradict one of the most tenacious of his convictions—and, as he will point out to you, if he should be something of a dialectician, you also contradict yourself. He may, under pressure from philosophers, surrender this conviction with regard to one and another limited class of the contents of his experience; surrender it wholly, neither he nor the most subjectivistic philosopher has ever really done.

And (4) this tenacity in believing that through what goes on within the individual's experience he can know what is other than that experience and as real as it is, is greatest with respect to his knowledge of the experiences of others of his kind. There are a few philosophers among us who profess not only to be satisfied with automatic sweethearts and mindless friends, but also to be unable to attach meaning to the proposition that these automata have any being beyond that which they have in the philosopher's own private and (as some would add) corporeal existence. (It is, of course, evident that if this philosophy is true—supposing the word "true" still to have meaning—there are not several such philosophers, but only one.) But this queer affectation, a hypertrophy of the logic of scientific empiricism, is manifestly belied at every moment by the behavior and speech of the philosophers who assume it; it denies the meaningfulness of a belief which every creature of our kind seems inevitably to hold and from which all the distinctive quality of man's moral consciousness and all the tang and poignancy of his social experience derive—the belief that he is surrounded by beings like himself but not himself, having inner lives of their own which are never in the same sense *his* own, but of which, nevertheless, he can attain some knowledge, and to whom, reciprocally, he can convey some understanding of that which is going on within himself. This social realism also, which is manifestly a piece of pure epistemology, seems to be one of the specific characters of *homo sapiens,* as properly a part of his zoölogical definition as his upright posture or his lack of a tail. It is implicit in all his most distinctive modes of feeling and behavior—his elaboration of language and art as means of expression, his craving for affection, the curious and immense potency over the individual's conduct which is possessed by his beliefs about the thoughts and feelings of others about himself, and his occasional ability to recognize the interests of other sentient creatures as ends in themselves. Apply the principle of relativity to men's apprehensions of one another, and you destroy the very idea of a society of the characteristically human type.

(5) Finally, the *cognoscenda* which the individual knower ascribes to places and times in the external world where his body is not, and in which his cognitive act is not occurring, he also conceives to be potentially, if not actually, apprehensible by these other knowers; they must be things capable of verification in experiences other than the one experience in which, at a given moment, they are in some sense before him. Out of his belief in a multiplicity of knowers other than himself, or a multiplicity of knowings which, though now knowable by him, are not *his present* knowing, he has framed the category of publicity, the notion of a world of objects for common knowledge; and he tends to treat this attribute of common verifiability

as the criterion of that independence of the percipient event or the cognitive act which he naturally attributes to the *cognoscendum.* In other words, his character as a social animal has profoundly and permanently infected his very notion of knowing, so that the experience of objects which he has when in dream or madness, he steps aside into a world of his own—be it never so vivid and never so coherent—is not, when seen to be thus private, taken as equivalent to that access to reality which he seeks.

These, then, are the five articles of the natural and spontaneous epistemological creed of mankind—a creed which, as I have said, contains its own apparent mysteries, or diverse aspects of the one mystery of the presence of the absent, the true apprehension, by a being remaining within certain fixed bounds, of things beyond those bounds. Epistemological dualism arises when reflection, initially accepting these articles, inquires about their implications and brings them into connection with certain familiar facts of experience. There is, indeed, as should be evident from what has already been said, a sense in which all realism is intrinsically dualistic; in all its forms, namely, it asserts that the thing known may be other in time and place and nature than the *event or act by means of which* the thing is known. Thus the event of seeing, as we have remarked, if conceived physiologically as a neuro-cerebral change, does not appear to occur either where the visual object is seen or where the real object is assumed to be. A happening inside of a given body somehow achieves the presentation, in the individual stream of experience connected with that particular body, of an entity outside the body. And even if the cognitive event be conceived as a purely psychic and non-spatial act of awareness, that act has at least a date which need not (e.g., in memory) be the date, and a *quale* which is by hypothesis not the *quale,* of the object known. But it is not this fundamental sort of dualism necessarily inherent in any realistic theory of knowledge which we shall here mean by "epistemological dualism"; the term stands for the assertion of quite another (though not unrelated) duality, that of the content or datum at a given moment immediately and indubitably presented, and the reality said to be known thereby. Even the datum, of course, *seems,* in the case of sight and touch, to be situated outside the body, though whether it truly is or not must be a matter for subsequent consideration. I do not actually see the desk inside the head of which I at the same time can see a small bit—namely, the tip of my nose—and to the rest of which I give in thought a spatial position definitely related to that bit. But epistemological dualism (as here understood) declares that not even the visible desk which is thus directly perceived as spatially external to the perceived body is the same existent as the "real" desk, i.e., the *cognoscendum.* And the existential distinctness of datum and *cognoscendum* which is thus held by the dualist to be exemplified in the case of visual perception is also asserted by him, *mutatis mutandis,* in the case of other modes of perception and other forms of cognitive experience; so that, in his view, all knowing is mediated through the presence "before the mind"—as the traditional phrase goes—of entities which must be distinguished from an ulterior reality which is the true objective of knowledge.

Now you obviously cannot discuss whether two particulars—two in the sense that they have been provisionally distinguished in discourse—are identical unless you already know or assume something about both. If you are in a state of blank ignorance about either one, no question concerning the nature of their relations can be raised. It is therefore necessary to know, or postulate, certain propositions about the class *cognoscenda* before we can compare it with the class "data" to ascertain whether the two satisfy our criteria of identity. To assert their non-identity is to ascribe to the one a spatial or a temporal or a spatio-temporal position, or a set of qualities, which is inconsistent with those empirically exhibited by the other. Philosophers, it is true, have often attempted to go about the matter in what seems a different way. They have begun by provisionally assuming that they know nothing whatever except the passing immediate datum, and have then sought to determine, by reflecting upon the nature or implications of this, how much knowledge of existents which are not immediate data they must, or may, suppose themselves to possess. This was, of course, essentially the method of Descartes, though he applied it confusedly and inconsistently. But it is not the natural road to epistemological dualism. That road starts from the position of natural realism—from the assumption that we already have certain information about realities which are not *merely* our immediate, private, and momentary data; and it leads to the discovery, or supposed discovery, that this very assumption forbids us to believe that our acquaintance with these realities is at first hand. The time, place, context, or qualities which we have ascribed to them prove inconsistent with those which belong to the data. Not only is this the natural approach to the dualism of datum and *cognoscendum,* but it is also the only approach which is at all likely to be persuasive to those averse to that theory. The argument starts from the premises of those who would, if possible, avoid its conclusion. We shall, then, in this and the next lecture, not attempt an affectation of universal doubt, but shall tentatively accept—with nearly all of the early and many even of the later insurgents—the broad outlines of the picture of nature familiar to common sense and sanctioned by the older physics. We shall, in particular, not initially question the supposition that there are extended external objects, such as pennies, tables, planets, and distant stars, having at least the primary and possibly also the secondary qualities; having determinable positions in a space like that of visual and tactual perception, whether or not it is identical with it; capable of motion and causal interaction; acting, by means of processes in space, upon our sense-organs; and thereby conditioning the presence in our experience of the data which, whether or not identical with the objects, are our sources of information about them. When these natural assumptions are provisionally adopted, there nevertheless prove to be at least five familiar aspects of experience in which it seems plain that the object of our knowing must be different in the time or place or mode of its existence, or in its character, from the perceptual or other content which is present to us at the moment when we are commonly said to be apprehending that object, and without which we should never apprehend it at all.

(1) Of these, the first is implicit in the second of the above-mentioned articles of man's natural realistic creed. Intertemporal cognition, the knowing at one time of things which exist or events which occur at another time, seems a patent example of a mode of knowledge which we are under the necessity of regarding as potentially genuine and yet as mediate. When I remember, for example, not only is there a present awareness distinct from the past memory-object (that alone would imply only the duality of act and content), but the present awareness manifestly has, and must have, a compresent content. But the past event which we say the memory is *of* cannot be this compresent content. In saying this I am, it is true, including among the natural grounds of epistomological dualism an assumption which some dualistic philosophers—and even some who repudiate the naïvely dualistic theory of memory—regard as unsound. Mr. Broad, for example, has said that there "is no general metaphysical objection to such a theory" on the ground that when an event is past it ceases to exist. "Once an event has happened it exists eternally"; past events, therefore, "are always 'there' waiting to be remembered; and there is no *a priori* reason why they should not from time to time enter unto such a relation with certain present events that they become objects of direct acquaintance." This view, however, implies an inconceivable divorce of the identity of an event from its date. The things which may be said to subsist eternally are essences; and the reason why they can so subsist is that, by definition, they have no dates. They do not "exist" at all, in the sense in which dated and located things do so; and if "events" eternally existed after they had "once happened" (and when they were no longer "happening"), they would likewise exist before they happened; eternalness can hardly be an acquired character. The pres-

ent image and the past event may be separate embodiments of the same essence; they are not identical particulars, because the particularity of each is undefinable apart from its temporal situation and relations. The duality of the memory-image and the bygone existence to which it refers seems to be inherent in what we *mean* by remembrance; if the two were one our intertemporal knowing would defeat its own aim of apprehending the beyond, by annulling its beyondness. The very wistfulness of memory implies such duality; the past, in being known, still inexorably keeps its distance. Plainest of all is it that a man's own experienc*ing* of yesterday, the event of his then *having* an experience, does not seem to him, in being remembered, to become to-day's experiencing. Common sense, however much inclined in its more self-confident moments to believe in direct perception, has never, I suppose, believed in direct memory; it has been well aware that what is present in retrospection is a duplicate which somehow and in some degree discloses to us the character, without constituting the existence, of its original.

(2) It is not alone in the case of memory that there is a temporal sundering, and therefore an existential duality, of the content given and the reality made known to us through that content. This second reason for dualism has not, it is true, like some of the others, always been discoverable by the simplest reflection upon everyday experience. But the fact upon which it rests has long been one of the elementary commonplaces of physical science; and the probability of it had suggested itself to acute minds long before its verification. There had at times occurred to him, wrote Bacon in the *Novum Organum,* " a very strange doubt," a *dubitatio plane monstrosa,* "namely, whether the face of a clear and starlight sky be seen at the instant at which it really exists, and not rather a little later; and whether there be not, as regards our sight of heavenly bodies, a real time and an apparent time (*tempus visum*), just as there is a real place and an apparent place taken account of by astronomers." For it had appeared to him "incredible that the images or rays of the heavenly bodies could be conveyed at once to the sight through such an immense space and did not rather take some appreciable time in travelling to us." Unfortunately for his reputation Lord Bacon was able to overcome this doubt by invoking against it several bad reasons, which need not be here recalled; but his subtler medieval namesake had not only propounded but embraced and defended the same conjecture three centuries earlier. Roemer's observation in 1675, through which it became established as one of the fundamental theorems of empirical science, is not usually mentioned in the histories of philosophy; but the omission merely shows how badly the history of

philosophy is commonly written, for the discovery was as significant for epistemology as it was for physics and astonomy. It appeared definitely to forbid that naïvely realistic way of taking the content of visual perception to which all men at first naturally incline. The doctrine of the finite velocity of light meant that the sense from which most of our information about the world beyond our epidermal surfaces is derived never discloses anything which (in Francis Bacon's phrase) "really exists" in that world, at the instant at which it indubitably exists in perception. It is with a certain phase in the history of a distant star that the astonomer, gazing through his telescope at a given moment, is supposed to become acquainted; but that phase, and perhaps the star itself, have, ages since, ceased to be; and the astronomer's present sense-data—it has therefore seemed inevitable to say—whatever else they may be, are not identical with the realities they are believed to reveal. They might perhaps be supposed to be identical with the peripheral effect produced by the light-ray on its belated arrival at the eye—in other words, with the retinal images; but two present and inverted retinal images *here* are obviously not the same as one extinct star formerly existing elsewhere, and the duality of datum and object would therefore remain. This particular hypothesis, moreover, is excluded by the now familiar fact established by the physiological psychologists, that there is a further lag—slight, but not theoretically negligible—in the transmission of the neural impulse to the cortical center, and therefore—since the percept does not appear until the impulse reaches the brain—a difference in time between the existence of a given pair of retinal images, or any other excitation of peripheral nerve-endings, and the existence of the corresponding percept. Never, in short, if both the physiologists and the physicists are right, can the datum or character-complex presented in the perception of a given moment be regarded as anything but the report of a messenger, more or less tardy and more or less open to suspicion, from the original object which we are said to know by virtue of that perception.

(3) Another class of empirical facts which are familiar, in their simpler forms, to all men have seemed by the plainest implication to show that perceptual content, even though it appears as external to the physical organs of perception, is not identical with the particular objects about which it is supposed to convey information. It is commonly assumed that the object, or objective, of a given perception can, first of all, be identified, at least roughly, by its position in space and time. What I am "perceiving" at a certain moment is the ink-bottle two feet away from my hand, or the star a hundred light-years distant. Even if the position

is defined only vaguely, the thing is at least supposed to be (or have been) "out there" somewhere. This identification of the object referred to is, obviously, possible only by means of the same perception; yet, assuming such identification, experience shows that what I perceive is determined by events or conditions intervening in space and time between that object and my so-called perception of it. The qualities sensibly presented vary with changes which appear to occur, not in the place where *the* object is supposed to exist, but in regions between it and the body itself, and, in particular, in the very organs of perception. The examples are trite: a man puts a lens before his eyes, and the size or shape or number or perceived distance of the objects presented is altered; he puts certain drugs into his stomach, and the colors of all the perceived objects external to his body change; he swallows other drugs in sufficient quantity, and sees outside his body objects which no one else can see, and which his own other senses fail to disclose. The discovery of this primary sort of physical relativity, which is really one of the most pregnant of philosophical discoveries, begins in infancy with the earliest experience of the illusions of perspective, or the observation that the objects in the visual field change their spatial relations when looked at with first one eye and then the other. If *homo sapiens* had at the outset been blind, the first seeing man, a paleolithic Einstein, when he reported this astonishing fact—the relativity of position to the motions of eyelids—to his fellow cave-men, would presumably have seemed to them a deviser of intolerable paradoxes, and have been made acquainted with those more effective methods for repressing strange doctrines which cave-men, no doubt, knew how to employ. The evidence of this dependence of the nature of what is perceived upon happenings which, as themselves experienced, do not happen in the right place to permit them to be regarded as changes in the *cognoscendum* itself, has constantly increased with the progress of the sciences of optics, neuro-cerebral physiology, and psychology; the eventual determination of the character of the percept has been removed farther and farther, not only from the external object, but even from the external organ of sense. As Professor Dewey remarked, in the preceding series of these lectures, "it is pure fiction that a 'sensation' or peripheral excitation, or stimulus, travels undisturbed in solitary state in its own coach-and-four to either the brain or consciousness in its purity. A particular excitation is but one of an avalanche of contemporaneously occurring excitations, peripheral and from proprioceptors; each has to compete with others, to make terms with them; what happens is an integration of complex forces." And even in the earliest and easiest phases of this discovery, the variability of the percept with conditions extrinsic to the object to be perceived manifestly affects those attributes by which the very identity of the individual object should be defined: it is not colors only but shapes, not shapes only but perceived positions, that prove to be functions of the processes spatially and temporally intervenient between the object and the perception, and therefore not attributable to the former. Thus what is actually perceived could be regarded only as the terminal effect of a more or less long and complex causal series of events happening at different places and times, only at the perceptually inaccessible other end of which series the *cognoscendum* was supposed to have—or rather, to have had—its being. Aside from any empirical evidences of the sort mentioned, it has apparently seemed to many minds virtually axiomatic that, if the *cognoscendum* in perception is conceived (as it is in ordinary thought and in most physical theory) as a "causal object" acting upon the bodily organs of perception in the determination of the character of the content experienced, that which is acted *upon* must also have a part—must, indeed, have the last and decisive word—in determining the character of that content. How under these circumstances the exterior causal object could be known at all is an obviously difficult question; this argument for epistemological dualism, and especially the rôle assigned in it to the organs of perception, gives rise to that "crux of realistic theories" which Mr. C. A. Strong has very precisely expressed: "to explain how a sensation which varies directly only with one physical object, the nervous system, can yet vary with another physical object sufficiently to give knowledge of it." But with these ulterior difficulties we are not for the moment concerned; whatever *their* solution, they obviously do not annul the difficulty, for any realistic philosophy, of identifying the end-term with the initial term of the physico-physiological causal series.

(4) This physical and physiological conditionedness of the data manifestly implies that the contents of the experience of percipients having different spatial and physical relations to a postulated external object cannot be wholly identical. But this implication is independently confirmed and extended through that communication and comparison of experiences which is supposed to be possible through language. While the many knowers are, by the fifth article of the natural epistemological creed, dealing with what is said to be one and the same object—and if they are not doing so are not achieving what is meant by knowledge—they notoriously are not experiencing the same sensible appearances. There is an assumed identity of the region of space at which the observers are all gazing, and this serves for the requisite antecedent identification of

the common *cognoscendum;* but what they severally find occupying this supposedly single locus consists of character-complexes which are not merely diverse but (according to the logic almost universally accepted until recently) contradictory. So long as it is assumed either that there are certain sets of sensible qualities—e.g., two or more colors—which are incompatible, i.e., cannot both occupy the same place or the same surface of a material object at the same time, or that there are in nature "things" which at a given moment have a single and harmonious outfit of geometrical and other properties, the conclusion has seemed inevitable that the many discrepant appearances cannot "really" inhabit the one place or be the one thing at that place. So soon as the dimmest notion that there is such a phenomenon as perspective distortion dawned upon men, they began *eo ipso* to be epistemological dualists. It is of course conceivable, so far as the present consideration goes, that *one* of the discordant appearances might be identical with the object-to-be-known or with some part of it; but even so, since all the other observers are also supposed to be apprehending the object, *their* apprehension, at least, must be mediated through data which are *not* identical with it. Nor does it seem a probable hypothesis that, while *almost* all percepton is mediate, a few privileged observers now and then attain direct access to the object.

(5) Finally, the experience of error and illusion, however difficult it may be to render philosophically intelligible, seems to have at least one direct and obvious implication: namely, that the thing which at any moment we err about—otherwise than by mere omission—cannot be a thing which is immediately present to us at that moment, since about the latter there can be no error. It, at least, *is* what it is experienced as. In so far as *cognoscendum* and content are identified, error is excluded; in so far as the possibility of error is admitted, *cognoscendum* and content are set apart from one another. It may perhaps seem that this reasoning applies only to the cases in which there *is* error, and that in true judgments (or in veridical perception) the content may still be the same as the *cognoscendum.* And if the term "true judgments" includes the mere awareness of an immediate datum, then in such judgments there is in fact no duality. But these constitute, at best, only a tiny part of the subject-matter of our claims to potential knowledge, the range of our possible judgments at any given time; and it is, indeed, an obviously inconvenient use of language to call them judgments at all. For the most part we are occupied, when judging, with matters conceived to be so related to us that we are not, from the very nature of that relation, necessarily immune against error; doubt as to the validity of our judgments about them is

assumed to be not meaningless. But where error is *conceivable,* the relation between content and *cognoscendum* must be the same as in the case of actual error. The generic nature of judgments-potentially-erroneous must be conceived in such a way as to permit the genus to have both judgments actually true and judgments actually false as its species—and to make it intelligible that the latter are aiming at the same mark as the former without hitting it. But a judgment is about something in particular; it has to do with a specific portion of reality. Since in actually erroneous judgments it is impossible that that portion can be the immediate datum, error must consist in attributing some character now present in perception or imagery, or represented by a verbal symbol, to *another* locus in reality, where it in fact is not present; and the species of actually true judgments will correspondingly be defined as the attribution of some such character to another locus in reality where it in fact *is* present. In all this, once more, I have only been putting explicitly the way of thinking about truth and error which seems to be common to all mankind, barring a few philosophers of more or less recent times. That bit of baldly dualistic epistemology known as the correspondence-theory of truth is one of the most deeply ingrained and persistent of human habits; there is much reason to doubt whether any of the philosophers who repudiate it actually dispense with it; yet *it* is not merely an instinctive faith, but has behind it certain simple and definite logical considerations which it appears absurd to deny. This also, among the five points of natural epistemological dualism, may plausibly be supposed to have been a part of the unformulated working epistemology of our race from an early stage in the progress of intelligence; for there can hardly have been many featherless bipeds so naïve as not to have learned that man is liable to error, and so dull as to be unable to see, at least dimly, that in direct contemplation there is no room for error.

C. D. Broad

Sense-Perception and Matter *

I think that I have now proved that we are tied down to three alternatives, each almost as distasteful to common-sense as the others. (*a*) We may try to keep the common-sense view that the objective constitutents of some visual situations are literally spatio-temporal parts of a certain physical object, which we are said to be "seeing". But, if we do this, we must hold either (α) that this physical object can be both constant and variable in its spatial characteristics within the same stretch of time; or (β) that the objective constituents of the visual situations can have qualities which are different from and inconsistent with those which they seem on careful inspection to have. Or (*b*) we may drop the common-sense view that the objective constituent of a visual situation may be, and in some cases actually is, literally a spatio-temporal part of a certain physical object which we are said to be "seeing". I will now take these alternatives in turn.

(a,α) *Theory of Multiple Inherence.* It might be held that this alternative is so absurd that it is not worth discussing. Is it not a plain contradiction that the same part of the same thing should be at once variable and constant in size, round and elliptical, and so on? It seems to me that this is possible, if and only if what we commonly regard as pure qualities are really relational properties. We all know that the same man can be at the same time generous (to his family) and stingy (to his workmen). The only question is whether we could possibly deal with such propositions as "This is round", "This is elliptical", etc., where "This" is an objective constituent in a visual situation, in a similar way. Let us first state what characteristics the objective constituent of a visual situation seems on careful inspection to have. I think we may fairly say that it seems to be a spatially extended patch, having a certain determinate size and

* From *The Mind and its Place in Nature* by C. D. Broad, pp. 160–174. Copyright 1929 by Harcourt, Brace and Company, Inc. Reprinted by permission of the Humanities Press, Inc.

shape, situated in a certain determinate position out from the body, and now occupied and marked out by a certain determinate shade of a certain colour. Of course, the colour need not be uniform throughout the region; but this raises no question of principle, so I will assume for simplicity that it is uniform. We have then four things to consider: the apparent colour, the apparent shape and size, the apparent position, and the apparent date at which the colour inheres in the place.

Now it has been suggested that the objective constituent of a visual situation can be regarded as a certain region of physical space which is pervaded by a certain determinate shade of colour at a certain time, *provided that* we recognise that the relation of "pervasion" is of a peculiar kind. It must not be a two-term relation, involving only the pervading colour and the pervaded region, as we commonly suppose. It must be at least a three-term relation, involving the pervading colour, the pervaded region, and another region which we might call the "region of projection". Theories of this kind have been suggested lately by Dr. Whitehead and by Professor Kemp Smith; and it seems to me that such a theory in a very crude form may be detected by a very charitable interpreter in the writings of Malebranche. I propose now to discuss it in my own way without further reference to the eminent men who have suggested it. I will call this type of theory "The Theory of Multiple Inherence".

The impression which it makes on me at the outset is that it can be made to work very well for secondary qualities, like colour, provided we raise no questions about shape, size, position, and date; but that it is more difficult to deal with these apparent characteristics of the objective constituents of perceptual situations in terms of the theory. Let us begin with colour. According to the theory the proposition "This is sensibly of such and such a shade of red" (where "this" is an objective constituent of a visual situation) *could not* be true if "this" were the only thing in the world, any more than "This is a shareholder" could be true if "this" were the only thing in the world. And by "could not" here I mean, not merely that it is *causally* impossible, but also that it is *logically* impossible. Red, on the present view, is a characteristic of such a kind that it cannot inhere in a place simply; it can only "inhere-in-a-place-from-a-place", and this relation, which needs such a complex phrase to express it, is simple and unanalysable. Now, supposing that this were true, it would be perfectly possible that one and the same region of physical Space should be pervaded at one and the same time by different determinate shades of red. For the minimum complete statement about pervasion by a colour would be of the form: "The determinate shade r_1 inheres in the place

s from the place s_1 at the time t". And this is perfectly compatible with: "The determinate share r_2 inheres in the place s from the place s_2 at the time t". What *would* be inconsistent with the first proposition is the proposition: "The determinate shade r_2 inheres in the place s from the place s_1 at the time t". But there is no reason to suppose that this complication ever arises, so it need not trouble us.

It would now be perfectly easy to define a meaning for the phrase "*s is* red" without reference to any other particular place. We might, e.g., define "*s is* red" to mean "From *every* place *some* shade of red inheres in s". This is no doubt only a first approximation to a satisfactory definition. For "every place" we should certainly have to substitute "every place that fulfils such and such conditions". But the general principle of the definition is obvious enough, and I do not think that there would be much difficulty in mentioning the conditions. The full statement would not, I think, differ very much from the following:—"s is physically red" means "From every place which is physically occupied by a normal human brain and nervous system in a normal condition and is near enough to s some shade of red sensibly inheres in s." The first condition is put in to deal with colour-blind men and men drugged with santonin; the second is put in to cut out complications about coloured spectacles, and so on.

The essence of the theory, so far as we have gone, is this: We must distinguish between the "sensible" and the "physical" inherence of a colour in a place. The former is the fundamental and indefinable relation; and it is irreducibly triadic, involving an essential reference to the pervading shade of colour, the pervaded region, and the region of projection. The latter is a two-term relation; but it is not ultimate, for it is definable in terms of the former. And the definition is of the following kind: "R inheres physically in s" means "From every place s_n, which fulfils certain conditions C, some determinate form r_n of the determinable R sensibly inheres in s". With these definitions we could perfectly well maintain the common-sense view that a physical object cannot have two different colours at once, and yet admit that it does have different colours at once. We should simply need to clear up the ambiguities of our statements. The truth will be (1) that two different colours cannot *sensibly* inhere in the same place *from the same place* at once; (2) that two different colours cannot *physically* inhere in the same place at once; but (3) that different colours or different shades of the same colour can *sensibly* inhere in the same place from *different* places at once. Perhaps I ought to say a word or two in further explanation of the second of these propositions. To say that the same place was at once physically red and physically green would be to say that from every one of a certain set of places this place was sensibly pervaded by some shade of red, and that from every one of the same set of places it is at the same time sensibly pervaded by some shade of green. This, I suppose, would be admitted to be impossible. But it does not cover all that we mean when we say that the same place could not at once be physically pervaded by two different colours. Under this head we should also include, e.g., two different shades of red as well as two different colours, such as red and green. This, however, raises no insuperable difficulty. We have defined the physical *colour* of a place in terms of the *colour* under which all the determinate shades which sensibly inhere in it from a certain set of places fall. It would be quite easy to define its physical *shade* in a similar way. We should say that a certain place was physically pervaded by purple if and only if all the shades which sensibly inhere in it from places which fulfil the required conditions fell within certain limits. If we were prepared to say that this place is physically pervaded by scarlet it is certain that it would have to be sensibly pervaded from the *same* places by *different* shades of red. Since it could not be sensibly pervaded at the same time and from the same place by different shades of the same colour any more than by shades of different colours, it would be impossible for it to be at once physically pervaded by scarlet and by purple on our definitions.

So far we have been discussing a question which may be called "logical", in a wide sense, and certainly not "causal". By this I mean that we have simply been considering the question: "What formal characteristics must the relation of inherence possess if it is to be logically possible to hold that a number of different colours or shades of colour inhere at the same time in the whole of the same region of Physical Space?" The *causal* question is: "Under what conditions will such and such a colour inhere in such and such a place from such and such a place?" To this question I now turn.

In view of what we know of geometrical and physical optics and of the physiology of vision, I think that the following answer is *almost* certain. The *independently* necessary and sufficient *material* conditions for a certain shade of colour to pervade a certain external region from a certain region of projection are all contained in or are close to the region of projection. (I will explain in a moment why I introduce the qualifications which I have italicised.) The direction of the pervaded region is the direction in which a normal human being, whose body is in the projecting region, has to look, in order to get the objective constituent under consideration into the middle of his visual field; and this is known to depend simply on what is going on in the immediate neighborhood of his eyes. When a number of people are said to be "seeing the same object directly under normal conditions", i.e., without complications due to mirrors, non-homogeneous transparent media, and so on, their respective lines of sight intersect within a fairly small determinate region. This is where the object is then said to be. But of course there often are mirrors and other complications, and we must be prepared to deal with the general case. When the medium is in fact non-homogeneous, or the vision is indirect, the place which is pervaded by a given shade of colour from a given region of projection is that place in which a suitable object *would* have to be put in order to present the same appearance *if* viewed directly and through a homogeneous medium. In actual fact nothing physically relevant may be going on in this region; this is the case with mirror images. If I look at the reflection of a luminous point in a plane mirror the region which is pervaded from where I am standing is somewhere behind the mirror; it is the place where a luminous point would have to be put in order to present the actual appearance, if viewed directly and without a mirror, from where I am standing. And of course nothing physically relevant is happening at this place behind the mirror. The direction of the place is determined by the direction in which the light enters my eye, i.e., by physical events in the immediate neighbourhood of the region of projection. Its distance along this direction is presumably determined by traces left in my brain by past visual situations and correlated bodily movements in cases where the vision really was direct and through a homogeneous medium. Thus I am justified in saying that the position of the pervaded region is immediately determined by events in or close to the region of projection.

Next, the facts which make us ascribe a velocity to light, and particularly the fact of aberration, make it almost certain that the date at which a certain place is pervaded by a certain shade of colour from a certain region of projection is the date at which certain events are happening within the region of projection. When I look at a distant star a certain shade of colour sensibly inheres in a certain distant region of Physical Space from the place which is physically occupied by my body, if the present theory be true. But we know quite well that the star may no longer be physically occupying this distant region; and that, whether it does so or not, the relevant physical events may have happened there hundreds of years ago.

Lastly, and in close connexion with this, we must notice that the particular colour and the particular shade of it which sensibly pervade an external place from a region of projection are almost certainly determined by specific events in the eyes, optic nerves, and brain which now physically occupy this region of projection. Facts about colour-blindness, about the effects of drugs like santonin, and of morbid bodily states like jaundice, make this practically certain.

I have now defended the statement that the *independently* necessary and sufficient *material* conditions which determine that such and such an external place shall be pervaded by such and such a shade of colour from a certain region of projection are physically present within or close to that region. I will now explain what I mean by the italicised qualifications in this statement. (1) The physical events within the region of projection of course have physical causes. Now a necessary condition of a necessary condition of an event may be called a "dependently" necessary condition of that event. There is every reason to believe that the pervasion of a certain region from a certain region by a certain shade of colour has generally *dependently* necessary conditions which are quite remote from the region of projection. When a certain place is pervaded by very similar shades of the same colour from all directions it is generally found that, on walking up to this place, tactual situations arise. And the objective constituents of these tactual situations are generally found to be closely correlated with the objective constituents of the successive visual situations which occur as we walk up to this place. We say then that this place is "tactually occupied". And we have very good reason to believe that such a region is physically occupied by certain microscopic events which are remote and dependently necessary conditions of the pervasion of this region by such and such a shade of colour from places round it. These events determine by physical causation certain events in our eyes, optic nerves, and brains; and the latter events are the immediately necessary and sufficient material conditions of the pervasion of the external region by such and such a shade of colour from the region of projection which contains our bodies. This may be regarded as the normal case; and it is expressed in common language by saying that we are then "looking directly at a certain physical object through a colourless homogeneous medium". But of course this sweet simplicity, though normal, is not universal. Suppose that a number of people "see the same mirror image". Then there is a certain set of microscopic physical events in a certain region of Space; and these do constitute the common dependently necessary condition of the pervasion of a place behind the mirror by similar shades of the same colour from a number of different regions of projection. But the region which contains these physical microscopic events is remote from the region in which these shades of colour sensibly inhere;

it is in fact as far in front of the mirror as the pervaded region is behind it.

Let us call the region which contains the common dependently necessary conditions "the emitting region". Then the position may be put as follows: In visual perception we have to consider an emitting region, a region of projection, a pervaded region, and a pervading shade of colour. The pervaded region is immediately determined by events in and near the region of projection. These events also determine immediately the pervading shade and colour. And they are themselves determined by microscopic events in the emitting region. In the cases that arise most often in everyday practical life the pervaded region and the emitting region roughly coincide. But, in the case of mirror-images and the visual situations which arise when we are surrounded by non-homogeneous media, the pervaded region and the emitting region cease to coincide and may be very distant from each other. The pervaded region may then contain no physical events at all; and, if it does, they will be quite irrelevant. In such cases there will always be a purely optical peculiarity too, viz., that the pervaded region will never be pervaded from *all* directions by similar shades of the same colour. (Cf. the sudden change which happens in the visual situation when we go to the back of a mirror in which we have been viewing the image of a certain object.)

Just as we have contrasted the prevaded region and the emitting region, so we must contrast the "date of pervasion" and the "date of emission". Owing to the very great velocity of light these generally coincide almost exacly in the visual situations of ordinary life. But, when we are concerned with very remote objects, such as stars, the date of emission (which is *always* earlier than the date of pervasion) may precede the latter by thousands of years. In the phenomenon of aberration we have a most interesting case in which the motion of the observer of a very distant object, and the difference between the *date* of emission and the *date* of pervasion, cause a difference between the *place* of emission and the *place* of pervasion.

(2) I have now explained why I used the phrase "*independently* necessary and sufficient conditions". It remains to explain why I introduced the word "material" before "conditions" in my original statement. This was simply a precaution. I cannot be completely certain that the sensible inherence of such and such a shade of colour in such and such a place from a given region of projection *may* not have psychical as well as physical conditions. Since we cannot get a brain and nervous system like ours working properly without a mind like ours, it is obviously impossible

to be sure that the latter is irrelevant for the present purpose and that the former is sufficient by itself. And, besides this general consideration, there is a more specific ground for caution. I do not think that the determination of the position of the pervaded region can be completely explained without reference to the persistent effect of past visual and tactual situations and bodily movements, and the associations between them. Now of course these factors *may* now be represented simply by persistent and suitably linked material modifications in the brain and nervous system. But, on the one hand, these material "traces" are purely hypothetical effects of certain causes and causes of certain effects. And, on the other hand, even if they be *now* purely material, it may be that they could not have been formed *originally* without the action of the mind, at least in the form of selective attention. If this be so, we might still say that the *independently* necessary conditions for a certain colour to pervade a certain place from a given region of projection are all material; but we should have to recognise that the past action of the mind is a *dependently* necessary condition, just as much as the past vibrations of distant electrons.

So far the Theory of Multiple Inherence seems to have worked fairly well. But we have left to the end the hardest question with which it is faced. This is the question of "physical" and "sensible" shape and size. We know that different observers, who say that they are all seeing the whole of the top of the same penny, find on careful inspection that the shapes and sizes of the objective constituents of their respective visual situations seem to be different. We know that the same complication arises if a single observer moves about whilst he claims all the time to be seeing the whole of the top of the same penny. And we know that it also arises when the same observer claims to be at once seeing and touching the whole of the top of the same penny. We have dealt with similar difficulties about shades of colour by suggesting that the relation of inherence between a colour and the place which it pervades is irreducibly triadic, and not dyadic, as has commonly been thought. But can we possibly deal with the difficulties about shape and size in the same way? Curiously enough. Dr. Whitehead does not, so far as I know, discuss this point. Yet no theory can claim to be satisfactory which does not make some answer to the question.

At first sight it seems evident that we cannot deal with variations in the apparent shape of the same surface in the way in which we have been dealing with variations in its apparent colour. It seems obvious that the proposition "This is round" *could* have been true, even if there had been nothing in the world but this area. In fact the shape of a region seems to be an intrinsic quality of it; and it seems nonsense to talk of various shapes inhering in a certain region from various places. Plausible as this argument sounds, I believe that it is mistaken. I think that it overlooks a very important distinction, viz., the distinction between a "sensible form" and a "geometrical property". I shall first try to explain the difference between the two, and to show that they must be distinguished quite apart from the present problem. And I shall then try to show that the distinction enables us to apply the Multiple Inherence Theory to the question of variations of apparent shape and size.

Let us consider circularity, for example. I find it necessary to distinguish a certain geometrical property called "circularity" and a certain sensible form called by the same name, for the following reasons. The geometrical property can be *defined.* To say that a certain area is geometrically circular *means* that all the points on its boundary are equidistant from a fixed point. But, if I wanted to make someone understand what I was referring to by the phrase "sensibly circular", it would be of no use whatever to offer this definition or any other definition. All that I could do would be to proceed by *exemplification,* just as I should have to do if I wanted to make him understand what I am referring to when I use the word "red". I should in fact have to proceed as follows: I might start by getting the man to look straight down on to a penny. I should then cut out geometrically circular bits of paper of various colours and sizes and get him to look straight down on them. I should also cut out bits of paper of the same colours and different geometrical shapes, and get him to look straight down on them. I should then say to him: "You notice that there was a certain resemblance between all the objective constituents of the first series of visual situations in which I placed you, in spite of the differences of colour, etc. And you notice that there was a certain unlikeness between every objective constituent of the first series of visual situations and every objective constituent of the second series. Very well; what I am referring to by the phrase "circular sensible form" is that feature which was present in all members of the first series and absent in all members of the second." In my view it is just as impossible to know *a priori* that a geometrically circular area, when pervaded by a colour and viewed normally, would have the sensible form called "circularity" as it is to know *a priori* that an area containing electrons moving in a certain way would be pervaded by a certain shade of red from a place occupied by a normal human body. Of course some *geometrical* properties are themselves indefinable, e.g., geometrical straightness. But it remains a fact that *all* sensible forms are indefinable, whilst *many* of the geometrical properties which are called by the same name are definable. It is therefore certain that geometrical properties and the sensible forms which are called by the same names must be distinguished.

Let us now apply this conclusion to our present problem. When it is said that the shape of a region is an intrinsic property, and that it is nonsense to talk of it having such and such a shape *from* such and such another region, this is true only of geometrical shape. If an area is geometrically circular it is so intrinsically, and there is an end of the matter. But, since geometrical shape and sensible form must always be distinguished, it does not follow that the sensible form of an area is an intrinsic property of it. It may be that one and the same area is "informed" by one sensible form from one place and by a different sensible form from another place. The relation of "informing" may be irreducibly triadic, as we have suggested that the relation of "pervading" is. If this be so, it may be that it is only from one place or one series of places that an area with a certain geometrical shape is informed by that sensible form which has the same name as the geometrical shape. A like distinction will have to be drawn between geometrical and physical size. The geometrical size of a region will be an intrinsic property of it; but the sensible size may be a property which it only has from another region. It will of course be just as necessary to distinguish tactual form from geometrical shape as to distinguish visual form from geometrical shape. But there may be good reasons for holding that tactual form is a safer indication of geometrical shape than is visual form.

There is every reason to believe that the visual form which informs a certain external region from a certain region of projection is causally determined by events which are physically contained within the region of projection. The determining factors would seem to be the geometrical shape and size of the part of the retina affected by light, and traces in the brain and nervous system left by past visual and tactual situations. Here again it seems to me that we cannot be sure that the mind does not play an essential part, if not as an independently necessary condition, yet perhaps as a remote and dependently necessary condition for the original formation and association of the traces.

A. J. Ayer

Perception *

. . . The phenomenalist need not deny that the occurrence and character of sense-data are to be explained in terms of entities which are not themselves observable. He must, however, maintain that to talk about such unobservable entities is, in the end, to talk about sense-data. His position is that every empirical statement about a physical object, whether it seems to refer to a scientific entity, or to an object of the more familiar kind which a naive realist would claim directly to perceive, is reducible to a statement, or set of statements, about sense-data. And what he is ordinarily taken to mean by saying that a statement S is reducible to a set of statements K is first that the members of K are on a lower epistemological level than S, that is that they refer to 'harder' data, and secondly that S and K are logically equivalent. The notion of logical equivalence is, in this context, not so clear as one could wish, but it requires at least that it should not be possible for us to find, or even to describe, a set of circumstances in which one statement would be true and its supposed equivalent false.

The first difficulty which the phenomenalist has to meet is that physical objects, unlike sense-data, can exist without being perceived. To say this is not to beg the question against Berkeley. It is simply that we so define our terms that it is a necessary condition for anything to be a physical object that it makes sense to say of it that it exists unperceived. This is not, in itself, to say that there are physical objects, and one might understand Berkeley as maintaining that there are not, or, more precisely, that there could not be. I doubt, however, if this would be an altogether just interpretation of Berkeley. He did allow that things, which commonly passed for physical objects, could continue to exist when only God perceived them; and to say of something that it is perceived only by God is to

* From "Perception" by A. J. Ayer, in *British Philosophy in the Mid-Century,* edited by C. A. Mace, pp. 228–236. Copyright 1936 by The Macmillan Company. Reprinted by permission of George Allen and Unwin Ltd. and The Macmillan Company.

say that it is not, in any ordinary sense, perceived at all. In any case the phenomenalist does not deny that there are physical objects; his contention is that they are constituted by sense-data. But the fact that they can exist unperceived obliges him to hold that the statements about sense-data, into which statements about physical objects are to be translated, are predominantly hypothetical. They will for the most part have to state not that any sense-data are actually occurring, but only that certain sense-data would occur if the appropriate conditions were fulfilled. Furthermore, these hypotheticals cannot be construed as statements of material implication; for in that case they would all be true provided that their antecedents were false, which would put the phenomenalist in the position of holding that anything whatsoever existed so long as it was unperceived. The hypotheticals which he mainly needs are subjunctive conditionals: but their correct analysis presents a problem.

Some critics base an objection to phenomenalism not so much on the difficulty of interpreting these unfulfilled conditionals as on the fact that they are brought in at all. They maintain that when statements about physical objects are categorical, as they very frequently are, no rendering of them, however complicated and ingenious, into merely hypothetical statements about sense-data can possibly be adequate. 'Such a categorical existential material object sentence', says Mr. Berlin, 'as, "the table is next door" or "there is a table next door", is used at the very least to describe something which is occurring or being characterized at the time of speaking . . . ; and being characterized or occurring, unless the contrary is specifically stated or implied, not intermittently but continuously, and in any case not "hypothetically". For to say that something is occurring hypothetically is a very artificial and misleading way of saying that it is not, in the ordinary sense, occurring at all . . .'[1] I cannot myself see that there is any logical force in this objection. It is quite true that sentences which express hypothetical statements about sense-data are not used to assert that any sense-data are occurring, but it does not follow that they are not used to assert that any physical events are occurring, or that any physical objects exist. On the contrary this is exactly what they do state if phenomenalism is correct. There is no more difficulty of principle in replacing categorical statements about chairs and tables by hypothetical statements about sense-data, than there is in replacing categorical statements about electrons by hypothetical statements about Geiger counters, or whatever it may be, or in replacing categorical statements about people's

[1] I. Berlin, 'Empirical Propositions and Hypothetical Statements', *Mind,* vol. LIX, no. 235, pp. 300–1.

unconscious feelings by hypothetical statements about their overt behaviour. Whether the translation can even theoretically be carried out in any of these cases is another question. As we shall see, there are strong reasons for concluding that the phenomenalist's 'reduction' is not feasible: but its possibility cannot be excluded merely on the ground that it substitutes hypothetical statements at one level for categorical statements at another.

What is puzzling about Mr. Berlin's position is that he is prepared to allow, at least for the sake of argument, that categorical statements about physical objects and hypothetical statements about sense-data may 'strictly entail' each other, which is surely all that any phenomenalist requires. He objects only that even if they do entail each other they are not identical in meaning, and in some legitimate sense of 'identical in meaning' he is no doubt right. His main point is, I think, that these different types of statement have, as it were, a different 'feel'. As he truly says, 'common sense and the philosophers who are in sympathy with it, have always felt dissatisfied (with phenomenalism). The reduction of material object sentences into what we may, for short, call sense-datum sentences, seemed to leave something out, to substitute something intermittent and attenuated for something solid and continuous'.[2] In fact, if the phenomenalists are right, nothing is left out: any statement which implies that there are solid and continuous objects in the world will re-appear in the form of the appropriate statements about sense-data. But even if nothing is left out, it is natural that something should seem to be. For there is no picture associated with phenomenalism in the way that the picture of things continuing to exist in much the same form as we perceive them is associated with a naive realist theory of perception, or the picture of things existing stripped of their disguise is associated with the causal theory. A permanent possibility of sensation is not something that can very well be pictured. In Plato's myth, the shadows in the cave are contrasted with substantial objects outside. Phenomenalism seems to leave us with nothing but the shadows.

This may account for the psychological resistance with which phenomenalists so very often meet, but it does not prove that their thesis is false. However hard they may make it for us to construct an imaginative picture of the physical world, they may still be right in claiming that statements about physical objects are reducible to statements about sense-data. To do them justice this claim must be submitted to a purely logical examination. But even so I do not think that it succeeds. It requires, among other things, the elimination from sense-datum statements of any explicit reference to

[2] Op. cit., p. 291.

an observer or to public space and time: and this raises serious difficulties, as I have remarked elsewhere.[3] But even if we suppose these difficulties to be overcome, there remains a more general objection which the phenomenalist is not, so far as I can see, in a position to meet. If phenomenalism is true, the existence of a physical object of a certain sort must be a sufficient condition for the occurrence, in the appropriate circumstances, of certain sense-data; there must be a deductive step from physical reality to possible, if not to actual, appearances. And conversely, the occurrence of the sense-data must be a sufficient condition for the existence of the physical object; there must be a deductive step from actual, or at any rate possible, appearances to physical reality. The objection is that neither of these requirements can be satisfied.

The denial that statements which imply the existence of physical objects can be logically deduced from any finite set of statements about sense-data is often expressed in the form that no statement about a physical object can be conclusively verified. The probability of illusion can be diminished to a point where it becomes negligible, but its possibility is never formally excluded. However far they may be extended, our sense-experiences can never put the truth of any statement about a physical object beyond question; it remains consistent with them that the statement be false. But is this really so? Is it not very paradoxical to suggest that there can be any doubt of the existence of the table at which I am seated, the pen with which I am writing, the hand which is holding the pen? Surely I know for certain that these physical objects exist. And if I do know this, I know it on the basis of my sense experiences. Admittedly my present experiences, taken by themselves, are not sufficient for the purpose: the mere fact that I now seem to see and feel a table does not conclusively prove that there is a table there: it does not prove it even in the case of my own right hand. But when they are taken in conjunction with all my past experiences, then, it may plausibly be argued, these experiences are sufficient. They put it beyond question that these physical objects exist. The run of favourable evidence may indeed come to an end; it is at any rate logically possible that from this moment onwards there ceases to be any indication in experience that these objects exist, or ever have existed. But even if this were to happen it would not follow that they do not exist now or even that their present existence has not been conclusively established. It would, according to this argument, be a contradiction to deny that these physical objects exist while allowing that I have had the sense-experiences that I have.

[3] 'Phenomenalism', *Proceedings of the Aristotelian Society,* 1947–48.

But what must these experiences have been for this result to obtain? The difficulty is that any description of the way things seem, whatever the number of its details and however much they may corroborate each other, would still appear to admit of their really being otherwise. No doubt there soon comes a point at which the suggestion that things are not what they seem ceases to be serious; but this is not to say that it is formally excluded. It would, indeed, be absurd for me to query the truth of such statements as that this is a piece of paper or that this is my right hand. I can at this moment quite properly claim to know that these statements are true. But from the fact that I know these statements to be true, and even that I know them to be true on the basis of my sense-experience, it does not follow that they are logically entailed by any set of statements which describe my sense-experience. But surely, it may be objected, if this is so it is only because your sense-experience is too limited; if it were suitably increased the entailment would hold. We speak of illusions only in the cases in which there is a conflict among our sense-experiences; that is, when the expectations to which some of them give rise are not fulfilled by the others. But when they are all mutually corroborative, not even the logical possibility of illusion remains; to speak of all human experience as illusory would be meaningless. It is a necessary truth that you cannot fool all the people all of the time. But the answer to this is that while it may be meaningless to assert in a general way that all experience is illusory, it is not meaningless to say this of any particular description of experience, however far it is extended. The statement that the experiences so described are as a whole illusory may be false and even certainly false, but it will not be self-contradictory. For the phenomenalist to succeed, it is not enough that he can establish the general thesis that if all experience is as if there are physical objects, then there are physical objects. He must be able to find at least one specimen set of statements about sense-data from which a statement which implies the existence of a given physical object logically follows. And this, it seems to me, he cannot do.

Neither, I now think, can he make good the converse claim that the existence of a given physical object is a sufficient condition for the occurrence of certain sense-data. It is sometimes asserted, as by Berkeley, that to say, for example, that the earth moves is to say that 'if we were placed in such and such circumstances, and such or such a position and distance, both from the earth and sun, we should perceive the former to move—.'[4] But it might happen that when we were placed in these circumstances we did not perceive this at all, not because the earth was

[4] *Principles of Human Knowledge,* LVIII.

not moving, but because we were inattentive, or looking in the wrong direction, or our view was in some way obscured, or because we suffered from some physiological or psychological disorder. It may be suggested that these difficulties can be provided for. We might, for instance, attempt to rule out the possibility of the observer's suffering from some physiological disorder by adding a further hypothetical to the effect that if a physiologist were to examine him, or rather were to seem to be examining him, it would seem to the physiologist that his vision was unimpaired. But then we should require a further hypothetical to guard against the possibility that the physiologist was undergoing an illusion; and so *ad infinitum*. This is not to say that the fact that some physical object fails to be observed is never to be counted as a proof that it does not exist; it is on the contrary the very best proof obtainable. But it is not a demonstrative proof. From the fact that in the specified conditions the requisite sense-data do not occur it does not follow logically that the physical object which is in question does not exist, or that it does not have the properties with which it has been credited. In many cases, this is the obvious, indeed the only reasonable, explanation of the apparent facts; but the possibility of an alternative explanation must always remain open.

It might seem that this difficulty could be met by stipulating that the test for the presence or absence of the physical object was to be carried out in normal conditions by a normal observer: and indeed this is an assumption that is generally made by those who maintain that to speak of such an object as existing unperceived is to imply that if one were in the appropriate situation one would be perceiving it. But this is merely a way of concealing the difficulty, not of resolving it. If we are to understand by 'normal' conditions those that permit an observer to perceive things as they really are, and by a 'normal' observer one who in such conditions does perceive things as they really are, then indeed it will follow from the fact that there is a physical object in such and such a place that if a normal observer were there he would under normal conditions by perceiving it. But it will follow only because it is made to follow by our definition of normality. And the difficulty which we are trying to avoid reappears immediately as the difficulty of making sure that the conditions and the observer really are, in this sense, normal. Again, we may attempt to make sure by stipulating that if tests were made for every known source of abnormality, their results would all appear to be negative. But once more we shall need an infinite series of further hypotheticals to guarantee the tests themselves. Nor is it logically necessary that the sources of abnormality that are known to us are all the sources that there are.

It follows that the step from physical reality to possible appearances cannot by this method be made formally deductive. Neither, so far as I can see, can it be made so by any other.

It appears then, if my reasoning is correct, that the phenomenalist's programme cannot be carried through. Statements about physical objects are not, in general, translatable into statements about sense-data. In itself, indeed, this conclusion is not startling. It is rather what we should expect if we reflected merely on the way in which sentences which refer to physical objects are actually used. That phenomenalism has commanded so strong an allegiance has been due not to its intrinsic plausibility but rather to the fact that the introduction of sense-data appears to leave no other alternative open. It has been assumed that since statements about physical objects can be verified or falsified only through the occurrence of sense-data, they must somehow be reducible to statements about sense-data. This is a natural assumption to make, but I now think that it is false. There is a parallel here with the case of scientific theories which ostensibly refer to such things as atomic particles or unconscious mental states. The cash value of such theories is to be sought in the lower-level statements on the truth or falsehood of which their validity depends: at the same time, the statements of the theory are not simply reformulations of these lower-level statements. In this sense, I suggest that statements about physical objects are theoretical with respect to statements about sense-data. The relation between them is not strictly deductive; and to say that it is inductive leaves its exact nature still to be explained. . . .

Universals

Bertrand Russell

*The World of Universals**

The problem with which we are now concerned is a very old one, since it was brought into philosophy by Plato. Plato's "theory of ideas" is an attempt to solve this very problem, and in my opinion it is one of the most successful attempts hitherto made. The theory to be advocated in what follows is largely Plato's, with merely such modifications as time has shown to be necessary.

The way the problem arose for Plato was more or less as follows. Let us consider, say, such a notion as *justice*. If we ask ourselves what justice is, it is natural to proceed by considering this, that, and the other just act, with a view to discovering what they have in common. They must all, in some sense, partake of a common nature, which will be found in whatever is just and in nothing else. This common nature, in virtue of which they are all just, will be justice itself, the pure essence the admixture of which with facts of ordinary life produces the multiplicity of just acts. Similarly with any other word which may be applicable to common facts, such as "whiteness" for example. The word will be applicable to a number of particular things because they all participate in a common nature or essence. This pure essence is what Plato calls an "idea" or "form." (It must not be supposed that "ideas," in his sense, exist in minds, though they may be apprehended by minds.) The "idea" *justice* is not identical with anything that is just: it is something other than particular things, which particular things partake of. Not being particular, it cannot itself exist in the world of sense. Moreover it is not fleeting or changeable like the things of sense: it is eternally itself, immutable and indestructible.

Thus Plato is led to a supra-sensible world, more real than the common world of sense, the unchangeable world of ideas, which alone gives to the world of sense whatever pale reflection of reality may belong to it. The

* From *The Problems of Philosophy* by Bertrand Russell, Chapter IX. Copyright 1912 by The Home University Library. Reprinted by permission of the Oxford University Press.

truly real world, for Plato, is the world of ideas; for whatever we may attempt to say about things in the world of sense, we can only succeed in saying that they participate in such and such ideas, which, therefore, constitute all their character. Hence it is easy to pass on into a mysticism. We may hope, in a mystic illumination, to *see* the ideas as we see objects of sense; and we may imagine that the ideas exist in heaven. These mystical developments are very natural, but the basis of the theory is in logic, and it is as based in logic that we have to consider it.

The word "idea" has acquired, in the course of time, many associations which are quite misleading when applied to Plato's "ideas." We shall therefore use the word "universal" instead of the word "idea," to describe what Plato meant. The essence of the sort of entity that Plato meant is that it is opposed to the particular things that are given in sensation. We speak of whatever is given in sensation, or is of the same nature as things given in sensation, as a *particular;* by opposition to this, a *universal* will be anything which may be shared by many particulars, and has those characteristics which, as we saw, distinguish justice and whiteness from just acts and white things.

When we examine common words, we find that, broadly speaking, proper names stand for particulars, while other substantives, adjectives, prepositions, and verbs stand for universals. Pronouns stand for particulars, but are ambiguous: it is only by the context or the circumstances that we know what particulars they stand for. The word "now" stands for a particular, namely the present moment; but like pronouns, it stands for an ambiguous particular, because the present is always changing.

It will be seen that no sentence can be made up without at least one word which denotes a universal. The nearest approach would be some such statement as "I like this." But even here the word "like" denotes a universal, for I may like other things, and other people may like things. Thus all truths involve universals, and all knowledge of truths involves acquaintance with universals.

Seeing that nearly all the words to be found in the dictionary stand for universals, it is strange that hardly anybody except students of philosophy ever realises that there are such entities as universals. We do not naturally dwell upon those words in a sentence which do not stand for particulars; and if we are forced to dwell upon a word which stands for a universal, we naturally think of it as standing for some one of the particulars that come under the universal. When, for example, we hear the sentence, "Charles I.'s head was cut off," we may naturally enough think of Charles I., of Charles I.'s head, and of the operation of cutting off *his* head, which are all particulars; but we do not naturally dwell upon what is meant by the word "head" or the word "cut", which is a universal. We feel such words to be incomplete and insubstantial; they seem to demand a context before anything can be done with them. Hence we succeed in avoiding all notice of universals as such, until the study of philosophy forces them upon our attention.

Even among philosophers, we may say, broadly, that only those universals which are named by adjectives or substantives have been much or often recognised, while those named by verbs and prepositions have been usually overlooked. This omission has had a very great effect upon philosophy; it is hardly too much to say that most metaphysics, since Spinoza, has been largely determined by it. The way this has occurred is, in outline, as follows: Speaking generally, adjectives and common nouns express qualities or properties of single things, whereas prepositions and verbs tend to express relations between two or more things. Thus the neglect of prepositions and verbs led to the belief that every proposition can be regarded as attributing a property to a single thing, rather than as expressing a relation between two or more things. Hence it was supposed that, ultimately, there can be no such entities as relations between things. Hence either there can be only one thing in the universe, or, if there are many things, they cannot possibly interact in any way, since any interaction would be a relation, and relations are impossible.

The first of these views, which was advocated by Spinoza, and is held in our own day by Mr. Bradley and many other philosophers, is called *monism;* the second, which was advocated by Leibniz, but is not very common nowadays, is called *monadism,* because each of the isolated things is called a *monad.* Both these opposing philosophies, interesting as they are, result, in my opinion, from an undue attention to one sort of universals, namely the sort represented by adjectives and substantives rather than by verbs and prepositions.

As a matter of fact, if any one were anxious to deny altogether that there are such things as universals, we should find that we cannot strictly prove that there are such entities as *qualities, i.e.* the universals represented by adjectives and substantives, whereas we can prove that there must be *relations, i.e.* the sort of universals generally represented by verbs and prepositions. Let us take in illustration the universal *whiteness.* If we believe that there is such a universal, we shall say that things are white because they have the quality of whiteness. This view, however, was strenuously denied by Berkeley and Hume, who have been followed in this by later empiricists. The form which their denial took was to deny that there are such things as "abstract ideas." When we want to think of whiteness, they said, we form an image of some particular white thing, and reason concerning this particular, taking care not to deduce anything concerning it which we cannot see to be equally true of any other white thing. As an account of our actual mental processes, this is no doubt largely true. In geometry, for example, when we wish to prove something about all triangles, we draw a particular triangle and reason about it, taking care not to use any characteristic which it does not share with other triangles. The beginner, in order to avoid error, often finds it useful to draw several triangles, as unlike each other as possible, in order to make sure that his reasoning is equally applicable to all of them. But a difficulty emerges as soon as we ask ourselves how we know that a thing is white or a triangle. If we wish to avoid the universals *whiteness* and *triangularity,* we shall choose some particular patch of white or some particular triangle, and say that anything is white or a triangle if it has the right sort of resemblance to our chosen particular. But then the resemblance required will have to be a universal. Since there are many white things, the resemblance must hold between many pairs of particular white things; and this is the characteristic of a universal. It will be useless to say that there is a different resemblance for each pair, for then we shall have to say that these resemblances resemble each other, and thus at last we shall be forced to admit resemblance as a universal. The relation of resemblance, therefore, must be a true universal. And having been forced to admit this universal, we find that it is no longer worth while to invent difficult and unplausible theories to avoid the admission of such universals as whiteness and triangularity.

Berkeley and Hume failed to perceive this refutation of their rejection of "abstract ideas," because, like their adversaries, they only thought of *qualities,* and altogether ignored *relations* as universals. We have therefore here another respect in which the rationalists appear to have been in the right as against the empiricists, although, owing to the neglect or denial of relations, the deductions made by rationalists were, if anything, more apt to be mistaken than those made by empiricists.

Having now seen that there must be such entities as universals, the next point to be proved is that their being is not merely mental. By this is meant that whatever being belongs to them is independent of their being thought of or in any way apprehended by minds. We have already touched on this subject at the end of the preceding chapter, but we must now consider more fully what sort of being it is that belongs to universals.

Consider such a proposition as "Edinburgh is north of London." Here we have a relation between two places, and it seems plain that the relation subsists independently of our knowledge of it. When we come to know that Edinburgh is north of London, we come to know something which has to do only with Edinburgh and London: we do not cause the truth of the proposition by coming to know it, on the contrary we merely apprehend a fact which was there before we knew it. The part of the earth's surface where Edinburgh stands would be north of the part where London stands, even if there were no human being to know about north and south, and even if there were no minds at all in the universe. This is, of course, denied by many philosophers, either for Berkeley's reasons or for Kant's. But we have already considered these reasons, and decided that they are inadequate. We may therefore now assume it to be true that nothing mental is presupposed in the fact that Edinburgh is north of London. But this fact involves the relation "north of," which is a universal; and it would be impossible for the whole fact to involve nothing mental if the relation "north of," which is a constituent part of the fact, did involve anything mental. Hence we must admit that the relation, like the terms it relates, is not dependent upon thought, but belongs to the independent world which thought apprehends but does not create.

This conclusion, however, is met by the difficulty that the relation "north of" does not seem to *exist* in the same sense in which Edinburgh and London exist. If we ask "Where and when does this relation exist?" the answer must be "Nowhere and nowhen." There is no place or time where we can find the relation "north of." It does not exist in Edinburgh any more than in London, for it relates the two and is neutral as between them. Nor can we say that it exists at any particular time. Now everything that can be apprehended by the senses or by introspection exists at some particular time. Hence the relation "north of" is radically different from such things. It is neither in space nor in time, neither material nor mental; yet it is something.

It is largely the very peculiar kind of being that belongs to universals which has led many people to suppose that they are really mental. We can think *of* a universal, and our thinking then exists in a perfectly ordinary sense, like any other mental act. Suppose, for example, that we are thinking of whiteness. Then *in one sense* it may be said that whiteness is "in our mind." We have here the same ambiguity as we noted in discussing Berkeley in Chapter IV. In the strict sense, it is not whiteness that is in our mind, but the act of thinking of whiteness. The connected ambiguity in the word "idea," which we noted at the same time, also causes confusion here. In one sense of this word, namely the sense in which it denotes the *object* of an act of thought, whiteness is an "idea." Hence, if the ambiguity is not guarded against, we may come to think that whiteness is an "idea" in the other sense, *i.e.* an act of thought; and thus we come to think that whiteness is mental. But in so thinking, we rob it of its essential quality of universality. One man's act of thought is necessarily a different thing from another man's; one man's act of thought at one time is necessarily a different thing from the same man's act of thought at another time. Hence, if whiteness were the thought as opposed to its object, no two different men could think of it, and no one man could think of it twice. That which many different thoughts of whiteness have in common is their *object,* and this object is different from all of them. Thus universals are not thoughts, though when known they are the objects of thoughts.

We shall find it convenient only to speak of things *existing* when they are in time, that is to say, when we can point to some time *at* which they exist (not excluding the possibility of their existing at all times). Thus thoughts and feelings, minds and physical objects *exist.* But universals do not exist in this sense; we shall say that they *subsist* or *have being,* where "being" is opposed to "existence" as being timeless. The world of universals, therefore, may also be described as the world of being. The world of being is unchangeable, rigid, exact, delightful to the mathematician, the logician, the builder of metaphysical systems, and all who love perfection more than life. The world of existence is fleeting, vague, without sharp boundaries, without any clear plan or arrangement, but it contains all thoughts and feelings, all the data of sense, and all physical objects, everything that can do either good or harm, everything that makes any difference to the value of life and the world. According to our temperaments, we shall prefer the contemplation of the one or of the other. The one we do not prefer will probably seem to us a pale shadow of the one we prefer, and hardly worthy to be regarded as in any sense real. But the truth is that both have the same claim on our impartial attention, both are real, and both are important to the metaphysician. Indeed no sooner have we distinguished the two worlds than it becomes necessary to consider their relations.

C. I. Lewis

The Pure Concept

The word "concept" is used, in philosophic discussion, in many different senses, three of which it is particularly important to distinguish. It may signify (1) the psychological state of mind when one uses a word or phrase to designate some individual thing or some class of objects. Or (2) it may refer to the meaning of a word or phrase throughout some period of the development of the individual's thought, or some period of the development of a science, of a given culture, or even of humanity altogether. Or, (3) it may signify the logical intension or connotation of a term. This third meaning is exemplified by dictionary definitions where these are satisfactory—and is the usual signification of "concept" in the study of logic.

The use of any substantive phrase or term ordinarily undergoes a process of development, both in the history of society and in the history of any individual who uses it. Usually, though not always, the denotation of the term remains unchanged throughout this process; we apply it to the same class of objects, but our realization of what is essential to these things reflects a process of learning. Such learning may consist in an enlargement of our experience of the class of things in question, or it may occasionally represent simply our more accurate apprehension of what are the universal properties and relations of the familiar objects thus classified. But if the meaning of a word or phrase undergo evolution, then, however normal or inevitable or commendable this process may be, we must, for the sake of clarity, recognize that this meaning is one unitary entity only in some generic and genetic sense, and that logically what we have is a succession of different meanings, related in ways which may be important. The recognition of their historical continuity must not obscure the fact of their logical distinctness.

* From *Mind and the World Order* by C. I. Lewis, Chapter III. Reprinted through permission by Dover Publications, Inc., New York 10, New York ($1.95).

The problem of the developing adequacy of thought is an interesting and important one; it requires as one of its fundamental categories the notion of just such historical and psychological continuities; and the selection of the word "concept" to designate this category is natural. No criticism of such genetic study or of this use of the term is intended. But this psychological and educational category must not be confused with "meaning" in the sense in which logic, for instance, requires that term. Here a meaning must be precise and clear, or be capable of being made so, and must remain unaltered throughout any discussion in which it occurs. No psychological or historical process is legislated out of existence by this restriction in the use of the word, but if there should be development or learning which affects the connotation of a term, then, from this point of view, we have *another* meaning; that is all.

Again, the psychological state is not the object in which we are here primarily interested. If a psychologist, thinking in terms of a context-theory of meaning, says, "Infinity means to me the image of the blue-black, dense, arched sky," [1] then we must observe that such a psychologist blurs over the distinction between what is essential and what is non-essential in meaning. He is in no danger of misunderstanding one who talks about what the symbol ∞ denotes to be referring to the heavens, nor does he, even in his own thinking, suppose that infinity is blue-black. To use "concept" to designate such a psychological state or association-complex, is to fail to mark the distinction between what is objective in meaning and what is adventitious or purely personal. Indeed, the question how meaning *can* be objective and shared, when the psychological states which are bearers of this meaning are separate existences and not even identical in their qualitative content, is one of the important problems of meaning.

Because it is our main interest here to isolate that element in knowledge which we can with certainty maintain to be objective and impersonal, we shall define the pure concept as "that meaning which must be common to two minds when they understand each other by the use of a substantive or its equivalent." (For brevity, the qualification "pure" will be omitted throughout the remainder of this chapter.) However, this designation of community of meaning as the distinguishing mark of the concept is, in part, merely an expository device for singling out that element in knowledge which, for reasons which will appear, I wish here to discuss.

That meanings may have this sort of objectivity, is a fundamental assumption of science or of any other intellectual enterprise. If there is nothing objective about propositions and concepts, then there is no such thing

[1] The reference is, of course, to Titchener.

as truth and there can be no serious purpose in reflection or discussion. There must be meanings which are common to minds when they coöperate in scientific or even in merely practical endeavors. Otherwise the coöperation is illusory; and one cannot escape the question how such common meaning stands related to different minds or psychological states which mean. One may follow Plato and cut the Gordian knot by removing these precise and logical meanings beyond our earthly sphere and establishing them as transcendent ideas or eternal objects. This reflects a judgment of their value but leaves our commerce with them a miracle; it substitutes adoration of a mystery for explanation of a fact. A similar remark would apply to any doctrine like that of the new realism, so far as this doctrine hypostatizes conceptual realities, such as those of mathematics, setting them up as objective realities without further ado and then explaining our apprehension of them as coincidence of mind and object. One does not answer the numerous objections which the nominalists and conceptualists in logic have urged—and very plausibly urged—by first setting up what they claim can exist only in a mind as something outside it and then offering coincidence of mind and object as explanation of the fact that these conceptual objects are also *in* minds. The new realist here follows the obvious analogy of the common-sense view concerning knowledge of the physical. There is the brick out there; we both see the brick, hence we have an idea in common. So—the new realist seems to say—there is the mathematical entity out there; we both apprehend this mathematical entity, hence we have an abstract mathematical concept in common. Even in the case of the physical object there are all sorts of difficulties to be met before community of knowledge can be understood. And in the case of the purely abstract or conceptual (if there be any purely conceptual entities) we have the added difficulty that such an object cannot arouse sensation. Undoubtedly the conceptual has its own appropriate kind of reality; but what that kind of reality is, is precisely the problem. It is not to be resolved by a phrase such as "neutral entity," or "eternal object," or "essence." We must assume the objectivity of conceptual meaning. But if in order to philosophize sensibly we must assume something to be true when we do not understand how it can be true, then our philosophy is, so far, a failure.

On the other hand, I see no necessity for resigning the problem of common meanings to the psychologist as his exclusive affair, especially since he, like the rest of us, must begin by assuming their existence. The meaning must be somehow identified before it can be correlated with behavior or motor-set or context or anything else. And it must be identified as somehow common to two minds before individual psychological differences will be pertinent to it; if what they are pertinent to is not somehow identical, but *A*'s state is pertinent of *x* and *B*'s to *y,* then there is no basis for comparison by which individual differences could be discovered as such.

Psychological differences of individuals are indeed impressive. Long before scientific psychology was thought of, the skeptic appealed to them to prove the impossibility of knowledge or the communication of ideas. For imagery and feeling, and even to some extent for sensation, idiosyncrasy is the rule. Furthermore, as the ancient skeptic was fond of pointing out, there can be no final verification of any community in these respects. The sense-quality of green cannot be conveyed to the congenitally blind; and if I suppose some idiosyncrasy of sense which makes my perception of green unique, I shall never discover that peculiarity provided it does not impair my powers to discriminate and relate as others do. In brief, there can be no verification of community between minds so far as it is a question of the feeling side of experience, though the assumption that there is no community here seems fantastic.

However, it is obvious that common meanings do transcend such individual differences of perception and imagery. We use language to convey thought. If language really conveys anything, then there must be something which is identical in your mind and in mine when we understand each other. And if our thought is objective and not merely a report of introspection, then what is identical in our two minds must also be somehow germane to that objective reality as we know it.

Suppose we talk of physical things in physical terms, and our discussion involves physical measurement. Presumably we have the same ideas of feet and pounds and seconds. If not, the thing is hopeless. But in psychological terms, my notion of a foot goes back to some immediate image of visual so-long-ness, or the movements which I make when I put my hands so far apart, or a relation between these two. Distances in general mean quite complex relationships between such visual images, muscle and contact-sensations, the feeling of fatigue, and so on. Weight goes back to muscle-sensations, the "heft" of the thing. And our direct apprehension of time is that feeling of duration which is so familiar but so difficult to describe.

Now in such terms, will your sensory image of a foot or a pound coincide with mine? I am nearsighted; your eyes are good. My arms are long; yours are short. If we lift a weight, there is the difference in strength between us to take into account. So it is with everything. In acuity of perception and power to discriminate, there is almost always some small difference between the senses of two individuals, and frequently these discrepancies are marked. It is only in rough and ready terms that we can reasonably suppose that our direct intuitions and images are alike. That so often theories of knowledge have ignored such differences, which are the rule and not the exception, or have proceeded as if our common and supposedly veridical knowledge depended on coincidence of such sensory content, is really a frightful scandal.

Even for the large and crude distinctions, what assurance is there that our impressions coincide? Suppose it should be a fact that I get the sensation you signalize by saying "red" whenever I look at what you call "green" and vice versa. Suppose that in the matter of immediate sense-qualities my whole spectrum should be exactly the reverse of yours. Suppose even that what are for you sensations of pitch, mediated by the ear, were identical with my feelings of color-quality, mediated by the eye. Since no one can look directly into another's mind, and the immediate feeling of red or of the middle C can never be conveyed, how should we find it out if such personal peculiarities should exist? We could never discover them so long as they did not impair the power to discriminate and relate as others do.

Furthermore, what difference to our common knowledge would it make? That is precisely the first point which needs to be emphasized: idiosyncrasy of intuition need not make any difference, except in the esthetic quality of the experience of one as compared with that of another. Let us take it for granted (it seems fairly sensible) that the sense-data of one are seldom precisely those of the other when we address ourselves to the same object. That, by itself, will in no way impede our common knowledge or the conveying of ideas. Why? Because we shall still agree that there are three feet to the yard; that yellow is lighter than blue; and that middle C means a vibration of 256 per second. In other words, if we *define* any one of the unit-ideas or concepts which enter into the expression of our thought, we shall define it in the same or equivalent fashion, and we shall apply the same substantives and adjectives to the same objects. So far as we fail in *these* two things, our knowledge will be really different and the attempt to convey our thought will break down. These, then, are the only practical and applicable criteria of common knowledge; that we should share common definitions of the terms we use, and that we should apply these terms identically to what is presented.

I am not, of course, trying to argue that individual feelings *are* thus unique. *Some* differences of subjective experience are attested by the inability of one person to discriminate where another can. For the rest, the question of such identity is, in the end, mere idle speculation because we have no possible means of investigating it. What I would point out is, rather, that in the determination of common concepts, the conveying of ideas, such possible idiosyncrasy in the correlated sense-feelings is entirely negligible. You and I mean the same by "red" if we both define it as the first band in the sun's spectrum, and if we both pronounce the same presented objects to be red. It does not matter if neither the red rug nor the first band of the spectrum give to the two of us identical sensations so long as we individually discover that same sense-quality in each thing which we agree in describing as "red."

Moreover, it is obvious that unless one have some peculiarity which both he and others will learn to recognize as a defect of his sense-perceptions, the very manner in which we learn the names of things will secure such unanimity in the ascription of terms, regardless of any idiosyncrasy of purely inner sense feelings.

Even those individual peculiarities which become recognized as inability to discriminate, limitation of the range of sensation, and so on, do not prevent us from sharing and conveying ideas, though they may impede the process of learning. We talk together and coöperate successfully about the vibration of 19,000 per second in the vacuum-tube, though for one of us this vibration is evidenced by a note and for the other it never can be. We both have a perfectly good concept of ultra-violet, though neither of us will ever see it, just as we know well enough what we mean by the other side of the moon. To be sure, no such concept would have a meaning if we could not, through the terms in which that meaning is explicated, get back eventually to concepts which are correlated for us with specific and identifiable qualities of sense. It is thus that we surmount our individual limitations. The pitch which is beyond my auditory range, I understand though the notion "vibration of 19,000," which is definitive both for me and for those who hear it as a note. This process of leading back, by which we understand what we can not directly perceive, may be quite complex and prolonged without defeating the purpose of sharing ideas and conveying thought. It is the same sort of process by which we must all of us understand what we mean by "ultra-violet" or "electron," and its objectivity is not affected by the fact that such indirection of understanding is, in this case of limitations of perception, necessary for some of us only.

The methods of verifying community of meaning are principally two, neither of which depends on any supposed community of feeling or imagery. Either we define our terms or, by our behavior, we exhibit their denotation. The second procedure is less conclusive for reasons which are fairly obvious. No collection of cases, or examples pointed to, is ever sufficient to determine uniquely the denotation of a term—to determine what other cases, not so far examined, would be included and what excluded. The meaning of the term will be what is common to the various examples pointed out as meant by it. In general, the larger the number of things so indicated, the smaller the chance that these will have in common other properties than those which are essential or comprehended within the conceptual meaning of the term. But that possibility can never be ruled out. Moreover, the exhibition of meaning in this way depends for success upon the ability of the person to whom the meaning is conveyed to make the analysis which will isolate correctly just that totality of properties which is common to the things indicated, not omitting to remark any which are essential. This is an important consideration, because concepts which stand in any need of being learned will represent analyses which are matters of some difficulty. On account of these shortcomings of it, the actual use of this method—of indicating a meaning by exemplifying its denotation—is confined almost exclusively to conveying the meaning of a *word* where the *concept* itself is already something shared; as, for instance, where teacher and taught have no language in common.

The method of definition specifies a meaning directly. In defining, we refer one concept to others; the typical definition equates the term defined with a complex of other terms in definite relations. To be sure, it may not be sufficient that you and I both define *A* in terms of *B* and *C,* since *B* and *C* may have for us different significations. But if *B* also is defined by both in the same or equivalent fashion, and *C,* and so on, that *is* sufficient to assure common meaning, regardless of all differences of imagery or any idiosyncrasy of sense. Such verification of community of meaning by comparison of definitions is obviously a process which must be incomplete, but it makes clear precisely what is essential to a genuine identity of meaning in two minds.

Speaking in terms of logic, these facts may be expressed by saying that sensation and imagery are essentially individual, and do not possess meaning in the sense in which meanings are common and shareable and expressible. The concept, which is the common, shareable and expressible meaning, must be distinguished from such feelings; it is constituted by that pattern which is set up by the expression of one concept in terms of others. These patterns must be identical and shared by all who really possess ideas in common and are capable of conveying them to one another.

Psychologically, this conceptual pattern of relations is, of course, an abstraction; no such concept ever existed, apart from imagery and sensory material, in any human mind. *For each individual* there must be a correlation of concept with specific sense-quality. But this correlation of concept and sense is intrinsically individual; if it, too, should be shared, we could not verify that fact, and it is not in the least essential to common understanding that it should be. The concept, so defined, is precisely that abstraction which it is *necessary* to make if we are to discover the basis of our common understanding of that reality which we all know. On a day which is terribly long to me and abominably short to you, we meet, by agreement, at three o'clock, and thus demonstrate that we have a world in common. An "hour" is not a feeling of tedium or vivacity, but sixty minutes, one round of the clock, a pattern of relations which we have established between chronometers and distances and rates of movement, and so on.

Defining, like logical analysis in general, sets up a pattern of relationships. We are all of us fond of what Bosanquet called the "linear" mode of thinking in such matters, and we might easily suppose that definition chases a conceptual meaning back into other such concepts, and these into still others, until finally it is brought to bay in some first (or last) identity of meaning which is identity of sensation or imagery. So far as meaning within the individual mind is concerned, I should suppose this is precisely what takes place; we analyze the meaning back until we come to rest in familiar imagery. But the end-terms, which for us are thus understood directly by reference to sense and feeling, have still a conceptual meaning; they are not indefinable. This conceptual meaning is shareable; our imagery essentially not. Thus the end-terms of such analysis are no different than the beginning terms; they have meaning in two senses—the logical, shareable meaning of further conceptual relations, and the direct, non-shareable meaning of reference to some complex of sense-qualities.

The notion that the analysis of meaning must, in linear fashion, go back eventually to ultimate constituents whose meaning *cannot* in turn be thus relational, is a prejudice which is very largely due to a false metaphor. Logical analysis is conceived after the fashion of the physical dissection of a whole into parts, or the chemical analysis of a compound into elements. But it will not escape the thoughtful reader that all definition is eventually circular. It is often the case that *A* can be defined in terms of *B* and *C*, *B* in terms of *A* and *C*, or *C* in terms of *A* and *B*. Where the circle is so small, and the defined meaning so promptly returns upon itself, the analysis is likely to be inadequate. But this circularity would never be possible at all, if the relation of defining to defined were that of part to whole. Moreover, the difference between a good and a bad definition, on this point, is only, so to speak, in the diameter of the circle. All the terms in the dictionary, however ideal its definitions, will be themselves defined.

Logical analysis is not dissection but relation; the analysis of *A* into *B* and *C* does not divide *A* into constituents *B* and *C* but merely traces a pattern of relations connecting *A* with *B* and *C*. As regards their conceptual meaning, terms are very closely analogous to points in space. A point is nothing whatever apart from its relation to other points; its very essence is relational. Likewise the conceptual meaning of a term is nothing whatever apart from other such meanings. Also it is true that if point *A* is located by reference to *B* and *C*, *B* and *C* in turn, and the other points in any spatial array, have their position eventually, in circularwise, in their relation to *A* and to one another. The positional relationships of any point are internal to its nature and constitute that nature. Likewise, the definitive relations of a term, signifying a concept, are internal to the meaning of that term and constitute it. The nature of a concept as such is its internal (essential or definitive) relationships with other concepts. All points have their positions eventually in terms of the array of all space: no point or set of points has any primal position in any other fashion; we merely choose as an arbitary basis of reference some set which is convenient or marks the place where we happen to be. All terms or concepts similarly have their meaning eventually in the array of all meanings, and no member of this array is intrinsically primal or privileged.

Concerning this interpretation of the concept as consisting in relational structures of meaning, there can be two doubts. We seldom "have in mind" any such conceptual pattern of definition. When we reflect upon the manner in which coincidence in the meaning of one term involves coincidence in the meaning of others, we see that such an ideal pattern of meaning goes far beyond what anyone could consciously have in mind at any one time. Again, we often coincide in our use of terms, and thus seem to possess meanings in common, when the definition of our terms would be a matter of some doubt and one holding possibility of disagreement.

Three points are here pertinent: First, that over and above the ambiguities of language commonly recognized, the same word may convey different concepts on different occasions; in particular, that it may convey a meaning which is more or less restricted. Second, when the denotation of a word rules, there are degrees of clearness about its meaning. Third, identity of meaning consists practically in implicit modes of behavior, and what is involved in these always runs beyond what can be explicit in consciousness at any one time.

If I talk with a chemist about helium or with a biologist about cells, we may understand each other perfectly. But without recourse to some reference book, I could not define "helium" or "cell" in a fashion which the specialist would accept as adequate. To me "helium" means "a non-inflammable gas a little lighter than hydrogen (or a little heavier—I forget which), produced in the disintegration of alpha-particles and found in the sun." I could not specify either atomic-weight or spectrum characteristics, one or other of which the chemist will regard as essential to a sufficiently guarded definition. But as long as we converse together without misunderstanding, the *common* meaning of "helium" is just what is set down above. This is a less specific meaning than the chemist's, but included in it, and sufficient for our present purposes. If our discussion should touch upon more recondite matters, he might need to instruct me about helium, and thus establish a more specific common concept, before we could go on. I recognize his authority to do so, and should accept his definition (which I cannot now give) as the "true" meaning of the word "helium." But this does not alter the fact that, for the time being, the common concept which serves our purposes is my looser understanding of the term. Such is quite commonly the case. Our actual meanings, the concepts we are concerned to convey, are more restricted than the true or full or dictionary meanings of the terms we use. Most words may convey any one of a whole range of more or less full and accurate meanings. It is, thus, quite possible that we may understand each other perfectly even when we should disagree about the definition of our terms, because only some restricted meaning, covered in both our definitions, is required by our discussion.

Second, it is obvious that in some sense or other we may have a meaning in mind when we could not state it without further thought. Any true account of thought and speech must recognize this. The ruling interest in knowledge is the practical interest of action. A meaning may be implicitly present in the consistency of behavior when confronted with experience of a certain type without the explicit recognition of what this behavior implies having come into consciousness or even been brought in question. Such we must suppose to be the child's early use of language. And in this sense, we may perhaps say that meanings must be implicit in the mind before they can become conscious. In fact, we may doubt whether any meaning would ever become conscious if it were not for the practical difficulties which arise when meanings are not thus explicit—the difficulties of hesitant or inconsistent behavior in border-line cases, and the social difficulty of misunderstanding, that is, of incongruous behavior when the same term has been used with apparently the same meaning.

Josiah Royce used to speak to his classes of the three grades of clearness about the meanings of terms.[2] We have the first grade of clearness when we are able appropriately to accept or reject any object of our acquaintance as belonging or not belonging to the class in question. The second grade of clearness involves, further, the preparedness to classify correctly objects not precisely like those with which we have previously been acquainted; that is, to make the dichotomy, *X* or not-*X*, not only for familiar but also for unfamiliar things, not only for all actual but also for all conceivable objects. The third grade of clearness consists in the ability to specify the criteria by which such classification is determined. This last, of course, is equivalent to definition, the explicit possession of the concept. That the mind may have the first or second grade of clearness without the third, is obvious. It is also evident without discussion, that even when we have, in the ordinary sense, this highest grade of clearness, we do not have this definition explicitly in mind whenever we use a term with understanding.

Any controversy as to whether a mind possesses a meaning whenever a term is used intelligently, would be useless because it would be verbal. The pertinent facts are sufficiently clear; that it may possess meaning in the sense of determining a consistent mode of behavior (such as the consistent use of a term) without our being able out of hand to specify the ground of our own discrimination, we can all of us testify. The psychology of this is doubtless a difficult and important topic; but with that we are not concerned. It would be an anomalous use of language to deny meaning to terms which are used without this explicit consciousness of what is essential, especially since the use of terms, like other modes of deliberate behavior, is most frequently a matter of habit, reflecting previous experience in which the mode of action was determined by clearer consciousness. It would also be anomalous to deny meaning where there is consistency of behavior or of consciously determined attitude which does not directly concern the use of language. In such cases the meaning is possessed by the mind both in the sense of this consistently determined attitude and in the further sense that *how* this meaning should become explicit and *what* would be recognized as essential, when the attitude became self-conscious, is already implicit in the attitude itself. There is such a thing as confusion of attitude, reflected in hesitation of behavior and self-frustration, just as there may be inconsistency in the use of terms and in our explicit concepts. It is such hesitation and dubiety which provides the spur to that self-consciousness and self-criticism which renders meanings explicit. If meanings could not

[2] He used to attribute this to Charles Peirce, but Peirce's discussion in "How to Make Our Ideas Clear," does not so precisely cover the point.

be present and determined in the attitude and behavior itself, there would be nothing to become conscious of. Objects do not classify themselves and come into experience with their tickets on them. The classifying attitude or mode of behavior which the mind brings to the given experience and which represents its meaning, dictates the explicit concept and implicitly possesses it already.

If, however, in the light of this, it should be charged that I have used the phrase "common to two minds" in a figurative and Pickwickian sense in the definition of "the concept," I shall plead guilty. I shall urge in extenuation that to begin the discussion by introducing all the qualification and explanation required for strict accuracy would have been confusing and impossible. I have but followed the custom to attributing to mind what is ideally determined by conscious attitude even though it is not explicitly present in consciousness. Whatever is merely convenient fiction in this can now be withdrawn in favor of an accurate equivalent. The concept is a definitive structure of meanings, which is what *would verify* completely the coincidence of two minds when they understand each other by the use of language. Such ideal community requires coincidence of a pattern of interrelated connotations, projected by and necessary to coöperative, purposeful behavior. It does *not* require coincidence of imagery or sensory apprehension. The concept is, thus, psychologically both an abstraction and an ideality, though in no greater degree or different sense than are most of things which are commonly attributed to mind. Both community of meaning and genuine understanding of reality are projected ideals more truly than realized actualities. We study them as what our purposes intend and as that the approximation to which gives value to our practice. It is concepts, as precisely such ideal abstractions, which must be implicity present in our practice, which constitute the element of interpretation which underlies our common understanding of our common world. . . .

W. V. Quine

Speaking of Objects *

I

We are prone to talk and think of objects. Physical objects are the obvious illustration when the illustrative mood is on us, but there are also all the abstracts objects, or so there purport to be: the states and qualities, numbers, attributes, classes. We persist in breaking reality down somehow into a multiplicity of identifiable and discriminable objects, to be referred to by singular and general terms. We talk so inveterately of objects that to say we do so seems almost to say nothing at all; for how else is there to talk?

It is hard to say how else there is to talk, not because our objectifying pattern is an invariable trait of human nature, but because we are bound to adapt any alien pattern to our own in the very process of understanding or translating the alien sentences.

Imagine a newly discovered tribe whose language is without known affinities. The linguist has to learn the language directly by observing what the natives say under observed circumstances, encountered or contrived. He makes a first crude beginning by compiling native terms for environing objects; but here already he is really imposing his own patterns. Let me explain what I mean. I will grant that the linguist may establish inductively, beyond reasonable doubt, that a certain heathen expression is one to which natives can be prompted to assent by the presence of a rabbit, or reasonable *facsimile,* and not otherwise. The linguist is then warranted in according the native expression the cautious translation 'There's a rabbit', 'There we have a rabbit', 'Lo! a rabbit', 'Lo! rabbithood again', insofar as the differences among these English sentences are counted irrelevant. This

* The Presidential Address to the American Philosophical Association, Eastern Division, 1957. From *Proceedings and Addresses of the American Philosophical Association,* Volume 31. Reprinted by permission of The American Philosophical Association and the author. The author thanks Burton Dreben for helpful criticism of the manuscript.

much translation can be objective, however exotic the tribe. It recognizes the native expression as in effect a rabbit-heralding sentence. But the linguist's bold further step, in which he imposes his own object-positing pattern without special warrant, is taken when he equates the native expression or any part of it with the *term* 'rabbit'.

It is easy to show that such appeal to an object category is unwarranted even though we cannot easily, in English, herald rabbits without objectification. For we can argue from indifference. Given that a native sentence says that a so-and-so is present, and given that the sentence is true when and only when a rabbit is present, it by no means follows that the so-and-so are rabbits. They might be all the various temporal segments of rabbits. They might be all the integral or undetached parts of rabbits. In order to decide among these alternatives we need to be able to ask more than whether a so-and-so is present. We need to be able to ask whether this is the same so-and-so as that, and whether one so-and-so is present or two. We need something like the apparatus of identity and quantification; hence far more than we are in a position to avail ourselves of in a language in which our high point as of even date is rabbit-announcing.

And the case is yet worse: we do not even have evidence for taking the native expression as of the form 'A so-and-so is present'; it could as well be construed with an abstract singular term, as meaning that rabbithood is locally manifested. Better just 'Rabbiteth', like 'Raineth'.

But if our linguist is going to be as cagey as all this, he will never translate more than these simple-minded announcements of observable current events. A cagey linguist is a caged linguist. What we want from the linguist as a serviceable finished product, after all, is no mere list of sentence-to-sentence equivalences, like the airline throwaways of useful Spanish phrases. We want a manual of instructions for custom-building a native sentence to roughly the purpose of any newly composed English sentence, within reason, and vice versa. The linguist has to resolve the potential infinity of native sentences into a manageably limited list of grammatical constructions and constituent linguistic forms, and then show how the business of each can be approximated in English; and vice versa. Sometimes perhaps he will translate a word or construction not directly but contextually, by systematic instructions for translating its containing sentences; but still he must make do with a limited lot of contextual definitions. Now once he has carried out this necessary job of lexicography, forwards and backwards, he has read our ontological point of view into the native language. He has decided what expressions to treat as referring to objects, and, within limits, what sorts of objects to treat them as referring to. He has had to decide, however *arbitrarily,* how to accommodate English idioms of identity and quantification in native translation.

The word 'arbitrary' needs stressing, not because those decisions are wholly arbitrary, but because they are so much more so than one tends to suppose. For, what evidence does the linguist have? He started with what we may call native observation sentences, such as the rabbit announcement. These he can say how to translate into English, provided we impute no relevance to the differences between 'Here a rabbit', 'Here rabbithood'; and the like. Also he can record further native sentences and settle whether various persons are prepared to affirm or deny them, though he find no rabbit movements or other currently observable events to tie them to. Among these untranslated sentences he may get an occasional hint of logical connections, by finding say that just the persons who are prepared to affirm *A* are prepared to affirm *B* and deny *C*. Thereafter his data leave off and his creativity sets in.

What he does in his creativity is attribute special and distinctive functions to component words, or conspicuously recurrent fragments, of the recorded sentences. The only ways one can appraise these attributions are as follows. One can see whether they add up to representing the rabbit sentence and the like as conforming to their previously detected truth conditions. One can see also how well they fit the available data on other sentences: sentences for which no truth conditions are known, but only the varying readiness of natives to affirm or deny them. Beyond this we can judge the attributions only on their simplicity and naturalness—to *us*.

Certainly the linguist will try out his theory on the natives, springing new sentences authorized by his theory, to see if they turn out right. This is a permuting of the time order: one frames the theory before all possible data are in, and then lets it guide one in the eliciting of additional data likeliest to matter. This is good scientific method, but it opens up no new kind of data. English general and singular terms, identity, quantification, and the whole bag of ontological tricks may be correlated with elements of the native language in any of various mutually incompatible ways, each compatible with all possible linguistic data, and none preferable to another save as favored by rationalization of the *native* language that is simple and natural to *us*.

It makes no real difference that the linguist will turn bilingual and come to think as the natives do—whatever that means. For the arbitrariness of reading our objectifications into the heathen speech reflects not so much the inscrutability of the heathen mind, as that there is nothing to scrute. Even we who grew up together and learned English at the same knee, or adjacent ones, talk alike for no other reason than that society coached us alike in a pattern of verbal response to externally observable cues. We have been beaten into an outward conformity to an outward standard; and thus it is that when I correlate your sentences with mine by the simple rule of phonetic correspondence, I find that the public circumstances of your affirmations and denials agree pretty well with those of my own. If I conclude that you share my sort of conceptual scheme, I am not adding a supplementary conjecture so much as spurning unfathomable distinctions; for, what further criterion of sameness of conceptual scheme can be imagined? The case of a Frenchman, moreover, is the same except that I correlate his sentences with mine not by phonetic correspondence but according to a traditionally evolved dictionary.[1] The case of the linguist and his newly discovered heathen, finally, differs simply in that the linguist has to grope for a general sentence-to-sentence correlation that will make the public circumstances of the heathen's affirmations and denials match up tolerably with the circumstances of the linguist's own. If the linguist fails in this, or has a hard time of it, or succeeds only by dint of an ugly and complex mass of correlations, then he is entitled to say—in the only sense in which one *can* say it—that his heathens have a very different attitude toward reality from ours; and even so he cannot coherently suggest what their attitude is. Nor, in principle, is the natural bilingual any better off.

When we compare theories, doctrines, points of view, cultures, on the score of what sorts of objects there are said to be, we are comparing them in a respect which itself makes sense only provincially. It makes sense only as far afield as our efforts to translate our domestic idioms of identity and quantification bring encouragement in the way of simple and natural-looking correspondences. If we attend to business we are unlikely to find a very alien culture with a predilection for a very outlandish universe of discourse, just because the outlandishness of it would detract from our sense of patness of our dictionary of translation. There is a notion that our provincial ways of positing objects and conceiving nature may be best appreciated for what they are by standing off and seeing them against a cosmopolitan background of alien cultures; but the notion comes to nothing, for there is no πoῦ στῶ.[2]

[1] See Richard von Mises, *Positivism,* Cambridge: Harvard, 1951, pp. 46 f.

[2] For a fuller development of the theme of §I, see my essay "Meaning and translation," in a forthcoming anthology on translation edited by Reuben Brower.

II

Yet, for all the difficulty of transcending our object-directed pattern of thought, we can examine it well enough from inside. Let us turn our attention from the heathen, who seemed to have a term for 'rabbit', to our own child at home who seems to have just acquired his first few terms in our own language: 'mama', 'water', perhaps 'red'. To begin with, the case of the child resembles that of the heathen. For though we may fully satisfy ourselves that the child has learned the trick of using the utterances 'mama' and 'water' strictly in the appropriate presences, or as means of inducing the appropriate presences, still we have no right to construe these utterances in the child's mouth as terms, at first, for things or substances.

We in our maturity have come to look upon the child's mother as an integral body who, in an irregular closed orbit, revisits the child from time to time; and to look upon red in a radically different way, viz., as scattered about. Water, for us, is rather like red, but not quite; things are red, stuff is water. But the mother, red, and water are for the infant all of a type; each is just a history of sporadic encounter, a scattered portion of what goes on. His first learning of the three words is uniformly a matter of learning how much of what goes on about him counts as the mother, or as red, or as water. It is not for the child to say in the first case 'Hello! mama again', in the second case 'Hello! another red thing', and in the third case 'Hello! more water'. They are all on a par: Hello! more mama, more red, more water. Even this last formula, which treats all three terms on the model of our provincial adult bulk term 'water', is imperfect; for it unwarrantedly imputes an objectification of matter, even if only as stuff and not as bits.

Progressively, however, the child is seen to evolve a pattern of verbal behavior that finally comes to copy ours too closely for there to be any sense in questioning the general sameness of conceptual scheme. For perspective on our own objectifying apparatus we may consider what steps of development make the difference between the 'mama'-babbling infant who cannot be said to be using terms for objects, and the older child who can.

It is only when the child has got on to the full and proper use of *individuative* terms like 'apple' that he can properly be said to have taken to using terms as terms, and speaking of objects. Words like 'apple', and not words like 'mama' or 'water' or 'red', are the terms whose ontological involvement runs deep. To learn 'apple' it is not sufficient to learn how much of what goes on counts as apple; we must learn how much counts as *an* apple, and how much as another. Such terms possess built-in modes of individuation.

Individuative terms are commonly made to double as bulk terms. Thus we may say 'There is some apple in the salad', not meaning 'some apple or other'; just as we may say 'Mary had a little lamb' in either of two senses. Now we have appreciated that the child can learn the terms 'mama', 'red', and 'water' quite well before he ever has mastered the ins and outs of our adult conceptual scheme of mobile enduring physical objects, identical from time to time and place to place; and in principle he might do the same for 'apple', as a bulk term for uncut apple stuff. But he can never fully master 'apple' in its individuative use, except as he gets on with the scheme of enduring and recurrent physical objects. He may come somewhat to grips with the individuative use of 'apple' before quite mastering the comprehensive physical outlook, but his usage will be marred by misidentifications of distinct apples over time, or misdiscriminations of identical ones.

He has really got on to the individuative use, one is tempted to suppose, once he responds with the plural 'apples' to a heap of apples. But not so. He may at that point have learned 'apples' as another bulk term, applicable to just so much apple as is taken up in apple heaps. 'Apples', for him, would be subordinated to 'apple' as is 'warm water' to 'water', and 'bright red' to 'red'.

The child might proceed to acquire 'block' and 'blocks', 'ball' and 'balls', as bulk terms in the same fashion. By the force of analogy among such pairs he might even come to apply the plural '-s' with seeming appropriateness to new words, and to drop it with seeming appropriateness from words first learned only with it. We might well not detect, for a while, his misconception: that '-s' just turns bulk terms into more specialized bulk terms connoting clumpiness.

A plausible variant misconception is this: 'apple' bulkwise might cover not apples generally, but just the lone ones, while 'apples' still figures as last suggested. Then apples and apple would be mutually exclusive rather than subordinate the one to the other. This variant misconception could likewise be projected systematically to 'block' and 'blocks', 'ball' and 'balls', and long escape exposure.

How can we ever tell, then, whether the child has really got the trick of individuation? Only by engaging him in sophisticated discourse of 'that apple', 'not that apple', 'an apple', 'same apple', 'another apple', 'these apples'. It is only at this level that a palpable difference emerges between genuinely individuative use and the counterfeits lately imagined.

Doubtless the child gets the swing of these peculiar adjectives 'same', 'another', 'an', 'that', 'not that', contextually: first he becomes attuned to various longer phrases or sentences that contain them, and then gradually he develops appropriate habits in relation to the component words as common parts and residues of those longer forms. His tentative acquisition of the plural '-s', lately speculated on, is itself a first primitive step of the kind. The contextual learning of these various particles goes on simultaneously, we may suppose, so that they are gradually adjusted to one another and a coherent pattern of usage is evolved matching that of one's elders. This is a major step in acquiring the conceptual scheme that we all know so well. For it is on achieving this step, and only then, that there can be any general talk of objects as such. Only at this stage does it begin to make sense to wonder whether the apple now in one's hand is the apple noticed yesterday.

Until individuation emerges, the child can scarcely be said to have general *or* singular terms, there being no express talk of objects. The pre-individuative term 'mama', and likewise 'water' and 'red' (for children who happen to learn 'water' and 'red' before mastering individuation), hark back to a primitive phase to which the distinction between singular and general is irrelevant.

Once the child has pulled through the individuative crisis, though, he is prepared to re-assess prior terms. 'Mama', in particular, gets set up retroactively as the name of a broad and recurrent but withal individual object, and thus as a singular term *par excellence.* Occasions eliciting 'mama' being just as discontinuous as those eliciting 'water', the two terms had been on a par; but with the advent of individuation the mother becomes integrated into a cohesive spatiotemporal convexity, while water remains scattered even in space-time. The two terms thus part company.

The mastery of individuation seems scarcely to affect people's attitude toward 'water'. For 'water', 'sugar', and the like the category of bulk terms remains, a survival of the pre-individuative phase, ill fitting the dichotomy into general and singular. But the philosophical mind sees its way to pressing this archaic category into the dichotomy. The bulk term 'water' after the copula can usually be smoothly reconstrued as a general term true of each portion of water, while in other positions it is usually more simply construed as a singular term naming that spatio-temporally diffuse object which is the totality of the world's water.

III

I have urged that we could know the necessary and sufficient stimulatory conditions of every possible act of utterance, in a foreign language, and still not know how to determine what objects the speakers of that language believe in. Now if objective reference is so inaccessible to observation, who is to say on empirical grounds that belief in objects of one or another description is right or wrong? How can there ever be empirical evidence against existential statements?

The answer is something like this. Grant that a knowledge of the appropriate stimulatory conditions of a sentence does not settle how to construe the sentence in terms of existence of objects. Still, it does tend to settle what is to count as empirical evidence for or against the truth of the sentence. If we then go on to assign the sentence some import in point of existence of objects, by arbitrary projection in the case of the heathen language or as a matter of course in the case of our own, thereupon what has already been counting as empirical evidence for or against the truth of the sentence comes to count as empirical evidence for or against the existence of the objects.

The opportunity for error in existential statements increases with one's mastery of the verbal apparatus of objective reference. In one's earliest phase of word-learning, terms like 'mama' and 'water' were learned which may be viewed retrospectively as names each of an observed spatiotemporal object. Each such term was learned by a process of reinforcement and extinction, whereby the spatiotemporal range of application of the term was gradually perfected. The object named is assuredly an observed one, in the sense that the reinforced stimuli proceeded pretty directly from it. Granted, this talk of name and object belongs to a later phase of language learning, even as does the talk of stimulation.

The second phase, marked by the advent of individuative terms, is where a proper notion of object emerges. Here we get general terms, each true of each of many objects. But the objects still are observable spatiotemporal objects. For these individuative terms, e.g. 'apple', are learned still by the old method of reinforcement and extinction; they differ from their predecessors only in the added feature of internal individuation.

Demonstrative singular terms like 'this apple' usher in a third phase, characterized by the fact that a singular term seriously used can now, through error, fail to name: the thing pointed to can turn out to be the mere façade of an apple, or maybe a tomato. But even at this stage anything that we do succeed in naming is still an observable spatiotemporal object.

A fourth phase comes with the joining of one general term to another in attributive position. Now for the first time we can get general terms which are not true of anything; thus 'blue apple', 'square ball'. But when there are things at all of which the thus formed general terms are true, they are nothing new; they are just some among the same old observables whereof the component terms are true.

It is a fifth phase that brings a new mode of understanding, giving access to new sorts of objects. When we form compounds by applying relative terms to singular terms, we get such compounds as 'smaller than that speck'. Whereas the non-existence of observable blue apples is tantamount to the non-existence of blue apples, the non-existence of observable objects smaller than that speck is not taken as tantamount to the non-existence of objects smaller than that speck. The notable feature of this fifth phase is not that it enables us to form meaningful singular terms devoid of reference, for that was already achieved on occasion with 'this apple'; nor that it enables us to form meaningful general terms true of nothing, for that was already achieved with 'blue apple'; but that it enables us, for the first time, to form terms whose references can be admitted to be forever unobservable without yet being repudiated, like blue apples, as non-existent.

Such applying of relative terms to singular terms is the simplest method of forming terms that purport to refer to unobservables, but there are also more flexible devices to much the same effect: the relative clause and description.

And there comes yet a sixth phase, when we break through to posits more drastically new still than the objects smaller than the smallest visible speck. For the objects smaller than the speck differ from observable objects only in a matter of degree, whereas the sixth phase ushers in abstract entities. This phase is marked by the advent of abstract singular terms like 'redness', 'roundness', 'mankind', purported names of qualities, attributes, classes. Let us speculate on the mechanism of this new move.

One wedge is the bulk term. Such terms can be learned at the very first phase, we saw, on a par with 'mama'. We saw them diverge from 'mama' at the second phase, simply on the score that the woman comes then to be appreciated as an integrated spatiotemporal thing while the world's water or red stuff ordinarily does not. For the child, thus, who is not on to the sophisticated idea of the scattered single object, the bulk term already has an air of generality about it, comparable to the individuative 'apple'; and still it is much like the singular 'mama' in form and function, having even been learned or learnable at the first phase on a par with 'mama'. So the bulk term already has rather the hybrid air of the abstract singular term. 'Water' might, from the very advent of individuation, even be said to name a shared *attribute* of the sundry puddles and glassfuls rather than a scattered portion of the world *composed* of those puddles and glassfuls; for the child of course adopts neither position.

Moreover, there is a tricky point about color words that especially encourages the transition to abstract reference. 'Red' can be learned as a bulk term, like 'water', but in particular it applies to apples whose insides are white. Before mastering the conceptual scheme of individuation and enduring physical object, the child sees the uncut red apple, like tomato juice, simply as so much red exposure in the passing show, and, having no sense of physical identity, he sees the subsequently exposed white interior of the apple as irrelevant. When eventually he does master the conceptual scheme of individuation and enduring physical object, then, he has to come to terms with a pre-acquired use of 'red' that has suddenly gone double: there is red stuff (tomato juice) and there are red things (apples) that are mostly white stuff. 'Red' both remains a bulk term of the ancient vintage of 'water' and 'mama', and becomes a concrete general term like 'round' or 'apple'. Since the child will still not clearly conceive of 'red' as suddenly two words, we have him somehow infusing singularity into the concrete general; and such is the recipe, however unappetizing, for the abstract singular. The analogy then spreads to other general terms, that were in no such special predicament as 'red', until they all deliver abstract singulars.

Another force for abstract terms, or for the positing of abstract objects, lies in abbreviated cross-reference. E.g., after an elaborate remark regarding President Eisenhower, someone says: "The same holds for Churchill." Or, by way of supporting some botanical identification, one says: "Both plants have the following attribute in common"—and proceeds with a double-purpose description. In such cases a laborious repetition is conveniently circumvented. Now the cross-reference in such cases is just to a form of words. But we have a stubborn tendency to reify the unrepeated matter by positing an attribute, instead of just talking of words.

There is indeed an archaic precedent for confusing sign and object; the earliest conditioning of the infant's babbling is ambiguous on the point. For suppose a baby rewarded for happening to babble something like 'mama' or 'water' just as the mother or water is looming. The stimuli which are thus reinforced are bound to be two: there is not only the looming of the object, there is equally the word itself, heard by the child from his own lips. Confusion of sign and object is original sin, coeval with the word.

We have seen how the child might slip into the community's ontology of attributes by easy stages, from bulk terms onward. We have also seen how talk of attributes will continue to be encouraged, in the child and the community, by a certain convenience of cross-reference coupled with a confusion of sign and object. We have in these reflections some materials for speculation regarding the early beginnings of an ontology of attributes in the childhood of the race. There is room, as well, for alternative or supplementary conjectures; e.g., that the attributes are vestiges of the minor deities of some creed outworn.[3] In a general way such speculation is epistemologically relevant, as suggesting how organisms maturing and evolving in the physical environment we know might conceivably end up discoursing of abstract objects as we do. But the disreputability of origins is of itself no argument against preserving and prizing the abstract ontology. This conceptual scheme may well be, however accidental, a happy accident; just as the theory of electrons would be none the worse for having first occurred to its originator in the course of some absurd dream. At any rate the ontology of abstract objects is part of the ship which, in Neurath's figure, we are rebuilding at sea.[4] We may revise the scheme, but only in favor of some clearer or simpler and no less adequate over-all account of what goes on in the world.

IV

By finding out roughly which non-verbal stimulations tend to prompt assent to a given existential statement, we settle, to some degree, what is to count as empirical evidence for or against the existence of the objects in question. This I urged at the beginning of § III. Statements, however, existential and otherwise, vary in the directness with which they are conditioned to non-verbal stimulation. Commonly a stimulation will trigger our verdict on a statement only because the statement is a strand in the verbal network of some elaborate theory, other strands of which are more directly conditioned to that stimulation. Most of our statements respond thus to reverberations across the fabric of intralinguistic associations, even when also directly conditioned to extralinguistic stimuli to some degree. Highly theoretical statements are statements whose connection with extralinguistic stimulation consists pretty exclusively in the reverberations across the fabric. Statements of the existence of various sorts of subvisible particles tend to be theoretical, in this sense; and, even more so, statements of

[3] Thus Ernst Cassirer, *Language and Myth,* pp. 95 ff.
[4] Otto Neurath, "Protokollsätze," Erkenntnis, vol 3 (1932), p. 206.

the existence of certain abstract objects. Commonly such statements are scarcely to be judged otherwise than by coherence, or by considerations of over-all simplicity of a theory whose ultimate contacts with experience are remote as can be from the statements in question. And, remarkably enough, there are abstract existence statements that do succumb to such considerations. We have had the wit to posit an ontology massive enough to crumble of its own weight.

For there are the paradoxes of classes. These paradoxes are usually stated for classes because classes are a relatively simple kind of abstract object to talk about, and also because classes, being more innocent on the face of them than attributes, are more fun to discredit. In any event, as is both well known and obvious, the paradoxes of classes go through *pari passu* for attributes, and again for relations.

The moral to draw from the paradoxes is not necessarily nominalism, but certainly that we must tighten our ontological belts a few holes. The law of attributes that was implicit in our language habits or that fitted in with them most easily was that *every* statement that mentions a thing attributes an attribute to it; and this cultural heritage, however venerable, must go. Some judicious *ad hoc* excisions are required at least.

Systematic considerations can press not only for repudiating certain objects, and so declaring certain *terms* irreferential; they can also press for declaring certain *occurences* of terms irreferential, while other occurrences continue to refer. This point is essentially Frege's,[5] and an example is provided by the sentence 'Tom believes that Tully wrote the *Ars Magna*'. If we assert this on the strength of Tom's confusion of Tully with Lully, and in full appreciation of Tom's appreciation that Cicero did not write the *Ars Magna,* then we are not giving the term 'Tully' purely referential occurrence in our sentence 'Tom believes that Tully wrote the *Ars Magna*'; our sentence is not squarely about Tully. If it were, it would have to be true of Cicero, who *is* Tully.

It was only after somehow deciding what heathen locutions to construe as identity and the like that our linguist could begin to say which heathen words serve as terms and what objects they refer to. It was only after getting the knack of identity and kindred devices that our own child could reasonably be said to be talking in terms and to be talking of objects. And it is to the demands of identity still, specifically the substitutivity of iden-

[5] See Frege, "On sense and reference," translated in *Philosophical Writings of Gottlob Frege* (Geach and Black, eds.), Oxford: Blackwell, 1952, and in *Readings in Philosophical Analysis* (Feigl and Sellars, eds.), New York: Appleton, 1949. See also my *From a Logical Point of View,* Cambridge: Harvard, 1953, Essay 8.

tity, that the adult Anglo-Saxon speaker remains answerable as long as he may be said to be using terms to refer.

We are free so to use the verb 'believes' as to allow ensuing terms full referential status after all. To do so is to deny 'Tom believes that Tully wrote the *Ars Magna*' in the light of Tom's knowledge of Cicero and despite his confusion of names. The fact is that we can and do use 'believes' both ways: one way when we say that Tom believes that Tully wrote the *Ars Magna,* and the other way when we deny this, or when, resorting to quantification, we say just that there is *someone* whom Tom believes to have done thus and so. Parallel remarks are suited also to others of the *propositional attitudes,* as Russell calls them: thus doubting, wishing, striving, along with believing.

Man in a state of nature is not aware of the doubleness of these usages of his, or of the strings attached to each; just as he is not aware of the paradoxical consequences of a naïve ontology of classes or attributes. Now yet another ontological weakness that we are likewise unaware of until, philosophically minded, we start looking to coherence considerations, has to do with the individuation of attributes.

The positing of attributes is accompanied by no clue as to the circumstances under which attributes may be said to be the same or different. This is perverse, considering that the very use of terms and the very positing of objects are unrecognizable to begin with except as keyed in with idioms of sameness and difference. What happens is that at first we learn general patterns of term-talk and thing-talk with help of the necessary adjuncts of identity; afterward we project these well-learned grammatical forms to attributes, without settling identity for them. We understand the forms as referential just because they are grammatically analogous to ones that we learned earlier, for physical objects, with full dependence on the identity aspect.

The lack of a proper identity concept for attributes is a lack that philosophers feel impelled to supply; for, what sense is there in saying that there are attributes when there is no sense in saying when there is one attribute and when two? Carnap and others have proposed this principle for identifying attributes: two sentences about x attribute the *same* attribute to x if and only if the two sentences are not merely alike in truth value for each choice of x, but necessarily and analytically so, by sameness of meaning.[6]

However, this formulation depends on a questionable notion, that of sameness of meaning. For let us not slip back into the fantasy of a gallery

[6] Rudolf Carnap, *Meaning and Necessity,* Chicago, 1947, p. 23.

of ideas and labels. Let us remember rather our field lexicographer's predicament: how arbitrary his projection of analogies from known languages. Can an empiricist speak seriously of sameness of meaning of two conditions upon an object *x*, one stated in the heathen language and one in ours, when even the singling out of an object *x* as object at all for the heathen language is so hopelessly arbitrary?

We could skip the heathen language and try talking of sameness of meaning just within our own language. This would degrade the ontology of attributes; identity of attributes would be predicated on frankly provincial traits of English usage, ill fitting the objectivity of true objects. Nor let it be said in extenuation that all talk of objects, physical ones included, is in a way provincial too; for the way is different. Our physics is provincial only in that there is no universal basis for translating it into remote languages; it would still never condone defining physical identity in terms of verbal behavior. If we rest the identity of attributes on an admittedly local relation of English synonymy, then we count attributes secondary to language in a way that physical objects are not.

Shall we just let attributes be thus secondary to language in a way that physical objects are not? But our troubles do not end here; for the fact is that I see no hope of making reasonable sense of sameness of meaning even for English. The difficulty is one that I have enlarged on elsewhere.[7] English expressions are supposed to mean the same if, vaguely speaking, you can use one for the other in any situation and any English context without *relevant* difference of effect; and the essential difficulty comes in delimiting the required sense of relevant.

V

There is no denying the access of power that accrues to our conceptual scheme through the positing of abstract objects. Most of what is gained by positing attributes, however, is gained equally by positing classes. Classes are on a par with attributes on the score of abstractness or universality, and they serve the purposes of attributes so far as mathematics and certainly most of science are concerned; and they enjoy, unlike attributes, a crystal-clear identity concept. No wonder that in mathematics the murky intensionality of attributes tends to give way to the limpid extensionality of

[7] "Two dogmas of empiricism," Philosophical Review, vol. 60 (1951), pp. 20–43; reprinted in my *From a Logical Point of View*. See further my "Carnap e la verità logica," Rivista di Filosofia, vol. 48 (1957), pp. 3–29, which is a translation of an essay part of which has appeared also in the original English under the title "Logical truth" in *American Philosophers at Work* (Sidney Hook, ed.), New York: Criterion, 1956.

classes; and likewise in other sciences, roughly in proportion to the rigor and austerity of their systematization.

For attributes one might still claim this advantage over classes: they help in systematizing what we may call the *attributary attitudes*—hunting, wanting, fearing, lacking, and the like. For, take hunting. Lion-hunting is not, like lion-catching, a transaction between men and individual lions; for it requires no lions. We analyze lion-catching, rabbit-catching, etc. as having a catching relation in common and varying only in the individuals caught; but what of lion-hunting, rabbit-hunting, etc.? If any common relation is to be recognized here, the varying objects of the relation must evidently be taken not as individuals but as kinds. Yet not kinds in the sense of classes, for then unicorn-hunting would cease to differ from griffin-hunting. Kinds rather in the sense of attributes.[8]

Some further supposed abstract objects that are like attributes, with respect to the identity problem, are the *propositions*—in the sense of entities that somehow correspond to sentences as attributes correspond to predicates. Now if attributes clamor for recognition as objects of the attributary attitudes, so do propositions as objects of the propositional attitudes: believing, wishing, and the rest.

Overwhelmed by the problem of identity of attributes and of propositions, however, one may choose to make a clean sweep of the lot, and undertake to manage the attributary and propositional attitudes somehow without them. Philosophers who take this austere line will perhaps resort to actual linguistic forms, sentences, instead of propositions, as objects of the propositional attitudes; and to actual linguistic forms, predicates, instead of attributes, as objects of the attributary attitudes.

Against such resort to linguistic forms one hears the following objection, due to Church and Langford.[9] If what are believed are mere sentences, then 'Edwin believes the English sentence *S*' goes correctly into German as 'Edwin glaubt den englischen Satz *S*', with *S* unchanged. But it also goes correctly into German as 'Edwin glaubt' followed by a German translation of *S* in indirect discourse. These two German reports, one quoting the English sentence and the other using German indirect discourse, must then be equivalent. But they are not, it is argued, since a German ignorant of English cannot equate them. Now I am not altogether satisfied with this argument. It rests on the notion of linguistic equivalence, or sameness of

[8] See my "Quantifiers and propositional attitudes," Journal of Philosophy, vol. 53 (1956), pp. 177–187.

[9] Alonzo Church, "On Carnap's analysis of statements of assertion and belief," Analysis, vol. 10 (1950), pp. 97–99. Reprinted in *Philosophy and Analysis* (Margaret Macdonald, ed.), Oxford and New York: Blackwell and Philosophical Library, 1954.

meaning; and this has seemed dubious as a tool of philosophical analysis. There is, however, another objection to taking linguistic forms as objects of the attributary and propositional attitudes; viz., simply that that course is discouragingly artificial. With this objection I sympathize.

Perhaps, after all, we should be more receptive to the first and least premeditated of the alternatives. We might keep attributes and propositions after all, but just not try to cope with the problem of their individuation. We might deliberately acquiesce in the old unregenerate positing of attributes and propositions without hint of a standard of identity. The precept "No entity without identity" might simply be relaxed. Certainly the positing of first objects makes no sense except as keyed to identity; but those patterns of thing talk, once firmly inculcated, have in fact enabled us to talk of attributes and propositions in partial grammatical analogy, without an accompanying standard of identity for them. Why not just accept them thus, as twilight half-entities to which the identity concept is not to apply? [10] If the disreputability of their origins is undeniable, still bastardy, to the enlightened mind, is no disgrace. This liberal line accords with the Oxford philosophy of ordinary language, much though I should regret, by my sympathetic reference, to cause any twinge of sorrow to my revered predecessor in this presidential chair.

What might properly count against countenancing such half-entities, inaccessible to identity, is a certain disruption of logic. For, if we are to tolerate the half-entities without abdication of philosophical responsibility, we must adjust the logic of our conceptual scheme to receive them, and th[illegible]ss to [illegible]ulting complexity against the benefits of the half-entities in the heath[illegible]sitional and attributary attitudes and elsewhere.

But [illegible] sure that even philosophical responsibility requires settling for one all-purpose system.[11] Propositional and attributary attitudes belong to daily discourse of hopes, fears, and purposes; causal science gets on well without them. The fact that science has shunned them and fared so well could perhaps encourage a philosopher of sanguine temper to try to include that erstwhile dim domain within an overhauled universal system, science-worthy throughout. But a reasonable if less ambitious alternative would be to keep a relatively simple and austere conceptual scheme, free of half-entities, for official scientific business, and then accommodate the half-entities in a second-grade system.

[10] Such might be said to be Frege's line in *Grundgesetze der Arithmetik* where he withholds identity from *Begriffe*. See also Peter Geach "Class and Concept," Philosophical Review, vol. 64 (1955), pp. 561–570.

[11] See James B. Conant, *Modern Science and Modern Man,* New York: Columbia University, 1952, pp. 98 ff.

In any event the idea of accommodating half-entities without identity illustrates how the individuative, object-oriented conceptual scheme so natural to us could conceivably begin to evolve away.

It seemed in our reflections on the child that the category of bulk terms was a survival of a pre-individuative phase. We were thinking ontogenetically, but the phylogenetic parallel is plausible too: we may have in the bulk term a relic, half vestigial and half adapted, of a pre-individuative phase in the evolution of our conceptual scheme. And some day, correspondingly, something of our present individuative talk may in turn end up, half vestigial and half adapted, within a new and as yet unimagined pattern beyond individuation.

Transition to some such radically new pattern could occur either through a conscious philosophical enterprise or by slow and unreasoned development along lines of least resistance. A combination of both factors is likeliest; and anyway the two differ mainly in degree of deliberateness. Our patterns of thought or language have been evolving, under pressure of inherent inadequacies and changing needs, since the dawn of language; and, whether we help guide it or not, we may confidently look forward to more of the same.

Translation of our remote past or future discourse into the terms we now know could be about as tenuous and arbitrary a projection as translation of the heathen language was seen to be. Conversely, even to speak of that remote medium as radically different from ours is, as remarked in the case of the heathen language, to say no more than that the translations do not come smoothly. We have, to be sure, a mode of acce[illegible] future stages of our own evolution that is denied us in the cas[illegible]en language: we can sit and evolve. But even those historical gradatio[illegible] if somehow traced down the ages and used as clues to translation between widely separated evolutionary stages, would still be gradations only, and in no sense clues to fixed ideas beneath the flux of language. For the obstacle to correlating conceptual schemes is not that there is anything ineffable about language or culture, near or remote. The whole truth about the most outlandish linguistic behavior is just as accessible to us, in our current Western conceptual scheme, as are other chapters of zoölogy. The obstacle is only that any one intercultural correlation of words and phrases, and hence of theories, will be just one among various empirically admissible correlations, whether it is suggested by historical gradations or by unaided analogy; there is nothing for such a correlation to be uniquely right or wrong about. In saying this I philosophize from the vantage point only of our own provincial conceptual scheme and scientific epoch, true; but I know no better.

Inference

Herbert Feigl

De Principiis Non Disputandum . . . *

Justification involving appeal to principles of formal logic. Justification or criticism of the processes or the results of reasoning may involve, *inter alia,* questions of meaningfulness, of truth (or of reliability), of consistency, and of formal correctness (or conclusiveness). We shall concentrate on the two last mentioned criteria in the present section.

In appraising the correctness of a deductive argument we confront it with the rules of deductive logic. Conformity with these rules establishes the correctness, violation establishes the incorrectness of our reasoning. In traditional logic we may prove the legitimacy or expose the illegitimacy of some argument by reference to the rules of the syllogism. In the more generalized disciplines of modern logic a much greater wealth of forms and standards becomes available.

A specific deductive argument such as a valid syllogism may then be justified by reference to the well-known rules of the syllogism. And these rules in turn may be justified by reference to definitions and more fundamental principles such as the *dictum de omni et nullo* or (in modern logic) the rules of substitution and inference. Here the logician qua logician usually rests his case. But if he is *philosophically* curious in regard to the justification or justifiability of those basic rules of formal deduction, he will involve himself in peculiar perplexities. If he assumes that the laws of logic are the most general laws of nature, he ascribes a factual content to them that, no matter how thin, would require inductive justification. But inductive justification, while irreducible to deductive justification, presupposes the rules of deductive logic and is therefore impossible without reliance upon them. It may be urged that those most general laws of the universe are known by a priori intuition and, thus being self-evident, are neither in need nor capable of validation. This reply, however, is unaccept-

* From "De Principiis Non Disputandum . . ." by Herbert Feigl, in *Philosophical Analysis,* edited by Max Black, pp. 123–139.

able for at least three reasons: The difficulties (Kant's heroic efforts notwithstanding) of accounting for the possibility of synthetic a priori knowledge are notoriously insurmountable. The reference to self-evidence involves us in the confusions of psychologism. Finally, closer analysis reveals a difference of kind (not merely of degree) between the laws of logic and the laws of nature.

The view (espoused by Mill and others) which construes the laws of logic as psychological laws of thought is merely a variant of the just criticized factualistic interpretation. Thought, as a matter of fact, does not generally conform to the rules of logic. Even if it were impossible to *think* a simple self-contradiction, it is only too painfully obvious that even a slight degree of complexity in argument often conceals just such an inconsistency to the thinker who then blithely asserts self-contradictions at least by way of implication.

A more promising view construes the rules of logic as the *norms* of correct reasoning. Leaving the question of the nature and status of rules or norms aside for the moment, we may say that the *rules* of logic in their totality *define what we mean by correct reasoning.* This view presupposes that we possess, at least implicitly, a criterion (or a set of criteria) by which we can tell whether reasoning is correct or incorrect. The formulation of the rules then merely explicates these criteria.

But this position provokes the question: What assures us of the adequacy of our explicandum, i.e., our pre-analytic notion of correct reasoning? The most widely accepted answer here refers us to the analytic character of all implication relations upon which correct deductive inference must be based. Deducibility, logical (or "strict") implication, entailment, or whatever else we may call it can be accounted for by reference to the *meaning* of the terms employed in deductive argument. We are then likely to say that whatever follows from propositions by virtue of the meaning of the terms they contain and by virtue of the meaning the propositions have as structured wholes follows *with necessity.* But how are we to decide what (if anything) follows from a given set of premises or is implied by given meanings unless we utilize the very rules of logic which we were going to justify? The emergence of circularity, here as well as elsewhere, is symptomatic of the fact that we have reached the limits of justification, that we are at least in the neighborhood of what are called "ultimate presuppositions."

More specifically, what is it that makes a presupposition ultimate? One well known reply to this question maintains that any attempt to deny, reject (or replace by alternatives) an ultimate principle involves its reaffirmation. This view appears indeed most plausible in the domain of formal logic; it is much less convincing in other domains of justification. Yet, even in regard to the laws of deductive logic, the argument, if intended as a *validation,* is specious. The denial of the law of noncontradiction leads to contradiction, that is, if we use all terms ("contradiction," "denial," etc.) in their customary sense. This sense is the "customary" one precisely because it conforms with the basic rules of ordinary (two-valued) logic. The argument therefore demonstrates only that a denial (in this sense!) of the laws of logic involves us in inconsistencies. These inconsistencies, however, are such only within the frame of the rules that determine the logic from which we expect to deviate and define the meaning of "denial" by means of which we attempt to deviate.

Let us then examine the widely held claims as to the legitimacy of *alternative logics.* The three-valued system of Łukasiewicz and Tarski, of Brouwer and Heyting, or the logic for quantum mechanics of von Neumann, etc., are called systems of *logic* not only because they, like the two-valued systems of Aristotle or of Whitehead and Russell, are capable of axiomatic deductive presentation, but also because (and this is much more important) they too provide us with rules of inference. We shall pass over in silence the rather confused claims of the disciples of Hegel, Marx, or Engels—not to mention Korzybski—in favor of a dialectical logic. If there are any tenable insights in these trends of thought, they would have to be first separated from a great deal of outright nonsense or egregious equivocation. Only by the most charitable interpretation can those tenable elements be assimilated to the aforementioned three-valued (or many-valued) systems.

Is it a matter of "arbitrary" decision whether or not to bestow the title of "logic" upon such alternative systems? An adequate discussion of this controversial question would take us too far afield. I can here only sketchily indicate what seems to me to be involved. First there is the question whether "deduction" or "deducibility" as defined in various alternative logics despite vague analogies is not something so radically different from what these terms signify in two-valued logic that the use of these terms without proper qualification is bound to lead to confusion. Secondly, there is the question whether the rules according to which we manipulate the symbols in a three- (or many-) valued calculus must not themselves be applied according to yes-or-no principles which in turn would impose two-valued character upon their metalinguistic formulation. No matter what the structure of a language or of a calculus, if we are to proceed according to constant rules at all, if we are to be able to answer questions, solve problems, etc., in a responsible manner, must we not at some level introduce the *definiteness* which has throughout the ages been regarded as the very essence of the logical? Is not the requirement of unambiguous designation the very root of the regulative principles of semantics? And is not *logic* as we customarily understand it predicated upon adherence to rules of univocal designation? Can communication from person to person, as well as with oneself, dispense with the principles that ensure self-consistency? Are we not continually trying to remove ambiguity and vagueness from our concepts precisely in order to safeguard ourselves against inconsistency?

These questions and their obvious answers seem also to imply a repudiation of a view of logic which has lately gained some currency especially among mathematically oriented philosophers. These thinkers take their cue from the conventionalism of Poincaré and from Duhem's views on scientific method. According to this outlook there is no way of justifying laws or principles in isolation. Only the total set of laws, hypotheses, and principles is capable of test by experience. The principles of logic are simply the ones we are unwilling to surrender or modify, except as the last resort if our total system proves inadequate. The principles of logic are thus considered as in no way sharply distinguishable from those that we ordinarily would call "empirical." The advocates of this view then deny that there is a sharp distinction between the analytic and the synthetic types of propositions, and they deny accordingly also the sharp distinction between the a priori and the a posteriori type of validity. While it is difficult to see how such a position can be maintained wherever analyticity depends upon explicit definitions (as in "All roans are horses"), it may be granted that the distinction between analytic and synthetic propositions within such systems as theoretical physics is more problematic. A given formula may represent an analytic or a synthetic proposition depending upon the context of inquiry. Or, more precisely speaking, it depends upon the specific interpretation (by way of co-ordinating definitions, or semantical designation rules) to which the given formula (or a whole postulate system) is subjected. But the admitted last-ditch-surrender policy in regard to logical principles would seem to indicate that it is the data of experience which have jurisdiction over the factual content of a theory, whereas criteria of a very different kind are relevant for the adoption (or rejection) of the logical principles. In the customary view of the theories of the factual sciences, the principles of logic and pure mathematics are silent partners, presupposed but not explicitly listed among the postulates of the given theory (geometry, mechanics, electrodynamics, quantum mechanics, etc.). They are, to use a Kantian phrase with greater propriety than we find it used by Kant himself, the necessary conditions for the very possibility of any theory whatsoever. To ensure definiteness of meaning for our symbols, to ensure (the related) conclusiveness of deductive inference we have no choice but to conform to the principles of identity, of noncontradiction, and of the excluded middle. No matter whether we understand these principles as tautologies of the object language (as we do in propositional and functional logic) or whether we understand them as semantical precepts (formulated in the metalanguage), it is impossible to abandon, e.g., the law of the excluded middle, without at the same time abandoning the other two principles (as well as the principle of double negation, or the principles "$p \vee p \equiv p$," "$p \cdot p \equiv p$," etc.). Only if we allow ourselves to tamper with the implicitly understood meanings of "proposition," "negation," "equivalence," "disjunction," "conjunction," etc., can we responsibly deviate from one principle without affecting the others. And even if, upon modifying some of these meanings, we arrive at an "alternative logic," we shall yet have achieved no more than if, for example, we had perversely decided to replace the numeral "4" by the numeral "5" in arithmetic. That under such conditions "$2 + 2 = 5$" becomes a true statement is not in the least surprising. Actually, the parallel with arithmetic is (as everybody should have realized, at least since Frege's contributions) not merely a superficial analogy but genuinely a consequence of the fact that arithmetic (in ordinary interpretation) is a branch of logic (in ordinary, i.e., in Frege-Russell-Whitehead interpretation). Even if in some other world putting two and two objects together resulted invariably in a total of five objects, we should need ordinary (good old) arithmetic in order to formulate the rather peculiar natural laws of that world. Thought experiments of this kind reveal that the fundamental principles of logic are indeed independent of the data of experience. They show that these principles are indispensable not because of some pervasive features of the world that is to be symbolized, but because of the requirements of the process of symbolization itself. Every symbolic system has its tautological equivalences, based on conventional synonymities.

What is it then that accounts for the unique and ineluctable character of the principles of logic? If it is not the data of experience or the facts of the universe at large, what is it that makes compliance with them imperative and their violation a sin against the spirit of Reason? Neither the Ten Commandments nor the Law of the Land prescribes any rules of logic or language. What then is the "authority," what are the "sanctions" that dictate conformity with these principles? It will be suggested that at least part of what we mean by "mental sanity" consists precisely in compliance with those laws. Assuredly so, but this merely shows that "mental sanity" is (in part) defined by conformity with logic. The appeal to sanity therefore amounts to begging the question.

It is obvious that we have reached the limits of justification. Justification in the sense of validation involves reliance upon the principles of logic and can thus not provide their validation. Justification in the sense of a pragmatic vindication of the adoption of, and compliance with, the rules of logic would then seem to offer itself as a further opening, if we insist on pursuing our quest to the bitter (because trivial) end. If we wish to give such a justification, it too must be given by reasoning and will thus have to rely upon the very standards whose adoption is now the issue at stake. Will this involve us in a vicious circle? It will not, if we are perfectly clear that we are not seeking a *validation* of the principles of logic. If pragmatic *vindication* is sharply distinguished from validation, then all it can provide amounts to a recommendation of a certain type of behavior with respect to certain ends. We may say to ourselves: If we wish to avoid the perplexities and discomforts that arise out of ambiguity and inconsistency, *then* we have to comply with the rules of semantics and logic. If we wish to derive true propositions from true premises then we must conform to the rules of inference and the rules of substitution. The reasoning concerning these means-ends relations utilizes, as any such reasoning must, the forms of deductive and inductive inference. Perhaps in the extreme case—the degenerate case, as it were—only deductive inference is required.

There is only one more question that the dialectical process will finally bring forth: Why should we accept the ends which we took for granted in the vindication of compliance with logical rules? If the end is a means to further ends, then the question merely shifts to those further ends. And just as in the reconstruction of validation we disclose ultimate validating principles, so in the reconstruction of vindication we encounter ultimate ends or purposes. Whether definiteness and conclusiveness of reasoning are to be viewed as ultimate ends or as means to certain other values is a question of psychology. The well known transformation process of means into ends has brought it about that for many persons, especially of the scientific type of mind, the virtues of logicality have become ends in themselves. But for the vast majority of mankind logicality is primarily a means in the struggle for existence and in the pursuit of more satisfactory ways of living. These ends we pursue as a matter of stark fact; they are part of our human nature. The question whether this ought to be our nature, if not altogether preposterous, falls at any rate outside the domain of logical justification. If there is a meaningful question here at all, it is one for *ethical* considerations to decide.

Justification involving appeal to principles of methodology. It is generally granted that consistency and conclusiveness of reasoning are necessary conditions for arguments purporting to substantiate knowledge claims. It is almost equally well agreed that while consistency and conclusiveness may be sufficient in the purely formal disciplines, they are not sufficient in the realm of factual knowledge. The sort of justification that the claims of factual knowledge require leads us then to a consideration of principles outside the domain of formal logic. These principles belong to the field of inductive logic.

One qualification may be in order here. Inductive logic is not required for a justification of factual-knowledge claims that involve no transcendence beyond the completely and directly given. Perhaps a better way to state this contention is in the subjunctive mood: If there were knowledge claims susceptible to complete and direct verification (or refutation), their justification would involve appeal only to immediate data, to designation rules, to definitions, and to the principles of formal logic. We shall not attempt here to clean up this particular corner of the Augean stables of philosophy. In any case the doctrine of immediate knowledge seems to me highly dubious. The very terms in which we formulate observation statements are used according to rules which involve reference beyond the occasion of direct experience to which they are applied. If they involve no such reference then they are not terms of a language as we usually conceive languages. Terms referring exclusively to the data of the present moment of a stream of experience could not fulfill the function of symbols in observation statements that are connected with symbols in other statements (of laws and/or other observation statements). If we are not be be reduced to mere signals indicating the individual occurrences of direct experience, we must formulate our statements regarding these individual occurrences in such a manner that they are capable of revision on the basis of other observation statements and of laws that are confirmable by observation.

Appeal to the justifying principles of inductive logic is inevitably made if the dialectic question "How do you know?" is pursued to the limit. An engineer may rest satisfied with reference to specific physical laws when he justifies his claims as to the efficiency (or inefficiency) of a particular machine. A physicist in turn may justify those specific laws by deduction from very general and basic laws, such as those of thermodynamics or electromagnetics. But when pressed for the reasons of his acceptance of those more (or most) general laws, he will invariably begin to speak of verification, of generalization, or of hypothetico-deductive confirmation. A researcher in medicine will proceed similarly. In order to justify a particular hypothesis, e.g., one according to which a certain disease is caused by a virus, he will quote evidence and/or will reason by analogy and induction. Justification of knowledge claims in the historical disciplines (natural as well as social) conforms to the same pattern.

A given item of observation is evidence not in and by itself, but only if viewed in the light of principles of inductive inference. On the level of common sense and on the more "empirical" levels of scientific inquiry those principles are simply the accepted laws of the relevant field. Utilizing some items of evidence and some pertinent laws we justify our assertions concerning past events in history, concerning the causes of diseases in pathology, concerning the existence of as yet unobserved heavenly bodies in astronomy, concerning motivations or learning-processes in psychology, and so on. The search for causes generally presupposes the assumption that events do have causes. The investigator of a crime would give us a queer look (if nothing worse) if we asked him how he could be so sure that the death under investigation must have had *some* cause or causes. He takes this for granted and it is not *his* business to justify the principle of causality. Philosophers however have felt that it is their business to justify the belief in causality.

We need not review in too much detail the variety of attempts that have been made in its behalf. The assimilation of causal to logical necessity was definitely refuted by Hume. Kant's transcedental deduction of a causal order depends on the premise that the human understanding impresses this order upon the data of the senses. Part of this premise is the tacit assumption that reason will remain constant throughout time and that it therefore can be relied upon invariably to bestow (the same) causal order upon the data. In this psychologistic version of Kant's epistemology we thus find that the lawfulness of the world is demonstrable only at the price of an assumption concerning the lawfulness of Reason. (We shall not press any further questions concerning the credibility of this ingenious but phantastic account of the nature of cognition.) Turning to the presuppositional version of the *Critique* we gladly acknowledge that Kant, more incisively than any of his predecessors, disclosed the frame of justifying principles within which the questions of natural science are raised as well as answered. But the elevation of strict determinism and of Newtonian mechanics to the rank of synthetic a priori principles proved to be a mistake. The development of recent science provides, if not a fully cogent refutation, at least a most serious counterargument against any such attempt at a rationalistic petrifaction of the laws of science of a given epoch. More crucial yet, Kant did not achieve what he proposed to do: overcome Hume's skepticism. The presuppositional analysis furnishes no more than this: "Knowledge" as we understand this term connotes explanation and prediction. Therefore, if knowledge of nature is to be possible, nature must be predictable. This is true enough. But do we establish in this fashion a synthetic a priori guarantee for the order of nature? Not in the least. All we have attained is an *analytic* proposition drawn from the definition of "knowledge."

Can *intuition* justify the belief in causality? Even if we granted that we have an intuitive acquaintance with causal necessity in some of its instantiations, how can we assure ourselves without *inductive* leap that the intuited samples are representative of the structure of the world at large?

It should scarcely be necessary to point out that the again fashionable attempts to rehabilitate the concept of Real Connections will not advance the problem of the justification of induction. We grant that problems such as those regarding the meaning of contrary-to-fact conditionals show that Hume's (and generally the radical empiricist) analysis of causal propositions is in need of emendation. Indeed, it seems inevitable to establish and clarify a meaning of "causal connection" that is stronger than Hume's constant conjunction and weaker than entailment or deducibility. Perhaps the distinction between laws (nomological statements) and initial conditions will help here. Our world, to the extent that it is lawful at all, is characterized by both: its laws and its initial condition. Counterfactual conditionals tamper with initial conditions. The frame of the laws is left intact in asking *this* kind of hypothetical question. The "real possibilities" which are correlative to the "real connections" are precisely the class of initial conditions compatible with the laws of our world (or of some other fancied world). These considerations show that the laws of a given world may be viewed as something stronger than can be formulated by means of general implication. They are the very principles of confirmation of any singular descriptive statement that is not susceptible to complete and direct verification. They are therefore constitutive principles of the conception of a given world, or rather of a class or family of worlds which are all characterized by the same laws.[1]

But the reconstruction of laws in terms of modal implications does not alter one whit their status in the methodology of science. Clearly, besides counterfactual hypotheticals we can equally easily formulate counternomological ones. Here we tamper with the laws. And the question of which *family* of worlds our world is a member can be answered only on grounds of empirical evidence and according to the usual rules of inductive procedure. Upon return from this excursion we are then confronted, just as before, with the problem of induction.

Obviously the next step in the dialectic must be the lowering of our level of aspiration. We are told that it is the quest for certainty that makes the justification of induction an insoluble problem. But we are promised a solution if only we content ourselves with probabilities. Let us see. "Probability" in the sense of a degree of expectation will not do. This is the psychological concept to which Hume resorted in his account of belief, or that Santayana has in mind when he speaks of "animal faith." What we want is a justifiable degree of expectation. And how do we justify the assignment of probability ratios to predictions and hypotheses? That depends on how we explicate the *objective* concept of probability. But here we encounter the strife of two schools of thought. According to the frequency interpretation there is no other meaning of "probability" than that of the limit of relative frequency. According to the logical interpretation "probability" (in the sense of strength of evidence, weight, degree of confirmation) consists in a logical relation between the evidence which bestows and the proposition upon which there is bestowed a certain degree of credibility. The adherents of this logical interpretation urge that the statistical concept of probability presupposes the logical one. For the ascription of a limit (within a certain interval) to a sequence of frequency ratios is itself an hypothesis and must therefore be judged according to the degree of confirmation that such hypotheses possess in the light of their evidence. Contrariwise, the frequency interpretation urges that locutions such as "degree of confirmation" or "weight," whether applied to predictions of single events or to hypotheses of all sorts, are merely *façons de parler.* Basically they all amount to stating frequency ratios which are generalized from statistical findings regarding the events concerned (the occurrence of successful predictions).

We shall not attempt to resolve the issue between these two schools

[1] Cp. W. Sellars, "Concepts as Involving Laws and Inconceivable without Them," *Phil. of Science,* XV (1948), 287.

of thought. Our concern is with the justification of induction. And here perhaps the divergence of interpretations makes no fundamental difference. Inductive probability in the sense of a degree of confirmation is a concept whose definition renders analytic every one of its specific applications. If we use this concept as our guide, that is if we believe that it will give us a maximum of successes in inductive guessing, then this could be explicated as an assertion about the (statistical) structure of the world. We are thus led to essentially the same rule of induction which the frequentists propose: Generalize on the basis of the broadest background of available evidence with a minimum of arbitrariness. This principle of straightforward extrapolation in sequences of frequency ratios applies to a world which need not display a deterministic order. Statistical regularity is sufficient. Does the application of the rule guarantee success? Of course not. Do the past successes of procedures according to this rule indicate, at least with probability, further successes? No again. Hume's arguments refuted this question-begging argument before Mill and others fell victims to the fallacy. Only if we utilize the *logical* concept of probability can we achieve a semblance of plausibility in the criticized argument. But for the reasons stated before, mere definitions cannot settle the issue as to whether our world will be good enough to continue to supply patterns of events in the future which will support this definition as a "useful" one.

The presuppositional analysis sketched thus far has merely disclosed one of the ultimate principles of all empirical inference. Any attempts to validate the principle itself involve question-begging arguments. Its ultimate and apparently ineluctable character can be forcefully brought out by considering how we would behave in a world that is so utterly chaotic and unpredictable that any anticipation of the future on the basis of past experience is doomed to failure. Even in such a world after countless efforts at inductive extrapolation had been frustrated we would (if by some miracle we managed to survive) abandon all further attempts to attain foresight. But would not even this yet be another inductive inference, viz., to the effect that the disorder will continue? The inductive principle thus is ultimately presupposed but in turn does not presuppose any further assumptions.

The various attempts (by Keynes, Broad, Nicod, Russell, and others) to deduce or render probable the principle of induction on the basis of some very general assumption concerning the structure of the world seem to me, if not metaphysical and hence irrelevant, merely to beg the question at issue. Assumptions of Permanent Kinds and of Limited Variety, provided they are genuine assertions regarding the constitution of the universe, themselves require inductive validation. To assign to such vast hypotheses a finite initial (or "antecedent") probability makes sense only if "probability" means subjective confidence. But nothing is gained in this manner. Any objective probability (logical or statistical) would presuppose a principle of induction by means of which we could ascertain the probability of such world hypotheses in comparison with the (infinite) range of their alternatives.

We have reached the limit of justification in the sense of validation. Can we then in any fashion provide a "reason" for this acknowledged principle of "reasonability"? Obviously not, if "reason" is meant in the sense of validating grounds. What we mean (at least in part, possibly as the most prominent part) by "reasonability" in practical life as well as in science consists precisely in the conformance of our beliefs with the probabilities assigned to them by a rule of induction or by a definition of degree of confirmation. We call expectations (hopes or fears) irrational if they markedly deviate from the best inductive estimates. The attempt to validate one of the major principles of all validation, it must be amply obvious by now, is bound to fail. We would be trying to lift ourselves by our own bootstraps.

The only further question that can be raised here concerns a justification of the *adoption* of the rule of induction (or rather of one of the various rules of induction, or one of the various definitions of inductive probability or of degree of confirmation). Such a justification must have the character of a vindication, a *justificatio actionis*. Our question then concerns the choice of means for the attainment of an end. Our end here is clearly successful prediction, more generally, true conclusions of nondemonstrative inference. No deductively necessary guarantee can be given for the success of such inferences even if we follow some rule of induction. The probability of success can be proved, but that is trivial because we here utilize the concept of probability which our rule of induction implicitly defines. This probability cannot be construed as an estimate of the limit of frequency. We do not know whether such a limit exists. Only if we grant hypothetically that there is such a limit can we assign weights to its various values (i.e., to intervals into which the limit may fall) on the basis of (always finite) statistical samples. What then justifies our optimistic belief in the convergence of statistical sequences toward a limit? Since any attempt at validation would inevitably be circular, we can only ask for a vindication of the rule according to which we posit the existence of limits. Reichenbach's well known but widely misunderstood justification of induction [2] consists, as I see it, in a vindication of the adoption of that rule. It amounts to the *deductive* proof that no method of attaining foresight could conceivably be successful if every sort of induction were bound to fail. Perhaps there are alternative techniques of foresight that might even be more efficient or reliable than the laborious method of scientific generalization. But such alternative methods (let us none too seriously mention crystal gazing, clairvoyance, premonitions, etc.) would themselves have to be appraised by their success; i.e., they would have to be accepted or rejected on the basis of statistical studies of the frequency ratio of correct predictions achieved by them. And our confidence in such "alternative" techniques of foresight would therefore ultimately be justifiable only on the basis of normal induction. *If* there is an order of nature at all (i.e., at least a statistical regularity), not too complex or deeply hidden, then a consistent application of the rule of induction will reveal it. This statement is of course a tautology. It should not be confused with such bolder and undemonstrable factual assertions as that the inductive procedure is the only reliable one, or that it is our best bet. Reliability and optimal wagering presuppose inductive probabilities and thus cannot be invoked for their justification. We cannot even say that straightforward generalization is a necessary condition (never known to be sufficient) for the success of predictions. The air of plausibility that this statement shares with its close relative, the common-sense slogan "Nothing ventured, nothing gained" arises only if we disregard (logically conceivable) alternative routes to predictive success, such as sheer inspiration, capricious guessing, intuition, premonition, etc. The unique character that the inductive procedure possesses in contrast with those alternatives rests exclusively in this: The method of induction is *the only one for which it can be proved* (deductively!) that it leads to successful predictions *if* there is an order of nature, i.e., *if* at least some sequences of frequencies do converge in a manner not too difficult to ascertain for human beings with limited experience, patience, and ingenuity. This is the tautology over again, in expanded form, but just as obvious and trivial as before. In the more ordinary contexts of pragmatic justification the validity of induction is invariably presupposed. If we want to attain a certain end, we must make "sure" (i.e., probable) that the means to be chosen will achieve that end. But if we ask for a vindication of the adoption of the very *principium* of all induction, we deal, so to speak, with

[2] H. Reichenbach, *Experience and Prediction* (1938). See also his article "On the Justification of Induction," *Jour. of Phil.*, XXXVII (1940), 101. Also reprinted in H. Feigl and W. Sellars (eds.), *Readings in Philosophical Analysis* (1949).

a degenerate case of justification. We have no assurance that inductive probabilities will prove a useful guide for our lives beyond the present moment. But equally we have no reason to believe that they will fail us. We know furthermore (as a matter of logical necessity or tautology) that *if* success can be had at all, in any manner whatsoever, it can certainly be attained by the inductive method. For this method is according to its very definition so designed as to disclose whatever order or regularity may be present to be disclosed. Furthermore, since the inductive method is self-corrective, it is the most flexible device conceivable for the adaptation and readaptation of our expectations.

The conclusion reached may seem only infinitesimally removed from Hume's skepticism. Philosophers do not seem grateful for small mercies. In their rationalist quest for certainty many still hope for a justification of a principle of uniformity of nature. We could offer merely a deductive (and trivial) vindication of the use of the pragmatic rule of induction. But for anyone who has freed himself from the wishful dreams of rationalism the result may nevertheless be helpful and clarifying. It is the final point which a consistent empiricist must add to his outlook. We refuse to countenance such synthetic a priori postulates as Russell (perhaps not with the best intellectual conscience) lately found necessary to stipulate regarding the structure of the universe. We insist that no matter how general or pervasive the assumptions, as long as they are about the *universe,* they fall under the jurisdiction of the rule of induction. This rule itself is not then a factual assertion but the maxim of a procedure or what is tantamount, a definition of inductive probability. In regard to rules or definitions we cannot raise the sort of doubt that is sensibly applicable to factual assertions. In order to settle doubts of the usual sort we must rely on some principles without which neither doubt nor the settlement of doubt makes sense. The maxim of induction is just such a principle.

Rudolf Carnap

The Two Concepts of Probability *

I. THE PROBLEM OF PROBABILITY

The problem of probability may be regarded as the task of finding an adequate definition of the concept of probability that can provide a basis for a theory of probability. This task is not one of defining a new concept but rather of redefining an old one. Thus we have here an instance of that kind of problem—often important in the development of science and mathematics—where a concept already in use is to be made more exact or, rather, is to be replaced by a more exact new concept. Let us call these problems (in an adaptation of the terminology of Kant and Husserl) problems of *explication;* in each case of an explication, we call the old concept, used in a more or less vague way either in every-day language or in an earlier stage of scientific language, the *explicandum;* the new, more exact concept which is proposed to take the place of the old one the *explicatum*. Thus, for instance, the definition of the cardinal number three by Frege and Russell as the class of all triples was meant as an explication; the explicandum was the ordinary meaning of the word 'three' as it appears in every-day life and in science; the concept of the class of all triples (defined not by means of the word 'triple' but with the help of existential quantifiers and the sign of identity) was proposed as an explicatum for the explicandum mentioned.

Using these terms, we may say that the problem of probability is the problem of finding an adequate explication of the word 'probability' in its ordinary meaning, or in one of its meanings if there are several.

II. THE LOGICAL CONCEPTS OF CONFIRMATION

In the preparation for our subsequent discussion of the problem of probability, let us examine some concepts which are connected with the

* From "The Two Concepts of Probability" by Rudolf Carnap, Section I–IV, in *Philosophy and Phenomenological Research,* 5, 1945. Reprinted by permission of *Philosophy and Phenomenological Research* and the author.

scientific procedure of confirming or disconfirming hypotheses on the basis of results found by observation.

The procedure of confirmation is a complex one consisting of components of different kinds. In the present discussion, we shall be concerned only with what may be called the logical side of confirmation, namely, with certain logical relations between sentences (or propositions expressed by these sentences). Within the procedure of confirmation, these relations are of interest to the scientist, for instance, in the following situation: He intends to examine a certain hypothesis *h;* he makes many observations of particular events which he regards as relevant for judging the hypothesis *h;* he formulates this evidence, the results of all observations made, or as many of them as are relevant, in a report *e,* which is a long sentence. Then he tries to decide whether and to what degree the hypothesis *h* is confirmed by the observational evidence *e*. It is with this decision alone that we shall be concerned. Once the hypothesis is formulated by *h* and the observational results by *e,* then this question as to whether and how much *h* is confirmed by *e* can be answered merely by a logical analysis of *h* and *e* and their relations. Therefore the question is a logical one. It is not a question of fact in the sense that knowledge of empirical fact is required to find the answer. Although the sentences *h* and *e* under consideration do themselves certainly refer to facts, nevertheless once *h* and *e* are given, the question of confirmation requires only that we are able to understand them, i.e., grasp their meanings, and to discover certain relations which are based upon their meanings. If by semantics [1] we understand the theory of the meanings of expressions, and especially of sentences, in a language then the relations to be studied between *h* and *e* may be regarded as semantical.

The question of confirmation in which we are here interested has just been characterized as a logical question. In order to avoid misunderstanding, a qualification should be made. The question at issue does not belong to deductive but to inductive logic. Both branches of logic have this in common: solutions of their problems do not require factual knowledge but only analysis of meaning. Therefore, both parts of logic (if formulated with respect to sentences rather than to propositions) belong to semantics. This similarity makes it possible to explain the logical character of the relations of confirmation by an analogy with a more familiar relation in deductive logic, viz., the relation of logical consequence or its converse,

[1] Compare Alfred Tarski, "The Semantic Conception of Truth and the Foundations of Semantics", *Philosophy and Phenomenological Research,* 4, 1944, pp. 341–376 [pp. 52–83 in the present collection]; and R. Carnap, *Introduction to Semantics,* 1942.

the relation of L-implication (i.e., logical implication or entailment in distinction to material implication). Let *i* be the sentence 'all men are mortal, and Socrates is a man,' and *j* the sentence 'Socrates is mortal.' Both *i* and *j* have factual content. But in order to decide whether *i* L-implies *j*, we need no factual knowledge, we need not know whether *i* is true or false, whether *j* is true or false, whether anybody believes in *i*, and if so, on what basis. All that is required is a logical analysis of the meanings of the two sentences. Analogously, to decide to what degree *h* is confirmed by *e* —a question in logic, but here in inductive, not in deductive, logic— we need not know whether *e* is true or false, whether *h* is true or false, whether anybody believes in *e*, and, if so, whether on the basis of observation or of imagination or of anything else. All we need is a logical analysis of the meanings of the two sentences. For this reason we call our problem the logical or semantical problem of confirmation, in distinction to what might be called the methodological problems of confirmation, e.g., how best to construct and arrange an apparatus for certain experiments in order to test a given hypothesis, how to carry out the experiments, how to observe the results, etc.

We may distinguish three logical concepts of confirmation, concepts which have to do with the logical side only of the problem of confirmation. They are all logical and hence semantical concepts. They apply to two sentences, which we call hypothesis and evidence and which in our example were designated by "*h*" and "*e*" respectively. Although the basis is usually an observational report, as in the application sketched above, and the hypothesis a law or a prediction, we shall not restrict our concepts of confirmation to any particular content or form of the two sentences. We distinguish the positive, the comparative, and the metrical concepts of confirmation in the following way.

(i) *The positive concept of confirmation* is that relation between two sentences *h* and *e* which is usually expressed by sentences of the following forms:

"*h* is confirmed by *e*."
"*h* is supported by *e*."
"*e* gives some (positive) evidence for *h*."
"*e* is evidence substantiating (or corroborating) the assumption of *h*."

Here *e* is ordinarily, as in the previous example, an observational report, but may also refer to particular states of affairs not yet known but merely assumed, and may even include assumed laws; *h* is usually a statement about an unknown state of affairs, e.g., a prediction, or it may be a law or any other hypothesis. It is clear that this concept of confirmation is a relation between two sentences, not a property of one of them. Customary formulations which mention only the hypothesis are obviously elliptical; the basis is tacitly understood. For instance, when a physicist says: "This hypothesis is well confirmed," he means ". . . on the evidence of the observational results known today to physicists."

(ii) *The comparative* (or topological) *concept of confirmation* is usually expressed in sentences of the following forms (*a*), (*b*), (*c*), or similar ones.

(*a*) "*h* is more strongly confirmed (or supported, substantiated, corroborated etc.) by *e* than *h′* by *e′*."

Here we have a tetradic relation between four sentences. In general, the two hypotheses *h* and *h′* are different from one another, and likewise the two evidences *e* and *e′*. Some scientists will perhaps doubt whether a comparison of this most general form is possible, and may, perhaps, restrict the application of the comparative concept only to those situations where two evidences are compared with respect to the same hypothesis [example (*b*)], or where two hypotheses are examined with respect to one evidence [example (*c*)]. In either case the comparative concept is a triadic relation between three sentences.

(*b*) "The general theory of relativity is more highly confirmed by the results of laboratory experiments and astronomical observations known today than by those known in 1905."

(*c*) "The optical phenomena available to physicists in the 19th century were more adequately explained by the wave theory of light than by the corpuscular theory; in other words, they gave stronger support to the former theory than to the latter."

(iii) *The metrical* (or quantitative) *concept of confirmation,* the concept of *degree of confirmation.* Opinion seems divided as to whether or not a concept of this kind ever occurs in the customary talk of scientists, that is to say, whether they ever assign a numerical value to the degree to which a hypothesis is supported by given observational material or whether they use only positive and comparative concepts of confirmation. For the present discussion, we leave this question open; even if the latter were the case, an attempt to find a metrical explicatum for the comparative explicandum would be worth while. (This would be analogous to many other cases of scientific explication, to the introduction, for example, of the metrical explicatum "temperature" for the comparative explicandum 'warmer', or of the metrical explicatum 'I.Q.' for the comparative explicandum 'higher intelligence.')

III. THE TWO CONCEPTS OF PROBABILITY

The history of the theory of probability is the history of attempts to find an explication for the pre-scientific concept of probability. The number of solutions which have been proposed for this problem in the course of its historical development is rather large. The differences, though sometimes slight, are in many cases considerable. To bring some order into the bewildering multiplicity, several attempts have been made to arrange the many solutions into a few groups. The following is a simple and plausible classification of the various conceptions of probability into three groups: [2] (i) the classical conception, originated by Jacob Bernoulli and Laplace, and represented by their followers in various forms; here, probability is defined as the ratio of the number of favorable cases to the number of all possible cases; (ii) the conception of probability as a certain objective logical relation between propositions (or sentences); the chief representatives of this conception are Keynes [3] and Jeffreys; [4] (iii) the conception of probability as relative frequency, developed most completely by von Mises [5] and Reichenbach.[6]

In this paper, a discussion of these various conceptions is not intended. While the main point of interest both for the authors and for the readers of the various theories of probability is normally the solutions proposed in those theories, we shall inspect the theories from a different point of view. We shall not ask what solutions the authors offer but rather which problems the solutions are intended to solve; in other words, we shall not ask what explicata are proposed but rather which concepts are taken as explicanda.

This question may appear superfluous, and the fact obvious that the explicandum for every theory of probability is the pre-scientific concept of probability, i.e., the meaning in which the word 'probability' is used in the pre-scientific language. Is the assumption correct, however, that there is only one meaning connected with the word 'probability' in its customary use, or at the least that only one meaning has been chosen by the authors as their explicandum? When we look at the formulations which the authors themselves offer in order to make clear which meanings of 'probability' they intend to take as their explicanda, we find phrases as

[2] See Ernest Nagel, "Principles of the Theory of Probability" (*International Encyclopedia of Unified Science,* Vol. I, 1939, No. 6).

[3] John Maynard Keynes, *A Treatise on Probability,* 1921.

[4] Harold Jeffreys, *Theory of Probability,* 1939.

[5] Richard von Mises, *Probability, Statistics, and Truth* (orig. 1928), 1939.

[6] Hans Reichenbach, *Wahrscheinlichkeitslehre,* 1935.

different as "degree of belief," "degree of reasonable expectation," "degree of possibility," "degree of proximity to certainty," "degree of partial truth," "relative frequency," and many others. This multiplicity of phrases shows that any assumption of a unique explicandum common to all authors is untenable. And we might even be tempted to go to the opposite extreme and to conclude that the authors are dealing not with one but with a dozen or more different concepts. However, I believe that this multiplicity is misleading. It seems to me that the number of explicanda in all the various theories of probability is neither just one nor about a dozen, but in all essential respects—leaving aside slight variations—very few, and chiefly two. In the following discussion we shall use subscripts in order to distinguish these two meanings of the term 'probability' from which most of the various theories of probability start; we are, of course, distinguishing between two explicanda and not between the various explicata offered by these theories, whose number is much greater. The two concepts are: (i) $probability_1 =$ degree of confirmation; (ii) $probability_2 =$ relative frequency in the long run. Strictly speaking, there are two groups of concepts, since both for (i) and for (ii) there is a positive, a comparative, and a metrical concept; however, for our discussion, we may leave aside these distinctions.

Let me emphasize again that the distinction made here refers to two explicanda, not to two explicata. That there is more than one explicatum is obvious; and indeed, their number is much larger than two. But most investigators in the field of probability apparently believe that all the various theories of probability are intended to solve the same problem and hence that any two theories which differ fundamentally from one another are incompatible. Consequently we find that most representatives of the frequency conception of probability reject all other theories; and, vice versa, that the frequency conception is rejected by most of the authors of other theories. These mutual rejections are often formulated in rather strong terms. This whole controversy seems to me futile and unnecessary. The two sides start from different explicanda, and both are right in maintaining the scientific importance of the concepts chosen by them as explicanda—a fact which does not, however, imply that on either side all authors have been equally successful in constructing a satisfactory explicatum. On the other hand, both sides are wrong in most of their polemic assertions against the other side.

A few examples may show how much of the futile controversy between representatives of different conceptions of probability is due to the blindness on both sides with respect to the existence and importance of the probability concept on the other side. We take as examples a prominent contemporary representative of each conception: von Mises, who constructed the first complete theory based on the frequency conception, and Jeffreys, who constructed the most advanced theory based on probability_1. Von Mises [7] seems to believe that probability_2 is the only basis of the Calculus of Probability. To speak of the probability of the death of a certain individual seems to him meaningless. Any use of the term "probability" in everyday life other than in the statistical sense of probability_2 has in his view nothing to do with the Calculus of Probability and cannot take numerical values. That he regards Keynes' conception of probability as thoroughly subjectivistic [8] indicates clearly his misunderstanding.

On the other hand, we find Jeffreys similarly blind in the other direction. Having laid down certain requirements which every theory of probability (and that means for him probability_1) should fulfill, he then rejects all frequency theories, that is, theories of probability_2, because they do not fulfill his requirements. Thus he says: [9] "No 'objective' definition of probability in terms of actual or possible observations . . . is admissible," because the results of observations are initially unknown and, consequently, we could not know the fundamental principles of the theory and would have no starting point. He even goes so far as to say that "in practice, no statistician ever uses a frequency definition, but that all use the notion of degree of reasonable belief, usually without ever noticing that they are using it." [10] While von Mises' concern with explicating the empirical concept of probability_2 by the limit of relative frequency in an infinite sequence has led him to apply the term "probability" only in cases were such a limit exists, Jeffreys misunderstands his procedure completely and accuses the empiricist von Mises of apriorism: "The existence of the limit is taken as a postulate by von Mises. . . . The postulate is an *a priori* statement about possible experiments and is in itself objectionable." [11] Thus we find this situation: von Mises and Jeffreys both assert that there is only one concept of probability that is of scientific importance and that can be taken as the basis of the Calculus of Probability. The first maintains that this concept is probability_2 and certainly not anything like probability_1; the second puts it just the other way round; and neither has anything but ironical remarks for the concept proposed by the other.

When we criticize the theory of probability proposed by an author, we

[7] *Op. cit.,* First Lecture.
[8] *Op. cit.,* Third Lecture.
[9] *Op. cit.,* p. 11.
[10] *Op. cit.,* p. 300.
[11] *Op. cit.,* p. 304.

must clearly distinguish between a rejection of his explicatum and a rejection of his explicandum. The second by no means follows from the first. Donald Williams, in his paper in this symposium,[12] raises serious objections against the frequency theory of probability, especially in von Mises' form. The chief objection is that von Mises' explicatum for probability, viz., the limit of the relative frequency in an infinite sequence of events with a random distribution, is not accessible to empirical confirmation—unless it be supplemented by a theory of inductive probability, a procedure explicitly rejected by von Mises. I think Williams is right in this objection. This, however, means merely that the concept proposed by von Mises is not yet an adequate explicatum. On the other hand, I believe the frequentists are right in the assertion that their explicandum, viz., the statistical concept of probability$_2$, plays an important rôle in all branches of empirical science and especially in modern physics, and that therefore the task of explicating this concept is of great importance for science.

It would likewise be unjustified to reject the concept of probability$_1$ as an explicandum merely because the attempts so far made at an explication are not yet quite satisfactory. It must be admitted that the classical Laplacean definition is untenable. It defines probability as the ratio of the number of favorable cases to the total number of equipossible cases, where equipossibility is determined by the principle of insufficient reason (or indifference). This definition is in certain cases inapplicable, in other cases it yields inadequate values, and in some cases it leads even to contradictions, because for any given proposition there are, in general, several ways of analyzing it as a disjunction of other, logically exclusive, propositions.[13] Modern authors, especially Keynes, Jeffreys, and Hosiasson,[14] proceed more cautiously, but at the price of restricting themselves to axiom systems which are rather weak and hence far from constituting an explicit definition. I have made an attempt to formulate an explicit definition of the concept of degree of confirmation (with numerical values) as an explicatum for probability$_1$, and to construct a system of metrical inductive logic based on that definition.[15] No matter whether this first at-

[12] "On the Derivation of Probabilities from Frequencies", *Philosophy and Phenomenological Research,* 5, 1945.

[13] Williams' indications (*op. cit,* pp. 450 and 469) to the effect that he intends to maintain Laplace's definition even in a simplified form and without the principle of indifference are rather puzzling. We have to wait for the full formulation of his solution, which his present paper does not yet give (*op. cit.,* p. 481), in order to see how it overcomes the well-known difficulties of Laplace's definition.

[14] Janina Hosiasson-Lindenbaum, "On Confirmation", *Journal of Symbolic Logic,* Vol. V, 1940, pp. 133–148.

[15] A book exhibiting this system is in preparation. The present paper is a modified version of a chapter of the book. The definition is explained and some of the theorems

tempt at an explication with the help of the methods of modern logic and in particular those of semantics will turn out to be satisfactory or not, I think there is no reason for doubting that an adequate explication will be developed in time through further attempts.

The distinction between the two concepts which serve as explicanda is often overlooked on both sides. This is primarily due to the unfortunate fact that both concepts are designated by the same familiar, but ambiguous word 'probability'. Although many languages contain two words (e.g., English 'probable' and 'likely', Latin *'probabilis'* and *'verisimilis'*, French *'probable'* and *'vraisemblable'*), these words seem in most cases to be used in about the same way or at any rate not to correspond to the two concepts we have distinguished. Some authors (e.g., C. S. Peirce and R. A. Fisher) have suggested utilizing the plurality of available words for the distinction of certain concepts (different from our distinction); however, the proposals were made in an artificial way, without relation to the customary meanings of the words. The same would hold if we were to use the two words for our two concepts; therefore, we prefer to use subscripts as indicated above.

Probability$_1$, in other words, the logical concept of confirmation in its different forms (positive, comparative, and metrical), has been explained in the preceding section. A brief explanation may here be given of probability$_2$, merely to make clear its distinction from probability$_1$. A typical example of the use of this concept is the following statement: "The probability$_2$ of casting an ace with this die is 1/6." Statements of this form refer to two properties (or classes) of events: (i) the reference property M_1, here the property of being a throw with this die; (ii) the specific property M_2, here the property of being a throw with any die resulting in an ace. The statement says that the probability$_2$ of M_2 with respect to M_1 is 1/6. The statement is tested by statistical investigations. A sufficiently long series of, say, n throws of the die in question is made, and the number m of these throws which yield an ace is counted. If the relative frequency m/n of aces in this series is sufficiently close to 1/6, the statement is regarded as confirmed. Thus, the other way round, the statement is understood as predicting that the relative frequency of aces thrown with this die in a sufficiently long series will be about 1/6. This formulation is admittedly inexact; but it intends no more than to indicate the meaning of 'probability$_2$' as an explicandum. To make this concept exact is the task of the explication; our discussion concerns only the two explicanda.

---

of my system of inductive logic are summarized in the paper "On Inductive Logic", which will appear in *Philosophy of Science,* Vol. XII, 1945.

IV. THE LOGICAL NATURE OF THE TWO PROBABILITY CONCEPTS

On the basis of the preceding explanations, let us now characterize the two probability concepts, not with respect to what they mean but merely with respect to their logical nature, more specifically, with respect to the kind of entities to which they are applied and the logical nature of the simplest sentences in which they are used. (Since the pre-scientific use of both concepts is often too vague and incomplete, e.g., because of the omission of the second argument [viz., the evidence or the reference class], we take here into consideration the more careful use by authors on probability. However, we shall be more concerned with their general discussions than with the details of their constructed systems.) For the sake of simplicity, let us consider the two concepts in their metrical forms only. They may be taken also in their comparative and in their positive forms (as explained for probability$_1$, i.e., confirmation, in section II), and these other forms would show analogous differences. Probability$_1$ and probability$_2$, taken as metrical concepts, have the following characteristics in common: each of them is a function of two arguments; their values are real numbers belonging to the interval 0 to 1 (according to the customary convention, which we follow here). Their characteristic differences are as follows:

1. *Probability*$_1$ (degree of confirmation).

(*a*) The *two arguments* are variously described as events (in the literal sense, see below), states of affairs, circumstances, and the like. Therefore each argument is expressible by a declarative sentence and hence is, in our terminology, a proposition. Another alternative consists in taking as arguments the sentences expressing the propositions, describing the events, etc. If we choose this alternative, probability$_1$ is a semantical concept (as in section II). (Fundamentally it makes no great difference whether propositions or sentences are taken as arguments; but the second method has certain technical advantages, and therefore we use it for our discussion.)

(*b*) A simple *statement* of probability$_1$, i.e., one attributing to two given arguments a particular number as value of probability$_1$, is either L-true (logically true, analytic) or L-false, (logically false, logically self-contradictory), hence in any case L-determinate, not factual (synthetic). Therefore, a statement of this kind is to be established by logical analysis alone, as has been explained earlier (section II). It is independent of the contingency of facts because it does not say anything about facts (although the two arguments do in general refer to facts).

2. *Probability*$_2$ (relative frequency).

(*a*) The *two arguments* are properties, kinds, classes, usually of events or things. [As an alternative, the predicate expressions designating the properties might be taken as arguments; then the concept would become a semantical one. In the present case, however, in distinction to (1), there does not seem to be any advantage in this method. On the contrary, it appears to be more convenient to have the probability$_2$ statements in the object language instead of the metalanguage; and it seems that all authors who deal with probability$_2$ choose this form.]

(*b*) A simple *statement* of probability$_2$ is factual and empirical, it says something about the facts of nature, and hence must be based upon empirical procedure, the observation of relevant facts. From these simple statements the theorems of a mathematical theory of probability$_2$ must be clearly distinguished. The latter do not state a particular value of probability$_2$ but say something about connections between probability$_2$ values in a general way, usually in a conditional form (for example: "if the values of such and such probabilities$_2$ are q_1 and q_2, then the value of a probability$_2$ related to the original ones in a certain way is such and such a function, say, product or sum, of q_1 and q_2"). These theorems are not factual but L-true (analytic). Thus a theory of probability$_2$, e.g., the system constructed by von Mises or that by Reichenbach, is not of an empirical but of a logico-mathematical nature; it is a branch of mathematics, like arithmetic, fundamentally different from any branch of empirical science, e.g., physics.

It is very important to distinguish clearly between *kinds of events* (war, birth, death, throw of a die, throw of this die, throw of this die yielding an ace, etc.) and *events* (Caesar's death, the throw of this die made yesterday at 10 A.M., the series of all throws of this die past and future). This distinction is doubly important for discussions on probability, because one of the characteristic differences between the two concepts is this: the first concept refers sometimes to two events, the second to two kinds of events [see 1 (*a*) and 2 (*a*)]. Many authors of probability use the word 'event' (or the corresponding words 'Ereignis' and 'évènement') when they mean to speak, not about events, but about kinds of events. This usage is of long standing in the literature on probability, but it is very unfortunate. It has only served to reinforce the customary neglect of the fundamental difference between the two probability concepts which arose originally out of the ambiguous use of the word 'probability', and thereby to increase the general confusion in discussions on probability. The authors who use the term 'event' when they mean kinds of events get into trouble, of course, whenever they want to speak about specific events. The traditional solution is to say 'the happenings (or occurrences) of a certain event' instead of 'the events of a certain kind'; sometimes the events are referred to by the term 'single events'. But this phrase is rather misleading; the important difference between events and kinds of events is not the same as the inessential difference between single events (the first throw I made today with this die) and multiple or compound events (the series of all throws made with this die). Keynes, if I interpret him correctly, has noticed the ambiguity of the term 'event'. He says [16] that the customary use of phrases like 'the happening of events' is "vague and unambiguous," which I suppose to be a misprint for "vague and ambiguous"; but he does not specify the ambiguity. He proposes to dispense altogether with the term 'event' and to use instead the term 'proposition'. Subsequent authors dealing with probability$_1$, like Jeffreys, for example, have followed him in this use.

Many authors have made a distinction between two (or sometimes more) kinds of probability, or between two meanings of the word 'probability'. Some of these distinctions are quite different from the distinction made here between probability$_1$ and probability$_2$. For instance, a distinction is sometimes made between mathematical probability and philosophical probability; their characteristic difference appears to be that the first has numerical values, the second not. However, this difference seems hardly essential; we find a concept with numerical values and one without, in other words, both a metrical and a comparative concept on either side of our distinction between the two fundamentally different meanings of 'probability'. Another distinction has been made between subjective and objective probability. However, I believe that practically all authors really have an objective concept of probability in mind, and that the appearance of subjectivist conceptions is in most cases caused only by occasional unfortunate formulations; this will soon be discussed.

Other distinctions which have been made are more or less similar to our distinction between probability$_1$ and probability$_2$. For instance, Ramsey [17] says: ". . . the general difference of opinion between statisticians who for the most part adopt the frequency theory of probability and logicians who mostly reject it renders it likely that the two schools are really discussing different things, and that the word 'probability' is used by logicians in one sense and by statisticians in another."

It seems that many authors have taken either probability$_1$ or probability$_2$ as their explicandum. I believe moreover that practically all authors

[16] *Op. cit.*, p. 5.

[17] F. P. Ramsey, *The Foundations of Mathematics*, 1931; see p. 157.

on probability have intended one of these two concepts as their explicandum, despite the fact that their various explanations appear to refer to a number of quite different concepts.

For one group of authors, the question of their explicandum is easily answered. In the case of all those who support a frequency theory of probability, i.e., who define their explicata in terms of relative frequency (as a limit or in some other way), there can be no doubt that their explicandum is probability$_2$. Their formulations are, in general, presented in clear and unambiguous terms. Often they state explicitly that their explicandum is relative frequency. And even in the cases where this is not done, the discussion of their explicata leaves no doubt as to what is meant as explicandum.

This, however, covers only one of the various conceptions, i.e., explicata proposed, and only one of the many different explanations of explicanda which have been given and of which some examples were mentioned earlier. It seems clear that the other explanations do not refer to the statistical, empirical concept of relative frequency; and I believe that practically all of them, in spite of their apparent dissimilarity, are intended to refer to probability$_1$. Unfortunately, many of the phrases used are more misleading than helpful in our efforts to find out what their authors actually meant as explicandum. There is, in particular, one point on which many authors in discussions on probability$_1$, or on logical problems in general, commit a certain typical confusion or adopt incautiously other authors' formulations which are infected by this confusion. I am referring to what is sometimes called psychologism in logic.

Many authors in their general remarks about the nature of (deductive) logic say that it has to do with ways and forms of thinking or, in more cautious formulations, with forms of correct or rational thinking. In spite of these subjectivistic formulations, we find that in practice these authors use an objectivistic method in solving any particular logical problem. For instance, in order to find out whether a certain conclusion follows from given premises, they do not in fact make psychological experiments about the thinking habits of people but rather analyze the given sentences and show their conceptual relations. In inductive logic or, in other words, the theory of probability$_1$, we often find a similar psychologism. Some authors, from Laplace and other representatives of the classical theory of probability down to contemporary authors like Keynes and Jeffreys, use subjectivistic formulations when trying to explain what they take as their explicandum; they say that it is probability in the sense of degree of belief or, if they are somewhat more cautious, degree of reasonable or justified belief. However, an analysis of the work of these authors comes to quite different results if we pay more attention to the methods the authors actually use in solving problems of probability than to the general remarks in which they try to characterize their own aims and methods. Such an analysis, which cannot be carried out within this paper, shows that most and perhaps all of these authors use objectivistic rather than subjectivistic methods. They do not try to measure degrees of belief by actual, psychological experiments, but rather carry out a logical analysis of the concepts and propositions involved. It appears, therefore, that the psychologism in inductive logic is, just like that in deductive logic, merely a superficial feature of certain marginal formulations, while the core of the theories remains thoroughly objectivistic. And, further, it seems to me that for most of those authors who do not maintain a frequency theory, from the classical period to our time, the objective concept which they take as their explicandum is probability$_1$, i.e., degree of confirmation. . . .

It has been the chief purpose of this paper to explain and discuss the two concepts of probability in their rôle as explicanda for theories of probability. I think that in the present situation clarification of the explicanda is the most urgent task. When every author has not only a clear understanding of his own explicandum but also some insight into the existence, the importance, and the meaning of the explicandum on the other side, then it will be possible for each side to concentrate entirely on the positive task of constructing an explication and a theory of the chosen explicatum without wasting energy in futile polemics against the explicandum of the other side.

Gilbert Ryle

Formal and Informal Logic *

Since Aristotle, there has existed a branch of inquiries, often entitled 'Formal Logic', which has always adhered more or less closely to general philosophical inquiries. It is not easy to describe this liaison between Formal Logic and philosophy. The systematic presentation of the rules of syllogistic inference is a very different sort of activity from, say, the elucidation of the concept of pleasure. The Aristotle who inaugurated the former is the same thinker as the Aristotle who considerably developed the latter, yet the kinds of thinking in which he was involved are very widely different. The technical problems in the theory of the syllogism have a strong resemblance to the problems of Euclidean geometry; the ideals of systematization and rigorous proof are at work, questions of switches and shades of significance are barred, false moves are demonstratable fallacies. The problems in, say, the theory of pleasure or perception or moral responsibility are not like this. Aristotle debates with Plato and Socrates, and the issues become better defined as the debate progresses, but the debate does not take the shape of a chain of theorems, nor do the arguments used in that debate admit of notational codification. Whether a given philosophical argument is valid or fallacious is, in general, itself a debatable question. Simple inspection cannot decide. More often it is a question of whether the argument has much, little or no force. Yet different though Formal Logic is from philosophy, the operations characteristic of Formal Logic exercise a detectable, if minor, control over the operations characteristic of philosophy. For good or for ill, the ways in which Aristotle debates the notion of *pleasure,* the *soul* or the *continuum* reflect lessons which he had taught himself in his logical inquiries. Nor is Aristotle peculiar in this. With a negligible number of exceptions, every philosopher of genius and nearly every philosopher of even high talent from Aristotle to the present day has given himself

* From *Dilemmas* by Gilbert Ryle. The Tarner Lectures, 1953, pp. 111–120. Copyright 1954 by The Syndics of the Cambridge University Press. Reprinted by permission of The Syndics of the University Press.

some schooling in some parts of Formal Logic, and his subsequent philosophical reasonings have exhibited the effects upon him of this self-schooling, including sometimes his revolts against it.

In some respects the following analogy holds. Fighting in battles is markedly unlike parade-ground drill. The best conducted drill-evolutions would be the worst possible battle-movements, and the most favourable terrain for a rearguard action would entirely forbid what the barrack-square is made for. None the less the efficient and resourceful fighter is also the well-drilled soldier. The ways in which he takes advantage of the irregularities of the ground show the marks of the schooling he had received on the asphalt. He can improvise operations in the dark and at the risk of his life now, partly because he had learned before to do highly stereotyped and formalized things in broad daylight and in conditions of unmitigated tedium. It is not the stereotyped motions of drill, but its standards of perfection of control which are transmitted from the parade-ground to the battlefield.

Aristotelian Formal Logic gave weapon-drill in only a limited variety of rather short-range inference-weapons. The supplementations given by the Megarian and Stoic logicians were, unfortunately, only slightly and belatedly influential. It was left to the nineteenth and twentieth centuries to generalize and systematize the discipline. In particular, the discipline was then in considerable measure mathematicized, and mathematicized in two separate ways. First, the new builders of Formal Logic, being themselves mathematicians, knew how to give mathematical shape, mathematical rigour and mathematical notations to this branch of abstract theory. Secondly, since their interest in Formal Logic derived from dissatisfaction with the logical foundations of mathematics itself, Formal Logic came to be not only mathematical in style but also mathematical in subject-matter; to be employed, that is, primarily in order to fix the logical powers of the terms or concepts on which hinged the proofs of propositions in pure mathematics.

Formal or Symbolic Logic has grown up into a science or discipline of such scope, such rigour and such fertility that it is now out of all danger of surviving only as the nursery-governess of philosophy. Indeed, philosophers are now complacent if they and their pupils are capable of doing their schoolroom sums in the subject, and gratified and flattered if original logicians are willing to join them, from time to time, in their own expeditions over the moors.

Now, perhaps, I can indicate in a very provisional way the nature of the dispute which has already begun between Formal Logic and general philosophy. Some properly zealous, if sometimes gratuitously jealous Formal Logicians are now beginning to say to the philosopher 'It is time that you stopped trying to solve your problems by your old-fashioned exercises in improvisation and trial-and-error. Your problems are, as you say yourself, logical problems, and we have now got the procedures for solving logical problems. Where you grope, we calculate. Where you haggle, we employ the cash-register. Where you ponder imponderable pros and cons, we work out the correct logical change.'

The natural response of the offended and also jealous philosopher is this. 'Yes, you have invented or hit upon a private game, with fewer pieces but more squares than are provided by chess. You have converted the words "logic" and "logical" to your private ends, and now you invite us to cease exploring the moors in order to become conductors on your trams. And for what? For nothing, apparently, but the proliferation of truistic formulae. No philosophical problem of any interest to anyone has yet been solved by reducing it to the shape or size that suits some slot in your slot-machine. Your cash-register is indeed quite impeccable and totally neutral, and for that reason it cannot be appealed to for aid in the settlement of any bargaining-disputes. There was the notion, once projected by Leibniz and later championed by Russell, that philosophers would soon be so equipped and drilled that they would be able to decide their issues by calculation. But now we have learned, what we should have foreseen, that questions which can be decided by calculation are different, *toto caelo* different, from the problems that perplex. There is one person to whom it is impertinence to give the advice that he should keep one foot on the kerb—and that is the pathfinder. Kerbs cannot exist where the road is unmade, and roads cannot be made where the route has not been found.'

You can guess for yourselves the abusive nouns which are now liable to be interchanged. 'Muddler-through', 'romantic', 'anti-scientist', 'hunch-rider', 'litterateur' and of course 'Platonist' come from the one side; from the other side there come 'Formalist', 'computer', 'reductionist', 'pseudo-scientist' and, of course, 'Platonist'.

As might be anticipated, neither party is right, though both are more nearly right than the appeasers who try to blend the operations of the one party with the operations of the other. The drill-sergeant is wrong who thinks that soldiering consists in going through the motions tabulated in the drill-book. The *franc-tireur* is wrong who thinks that soldiering consists in outbursts of amateur gunmanship. But neither is so wrong as the scenario-writer who represents fighting soldiers as heroes going berserk in close column of platoons.

Let us examine, rather more closely, the actual work, as distinct from the intermittent promises of Formal Logicians. Aristotle, it is nearly enough correct to say, examined certain ranges of inferences, namely those which pivot on the notions of *all, some,* and *not.* He saw that from two premisses like 'some men are blue-eyed' and 'some men are red-haired' it does not follow that any men are both blue-eyed and red-haired, or, of course, that none are. On the other hand from 'all men are mortal' and 'all philosophers are men' it does follow that all philosophers are mortal. There are rules governing the employment of *all, some* and *not* such that all inferences pivoting on two or all three of these concepts, arranged in certain ways, are valid, while all inferences pivoting on them arranged in certain other ways are invalid. These rules are perfectly general, anyhow in this sense, that differences of concrete subject-matter make no difference to the validity or fallaciousness of the inferences. The quantifier-words 'all' and 'some' can be followed indifferently by 'men', 'cows', 'gods' or what you will, without affecting our decision that the inference holds or does not hold. What determines whether a proposed syllogism is valid or fallacious is the work given to 'all', 'some' and 'not', irrespective of the concrete topics of its premises and conclusion. So, for brevity, we can say that Aristotle was investigating the logical powers of certain topic-neutral concepts, namely those of *all, some* and *not.* These are sometimes listed among what are nowadays called the 'logical constants'.

In a similar way the Megarian and Stoic logicians began the investigation of the logical powers of the equally topic-neutral concepts of *and, or,* and *if;* they concentrated on certain propositional conjunctions or connectives, where Aristotle had concentrated on certain quantifiers. They were studying the legitimacy and illegitimacy of possible arguments in so far as they hinged on these particular topic-neutral conjunctions.

These studies yielded a modest degree of codification of the inference-patterns that were examined, and even a semi-Euclideanization of the rules of these inferences. Certain crucial fallacy-patterns were classified. So it was natural, though, as we now know, quite mistaken to suppose that any piece of valid reasoning whatsoever was, by some device or other of re-wording, reducible to one of the already scheduled patterns, and every piece of fallacious reasoning reducible to one of the already registered howlers. Some terms like 'all', 'some' and 'not', and perhaps also 'and', 'or' and 'if' do carry inferences; the rest, it was mistakenly supposed, do not.

Part of what characterizes the terms which do, on this view, carry inferences is that these terms or 'logical constants' are indifferent to subject-matter or are topic-neutral; so part of what characterizes all the other terms which were supposed not to carry inferences is that they are not topic-neutral. Inferences are valid or invalid in virtue of their forms, and to say this, it was supposed, was to say that they were valid or invalid because of the ways in which certain topic-neutral or purely formal expressions occurred in certain positions and arrangements in their premises and conclusions. This temptingly crisp doctrine, whose obituary notice has yet to be written, might easily suggest the following demarcation of Formal Logic from philosophy. Formal Logic, it might be said, maps the inference-powers of the topic-neutral expressions or logical constants on which our arguments pivot; philosophy has to do with the topical or subject-matter concepts which provide the fat and the lean, but not the joints or the tendons of discourse. The philosopher examines such notions as *pleasure, colour, the future,* and *responsibility,* while the Formal Logician examines such notions as *all, some, not, if* and *or.*

But this way of making the division quickly breaks down. To begin with, topic-neutrality is not enough to qualify an expression as a logical constant. European languages, ancient and modern, and especially the largely uninflected languages, are rich in topic-neutral expressions, most of which have, for very good reasons, received no attention at all from Formal Logicians. We may call English expressions 'topic-neutral' if a foreigner who understood them, but only them, could get no clue at all from an English paragraph containing them what that paragraph was about. Such expressions can or must occur in any paragraph about any topic, abstract or concrete, biographical or legal, philosophical or scientific. They are not dedicated to this topic as distinct from that. They are like coins which enable one to bargain for any commodity or service whatsoever. You cannot tell from the coins in the customer's hand what he is going to buy. In this way 'not', 'and', 'all', 'some', 'a', 'the', 'is', 'is a member of ', etc., certainly are topic-neutral, but so are 'several', 'most', 'few', 'three', 'half', 'although', 'because', 'perhaps', 'may', as well as hosts of other conjunctions, particles, prepositions, pronouns, adverbs, etc. Some expressions seem to be nearly but not quite topic-neutral. The temporal conjunctions 'while', 'after' and 'before', and the spatial conjunction 'where' could be used not in all, but only in nearly all sorts of discourse. Our foreigner could tell from the occurrence of temporal conjunctions in the paragraph that no purely geometrical matter was being discussed.

But not only do Formal Logicians very properly ignore the great majority of topic-neutral expressions, as not being in their beat; they also, very properly, bestow their professional attentions upon the logical powers of certain classes of expressions which are by no means topic-neutral. Relational expressions like 'north of', 'taller than' and 'encompasses' are pivots of strict inferences, and it has proved necessary and feasible to divide such expressions up into families according to the sorts of inferences which they do and do not carry. 'Taller-than', for example, is transitive, in the sense that if *A* is taller than *B,* and *B* than *C,* then *A* is taller than *C*. But 'next to' and 'mother of' are not transitive. *A* can be next to *B* and *B* to *C* without *A* being next to *C;* and Sarah cannot be the mother of the child of her own daughter. This does not prevent us from discovering rigorous parities of reasoning between, for example, inferences hinging on 'north of' and inferences hinging on 'encompasses'. But the feature of parity cannot always be detached for separate examination by publication of some elided topic-neutral expression. Sometimes it can. 'Fatter than' works, in some directions, like 'hotter than', and what is common to the two can be brought out by the rewording 'more fat than' and 'more hot than', where the expression 'more so and so than' is a detachable topic-neutral expression.

So we should say, perhaps, with considerable loss of crispness and misleadingness, that Formal Logic is a certain sort of study of parities of reasoning or certain special kinds of parities of reasoning; and that it is convenient, when possible, to exhibit these parities by operations with topic-neutral expressions detached from any particular topical contexts; but that this is not essential and is not always possible. Not all strict inferences pivot on the recognized logical constants, and not all topic-neutral expressions qualify for treatment as logical constants.

A further amendment is required. I have spoken as if our ordinary 'and', 'or', 'if', 'all', 'some' and so on are identical with the logical constants with which the Formal Logician operates. But this is not true. The logician's 'and', 'not', 'all', 'some' and the rest are not our familiar civilian terms; they are conscript terms, in uniform and under military discipline, with memories, indeed, of their previous more free and easy civilian lives, though they are not living those lives now. Two instances are enough. If you hear on good authority that she took arsenic and fell ill you will reject the rumour that she fell ill and took arsenic. This familiar use of 'and' carries with it the temporal notion expressed by 'and subsequently' and even the causal notion expressed by 'and in consequence'. The logicians' conscript 'and' does only its appointed duty—a duty in which 'she took arsenic and fell ill' is an absolute paraphrase of 'she fell ill and took arsenic'. This might be called the minimal force of 'and'. In some cases the overlap between the military duties and the civilian work and play of an expression is even slighter. What corresponds in the glossary of Formal Logic to the civilian word 'if' is an expression which plays only a very small, though certainly cardinal part of the role or roles of that civilian word.

This point that Formal Logic operates (1) only with some, and not with all topic-neutral expressions, and (2) only with artificial extracts from the selected few topic-neutral expressions of ordinary discourse is sometimes used by philosophers as a criticism of the programme of Formal Logic. Where the philosopher concerns himself with full-blooded concepts like that of *pleasure* or *memory,* the Formal Logician concerns himself only with meatless concepts like those of *not* and *some;* and even these have to be filed down to reduced size and unnatural shape before the Formal Logician will deign to inspect them. Moreover, the philosopher investigates concepts which, in one way or another, generate genuine perplexities. He investigates the concepts, say, of *seeing* and not that of, say, *perspiring,* since the former is charged with paradoxes where the latter is not. But, the criticism goes, the Formal Logician investigates the inference-carrying labours of concepts which engender no paradoxes whatsoever; what he finds out about *and* and *not* are only elaborations of what every child has completely mastered in his early talking years.

I mention this allegation here because it makes the right opening for me. It is quite false that doing Formal Logic is doing gratuitous and profitless philosophy upon philosophically transparent concepts. It is quite false, equally, that the philosopher is doing makeshift and amateurish Formal Logic upon wrongly chosen because non-logical concepts. The battlefield is not a makeshift parade-ground; and the parade-ground is not a sham battlefield.

None the less, there remains a very important way in which the adjective 'logical' is properly used to characterize both the inquiries which belong to Formal Logic and the inquiries which belong to philosophy. The Formal Logician really is working out the logic of *and, not, all, some,* etc., and the philosopher really is exploring the logic of the concepts of *pleasure, seeing, chance,* etc., even though the work of the one is greatly unlike the work of the other in procedure and in objectives. Neither is doing what the other is doing, much less is either doing improperly what the other is doing properly. Yet we are not punning when we say, for example, that the considerations which are decisive for both are 'logical' considerations, any more than we are punning if we say that the choice of drill-evolutions and the choice of battle-evolutions are both decided by 'military' considerations. How can this be?

I find the following partial parallel of some assistance. Trading begins with barter of goods for goods, and, by means of fixed places and times for markets, such barter-dealings can reach a fairly high degree of systematization. Though the relative exchange-values of different sorts of goods vary with times and places, some measure of stabilization can be achieved by tacit or explicit convention. There is, however, even at this stage, a strong pressure upon traders to use just a few kinds of consumable goods not only for consumption, but also, at least for a short time, as a sort of informal currency. Dried fishes, cigarettes or iron bars, though wanted for use, come also to be wanted because any other trader can be relied on to accept them, whether he himself wants to use them or not, because they will always be exchangeable anywhere for consumable goods. So long as they are reasonably imperishable, easy to store and handle, easy to count or weigh, and certain to be wanted some day by someone for consumption purposes, they are negotiable as exchange-tokens. From this stage to the stage of operating with a conventional currency or legal tender is a relatively short step. Though no one, perhaps, can be expected to want to use metal discs for any consumption purpose, everyone can be expected to want to use them for exchange-purposes. They might be described as auxiliary goods, goods which are of little or no utility in themselves, but of great utility for getting and disposing of other goods which are wanted for themselves.

For future purposes we should notice another kind of auxiliary goods. Baskets, pitchers, sacks, brown paper and string are, to exaggerate a little, of no use in themselves, but only for the collection and housing of goods which we do want for themselves. But clearly the way in which baskets and string are auxiliary to marketing and storing is different from the way in which coins are auxiliary. A basket or keg is only being actually useful to us when we are in possession of goods for it to contain. A coin is useful to us in another way. While we possess the coin, we do not possess what we shall buy with it. But still there is a certain similiarity between them. A coin is commodity-neutral, for I can buy any sort of commodity with it. A sack or a piece of string is, in lower degree, commodity-neutral. You cannot tell from the fact that I go to market with a sack or some string precisely what kinds of goods I shall bring back with its aid. It would be useful for any of a fairly wide range of goods, though not, of course, for all kinds of goods.

Linguistic dealings between men have some of the features of market-dealings between men. There is a comparable pressure upon language to evolve idioms, which may or may not be separate words, to subserve in stabilized ways different kinds of constantly recurring linguistic negotiations. We need and therefore we get a variety of topic-neutral words, inflections, constructions, etc., some of which function rather like baskets, pitchers, string and wrapping-paper, while others function rather like the dried fishes, cigarettes or iron bars and, later on, rather like the coins and currency notes, part or the whole of whose utility is to serve as instruments of exchange.

Truth

Henri Bergson

An Introduction to Metaphysics *

A comparison of the definitions of metaphysics and the various concepts of the absolute leads to the discovery that philosophers, in spite of their apparent divergencies, agree in distinguishing two profoundly different ways of knowing a thing. The first implies that we move round the object; the second, that we enter into it. The first depends on the point of view at which we are placed and on the symbols by which we express ourselves. The second neither depends on a point of view nor relies on any symbol. The first kind of knowledge may be said to stop at the *relative;* the second, in those cases where it is possible, to attain the *absolute.*

Consider, for example, the movement of an object in space. My perception of the motion will vary with the point of view, moving or stationary, from which I observe it. My expression of it will vary with the systems of axes, or the points of reference, to which I relate it; that is, with the symbols by which I translate it. For this double reason I call such motion *relative:* in the one case, as in the other, I am placed outside the object itself. But when I speak of an *absolute* movement, I am attributing to the moving object an interior and, so to speak, states of mind; I also imply that I am in sympathy with those states, and that I insert myself in them by an effort of imagination. Then, according as the object is moving or stationary, according as it adopts one movement or another, what I experience will vary. And what I experience will depend neither on the point of view I may take up in regard to the object, since I am inside the object itself, nor on the symbols by which I may translate the motion, since I have rejected all translations in order to possess the original. In short, I shall no longer grasp the movement from without, remaining where I am, but from where it is, from within, as it is in itself. I shall possess an absolute.

Consider, again, a character whose adventures are related to me in a

* From *An Introduction to Metaphysics* by Henri Bergson, translated by T. E. Hulme, pp. 21–30. (The Library of Liberal Arts, No. 10, New York, 1955.) Reprinted by permission of the publishers, The Liberal Arts Press, Inc.

novel. The author may multiply the traits of his hero's character, may make him speak and act as much as he pleases, but all this can never be equivalent to the simple and indivisible feeling which I should experience if I were able for an instant to identify myself with the person of the hero himself. Out of that indivisible feeling, as from a spring, all the words, gestures, and actions of the man would appear to me to flow naturally. They would no longer be accidents which, added to the idea I had already formed of the character, continually enriched that idea, without ever completing it. The character would be given to me all at once, in its entirety, and the thousand incidents which manifest it, instead of adding themselves to the idea and so enriching it, would seem to me, on the contrary, to detach themselves from it, without, however, exhausting it or impoverishing its essence. All the things I am told about the man provide me with so many points of view from which I can observe him. All the traits which describe him, and which can make him known to me only by so many comparisons with persons or things I know already, are signs by which he is expressed more or less symbolically. Symbols and points of view, therefore, place me outside him; they give me only what he has in common with others, and not what belongs to him and to him alone. But that which is properly himself, that which constitutes his essence, cannot be perceived from without, being internal by definition, nor be expressed by symbols, being incommensurable with everything else. Description, history, and analysis leave me here in the relative. Coincidence with the person himself would alone give me the absolute.

It is in this sense, and in this sense only, that *absolute* is synonymous with *perfection*. Were all the photographs of a town, taken from all possible points of view, to go on indefinitely completing one another, they would never be equivalent to the solid town in which we walk about. Were all the translations of a poem into all possible languages to add together their various shades of meaning and, correcting each other by a kind of mutual retouching, to give a more and more faithful image of the poem they translate, they would yet never succeed in rendering the inner meaning of the original. A representation taken from a certain point of view, a translation made with certain symbols, will always remain imperfect in comparison with the object of which a view has been taken, or which the symbols seek to express. But the absolute, which is the object and not its representation, the original and not its translation, is perfect, by being perfectly what it is.

It is doubtless for this reason that the *absolute* has often been identified with the *infinite*. Suppose that I wished to communicate to some one who did not know Greek the extraordinarily simple impression that a passage in Homer makes upon me; I should first give a translation of the lines, I should then comment on my translation, and then develop the commentary; in this way, by piling up explanation on explanation, I might approach nearer and nearer to what I wanted to express; but I should never quite reach it. When you raise your arm, you accomplish a movement of which you have, from within, a simple perception; but for me, watching it from the outside, your arm passes through one point, then through another, and between these two there will be still other points; so that, if I began to count, the operation would go on forever. Viewed from the inside, then, an absolute is a simple thing; but looked at from the outside, that is to say, relatively to other things, it becomes, in relation to these signs which express it, the gold coin for which we never seem able to finish giving small change. Now, that which lends itself at the same time both to an indivisible apprehension and to an inexhaustible enumeration is, by the very definition of the word, an infinite.

It follows from this that an absolute could only be given in an *intuition,* whilst everything else falls within the province of *analysis.* By intuition is meant the kind of *intellectual sympathy* by which one places oneself within an object in order to coincide with what is unique in it and consequently inexpressible. Analysis, on the contrary, is the operation which reduces the object to elements already known, that is, to elements common both to it and other objects. To analyze, therefore, is to express a thing as a function of something other than itself. All analysis is thus a translation, a development into symbols, a representation taken from successive points of view from which we note as many resemblances as possible between the new object which we are studying and others which we believe we know already. In its eternally unsatisfied desire to embrace the object around which it is compelled to turn, analysis multiplies without end the number of its points of view in order to complete its always incomplete representation, and ceaselessly varies its symbols that it may perfect the always imperfect translation. It goes on, therefore, to infinity. But intuition, if intuition is possible, is a simple act.

Now it is easy to see that the ordinary function of positive science is analysis. Positive science works, then, above all, with symbols. Even the most concrete of the natural sciences, those concerned with life, confine themselves to the visible form of living beings, their organs and anatomical elements. They make comparisons between these forms, they reduce the more complex to the more simple; in short, they study the workings of life in what is, so to speak, only its visual symbol. If there exists any means of possessing a reality absolutely instead of knowing it relatively, of placing oneself within it instead of looking at it from outside points of view, of having the intuition instead of makng the analysis: in short, of seizing it without any expression, translation, or symbolic representation—metaphysics is that means. *Metaphysics, then, is the science which claims to dispense with symbols.*

There is one reality, at least, which we all seize from within, by intuition and not by simple analysis. It is our own personality in its flowing through time—our self which endures. We may sympathize intellectually with nothing else, but we certainly sympathize with our own selves.

When I direct my attention inward to contemplate my own self (supposed for the moment to be inactive), I perceive at first, as a crust solidified on the surface, all the perceptions which come to it from the material world. These perceptions are clear, distinct, juxtaposed or juxtaposable one with another; they tend to group themselves into objects. Next, I notice the memories which more or less adhere to these perceptions and which serve to interpret them. These memories have been detached, as it were, from the depth of my personality, drawn to the surface by the perceptions which resemble them; they rest on the surface of my mind without being absolutely myself. Lastly, I feel the stir of tendencies and motor habits—a crowd of virtual actions, more or less less firmly bound to these perceptions and memories. All these clearly defined elements appear more distinct from me, the more distinct they are from each other. Radiating, as they do, from within outwards, they form, collectively, the surface of a sphere which tends to grow larger and lose itself in the exterior world. But if I draw myself in from the periphery towards the center, if I search in the depth of my being that which is most uniformly, most constantly, and most enduringly myself, I find an altogether different thing.

There is, beneath these sharply cut crystals and this frozen surface, a continuous flux which is not comparable to any flux I have ever seen. There is a succession of states, each of which announces that which follows and contains that which precedes it. They can, properly speaking, only be said to form multiple states when I have already passed them and turn back to observe their track. Whilst I was experiencing them they were so solidly organized, so profoundly animated with a common life, that I could not have said where any one of them finished or where another commenced. In reality no one of them begins or ends, but all extend into each other.

This inner life may be compared to the unrolling of a coil, for there is no living being who does not feel himself coming gradually to the end of his rôle; and to live is to grow old. But it may just as well be compared to a continual rolling up, like that of a thread on a ball, for our past follows us, it swells incessantly with the present that it picks up on its way; and consciousness means memory.

But actually it is neither an unrolling nor a rolling up, for these two similes evoke the idea of lines and surfaces whose parts are homogeneous and superposable on one another. Now, there are no two identical moments in the life of the same conscious being. Take the simplest sensation, suppose it constant, absorb in it the entire personality: the consciousness which will accompany this sensation cannot remain identical with itself for two consecutive moments, because the second moment always contains, over and above the first, the memory that the first has bequeathed to it. A consciousness which could experience two identical moments would be a consciousness without memory. It would die and be born again continually. In what other way could one represent unconsciousness?

It would be better, then, to use as a comparison the myriad-tinted spectrum, with its insensible gradations leading from one shade to another. A current of feeling which passed along the spectrum, assuming in turn the tint of each of its shades, would experience a series of gradual changes, each of which would announce the one to follow and would sum up those which preceded it. Yet even here the successive shades of the spectrum always remain external one to another. They are juxtaposed; they occupy space. But pure duration, on the contrary, excludes all idea of juxtaposition, reciprocal externality, and extension.

Let us, then, rather, imagine an infinitely small elastic body, contracted, if it were possible, to a mathematical point. Let this be drawn out gradually in such a manner that from the point comes a constantly lengthening line. Let us fix our attention not on the line as a line, but on the action by which it is traced. Let us bear in mind that this action, in spite of its duration, is indivisible if accomplished without stopping, that if a stopping-point is inserted, we have two actions instead of one, that each of these separate actions is then the indivisible operation of which we speak, and that it is not the moving action itself which is divisible, but, rather, the stationary line it leaves behind it as its track in space. Finally, let us free ourselves from the space which underlies the movement in order to consider only the movement itself, the act of tension or extension; in short, pure mobility. We shall have this time a more faithful image of the development of our self in duration.

However, even this image is incomplete, and, indeed, every comparison will be insufficient, because the unrolling of our duration resembles in some of its aspects the unity of an advancing movement and in others the multiplicity of expanding states; and, clearly, no metaphor can express one of these two aspects without sacrificing the other. If I use the comparison of the spectrum with its thousand shades, I have before me a thing already made, whilst duration is continually in the making. If I think of an elastic which is being stretched, or of a spring which is extended or relaxed, I forget the richness of color, characteristic of duration that is lived, to see only the simple movement by which consciousness passes from one shade to another. The inner life is all this at once: variety of qualities, continuity of progress, and unity of direction. It cannot be represented by images.

But it is even less possible to represent it by *concepts,* that is by abstract, general, or simple ideas. It is true that no image can reproduce exactly the original feeling I have of the flow of my own conscious life. But it is not even necessary that I should attempt to render it. If a man is incapable of getting for himself the intuition of the constitutive duration of his own being, nothing will ever give it to him, concepts no more than images. Here the single aim of the philosopher should be to promote a certain effort, which in most men is usually fettered by habits of mind more useful to life. Now the image has at least this advantage, that it keeps us in the concrete. No image can replace the intuition of duration, but many diverse images, borrowed from very different orders of things, may, by the convergence of their action, direct consciousness to the precise point where there is a certain intuition to be seized. By choosing images as dissimilar as possible, we shall prevent any one of them from usurping the place of the intuition it is intended to call up, since it would then be driven away at once by its rivals. By providing that, in spite of their differences of aspect, they all require from the mind the same kind of attention, and in some sort the same degree of tension, we shall gradually accustom consciousness to a particular and clearly-defined disposition—that precisely which it must adopt in order to appear to itself as it really is, without any veil. But, then, consciousness must at least consent to make the effort. For it will have been shown nothing: It will simply have been placed in the attitude it must take up in order to make the desired effort, and so come by itself to the intuition. Concepts on the contrary—especially if they are simple—have the disadvantage of being in reality symbols substituted for the object they symbolize, and demand no effort on our part. Examined closely, each of them, it would be seen, retains only that part of the object which is common to it and to others, and expresses, still more than the image does, a *comparison* between the object and others which resemble it. But as the comparison has made manifest a resemblance, as the resemblance is a property of the object, and as a property has every appearance of being a *part* of the object which possesses it, we easily persuade ourselves that by setting concept beside concept we are reconstructing the whole of the object with its parts, thus obtaining, so to speak, its intellectual equivalent. In this way we believe that we can form a faithful representation of duration by setting in line the concepts of unity, multiplicity, continuity, finite or infinite divisibility, etc. There precisely is the illusion. There also is the danger. Just in so far as abstract ideas can render service to analysis, that is, to the scientific study of the object in its relations to other objects, so far are they incapable of replacing intuition, that is, the metaphysical investigation of what is essential and unique in the object. For on the one hand these concepts, laid side by side, never actually give us more than an artificial reconstruction of the object, of which they can only symbolize certain general, and, in a way, impersonal aspects; it is therefore useless to believe that with them we can seize a reality of which they present to us the shadow alone. And, on the other hand, besides the illusion there is also a very serious danger. For the concept generalizes at the same time as it abstracts. The concept can only symbolize a particular property by making it common to an infinity of things. It therefore always more or less deforms the property by the extension it gives to it. Replaced in the metaphysical object to which it belongs, a property coincides with the object, or at least moulds itself on it, and adopts the same outline. Extracted from the metaphysical object, and presented in a concept, it grows indefinitely larger, and goes beyond the object itself, since henceforth it has to contain it, along with a number of other objects. Thus the different concepts that we form of the properties of a thing inscribe round it so many circles, each much too large and none of them fitting it exactly. And yet, in the thing itself the properties coincided with the thing, and coincided consequently with one another. So that if we are bent on reconstructing the object with concepts, some artifice must be sought whereby this coincidence of the object and its properties can be brought about. For example, we may choose one of the concepts and try, starting from it, to get round to the others. But we shall then soon discover that according as we start from one concept or another, the meeting and combination of the concepts will take place in an altogether different way. According as we start, for example, from unity or from multiplicity, we shall have to conceive differently the multiple unity of duration. Everything will depend on the weight we attribute to this or that concept, and this weight will always be arbitrary, since the concept extracted from the object has no weight, being only the shadow of a body. In this way, as many different *systems* will spring up as there are external points of view from which the reality can be examined, or larger circles in which it can be enclosed. Simple concepts have, then, not only the inconvenience of dividing the concrete unity of the object into so many symbolical expressions; they also divide philosophy into distinct schools, each of which takes its seat, chooses its counters, and carries on with the others a game that will never end. Either metaphysics is only this play of ideas, or else, if it is a serious occupation of the mind, if it is a science and not simply an exercise, it must transcend concepts in order to reach intuition. Certainly, concepts are necessary to it, for all the other sciences work as a rule with concepts, and metaphysics cannot dispense with the other sciences. But it is only truly itself when it goes beyond the concept, or at least when it frees itself from rigid and ready-made concepts in order to create a kind very different from those which we habitually use; I mean supple, mobile, and almost fluid representations, always ready to mould themselves on the fleeting forms of intuition. We shall return later to this important point. Let it suffice us for the moment to have shown that our duration can be presented to us directly in an intuition, that it can be suggested to us indirectly by images, but that it can never—if we confine the word concept to its proper meaning—be enclosed in a conceptual representation.

William James

Pragmatism's Conception of Truth *

When Clerk-Maxwell was a child it is written that he had a mania for having everything explained to him, and that when people put him off with vague verbal accounts of any phenomenon he would interrupt them impatiently by saying, 'Yes; but I want you to tell me the *particular go* of it!' Had his question been about truth, only a pragmatist could have told him the particular go of it. I believe that our contemporary pragmatists, especially Messrs. Schiller and Dewey, have given the only tenable account of this subject. It is a very ticklish subject, sending subtle rootlets into all kinds of crannies, and hard to treat in the sketchy way that alone befits a public lecture. But the Schiller-Dewey view of truth has been so ferociously attacked by rationalistic philosophers, and so abominably misunderstood, that here, if anywhere, is the point where a clear and simple statement should be made.

I fully expect to see the pragmatist view of truth run through the classic stages of a theory's career. First, you know, a new theory is attacked as absurd; then it is admitted to be true, but obvious and insignificant; finally it is seen to be so important that its adversaries claim that they themselves discovered it. Our doctrine of truth is at present in the first of these three stages, with symptoms of the second stage having begun in certain quarters. I wish that this lecture might help it beyond the first stage in the eyes of many of you.

Truth, as any dictionary will tell you, is a property of certain of our ideas. It means their 'agreement', as falsity means their disagreement, with 'reality.' Pragmatists and intellectualists both accept this definition as a matter of course. They begin to quarrel only after the question is raised as to what may precisely be meant by the term 'agreement,' and what by the

* From *Pragmatism* by William James. New York: Longmans, Green and Co., 1907, pp. 197–217. Copyright 1907 by William James. Reprinted by permission of Paul R. Reynolds & Son, 599 Fifth Avenue, New York 17, New York.

term 'reality,' when reality is taken as something for our ideas to agree with.

In answering these questions the pragmatists are more analytic and painstaking, the intellectualists more offhand and irreflective. The popular notion is that a true idea must copy its reality. Like other popular views, this one follows the analogy of the most usual experience. Our true ideas of sensible things do indeed copy them. Shut your eyes and think of yonder clock on the wall, and you get just such a true picture or copy of its dial. But your idea of its 'works' (unless you are a clock maker) is much less of a copy, yet it passes muster, for it in no way clashes with the reality. Even though it should shrink to the mere word 'works,' that word still serves you truly; and when you speak of the 'time-keeping function' of the clock, or of its spring's 'elasticity,' it is hard to see exactly what your ideas can copy.

You perceive that there is a problem here. Where your ideas cannot copy definitely their object, what does agreement with that object mean? Some idealists seem to say that they are true whenever they are what God means that we ought to think about that object. Others hold the copy-view all through, and speak as if our ideas possessed truth just in proportion as they approach to being copies of the Absolute's eternal way of thinking.

These views, you see, invite pragmatistic discussion. But the great assumption of the intellectualists is that truth means essentially an inert static relation. When you've got your true idea of anything, there's an end of the matter. You're in possession, you *know:* you have fulfilled your thinking destiny. You are where you ought to be mentally; you have obeyed your categorical imperative; and nothing more need follow on that climax of your rational destiny. Epistemologically you are in stable equilibrium.

Pragmatism, on the other hand, asks its usual question. "Grant an idea or belief to be true," it says, "what concrete difference will its being true make in any one's actual life? How will the truth be realized? What experiences will be different from those which would obtain if the belief were false? What, in short, is the truth's cash-value in experimental terms?"

The moment pragmatism ask this question, it sees the answer: *True ideas are those that we can assimilate, validate, corroborate and verify. False ideas are those that we can not.* That is the practical difference it makes to us to have true ideas; that, therefore, is the meaning of truth, for it is all that truth is known-as.

This thesis is what I have defended. The truth of an idea is not a stagnant property inherent in it. Truth *happens* to an idea. It *becomes* true, is *made* true by events. Its verity *is* in fact an event, a process; the process namely of its verifying itself, its veri-*fication*. Its validity is the process of its valid-*ation*.

But what do the words verification and validation themselves pragmatically mean? They again signify certain practical consequences of the verified and validated idea. It is hard to find any one phrase that characterizes these consequences better than the ordinary agreement-formula—just such consequences being what we have in mind whenever we say that our ideas 'agree' with reality. They lead us, namely, through the acts and other ideas which they instigate, into or up to, or towards, other parts of experience with which we feel all the while—such feeling being among our potentialities—that the original ideas remain in agreement. The connexions and transitions come to us from point to point as being progressive, harmonious, satisfactory. This function of agreeable leading is what we mean by an idea's verification. Such an account is vague and it sounds at first quite trivial, but it has results which it will take the rest of my hour to explain.

Let me begin by reminding you of the fact that the possession of true thoughts means everywhere the possession of invaluable instruments of action; and that our duty to gain truth, so far from being a blank command from out of the blue, or a 'stunt' self-imposed by our intellect, can account for itself by excellent practical reasons.

The importance to human life of having true beliefs about matters of fact is a thing too notorious. We live in a world of realities that can be infinitely useful or infinitely harmful. Ideas that tell us which of them to expect count as the true ideas in all this primary sphere of verification, and the pursuit of such ideas is a primary human duty. The possession of truth so far from being here an end in itself is only a preliminary means towards other vital satisfactions. If I am lost in the woods and starved, and find what looks like a cow-path, it is of the utmost importance that I should think of a human habitation at the end of it, for if I do so and follow it, I save myself. The true thought is useful here because the house which is its object is useful. The practical value of true ideas is thus primarily derived from the practical importance of their objects to us. Their objects are, indeed, not important at all times. I may on another occasion have no use for the house; and then my idea of it, however verifiable, will be practically irrelevant, and had better remain latent. Yet since almost any object may some day become temporarily important, the advantage of having a general stock of *extra* truths, of ideas that shall be true of merely possible situations, is obvious. We store such extra truths away in our memories, and with the overflow we fill our books of reference. Whenever such an extra truth becomes practically relevant to one of our emergencies, it passes from cold-storage to do work in the world and our belief in it grows active. You can say of it then either that 'it is useful because it is true' or that 'it is true because it is useful.' Both of these phrases mean exactly the same thing, namely that here is an idea that gets fulfilled and can be verified. True is the name for whatever idea starts the verification-process, useful is the name for its completed function in experience. True ideas would never have been singled out as such, would never have acquired a class-name, least of all a name suggesting value, unless they had been useful from the outset in this way.

From this simple cue pragmatism gets her general notion of truth as something essentially bound up with the way in which one moment in our experience may lead us towards other moments which it will be worth while to have been led to. Primarily, and on the common-sense level, the truth of a state of mind means this function of *a leading that is worth while*. When a moment in our experience, of any kind whatever, inspires us with a thought that is true, that means that sooner or later we dip by that thought's guidance into the particulars of experience again and make advantageous connexion with them. This is a vague enough statement, but I beg you to retain it, for it is essential.

Our experience meanwhile is all shot through with regularities. One bit of it can warn us to get ready for another bit, can 'intend' or be 'significant of' that remoter object. The object's advent is the significance's verification. Truth, in these cases, meaning nothing but eventual verification, is manifestly incompatible with waywardness on our part. Woe to him whose beliefs play fast and loose with the order which realities follow in his experience; they will lead him nowhere or else make false connexions.

By 'realities' or 'objects' here, we mean either things of common sense, sensibly present, or else common-sense relations, such as dates, places, distances, kinds, activities. Following our mental image of a house along the cow-path, we actually come to see the house; we get the image's full verification. *Such simply and fully verified leadings are certainly the originals and prototypes of the truth-process.* Experience offers indeed other forms of truth-process, but they are all conceivable as being primary verifications arrested, multiplied or substituted one for another.

Take, for instance, yonder object on the wall. You and I consider it to be a 'clock,' altho no one of us has seen the hidden works that make it one. We let our notion pass for true without attempting to verify. If truths mean verification-process essentially, ought we then to call such unverified truths as this abortive? No, for they form the overwhelmingly large number of the truths we live by. Indirect as well as direct verifications pass muster.

Where circumstantial evidence is sufficient, we can go without eye-witnessing. Just as we here assume Japan to exist without ever having been there, because it *works* to do so, everything we know conspiring with the belief, and nothing interfering, so we assume that thing to be a clock. We *use* it as a clock, regulating the length of our lecture by it. The verification of the assumption here means its leading to no frustration or contradiction. Veri*fiability* of wheels and weights and pendulum is as good as verification. For one truth-process completed there are a million in our lives that function in this state of nascency. They turn us *towards* direct verification; lead us into the *surroundings* of the objects they envisage; and then, if everything runs on harmoniously, we are so sure that verification is possible that we omit it, and are usually justified by all that happens.

Truth lives, in fact, for the most part on a credit system. Our thoughts and beliefs 'pass' so long as nothing challenges them just as bank-notes pass so long as nobody refuses them. But this all points to direct face-to-face verifications somewhere, without which the fabric of truth collapses like a financial system with no cash-basis whatever. You accept my verification of one thing, I yours of another. We trade on each other's truth. But beliefs verified concretely by *somebody* are posts of the whole superstructure.

Another great reason—beside economy of time—for waiving complete verification in the usual business of life is that all things exist in kinds and not singly. Our world is found once for all to have that peculiarity. So that when we have once directly verified our ideas about one specimen of a kind, we consider ourselves free to apply them to other specimens without verification. A mind that habitually discerns the kind of thing before it, and acts by the law of the kind immediately, without pausing to verify, will be a 'true' mind in ninety-nine out of a hundred emergencies, proved so by its conduct fitting everything it meets, and getting no refutation.

Indirectly or only potentially verifying processes may thus be true as well as full verification-processes. They work as true processes would work, give us the same advantages, and claim our recognition for the same reasons. All this on the common-sense level of matters of fact, which we are alone considering.

But matters of fact are not our only stock in trade. *Relations among purely mental ideas* form another sphere where true and false beliefs obtain, and here the beliefs are absolute, or unconditional. When they are true they bear the name either of definitions or of principles. It is either a principle or a definition that 1 and 1 make 2, that 2 and 1 make 3, and so on; that white differs less from gray than it does from black; that when the cause begins to act the effect also commences. Such propositions hold of all possible 'ones,' of all conceivable 'whites' and 'grays' and 'causes.' The objects here are mental objects. Their relations are perceptually obvious at a glance, and no sense-verification is necessary. Moreover, once true, always true, of those same mental objects. Truth here has an 'eternal' character. If you can find a concrete thing anywhere that is 'one' or 'white' or 'gray' or an 'effect,' then your principles will everlastingly apply to it. It is but a case of ascertaining the kind, and then applying the law of its kind to the particular object. You are sure to get truth if you can but name the kind rightly, for your mental relations hold good of everything of that kind without exception. If you then, nevertheless, failed to get truth concretely, you would say that you had classed your real objects wrongly.

In this realm of mental relations, truth again is an affair of leading. We relate one abstract idea with another, framing in the end great systems of logical and mathematical truth, under the respective terms of which the sensible facts of experience eventually arrange themselves, so that our eternal truths hold good of realities also. This marriage of fact and theory is endlessly fertile. What we say is here already true in advance of special verification, *if we have subsumed our objects rightly.* Our ready-made ideal framework for all sorts of possible objects follows from the very structure of our thinking. We can no more play fast and loose with these abstract relations than we can do so with our sense-experiences. They coerce us; we must treat them consistently, whether or not we like the results. The rules of addition apply to our debts as rigorously as to our assets. The hundredth decimal of π, the ratio of the circumference to its diameter, is predetermined ideally now, tho no one may have computed it. If we should ever need the figure in our dealings with an actual circle we should need to have it given rightly, calculated by the usual rules; for it is the same kind of truth that those rules elsewhere calculate.

Between the coercions of the sensible order and those of the ideal order, our mind is thus wedged tightly. Our ideas must agree with realities, be such realities concrete or abstract, be they facts or be they principles, under penalty of endless inconsistency and frustration.

So far, intellectualists can raise no protest. They can only say that we have barely touched the skin of the matter.

Realities mean, then, either concrete facts, or abstract kinds of things and relations perceived intuitively between them. They furthermore and thirdly mean, as things that new ideas of ours must no less take account of, the whole body of other truths already in our possession. But what now does 'agreement' with such threefold realities mean?—to use again the definition that is current.

Here it is that pragmatism and intellectualism begin to part company. Primarily, no doubt, to agree means to copy, but we saw that the mere word 'clock' would do instead of a mental picture of its works, and that of many realities our ideas can only be symbols and not copies. 'Past time,' 'power,' 'spontaneity',—how can our mind copy such realities?

To 'agree' in the widest sense with a reality *can only mean to be guided either straight up to it or into its surroundings, or to be put into such working touch with it as to handle either it or something connected with it better than if we disagreed.* But either intellectually or practically! And often agreement will only mean the negative fact that nothing contradictory from the quarter of that reality comes to interfere with the way in which our ideas guide us elsewhere. To copy a reality is, indeed, one very important way of agreeing with it, but it is far from being essential. The essential thing is the process of being guided. Any idea that helps us to *deal,* whether practically or intellectually, with either the reality or its belongings, that doesn't entangle our progress in frustrations, that *fits,* in fact, and adapts our life to the reality's whole setting, will agree sufficiently to meet the requirement. It will hold true of that reality.

Thus, *names* are just as 'true' or 'false' as definite mental pictures are. They set up similar verification-processes, and lead to fully equivalent practical results.

All human thinking gets discursified; we exchange ideas, we lend and borrow verifications, get them from one another by means of social intercourse. All truth thus gets verbally built out, stored up, and made available for every one. Hence, we must *talk* consistently just as we must *think* consistently; for both in talk and thought we deal with kinds. Names are arbitrary, but once understood they must be kept so. We mustn't now call Abel 'Cain' or Cain 'Abel.' If we do, we ungear ourselves from the whole book of Genesis, and from all its connexions with the universe of speech and fact down to the present time. We throw ourselves out of whatever truth that entire system of speech and fact may embody.

The overwhelming majority of our true ideas admit of no direct or face-to-face verification—those of past history, for example, as of Cain and Abel. The stream of time can be remounted only verbally, or verified indirectly by the present prolongations or effects of what the past harbored. Yet if they agree with these verbalities and effects, we can know that our ideas of the past are true. *As true as past time itself was,* so true was Julius Caesar, so true were antediluvian monsters, all in their proper dates and settings. That past time itself was, is guaranteed by its coherence with everything that's present. True as the present *is,* but the past *was* also.

Agreement thus turns out to be essentially an affair of leading—leading that is useful because it is into quarters that contain objects that are important. True ideas lead us into useful verbal and conceptual quarters as well as directly up to useful sensible termini. They lead to consistency, stability and flowing human intercourse. They lead away from excentricity and isolation, from foiled and barren thinking. The untrammelled flowing of the leading-process, its general freedom from clash and contradiction, passes for its indirect verification; but all roads lead to Rome, and in the end eventually, all true processes must lead to the face of directly verifying sensible experience *somewhere,* which somebody's ideas have copied.

Such is the large loose way in which the pragmatist interprets the word agreement. He treats it altogether practically. He lets it cover any process of conduction from a present idea to a future terminus, provided only it run prosperously. It is only thus that 'scientific' ideas, flying as they do beyond common sense, can be said to agree with their realities. It is, as I have already said, *as if* reality were made of ether, atoms or electrons, but we mustn't think so literally. The term 'energy' doesn't even pretend to stand for anything 'objective.' It is only a way of measuring the surface of phenomena so as to string their changes on a simple formula.

Yet in the choice of these man-made formulas we can not be capricious with impunity any more than we can be capricious on the common-sense practical level. We must find a theory that will *work;* and that means something extremely difficult; for our theory must mediate between all previous truths and certain new experiences. It must derange common sense and previous belief as little as possible, and it must lead to some sensible terminus or other that can be verified exactly. To 'work' means both these things; and the squeeze is so tight that there is little loose play for any hypothesis. Our theories are wedged and controlled as nothing else is. Yet sometimes alternative theoretic formulas are equally compatible with all the truths we know, and then we choose between them for subjective reasons. We choose the kind of theory to which we are already partial; we follow 'elegance' or 'economy.' Clerk-Maxwell somewhere says it would be 'poor scientific taste' to choose the more complicated of two equally well-evidenced conceptions; and you will all agree with him. Truth in science is what gives us the maximum possible sum of satisfactions, taste included, but consistency both with previous truth and with novel fact is always the most imperious claimant.

Harold H. Joachim

Truth as Coherence *

We may start with the following as a provisional and rough formulation of the coherence-notion. 'Anything is true which can be conceived. It is true because, and in so far as, it can be conceived. Conceivability is the essential nature of truth.' And we may proceed at once to remove a possible misunderstanding of the term 'conceive'. We do not mean by 'conceive' to form a mental picture; and we shall not be dismayed when we hear that the Antipodes were once 'inconceivable', or that a Centaur can be 'conceived.' For it may be difficult—or even, if you like, impossible—to 'image' people walking head downwards; and to 'picture' a horse with the head and shoulders of a man may be as easy as you please. All this is quite irrelevant, and does not touch our position. To 'conceive' means for us to think out clearly and logically, to hold many elements together in a connexion necessitated by their several contents. And to be 'conceivable' means to be a 'significant whole', or a whole possessed of meaning for thought. A 'significant whole' is such that all its constituent elements reciprocally involve one another, or reciprocally determine one another's being as contributory features in a single concrete meaning. The elements thus cohering constitute a whole which may be said to control the reciprocal adjustment of its elements, as an end controls its constituent means. And in this sense a Centaur is 'inconceivable', whilst the Antipodes are clearly 'conceivable.' For the elements constitutive of the Centaur refuse to enter into reciprocal adjustment. They collide amongst themselves, or they clash with some of the constitutive elements in that wider sphere of experience, that larger significant whole, in which the Centaur must strive for a place. The horse-man might pass externally as a convenient shape for rapid movement; but how about his internal economy,

* From *The Nature of Truth* by Harold H. Joachim. Oxford: At the Clarendon Press, 1906, pp. 66–84. Reprinted by permission of The Clarendon Press, Oxford, on behalf of Mrs. Joachim.

Note: Footnotes are here omitted.

the structure, adjustment and functioning of his inner organs? If he is to be 'actual', the animal kingdom is his natural home. But if we persisted in our attempt to locate the creature there, we should inevitably bring confusion and contradiction into that sphere of significant being—so far at least as it is manifest to us in our anatomical and physiological knowledge. And, on the other hand, the being of the Antipodes is a necessary interconnected piece in that puzzle of which our astronomical science is the coherent exposition. The Antipodes are 'conceivable' in the sense that they are *forced* upon any thinker for whom the earth and the solar system are to possess significance; i.e. the Antipodes are a necessary constituent of a significant whole, as that whole must be conceived.

Thus 'conceivability' means for us *systematic coherence,* and is the determining characteristic of a 'significant whole.' The systematic coherence of such a whole is expressed most adequately and explicitly in the system of reasoned knowledge which we call a science or a branch of philosophy. Any element of such a whole shares in this characteristic to a greater or less degree—i.e. is more or less 'conceivable'—in proportion as the whole, with its determinate inner articulation, shines more or less clearly through that element; or in proportion as the element, in manifesting itself, manifests also with more or less clearness and fullness the remaining elements in their reciprocal adjustment.

It is obvious that this rough sketch suggests many difficult problems. Truth, we have said, *is* in its essence conceivability or systematic coherence; and now we seem to have severed 'the conceivable' from its expression, the 'significant whole' from the forms in which its significance is revealed. The truth, therefore, would apparently fall on the side of the Real; and would stand over against science or reasoned knowledge, faith, emotion, volition, etc., as the various subjective modes in which it obtains actuality and recognition. But this severance of the experienced Real from the experiencing of it, is the very mistake against which the main discussions of our second chapter were directed; whilst, if truth be thus located in a sphere of being apart from mind, it is difficult to see how science can in any sense be 'true.' We spoke of science as an explicit analysis and reasoned reconstruction of the systematic coherence of a significant whole; but this sounds uncommonly like a reversion to the correspondence-notion. Science would be 'true', so far as its system of demonstrations reconstructs—i.e. *repeats or corresponds to*—the systematic coherence which *is* the truth as a character of the Real.

Moreover, we have admitted degrees of conceivability, and therefore also degrees of truth. But we have not explained, and perhaps could not explain, the ideal of perfect conceivability and perfect truth by reference to which these degrees are to be estimated.

Before I turn to the consideration of these problems, let me endeavour to throw further light on the theory just sketched, by contrasting it with two very different views to which it bears some superficial resemblance. The time and labour occupied in this comparison will not be wasted; for it will enable us to develop a more adequate formulation of the coherence-notion, and we shall approach the problems to be solved with a more just appreciation of their precise difficulty.

When Descartes laid it down as a principle for the seeker after truth 'to affirm nothing as true except that which he could clearly and distinctly perceive', he was in reality presupposing a very definite theory of knowledge and a correspondingly determinate metaphysics. If we wish to pass a true judgement, we must affirm or deny only that content which we clearly and distinctly apprehend. Inner affirmation, or denial, which is the characteristic of judgement, is an act in which we exhibit our free choice or will. But this act is exercised upon a material in the acceptance of which we are passive. The intellect—a passive recipient—apprehends a content, which the will—an active faculty—may affirm or deny. And if this affirmation is to constitute a true judgement, the content affirmed must force itself upon our intellect as a self-evident *datum,* which we immediately recognize as indubitable. Thus the immediate apprehension of indubitable truth, an 'intuition', is the necessary pre-condition of truth of judgement. The content of such an 'intuition', viz. that which we apprehend intuitively as self-evident, is a 'simple idea', or rather (as Descartes sometimes more clearly expresses it) a 'simple proposition.' Its 'simplicity' does not exclude inner distinction; for it is the immediate, but necessary, cohesion of two elements or two constituent ideas. In other words, the self-evident *datum,* which Descartes calls a 'simple idea' or a 'simple proposition', is a hypothetical judgement so formulated that the antecedent immediately necessitates the consequent, though the consequent need not reciprocally involve the antecedent.

The elements in the content of an 'intuition' cohere by the immediate necessity which binds consequent to antecedent in a hypothetical judgement of the kind explained. But the content *as a whole* is grasped intuitively, or immediately, as an indubitable self-evident *datum.* Such self-evident indubitable truths constitute the foundation on which the structure of scientific and philosophical knowledge is built. They are the principles, from which the whole system of demonstrated and demonstrable truth must be derived. And this system is, so to say, a network of chains of propositions. The links in each chain form an uninterrupted sequence from its first link. They follow with unbroken logical coherence from a self-evident *datum,* a 'simple proposition' apprehended intuitively. Each derivative link is grasped by the intellect as the necessary consequent of a link or links intuited as indubitable truths, and *as thus grasped* itself is manifest as an indubitable truth.

Thus, the ideal of knowledge for Descartes is a coherent system of truths, where each truth is apprehended in its logical position: the immediate as the basis, and the mediate truths in their necessary dependence on the immediate. Each truth in this ideal system is a cohesion of different elements united by a logical nexus; and every truth is true *per se* absolutely and unalterably.

But the theory which I am trying to expound is committed, for good or for evil, to a radically different view of the systematization of knowledge. The image of a chain, admirably suited to illustrate the theory of Descartes, is a sheer distortion of the conception of 'coherence' or 'conceivability', which, on my view, characterizes truth. The ideal of knowledge for me is a system, not of *truths,* but of *truth.* 'Coherence' cannot be attached to propositions from the outside: it is not a property which they can acquire by colligation, whilst retaining unaltered the truth they possessed in isolation. And whereas for Descartes ideally certain knowledge (indubitable truth) is typified in the intuitive grasp of the immediately cohering elements of a 'simple proposition', such a content is for me so remote from the ideal as hardly to deserve the name of 'truth' at all. For it is the smallest and most abstracted fragment of knowledge, a mere mutilated shred torn from the living whole in which alone it possessed its significance. The typical embodiments of the ideal must be sought, not in such isolated intuitions, but rather in the organized whole of a science: for that possesses at least *relative* self-dependence, and its significance is at least *relatively* immanent and self-contained.

The second view with which I propose to contrast the coherence-theory may be regarded as a corollary of the first. For, if there are certain judgements indubitably true, then these are the *materials* of knowledge. And, in the progress of thought, a *form* is imposed upon these materials which arranges without altering them. Truth is linked to truth until the arrangement constitutes that network of chains of truths which is the system of ideally complete knowledge. The form under which the infinitely various materials are ordered, is the universal form of all thinking. It is the characteristic grey of formal consistency, which any and every thinking monotonously paints over all its materials to stamp them as its own. This arrangement under the form of thinking cannot of *itself* guarantee the truth of the result. For false materials, as well as true, may be painted with the royal colour. But the result cannot be true *without* this arrangement, which is thus a *sine qua non* or a 'negative condition' of truth. We may christen the observance of this condition 'validity'; and we may then draw the conclusion that the completely true must also be valid, though the valid may be false. Or if we prefer the term 'consistency' we shall point out that consistent lying and consistent error are occasionally achieved, and that a man may be a consistent scoundrel; but that the truth requires for its apprehension and utterance the same consistency of thought and purpose, which must also be expressed in the actions of the morally good man. The consistent, in short, need be neither true nor good; but the good and the true must be consistent.

This distinction between the universal form and the particular materials of thought has, in various modifications, played a great part in the history of philosophy. I am here concerned with it in its barest and most extreme shape, as the fundamental assumption of the traditional 'formal' logic. Pressed beyond the limits of legitimate provisional abstraction until it has become a mere caricature, the antithesis between form and matter has in that 'science' been worked out through the whole domain and through all the functions of thinking. Judgement e.g. is that function of thought whereby two conceptions are combined; and whatever the materials, the form of combination exhibits a character of its own, which is to be studied apart. Hence those classifications of 'formal' logic which we have all of us learnt, and learnt to unlearn again: those rigid groupings of Judgements as Universal, Individual, Particular; as Negative, Affirmative, Infinite; as Categorical, Hypothetical, Necessary, &c., &c. So, Syllogism is the function of thought whereby two judgements are combined to generate a third; and 'formal' logic gives you the rules of 'valid' combination irrespective of *what* is combined, and impotent therefore to determine the truth of the result.

Formal logic, in this sense of the term, might be called 'the analysis of low-grade thinking'; but all thinking, even at its lowest, is a living process, which the mechanical methods of such an analysis are too crude to grasp. Yet all thinking—the most complicated and profound, as well as the most shallow and rudimentary—exhibits a certain unity of character. And the formal logician has followed a sound instinct in emphasizing the necessity of analysing and grasping this unity, if thinking is to understand itself. But he has erred in looking for the unity as an abstract common feature, to be found in the actual processes of thinking by stripping them of their concrete differences. And it is the same error which has led him to conceive thinking as a dead and finished product instead of a living and moving process. In the end and in principle his error is the failure to conceive a universal except as one element along with others in the particular: a failure which is tantamount to the negation of all universals. Or it is the failure to conceive a whole except as the sum of its parts: a failure which is the denial of unity and individual character to that which develops and lives. Hence formal logic assumes that the essential nature of thought is to be found in an abstractly self-identical form; in a tautologous self-consistency, where the 'self' has no diversity of content in which a genuine consistency could be manifested, or where diversity of content is cast aside as mere irrelevant material. But the essential nature of thought is a concrete unity, a living individuality. Thought is a form, which moves and expands, and exhibits its consistent character precisely in those ordered articulations of its structure which formal logic impotently dismisses as *mere* materials.

The 'systematic coherence', therefore, in which we are looking for the nature of truth, must not be confused with the 'consistency' of formal logic. A piece of thinking might be free from self-contradiction, might be 'consistent' and 'valid' as the formal logician understands those terms, and yet it might fail to exhibit that systematic coherence which is truth.

We may now proceed to formulate the coherence-theory afresh in the following terms. Truth in its essential nature is that systematic coherence which is the character of a significant whole. A 'significant whole' is an organized individual experience, self-fulfilling and self-fulfilled. Its organization *is* the process of its self-fulfilment, and the concrete manifestation of its individuality. But this process is no mere surface-play between static parts within the whole: nor *is* the individuality of the whole, except in the movement which is its manifestation. The whole *is* not, if 'is' implies that its nature is a finished product prior or posterior to the process, or in any sense apart from it. And the whole *has* no parts, if 'to have parts' means to consist of fixed and determinate constituents, from and to which the actions and inter-actions of its organic life proceed, much as a train may travel backwards and forwards between the terminal stations. Its 'parts' are through and through in the process and constituted by it. They are 'moments' in the self-fulfilling process which is the individuality of the whole. And the individuality of the whole is *both* the pre-supposition of the distinctive being of its 'moments' or parts *and* the resultant which emerges as their co-operation, or which they make and continuously sustain.

It is this process of self-fufilment which is truth, and it is *this* which the theory means by 'systematic coherence.' The process is not a movement playing between static elements, but the very substance of the moving elements. And the coherence is no abstract form imposed upon the surface of materials, which retain in their depths a nature untouched by the imposition. The coherence—if we call it a 'form'—is a form which through and through interpenetrates its materials; and they—if we call them 'materials'—are materials, which retain no inner privacy for themselves in independence of the form. They hold their distinctive being in and through, and not in sheer defiance of, their identical form; and its identity is the concrete sameness of different materials. The materials *are* only as moments in the process which is the continuous emergence of the coherence. And the form *is* only as the sustained process of self-fulfilment, wherein just these materials reveal themselves as constitutive moments of the coherence.

In the above formulation I have endeavoured to express the coherence-notion so as to emphasize the *concreteness* of the coherence which is truth, as against the view which found truth in formal consistency; and I have insisted upon the conception of truth as a living and moving whole, as against the Cartesian view of fixed truths on which the structure of knowledge is built. But the result at present is a mere vague sketch, which cannot pretend to be satisfactory. Even the well-disposed reader will regard it as the description of a mystical ideal with no obvious application to the actual problems of human knowledge; whilst the hostile critic will view it as a dishonest evasion of the difficulties, as mere words in place of a solid discussion. I shall accordingly attempt to work out my sketch in detail, so as to show the precise bearing of this conception of truth on the truth in human judgement and inference, and so as to defend it against the charge of mysticism or evasion of the difficulties.

If we are to develop our vague sketch into a definite theory, we must make it clear *what* truth we are professing to describe. Was our sketch intended as an exposition of truth as it is for human knowledge? or were we describing an ideal experience, which no finite mind can ever actually enjoy?

This manner of formulating the question seems to challenge a choice between two unambiguous alternatives, and thus to put a clear issue before us. But in reality it involves certain assumptions which are open to debate, and which—as I think, and hope to show—are false. For it is assumed that finite experience is sundered by a gulf from ideal experience. It is implied that an ideal experience is as such debarred from actuality, and it is suggested that knowledge which is severed from ideal experience can yet be true. But, whilst refusing to commit myself to these implications, I should reply that my sketch was intended to describe the nature of truth as an ideal, as the character of an ideally complete experience. Truth, we said, was the systematic coherence which characterized a significant whole. And we proceeded to identify a sigificant whole with 'an organized individual experience, self-fulfilling and self-fulfilled.' Now there can be one *and only one* such experience: or *only one* significant whole, the significance of which is self-contained in the sense required. For it is *absolute* self-fulfilment, *absolutely* self-contained significance, that is postulated; and nothing short of *absolute* individuality—nothing short of *the* completely whole experience—can satisfy this postulate. And human knowledge—not merely *my* knowledge or *yours,* but the best and fullest knowledge in the world at any stage of its development—is clearly not a significant whole in this ideally complete sense. Hence the truth, which our sketch described, is—*from the point of view of the human intelligence*—an Ideal, and an Ideal which can never *as such,* or in its completeness, be actual as human experience.

But it will be contended that such an Ideal cannot be expressed in terms of human thought, and is strictly inconceivable. 'All attempts to conceive your Ideal', we shall be told, 'are foredoomed to failure. For we cannot conceive, except under categories whose meaning is moulded and restricted by the limitations of that finite experience in which alone they have any legitimate application. We employ categories with a determinate meaning in their application to the incomplete experience, which is actually ours: but their meaning is determinate, only in so far as it is relative to the area in which the restricting conditions hold. Yet the conception of your Ideal requires the absolute and unrestricted use of these categories. But, if they are used absolutely, we can conceive nothing determinate under them: we are playing with empty words. Whilst, if they are used under the restrictions which condition their application in finite experience, they are inadequate to express the Ideal, and distort instead of describing its nature. Thus you made use e.g. of the notions of Life, Organism, Self-fulfilling Process. These notions have a determinate meaning in their application to the objects of our limited experience; but their meaning is itself restricted in that application. The life of any object of our experience is far from being a self-sustaining process, a closed circle of functions revolving free from all external conditions. It is limited in every way, dependent in origin, extent, intensity and duration, and conditioned throughout by what is other and perhaps hostile. No object of our experience *is* Life; and the Life, which some of them manifest, is conditioned by the sources from which it was derived, and by the bodily organs and the environment in and through which it is maintained. Yet the "living whole", which is your Ideal, is to be limited in no way, and in no way dependent upon anything other than itself. Or did you intend to suggest that it came to be, and grew, and would pass away; that it maintained itself in this its bodily vehicle over against an environment not itself? Nor again can the notion of Organism find absolute expression in any of the objects of our experience. No whole is through and through organic, an organism pure and simple. We never find a whole whose parts are what they are as reciprocally ends and means to one another, and such that the plan of coherence (which is the whole) determines absolutely the nature and the being of the parts which in turn constitute it. The idea of such a purely organic whole remains an empty conception, a shadowy notion with no positive significance. To describe your ideal as an "organized experience", if "organized" is used in this absolute sense, in no way elucidates your meaning. And Self-fulfilment, where it applies in our experience, expresses a process which starts with given materials and a given and limited power of working upon them. At best, the process culminates in a limited achievement; and, after a shorter or a longer period of effort and relative success, the Self and its Fulfilment vanish together. Yet you used all these notions to describe your Ideal, with an utter disregard of the restrictions under which alone they convey a determinate meaning. And the result was meaningless phrases—words such as "a process, whose moments sustain the whole, and themselves are made and constituted by the process", or "a movement, which is the very substance of the moving elements." '

Now it may be admitted that conceptions derived from partial wholes cannot adequately express *the* whole; and that what we experience is in a sense always a partial whole, or the whole from a finite and partial point of view. We cannot experience the whole completely and adequately, just in so far as we are not ourselves complete. But because we are not complete, it does not follow that we are divorced from the complete and in sheer opposition to it. We are not absolutely real, but neither are we utterly unreal. And because our apprehension is restricted, and in part confused, it does not follow that it is utterly false and an entire distortion of the nature of things. The categories which we have to employ are no doubt inadequate to express the complete reality; but this is no reason for not employing them at all, or for employing them all alike and indifferently. For they all to some extent express the whole; and there are degrees in the relative adequacy of the expression. The categories of Life, Organism, and Self-fulfilment express in our experience wholes of a more concrete, more developed and relatively more self-contained individuality than e.g. the categories under which we conceive a whole of aggregation, or a whole constituted by the limiting outline of its continent environment, or again a whole whose inner being is a static adjustment of parts or a surface-play of movements between fixed constituent elements. And for this reason I employed these categories as relatively more adequate notions under which to conceive the Ideal. Still more adequate notions might perhaps have been found within our finite experience. For it would seem that the significant whole, which is truth, can in the end be most adequately described only in terms of the categories of self-conscious thought. But it is worth while to describe it in terms of the categories of Life, Organism, and Self-fulfilling Process as against those lower grades of theory which we have been criticizing—theories which conceive it under the notions of a static whole, like a 'building'; or of an aggregation of units, like a 'sum of truths'; or of a static adjustment of two wholes of fixed elements, like a 'correspondence' between original and copy.

But the real way to meet the charge that the Ideal is inconceivable is to challenge the 'common-sense' attitude of the critic. The Ideal, he is in effect maintaining, is not in its completeness *here* and *now,* and therefore is not actual: it cannot be adequately expressed in terms of finite experience, and therefore is inconceivable. And this criticism betrays an amazing acquiescence in the first hasty assumptions of the unreflecting consciousness. For the critic assumes that finite experience is solid and fully real and clearly conceivable, an unshaken *datum* here and now; and that we must accept it without question as, so to say, a pier from which to throw a bridge across to the cloudland Ideal. But we have been demanding all along an entire reversal of this attitude. In our view it is the Ideal which is solid and substantial and fully actual. The finite experiences are rooted in the Ideal. They share its actuality, and draw from it whatever being and conceivability they possess. It is a perverse attitude to condemn the Ideal because the conditions, under which the finite experiences exhibit their fragmentary actuality, do not as such restrict its being; or to deny that it is conceivable, because the conceivability of such incomplete expressions is too confused and turbid to apply to it.

That nothing in our partial experience answers precisely to the demands of the Ideal, cannot show that the Ideal is an unsubstantial dream, an idle play of words. The question is whether our partial experience through and through involves the being of the ideally-complete experience which we have postulated. And the way to answer this question is to examine the implications of our partial experience, or on the other hand to trace the Ideal in its manifestations.

But this is precisely where our critics will join issue with us. For they will fasten on the term 'experience', and they will demand, '*Whose* is this Ideal Experience? *Where* and *when* is it actual? What is its precise *relation* to the finite experiences?'

Now one answer to such questions is, 'Such an experience is nowhere and at no time, no one possesses it, and it is related to nothing save itself'. For the questions assume that the Truth is a finished product, a static consummated whole of experience, which *is* somewhere and at some time, exclusive of the finite experiences as occurrences in time and place, and yet related to them. But this is not what was meant. And again they assume that the Truth is the possession of a finite being. They regard it as the experience of a 'this-now', much as I may here and now experience this toothache. But this again was not meant, though the misleading associations of the term 'experience' to some extent justify the misunderstanding.

It is not, however, of much value to make a negative answer of this kind. On the other hand, if we answered, 'Such an Ideal Experience is everywhere and at all times; it is the partial possession of all finite beings, and they are the incomplete vehicles of it', we should merely be repeating more explicitly what we have already asserted. The mere assertion is useless; but nothing short of an entire system of metaphysics could serve as its justification. The difficulty, in short, is that our problem is expanding into the whole problem of philosophy, and that the discussion threatens to become unmanageable.

Ledger Wood

Knowledge, Meaning, and Truth *

The *extrinsic* theory of truth assumes a variety of forms of which the correspondence theory and the pragmatic theory are the most familiar. The correspondence theory, in its most familiar version, defines truth as a correspondence between ideas in the mind and real physical objects external to the mind. The theory is associated historically with the theory of representative perception, but this affiliation of the correspondence theory of truth with a particular epistemological theory of perception is the result of historical accident and not of any necessary logical affinity between the two theories. Because of this accidental association, the correspondence theory has been subjected to an unfair type of critcism which, though perhaps damaging to a crude representative perceptionism, is not pertinent to the conception of truth as correspondence. The conventional criticism of the correspondence theory is that if truth is a relation between ideas or sense-data as immediately given and an extra-mental object, the correspondence could never be confirmed, since its confirmation would require the direct comparison of the idea with its object—a comparison which is precluded by the inaccessibility of the object to direct inspection. In other words truth is defined by the correspondence theory in such a way that its presence in any cognitive situation could not possibly be ascertained; it therefore affords a conception of truth which is useless and meaningless. Now the difficulty embodied in this criticism arises solely from the adoption of the theory of representative perception—which, although to be sure it may and in the past frequently has been combined with the correspondence theory of truth, is not essential to it. When, however, the correspondence theory is entirely dissociated from the theory of representative perception, it is no longer open to this criticism, and it is such a theory of correspondence which I shall now attempt to formulate.

Truth may be defined as the correspondence—or as I shall prefer to designate it, the congruence—between the meaning of a proposition and a factual situation. Congruence, the crucial conception in the definition, is an unique harmony or accord between meaning and fact which eludes precise definition and description. When a propositional meaning is confronted with the crucial fact, the fact is recognized as either conformable to or discordant with the meaning intended. The confronting of a meaning with a fact, which is the crux of verification, is, in its psychological aspect, an act of recognition not essentially different from the recognition of a familiar face or a familiar voice. In ordinary recognition, the memory of the object of an earlier perception is confronted by a present perception of the same object, whereas, in verification, a propositional meaning—achieved by abstract conceptual processes—is confronted by a perceptual object which ordinarily is encountered for the first time. Verification is the recognition that a perceptual object is conformable to the propositional anticipation of. The psychological mechanism of recognition, and hence of verification, varies greatly from individual to individual. Individuals, whose imagination is exceptionally vivid, perhaps achieve recognition by a comparison of a memory image with the present perception to determine whether or not the two resemble each other; usually, however, the recognition depends upon a felt-congruence between the expectation and the fulfilment. When I meet a friend on the street I do not, in order to recognize him, have to conjure up a memory image in order to compare it with my present perceptual experience; I simply "feel" that his appearance conforms to a familiar pattern. Similarly a propositional meaning may for certain minds be clothed in sensuous imagery, such that it can be directly compared with the sensuous ingredients of the verifying percept, but usually the congruence between the meaning of the proposition and the percept which verifies it is directly felt. When the propositional meaning is confronted with the fact which verifies it, the mind recognizes without any explicit comparison that the fact is conformable to the meaning. The process of discovering the conformity is analogous to the successive trying of keys in a lock to see which fits. We do not reject certain keys and identify the "right" one by comparing the shape of the keys with the internal structure of the lock, but by successively trying the keys to see which "fits". The term congruency—rather than correspondence or resemblance—is employed because of its greater generality; the agreement between a propositional meaning and the crucial fact which supposedly verifies it is analogous to the congruence between two geometrical figures which admit of superposition or to the agreement between the shape of the key and the arrangement of the inside of the lock. When the facts "fit" the proposition, the proposition is true, but when the facts do not "fit" the preconceived meaning, the proposition is thereby falsified.

The proposition to which truth accrues by virtue of its congruence with a factual situation is not the proposition considered as a mere verbal statement, but the proposition as conveying a determinate meaning. A propositional meaning may be defined as a propositional statement plus its meaning or intentionality. Now the meaning of a proposition is always embodied in concepts which are individually empirical in their orgin and which are combined in a novel way in the proposition. Until the proposition is verified by the appeal to experience, it is not known whether the composite meaning expressed by the proposition is or is not exemplified in fact. When, for example, I assert that the ash-tray on the table before me will produce a metallic ring if I strike it, the meaning of the proposition is conveyed by the concepts, "table", "in front of", "I" or "self", and "metallic ring", each empirical in origin. The truth or falsity of the statement hinges upon whether the actual state of affairs is or is not congruent with this total propositional meaning. If, when I actually strike the ash-tray, the sound emitted exemplifies my empirical concept, "metallic ring", then the proposition is verified; if it does not conform to my preconception, the proposition is falsified. This example, which is typical of the process of direct verification of a proposition, illustrates the important rôle played by empirical concepts in the constitution of propositional meanings and in their verification. Apart from the meaning which accrues to a proposition from its constituent empirical concepts, a proposition is an empty, verbal statement incapable of verification or falsification; moreover, the verification itself consists in exemplifying in the factual state of affairs one or more of the concepts embodied in the proposition.

There remains to be considered the nature of the fact by reference to which the truth of a proposition is determinable. Empiricists commonly supposed that a proposition is verified by reference to a bare datum in its character of brute fact, but such an account of the verificatory situation is unintelligible. How can a meaningless fact entirely devoid of conceptualization and interpretation be assimilated to a meaningful proposition? It was this very difficulty which Kant formulated and attempted to solve in the chapter on "The Schematism of the Pure Concepts of Understanding". Kant is confronted with the question: "How is the *subsumption* of intuitions under pure concepts . . . possible?" because of his contention that "the pure concepts of the understanding are quite heterogeneous from empirical intuitions".[1] His own solution to this difficulty, which was to invoke time as a *tertium quid* mediating between the conceptual and the factual, was highly artificial and unsuccessful, but the problem posed by the "Schematism" is genuine and unavoidable. Bare facts cannot be subsumed under or assimilated to pure meanings, and hence the fact which constitutes the verification or falsification of a propositional meaning is not a bare fact, but a fact suffused with conceptual meanings. Accordingly, verification involves the confronting of a propositional meaning with another meaning, usually a perceptual meaning, and the congruence or incongruence between the two meanings determines the truth or falsity of the proposition. The "metallic ring" which verifies my assertion that the ash-tray is metallic rather than wooden is no mere sound-datum, but is a sound perceived and recognized by me as conforming to my concept, "metallic sound". The congruence by means of which truth is established is then neither a correspondence between data of sense and a physical object—as the theory of representative perception holds—nor between a statement and a brute factual datum—as certain positivistic theories seem to maintain—but between a propositional meaning and a non-propositional, usually a perceptual meaning. But it will be objected: "If *verification* is the assimilation of a perceptual meaning to an anticipatory meaning, is not the correspondence theory thereby transformed into a coherence theory which moves endlessly within a circumscribed system of meanings?" "Is not the *conceptualization* of fact tantamount to the denial of factuality?" In reply to this objection I should urge that the denial of *bare* factuality and the insistence that factuality as encountered in experience is suffused with meaning and interpretation is not to deny factuality altogether. Every percept contains a sensuous core in addition to its conceptual, interpretational, and constructional ingredients; the sensuous core of the percept itself is the factual element in the perceptual situation by reference to which the perceptual proposition is verified or falsified. No perceptual proposition can acquire truth and no perceptual concept can be shown to be exemplified except by exhibiting an actual percept having a core of factuality. An ingredient of factuality is similarly contained in non-perceptual knowledge, for example in introspection.

The direct verification of any proposition consists in exhibiting in experience actual objects which exemplify the concepts specified by the propo-

[1] Immanuel Kant, *Critique of Pure Reason,* A 137–8, B 176–7. Norman Kemp Smith's translation, p. 180.

sition. If actual entities can be found conformable to all the conceptual conditions embraced within the total propositional meaning, the proposition is true, otherwise it is false. Besides direct verification by appeal to perception, memory, introspection, and other modes of factual cognition, there is an indirect verification by means of inference and hypothesis. Historical propositions, propositions about the future and other propositions about inaccessible objects admit of indirect or inferential verification, but all such indirect verification relies, at some point, on perceptual or quasi-perceptual evidence.

Certain empiricists in philosophy, for example logical positivists and pragmatists, would challenge the distinction between direct and indirect verification, or rather would urge that all genuine verification is direct verification and that propositions about inaccessible objects, for example, the contents of another's mind, are meaningless, because unverifiable. This view is an exaggerated expression of the important truth that there is no indirect verification which does not entail at some juncture the employment of direct verification, either perceptual, mnemic, or introspective. The rejection as meaningless of all statements incapable of direct verification rests on too narrow a definition of the meaningful. The definition of the meaningful as the directly verifiable arbitrarily contracts the domain of the meaningful and proportionately enlarges the domain of the meaningless in a way which does violence to ordinary linguistic usage, thereby relegating many genuinely significant and communicable propositions to a limbo of the meaningless. The line of demarcation between the meaningful and the meaningless may be drawn in another way with logical precision, and yet in much closer conformity with the usages of language, by defining a meaningful proposition as the description of a factual state of affairs by a set of concepts each of which is empirically definable or exemplifiable. A concept in order to possess empirical meaning need not actually be exemplified in experience, as are the generic concepts ash-tray, colour, sound, etc., but it must be resolvable into concepts and operations which are exemplified or exemplifiable. When the meaningfulness of propositions is thus broadly conceived, many so-called "metaphysical" propositions fulfil the conditions of meaningfulness, even though they do not admit of direct verification. For example, propositions regarding the contents of another's mind cannot in the nature of the situation be directly verified, and yet I can meaningfully assert that another mind has an emotion, say of anger, because the component concepts, "other", "mind", "emotion", "anger", and the relation asserted by the proposition to obtain between them are individually exemplified in immediate experience, and thus their conceptual amalgamation, though not exemplifiable, is, nevertheless, meaningful. Not only are such propositions *meaningful,* but they may often be *true,* even though the evidence for them is indirect and their truth merely problematic.

III. BEING

Being

I

To attain a comprehensive understanding of the nature of existence has been a perennial interest of the human mind. What is our cosmic background? What is our place in this larger context? What are the powers that determine our destiny? These and similar questions have always been of deep concern and have always fascinated reflective minds. However difficult it may be to answer such questions, we all try to answer them with the hope of arriving at some ultimate view.

Traditionally this pursuit has been called metaphysics, and we are all more or less metaphysicians. As Gilson says, "By his very nature, man is a metaphysical animal." The word "metaphysics" was derived from the fact that Aristotle's writings on what he called "First Philosophy," in which he considered the generic traits manifested by existence of any kind, were placed by his earliest editor after the books on physics. Probably Aristotle had never heard the word "metaphysics," which was for many centuries connected with his name. This word, in the meantime, has acquired a variety of meanings. Sometimes it has stood for the study of some hidden reality beyond all possible experience, and therefore not empirically verifiable; sometimes it has stood for knowledge of the first causes of what is given in sensible experience; sometimes it has stood for the search for the "Real" or the "Whole"; and sometimes it has stood for the inquiry into the generic traits of existence as such.

And yet there is a common core to all these meanings of the term which may be focused on without involving one in the intricate disputes over the definition of the term. What is common to all metaphysical pursuits is the desire to arrive at a generalized understanding of existence. Given this aim, we are concerned with the generic traits of limited phases of existence—such as matter, life, mind, society—and also with their relational context—such as space, time, causality, teleology—and it is through a knowledge of these that we expect to arrive at a synthetic map of existence. There is nothing trivial about this aim however much one might object to the traditional findings. And the aim is inescapable; the most anti-metaphysical philosophers have their implicit metaphysics. Should one wish to discard the term because of its unsatisfactory traditional associations, one is privileged to substitute some other expression, such as speculative philosophy, or philosophy of existence, or philosophy of nature.

Metaphysics as a generalized view of existence has a vital bearing on other phases of human activity. As an attempt to get an over-all knowledge of existence, it is akin to the investigations of the scientist; as a search for the final source of power in existence, it is akin to religion; as a pursuit that deals with such themes as eternity and transiency, which involve the deepest human feelings, it is akin to art; as an attempt to discern man's place in the universe and thus provide a background that may help one to conduct his life, it is pertinent to morals.

Though related to other human activities metaphysics has its own distinctive aim. Because this aim is difficult, one can expect only a tentative and growing achievement. Throughout the centuries some of the great minds have grappled with metaphysical problems. Plato's integration of the whole of knowledge in the Idea of the Good, Aristotle's sober reflections on "the first principles and causes" of existence, Plotinus's vision of "the One" as the source of all creation and being, Lucretius's praise of matter in his famous poem "Concerning the Nature of Things," St. Thomas Aquinas's synthetic metaphysics with its First Cause and the grades of being—these are among the notable metaphysical achievements of antiquity and the Middle Ages. Coming to the early modern period, one thinks of Spinoza's majestic concept of the infinite substance and of Leibniz's fascinating monadology.

The nineteenth century also had its full share of metaphysical theories. Bold attempts were made to break through the phenomenal world to which Kant had confined human knowledge and thus in effect annulled the possibility of metaphysics. Schopenhauer tried to break through the phenomenal world with his Will; Fichte with his Ego; and, above all, Hegel with his rational Absolute. Hegel's famous pronouncement that "what is real is rational" and that "what is rational is real" was supposed to be the golden key to a complete and final metaphysics. In the latter part of the nineteenth century Hegel's influence was very great; the Hegelians dominated the philosophic scene with their idealistic metaphysics. At the turn of the century there was profound dissatisfaction with such sweeping idealistic systems. Realism and pragmatism and later the analytic school and logical positivism challenged the supremacy of idealism. Idealistic metaphysics was considered to be intellectually questionable, and the criticism of idealistic metaphysics led to the criticism of metaphysics itself. Not that criticism of metaphysics was something new—Kant, and before him Hume, had challenged the possibility of metaphysics—but the attacks became more widespread and persistent.

II

Some criticized metaphysics primarily on psychological grounds. It was considered an idealized, illusory expression of human wishes and prejudices, akin to art, if you like, but having no epistemic value. This kind of criticism was given even greater impetus with the development of the Freudian, behavioristic, and functional psychologies. For the Freudians, reason when employed in areas like religion and metaphysics was identified with rationalization, and rationalization was the unwitting mendacity of unconscious desires. For the behaviorists and functionalists, religious and metaphysical pursuits were modes of compensatory adjustment to a difficult and alien environment.

Others criticized metaphysics on the principle of the relativity of cultural and social patterns. From this perspective one's world view was considered merely an expression of the desire to unify cultural tensions and demands. Different cultures had to have different world views. The objectivity of metaphysical claims was denied. The Marxian view of social development in terms of economic demands and the new growth of anthropology and sociology gave additional force to these arguments.

Still others attacked metaphysics on pragmatic grounds. Pragmatism, especially in America, wished to apply philosophy to practical, social issues. The metaphysical preoccupation with "Reality" and "the Whole" was regarded as utterly fruitless.

But the most violent and uncompromising attack on metaphysics was pressed by the analysts and logical positivists, powerful schools of thought in Britain and America during the second quarter of this century. For these schools, the function of philosophy was primarily, if not solely, to clarify common-sense ideas and scientific concepts. The pursuit of metaphysics, with its frequent claim of super-empirical knowledge, was regarded as not only wasteful but basically meaningless.

These and similar objections to metaphysics and the counterclaims of metaphysicians to these objections form a large bulk of contemporary philosophic literature.

III

Yet despite these critical claims the metaphysical drive has not been stopped. Indeed, we have recently witnessed a metaphysical renaissance. It is hardly possible to give briefly a clear and precise account of the fundamental trends in contemporary metaphysics. They are many and the interrelations are complex, and we are too much in the swim of events to be able to give an adequate description. It will be feasible to describe only certain of the major trends, and only those, moreover, whose more precise formulation is rather recent. One must not get the impression, however, that the traditional forms of metaphysics, like the idealistic and the Thomistic, are not alive or influential at present, but since their classic formulation was given in the past, they need not be described afresh. What, then, are some of the recent distinctive trends in metaphysics?

One of these is the trend toward an empirical metaphysics. Some of the greatest metaphysical systems of the past were developed in a purely deductive way. Starting from certain allegedly self-evident premises, the philosophers in question built what they considered strictly rationalistic systems. Spinoza and Hegel are examples from the past, and McTaggart from the recent past. The strictly deductive claim is not wholly convincing. Even the most rationalistic philosophers were not devoid of empiricism; they were anchored in some aspect of experience. But be this as it may, the modern temper is explicitly, insistently empirical. There is hardly a place for a purely rationalistic metaphysics at present. Idealists, as well as naturalists and existentialists, claim to be empiricists. We are all in some sense empiricists.

Yet the notion of empiricism is ambiguous and the different meanings given to this term have different philosophic consequences. For some, empiricism means that only concrete personal experience can be accepted as reality. This view has usually led to subjective idealism. For others, empiricism stands for the Humean "impressions," or sense-experience. Usually phenomenalists have given such an interpretation to empiricism. And for still others, empiricism means experimentalism. The traditional usages of the term are not considered to be sufficiently responsible in spirit nor fruitful in consequence. The more recent usage identifies empiricism with objectively and socially verifiable claims. On the whole, naturalists and logical empiricists emphasize this meaning of empiricism.

Empiricism, especially as experimentalism, does not deny the significance of and the necessity for reason or concepts. Without concepts one could not formulate hypotheses or theories. And yet concepts, to have empirical meaning, must at some point be relevant to sense-experience and be confirmable through sense-experience.

Another recent contemporary trend in metaphysics exhibits the naturalistic temper. In modern times the desire to give a naturalistic account of all phases of experience has been greatly strengthened by the growth of the sciences and by the consequent growth of a technological and industrial civilization. Naturalism has become, in one form or other, a widely held view in many circles, especially in the universities. For many it is the philosophy that is most pertinent to modern life. The early philosophical formulations of this outlook were elaborated by George Santayana, Samuel Alexander, John Dewey, F. J. E. Woodbridge, Roy Wood Sellars, Morris R. Cohen, and others.

The naturalists insist that all phases of our experience should be explained by use of the empirical method. One does not achieve philosophic knowledge through some special mode of mental action, such as the intuitive or the purely rationalistic, but through critical reflection akin to our daily thinking and the empirical and rational procedures of the sciences. There exists no specially privileged domain immune to empirical inquiry. Matter, life, mind, history, and deity are all amenable to such a method.

Yet naturalism is not merely a doctrine of method, but a generalized outlook on existence. Naturalism as a world-outlook is opposed to supernaturalism. It regards nature as a self-contained system and as the whole of reality, a system operating according to its own laws without extranatural intrusions. In this conception of nature one assumes, as Ernest Nagel expresses it, that the occurrence of events is "contingent on the organization of spatio-temporally located bodies." Thus in naturalism there is no place for the Bergsonian élan vital or for disembodied spirits directing the course of events.

Naturalism also insists that qualities and values are irreducible aspects of existence. It is true that these aspects have developed from physical conditions, yet they are not mere illusions but are as much part of the natural world as the physical or chemical conditions. Yet one must not infer from this statement that values, like good and evil and purposive design, are applicable to the cosmos as a whole, as many traditional philosophies have argued.

The naturalistic temper has its strong critics in contemporary thought. Many have accused naturalism of being the destroyer of values, especially of moral and religious values. Values, it is claimed, have no basis for our loyalty apart from some supernatural ground. The naturalists, on the other hand, find the natural world and its possibilities a sufficient ground for these values, and the natural means of intelligence and human morality an adequate one for dealing with life.

Another contemporay metaphysical trend is the emphasis on change, process, events. This emphasis has been developed into what might be called process philosophy, which is a wide philosophic movement with varied formulations. In many respects the concern with process is the most distinctive trait of recent philosophy. The transitoriness of everyday events, the new theories of matter and astronomical evolution, the recent experimental work on growth in biology and psychology, and the new pace of technological, business, and political activities—all these emphasize change.

The notion of change or process is, of course, not a new concept in human thought. In the ancient past, Buddha and Heraclitus declared that everything is in flux and perishing. In the seventeenth and eighteenth century, Leibniz and Condorcet introduced the modern notion of progress. And in the nineteenth century, the Darwinian theory of evolution and the Hegelian and Marxian theories of historical dialectic gave dramatic emphasis to the idea of change. Yet the notion of process was never used in philosophy as widely and fruitfully as by such moderns as Bergson, Alexander, Whitehead, Dewey, and Mead, to mention only a few of the process philosophers. The most vigorous development of this philosophy has been in this country. The two great books of recent American philosophy —Dewey's EXPERIENCE AND NATURE, and Whitehead's PROCESS AND REALITY —expound the philosophy of process.

Process philosophy is so broad and varied that all process philosophers can scarcely be said to belong to the same school, yet they do have certain common traits.

First of all, process philosophy asserts the universality and ultimacy of change. For Whitehead becoming is a more basic concept than being. The actual world is process, it is "always becoming and as it becomes it passes and perishes." Creativity is his key concept. Creativity holds for every phase of existence, even God is in the grip of creative novelty. Dewey's philosophy is equally important in this connection; he is as emphatic as Whitehead on the notion of change. "Every existence is an event."

For most members of this movement process is of one piece. There are no gaps, no dualisms, no hidden caves or privacy in nature. Dewey strongly emphasizes this point. Nature thus conceived makes possible a new approach to the age-old problem of the relation between body and mind. The difference between the two does not lie in substance, as traditionally maintained, but in process, function, behavior. Nature is continuous throughout. Whitehead emphasizes the notion of continuity even more daringly and imaginatively. An actual entity, the ultimate for him, is a process and not describable as a "stuff"; it is a pulse of experience, a miniature, if you like, of human experience.

Yet the process of which they speak is not mere change: it is incremental. Change is not necessarily purposive; yet there is a cumulative, creative drift to events. Nature preserves the old as it adds the new, the unpredictable. The contrast here with Thomistic philosophy is striking. Thomism has rigid levels of being and an unchanging perfect God; process philosophy has novelty and emergent evolution, nature developing by itself. Alexander, Sellars, and Lovejoy were among the early emergent evolutionists in contemporary thought. Even if some process philosophers entertain the notion of God, he is not omnipotent nor the creator of the world, but the lure of ideal possibilities. Process philosophy is a philosophy of progress. Even if progress should not be inevitable, yet it is possible. As Bergson, one of the early prophets of this philosophy, expresses it, "Before the evolution of life the portals of the future remain wide open."

Process philosophy is the metaphysics of many contemporary philosophers. We have mentioned some of the leading names; many others could be mentioned who are in this current. As to what more specific form this philosophy will take, this too is in process.

Still another trend in contemporary metaphysics is that of irrationalism. In their attempt to build a metaphysical system many philosophers have been critical of the scope of reason. In the past, metaphysicians have usually been rationalists, with only a few exceptions; but today there are vigorous philosophical schools that insist on the basic limitations of reason in dealing with metaphysics. This disparagement of reason has taken different forms.

Santayana, who can hardly be called an irrationalist and whose praise of the life of reason is still one of his major contributions, insists, in his later writings, on the incapacity of reason to apprehend reality. Like Kant, he places faith above knowledge, but, unlike Kant, he substitutes for the latter's religious faith what he calls animal faith. Santayana is a metaphysician, though he regards metaphysics as a poetic myth.

Bergson, an avowed metaphysician, is more radical in his rejection of reason and concepts. "Metaphysics," he writes, "is the science which claims to dispense with symbols." Metaphysics, for him, rests upon intuition and not upon conceptual analysis. And intuition, unlike intellect, is the apprehension of reality from within and hence as it is in itself and not as seen from without. For this reason Bergson writes his philosophy as a literary artist rather than as a vigorous analyst.

Existentialism similarly disparages reason. Existentialism has been a revolt against all attempts to construct rational systems of thought. Contemporary existentialists claim that it is not reason but the free decision of man's will that determines the purview of reality. This is the key which may open the door to a right insight, or even the chisel that carves out the shape of reality itself. Reality is to be grasped through action; it is the experience undergone in action. For reason, the world is either, as Jasper maintains, a series of ciphers, of mysteries beyond understanding, or, as Sartre maintains, just sheer futility.

One final trend deserves to be mentioned. On the whole, most of the contemporary philosophers, especially the important ones, have regarded their philosophic systems as tentative and provisional. Philosophic constructions are like scientific constructions—inherently incomplete, lacking finality. Peirce had earlier given expression to this spirit in his idea of fallibilism. "Fallibilism," as he writes, "is the doctrine that our knowledge is never absolute but always swims, as it were, in a continuum of uncertainty and indeterminacy." More recently, Edgar A. Singer, Jr., expressed the same attitude: "We formulate in order to revise and when one of us is asked . . . to account for his creed . . . , what is left for him to do . . . but to recall the dissatisfactions that have pushed him on, and are still pushing?"

For this dissatisfaction there are several reasons: the limitation of experience, defect of insight, and the obscurities of language. Recently we have become especially aware of the treacheries involved in language. And, in some cases, as in that of Whitehead, the very nature of a philosophic system may impose the provisional character. If reality is process, and its basic character is creation of novelty, our philosophic formulations are always bound to be incomplete.

Yet despite fallibilism some metaphysical systems are better than others. What, then, are some of the characteristics of a good metaphysics?

The first is consistency. The argument must, so far as can be ascertained, be logically sound. If the parts of a metaphysical system do not hang together it stands self-condemned. But logical consistency is not sufficient. A system may be self-consistent and yet a very bad metaphysics. A metaphysical system is not merely a deductive, logical system; it must have relevancy to existence. Another necessary characteristic is comprehensiveness. One's philosophy should provide an interpertation of every aspect of our complex experience and not of a fragment only. One must do justice to common sense experience, to science, to religion, to art, to morals, to good and to evil, to every phase of existence. Finally, a good metaphysics must be adequate. This characteristic is the most ambiguous, yet the most important criterion. One's metaphysics must make sense to common sense as well as to critical reflection. It is plain that a fully consistent, comprehensive, and adequate philosophy can be no more than a regulative idea. All actual philosophies must be content with an approximation to the ideal.

Despite the intrinsic difficulties of the enterprise, contemporary metaphysics has been a vigorous and many-sided growth. No system has a monopoly; each has added its individual insight. There have been some attempts, of course, to arrive at a final synthesis; but such a synthesis does not seem feasible at present.

IV

In the selections of this part the aim has been to present some of the significant literature in contemporary metaphysics. The first group considers the nature of metaphysics, the various conceptions of its task, and the controversy about its possibility. In the second group, some of the most general traits of being and existence are analyzed. The last group deals with the relations and modes of being; the readings include discussions of causality, teleology, emergence, matter, life, mind, community, history and God. The hierarchy of concepts from matter to God need not lead to the conclusion that there is such a hierarchy in reality, though some may wish to entertain this conclusion; the so-called hierarchy may be considered a useful methodological classification of the different phases of reality.

Metaphysics

F. J. E. Woodbridge

Metaphysics *

. . . "There is," so we are told by the Stagirite, "a science which investigates existence as existence and whatever belongs to existence as such. It is identical with none of the sciences which are defined less generally. For none of these professedly considers existence as existence, but each, restricting itself to some aspect of it, investigates the general aspect only incidentally, as do the mathematical sciences." The emphasis is thus put by Aristotle on fact and on nature, but it is put on fact and nature as we attempt to view them with at once the least and with the greatest restriction: with the least restriction, because we are invited to view nature in the light of her most comprehensive characters; with the greatest restriction, because we are invited to view her stripped of her wonderful diversity.

In thus conceiving a science whose distinguishing mark should be that it applies to all existence, Aristotle noted a fact which the history of intellectual progress has abundantly illustrated, the fact, namely, that knowledge grows in extent and richness only through specialization. Nature herself is a specialized matter. She does things by producing differences, individuals, variations. To grasp this variety, a variety of sciences is necessary. Indeed, as Aristotle estimates the achievements of his predecessors, he finds the source of their confusion, inadequacy, and limitation to lie in their habit of regarding each his own special science as a sufficient account of the cosmos. What they said may have been true under the restrictions which their limited field imposed upon their utterance; but it became false when it was transferred to other fields differently limited. Following his own illustrations we may say, for instance, that the Pythagoreans were quite right in trying to formulate the undoubted numerical relations which obtain in nature; but they were quite wrong if they conceived arithmetic to be an

* From *Nature and Mind* by F. J. E. Woodbridge, pp. 96–108. Copyright 1937 by Columbia University Press. Reprinted by permission of the publishers.

adequate astronomy. The soul may be a harmony of the body and thus capable of numerical expression, but to think one has exhausted its nature by defining it as a moving number is to forget the natural limitations of inquiry and to make a rhetorical phrase the substitute for scientific insight. We may properly speak of a sick soul as out of tune, but we should not thereby become either psychologists or physicians. No; knowledge is a matter of special sciences, each growing sanely as it clearly recognizes the particular and specialized aspect of nature with which it deals, but becoming confused when it forgets that it is one of many. Accordingly what we call the philosophy of Aristotle is not a single science to be described by a picturesque or a provoking name, but a system of sciences the members of which should be related to one another in the way nature rather than desire permits.

If knowledge increases thus through limitation, restriction, and specialization, if science grows through the multiplication of different sciences, must our final view of nature reveal her as a parcelled and disjointed thing? Is the desire to say something about the universe as a whole which may none the less be true of it, is that desire without warrant, something utterly condemned? Not, thought Aristotle, if that desire is checked and controlled by fact. We should indeed err if we thought to attain unity through any artificial combination of special truths, or by attempting so to reduce the diversity of the sciences that their individual differences should disappear. Yet we may approach unity through the same method by which the special sciences gain their individual coherence and stability, that is, by limitation and restriction of field. All things somehow exist; and because they so obviously do, we can never lose sight of the fact that existence itself is a problem irrespective of the fact whether a particular existence is that of a stone, a man, or a god. Particular existences may carry us at last to some exclusive and inalienable core of individuality, hidden somewhere and possibly discoverable, but existence itself is possessed by nothing exclusively. It is rather the common feature of everything that can be investigated, and as such is something to be looked into. Whether such looking is fruitful is a question not to be prejudiced. The fruitfulness of the inquiry depends upon the discovery whether existence as such has anything to reveal. We thus return to Aristotle's conception of a science of existence as existence, a specialized and restricted science, doing its own work and not that of the mathematician or the physicist or the biologist, or of any other investigator, a science which should take its place in that system of sciences the aim of which is to reveal to us with growing clearness the world in which we live. It was that science which Andronicus of Rhodes called "Metaphysics," baptizing it in the name of ambiguity, confusion, and idiosyncrasy.

For me it would be a congenial task to devote the remainder of this lecture to a detailed exposition of the metaphysics of Aristotle. It would be the more congenial, since the lecturer on history, by making the ancients our contemporaries, has saved enthusiasm for the Stagirite from being condemned as a mere anachronism. To call Aristotle, as Dante is supposed to have done, the master of them that know, even if they know no less than others, is still a privilege in the twentieth century. And this privilege is the one *ad hominem* argument in justification of the study of metaphysics which I would venture to suggest to an audience already made somewhat familiar with the inadequacies and limitations of human knowledge. As the congenial, however, may not be the appropriate, I proceed to sketch the general bearings of metaphysics, pointing out how, beginning with analysis and description, it tends to become speculative, and to construct systems of metaphysics which aim at complete conceptions of the universe and have a certain relevancy to science, morals, and religion. Then I will indicate how metaphysics, influenced by modern idealistic speculation, became arrogant as a theory of knowledge, and how there are present signs of its return to its ancient place as a science co-ordinated with the rest of knowledge. In concluding, I will consider how, with this return, it finds a new interest in the interpretation of the process of evolution.

Either because Aristotle developed his science of existence with so much skill or because the science is to be reckoned, as he reckoned it, among those intellectual performances which are excellent, its unfortunate name has never completely obscured its professed aims and restrictions. Too often, indeed, metaphysics has been made the refuge of ignorance, and inquirers in other fields have been too ready to bestow upon it their own unsolved problems and inconsistencies. Many have thus been led to refuse discussion of certain difficulties for the reason that they are metaphysical, a reason which may indicate that one is tired rather than that one is wise. It has even been suggested that so long as problems are unsolved they are metaphysical. Even so, the study, on account of the comprehensiveness thus given to it, might advance itself, imposing and commanding, a guarantor of intellectual modesty. Yet metaphysicians, as a rule, have not regarded their work as that of salvation. They have viewed their problems as the result of reflection rather than of emergency. And their reflection has ever seized upon the fact that nature's great and manifold diversities do, none the less, in spite of that diversity, consent to exist together in some sort of union, and that, consequently, some understanding of that unity is a thing to attempt. Metaphysics, therefore, may still adopt the definition and limitations set for it by Aristotle. We may, indeed, define it in other terms, calling it, for instance, the science of reality, but our altered words still point out that metaphysical interest is in the world as a world of connected things, a world with a general character in addition to those specific characters which give it its variety and make many sciences necessary for its comprehension.

The term "reality," however, is intellectually agile. It tends to play tricks with one's prejudices and to lead desire on a merry chase. For to denominate anything real is usually to import a distinction, and to consign, thereby, something else to the region of appearance. Could we keep the region of appearance from becoming populated, it might remain nothing more than the natural negative implication of a region of positive interest. But reality, once a king, makes many exiles who crave and seek citizenship in the land from which they have been banished. The term "reality," therefore, should inspire caution instead of confidence in metaphysics—a lesson which history has abundantly illustrated, but which man is slow to learn. Contrast those imposing products of human fancy which we call materialism and idealism, each relegating the other to the region of appearance, and what are they at bottom but an exalted prejudice for matter and an exalted prejudice for mind? And had not their conflict been spectacular, as armies with banners, what a pitiable spectacle it would have presented, since a child's first thought destroys the one, and every smallest grain of sand the other? No; everything is somehow real; and to make distinctions within that realm demands caution and hesitation.

Thus it is that the concept of reality has become an important theme in a great part of metaphysical inquiry, and that a keen appreciation of its varieties is essential to the historian of metaphysics. That science has been thought to suffer from a too close scrutiny into the idiosyncrasies of its past; but being somewhat ancient and robust, and, withal, decidedly human, it may consult the reflection that more youthful sciences have not always walked in wisdom's path, and so bear its own exposure with some consequent consolation. Yet what it has to reveal in the light of the shifting concept of reality is significant indeed. For we have come to learn that to call anything real exclusively, is to imply a preference, and that preference is largely a matter of the time in which it is born. It reflects an age, an occasion, a society, a moral, intellectual, or economic condition. It does not reflect an absolute position which knows no wavering. For me, just now, metaphysics is the most real thing imaginable, more real than chemistry or the stock exchange. In displaying some enthusiasm for it, I care not if the elements revert to ether or how the market goes. To be invited just now to consider the periodic law of the latest market quotations would irritate me. An altered situation would find me, doubtless, possessed of an altered preference, indifferent no longer to another science or to the Street. So much does occasion determine preference, and preference reality.

The historical oppositions in metaphysics present themselves, therefore, not as a mass of conflicting and contradictory opinions about the absolutely real, but as a too exclusive championship of what their exponents have believed to be most important for their times. In such metaphysicians the enthusiasm of the prophet has outrun the disinterestedness of the scientist. We may describe them as men of restricted vision, but we may not, therefore, conclude that their vision was not acute. Plato was not an idle dreamer, assigning to unreality the bed on which you sleep in order that he might convince you that the only genuinely real bed is the archetype in the mind of God, the ideal bed of which all others are shadows. Undoubtedly he converses thus about beds in his *Republic,* but he does not advise you, as a consequence, to go to sleep in heaven. He tells you, rather, that justice is a social matter which you can never adequately administer so long as your attention is fixed solely on individual concerns. You must seek to grasp justice as a principle, in the light of which the different parts of the body politic may find their most fruitful interplay and co-ordination. His metaphysics of the ideal was born in Athens' need, but his dialogues remain instructive reading for the modern man. We may confound him by pointing out the obvious fact that men, not principles, make society, and yet accept his teaching that men without principles make a bad society, exalting principles thus to the position of the eminently real.

Similarly, he who reads Fichte's *Science of Knowledge* should not forget that Fichte spoke to the German people, calling them a nation. And the response he met must have seemed, in his eyes, no small justification of his view that reality is essentially a self-imposed moral task. And Spencer, influenced by social and economic reorganization and consolidation, could force the universe into a formula and think that he had said the final word about reality. Thus any exclusive conception of reality is rendered great, not by its finality for all times, but by its historical appropriateness.

Such questions, therefore, as, What is real? Is there any reality at all? Is not everything illusion, or at least part of everything? and such statements as, Only the good is real, Only matter is real, Only mind is real, Only energy is real, are questions and statements to be asked and made only by persons with a mission. For reality means either everything whatsoever or that a distinction has been made, a distinction which indicates not a difference in the fact of existence, but a difference in point of view, in value, in preference, in relative importance for some desire or choice. Yet it is doubtless the business of metaphysics to undertake an examination and definition of the different points of view from which those questions can be asked and those statements made. Indeed, that undertaking may well be regarded as one of the most important in metaphysics. The outcome of it is not a superficial doctrine of the relativity of the real, with the accompanying advice that each of us select his own reality and act accordingly. Nor is it the doctrine that since nothing or everything is absolutely real, there is no solid basis for conduct and no abiding hope for man. That individualism which is willful and that kind of agnosticism which is not intellectual reserve, but which is intellectual complacency, have no warrant in metaphysics. On the contrary, the doctrine of metaphysics is much more obvious and much more sane. It is that existence, taken comprehensively, is an affair of distinctions; that existence is shot through and through with variety.

But this is not all. Metaphysics discovers in the fact of variety a reason for the world's onward movement. For a world without variety would be a world eternally still, unchanged and unchanging through all the stretches of time. We might endow such a world with unlimited power, capable, if once aroused, of a marvelous reaction; but unless there existed somewhere within it a difference, no tremor of excitement would ever disturb its endless slumber. All the sciences teach this doctrine. Even logic and mathematics, the most static of them all, require variables, if their formulations are to have any significance or application. Knowledge thus reflects the basal structure of things. And in this fact that differences are fundamental in the constitution of our world, we discover the reason why all those systems of metaphysics eventually fail which attempt to reduce all existence to a single type of reality devoid of variety in its internal make-up.

The variety in our world involves a further doctrine. While all varieties as such are equally real, they are not all equally effective. They make different sorts of differences, and introduce, thereby, intensive and qualitative distinctions. The onward movement of the world is thus, not simply successive change, but a genuine development or evolution. It creates a past the contents of which must forever remain what they were, but it proposes a future where variety may still exercise its difference-making function. And that is why we human beings, acting our part in some cosmic comedy or tragedy, may not be indifferent to our performance or to the preferences we exalt. The future makes us all reformers, inviting us to meddle with the world, to use it and change it for our ends. The invitation is genuine and made in good faith, for all man's folly is not yet sufficient to prove it insincere. That is why it has been easy to believe that God once said to man: "Be fruitful and multiply, and replenish the earth, and subdue it; and have dominion over the fish of the sea, and over the fowl of the air, and over every living thing that moveth upon the earth." That is why, also, willful individualism and complacent agnosticism have no warrant in metaphysics. Since all things are equally real, but all not equally important, the world's evolution presents itself as a drift towards results, as something purposeful and intended. While we may not invoke design to explain this relative importance of things, the world's trend puts us under the natural obligation of discovering how it may be controlled, and enforces the obligation with obvious penalties. Thus willfulness receives natural punishment and the universe never accepts ignorance as an excuse.

It seems difficult, therefore, not to describe evolution as a moral process. By that I do not mean that nature is especially careful about the kinds of things she does or that she is true and just in all her dealings. But evolution is movement controlled by the relative importance of things. We consequently find such terms as "struggle," "survival," "adaptation," useful in the description of it. And although these terms may appear more appropriate to the development of living things than to that of inorganic nature, we may not overlook the fact that the physical world also begets varieties and has its character determined by their relative importance.

Thus it is that the metaphysical doctrine of final causes appears to be fundamentally sound. It is easy to render it ridiculous by supposing that things were once made on purpose to exhibit the features and manners of action which we now discover in them, or by conceiving adaptation as an efficient cause of events, as if the fact that we see were the reason why we have eyes. So conceived the doctrine of final causes is justly condemned. On the other hand, however, how superficial is the opinion that in nature there is entire indifference to results, and that there are no natural goods! Today is not simply yesterday rearranged or twenty-four hours added to a capricious time; it is yesterday reorganized, with yesterday's results carried on and intensified. So that we might say that nature, having accidentally discovered that the distinction between light and darkness is a natural good, stuck to the business of making eyes. We should thus express a natural truth, but should not thereby free ourselves from the obligation of discovering how nature had achieved so noteworthy a result. That obligation the doctrine of final causes most evidently does not discharge, because final causes have never been found adequate to reveal the method of nature's working. Again and again, some investigator, impressed by the undoubted fact of nature's continuity, by her carefulness of the type, by her preservation of forms, by that character of hers which we can properly describe only by calling it preferential or moral, impressed by these things he has attempted to turn them into efficient causes, factors operative in the mechanism of the world. And he has repeatedly failed. It is, consequently, not prejudice which leads many students of nature's processes to insist that these are ultimately what we call mechanical. It is metaphysical insight. Yet that insight may readily degenerate into the most superficial philosophy, if it leads us to forget that mechanism is the means by which the ends of nature are reached. For nature undoubtedly exists for what she accomplishes, and it is that fact which gives to mechanism its relevancy, its importance, and its high value. Thus metaphysics, true to its early formulations, finds the world to be both mechanical and teleological, both a quantitative relation of parts and a qualitative realization of goods. Some indication that this finding is correct may be discovered in our instinctive recognition that nature is appropriately described both in the formulations of science and in the expressions of poetry.

Metaphysical analysis tends thus to disclose existence as a process motivated by the variety of its factors, as an evolution characterized, not by indifference, but by selection based on the relative importance of its factors for the maintenance of natural goods, as a development executed through an elaborate mechanism. It is natural that metaphysics should become speculative and attempt the construction of a system of things wherein its obvious disclosures may be envisaged with coherence and simplicity, and thus be rationally comprehended and explained. It is in such attempts that metaphysics has historically scored its greatest successes and its greatest failures. The lesson to be derived from a survey of them is, doubtless, one of grave caution, but it would be idle to affirm that we have seen the last of great systems of metaphysics. Democritus, Plato, Aristotle, Bruno, Descartes, Hobbes, Spinoza, Newton, Leibniz, Berkeley, Kant, Laplace, Hegel, Spencer—to mention only the greatest names—each has had his system of the world which still has power to affect the thought and lives of men. System is beloved of man's imagination and his mind is restless in the presence of unconnected and unsupported details. He will see things *sub specie æternitatis* even while time counts out his sands of life. It is a habit begotten of nature, to be neither justified nor condemned. It would be absurd consequently, to regard any system of metaphysics as absolutely true, but it would be more absurd to refuse to make one on that account. For such systems constitute the supreme attempts of intelligence at integration. They propose to tell us what our world would be like if our present restricted knowledge were adequate for its complete exposition. They are not, therefore, to be abandoned because they are always inadequate, incomplete, and provisional; they are rather to be pursued, because, when constructed by the wise, they are always ennobling and minister faithfully to the freedom of the mind.

Protests against metaphysical systems are, consequently, apt to be proofs of an impatient temper rather than of sound judgment. Yet such systems often grow arrogant, and become, thereby, objects of justified suspicion. Being the crowning enterprise of intelligence, to be worn, one might say, as an indication of a certain nobility of mind, they forfeit the claim to be thus highly regarded if they are made the essential preliminaries of wisdom. Yet the too eager and the too stupid have often claimed that the only possible foundation for the truth and value of science, and the only possible warrant for morality and human aspiration, are to be found in a system of metaphysics. If such a claim meant only that with a perfect system, could we attain it, would riddles all be solved and life's darkness made supremely clear, it would express an obvious truth. But made with the intent of laying metaphysics down as the foundation of science, of morality, and of religion, it is obviously false and iniquitous. In our enthusiasm we may indeed speak of metaphysics as the queen of all the sciences, but she can wear the title only if her behavior is queenly; she forfeits it when, ceasing to reign, she stoops to rule.

Yet there is justice in the notion that metaphysics, especially in its systematic shape, should contribute to the value of science, and be a source of moral and religious enlightenment. Its greatest ally is logic. In the systematic attempt to reduce to order the business of getting and evaluating knowledge, in distinguishing fruitful from fruitless methods, and, above all, in attempting to disclose the sort of conquest knowledge makes over the world, the aims and achievements of science should become better appreciated and understood. It is still true, as Heraclitus of old remarked, that much information does not make a man wise, but wisdom is intelligent understanding.

The disclosures of metaphysics are equally significant for ethics. The great systems have usually eventuated in a theory of morals. And this is natural. Metaphysics, disclosing the fact that behavior is a primary feature of things, raises inevitably the question of how to behave effectively and well. Emphasizing the relative importance of the factors of evolution, it encourages the repeated valuation of human goods. It can make no man moral, nor give him a rule to guide him infallibly in his choices and acts;

but it can impress upon him the fact that he is under a supreme obligation, that of living a life controlled, not by passion, but by reason, and of making his knowledge contribute to the well-being of society. It will still preach its ancient moral lesson, that, since with intelligence has arisen some comprehension of the world, the world is best improved, not by passion or by parties, not by governments or by sects, but by the persistent operation of intelligence itself.

After a somewhat similar manner, metaphysics in its systematic character has significance for theology. To speak of existence as a riddle is natural, because so much of its import can be only guessed. That it has import most men suspect, and that this import is due to superior beings or powers is the conviction of those who are religious. Metaphysics is seldom indifferent to such suspicions and convictions. As it has a lively sense of the unity of things, it is led to seek ultimate reasons for the world's stability. And as it deals with such conceptions as "the infinite" and "the absolute," it has a certain linguistic sympathy with faith. Consequently, while it has never made a religion, it has been used as an apology for many. This fact witnesses, no doubt, more profoundly to the adaptability of metaphysics than it does to the finality of the ideas it has been used to sustain. Yet metaphysics, tending to keep men ever close to the sources of life, fosters a whole-hearted acceptance of life's responsibilities and duties. It is thus the friend of natural piety. And in superimposing upon piety systematic reflection on what we call the divine, it follows a natural instinct, and seeks to round out man's conception of the universe as the source of his being, the place of his sojourning, the begettor of his impulses and his hopes, and the final treasury of what he has been and accomplished.

Such, then, are the general nature and scope of metaphysical inquiry. With Aristotle we may define metaphysics as the science of existence and distinguish it from other departments of knowledge by its generality and its lack of attention to those specific features of existence which make many sciences an intellectual necessity. Existence, considered generally, presents itself as an affair of connected varieties and, consequently, as an onward movement. Because the varieties have not all the same efficacy, the movement presents those selective and moral characters which we ascribe to a development or evolution. While the efficient causes of this evolution appear to be mechanical, the mechanism results in the production of natural goods, and thus justifies a doctrine of final causes. Upon such considerations metaphysics may superimpose speculative reflection, and attempt to attain a unified system of the world. It may also attempt to evaluate science in terms of logical theory, to enlarge morality through a theory of ethics, and to interpret natural piety and religion in terms of theological conceptions. Metaphysics proposes thus both an analysis and a theory of existence; it is descriptive and it is systematic. If metaphysicians often forget that theory is not analysis, that system is not description, it is not because they are metaphysicians, but because they are human. For my part, therefore, I do not see why they should not be allowed to entertain at least as many absurdities as the average reflective inquirer. Greater indulgence is neither desired nor necessary. And while metaphysicians may be hard to understand, they do not like to be misunderstood. So I emphasize again the fact that it appears to be the greatest abuse of metaphysical theories to use them to justify natural excellence or to condone natural folly. It is their business to help clarify existence. It is not their business to constitute an apology for our prejudices or for our desires.

Etienne Gilson

The Nature and Unity of Philosophical Experience *

By his very nature, man is a metaphysical animal. . . . Since man is essentially rational, the constant recurrence of metaphysics in the history of human knowledge must have its explanation in the very structure of reason itself. In other words, the reason why man is a metaphysical animal must lie somewhere in the nature of rationality. Many centuries before Kant, philosophers had stressed the fact that there is more in rational knowledge than we find in sensible experience. The typical attributes of scientific knowledge, that is universality and necessity, are not to be found in sensible reality, and one of the most generally received explanations is that they come to us from our very power of knowing. As Leibniz says, there is nothing in the intellect that has not first been in sense, except the intellect itself. As Kant was the first both to distrust metaphysics and to hold it to be unavoidable, so was he also the first to give a name to human reason's remarkable power to overstep all sensible experience. He called it the *transcendent* use of reason and denounced it as the permanent source of our metaphysical illusions. Let us retain the term suggested by Kant; it will then follow that whether such knowledge be illusory or not, there is, in human reason, a natural aptness, and consequently a natural urge, to transcend the limits of experience and to form transcendental notions by which the unity of knowledge may be completed. These are metaphysical notions, and the highest of them all is that of the cause of all causes, or first cause, whose discovery has been for centuries the ambition of the metaphysicians. . . . *Metaphysics is the knowledge gathered by a naturally transcendent reason in its search for the first principles, or first causes, of what is given in sensible experience.*

This is, in fact, what metaphysics is, but what about its validity? The Kantian conclusion that metaphysical knowledge is illusory by its own

* From *The Unity of Philosophical Experience* by Etienne Gilson, pp. 307–316.

nature was not a spontaneous offspring of human reason. If metaphysical speculation is a shooting at the moon, philosophers have always begun by shooting at it; only after missing it have they said that there was no moon, and that it was a waste of time to shoot at it. Scepticism is defeatism in philosophy, and all defeatisms are born of previous defeats. When one has repeatedly failed in a certain undertaking, one naturally concludes that it was an impossible undertaking. I say naturally, but not logically, for a repeated failure in dealing with a given problem may point to a repeated error in discussing the problem rather than to its intrinsic insolubility.

The question then arises: should the repeated failures of metaphysics be ascribed to metaphysics itself, or to metaphysicians? It is a legitimate question, and one that can be answered in the light of philosophical experience. For indeed that experience itself exhibits a remarkable unity. If our previous analyses are correct, they all point to the same conclusion, that metaphysical adventures are doomed to fail when their authors substitute the fundamental concepts of any particular science for those of metaphysics. Theology, logic, physics, biology, psychology, sociology, economics, are fully competent to solve their own problems by their own methods; on the other hand, however, and this must be our . . . conclusion: *as metaphysics aims at transcending all particular knowledge, no particular science is competent either to solve metaphysical problems, or to judge their metaphysical solutions.*

Of course, Kant would object that, so far, his own condemnation of metaphysics still holds good, for he never said that metaphysical problems could be solved in that way; he merely said that they could not be solved at all. True, but it is also true that his condemnation of metaphysics was not the consequence of any personal attempt to reach the foundations of metaphysical knowledge. Kant busied himself with questions about metaphysics, but he had no metaphysical interests of his own. Even during the first part of his career there was always some book between this professor and reality. To him, nature was in the books of Newton, and metaphysics in the books of Wolff. Anybody could read it there; Kant himself had read it, and it boiled down to this, that there are three metaphysical principles or transcendental ideas of pure reason: an immortal soul to unify psychology; freedom to unify the laws of cosmology; and God to unify natural theology. Such, to Kant, was metaphysics; a second-hand knowledge, for which he was no more personally responsible than for the physics of Newton. Before allowing Kant to frighten us away from metaphysics, we should remember that what he knew about it was mere hearsay.

In fact, what Kant considered as the three principles of metaphysics were not principles, but conclusions. The real principles of metaphysics are the first notions through which all the subsequent metaphysical knowledge has to be gathered. What these first notions are cannot be known unless we begin by bringing forth some metaphysical knowledge; then we can see how it is made and, lastly, we can form an estimate of its value. Now our analysis of the concrete working of various metaphysical minds clearly suggests that the principles of metaphysics are very different from the three transcendental ideas of Kant. The average metaphysician usually overlooks them because, though he aims at the discovery of the ultimate ground of reality as a whole, he attempts to explain the whole by one of its parts. Then he fails and he ascribes his failure to metaphysics, little aware of the fact that now is the proper time for him to metaphysicize, for the most superficial reflection on his failure would take him to the very root of metaphysics.

When Thales said, six centuries before Christ, that everything is water, though he certainly did not prove his thesis, he at least made it clear that reason is naturally able to conceive all that is as being basically one and the same thing, and that such a unification of reality cannot be achieved by reducing the whole to one of its parts. Instead of drawing that conclusion, the successors of Thales inferred from his failure that he had singled out the wrong part. Thus Anaximenes said that it was not water, but air. It still did not work. Then Heraclitus said it was fire, and as there were always objections, the Hegel of the time appeared, who said that the common stuff of all things was the *indeterminate,* that is, the initial fusion of all the contraries from which all the rest had been evolved. Anaximander thus completed the first philosophical cycle recorded by the history of Western culture. The description of the later cycles could not take us further, for it is already clear, from a mere inspection of the first, that the human mind must be possessed of a natural aptitude to conceive all things as the same, but always fails in its endeavor to conceive all things as being the same as one of them. In short, *the failures of the metaphysicians flew from their unguarded use of a principle of unity present in the human mind.*

This new conclusion brings us face to face with the last and truly crucial problem: what is it which the mind is bound to conceive both as belonging to all things and as not belonging to any two things in the same way? Such is the riddle which every man is asked to read on the threshold of metaphysics. It is an easy one, as, after all, was that of the Sphinx; yet many a good man has failed to say the word, and the path to the metaphysical Sphinx is strewn with the corpses of philosophers. The word is—Being. Our mind is so made that it cannot formulate a single proposition without relating it to some being. Absolute nothingness is strictly unthinkable, for we cannot even deny an existence unless we first posit it in the mind as something to be denied. "If any man," says J. Edwards, "thinks that he can conceive well enough how there should be nothing, I will engage, that what he means by nothing, is as much something, as anything that he ever thought of in his life." This, I think, is true. But if it is true that human thought is always about being; that each and every aspect of reality, or even of unreality, is necessarily conceived as being, or defined in reference to being, it follows that the understanding of being is the first to be attained, the last into which all knowledge is ultimately resolved and the only one to be included in all our apprehensions. What is first, last and always in human knowledge is its first principle, and its constant point of reference. Now if metaphysics is knowledge dealing with the first principles and the first causes themselves, we can safely conclude that *since being is the first principle of all human knowledge, it is a fortiori the first principle of metaphysics.*

The classical objection to this statement is that, from such a vague idea as that of being, no distinct knowledge can be deduced. This is true, but it is not an objection. To describe being as the "principle of knowledge," does not mean that all subsequent knowledge can be analytically deduced from it, but rather that being is the first knowledge through which all subsequent knowledge can be progressively acquired. As soon as it comes into touch with sensible experience the human intellect elicits the immediate intuition of being: X is, or exists; but from the intuition *that* something is, the knowledge of *what* it is, beyond the fact that it is something, cannot possibly be deduced, nor is it the task of the intellect to deduce it. The intellect does not deduce, it intuits, it sees, and, in the light of intellectual intuition, the discursive power of reason slowly builds up from experience a determinate knowledge of concrete reality. Thus, in the light of immediate evidence, the intellect sees that something is, or exists; that what exists is that which it is; that that which is, or exists, cannot be and not be at one and the same time; that a thing either is, or it is not, and no third supposition is conceivable; last, but not least, that being only comes from being, which is the very root of the notion of causality. Reason has not to prove any one of these principles, otherwise they would not be principles, but conclusions; but it is by them that reason proves all the rest. Patiently weaving the threads of concrete knowledge, reason adds to the intellectual evidence of being and of its properties the science of *what* it is. The first principle brings with it, therefore, both the certitude that metaphysics is the science of being as being, and the abstract laws according to which that science has to be constructed. Yet the principle of a certain knowledge is not that knowledge; and the first principle of human knowledge does not bring us a ready-made science of metaphysics, but its principle and its object.

The twofold character of the intellectual intuition of being, to be given in any sensible experience, and yet to transcend all particular experience, is both the origin of metaphysics and the permanent occasion of its failures. If being is included in all my representations, no analysis of reality will ever be complete unless it culminates in a science of being, that is in metaphysics. On the other hand, the same transcendency which makes the first principle applicable to all experience entails at least the possibility of overstepping the limits by which concrete and particular existences are distinguished. This indeed is more than an abstract possibility, it is a temptation, precisely because it is true that the notion of Being applies to all real or possible experience. Yet, if it is also true that everything is what it is, and nothing else, existence belongs to each and every thing in a truly unique manner, as its own existence, which can be shared in by nothing else. Such is the first principle, both universally applicable, and never applicable twice in the same way. When philosophers fail to perceive either its presence or its true nature, their initial error will pervade the whole science of being, and bring about the ruin of philosophy.

When, owing to some fundamental scientific discovery, a metaphysically minded man first grasps the true nature of a whole order of reality, what he is thus grasping for the first time is but a particular determination of being at large. Yet the intuition of being is always there, and if our philosopher fails to discern its meaning, he will fall a victim to its contagious influence. That which is but a particular determination of being, or *a* being, will be invested with the universality of being itself. In other words, a particular essence will be credited with the universality of being, and allowed to exclude all the other aspects of reality. This is precisely what happened to Abailard, to Ockham, to Descartes, to Kant and to Comte. They were truly labouring under a transcendental delusion; Kant himself knew it, but he was wrong in thinking that such an illusion was unavoidable, for it can be avoided; and he was still more wrong in viewing that illusion as the source of metaphysics, for it is not its source but the cause of its destruction; and not only of the destruction of metaphysics, but, for the same reason and at the same time, of the ruin of the very science which has thus been unduly generalized. If every order of reality is defined by its own essence, and every individual is possessed of its own existence, to encompass the universality of being within the essence of this or that being is to destroy the very object of metaphysics; but to ascribe to the essence of this or that being the universality of being itself, is to stretch a particular science beyond its natural limits and to make it a caricature of metaphysics. In short, and this will be our last conclusion: *all the failures of metaphysics should be traced to the fact, that the first principle of human knowledge has been either overlooked or misused by the metaphysician.*

A. J. Ayer

The Elimination of Metaphysics *

The traditional disputes of philosophers are, for the most part, as unwarranted as they are unfruitful. The surest way to end them is to establish beyond question what should be the purpose and method of a philosophical enquiry. And this is by no means so difficult a task as the history of philosophy would lead one to suppose. For if there are any questions which science leaves it to philosophy to answer, a straightforward process of elimination must lead to their discovery.

We may begin by criticising the metaphysical thesis that philosophy affords us knowledge of a reality transcending the world of science and common sense. Later on, when we come to define metaphysics and account for its existence, we shall find that it is possible to be a metaphysician without believing in a transcendent reality; for we shall see that many metaphysical utterances are due to the commission of logical errors, rather than to a conscious desire on the part of their authors to go beyond the limits of experience. But it is convenient for us to take the case of those who believe that it is possible to have knowledge of a transcendent reality as a starting-point for our discussion. The arguments which we use to refute them will subsequently be found to apply to the whole of metaphysics.

One way of attacking a metaphysician who claimed to have knowledge of a reality which transcended the phenomenal world would be to enquire from what premises his propositions were deduced. Must he not begin, as other men do, with the evidence of his senses? And if so, what valid process of reasoning can possibly lead him to the conception of a transcendent reality? Surely from empirical premises nothing whatsoever concerning the properties, or even the existence, of anything super-empirical can legitimately be inferred. But this objection would be met by a denial on the part of the metaphysician that his assertions were ultimately based on the evi-

* From *Language, Truth and Logic* by Alfred Jules Ayer, pp. 33–35, 38–45. Reprinted through permission by Dover Publications, Inc., New York 10, New York ($1.25).

dence of his senses. He would say that he was endowed with a faculty of intellectual intuition which enabled him to know facts that could not be known through sense-experience. And even if it could be shown that he was relying on empirical premises, and that his venture into a non-empirical world was therefore logically unjustified, it would not follow that the assertions which he made concerning this non-empirical world could not be true. For the fact that a conclusion does not follow from its putative premise is not sufficient to show that it is false. Consequently one cannot overthrow a system of transcendent metaphysics merely by criticising the way in which it comes into being. What is required is rather a criticism of the nature of the actual statements which comprise it. And this is the line of argument which we shall, in fact, pursue. For we shall maintain that no statement which refers to a "reality" transcending the limits of all possible sense-experience can possibly have any liberal significance; from which it must follow that the labours of those who have striven to describe such a reality have all been devoted to the production of nonsense.

It may be suggested that this is a proposition which has already been proved by Kant. But although Kant also condemned transcendent metaphysics, he did so on different grounds. For he said that the human understanding was so constituted that it lost itself in contradictions when it ventured out beyond the limits of possible experience and attempted to deal with things in themselves. And thus he made the impossibility of a transcendent metaphysic not, as we do, a matter of logic, but a matter of fact. He asserted, not that our minds could not conceivably have had the power of penetrating beyond the phenomenal world, but merely that they were in fact devoid of it. And this leads the critic to ask how, if it is possible to know only what lies within the bounds of sense-experience, the author can be justified in asserting that real things do exist beyond, and how he can tell what are the boundaries beyond which the human understanding may not venture, unless he succeeds in passing them himself. As Wittgenstein says, "in order to draw a limit to thinking, we should have to think both sides of this limit," [1] a truth to which Bradley gives a special twist in maintaining that the man who is ready to prove that metaphysics is impossible is a brother metaphysician with a rival theory of his own.[2]

Whatever force these objections may have against the Kantian doctrine, they have come none whatsoever against the thesis that I am about to set forth. It cannot here be said that the author is himself overstepping the bar-

[1] *Tractatus Logico-Philosophicus,* Preface.
[2] Bradley, *Appearance and Reality,* 2nd ed., p. 1.

rier he maintains to be impassable. For the fruitlessness of attempting to transcend the limits of possible sense-experience will be deduced, not from a psychological hypothesis concerning the actual constitution of the human mind, but from the rule which determines the literal significance of language. Our charge against the metaphysician is not that he attempts to employ the understanding in a field where it cannot profitably venture, but that he produces sentences which fail to conform to the conditions under which alone a sentence can be literally significant. Nor are we ourselves obliged to talk nonsense in order to show that all sentences of a certain type are necessarily devoid of literal significance. We need only formulate the criterion which enables us to test whether a sentence expresses a genuine proposition about a matter of fact, and then point out that the sentences under consideration fail to satisfy it. And this we shall now proceed to do. We shall first of all formulate the criterion in somewhat vague terms, and then give the explanations which are necessary to render it precise.

The criterion which we use to test the genuineness of apparent statements of fact is the criterion of verifiability. We say that a sentence is factually significant to any given person, if, and only if, he knows how to verify the proposition which it purports to express—that is, if he knows what observations would lead him, under certain conditions, to accept the proposition as being true, or reject it as being false. If, on the other hand, the putative proposition is of such a character that the assumption of its truth, or falsehood, is consistent with any assumption whatsoever concerning the nature of his future experience, then, as far as he is concerned, it is, if not a tautology, a mere pseudo-proposition. The sentence expressing it may be emotionally significant to him; but it is not literally significant. And with regard to questions the procedure is the same. We enquire in every case what observations would lead us to answer the question, one way or the other; and, if none can be discovered, we must conclude that the sentence under consideration does not, as far as we are concerned, express a genuine question, however, strongly its grammatical appearance may suggest that it does. . . .

To make our position clearer, we may formulate it in another way. Let us call a proposition which records an actual or possible observation an experiential proposition. Then we may say that it is the mark of a genuine factual proposition, not that it should be equivalent to an experiential proposition, or any finite number of experiential propositions, but simply that some experiential propositions can be deduced from it in conjunction with certain other premises without being deducible from those other premises alone.*

This criterion seems liberal enough. In contrast to the principle of conclusive verifiability, it clearly does not deny significance to general propositions or to propositions about the past. Let us see what kinds of assertion it rules out.

A good example of the kind of utterance that is condemned by our criterion as being not even false but nonsensical would be the assertion that the world of sense-experience was altogether unreal. It must, of course, be admitted that our senses do sometimes deceive us. We may, as the result of having certain sensations, expect certain other sensations to be obtainable which are, in fact, not obtainable. But, in all such cases, it is further sense-experience that informs us of the mistakes that arise out of sense-experience. We say that the senses sometimes deceive us, just because the expectations to which our sense-experiences give rise do not always accord with what we subsequently experience. That is, we rely on our senses to substantiate or confute the judgements which are based on our sensations. And therefore the fact that our perceptual judgements are sometimes found to be erroneous has not the slightest tendency to show that the world of sense-experience is unreal. And, indeed, it is plain that no conceivable observation, or series of observations, could have any tendency to show that the world revealed to us by sense-experience was unreal. Consequently, anyone who condemns the sensible world as a world of mere appearance, as opposed to reality, is saying something which, according to our criterion of significance, is literally nonsensical.

An example of a controversy which the application of our criterion obliges us to condemn as fictitious is provided by those who dispute concerning the number of substances that there are in the world. For it is admitted both by monists, who maintain that reality is one substance, and by pluralists, who maintain that reality is many, that it is impossible to imagine any empirical situation which would be relevant to the solution of their dispute. But if we are told that no possible observation could give any probability either to the assertion that reality was one substance or to the assertion that it was many, then we must conclude that neither assertion is significant. We shall see later on that there are genuine logical and empirical questions involved in the dispute between monists and pluralists. But the metaphysical question concerning "substance" is ruled out by our criterion as spurious.

* [Ayer sees this as over-simplified, and revised it in the Introduction to the revised edition of the book.—EDITORS]

A similar treatment must be accorded to the controversy between realists and idealists, in its metaphysical aspect. A simple illustration, which I have made use of in a similar argument elsewhere [3] will help to demonstrate this. Let us suppose that a picture is discovered and the suggestion made that it was painted by Goya. There is a definite procedure for dealing with such a question. The experts examine the picture to see in what way it resembles the accredited works of Goya, and to see if it bears any marks which are characteristic of a forgery; they look up contemporary records for evidence of the existence of such a picture, and so on. In the end, they may still disagree, but each one knows what empirical evidence would go to confirm or discredit his opinion. Suppose, now, that these men have studied philosophy, and some of them proceed to maintain that this picture is a set of ideas in the perceiver's mind, or in God's mind, others that it is objectively real. What possible experience could any of them have which would be relevant to the solution of this dispute one way or the other? In the ordinary sense of the term "real," in which it is opposed to "illusory," the reality of the picture is not in doubt. The disputants have satisfied themselves that the picture is real, in this sense, by obtaining a correlated series of sensations of sight and sensations of touch. Is there any similiar process by which they could discover whether the picture was real, in the sense in which the term "real" is opposed to "ideal"? Clearly there is none. But, if that is so, the problem is fictitious according to our criterion. This does not mean that the realist-idealist controversy may be dismissed without further ado. For it can legitimately be regarded as a dispute concerning the analysis of existential propositions, and so as involving a logical problem which, as we shall see, can be definitively solved. What we have just shown is that the question at issue between idealists and realists becomes fictitious when, as is often the case, it is given a metaphysical interpretation.

There is no need for us to give further examples of the operation of our criterion of significance. For our object is merely to show that philosophy, as a genuine branch of knowledge, must be distinguished from metaphysics. We are not now concerned with the historical question how much of what has traditionally passed for philosophy is actually metaphysical. We shall, however, point out later on that the majority of the "great philosophers" of the past were not essentially metaphysicians, and thus reassure those who would otherwise be prevented from adopting our criterion by considerations of piety.

As to the validity of the verification principle, in the form in which we

[3] Vide "Demonstration of the Impossibility of Metaphysics," *Mind,* 1934, p. 339.

have stated it, a demonstration will be given in the course of this book. For it will be shown that all propositions which have factual content are empirical hypotheses; and that the function of an empirical hypothesis is to provide a rule for the anticipation of experience. And this means that every empirical hypothesis must be relevant to some actual, or possible, experience, so that a statement which is not relevant to any experience is not an empirical hypothesis, and accordingly has no factual content. But this is precisely what the principle of verifiability asserts.

It should be mentioned here that the fact that the utterances of the metaphysician are nonsensical does not follow simply from the fact that they are devoid of factual content. It follows from that fact, together with the fact that they are not *a priori* propositions. And in assuming that they are not *a priori* propositions, we are once again anticipating the conclusions of a later chapter in this book. For it will be shown there that *a priori* propositions, which have always been attractive to philosophers on account of their certainty, owe this certainty to the fact that they are tautologies. We may accordingly define a metaphysical sentence as a sentence which purports to express a genuine proposition, but does, in fact, express neither a tautology nor an empirical hypothesis. And as tautologies and empirical hypotheses form the entire class of significant propositions, we are justified in concluding that all metaphysical assertions are nonsensical. Our next task is to show how they come to be made.

The use of the term "substance," to which we have already referred, provides us with a good example of the way in which metaphysics mostly comes to be written. It happens to be the case that we cannot, in our language, refer to the sensible properties of a thing without introducing a word or phrase which appears to stand for the thing itself as opposed to anything which may be said about it. And, as a result of this, those who are infected by the primitive superstition that to every name a single real entity must correspond assume that it is necessary to distinguish logically between the thing itself and any, or all, of its sensible properties. And so they employ the term "substance" to refer to the thing itself. But from the fact that we happen to employ a single word to refer to a thing, and make that word the grammatical subject of the sentences in which we refer to the sensible appearances of the thing, it does not by any means follow that the thing itself is a "simple entity," or that it cannot be defined in terms of the totality of its appearances. It is true that in talking of "its" appearances we appear to distinguish the thing from the appearances, but that is simply an accident of linguistic usage. Logical analysis shows that what makes these "appearances" the "appearances of" the same thing is not their relationship to an entity other than themselves, but their relationship to one another. The metaphysician fails to see this because he is misled by a superficial grammatical feature of his language.

A simpler and clearer instance of the way in which a consideration of grammar leads to metaphysics is the case of the metaphysical concept of Being. The origin of our temptation to raise questions about Being, which no conceivable experience would enable us to answer, lies in the fact that, in our language, sentences which express existential propositions and sentences which express attributive propositions may be of the same grammatical form. For instance, the sentences "Martyrs exist" and "Martyrs suffer" both consist of a noun followed by an intransitive verb, and the fact that they have grammatically the same appearance leads one to assume that they are of the same logical type. It is seen that in the proposition "Martyrs suffer," the members of a certain species are credited with a certain attribute, and it is sometimes assumed that the same thing is true of such a proposition as "Martyrs exist." If this were actually the case, it would indeed, be as legitimate to speculate about the Being of martyrs as it is to speculate about their suffering. But, as Kant pointed out,[4] existence is not an attribute. For, when we ascribe an attribute to a thing, we covertly assert that it exists: so that if existence were itself an attribute, it would follow that all positive existential propositions were tautologies, and all negative existential propositions self-contradictory; and this is not the case.[5] So that those who raise questions about Being which are based on the assumption that existence is an attribute are guilty of following grammar beyond the boundaries of sense.

A similar mistake has been made in connection with such propositions as "Unicorns are fictitious." Here again the fact that there is a superficial grammatical resemblance between the English sentences "Dogs are faithful" and "Unicorns are fictitious," and between the corresponding sentences in other languages, creates the assumption that they are of the same logical type. Dogs must exist in order to have the property of being faithful, and so it is held that unless unicorns in some way existed they could not have the property of being fictitious. But, as it is plainly self-contradictory to say that fictitious objects exist, the device is adopted of saying that they are real in some non-empirical sense—that they have a mode of real being which is different from the mode of being of existent things. But since there is no way of testing whether an object is real in this sense, as there

[4] Vide *The Critique of Pure Reason,* "Transcendental Dialectic," Book II, Chapter iii, section 4.

[5] This argument is well stated by John Wisdom, *Interpretation and Analysis,* pp. 62, 63.

is for testing whether it is real in the ordinary sense, the assertion that fictitious objects have a special non-empirical mode of real being is devoid of all literal significance. It comes to be made as a result of the assumption that being fictitious is an attribute. And this is a fallacy of the same order as the fallacy of supposing that existence is an attribute, and it can be exposed in the same way.

In general, the postulation of real non-existent entities results from the superstition, just now referred to, that, to every word or phrase that can be the grammatical subject of a sentence, there must somewhere be a real entity corresponding. For as there is no place in the empirical world for many of these "entities" a special non-empirical world is invoked to house them. To this error must be attributed, not only the utterances of a Heidegger, who bases his metaphysics on the assumption that "Nothing" is a name which is used to denote something peculiarly mysterious,[6] but also the prevalence of such problems as those concerning the reality of propositions and universals whose senselessness, though less obvious, is no less complete.

These few examples afford a sufficient indication of the way in which most metaphysical assertions come to be formulated. They show how easy it is to write sentences which are literally nonsensical without seeing that they are nonsensical. And thus we see that the view that a number of the traditional "problems of philosophy" are metaphysical, and consequently fictitious, does not involve any incredible assumptions about the psychology of philosophers.

Among those who recognise that if philosophy is to be accounted a genuine branch of knowledge it must be defined in such a way as to distinguish it from metaphysics, it is fashionable to speak of the metaphysician as a kind of misplaced poet. As his statements have no literal meaning, they are not subject to any criteria of truth or falsehood: but they may still serve to express, or arouse, emotion, and thus be subject to ethical or æsthetic standards. And it is suggested that they may have considerable value, as means of moral inspiration, or even as works of art. In this way, an attempt is made to compensate the metaphysician for his extrusion from philosophy.[7]

I am afraid that this compensation is hardly in accordance with his deserts. The view that the metaphysician is to be reckoned among the poets

[6] Vide *Was ist Metaphysik,* by Heidegger: criticised by Rudolf Carnap in his "Überwindung der Metaphysik durch logische Analyse der Sprache," *Erkenntnis,* Vol. II, 1932.

[7] For a discussion of this point, see also C. A. Mace, "Representation and Expression," *Analysis,* Vol. I, No. 3; and "Metaphysics and Emotive Language," *Analysis,* Vol. II, Nos. 1 and 2.

appears to rest on the assumption that both talk nonsense. But this assumption is false. In the vast majority of cases the sentences which are produced by poets do have literal meaning. The difference between the man who uses language scientifically and the man who use it emotively is not that the one produces sentences which are incapable of arousing emotion, and the other sentences which have no sense, but that the one is primarily concerned with the expression of true propositions, the other with the creation of a work of art. Thus, if a work of science contains true and important propositions, its value as a work of science will hardly be diminished by the fact that they are inelegantly expressed. And similarly, a work of art is not necessarily the worse for the fact that all the propositions comprising it are literally false. But to say that many literary works are largely composed of falsehoods, is not to say that they are composed of pseudo-propositions. It is, in fact, very rare for a literary artist to produce sentences which have no literal meaning. And where this does occur, the sentences are carefully chosen for their rhythm and balance. If the author writes nonsense, it is because he considers it most suitable for bringing about the effects for which his writing is designed.

The metaphysician, on the other hand, does not intend to write nonsense. He lapses into it through being deceived by grammar, or through committing errors of reasoning, such as that which leads to the view that the sensible world is unreal. But it is not the mark of a poet simply to make mistakes of this sort. There are some, indeed, who would see in the fact that the metaphysician's utterances are senseless a reason against the view that they have æsthetic value. And, without going so far as this, we may safely say that it does not constitute a reason for it.

It is true, however, that although the greater part of metaphysics is merely the embodiment of humdrum errors, there remain a number of metaphysical passages which are the work of genuine mystical feeling; and they may more plausibly be held to have moral or æsthetic value. But, as far as we are concerned, the distinction between the kind of metaphysics that is produced by a philosopher who has been duped by grammar, and the kind that is produced by a mystic who is trying to express the inexpressible, is of no great importance: what is important to us is to realise that even the utterances of the metaphysician who is attempting to expound a vision are literally senseless; so that henceforth we may pursue our philosophical researches with as little regard for them as for the more inglorious kind of metaphysics which comes from a failure to understand the workings of our language.

H. H. Price

Clarity Is Not Enough *

I think that there is one historical fact upon which we can all agree. In the period between the two wars it came to be very widely accepted, among professional philosophers at any rate, that clarification is the fundamental aim of Philosophy. Philosophy, it was often said, gives us no new knowledge; it only makes clear to us what we know already. The philosopher's task is to analyse the statements of science, of history and of common sense, including of course ethical statements, and I suppose religious statements too, though in practice not much attention was paid to these. The word "analysis," it is true, was sometimes associated with a particular school of philosophers, the so-called Cambridge school. But many Philosophers who did not subscribe to all the tenets and methods of that school would have agreed with this conception of Philosophy. For the purposes of this discussion, then, I propose to use the words "clarification" and "analysis" (both of which are metaphors after all) as if they were synonyms; and I do not think that this will lead to any serious injustice or confusion.

But the statement that Philosophy "makes clear to us what we already know" is itself in need of interpretation. For in one sense of the word "know", what the philosopher had to clarify was not necessarily something known. It need not even be something true; it might just as well be something false. We start, for instance, by asking ourselves what exactly we are knowing when we know that there is a chair in the bedroom which is not at the moment observed by anyone. But it soon occurs to us that it makes no difference whether we do know this or not, or whether there is or is not as a matter of fact an unobserved chair there. What matters is merely what is *meant* by the statement "there is an unobserved chair in the bedroom." It does not matter whether this statement is true or false; whether it is known to be true, or only believed, or merely considered with-

* From *Proceedings of the Aristotelian Society,* Supplementary Volume XIX, 1945, pp. 3–9, 20–30. Reprinted by permission of the Aristotelian Society and the author.

out either belief or disbelief. And a sentence of similar meaning which we are quite sure is false, e.g. "there is an unobserved crocodile on the roof", would do just as well. Thus the knowledge which has to be clarified is not, or not mainly, a knowledge of facts, but a knowledge of the meanings of statements. Similarly, it would be said that the moral philosopher's task is to ask what I *mean* by saying "I ought to keep the promise I have made to Jones"; even though in fact I have made no promise to Jones and know that I have not, or even though, knowing that I have made one, I know also that I ought not to keep it, owing to the demands of some more urgent duty.

Such is the programme of analytic or clarificatory philosophy. A very simple-minded person might feel some surprise at it. Is there any point in asking what such statements mean, since admittedly we already know their meaning to begin with? I remember a story about a celebrated authoress who addressed a meeting in Oxford, and made some very peculiar statements about the nature of literature. At the end an undergraduate got up and asked her what she had meant by one of them. She replied "You know English, don't you?" He had to admit that he did, and was silenced. But of course he ought not to have been silenced. (I do not think he can have been a student of Philosophy.) He ought to have said "Oh yes, in one sense I know perfectly well what you meant: but in another sense I do not, because I do not know it clearly." The original statement was puzzling or muddling in some way; and what he wanted was an equivalent statement, or set of statements which would not be puzzling or muddling. The new understanding with which the Analytic Philosopher provides us is not like that which we get when we learn a new technical terminology, e.g. that of Navigation or of Chemistry, though incidentally we may find ourselves acquiring one. It is like the new understanding which we got when a puzzle is solved. The darkness, out of which we are to advance into light, is the darkness of perplexity, not of ignorance.

Hence the analytic conception of Philosophy developed very naturally into a "therapeutic" conception of it. The philosopher's job, it was said, is to cure us of muddles or headaches, generated by language; either by everyday language, or by the technical language of some science. But it would appear that nobody could suffer from headaches of that particular sort unless he were already a philosopher. The word "I" for example has caused many headaches, but the plain man does not suffer from any of them. And so we witness the curious spectacle of the professional philosopher deliberately and methodically causing the headaches which he is subsequently going to cure. The student spends the first year of his Philosophy course laboriously catching the disease, and then he spends the second year being cured of it. A strange sort of therapy! But unless things were done that way, the therapist would have no patients.

To this it would be replied that *some* of the headaches are sure to arise spontaneously, sooner or later, in almost everybody. To that extent everybody is by nature a philosopher. The disease, in a mild form, is endemic. But you can only be cured of it, if you catch it "good and proper." To say the same thing in a more old-fashioned way: philosophical problems arise spontaneously in everyone's mind sooner or later, when he begins to reflect upon himself and upon the world. But other people must teach us to state these problems in their most general form, to grasp the full implications of each problem and the connexion between one problem and another; that is why we study the History of Philosophy. When we have learned these things, but not before, we can profitably consider what solutions are possible.

But however the Analytic conception of Philosophy should be formulated—whether in a "therapeutic" way or in some other—it is clear that a good many people have become dissatisfied with it. Perhaps, as I have hinted already, this is one result of the general change in the climate of opinion which the second world-war has brought about. Our main task is to consider this dissatisfaction and to ask ourselves whether there are any good grounds for it. Perhaps those who feel it might state their case as follows. Philosophy, they might say, is admittedly a very difficult subject. To master it—if it can be mastered at all—takes a lifetime. To attain even a reasonable Honours standard in it takes two or three years. Now the individual, and the community as a whole, have only a limited amount of time and energy to spare. Is it really wise to spend so much of it on something so trivial as the analysis of sentences? It is a question of "priorities," of the optimum allocation of scarce resources. This spring-cleaning, this clearing up of the muddles which some of these sentences engender, is no doubt quite a good thing. But is it really a very important occupation? Should it not be left to a few, a very few, specialists who happen to have a talent for it? Is it a thing which every educated man should know something about, and quite a large number should know quite a lot? If Philosophy is only clarification, does it deserve the place it has traditionally had in a liberal education? It acquired that place on the strength of a claim to be something much more than this. If that claim has now been abandoned, would it not be well for the claimant to stand down? Was it originally made at a time when Philosophy included much of what would be called

Science today, and not only natural science, but also "human" sciences such as Psychology, Sociology, Economics?

To say the same thing less politely, we are being told that there is a danger that we shall lose both our readers and our pupils, if things go on as they have been going; that by our own confession, we ought to lose most of them; and that with the gradual spread of enlightened views of what Philosophy is, Philosophy will extinguish itself. Or at least, it will have to retire into a small and remote corner of the intellectual world, and an even smaller corner of the educational world, and there be left to cultivate its little garden, by the curious method of first planting weeds and then pulling them up again. And if the analysis of sentences is its sole job, can we honestly maintain that it deserves a more important place than this?

What answer shall we make to these candid friends? Up to a point, I think they can be answered. They have blackened the picture too much. Let us see what can be said on the other side.

In the first place, the complaint which is often made that "philosophers nowadays talk about nothing but words" is not altogether just. For one thing, the clarificatory conception of Philosophy need not be stated in a linguistic form at all. The analytical philosopher is not bound to maintain that the aim of Philosophy is just to analyse the meaning of sentences. He can equally well say that its aim is to analyse our experience, or again to analyse certain types or forms of fact: not of course certain individual facts, for example the fact that there is a table in the next room, but certain *types* of fact, of which this one is an instance. The antithesis between non-philosophical knowledge which is concerned "with the world," and philosophical knowledge which is concerned "only with the sentences in which we talk about the world," is liable to mislead us; as if Philosophy were just Grammar or Lexicography, which no analytic philosopher really believes that it is. Words only matter because words are what we think with. So you could equally well say, as some clarificatory philosophers do say, that Philosophy is the analysis of certain very general and very fundamental concepts—such as Thing, Self, Cause, Duty—or that it is an analysis of categories. And then, in your definition of Philosophy, you need not mention words or sentences at all.

If however you do think fit to mention them, there is nothing to be ashamed of in that. In all ages, philosophers have in fact been greatly concerned about words, whatever their official definition of Philosophy might be. I need only mention Socrates. If anyone was ever a "linguistic analyst," surely Socrates was. No one was more concerned with the unravelling of linguistically generated muddles, the curing of "headaches" arising from linguistic usages. Nor were his therapeutic methods very different from those which are practised today. We even observe that, like our modern practitioners, he usually began by exacerbating the headaches which he then proceeded to cure. To be sure, he got little thanks for it from his contemporaries. We may suppose that a lot of them said "This verbal stuff is not Philosophy at all; it is not at all the sort of thing we used to get in the good old Ionian days." And persons who were concerned about the future of higher education accused him of corrupting the youth. Nevertheless, his successors have thought him not unworthy of admiration.

This brings me to another point which I have not hitherto mentioned. The clarificatory philosophers of the inter-war period were often accused of writing and speaking as if Philosophy had begun in the year 1900. It was said that they neglected the History of Philosophy; that they altogether ignored the "great problems" which our predecessors have handed down to us, and the solutions of them which our predecessors have offered; and that instead they concentrated on trivial and new-fangled puzzles of their own devising. Now perhaps some of them did neglect the History of Philosophy, though I do not think they all did (I seem to remember hearing a good deal of discussion of the views of Locke, Berkeley, Hume and Kant, for instance). But there was nothing in their principles which obliged them to neglect it. For clarification or analysis, even in the most strictly "verbalistic" interpretation of it, is as old, or almost as old, as Philosophy itself. In all periods from Socrates' time to our own, with the possible exception of the darkest part of the Dark Ages, clarification has been regarded as an essential part of the philosopher's job, though not generally as the whole of it. The practice of clarification has a long and very honourable history. And that history is relevant to our modern clarificatory techniques in two ways. It is worth studying for its own sake, as one of the monuments of human genius, and we shall study it more effectively if we have been taught to do some clarification for ourselves. The student of the Socratic dialogues will benefit from a reading of the works of Lord Russell or Professor Moore. Conversely, the modern clarifier who really wants to know the answers to the philosophical problems or muddles which puzzle him—some people speak as if there were something unscholarly and almost indecent in this desire for an answer, but for my part I disagree—the modern clarifier is surely very foolish if he neglects what has been said on the subject by the clarifiers of previous ages. Nor will he necessarily suppose that the analysts of the 19th or early 20th century have more to teach him than the analysts of the 4th or 5th century B.C. He will gladly accept any illumination he can get from any writer, however old or however new. Thus if the traditional "great problems" of Philosophy be problems of clarification—as many of them undoubtedly are—our modern clarifiers have every reason for studying them, and every reason also for studying what the great philosophers of the past have had to say about them. It is fair to add that if some modern clarifiers have looked with some suspicion on the History of Philosophy, their mistake has not been without excuse. For too often the History of Philosophy has been confounded with mere *Quellenforschung*. The clarifying philosopher is not interested in the question whether A borrowed such and such a theory from B or from C or from D. Why should he be? It is no concern of his. He only wants to know what the theory in question is, and whether it is illuminating, no matter who invented it or when. . . .

In my opinion, the most that we can fairly say against our modern clarifiers on this head, is that they have sometimes paid too little attention to pre-verbal or non-verbal thinking. For we do also think in images as well as in words, and there is even a sense (I believe) in which we may be said to think "in" actions and motor attitudes, without even using images. And such pre-verbal thinking seems to me important, both in the Theory of Knowledge and in the Theory of Conduct. Of course you may refuse to call it thinking if you like, but it does seem to be a very important kind of symbolic cognition. Perhaps it has also been forgotten sometimes that when we do think in words, the language we use is by no means always the "full dress" language which would satisfy a grammarian or a governess; for example syntactical words like "and," "if," "some" are not always present. I do not think that these considerations are merely psychological (whatever exactly is meant by that abusive epithet) since they may well throw valuable light on what thinking is. Even if they were, it seems to me that they are not likely to be much studied in psychological laboratories, and if philosophers think it beneath them to discuss such subjects, they will not be discussed by any one at all.

Are we to conclude then that clarity *is* enough, and that the dissatisfaction widely aroused by the "clarificatory" conception of Philosophy is wholly, or almost wholly, unjustified? I do not think so. I think that clarification is a part of the philosopher's task; an indispensable part moreover, and one which he must be allowed to fulfil by whatever methods—verbalistic or other—may seem good to him. But I do not think that it is the whole of his task. And certainly clarification is not all that the educated public demands of him. Then what else does it demand, if clarification is the primary function alike of Moral Philosophy, Logic, and Theory of

Knowledge? The simplest answer is "Metaphysics." Let us consider whether it is the right one.[1]

As we all know, Metaphysics was sadly blown upon in the second half of the inter-war period. Metaphysical statements were declared to be meaningless, not even false; indeed the adjective "metaphysical" became almost a term of abuse. To be sure, a number of the subjects previously included under Metaphysics might still be studied under other names, even by the most advanced thinkers. It was quite proper to study the notions of Substance and Cause, for example, provided one said one was studying the analysis of thing-propositions and causal propositions. You might still discuss the nature of the self or of Personal Identity, provided you called it "the analysis of 'I' sentences." You might even have been allowed to discuss the relation of Mind and Body, if you were prepared to change the label and say you wanted to talk about the relation between psychological statements and physiological statements. Thus although many of our modern Analysts would profess to have abolished Metaphysics, this revolution —like others—is not quite such a clean sweep as it appears. And I think the revolutionaries themselves would admit this.

Nevertheless, they would insist that something has been abolished; and certainly there is something which has been rendered very unpopular among professional philosophers. It is *speculative* Metaphysics, the construction of metaphysical systems: what has been called "Philosophy in the grand manner." And perhaps those who tell use that clarity is not enough are really saying that the attempt to abolish speculative Metaphysics was a fundamental mistake, indeed a kind of intellectual suicide.

Is this because they are not convinced by the reasoning which purports to show that the sentences written by the speculative metaphysicians are meaningless? Partly, no doubt. It is indeed very difficult to decide just how much this reasoning establishes. I am inclined to think that in the last resort it only establishes this much: that it is illegitimate to argue to a conclusion concerning matters of fact if there are no matters of fact among your premises. But so far as I can see, the only important metaphysical argument which would be put out of court by this is the Ontological Argument for the existence of God. And although many constructors of metaphysical systems have used this argument, in one form or another, it is not true that they all have; and even when a speculative metaphysician does use the Ontological Argument, it is not necessarily true that his whole metaphys-

[1] Miss D. M. Emmet's recent book "The Nature of Metaphysical Thinking" (especially ch. 9, on Metaphysical Analogies) contains a number of points which are highly relevant to this section of my paper, which was unfortunately written before her book came into my hands.

ical system depends on it, so that a part of his system might still be sense even though another part might be nonsensical.

I think however that the main reason, or motive, behind these protests against the abolition of speculative Metaphysics is a different one. When the critics say that a philosopher ought to concern himself with the construction of metaphysical systems, or at least with the exposition of other people's metaphysical systems if he can construct none of his own, I think they mainly have in mind what I have called the interests of the consumer; that is, the needs of the educated public which reads philosophical books or is influenced by those who do, and sends its sons and daughters to philosophical lectures at universities. Now of course it is conceivable that even though the educated public does have these needs, it is impossible in principle that they should be satisfied; and the speculative metaphysicians who have professed to satisfy them in the past may have been confusing both themselves and their readers. But when we consider the long line of speculative metaphysicians from Plato to Whitehead, when we reflect that many of them were admittedly men of the very highest genius, can we really feel very comfortable about this conclusion? Or if we do feel comfortable about it, may we not be the victims of a kind of temporal parochialism? *Securus judicat orbis terrarum.* Is it not more likely that such men were talking sense (in *some* good sense of the word "sense") than that the arguments which purport to prove that they were talking nonsense are correct?

Moreover, this is not the first time that speculative Metaphysics has been abolished. The sceptics of the later Classical period abolished it. It revived in the form of Neoplatonism and of Christian metaphysical theology. In the 18th century Hume abolished it, and Kant imposed the most drastic restrictions on it. But not for long. It arose again, more vigorous than ever, in the great speculative systems of the Romantic period. The Positivists and Agnostics of the later 19th century abolished it once more; and once more it revived in the speculative systems of Bergson, Alexander and Whitehead. If what I called the needs of the consumer are in principle incapable of being satisfied (as the modern anti-speculators assert) we may nevertheless be pretty confident that fresh attempts will in fact be made to satisfy them in the future, whether we like it or not. It looks as if there were a kind of rhythm in the history of human thought on metaphysical subjects. A long period of speculative thinking is followed by a shorter period of criticism and agnosticism, and then speculative thinking begins again in a different form. At the moment we happen to be living in one of the critical and agnostic periods; and perhaps the widespread complaint that "clarity is not enough" is itself one of the symptoms that the period is approaching its end. Certainly in other departments of human thought and culture the "debunking" which went on in the inter-war period has begun to look a little old-fashioned; as the saying is, it begins to "date." I suspect that if the complainants are asking for a revival of speculative metaphysics, they will in fact get what they want in the end, though they may not get it from the present generation of professional philosophers; and perhaps they will not get it from professional philosophers at all, but from other and less well-qualified persons.

But what exactly are these "needs of the consumer" which—if I am right—are what the critics of the purely clarificatory conception of Philosophy are mainly concerned about? And how would these needs be satisfied by a system of speculative metaphysics? What the consumer mainly needs, I think, is a *Weltanschauung,* a unified outlook on the world. This is what he is asking for when he asks the philosopher for wisdom or guidance, or a clue to "the meaning of the Universe"; and this is what the analytic philosophers are failing to give him. I am afraid he is not particularly interested in the arguments by which this or that world-outlook is recommended; at any rate not in the detail of them. But he is not wholly disinterested in them either. For the outlook which he demands has to be a *reasoned* outlook. If it is supported merely by the *ipse dixit* of some authority, or by the dictates of the heart, it will not satisfy him, or not for long. But the reasoning which supports it need not be the sort of reasoning which the anti-metaphysical philosophers disapprove of. It need not be that "pure thought" which tries to establish existential conclusions by means of wholly *a priori* premises. In every one of his arguments, the speculator might use one empirical premise at least. Nor is it at all necessary that any of his arguments should be completely demonstrative. His conclusions must be recommended by reasoning; but they need not be strictly proved, in a way which would satisfy a professor of Formal Logic.

Does this amount to saying that what is demanded of the speculative metaphysician is a kind of explanatory hypothesis, capable of accounting for all the main types of facts which are empirically known to us? That is one way of putting it, but perhaps the word "hypothesis" may mislead us. For one thing, his hypothesis—if you call it that—must be more comprehensive than any scientific or historical hypothesis. It must cover all the main departments of human experience, including experiences which it is not fashionable nowadays for philosophers to talk about: religious and mystical experience, for instance, and the queer or "supernormal" experiences which psychical researchers investigate, such as telepathy and precognition. Moreover his theory will not, I think, be capable of conclusive refutation by future empirical data. New empirical facts may turn up which are (as we say) "difficult to reconcile with it"; but by sufficiently ingenious interpretation it will always be possible to explain them away. Indeed even the word "theory" is not altogether a suitable one, for it has come to be used mainly in a scientific sense ("the Evolution Theory" "the Quantum Theory"). For the same reason words like "explain" and "account for" may be misleading. "Explanation" has come to mean primarily *causal* explanation, or at any rate explanation in terms of inductively established regularities of sequence, whether deterministic or statistical. And this is not the speculative metaphysician's business. It would be better to say that what we demand of him is just a unifying conception, or to use some still vaguer expression like "point of view" or "outlook": thus we speak of the theocentric point of view of the Mediaeval Schoolmen, or the biocentric outlook of Bergson.

This has some bearing on a very puzzling question: in what sense can a system of speculative metaphysics be called true or false? I do not think that the words "true" and "false" are rightly applicable to the sentences in which the metaphysician formulates his speculative theses, though they do of course apply to the statements which he makes in support of them. In saying this, I am not agreeing with those who maintain that a system of speculative metaphysics is just an expression of emotion, akin to a work of art. There is some force in this analogy, no doubt. But I think a much better one would be a map or chart. This is a kind of picture, if you like, and it may well have aesthetic merits. But it is also something more. It is a systematic representation of a certain set of geographical facts. And the question whether this or that stretch of green paint or blue ink shall be put in or left out, or what shape it shall have, is not settled by the emotions of the map-maker. It is settled by two considerations in conjunction: by the geographical facts on the one hand (is it empirically true that there is a wood here, and a brook there?) and on the other by the principle of representation which he has adopted.

Now two maps of the same tract of territory may be very different indeed. If your map of the world is a schoolroom globe, it will differ in many ways from a flat map constructed according to Mercator's projection; on a one-inch map a main road may be broader than the river Thames, whereas on a six-inch map it will be the other way round. But we do not say on that account that the Mercator map is "wrong" and the Schoolroom globe "right," nor that the six-inch map is "right" and the one-inch map is "wrong."

It seems to me that systems of speculative metaphysics differ from each other in somewhat the same way. We may regard them as alternative modes of conceptual arrangement by which the body of empirical data is systematically ordered: for example, the speculative system of Alexander is a mode of conceiving the universe as a hierarchical arrangement, ordered by means of the three notions of space-time, quality and emergence. What the metaphysician has to show is that his method or arrangement—his principle of systematic representation—is a possible one, that the facts can be ordered in accordance with it, but not that it is the only one possible; no more than Mercator has to show that his method of projection is the one and only "right" one and all the others "wrong." We may of course find that a particular metaphysical system leaves out some of the facts altogether; not because the metaphysician was unaware of them (if that is all, the defect can be remedied by his successors) but because in the system of representation which he has adopted they cannot be put in, just as in some types of maps there is no way of representing telegraph lines or level-crossings. Religious experience has been omitted by some metaphysicians in this way, moral experience by others; while "supernormal" experiences, such as telepathy, have been omitted by almost all. Or we may find that his system of representation is so obscure that we cannot see how to apply it to new facts which he himself did not know; or still worse, we cannot see how he applied it himself to the old ones he did know. But though we may discover defects of these sorts in a particular metaphysical system, we ought not to say on that account that it is wrong, or false, or that it has been refuted (as the Phlogiston Theory has been refuted). We ought rather to say, and indeed we often do say, that it is inadequate or unsatisfactory in this or that respect, though perhaps satisfactory in others; which is much like what we say of Mercator's map of Greenland. And we shall then look about for another metaphysical system which is more illuminating. But in the meantime we shall not just throw the old one into the waste-paper basket, on the ground that it has been "refuted," for the notion of refutation does not apply in this case. On the contrary, we shall continue to study it carefully, in order to get all the illumination out of it that we can; only, we shall hope to invent another (or rediscover an ancient one) which will illuminate more comprehensively. Thus the choice between different systems of speculative metaphysics is not a choice between the true and the false, at least in the ordinary sense of those words. It is rather a choice between the less good and the better, or even between several things which are good, but good in different ways. And even a little illumination is much better than none at all.

Let us now return to the needs of the consumer. What he is alleged to need is a unified conceptual scheme of the sort I have been trying to describe. And I think it is true that he does need it. When the ordinary educated man speaks of "a philosophy," it is a conceptual scheme of this kind which he has in mind. Such a scheme, he thinks, will provide him with the wisdom which philosophers are traditionally supposed to supply. He needs, as it were, a map of the universe so far as our empirical information has disclosed it; and not a map of the physical world only, but one which makes room for all the known aspects of the universe, physical, spiritual, and whatever others there may be. He needs it nowadays more than ever, since for good reasons or bad the Christian metaphysical scheme has lost its hold over him; and Science does not give him what he wants either, since he feels (in my opinion rightly) that there are a number of very important questions on which Science has nothing to say. And he complains that just when his need is greatest, the philosophers are refusing to satisfy it. The prevalence of the purely clarificatory conception of Philosophy prevents them from even making the attempt. They will not even discuss and expound for his benefit the speculative systems of the past, so that he may avail himself of such illumination and guidance as these old fashioned "maps of the universe" have to offer. It is true that they are not by any means uninterested in the history of Philosophy, as I have argued already. But they *are* uninterested in the history of speculative Metaphysics.

It would seem then that the complaint "clarity is not enough" is in one important respect justified, in so far as the contemporary clarifying philosophers have neglected speculative Metaphysics, which is one of the things which philosophers are traditionally paid to know about. They have neglected it, not of course through mere laziness or inadvertence, but on principle, because they have thought that the speculative metaphysician is trying to do something which is from the nature of the case impossible: namely, to establish conclusions about matters of fact by means of purely *a priori* premises. But if I am right, that is not what he is trying to do, except in occasional moments of aberration. He is trying to do something much less extravagant and much more important: to produce a unified conceptual scheme under which all the known types of empirical fact may be systematically arranged. And there is nothing in this enterprise which even the most sensitive philosophical conscience need object to.

Yet if this be so, it might be said, the statement that clarity is not enough is hardly the best way of formulating the legitimate complaints of the consumer. For, it may be suggested, there are more sorts of clarity than one. The function of the map-maker, to whom I have compared the speculative metaphysician, is surely in a sense to make things clear which were not clear before. And the speculative metaphysician, at least as I have conceived him, could even accept the dictum that "Philosophy gives us no new knowledge, but only makes clear to us what we already know." For certainly it is not his function to give us new information about matters of fact, but rather to devise a conceptual scheme which brings out certain systematic relationships between the matters of fact we know already—including those queer and puzzling ones about which we know only a little. His job is to make things comprehensible, not to establish what things are. In short, is there not such a thing as *synoptic* clarity, as well as analytical clarity? And if we are careful to remember that the word "clarity" covers both of them, could we not conclude that clarity *is* enough after all?

Perhaps we could. But I should like to add a final word of caution, and it is probably the most shocking of all the shocking things I have said this evening. It has been maintained that whatever can be said at all, can be said clearly; from which it follows that if a thing cannot be said clearly, then it cannot be said at all. We should all like to believe this. It presents itself as a kind of charter of liberation, lifting a vast load of twaddle and muddle from our shoulders. But I think we ought not to accept this freedom which is offered to us, until we have considered carefully what the word "can" means in this context. I am afraid that it only means "can in principle," not "can in practice." A man may be saying something, even something of fundamental importance, and yet it may be quite impossible for *him* to say it clearly, and impossible equally for any of his contemporaries; and this not through lack of cleverness on his part of theirs, but simply because the existing terminology is not adequate for the task. We must not however allow ourselves to conclude—as this dictum might tempt us to, unless carefully interpreted—that he would have done better not to speak at all. There may very well be some things which in the terminology available at the time can only be said obscurely; either in a metaphor, or (still more disturbing) in an oxymoron or a paradox, that is, in a sentence which breaks the existing terminological rules and is in its literal meaning absurd. The man who says them may of course be just confused. But it is possible that he is saying something important; or he may be confused in some degree, and yet he may at the same time be saying something important. Nevertheless, his successors may be able to divine what he is trying to convey. The terminological rules may eventually be changed. And the wild metaphor or outrageous paradox of today may become the platitude of the day after tomorrow. The old saying that a philosopher's reach should exceed his grasp has no doubt been grossly abused in the past, and has enabled many solemn muddles to masquerade as profound truths. But it is not a wholly silly statement all the same. And the denial or neglect of it may be even more deleterious than the abuse of it. I think we are in danger of neglecting it. If we do, we shall only succeed in being clear at the expense of being superficial; and in our zeal to "disinfect" our language from muddles, we shall only succeed in sterilising it. To use another analogy, we shall have made its rules so rigid that it becomes a strait jacket, and prevents us even from asking questions which ought to be asked and from understanding the non-professional outsider who (in a confused way, very likely) is trying to ask them. Has it not happened sometimes that an important question was first asked by poets and religious teachers and other unphilosophical persons, who were blissfully ignorant of the terminological rules which the philosophers of their day had laid down? "Nonsense! Nonsense!" says the professional philosopher, when he is told of the question these people have asked. But his successors a generation or two later may call it unconscious wisdom or untutored insight; and having altered the terminological rules so as to make the question a permissible one, they may spend their professional lives in looking for the answer. In that case the philosopher who said "Nonsense!" will appear a little ridiculous. Let us take care that this does not happen to ourselves, and let us not allow our zeal for "tightening up language," to run away with us. Even though we allow for the distinction between analytic clarity and synoptic clarity, it may still be true that clarity is not enough.

Being and Becoming

George Santayana

Pure Being *

Of all essences the most lauded and the most despised, the most intently studied in some quarters and the most misunderstood in others, is pure Being. It has been identified with nothing, with matter, and with God; and even among those who regard it in its logical purity, it is sometimes said to be the richest and most comprehensive of essences and sometimes the poorest and most abstract.

No essence, as we have seen, is abstract essentially, since it defines itself and might appear alone to an intellect strung to that key: and in the case of pure Being we have high testimony (which there is no reason to distrust) assuring us that, in fact, it appears alone to the human intellect in its ultimate reaches; and even when not realised separately in intuition, it can be discerned both analytically and intuitively in every essence whatsoever. Pure Being supplies, as it were, the logical or æsthetic matter which all essences have in common, and which reduces them to comparable modes on one plane of reality. Pure Being is thus found in all essences somewhat as light is in all colours or life in all feeling and thought; and philosophers like Parmenides and Spinoza (not to speak here of the Indians) assure us that we always have an adequate intuition of this pure Being, usually buried under vain illusions, but when unearthed and isolated seen to be very mighty in itself and easily recognisable. Nevertheless such assurances may mean little to other mortals. Language at these depths of attentiveness is perforce the language of solitaries. When repeated it may not carry with it the intuition which it was first meant to record. The very logicians who distinguish this essence, because they call it Being, may conclude that nothing else can *be*—a most perplexing inference and, in view of the many meanings of the word *is,* a most misleading one; while other logicians, because pure Being is different from

* From *The Realm of Essence* by George Santayana. In *Realms of Being,* pp. 45–57. Reprinted by permission of Charles Scribner's Sons, and Constable and Company Limited.

all other essences, may hastily identify it with nothing, by a strange equivocation between nothing and nothing else.

Confusion in this matter comes chiefly from the equivocation between being and existence. Initially this equivocation is normal, innocent, and even expedient, like any substitution of names for things: it is only when defended theoretically that it becomes perverse. Intelligence begins with it: animals are surrounded by things that affect their condition and prompt their reactions, so that their attention is necessarily intent upon existing things; yet the intellectual transcript of their condition, in that agony of attention, is only some intuited essence, some sensuous or logical term, which being their sole description for the object before them, they take to be that object itself in its whole existing nature. So individual forms of being stand in discourse for particular things. But sometimes, rather than some specific thing, a certain equilibrium of influences absorbs attention: a noon pause comes in our labour; and more special sensations being fused and blurred, we endure dull strain and duration without diversity—a vast, strange feeling. We return, then, as it were, to the sleep preceding life, to the peace of the womb: there is vitality without urgency, pressure without light, potential movement without object or express direction. Such, we may fancy, might be the inner sense of matter: perhaps some forms of animal or vegetable life never yield any other experience. A vague world is posited as existing; for in expectation and intent, as in memory and the sense of movement, there is a tacit assumption of things removed, threatening, eventual, as yet unknown. There is accordingly nothing pure in this sense of existence, simple or vague as its deliverance may seem; for this vagueness and simplicity are uneasy. The peace of the womb is precarious; it is but a muffled and initial phase of distraction, confusion, hope, and fear. Care fills its heart, as it does our dreams; and we might identify it with the Universal Will of German transcendentalism, vaguely pregnant with worlds and worlds. But slumber is not contemplation, and the buzz of matter is not the beatific vision. The pleasure, if pleasure be found in it, is that of original sin: the father of lies is whispering in that paradise. The intuition of pure Being looks in the opposite direction. In order to reach it, attention would need to abandon all concern for transitions, events, ulterior or external facts, and to concentrate all its light on the positive intrinsic nature of the present datum; nor would that suffice, but from this special essence it would need to pass to the inner essence of all those alien half-known things, all those absent times, and eventual passions, which animal faith may posit, or fancy may conceive; since pure Being resides in them all equally, no less than in the here and now. The force of insight would thus have to vanquish all will and transcend all animal limitations, cancelling every fear, preference, or private perspective which a station now and here would involve. In other words, in order to reach the intuition of pure Being, it is requisite to rise altogether above the sense of existence.

The reason for this lies in the very nature of existence, which is flux and, as Plato would say, non-being. The more truly existence is felt, therefore, the less possible it is to concentrate attention on anything, and to say, Existence is this. He is closest to existence, and most at its heart, who lives on the wing, intent always on the not-given; and even when the present fact is atrociously absorbing, as in pain, the sense of existence remains empty essentially and indescribable, by the very force and distraction of its presence. If we are asked to describe it, we are reduced to naming the circumstances or using some metaphor; and if in the midst of it we pause to consider the internal character of that which we feel, raising it thereby for the first time to distinct intuition, the distraction, the belief, the assurance of existence which filled us before have *ipso facto* disappeared: some image, some word, some finely shaded sensible essence alone is left. In other words, the proper nature of existence is distraction itself, transition at least virtual; so that it cannot be synthesised in intuition without being sublimated into a picture of itself, and washed clean of its contradiction and urgency. The relations which were external from the station of each of the parts as it arose separately, now become internal to the system of the whole; and the intuition in which this whole is synthesised drops the flux of existence in order to retain only its form and the truth about it.

If, then, being and existence seem in common parlance almost interchangeable terms, it is only so long as their respective objects are merely named or designated from the outside: when they are conceived positively and at close quarters they turn out to be exact opposites. Existence exists by virtue of oppositions in the place, time, and exclusive characters of particulars: being has being by virtue of its universal identity. This is true of the being of each individual essence; and it is true preeminently of pure Being. Its identity is omnipresent and internal everywhere; it equalises those centres of existence which in their single blindness become nests for external relations; it makes all times simultaneous; and by excluding change renders existence, from its point of view, inconceivable. Moreover, in reducing all things and all external relations to their internal being, that is, to their essences, it transports them into a realm of being which is necessarily infinite, in which their presence, therefore, is no temporary accident, as is their existence in the world: so that the existent becomes continuous with the non-existent, and neither more nor less real than any other eternal essence.

This contrast between being and existence is indicated by calling being pure. "Pure" is an epithet proper to all essences. Objects become pure when intuition permeates them and rests in them without the intervention of any ulterior intent or cross-lights, as we speak of pure mathematics or pure pleasure. Purity of this sort is no thinness of form, but the perfection of it. It admits any amount of detail, if it is all overt and clear, on the plane of actuality, and not latent. In this acceptation of the word "pure", pure Being is no purer than any other essence, but all are pure in so far as they are considered in their proper character, freed from the irrelevancies that may encumber them when they figure for a moment in some material world or in some labouring mind.

It would therefore be useless and redundant habitually to speak of "pure Being" if nothing were meant save that Being is an essence. What is indicated is the pure Being is related to other essences very much as any essence is related to its existing manifestations; for whereas any special essence, such as colour or sound, sky-blue or B flat, is exclusive and definable by contrast, pure Being is present in them all, somewhat as space is in all geometrical figures, at once permeating and transcending each of them; for this essence, if not fertile casually as facts are fertile, is in its own way infinitely pregnant. The nature of pure Being anywhere implies the whole realm of essence, since being could not possess its full extension if any sort of being were forbidden to be.

That pure Being, in the sphere of essence, should have this simple, intense, and pervasive sort of reality, provokes afresh in the minds of dialecticians that tendency to identify essence with existence which is native to the animal mind. For in the natural world too there seems to be an omnipresent, simple, intensely real something which dwells in particular things, is transmitted from one to another, and compels them to arise in their infinite variety and endless succession. This omnipresent something is called substance. Might not then pure Being, which lies in all essences and therefore also in all existing things, be the substance of these things, and the universal internal cause of their existence? This is a suggestion which has worked powerfully in the thoughts of those metaphysicians, like the Eleatics, whose physics has been dominated by dialectic. Nor is the suggestion altogether false. That something exists, that there is a world, is very true; also that whatever else this world may be, it is substantial—that is, exists in itself independently of all report or opinion. The hypostasis of being into substance is therefore no error, but a first awakening of curiosity and belief, which in so far as it posits the existence of something errs only by its extreme inadequacy. It honestly sets about using the category of substance, but without any notion of what, in detail, this substance is. This inadequacy itself is inevitable: how should animals in the womb, or just out of it, conceive truly that constitution of the world which is not disentangled even to-day by science or philosophy? Positive error only appears when this natural inadequacy of our ideas is denied, and when mere being is deputed to reveal the whole substance and complete reality of things. The belief in substance, which should have been the beginning of art and science, then suddenly makes an end of them; for if there were truly nothing in nature or in experience except mere being, all events and appearances would be sheer illusions, since in reality they would be all identical.

I shall return to this subject in considering the properties requisite in any substance fit to subtend appearances and the life of nature; such a substance must be unequally distributed and in motion; its proper name is matter. Here I will only notice in passing how the notion of pure Being is likely to be contaminated in the effort to identify it with substance. Pure Being—as is indicated by calling it infinite and eternal, if we ponder these epithets—is utterly absolved from all subservience to contingent facts and to the momentary casual forms of human experience; it is the most immaterial, untameable, inexhaustible of essences. Yet Parmenides—no tyro in dialectic—denied that it was infinite, because it had to give body to an existing spherical cosmos; and indeed, apart from ancient astronomy, existence always involves a certain concentration and contrast with what is not, and thereby excludes infinity. Again, we find Spinoza asserting that the entire nature of being—which he actually calls substance—must be manifested in existence, and that all these manifestations must be parallel to the forms of the material world, of which indeed those other manifestations can be only complementary aspects, by chance unknown to us. Here is the cosmic frog prodigiously swollen in rivalry with the ontological ox; but the ox, lest that ambition should seem too absurd, is accommodated to the frog nature, and pure Being is thought of as a sort of matter or force resident in natural things and lending them their existence, while at the same time enriching them with an infinite number of attributes which they hide from view.

On the one hand, then, if pure Being is substance, existence must be illusion; and on the other hand pure Being must be, not the infinite essence which it is, but a hard kernel for existence. Hence the see-saw in the views of those metaphysicians who hypostatise pure Being; sometimes their substance annuls all particulars, and sometimes it supports them. Pure Being excludes particular determinations within its own bosom, but it does not annul them in the world, because it is not on the plane of existence at all: it is by no means a matter within particulars which lends them existence. Substance, on the other hand, is such a matter; and by its movements and redistribution it gives rise in turn to every fact and relation in the natural world. Were pure Being an existing substance, nothing else could exist or arise, not even the occasional intuition of pure Being. All that exists exists by being other than pure Being, under circumstances which themselves are particular and contingent; and if substance were not contingent, unequally distributed, and in motion, it would evidently not be the ground of any event or of any actual appearance.

Thus the hypostasis of pure Being, after being fatal to the reality of all facts, is fatal to respect for pure Being itself; because, considered as a substance, it would be useless, unknowable, and nowhere to be found. Pure Being, although a supreme degree of detachment and concentration be requisite to conceive it adequately, is, like any other essence, perfectly open to intuition; its sublimity is not obscurity; and it is excluded from "knowledge" only in the sense in which any immediate object, being an object of intuition, need not and should not be posited as a removed existence, by the transitive and precarious sort of knowledge by which facts may be known. But pure Being hypostatised into substance is a metaphysical spectre: matter congealed, arrested, emptied, and deprived of its cosmic fertility.

Pure Being, conceived as a substance or an existence, might indeed almost justify the well-known gibe that pure Being and pure nothing are identical. This sophism is complementary to those misunderstandings; the same misplaced preoccupation with physics has ended in impatience of logic and of honest intent. Of pure Being, which is not a romantic object, the moderns have little experience: the idea of nothing is easier and far more familiar to them. We all know the feeling of contrast and disappointment which comes over the senses when they are robbed of their habitual entertainment, as, for instance, the sensation of darkness when the lights suddenly go out. The psyche, continuing to live her incessant life, feels cheated of her food and bereft of her employment. This is perhaps the origin of that horror of non-existence which afflicts so many mortals; a horror which would be evidently objectless and impossible if really nothing existed, and the poor wights were not there to shiver in the cold. But the psyche, feeling or imagining the sudden disappearance of her supports, finds her own existence empty and abortive: she does not know where to turn or what to expect, and this anguish is her acquaintance with nothingness.

For experience, then, "nothing" means a void caused by the absence of some expected thing. The fact that such a thing fails to exist is logically dependent on the reality of its form of being, its designated and recognisable essence; and the sense that there is nothing there, is dependent for its existence on a psyche missing some particular thing, and feeling a specific emptiness. Negation, no less than doubt, assertion, or faith, requires the prior individuality of ideal terms; and to predicate non-existence is in that measure to recognise essence. Being and the non-existent here actually coincide; not because both are nothing, but because both are being. If all existence could be abolished, all essence would resume its equable reign: and the absence of rude emphasis or blind exclusion would leave the infinite variety of being subsisting in peace: although this fullness, even if an animal imagination could conceive it, might seem nothing to it, singly preoccupied as it must be with the flux of facts.

The fact of non-existence, then, is a natural alternative to that of existence, in many cases familiar, and in others feared or desired. Like every fact, it is contingent, coming and going at will, and leaving the eternal manifold of being exactly as it was. "The non-existent" is accordingly not a bad name for the realm of essence, seen from the point of view of existence. But this point of view is adventitious; no essence is non-existent intrinsically, since for all it contains or suggests it may very well exist; that is, some existence somewhere may for a time embody or manifest it; and even if this contingent occurrence were by chance perpetual—if, for instance, the essence of Euclidean space were frozen into an omnipresent everlasting fact in nature—this persistent accident would not touch the status of mathematical space in its own realm, a status which is simply irrelevant to existence and not contrary to it.

When the word "nothing" denotes non-existence it is fundamentally exclamatory: it expresses a feeling or an encounter rather than an idea. But the same word may be applied descriptively within the realm of essence, to express non-being or privation of essence; "nothing", then, means "nothing of that sort". This mixture of privation distinguishes every essence, since in being itself it is necessarily no other. This is true even of the most comprehensive essences. A statue which includes the head excludes the special individuality of the same head reproduced in a bust:

the different limits individuate not only the two material blocks but the two compositions. So the realm of essence, which is the full-length portrait of being, while it contains everything, drops in everything that isolation which makes it, when taken singly, seem the whole of being: it shatters the illusion of so many philosophers that they have found "the only possible" this or "the only possible" that.

Indeed, the essential mixture of privation in all being is more uncompromisingly evident among essences than among existences, because existence, in admitting change, seems to have found a way of circumventing definition. The expedient is not successful, save in so defining an existence that it may include successive phases, as a man's life does: but both the incidents and the life still depend for their being on their essential exclusions. The bachelor becoming a Benedict does not succeed in combining contraries; his singleness is gone; any backward glances or truancies which he may indulge in only spoil and deepen his married state, in which he then feels henpecked or adulterous. Wisdom lies in voluntary finitude and a timely change of heart: until maturity, multiplying the inclusions, up to the limit of natural faculty and moral harmony; afterwards, gladly relinquishing zone after zone of vegetation, and letting the snow-peak of integrity rise to what height it may. Becoming, therefore, does not unite being and privation more closely than being unites them in itself, even without change or existence. The full character of each essence is inevitably absent from every other essence; but this relative privation or absence of what is alien is the consequence of possessing a positive character. Had each term no private, indefinable, positive essence of its own, it could not justify those exclusions by which we define it, nor could it fill its appointed place and spread out its eternal intrinsic relations in the realm of essence.

Pure Being, like any other essence, is individual and distinguished by exclusions, for it excludes those limitations which render all other essences specific; somewhat as light, which fills up and dynamically constitutes all colours, nevertheless excludes each particular tint. This is far from being a reason for calling pure Being a non-entity: the exclusion of all exclusions renders it infinite, not vacant. Vacancy and nothingness are terms applicable to existence, to which external relations are indispensable, and which at any moment may lapse, so that the place thereof knows it no more; they are meaningless in respect to essences each of which, including pure Being, is grounded in itself, and like a jewel or a star, shines all the brighter in isolation. Non-entity figures, indeed, in the realm of essence, because it is eternally impossible that anything there should be anything else; there are therefore always many things which anything is not. This non-entity is purely relative; an absolute non-entity would be self-contradictory, a false suggestion of discourse like the round square or the son of the barren woman. You cannot make a void of the realm of essence, as you so easily might of existence, by waving a magic wand. Its indestructibility is not an accident, a stubborn matter of fact, like that of matter or of God. If you flatter yourself to abolish the realm of essence, you actually refer to it and reinstate it; if you deny it, you affirm it. The only negation of it which, in one sense, might be staunch, would be utter oblivion; but oblivion is subjective. It destroys nothing save the feeling or thought by which something was formerly recognised.

William James

The One and the Many *

Philosophy has often been defined as the quest or the vision of the world's unity. Few persons ever challenge this definition, which is true as far as it goes, for philosophy has indeed manifested above all things its interest in unity. But how about the *variety* in things? Is that such an irrelevant matter? If instead of using the term philosophy, we talk in general of our intellect and its needs, we quickly see that unity is only one of them. Acquaintance with the details of fact is always reckoned, along with their reduction to system, as an indispensable mark of mental greatness. Your 'scholarly' mind, of encyclopedic, philological type, your man essentially of *learning,* has never lacked for praise along with your philosopher. What our intellect really aims at is neither variety nor unity taken singly, but *totality.* In this, acquaintance with reality's diversities is as important as understanding their connexion. Curiosity goes *pari passu* with the systematizing passion.

In spite of this obvious fact the unity of things has always been considered more *illustrious,* as it were, than their variety. When a young man first conceives the notion that the whole world forms one great fact, with all its parts moving abreast, as it were, and interlocked, he feels as if he were enjoying a great insight, and looks superciliously on all who still fall short of this sublime conception. Taken thus abstractly as it first comes to one, the monistic insight is so vague as hardly to seem worth defending intellectually. Yet probably every one in this audience in some way cherishes it. A certain abstract monism, a certain emotional response to the character of oneness, as if it were a feature of the world not coordinate with its manyness, but vastly more excellent and eminent, is so prevalent in educated circles that we might almost call it a part of philosophic common sense. Of *course* the world is One, we say. How else could

* From *Pragmatism* by William James. New York: Longmans, Green and Co., 1907, pp. 129–149.

it be a world at all? Empiricists as a rule, are as stout monists of this abstract kind as rationalists are.

The difference is that the empiricists are less dazzled. Unity doesn't blind them to everything else, doesn't quench their curiosity for special facts, whereas there is a kind of rationalist who is sure to interpret abstract unity mystically and to forget everything else, to treat it as a principle; to admire and worship it, and thereupon to come to a full stop intellectually.

'The world is One!'—the formula may become a sort of number-worship. 'Three' and 'seven' have, it is true, been reckoned sacred numbers; but, abstractly taken, why is 'one' more excellent than 'forty-three,' or than 'two million and ten'? In this first vague conviction of the world's unity, there is so little to take hold of that we hardly know what we mean by it.

The only way to get forward with our notion is to treat it pragmatically. Granting the oneness to exist, what facts will be different in consequence? What will the unity be known as? The world is One—yes, but *how* one. What is the practical value of the oneness for *us*.

Asking such questions, we pass from the vague to the definite, from the abstract to the concrete. Many distinct ways in which a oneness predicated of the universe might make a difference, come to view. I will note successively the more obvious of these ways.

1. First, the world is at least *one subject of discourse*. If its manyness were so irremediable as to permit *no* union whatever of its parts, not even our minds could 'mean' the whole of it at once: they would be like eyes trying to look in opposite directions. But in point of fact we mean to cover the whole of it by our abstract term 'world' or 'universe,' which expressly intends that no part shall be left out. Such unity of discourse carries obviously no farther monistic specifications. A 'chaos,' once so named, has as much unity of discourse as a cosmos. It is an odd fact that many monists consider a great victory scored for their side when pluralists says 'the universe is many.' " 'The Universe'!" they chuckle—"his speech betrayeth him. He stands confessed of monism out of his own mouth." Well, let things be one in so far forth! You can then fling such a word as universe at the whole collection of them, but what matters it? It still remains to be ascertained whether they are one in any further or more valuable sense.

2. Are they, for example, *continuous?* Can you pass from one to another, keeping always in your one universe without any danger of falling out? In other words, do the parts of our universe *hang together*, instead of being like detached grains of sand?

Even grains of sand hang together through the space in which they are embedded, and if you can in any way move through such space, you can pass continuously from number one of them to number two. Space and time are thus vehicles of continuity by which the world's parts hang together. The practical difference to us, resultant from these forms of union, is immense. Our whole motor life is based upon them.

3. There are innumerable other paths of practical continuity among things. Lines of *influence* can be traced by which they hang together. Following any such line you pass from one thing to another till you may have covered a good part of the universe's extent. Gravity and heat-conduction are such all-uniting influences, so far as the physical world goes. Electric, luminous and chemical influences follow similar lines of influence. But opaque and inert bodies interrupt the continuity here, so that you have to step round them, or change your mode of progress if you wish to get farther on that day. Practically, you have then lost your universe's unity, *so far as it was constituted by those first lines of influence.*

There are innumerable kinds of connexion that special things have with other special things; and the *ensemble* of any one of these connexions forms one sort of *system* by which things are conjoined. Thus men are conjoined in a vast network of *acquaintanceship*. Brown knows Jones, Jones knows Robinson, etc.; and *by choosing your farther intermediaries rightly* you may carry a message from Jones to the Empress of China, or the Chief of the African Pigmies, or to any one else in the inhabited world. But you are stopped short, as by a nonconductor, when you choose one man wrong in this experiment. What may be called love-systems are grafted on the acquaintance-system. A loves (or hates) B; B loves (or hates) C, etc. But these systems are smaller than the great acquaintance-system that they presuppose.

Human efforts are daily unifying the world more and more in definite systematic ways. We found colonial, postal, consular, commercial systems, all the parts of which obey definite influences that propagate themselves within the system but not to facts outside of it. The result is innumerable little hangings-together of the world's parts within the larger hangings-together, little worlds, not only of discourse but of operation, within the wider universe. Each system exemplifies one type or grade of union, its parts being strung on that peculiar kind of relation, and the same part may figure in many different systems, as a man may hold various offices and belong to several clubs. From this 'systematic' point of view, therefore, the pragmatic value of the world's unity is that all these definite networks actually and practically exist. Some are more enveloping and extensive, some less so; they are superposed upon each other; and between them all they let no individual elementary part of the universe escape. Enormous as is the amount of disconnexion among things (for these systematic influences and conjunctions follow rigidly exclusive paths), everything that exists is influenced in *some* way by something else, if you can only pick the way out rightly. Loosely speaking, and in general, it may be said that all things cohere and adhere to each other *somehow,* and that the universe exists practically in reticulated or concatenated forms which make of it a continuous or 'integrated' affair. Any kind of influence whatever helps to make the world one, so far as you can follow it from next to next. You may then say that 'the world *is* One,'—meaning in these respects, namely, and just so far as they obtain. But just as definitely is it *not* One, so far as they do not obtain; and there is no species of connexion which will not fail, if, instead of choosing conductors for it you choose non-conductors. You are then arrested at your very first step and have to write the world down as a pure *many* from that particular point of view. If our intellect had been as much interested in disjunctive as it is in conjunctive relations, philosophy would have equally successfully celebrated the world's *disunion.*

The great point is to notice that the oneness and the manyness are absolutely co-ordinate here. Neither is primordial or more essential or excellent than the other. Just as with space, whose separating of things seems exactly on a par with its uniting of them, but sometimes one function and sometimes the other is what comes home to us most, so, in our general dealings with the world of influences, we now need conductors and now need non-conductors, and wisdom lies in knowing which is which at the appropriate moment.

4. All these systems of influence or non-influence may be listed under the general problem of the world's *causal unity.* If the minor causal influences among things should converge towards one common causal origin of them in the past, one great first cause for all that is, one might then speak of the absolute causal unity of the world. God's *fiat* on creation's day has figured in traditional philosophy as such an absolute cause and origin. Transcendental Idealism, translating 'creation' into 'thinking' (or 'willing to think') calls the divine act 'eternal' rather than 'first,' but the union of the many here is absolute, just the same—the many would not *be,* save for the One. Against this notion of the unity of origin of all things there has always stood the pluralistic notion of an eternal self-existing many in the shape of atoms or even of spiritual units of some sort. The alternative

has doubtless a pragmatic meaning, but perhaps as far as these lectures go, we had better leave the question of unity of origin unsettled.

5. The most important sort of union that obtains among things, pragmatically speaking, is their *generic unity.* Things exist in kinds, there are many specimens in each kind, and what the 'kind' implies for one specimen, it implies also for every other specimen of that kind. We can easily conceive that every fact in the world might be singular, that is, unlike any other fact and sole of its kind. In such a world of singulars our logic would be useless, for logic works by predicating of the single instance what is true of all its kind. With no two things alike in the world, we should be unable to reason from our past experiences to our future ones. The existence of so much generic unity in things is thus perhaps the most momentous pragmatic specification of what it may mean to say 'the world is One.' *Absolute* generic unity would obtain if there were one *summum genus* under which all things without exception could be eventually subsumed. 'Beings,' 'thinkables,' 'experiences,' would be candidates for this position. Whether the alternatives expressed by such words have any pragmatic significance or not, is another question which I prefer to leave unsettled just now.

6. Another specification of what the phrase 'the world is one' may mean is *unity of purpose.* An enormous number of things in the world subserve a common purpose. All the man-made systems, administrative, industrial, military, or what not, exist each for its controlling purpose. Every living being pursues its own peculiar purposes. They co-operate, according to the degree of their development, in collective or tribal purposes, larger ends thus enveloping lesser ones, until an absolutely single, final and climacteric purpose subserved by all things without exception might conceivably be reached. It is needless to say that the appearances conflict with such a view. Any resultant, as I said in my third lecture, *may* have been purposed in advance, but none of the results we actually know in this world have in point of fact been purposed in advance in all their details. Men and nations start with a vague notion of being rich, or great, or good. Each step they make brings unforeseen chances into sight, and shuts out older vistas, and the specifications of the general purpose have to be daily changed. What is reached in the end may be better or worse than what was proposed, but it is always more complex and different.

Our different purposes also are at war with each other. Where one can't crush the other out, they compromise; and the result is again different from what any one distinctly proposed beforehand. Vaguely and generally, much of what was purposed may be gained; but everything makes strongly for the view that our world is incompletely unified teleologically and is still trying to get its unification better organized.

Whoever claims *absolute* teleological unity, saying that there is one purpose that every detail of the universe subserves, dogmatizes at his own risk. Theologians who dogmatize thus find it more and more impossible, as our acquaintance with the warring interests of the world's parts grows more concrete, to imagine what the one climacteric purpose may possibly be like. We see indeed that certain evils minister to ulterior goods, that the bitter makes the cocktail better, and that a bit of danger or hardship puts us agreeably to our trumps. We can vaguely generalize this into the doctrine that all the evil in the universe is but instrumental to its greater perfection. But the scale of the evil actually in sight defies all human tolerance; and transcendental idealism, in the pages of a Bradley or a Royce, brings us no farther than the book of Job did—God's ways are not our ways, so let us put our hands upon our mouth. A God who can relish such superfluities of horror is no God for human beings to appeal to. His animal spirits are too high. In other words the 'Absolute' with his one purpose, is not the man-like God of common people.

7. *Æsthetic union* among things also obtains, and is very analogous to teleological union. Things tell a story. Their parts hang together so as to work out a climax. They play into each other's hands expressively. Retrospectively, we can see that altho no definite purpose presided over a chain of events, yet the events fell into a dramatic form, with a start, a middle, and a finish. In point of fact all stories end; and here again the point of view of a many is the more natural one to take. The world is full of partial stories that run parallel to one another, beginning and ending at odd times. They mutually interlace and interfere at points, but we can not unify them completely in our minds. In following your life-history, I must temporarily turn my attention from my own. Even a biographer of twins would have to press them alternately upon his reader's attention.

It follows that whoever says that the whole world tells one story utters another of those monistic dogmas that a man believes at his risk. It is easy to see the world's history pluralistically, as a rope of which each fibre tells a separate tale; but to conceive of each cross-section of the rope as an absolutely single fact, and to sum the whole longitudinal series into one being living an undivided life, is harder. We have indeed the analogy of embryology to help us. The microscopist makes a hundred flat cross-sections of a given embryo, and mentally unites them into one solid whole. But the great world's ingredients, so far as they are beings, seem like the rope's fibres, to be discontinuous, cross-wise, and to cohere only in the longitudinal direction. Followed in that direction they are many. Even the embryologist, when he follows the *development* of his object, has to treat the history of each single organ in turn. *Absolute* æsthetic union is thus another barely abstract ideal. The world appears as something more epic than dramatic.

So far, then, we see how the world is unified by its many systems, kinds, purposes, and dramas. That there is more union in all these ways than openly appears is certainly true. That there *may* be one sovereign purpose, system, kind, and story, is a legitimate hypothesis. All I say here is that it is rash to affirm this dogmatically without better evidence than we possess at present.

8. The *great* monistic *denkmittel* for a hundred years past has been the notion of *the one Knower*. The many exist only as objects for his thought—exist in his dream, as it were; and *as he knows* them, they have one purpose, form one system, tell one tale for him. This notion of an *all enveloping noetic unity* in things is the sublimest achievement of intellectualist philosophy. Those who believe in the Absolute, as the All-Knower is termed, usually say that they do so for coercive reasons, which clear thinkers can not evade. The Absolute has far-reaching practical consequences, to some of which I drew attention in my second lecture. Many kinds of difference important to us would surely follow from its being true. I can not here enter into all the logical proofs of such a Being's existence, farther than to say that none of them seem to me sound. I must therefore treat the notion of an All-Knower simply as an hypothesis, exactly on a par logically with the pluralist notion that there is no point of view, no focus of information extant, from which the entire content of the universe is visible at once. "God's conscience," says Professor Royce,[1] "forms in its wholeness one luminously transparent conscious moment"—this is the type of noetic unity on which rationalism insists. Empiricism on the other hand is satisfied with the type of noetic unity that is humanly familiar. Everything gets known by *some* knower along with something else; but the knowers may in the end be irreducibly many, and the greatest knower of them all may yet not know the whole of everything, or even know what he does know at one single stroke:—he may be liable to forget. Whichever type obtained, the world would still be a universe noetically. Its parts would be conjoined by knowledge, but in the one case the knowl-

[1] *The Conception of God* (New York, 1897), p. 292.

edge would be absolutely unified, in the other it would be strung along and overlapped.

The notion of one instantaneous or eternal Knower—either adjective here means the same thing—is, as I said, the great intellectualist achievement of our time. It has practically driven out that conception of 'Substance' which earlier philosophers set such store by, and by which so much unifying work used to be done—universal substance which alone has being in and from itself, and of which all the particulars of experience are but forms to which it gives support. Substance has succumbed to the pragmatic criticisms of the English school. It appears now only as another name for the fact that phenomena as they come are actually grouped and given in coherent forms, the very forms in which we finite knowers experience or think them together. These forms of conjunction are as much parts of the tissue of experience as are the terms which they connect; and it is a great pragmatic achievement for recent idealism to have made the world hang together in these directly representable ways instead of drawing its unity from the 'inherence' of its parts—whatever that may mean—in an unimaginable principle behind the scenes.

'The world is One,' therefore, just so far as we experience it to be concatenated, One by as many definite conjunctions as appear. But then also *not* One by just as many definite *dis*-junctions as we find. The oneness and the manyness of it thus obtain in respects which can be separately named. It is neither a universe pure and simple nor a multiverse pure and simple. And its various manners of being One suggest, for their accurate ascertainments, so many distinct programs of scientific work. Thus the pragmatic question 'What is the oneness known as? What practical difference will it make?' saves us from all feverish excitement over it as a principle of sublimity and carries us forward into the stream of experience with a cool head. The stream may indeed reveal far more connexion and union than we now suspect, but we are not entitled on pragmatic principles to claim absolute oneness in any respect in advance.

John Dewey

Existence as Precarious and as Stable *

A feature of existence which is emphasized by cultural phenomena is the precarious and perilous. Sumner refers to Grimm as authority for the statement that the Germanic tribes had over a thousand distinct sayings, proverbs and apothegms, concerning luck. Time is brief, and this statement must stand instead of the discourse which the subject deserves. Man finds himself living in an aleatory world; his existence involves, to put it baldly, a gamble. The world is a scene of risk; it is uncertain, unstable, uncannily unstable. Its dangers are irregular, inconstant, not to be counted upon as to their times and seasons. Although persistent, they are sporadic, episodic. It is darkest just before dawn; pride goes before a fall; the moment of greatest prosperity is the moment most charged with ill-omen, most opportune for the evil eye. Plague, famine, failure of crops, disease, death, defeat in battle, are always just around the corner, and so are abundance, strength, victory, festival and song. Luck is proverbially both good and bad in its distributions. The sacred and the accursed are potentialities of the same situation; and there is no category of things which has not embodied the sacred and accursed: persons, words, places, times, directions in space, stones, winds, animals, stars.

Anthropologists have shown incontrovertibly the part played by the precarious aspect of the world in generating religion with its ceremonies, rites, cults, myths, magic; and it has shown the pervasive penetration of these affairs into morals, law, art, and industry. Beliefs and dispositions connected with them are the background out of which philosophy and secular morals slowly developed, as well as more slowly those late inventions, art for art's sake, and business is business. Interesting and instructive as is this fact, it is not the ramifications which here concern us. We must not be diverted to consider the consequences for philosophy, even for doctrines

* From *Experience and Nature* by John Dewey, pp. 41–48, 62–72.

reigning today, of facts concerning the origin of philosophies. We confine ourselves to one outstanding fact: the evidence that the world of empirical things includes the uncertain, unpredictable, uncontrollable and hazardous.

It is an old saying that the gods were born of fear. The saying is only too likely to strengthen a misconception bred by confirmed subjective habits. We first endow man in isolation with an instinct of fear and then we imagine him irrationally ejecting that fear into the environment, scattering broadcast as it were, the fruits of his own purely personal limitations, and thereby creating superstition. But fear, whether an instinct or an acquisition, is a function of the environment. Man fears because he exists in a fearful, an awful world. The world is precarious and perilous. It is as easily accessible and striking evidence of this fact that primitive experience is cited. The voice is that of early man; but the hand is that of nature, the nature in which we still live. It was not fear of gods that created the gods.

For if the life of early man is filled with expiations and propitiations, if in his feasts and festivals what is enjoyed is gratefully shared with his gods, it is not because a belief in supernatural powers created a need for expiatory, propitiatory and communal offerings. Everything that man achieves and possesses is got by actions that may involve him in other and obnoxious consequences in addition to those wanted and enjoyed. His acts are trespasses upon the domain of the unknown; and hence atonement, if offered in season, may ward off direful consequences that haunt even the moment of prosperity—or that most haunt that moment. While unknown consequences flowing from the past dog the present, the future is even more unknown and perilous; the present by that fact is ominous. If unknown forces that decide future destiny can be placated, the man who will not study the methods of securing their favor is incredibly flippant. In enjoyment of present food and companionship, nature, tradition and social organization have cooperated, thereby supplementing our own endeavors so petty and so feeble without this extraneous reinforcement. Goods are by grace not of ourselves. He is a dangerous churl who will not gratefully acknowledge by means of free-will offerings the help that sustains him.

These things are as true today as they were in the days of early culture. It is not the facts which have changed, but the methods of insurance, regulation and acknowledgment. Herbert Spencer sometimes colored his devotion to symbolic experiences with a fact of direct experience. When he says that every fact has two opposite sides, "the one its near or visible side and the other its remote or invisible side," he expresses a persistent trait of every object in experience. The visible is set in the invisible; and in the end what is unseen decides what happens in the seen; the tangible rests precariously upon the untouched and ungrasped. The contrast and the potential maladjustment of the immediate, the conspicuous and focal phase of things, with those indirect and hidden factors which determine the origin and career of what is present, are indestructible features of any and every experience. We may term the way in which our ancestors dealt with the contrast superstitious, but the contrast is no superstition. It is a primary datum in any experience.

We have substituted sophistication for superstition, at least measurably so. But the sophistication is often as irrational and as much at the mercy of words as the superstition it replaces. Our magical safeguard against the uncertain character of the world is to deny the existence of chance, to mumble universal and necessary law, the ubiquity of cause and effect, the uniformity of nature, universal progress, and the inherent rationality of the universe. These magic formulae borrow their potency from conditions that are not magical. Through science we have secured a degree of power of prediction and of control; through tools, machinery and an accompanying technique we have made the world more conformable to our needs, a more secure abode. We have heaped up riches and means of comfort between ourselves and the risks of the world. We have professionalized amusement as an agency of escape and forgetfulness. But when all is said and done, the fundamentally hazardous character of the world is not seriously modified, much less eliminated. Such an incident as the last war and preparations for a future war remind us that it is easy to overlook the extent to which, after all, our attainments are only devices for blurring the disagreeable recognition of a fact, instead of means of altering the fact itself.

What has been said sounds pessimistic. But the concern is not with morals but with metaphysics, with, that is to say, the nature of the existential world in which we live. It would have been as easy and more comfortable to emphasize good luck, grace, unexpected and unwon joys, those unsought for happenings which we so significantly call happiness. We might have appealed to good fortune as evidence of this important trait of hazard in nature. Comedy is as genuine as tragedy. But it is traditional that comedy strikes a more superficial note than tragedy. And there is an even better reason for appealing to misfortunes and mistakes as evidence of the precarious nature of the world. The problem of evil is a well recognized problem, while we rarely or never hear of a problem of good. Goods we take for granted; they are as they should be; they are natural and proper. The good is a recognition of our deserts. When we pull out a plum we treat it as evidence of the real order of cause and effect in the world. For this reason it is difficult for the goods of existence to furnish as convincing evidence of the uncertain character of nature as do evils. It is the latter we term accidents, not the former, even when their adventitious character is as certain.

What of it all, it may be asked? In the sense in which an assertion is true that uncontrolled distribution of good and evil is evidence of the precarious, uncertain nature of existence, it is a truism, and no problem is forwarded by its reiteration. But it is submitted that just this predicament of the inextricable mixture of stability and uncertainty gives rise to philosophy, and that it is reflected in all its recurrent problems and issues. If classic philosophy says so much about unity and so little about unreconciled diversity, so much about the eternal and permament, and so little about change (save as something to be resolved into combinations of the permanent), so much about necessity and so little about contingency, so much about the comprehending universal and so little about the recalcitrant particular, it may well be because the ambiguousness and ambivalence of reality are actually so pervasive. Since these things form the problem, solution is more apparent, (although not more actual) in the degree in which whatever of stability and assurance the world presents is fastened upon and asserted.

Upon their surface, the reports of the world which form our different philosophies are various to the point of stark contrariness. They range from spiritualism to materialism, from absolutism to relativistic phenomenalism, from transcendentalism to positivism, from rationalism to sensationalism, from idealism to realism, from subjectivism to bald objectivism, from Platonic realism to nominalism. The array of contraditions is so imposing as to suggest to sceptics that the mind of man has tackled an impossible job, or that philosophers have abandoned themselves to vagary. These radical oppositions in philosophers suggest however another consideration. They suggest that all their different philosophies have a common premise, and that their diversity is due to acceptance of a common premise. Variant philosophies may be looked at as different ways of supplying recipes for denying to the universe the character of contingency which it possesses so integrally that its denial leaves the reflecting mind without a clew, and puts subsequent philosophising at the mercy of temperament, interest and local surroundings.

Quarrels among conflicting types of philosophy are thus family quarrels. They go on within the limits of a too domestic circle, and can be settled only by venturing further afield, and out of doors. Concerned with imputing complete, finished and sure character to the world of real existence, even if things have to be broken into two disconnected pieces in order to accomplish the result, the character desiderated can plausibly be found in reason or in mechanism; in rational conceptions like those of mathematics, or brute things like sensory data; in atoms or in essences; in consciousness or in a physical externality which forces and overrides consciousness.

As against this common identification of reality with what is sure, regular and finished, experience in unsophisticated forms gives evidence of a different world and points to a different metaphysics. We live in a world which is an impressive and irresistible mixture of sufficiencies, tight completenesses, order, recurrences which make possible prediction and control, and singularities, ambiguities, uncertain possibilities, processes going on to consequences as yet indeterminate. They are mixed not mechanically but vitally like the wheat and tares of the parable. We may recognize them separately but we cannot divide them, for unlike wheat and tares they grow from the same root. Qualities have defects as necessary conditions of their excellencies; the instrumentalities of truth are the causes of error; change gives meaning to permanence and recurrence makes novelty possible. A world that was wholly risky would be a world in which adventure is impossible, and only a living world can include death. Such facts have been celebrated by thinkers like Heracleitus and Laotze; they have been greeted by theologians as furnishing occasions for exercise of divine grace; they have been elaborately formulated by various schools under a principle of relativity, so defined as to become itself final and absolute. They have rarely been frankly recognized as fundamentally significant for the formation of a naturalistic metaphysics. . . .

The union of the hazardous and the stable, of the incomplete and the recurrent, is the condition of all experienced satisfaction as truly as of our predicaments and problems. While it is the source of ignorance, error and failure of expectation, it is the source of the delight which fulfillments bring. For if there were nothing in the way, if there were no deviations and resistances, fulfillment would be at once, and in so being would fulfill nothing, but merely be. It would not be in connection with desire or satisfaction. Moreover when a fulfillment comes and is pronounced good, it is judged good, distinguished and asserted, simply because it is in jeopardy, because it occurs amid indifferent and divergent things. Because of this mixture of the regular and that which cuts across stability, a good object once experienced acquires ideal quality and attracts demand and effort to itself. A particular ideal may be an illusion, but having ideals is no illusion. It embodies features of existence. Although imagination is often fantastic it is also an organ of nature; for it is the appropriate phase of indeterminate events moving toward eventualities that are now but possibilities. A purely stable world permits of no illusions, but neither is it clothed with ideals. It just exists. To be good is to be better than; and there can be no better except where there is shock and discord combined with enough assured order to make attainment of harmony possible. Better objects when brought into existence are existent not ideal; they retain ideal quality only retrospectively as commemorative of issue from prior conflict and prospectively, in contrast with forces which make for their destruction. Water that slakes thirst, or a conclusion that solves a problem has ideal character as long as thirst or problem persists in a way which qualifies the result. But water that is not a satisfaction of need has no more ideal quality than water running through pipes into a reservoir; a solution ceases to be a solution and becomes a bare incident of existence when its antecedent generating conditions of doubt, ambiguity and search are lost from its context. While the precarious nature of existence is indeed the source of all trouble, it is also an indispensable condition of ideality, becoming a sufficient condition when conjoined with the regular and assured.

We long, amid a troubled world, for perfect being. We forget that what gives meaning to the notion of perfection is the events that create longing, and that, apart from them, a "perfect" world would mean just an unchanging brute existential thing. The ideal significance of esthetic objects is no exception to this principle. Their satisfying quality, their power to compose while they arouse, is not dependent upon definite prior desire and effort as is the case with the ideally satisfying quality of practical and scientific objects. It is part of their peculiar satisfying quality to be gratuitous, not purchased by endeavor. The contrast to other things of this detachment from toil and labor in a world where most realizations have to be bought, as well as the contrast to trouble and uncertainty, give esthetic objects their peculiar traits. If all things came to us in the way our esthetic objects do, none of them would be a source of esthetic delight.

Some phases of recent philosophy have made much of need, desire and satisfaction. Critics have frequently held that the outcome is only recurrence to an older subjective empiricism, though with substitution of affections and volitional states for cognitive sensory states. But need and desire are exponents of natural being. They are, if we use Aristotelian phraseology, actualizations of its contingencies and incompletenesses; as such nature itself is wistful and pathetic, turbulent and passionate. Were it not, the existence of wants would be a miracle. In a world where everything is complete, nothing requires anything else for its completion. A world in which events can be carried to a finish only through the coinciding assistance of other transitory events, is already necessitous, a world of begging as well as of beggarly elements. If human experience is to express and reflect this world, it must be marked by needs; in becoming aware of the needful and needed quality of things it must project satisfactions or completions. For irrespective of whether a satisfaction is conscious, a satisfaction or non-satisfaction is an objective thing with objective conditions. It means fulfillment of the demands of objective factors. Happiness may mark an awareness of such satisfaction, and it may be its culminating form. But satisfaction is not subjective, private or personal: it is conditioned by objective partialities and defections and made real by objective situations and completions.

By the same logic, necessity implies the precarious and contingent. A world that was all necessity would not be a world of necessity; it would just be. For in its being, nothing would be necessary for anything else. But where some things are indigent, other things are necessary if demands are to be met. The common failure to note the fact that a world of complete being would be a world in which necessity is meaningless is due to a rapid shift from one universe of discourse to another. First we postulate a whole of Being; then we shift to a part; now since a "part" is logically dependent as such in its existence and its properties, it is necessitated by other parts. But we have unwittingly introduced contingency in the very fact of marking off something as just a part. If the logical implications of the original notion are held to firmly, a part is already a part-of-a-whole. Its being what it is, is not necessitated by the whole or by other parts: its being what it is, is just a name for the whole being what it is. Whole and parts alike are but names for existence there as just what it is. But wherever we can say if so-and-so, then something else, there is necessity, because partialities are implied which are not just parts-of-a-whole. A world of "ifs" is alone a world of "musts"—the "ifs" express real differences; the "musts" real connections. The stable and recurrent is needed for the fulfillment of the possible; the doubtful can be settled only through its adaptation to stable objects. The necessary is always necessary for, not necessary in and of itself; it is conditioned by the contingent, although itself a condition of the full determination of the latter.

One of the most striking phases of the history of philosophic thought is the recurrent grouping together of unity, permanence (or "the eternal"), completeness and rational thought, while upon another side full multiplicity, change and the temporal, the partial, defective, sense and desire. This division is obviously but another case of violent separation of the precarious and unsettled from the regular and determinate. One aspect of it, however, is worthy of particular attention: the connection of thought and unity. Empirically, all reflection sets out from the problematic and confused. Its aim is to clarify and ascertain. When thinking is successful, its career closes in transforming the disordered into the orderly, the mixed-up into the distinguished or placed, the unclear and ambiguous into the defined and unequivocal, the disconnected into the systematized. It is empirically assured that the goal of thinking does not remain a mere ideal, but is attained often enough so as to render reasonable additional efforts to achieve it.

In these facts we have, I think, the empirical basis of the philosophic doctrines which assert that reality is really and truly a rational system, a coherent whole of relations that cannot be conceived otherwise than in terms of intellect. Reflective inquiry moves in each particular case from differences toward unity; from indeterminate and ambiguous position to clear determination, from confusion and disorder to system. When thought in a given case has reached its goal of organized totality, of definite relations of distinctly placed elements, its object is the accepted starting point, the defined subject matter, of further experiences; antecedent and outgrown conditions of darkness and of unreconciled differences are dismissed as a transitory state of ignorance and inadequate apprehensions. Retain connection of the goal with the thinking by which it is reached, and then identify it with true reality in contrast with the merely phenomenal, and the outline of the logic of rational and "objective" idealisms is before us. Thoughtlike Being, has two forms, one real; the other phenomenal. It is compelled to take on reflective form, it involves doubt, inquiry and hypothesis, because it sets out from a subject-matter conditioned by sense, a fact which proves that thought, intellect, is not pure in man, but restricted by an animal organism that is but one part linked with other parts, of nature. But the conclusion of reflection affords us a pattern and guarantee of thought which is constitutive; one with the system of objective reality. Such in outline is the procedure of all ontological logics.

A philosophy which accepts the denotative or empirical method accepts at full value the fact that reflective thinking transforms confusion, ambiguity and discrepancy into illumination, definiteness and consistency. But it also points to the contextual situation in which thinking occurs. It notes that the starting point is the actually problematic, and that the problematic phase resides in some actual and specifiable situation.

It notes that the means of converting the dubious into the assured, and the incomplete into the determinate, is use of assured and established things, which are just as empirical and as indicative of the nature of experienced things as is the uncertain. It thus notes that thinking is no different in kind from the use of natural materials and energies, say fire and tools, to refine, re-order, and shape other natural materials, say ore. In both cases, there are matters which as they stand are unsatisfactory and there are also adequate agencies of dealing with them and connecting them. At no point or place is there any jump outside empirical, natural objects and their relations. Thought and reason are not specific powers. They consist of the procedures intentionally employed in the application to each other of the unsatisfactorily confused and indeterminate on one side and the regular and stable on the other. Generalizing from such observations, empirical philosophy perceives that thinking is a continuous process of temporal re-organization within one and the same world of experienced things, not a jump from the latter world into one of objects constituted once for all by thought. It discovers thereby the empirical basis of rational idealism, and the point at which it empirically goes astray. Idealism fails to take into account the specified or concrete character of the uncertain situation in which thought occurs; it fails to note the empirically concrete nature of the subject-matter, acts, and tools by which determination and consistency are reached; it fails to note that the conclusive eventual objects having the latter properties are themselves as many as the situations dealt with. The conversion of the logic of reflection into an ontology of rational being is thus due to arbitrary conversion of an eventual natural function of unification into a causal antecedent reality; this in turn is due to the tendency of the imagination working under the influence of emotion to carry unification from an actual, objective and experimental enterprise, limited to particular situations where it is needed, into an unrestricted, wholesale movement which ends in an all-absorbing dream.

The occurrence of reflection is crucial for dualistic metaphysics as well as for idealistic ontologies. Reflection occurs only in situations qualified by uncertainty, alternatives, questioning, search, hypotheses, tentative trials or experiments which test the worth of thinking. A naturalistic metaphysics is bound to consider reflection as itself a natural event occurring within nature because of traits of the latter. It is bound to inference from the empirical traits of thinking in precisely the same way as the sciences make inferences from the happening of suns, radio-activity, thunder-storms or any other natural event. Traits of reflection are as truly indicative or evidential of the traits of other things as are the traits of these events. A theory of the nature of the occurrence and career of a sun reached by denial of the obvious traits of the sun, or by denial that these traits are so connected with the traits of other natural events that they can be used as evidence concerning the nature of these other things, would hardly possess scientific standing. Yet philosophers, and strangely enough philosophers who call themselves realists, have constantly held that the traits which are characteristic of thinking, namely, uncertainty, ambiguity, alternatives, inquiring, search, selection, experimental reshaping of external conditions, do not possess the same existential character as do the objects of valid knowledge. They have denied that these traits are evidential of the character of the world within which thinking occurs. They have not, as realists, asserted that these traits are mere appearances; but they have often asserted and implied that such things are only personal or psychological in contrast with a world of objective nature. But the interests of empirical and denotative method and of naturalistic metaphysics wholly coincide. The world must actually be such as to generate ignorance and inquiry; doubt and hypothesis, trial and temporal conclusions; the latter being such that they develop out of existences which while wholly "real" are not as satisfactory, as good, or as significant, as those into which they are eventually re-organized. The ultimate evidence of genuine hazard, contingency, irregularity and indeterminateness in nature is thus found in the occurrence of thinking. The traits of natural existence which generate the fears and adorations of superstitious barbarians generate the scientific procedures of disciplined civilization. The superiority of the latter does not consist in the fact that they are based on "real" existence, while the former depend wholly upon a human nature different from nature in general. It consists in the fact that scientific inquiries reach objects which are better, because reached by method which controls them and which adds greater control to life itself, method which mitigates accident, turns contingency to account, and releases thought and other forms of endeavor.

The conjunction of problematic and determinate characters in nature renders every existence, as well as every idea and human act, an experiment in fact, even though not in design. To be intelligently experimental is but to be conscious of this intersection of natural conditions so as to profit by it instead of being at its mercy. The Christian idea of this world and this life as a probation is a kind of distorted recognition of the situation; distorted because it applied wholesale to one stretch of existence in contrast with another, regarded as original and final. But in truth anything which can exist at any place and at any time occurs subject to tests imposed upon it by surroundings, which are only in part compatible and reinforcing. These surroundings test its strength and measure its endurance. As we can discourse of change only in terms of velocity and acceleration which involve relations to other things, so assertion of the permanent and enduring is comparative. The stablest thing we can speak of is not free from conditions set to it by other things. That even the solid earth mountains, the emblems of constancy, appear and disappear like the clouds is an old theme of moralists and poets. The fixed and unchanged being of the Democritean atom is now reported by inquirers to possess some of the traits of his non-being, and to embody a temporary equilibrium in the economy of nature's compromises and adjustments. A thing may endure *secula seculorum* and yet not be everlasting; it will crumble before the gnawing tooth of time, as it exceeds a certain measure. Every existence is an event.

This fact is nothing at which to repine and nothing to gloat over. It is something to be noted and used. If it is discomfiting when applied to good things, to our friends, possessions and precious selves, it is consoling also to know that no evil endures forever; that the longest lane turns sometime, and that the memory of loss of nearest and dearest grows dim in time. The eventful character of all existences is no reason for consigning them to the realm of mere appearance any more than it is a reason for idealizing flux into a deity. The important thing is measure, relation, ratio, knowledge of the comparative tempos of change. In mathematics some variables are constants in some problems; so it is in nature and life. The rate of change of some things is so slow, or is so rhythmic, that these changes have all the advantages of stability in dealing with more transitory and irregular happenings—if we know enough. Indeed, if any one thing that concerns us is subject to change, it is fortunate that all other things change. A thing "absolutely" stable and unchangeable would be out of the range of the principle of action and reaction, of resistance and leverage as well as of friction. Here it would have no applicability, no potentiality of use as measure and control of other events. To designate the slower and the regular rhythmic events structure, and more rapid and irregular ones process, is sound practical sense. It expresses the function of one in respect to the other.

Martin Heidegger

The Way Back into the Ground of Metaphysics *

Descartes, writing to Picot, who translated the *Principia Philosophiae* into French, observed: "Thus the whole of philosophy is like a tree: the roots are metaphysics, the trunk is physics, and the branches that issue from the trunk are all the other sciences . . ." (*Opp. ed. Ad. et Ta.* IX, 14)

Sticking to this image, we ask: In what soil do the roots of the tree of philosophy have their hold? Out of what ground do the roots—and through them the whole tree—receive their nourishing juices and strength? What element, concealed in the ground, enters and lives in the roots that support and nourish the tree? What is the basis and element of metaphysics? What is metaphysics, viewed from its ground? What is metaphysics itself, at bottom?

Metaphysics thinks about beings as beings. Wherever the question is asked what beings are, beings as such are in sight. Metaphysical representation owes this sight to the light of Being. The light itself, i.e., that which such thinking experiences as light, does not come within the range of metaphysical thinking; for metaphysics always represents beings only as beings. Within this perspective, metaphysical thinking does, of course, inquire about the being which is the source and originator of this light. But the light itself is considered sufficiently illuminated as soon as we recognize that we look through it whenever we look at beings.

In whatever manner beings are interpreted—whether as spirit, after the fashion of spiritualism; or as matter and force, after the fashion of materialism; or as becoming and life, or idea, will, substance, subject, or *energeia;* or as the eternal recurrence of the same events—every time, beings as beings appear in the light of Being. Wherever metaphysics repre-

* From "The Way Back into the Ground of Metaphysics" by Martin Heidegger, translated by Walter Kaufmann. In *Existentialism from Dostoevsky to Sartre,* edited by Walter Kaufmann.

sents beings, Being has entered into the light. Being has arrived in a state of unconcealedness (᾿Αλήθεια.). But whether and how Being itself involves such unconcealedness, whether and how it manifests itself in, and as, metaphysics, remains obscure. Being in its revelatory essence, i.e. in its truth, is not recalled. Nevertheless, when metaphysics gives answers to its question concerning beings as such, metaphysics speaks out of the unnoticed revealedness of Being. The truth of Being may thus be called the ground in which metaphysics, as the root of the tree of philosophy, is kept and from which it is nourished.

Because metaphysics inquires about beings as beings, it remains concerned with beings and does not devote itself to Being as Being. As the root of the tree, it sends all nourishment and all strength into the trunk and its branches. The root branches out in the soil to enable the tree to grow out of the ground and thus to leave it. The tree of philosophy grows out of the soil in which metaphysics is rooted. The ground is the element in which the root of the tree lives, but the growth of the tree is never able to absorb this soil in such a way that it disappears in the tree as part of the tree. Instead, the roots, down to the subtlest tendrils, lose themselves in the soil. The ground is ground for the roots, and in the ground the roots forget themselves for the sake of the tree. The roots still belong to the tree even when they abandon themselves, after a fashion, to the element of the soil. They squander themselves and their element on the tree. As roots, they do not devote themselves to the soil—at least not as if it were their life to s[illegible] into this element and to spread out in it. Presumably, the elem[illegible]e the same element either if the roots did not live in it.

Metaphysics, insofar as it always represents only beings as beings, does not recall Being itself. Philosophy does not concentrate on its ground. It always leaves its ground—leaves it by means of metaphysics. And yet it never escapes its ground.

Insofar as a thinker sets out to experience the ground of metaphysics, insofar as the attempts to recall the truth of Being itself instead of merely representing beings as beings, his thinking has in a sense left metaphysics. From the point of view of metaphysics, such thinking goes back into the ground of metaphysics. But what still appears as ground from this point of view is presumably something else, once it is experienced in its own terms—something as yet unsaid, according to which the essence of metaphysics, too, is something else and not metaphysics.

Such thinking, which recalls the truth of Being, is no longer satisfied with mere metaphysics, to be sure; but it does not oppose and think against metaphysics either. To return to our image, it does not tear up the root of philosophy. It tills the ground and plows the soil for this root. Metaphysics remains the basis of philosophy. The basis of thinking, however, it does not reach. When we think of the truth of Being, metaphysics is overcome. We can no longer accept the claim of metaphysics that it takes care of the fundamental involvement in "Being" and that it decisively determines all relations to beings as such. But this "overcoming of metaphysics" does not abolish metaphysics. As long as man remains the *animal rationale* he is also the *animal metaphysicum.* As long as man understands himself as the rational animal, metaphysics belongs, as Kant said, to the nature of man. But if our thinking should succeed in its efforts to go back into the ground of metaphysics, it might well help to bring about a change in human nature, accompanied by a transformation of metaphysics.

If, as we unfold the question concerning the truth of Being, we speak of overcoming metaphysics, this means: recalling Being itself. Such recalling goes beyond the tradition of forgetting the ground of the root of philosophy. The thinking attempted in *Being and Time* (1927) sets out on the way to prepare an overcoming of metaphysics, so understood. That, however, which prompts such thinking can only be that which is to be recalled. That Being itself and how Being itself concerns our thinking does not depend upon our thinking alone. That Being itself, and the manner in which Being itself, strikes a man's thinking, that rouses his thinking and stirs it to rise from Being itself to respond and correspond to Being as such.

Why, however, should such an overcoming of metaphysics be necessary? Is the point merely to underpin that discipline of philosophy which was the root hitherto, or to supplant it with a yet more basic discipline? Is it a question of changing the philosophic system of instruction? No. Or are we trying to go back into the ground of metaphysics in order to uncover a hitherto overlooked presupposition of philosophy, and thereby to show that philosophy does not yet stand on an unshakable foundation and therefore cannot yet be the absolute science? No.

It is something else that is at stake with the arrival of the truth of Being or its failure to arrive: it is neither the state of philosophy nor philosophy itself alone, but rather the proximity or remoteness of that from which philosophy, insofar as it means the representation of beings as such, receives its nature and its necessity. What is to be decided is nothing less than this: can Being itself, out of its own unique truth, bring about its involvement in human nature; or shall metaphysics, which turns its back to its ground, prevent further that the involvement of Being in man may generate a radiance out of the very essence of this involvement itself—a radiance which might lead man to belong to Being?

In its answers to the question concerning beings as such, metaphysics operates with a prior conception of Being. It speaks of Being necessarily and hence continually. But metaphysics does not induce Being itself to speak, for metaphysics does not recall Being in its truth, nor does it recall truth as unconcealedness, nor does it recall the nature of unconcealedness. To metaphysics the nature of truth always appears only in the derivative form of the truth of knowledge and the truth of propositions which formulate our knowledge. Unconcealedness, however, might be prior to all truth in the sense of *veritas*. 'Αλήθεια might be the word that offers a hitherto unnoticed hint concerning the nature of *esse* which has not yet been recalled. If this should be so, then the representational thinking of metaphysics could certainly never reach this nature of truth, however zealously it might devote itself to historical studies of pre-Socratic philosophy; for what is at stake here is not some renaissance of pre-Socratic thinking: any such attempt would be vain and absurd. What is wanted is rather some regard for the arrival of the hitherto unexpressed nature of unconcealedness, for it is in this form that Being has announced itself. Meanwhile the truth of Being has remained concealed from metaphysics during its long history from Anaximander to Nietzsche. Why does metaphysics not recall it? Is the failure to recall it merely a function of some kinds of metaphysical thinking? Or is it an essential feature of the fate of metaphysics that its own ground eludes it because in the rise of unconcealedness its very core, namely concealedness, stays away in favor of the unconcealed which appears in the form of beings?

Metaphysics, however, speaks continually and in the most various ways of Being. Metaphysics gives, and seems to confirm, the appearance that it asks and answers the question concerning Being. In fact, metaphysics never answers the question concerning the truth of Being, for it never asks this question. Metaphysics does not ask this question because it thinks of Being only by representing beings as beings. It means all beings as a whole, although it speaks of Being. It refers to Being and means beings as beings. From its beginning to its completion, the propositions of metaphysics have been strangely involved in a persistent confusion of beings and Being. This confusion, to be sure, must be considered an event and not a mere mistake. It cannot by any means be charged to a mere negligence of thought or a carelessness of expression. Owing to this persistent confusion, the claim that metaphysics poses the question of Being lands us in utter error.

Due to the manner in which it thinks of beings, metaphysics almost seems to be, without knowing it, the barrier which keeps man from the original involvement of Being in human nature.

What if the absence of this involvement and the oblivion of this absence determined the entire modern age? What if the absence of Being abandoned man more and more exclusively to beings, leaving him forsaken and far from any involvement of Being in his nature, while this forsakenness itself remained veiled? What if this were the case—and had been the case for a long time now? What if there were signs that this oblivion will become still more decisive in the future?

Would there still be occasion for a thoughtful person to give himself arrogant airs in view of this fateful withdrawal with which Being presents us? Would there still be occasion, if this should be our situation, to deceive ourselves with pleasant phantasms and to indulge, of all things, in an artificially induced elation? If the oblivion of Being which has been described here should be real, would there not be occasion enough for a thinker who recalls Being to experience a genuine horror? What more can his thinking do than to endure in dread this fateful withdrawal, while first of all facing up to the oblivion of Being? But how could thought achieve this as long as its fatefully granted dread seems to it no more than a mood of depression? What does such dread, which is fated by Being, have to do with psychology or psychoanalysis?

Suppose that the overcoming of metaphysics involved the endeavor to commence with a regard for the oblivion of Being—the attempt to learn to develop such a regard, in order to experience this oblivion and to absorb this experience into the involvement of Being in man, and to preserve it there: then, in the distress of the oblivion of Being, the question "What is metaphysics?" might well become the most necessary necessity for thought.

Thus everything depends on this: that our thinking should become more thoughtful in its season. This is achieved when our thinking, instead of implementing a higher degree of exertion, is directed toward a different point of origin. The thinking which is posited by beings as such, and therefore representational and illuminating in that way, must be supplanted by a different kind of thinking which is brought to pass by Being itself and, therefore, responsive to Being.

All attempts are futile which seek to make representational thinking which remains metaphysical, and only metaphysical, effective and useful for immediate action in everyday public life. The more thoughtful our thinking becomes and the more adequate it is to the involvement of Being in it, the purer our thinking will stand *eo ipso* in the one action appropriate to it: recalling what is meant for it and thus, in a sense, what is already meant.

But who still recalls what is meant? One makes inventions. To lead our thinking on the way on which it may find the involvement of the truth of Being in human nature, to open up a path for our thinking on which it may recall Being itself in its truth—to do that the thinking attempted in *Being and Time* is "on its way." On this way—that is, in the service of the question concerning the truth of Being—it becomes necessary to stop and think about human nature; for the experience of the oblivion of Being, which is not specifically mentioned because it still had to be demonstrated, involves the crucial conjecture that in view of the unconcealedness of Being the involvement of Being in human nature is an essential feature of Being. But how could this conjecture, which is experienced here, become an explicit question before every attempt had been made to liberate the determination of human nature from the concept of subjectivity and from the concept of the *animal rationale?* To characterize with a single term both the involvement of Being in human nature and the essential relation of man to the openness ("there") of Being as such, the name of "being there [*Dasein*]" was chosen for that sphere of being in which man stands as man. This term was employed, even though in metaphysics it is used interchangeably with *existentia,* actuality, reality, and objectivity, and although this metaphysical usage is further supported by the common [German] expression *"menschliches Dasein."* Any attempt, therefore, to re-think *Being and Time* is thwarted as long as one is satisfied with the observation that, in this study, the term "being there" is used in place of "consciousness." As if this were simply a matter of using different words! As if it were not the one and only thing at stake here: namely, to get men to think about the involvement of Being in human nature and thus, from our point of view, to present first of all an experience of human nature which may prove sufficient to direct our inquiry. The term "being there" neither takes the place of the term "consciousness" nor does the "object" designated as "being there" take the place of what we think of when we speak of "consciousness." "Being there" names that which should first of all be experienced, and subsequently thought of, as a place—namely, the location of the truth of Being.

What the term "being there" means throughout the treatise on *Being and Time* is indicated immediately (page 42) by its introductory key sentence: *"The 'essence' of being there lies in its existence."* [*Das "Wesen" des Daseins liegt in seiner Existenz.*]

To be sure, in the language of metaphysics the word "existence" is a synonym of "being there": both refer to the reality of anything at all that is real, from God to a grain of sand. As long, therefore, as the quoted sentence is understood only superficially, the difficulty is merely transferred from one word to another, from "being there" to "existence." In *B.&T.* the term "existence" is used exclusively for the being of man. Once "existence" is understood rightly, the "essence" of being there can be recalled: in its openness, Being itself manifests and conceals itself, yields itself and withdraws; at the same time, this truth of Being does not exhaust itself in being there, nor can it by any means simply be identified with it after the fashion of the metaphysical proposition: all objectivity is as such also subjectivity.

What does "existence" mean in *B.&T.*? The word designates a mode of Being; specifically, the Being of those beings who stand open for the openness of Being in which they stand, by standing it. This "standing it," this enduring, is experienced under the name of "care." The ecstatic essence of being there is approached by way of care, and, conversely, care is experienced adequately only in its ecstatic essence. "Standing it," experienced in this manner, is the essence of the *ekstasis* which must be grasped by thought. The ecstatic essence of existence is therefore still understood inadequately as long as one thinks of it as merely "standing out," while interpreting the "out" as meaning "away from" the inside of an immanence of consciousness and spirit. For in this manner, existence would still be understood in terms of "subjectivity" and "substance"; while, in fact, the "out" ought to be understood in terms of the openness of Being itself. The *stasis* of the ecstatic consists—strange as it may sound—in standing in the "out" and "there" of unconcealedness in which Being itself is present. What is meant by "existence" in the context of an inquiry that is prompted by, and directed toward, the truth of Being, can be most beautifully designated by the word "instancy [*Inständigkeit*]." We must think at the same time, however, of standing in the openness of Being, of enduring and out-standing this standing-in (care), and of out-braving the utmost (Being toward death); for it is only together that they constitute the full essence of existence.

The being that exists is man. Man alone exists. Rocks are, but they do not exist. Trees are, but they do not exist. Horses are, but they do not exist. Angels are, but they do not exist. God is, but he does not exist. The proposition "man alone exists" does not mean by any means that man alone is a real being while all other beings are unreal and mere appearances or human ideas. The proposition "man exists" means: man is that being whose

Being is distinguished by the open-standing standing-in in the unconcealedness of Being, from Being, in Being. The existential nature of man is the reason why man can represent beings as such, and why he can be conscious of them. All consciousness presupposes ecstatically understood existence as the *essentia* of man—*essentia* meaning that as which man is present insofar as he is man. But consciousness does not itself create the openness of beings, nor is it consciousness that makes it possible for man to stand open for beings. Whither and whence and in what free dimension could the intentionality of consciousness move, if instancy were not the essence of man in the first instance? What else could be the meaning—if anybody has ever seriously thought about this—of the word *sein* in the [German] words *Bewusstsein* ["consciousness"; literally: "being conscious"] and *Selbstbewusstsein* ["self-consciousness"] if it did not designate the existential nature of that which is in the mode of existence? To be a self is admittedly one feature of the nature of that being which exists; but existence does not consist in being a self, nor can it be defined in such terms. We are faced with the fact that metaphysical thinking understands man's selfhood in terms of substance or—and at bottom this amounts to the same—in terms of the subject. It is for this reason that the first way which leads away from metaphysics to the ecstatic existential nature of man must lead through the metaphysical conception of human selfhood (*B.&T.*, §§63 and 64).

The question concerning existence, however, is always subservient to that question which is nothing less than the only question of thought. This question, yet to be unfolded, concerns the truth of Being as the concealed ground of all metaphysics. For this reason the treatise which sought to point the way back into the ground of metaphysics did not bear the title "Existence and Time," nor "Consciousness and Time," but *Being and Time.* Nor can this title be understood as if it were parallel to the customary juxtapositions of Being and Becoming, Being and Seeming, Being and Thinking, or Being and Ought. For in all these cases Being is limited, as if Becoming, Seeming, Thinking, and Ought did not belong to Being, although it is obvious that they are not nothing and thus belong to Being. In *Being and Time,* Being is not something other than Time: "Time" is called the first name of the truth of Being, and this truth is the presence of Being and thus Being itself. But why "Time" and "Being"?

By recalling the beginnings of history when Being unveiled itself in the thinking of the Greeks, it can be shown that the Greeks from the very beginning experienced the Being of beings as the presence of the present. When we translate εἶναι as "being," our translation is linguistically correct. Yet we merely substitute one set of sounds for another. As soon as we examine ourselves it becomes obvious that we neither think εἶναι, as it were, in Greek nor have in mind a correspondingly clear and univocal concept when we speak of "being." What, then, are we saying when instead of εἶναι we say "being," and instead of "being," εἶναι and *esse?* We are saying nothing. The Greek, Latin, and German word all remain equally obtuse. As long as we adhere to the customary usage we merely betray ourselves as the pacemakers of the greatest thoughtlessness which has ever gained currency in human thought and which has remained dominant until this moment. This εἶναι, however, means: to be present [*anwesen;* this verb form, in place of the idiomatic *"anwesend sein,"* is Heidegger's neology]. The true being of this being present [*das Wesen dieses Anwesens*] is deeply concealed in the earliest names of Being. But for us εἶναι and οὐσία as παρῖ and ἀπουσία means this first of all: in being present there moves, unrecognized and concealed, present time and duration—in one word, Time. Being as such is thus unconcealed owing to Time. Thus Time points to unconcealedness, i.e., the truth of Being. But the Time of which we should think here is not experienced through the changeful career of beings. Time is evidently of an altogether different nature which neither has been recalled by way of the time concept of metaphysics nor ever can be recalled in this way. Thus Time becomes the first name, which is yet to be heeded, of the truth of Being, which is yet to be experienced.

A concealed hint of Time speaks not only out of the earliest metaphysical names of Being but also out of its last name, which is "the eternal recurrence of the same events." Through the entire epoch of metaphysics, Time is decisively present in the history of Being, without being recognized or thought about. To this Time, space is neither co-ordinated nor merely subordinated.

Suppose one attempts to make a transition from the representation of beings as such to recalling the truth of Being: such an attempt, which starts from this representation, must still represent, in a certain sense, the truth of Being, too; and any such representation must of necessity be heterogeneous and ultimately, insofar as it is a representation, inadequate for that which is to be thought. This relation, which comes out of metaphysics and tries to enter into the involvement of the truth of Being in human nature, is called understanding. But here understanding is viewed, at the same time, from the point of view of the unconcealedness of Being. Understanding is a pro-ject thrust forth and ecstatic, which means that it stands in the sphere of the open. The sphere which opens up as we project, in order that something (Being in this case) may prove itself as something (in this case, Being as itself in its unconcealedness), is called the sense.

(Cf. *B.&T.*, p. 151) "The sense of Being" and "the truth of Being" mean the same.

Let us suppose that Time belongs to the truth of Being in a way that is still concealed: then every project that holds open the truth of Being, representing a way of understanding Being, must look out into Time as the horizon of any possible understanding of Being. (Cf. *B.&T.*, §§ 31–34 and 68.)

The preface to *Being and Time,* on the first page of the treatise, ends with these sentences: "To furnish a concrete elaboration of the question concerning the sense of 'Being' is the intention of the following treatise. The interpretation of Time as the horizon of every possible attempt to understand Being is its provisional goal."

All philosophy has fallen into the oblivion of Being which has, at the same time, become and remained the fateful demand on thought in *B.&T.*; and philosophy could hardly have given a clearer demonstration of the power of this oblivion of Being than it has furnished us by the somnambulistic assurance with which it has passed by the real and only question of *B.&T.* What is at stake here, is, therefore, not a series of misunderstandings of a book but our abandonment by Being.

Metaphysics states what beings are as beings. It offers a λόγος (statement) about the ὄντα (beings). The later title "ontology" characterizes its nature, provided, of course, that we understand it in accordance with its true significance and not through its narrow scholastic meaning. Metaphysics moves in the sphere of the ὄν ᾗ ὄν: it deals with beings as beings. In this manner, metaphysics always represents beings as such in their totality; it deals with the beingness of beings (the οὐσία of the ὄν). But metaphysics represents the beingness of beings [*die Seiendheit des Seienden*] in a twofold manner: in the first place, the totality of beings as such with an eye to their most universal traits ὄν καθόλου, κοινόν;) but at the same time also the totality of beings as such in the sense of the highest and therefore divine being ὄν καθόλου, ἀκρότατον, θεῖον). In the metaphysics of Aristotle, the unconcealedness of beings as such has specifically developed in this twofold manner. (Cf. Met. Γ, E, K.)

Because metaphysics represents beings as beings, it is, two-in-one, the truth of beings in their universality and in the highest being. According to its nature, it is at the same time ontology in the narrower sense and theology. This onto-theological nature of philosophy proper (πρώτη φιλοσοφία) is, no doubt, due to the way in which the ὄν opens up in it, namely as ὄν. Thus the theological character of ontology is not merely due to the fact that Greek metaphysics was later taken up and transformed by the ecclesiastic theology of Christianity. Rather it is due to the manner in which beings as beings have from the very beginning disconcealed themselves. It was this unconcealedness of beings that provided the possibility for Christian theology to take possession of Greek philosophy—whether for better or for worse may be decided by the theologians, on the basis of their experience of what is Christian; only they should keep in mind what is written in the First Epistle of Paul the Apostle to the Corinthians: "οὐχὶ ἐμώρανεν ὁ θεὸς τὴν σοφίαν τοῦ κόσμου; Has not God let the wisdom of this world become foolishness?" (I Cor. 1:20) The *σοφία τοῦ κόσμου* [wisdom of this world], however, is that which, according to 1:22, the Ἕλληνες ζητοῦσιν, the Greeks seek. Aristotle even calls the πρώτη φιλοσοφία (philosophy proper) quite specifically ζητουμένη—what is sought. Will Christian theology make up its mind one day to take seriously the word of the apostle and thus also the conception of the philosophy of foolishness?

As the truth of beings as such, metaphysics has a twofold character. The reason for this twofoldedness, however, let alone its origin, remains unknown to metaphysics; and this is no accident, nor due to mere neglect. Metaphysics has this twofold character because it is what it is: the representation of beings as beings. Metaphysics has no choice. Being metaphysics, it is by its very nature excluded from the experience of Being; for it always represents beings (ὄν) only with an eye to what of Being has already manifested itself as beings (ᾗ ὄν). But metaphysics never pays attention to what has concealed itself in this very ὄν insofar as it became unconcealed.

Thus the time came when it became necessary to make a fresh attempt to grasp by thought what precisely is said when we speak of ὄν or use the word "being" [*seiend*]. Accordingly, the question concerning the ὄν was reintroduced into human thinking. (Cf. *B.&T.*, Preface.) But this reintroduction is no mere repetition of the Platonic-Aristotelian question; instead it asks about that which conceals itself in the ὄν.

Metaphysics is founded upon that which conceals itself here as long as metaphysics studies the ὂν ᾗ ὄν. The attempt to inquire back into what conceals itself here seeks, from the point of view of metaphysics, the fundament of ontology. Therefore this attempt is called, in *Being and Time* (page 13) "fundamental ontology" [*Fundamentalontologie*]. Yet this title, like any title, is soon seen to be inappropriate. From the point of view of metaphysics, to be sure, it says something that is correct; but precisely for that reason it is misleading, for what matters is success in the transition from metaphysics to recalling the truth of Being. As long as this thinking calls itself "fundamental ontology" it blocks and obscures its own way with this title. For what the title "fundamental ontology" suggests is, of course, that the attempt to recall the truth of Being—and not, like all ontology, the truth of beings—is itself (seeing that it is called "fundamental ontology") still a kind of ontology. In fact, the attempt to recall the truth of Being sets out on the way back into the ground of metaphysics, and with its first step it immediately leaves the realm of ontology. On the other hand, every philosophy which revolves around an indirect or direct conception of "transcendence" remains of necessity essentially an ontology, whether it achieves a new foundation of ontology or whether it assures us that it repudiates ontology as a conceptual freezing of experience.

Coming from the ancient custom of representing beings as such, the very thinking that attempted to recall the truth of Being became entangled in these customary conceptions. Under these circumstances it would seem that both for a preliminary orientation and in order to prepare the transition from representational thinking to a new kind of thinking recalls [*das andenkende Denken*], that nothing could be more necessary than the question: What is metaphysics?

The unfolding of this question in the following lecture culminates in another question. This is called the basic question of metaphysics: Why is there any being at all and not rather Nothing? Meanwhile [since this lecture was first published in 1929], to be sure, people have talked back and forth a great deal about dread and the Nothing, both of which are spoken of in this lecture. But one has never yet deigned to ask oneself why a lecture which moves from thinking of the truth of Being to the Nothing, and then tries from there to think into the nature of metaphysics, should claim that this question is the basic question of metaphysics. How can an attentive reader help feeling on the tip of his tongue an objection which is far more weighty than all protests against dread and Nothing? The final question provokes the objection that an inquiry which attempts to recall Being by way of the Nothing returns in the end to a question concerning beings. On top of that, the question even proceeds in the customary manner of metaphysics by beginning with a causal "Why?" To this extent, then, the attempt to recall Being is repudiated in favor of representational knowledge of beings on the basis of beings. And to make matters still worse, the final question is obviously the question which the metaphysician Leibniz posed in his *Principes de la nature et de la grace: "Pourquoi il y a plutôt quelque chose que rien?"* (Opp. ed. Gerh. tom. VI, 602.n. 7).

Does the lecture, then fall short of its intention? After all, this would be quite possible in view of the difficulty of effecting a transition from metaphysics to another kind of thinking. Does the lecture end up by asking Leibniz's metaphysical question about the supreme cause of all things that have being? Why, then, is Leibniz's name not mentioned, as decency would seem to require?

Or is the question asked in an altogether different sense? If it does not concern itself with beings and inquire about their first cause among all beings, then the question must begin from that which is not a being. And this is precisely what the question names, and it capitalizes the word: the Nothing. This is the sole topic of the lecture. The demand seems obvious that the end of the lecture should be thought through, for once, in its own perspective which determines the whole lecture. What has been called the basic question of metaphysics would then have to be understood and asked in terms of fundamental ontology as the question that comes out of the ground of metaphysics and as the question about this ground.

But if we grant this lecture that in the end it thinks in the direction of its own distinctive concern, how are we to understand this question?

The question is: Why is there any being at all and not rather Nothing? Suppose that we do not remain within metaphysics to ask metaphysically in the customary manner; suppose we recall the truth of Being out of the nature and the truth of metaphysics; then this might be asked as well: How did it come about that beings take precedence everywhere and lay claim to every "is" while that which is not a being is understood as Nothing, though it is Being itself, and remains forgotten? How did it come about that with Being it really is nothing and the Nothing really is not? Is it perhaps from this that the as yet unshaken presumption has entered into all metaphysics that "Being" may simply be taken for granted and that Nothing is therefore made more easily than beings? That is indeed the situation regarding Being and Nothing. If it were different, then Leibniz could not have said in the same place by way of an explanation: "*Car le rien est plus simple et plus facile que quelque chose* [For the nothing is simpler and easier than any thing]."

What is more enigmatic: that things are, or that Being is? Or does even this reflection fail to bring us close to that enigma what has occurred with the Being of beings?

Whatever the answer may be, the time should have ripened meanwhile for thinking through the lecture "What is Metaphysics?" which has been subjected to so many attacks, from its end, for once—from *its* end and not from an imaginary end.

Sarvepalli Radhakrishnan

Saṁsāra or the World of Change *

Philosophical Explanation. Whereas the scientific mind is satisfied with secondary causes, the philosophic mind demands final causes. Philosophy is an attempt to explain the world to which we belong. It is experience come to an understanding with itself. Experience relates to the world of objects, of things, of nature studied by the natural sciences; the world of individual subjects, their thoughts and feelings, their desires and decisions, studied by the social sciences, like psychology and history; the world of values, studied by literature, philosophy and religion. We must weave into a consistent pattern the different sides of our experience. There can be no bifurcation between them. We must endeavour to frame a coherent system of general ideas in terms of which the different types of experience can be interpreted. Even if we may not be able to reach a final and adequate answer, it is useful to make the attempt. After all, the wisest of us, like Socrates, are ignorant men thinking aloud, faced by the infinitude and complexity of the world.

A spiritual interpretation of the universe is based on a number of arguments, which may not be separately infallible, but they do strengthen one another. We may indicate them by looking at the question from the three different angles of the object, the subject and the spirit.

The World as Saṁsāra. It is interesting to know that the Indian thinkers, Hindu and Buddhist, viewed the world as a stream of happenings, a perpetual flow of events. Change is the essence of existence. The ultimate units of the concrete flow of experience are neither points of space nor instants of time nor particles of matter. They are events which have a three-dimensional character, a concrete content occupying a point of space at an instant of time. Śivāditya (eleventh century) in his *Saptapadārthi* observes that the concrete filling, space and time are in reality one only.[1] Space,

* From *The Philosophy of Sarvepalli Radhakrishnan,* edited by P. A. Schilpp. Tudor Publishing Co., n. d., pp. 26–32, 38–47. Copyright 1952 by The Library of Living Philosophers. Reprinted by permission of The Library of Living Philosophers, Inc.

[1] *ākāśāditrayaṁ tu vastuta ekam eva.* 27.

time, matter or life are always abstractions from a happening with a qualitative character and a spatio-temporal setting. This world or saṁsāra is a process consisting of events, to use Whitehead's expressions.

Cosmic Evolution. The world process is not an incessant fluctuation comparable to a surging sea. It is a movement with a direction and a goal. Aristotle said that, if nothing depended on time for its realisation, everything would already have happened. If time is a necessary element in the structure of the cosmic process then nature is a creative advance. The idea of evolution is not unknown to Indian thinkers, though they conceived it as a metaphysical hypothesis rather than as an empirically verified theory.

If the cosmos is a process, what is it that proceeds, and what is its destination? In the ancient Upaniṣad, the *Taittirīya* (eighth century B.C.), cosmic evolution is represented by the five stages of matter (anna), life (prāṇa), perceptual-instinctive consciousness (manas), reflective consciousness (vijñāna), and spiritual or creative consciousness (ānanda). In the cosmic process we have the successive emergence of the material, the organic, the animal, the human and the spiritual orders of existence.

Matter and Life. Materiality is the first manifested form of cosmic existence. From unmanifested being we get the material manifestation. If matter grows into life, is there anything in matter compelling it to grow into life? Can the emergence of life be traced to the working of the principle of matter? It is assumed that it is the work of life itself energising in and on the conditions of matter and applying to it its own laws and principles. Life exhibits characteristics which go beyond the general laws of inorganic processes. Living organisms respond to situations in a way that they preserve and perpetuate themselves. Their nutritive, reparatory and reproductive functions are 'intelligent,' though not guided by intelligence. They are full of "prospective adaptations." Their actions tend to produce results which are beneficial to the individual and the species. Such actions, on the part of human individuals, are due to foresight. We need not postulate any mysterious vital force; but we must recognise that life is a unique kind of activity for which the formulas of matter and energy are not adequate.

Life and Mind. Similarly when mind emerges out of life, it is due to the principle of mind working with its own impulses and necessities in life. Mind is not a kind of ghost introduced into the living organism. The principles of life and mind are not to be treated as working on independent lines in the conscious being. The unity of the living whole is preserved when the quality of mind arises.

Mind and Intelligence. Animals are conscious; men are self-conscious, and so have greater dignity than stones, or plants or animals. By overlooking the distinction between men and animals, Hitler, for example, argued that the individual is nothing, it is the group that counts. Nature, he argued in his *Mein Kampf,* is ruthless in regard to individual lives and considerate only for the development of the species. He thought of man as merely the highest of the animals. "It is not necessary that any of us should live," he said. "It is only necessary that Germany should live." Even John Dewey argues in a similar vein:

> Within the flickering inconsequential acts of separate selves dwells a sense of the whole which claims and dignifies them. In its presence we put off mortality and live in the universal. The life of the community in which we live and have our being is the fit symbol of this relationship. The acts in which we express the perception of ties which bind us to others are only rites and ceremonies.[2]

History is not a branch of biology. The drama of human personalities is distinct from life in the animal kingdom. Social sciences which deal with the story of man in society are a separte category from natural sciences.

Men have a restless reaching out for ideals. The human individual has to work his evolution consciously and deliberately. His growth is not effected fortuitously or automatically. He has to act responsibly and co-operate willingly with the purpose of evolution. If he falls into the external sphere, if he does not recognise his own dignity, the law of Karma rules. If he withdraws from the external, he can participate creatively in the cosmic development.

Intelligence and Spirit. Looking back on the millions of years of the steady climb of life on the path of evolution, it seems presumptuous for us to imagine that with thinking man evolution has come to an end. The Upaniṣad affirms that there is a further step to be taken. Animal cunning has become human foresight; human self-consciousness must grow into comprehensive vision, into illumined consciousness.[3] We must pass beyond the dualities and discords of intellect and possess truth as our inherent right. Ānanda, or joy, which is, according to St. Paul, one of the fruits of the spirit, is the stage we have to reach. The new spiritual man differs from the present intellectual man as much as the latter differs from the animal and the animal from the plant. Every human individual is a historical becoming. What we are here and now is the result of what we were, what we

[2] John Dewey, *Human Nature and Conduct,* 332.

[3] Cp. *Jalālu'd Dīn Rūmī:* "First came he from the realm of the inorganic, long years dwelt he in the vegetable state, passed into the animal condition, thence towards humanity; whence again, there is another migration to be made." *Mathnawī* 4.3637f.

thought, what we felt and willed, what we did during earlier periods of our personal history. We cannot understand a human individual except as a process in time. There is no such thing as an I-substance. When we speak of the essence of the human individual, we refer not to his existence or the series of changes through which he passes, but to the plan or pattern of behaviour which he is attempting to realise. Human life presses forward through blood and tears to realise its form. As progress at the human level is willed, not determined, we are participants in history, not mere spectators of it. We can do much to determine our own future. If we follow false lights and seek for finite and relative progress, which is often precarious and disappointing, we do not further our own evolution. If, on the other hand, we overcome the narrowness of our ego, open out to others, overflow and communicate love and joy, we foster our growth. By our freely chosen activities we may retard or further the march of the world to its consummation. We are living our lives in the process of a great gestation. The slowness of the process, the occasional backslidings in any historical period do not disprove the possibility of development. History is neither a chapter of accidents, nor a determined drift. It is a pattern of absolute significance.

There is as much discontinuity between the human and the spiritual as there is between the human and the animal. Spiritual life is not only the negation but the fulfilment of the human life. We sometimes stress the continuity, sometimes the newness of it. "Behold, I make all things new."

The Goal of the Cosmic Process. The meaning of history is to make all men prophets, to establish a kingdom of free spirits. The infinitely rich and spiritually impregnated future, this drama of the gradual transmutation of intellect into spirit, of the son of man into the son of God, is the goal of history. When death is overcome, when time is conquered, the kingdom of the eternal spirit is established.

Ānanda, spirit, which is the goal of evolution, comprises all the rest. It is not unrelated to the others which it has superseded and resolved into itself. All of them are activities of the Spirit. Each of them in its operation in the whole presupposes the others. Since all are necessary to the whole, no one can claim a primacy which belongs to the whole or the Spirit itself. We cannot unify the categories by annihilating them. Matter and life are different. The different levels of existence are not to be treated as inferior or degraded. In its place everything has value. The world is of one piece, though it has different stages which cannot be partitioned.

In the cosmic evolution, the different stages are not opposed as good and evil. It is an evolution from one stage to another and the different stages are distinguishable only within a unity. The one Spirit is manifesting itself in its various activities which are all partial and therefore inadequate. Wholeness belongs to the Spirit itself.

Spirit and Body. It follows that we should not assume that body is the lower element out of which evil arises. The whole man, body, mind and spirit, is one; Spirit is not to be delivered out of entanglement with the body. In the Rabbinical phrase the body is the "scabbard of the soul." It is "the temple of the Holy Spirit." [4] It is, according to Hindu thought, the instrument of ethical life, *dharma-sādhanam.* Even the lowest form of manifestation is an expression of the Divine, *annaṁ brahmeti vyajānāt.*

Philosophy as Criticism of the Categories. There is a tendency to apply categories, which have proved helpful and even necessary in certain areas, to others by the sheer impetus of the search for a comprehensive theory of being. In the eighteenth century Laplace conceived a theory of world mechanics. In the nineteenth century the Darwinian principle of natural selection was extended to all phenomena, living, minded and purposive. We can explain the lower by the higher, not *vice versa.* There is not a single type of law to which all existence conforms.

Spirit, the Explanation. The Upaniṣads believe that the principle of Spirit is at work at all levels of existence, moulding the lower forms into expressions of the higher. The splendour of Spirit, which in Greek philosophy was identified with the transcendental and timeless world of Ideas, or in Christian thought is reserved for the divine supernatural sphere, is making use of natural forces in the historical world. The highest product of cosmic evolution, ānanda or spiritual freedom, must also be the hidden principle at work, slowly disclosing itself. Spirit creates the world and controls its history by a process of perpetual incarnation. Spirit is working in matter that matter may serve the Spirit.

Puruṣa and Prakṛti. To account for the world of change, which is a progressive manifestation of the values of spirit, we assume not only the principle of spirit but also the principle of non-being which is being gradually overcome. We struggle with chaos, we mould crude primordial being into forms expressive of spirit. Spirit represents all that is positive in becoming. The things of the world are struggling to reach the spirit by overcoming their inner void, the interval between what they are and what they aim to be. This negative principle measures the distance between being and becoming. The world process can only be conceived as a struggle between two antagonistic but indispensable principles of being and non-being. What is called non-being is the limiting concept on the object side, the name for the unknown, the hypothetical cause of the object world. This

[4] 1. *Corinthians.* III. 6, 18; VI. 19.

non-being is an abstraction, that which remains when we abstract from the world all that gives it existence, form and meaning. It is the unmanifested, imperceptible, all but nothing, capable of receiving, though not without resistance, existence, form and meaning. It is a demand of thought more than a fact of existence, the limit of the downward movement, the lowest form which is all but nonexistent. It is the absence of form, though there is nothing in the actual world which is completely devoid of form. In Indian thought it is called *prakṛti,* the *avyakta,* the unmanifested, the formless substrate of things. It is potentially all things. The two, spirit and nature, puruṣa and prakṛti, are not two ultimate principles. They are parts of one World-Spirit, which divided into two, *dvedhā apātayat,* for the sake of cosmic development.[5] The two are opposite, yet complementary poles of all existence. They are not altogether independent of each other. The principle of non-being is dependent on being. It is that without which no effort would be possible or necessary. It is essential for the unfolding of the divine possibility. It is the material through which ideals are actualised. Proclus says that matter is a "child of God." So it is able to reveal spirit.

Prakṛti is not absolute non-being. It is unformed non-being which is powerless to form itself into being without the guidance of puruṣa, or the self. The existential development is not out of utter nothing or the absolute absence of all being Nothing is the conceptual opposite of what truly and authentically is. If God creates out of nothing, he must be able to relate himself to nothing. But he cannot know nothing, for Pure Being excludes from itself all nullity. There is an inconscient world of being from out of which different worlds form themselves under the guidance of spirit. The dualism of puruṣa and prakṛti cannot be ultimate. The World-Spirit confronted by chaos or the waters over which the Spirit broods are both the expressions of the Supreme Being. . . .

Metaphysical Implications. Philosophy is a quest of truth which underlies existence. The very name *metaphysics* characterises the type of inquiry which goes beyond what is given to us. Whereas science deals with existent objects, philosophy tries to envisage the hidden structure, discover and analyse the guiding concepts of ontological reality. Why is there something rather than nothing? Why is there this world rather than another?

The Primacy of Being. The very existence of this world implies the existence of Being from which the world derives. Being is the foundation of all existence, though it is not itself anything existent. It is not something like a stone or a plant, an animal or a human individual. Whenever we say that anything is, we make use of the concept of Being. It is therefore

[5] *Bṛhad-āraṇyaka Upaniṣad.* I. 4. 3.

the most universal and the most comprehensive concept. We unfold the nature of Being by the study of existences, though we cannot prove it. It is self-evident. If Being were not, nothing can possibly exist. Being is in all that exists. We live in the world of existence, we think of some kind of existence or other, but in metaphysics we get beyond the sphere of daily life, the objects of science, and rise to the transcendent conception of Being itself. Being posits everything but is not itself posited. It is not an object of thought, it is not the result of production. It forms an absolute contrast to and is fundamentally different from all that is. If anything exists, then Being is. As this world exists, Being is. *Aseitas* means the power of Being to exist absolutely in virtue of itself, requiring no cause, no other justification for its existence except that its very nature is to be. There can be only one such Being and that is the Divine Spirit. To say that God exists *a se,* of and by reason of Himself, is to say that God is Being itself.

This is the concept of Brahman as it is formulated in the Upaniṣads. It is the *I am that I am* of the Christian Scripture. It is also the central doctrine of Catholic Christianity. St. Thomas Aquinas describes God as *Esse* or Being, pure and simple. In Him there is no distinction whatever. Even the distinction between the knowing subject and the known object is lost. God knows Himself, not through representations of Himself, but without mediation, through His own being. God is absolute as distinct from dependent or conditioned being. As the ground of an ordered multiplicity He is one and not multiple. That which is to make all conditions possible cannot itself be subject to conditions.

Being and Freedom. Why has evolution taken this direction and not another? Why has the world this character and not any other? In other words, why is the world what it is and not another? Being which is the ultimate basis of all existence, which is independent and has nothing outside it to control it, has freely willed to realise this world, to actualise this possibility. Absolute Being is also absolute freedom. To the question, why should such an order exist at all, the only answer is because the Absolute is both Being and Freedom. He is *actus purus,* unconditional activity. All the worlds would collapse into nothingness if He were not active. His will prevents Being from being the abyss of nothingness. The 'given' fact of the world in which we are all involved is a mystery. The genesis of the universe with its specific character is traced to Being-Activity. As to why this possibility and not another is selected, is intelligible solely as mystery which we have only to acknowledge. It is the will of God. There are two sides of the Supreme, Essential Transcendent Being which we call Brahman; free activity which we call Īśvara: the timeless, spaceless reality and the conscious active delight creatively pouring out its powers and qualities, the timeless calm and peace and the timeful joy of activity freely, infinitely expressing itself without any lapse into unrest or bondage. When we refer to the free choice of this specific possibility, we deal with the Īśvara side of the Absolute. Pure Being without any expression or variation moves out of its primal poise so that worlds may spring into existence. Pure Being is not locked up in its own transcendence. Īśvara is the Absolute in action as Lord and Creator.[6] The created world is contingent because it depends on the free will of the Supreme. Possible realities have potential being in the Absolute, existent realities have actual being though they are contingent. The Supreme has necessary being or, more accurately, it is its own being (svayambhu) and it is infinite because it possesses infinite possibilities. The mystery of the world abides in freedom. Freedom is the primordial source and condition of all existence. It precedes all determination.

Infinite Possibility and the Actual World. This world, we have seen, is not a machine. It is an act of worship. It is in love with God, as Aristotle said, and is working towards Him. Its possibility, the eternal idea which it is accomplishing, is conceived by the Greeks as an abstract principle, the timeless Logos. The words of the Prologue to St. John's Gospel make out that it is a personal being who is the moving dynamism of history. "In the beginning was the Logos, and the Logos was with God and the Logos was God. The same was in the beginning with God. All things were made by Him. . . . In Him was life; and the life was the light of men." It is a definite manifestation of that which in the end of time brings with it the victory of the divine will over the powers that threaten the meaning of life. It perfects the historical revelation and completes the meaning of earthly existence. It is the Divine Logos which permeates the world and forms it into a cosmos. According to Hindu thought, the God who is shaping the universe is not the Absolute, free from all relativity, but the active personal being who shares in the life of his finite creatures. He bears in them and with them the whole burden of their finitude. The Spirit has entered into the world of non-spirit to realise one of the infinite possibilities that exist potentially in Spirit. Unconditioned Being becomes conditioned by the assumption of the creation of a specific possibility. A further definition of the Supreme Being's relation to the world is given by stating that the World Spirit creates, sustains and ultimately resolves the universe. These three aspects are brought out by the names, Brahmā, Viṣṇu and Śiva.

[6] Cp. *Origen's* account of the coeternity of the Son with the Father. "There never can have been a time when He was not. For when was the Divine Light destitute of its effulgence?" *De Principiis,* IV, 28.

They represent the three sides of God's activity in regard to the world. These three represent different functions of the one Supreme and are not, except figuratively, to be regarded as different persons. God the conceptual is logically prior to God the cosmic, who is logically prior to God the consequent or the final perfection. The Ideas of Brahmā are seeking concrete expression and Viṣṇu is assisting the world's striving for perfection.[7] During the process all his qualities of wisdom, love and patience find expression and help the fluent world to reach its end. God is spiritual Reality, unconditioned freedom and absolute love.

In the Upaniṣads, a fourfold distinction of the Supreme Being is set forth.[8] (1) Brahman, the Absolute Being (2) Iṣvara, the unconditioned free activity (3) Hiraṇya-garbha, Prajă-pati, Brahmā, the World-Spirit in its subtle form and (4) Virāj, the World-Spirit in its gross form.

These bring out different aspects of the Supreme. There is a tendency to regard the Supreme as Īṣvara or God as subordinate to the Supreme as Brahman or Godhead. For Eckhart God is secondary, not primary, for it assumes the distinction of subject and object while Godhead transcends this distinction. A being is different from what he does. I feel that these disclose great depths in the Supreme Being and only logically can we distinguish them. They are all united in the Supreme.

The Status of the World. This world is not an illusion; it is not nothingness, for it is willed by God and therefore is real. Its reality is radically different from the being of Absolute-God. The Absolute alone has non-created divine reality; all else is dependent, created reality. This is the significance of the doctrine of māyā. It does not mean that the temporal process is a tragedy or an aberration. The reality of the world is not in itself but it is in the thought and being of the Creator. It is what God thought and willed it to be before it was.

There is a beginning to time as well as an end. When we say that time is infinite, all that we mean is that its future is indifinite or incalculable. Between these two points, the beginning and the end, between the start and the finish, what happens is real and significant, not only for us but for the World-Spirit. God is so intensely concerned with this history

[7] Cp. *Whitehead:* "One side of God's nature is constituted by his conceptual experience. This experience is the primordial fact in the world, limited by no actuality which it presupposes. It is therefore infinite, devoid of all negative prehensions. This side of his nature is free, completely primordial, eternal, actually deficient and unconscious. The other side originates with physical experience, derived from the temporal world and then acquires integration with the primordial side. It is determined, incomplete, consequent, everlasting, fully actual and conscious." *Process and Reality* (1929), 488f.

[8] *See Ind P,* I (1923), 169–173. *Māṇḍūkya Upaniṣad* gives us a two-fold dialectic, relating not only to Reality but also to the being who apprehends it.

that He not only looks on the human life as an interested spectator but He actively intervenes in it. It is not correct to say that this intervention took place only once. Every moment in the temporal process is a moment of decision. It is charged with an extreme tension. History is not a cyclic movement. It is full of new things, because God works in it and reveals Himself in it. The end of the time process is the triumph of the World-Spirit, or to use the phrases of Greek classical thought, the triumph of *Nous* over chaos.

Laws of Nature. There are laws of nature, physical, biological and psychological. These laws are comprehensively designated Karma. The Creator does not use the forces of nature to reward virtue or punish sin. Jesus said: "Think you that the eighteen upon whom the Tower in Siloam fell were sinners above all that dwelt in Jerusalem? I tell you nay. He maketh his sun to rise on the evil and on the good and sendeth rain on the just and on the unjust." [9] In this world there are no rewards or punishments but only consequences. There is no arbitrariness in the world. The laws of nature are the expression of the divine mind. The *Śvetāśvatara Upaniṣad* states that God is the ordainer or overlord of Karma, *karmādhyakṣaḥ*. Karma is not ultimate or absolute. It is the expression of God's will and purpose. It has an important and indispensable function in the divine economy. It belongs to the created world. If God is bound up to the order of nature, if He is responsible for the world without the power of redeeming it, if His will is inflexible that no prayer can reach, if He sanctions all the evil as well as the good in the world, if He treats the tears of the children of and the agony of the innocents as just ingredients in a world of sacred necessity, the world becomes meaningless. The Supreme is love and knowledge, goodness and power. He is related to everything and every one in the universe. He responds to everything and to everything's response to Him.

Human Freedom. God is not fate, nor an impersonal, abstract determining power. We are not puppets moved hither and thither by the blind impersonal necessity of omnipotent matter or the sovereignty of divine providence. We cannot say that everything is finished before it starts and the last day of reckoning will read what the first day of creation wrote. In that case nothing new can happen and there is no room for contingency. The future has yet to be made. Our present choices give a new form even to the past so that what it means depends on what we do now.

The freedom of will possessed by self-conscious individuals makes possible sin and discord. They are not willed by the Divine, though they fall within His purpose. When we are self-willed we surrender to the restraint exercised by the play of mechanical forces. We are then the victims of

[9] *Matthew* V, 45.

Karma. We are free to do differently. We can turn our eyes towards the Light in prayer, make an effort of genuine attention to empty our mind of selfish desires and let the thought of the Eternal fill it. We will then bear within us the very power to which necessity or Karma is in subjection. It is our community with the Eternal that endows us with creative quality. It helps us to remake our environment and realise new types of achievement which will enrich the experience of the human race. Keats spoke of the world as the 'veil of soul-making' and declared in the same letter [10] that "as various as the lives of men are—so various become their souls and thus does God make individual beings, Souls, Identical Souls, of the sparks of his own essence."

Meaning of Liberation. An individual is free when he attains universality of spirit, but his liberated self retains its individuality as a centre of action so long as the cosmic process lasts. For complete liberation implies not only harmony within the self but also harmony with the environment. Complete freedom is therefore impossible in an imperfect world. Those who have attained to the consciousness of the Eternal work within the world to set other men forward in their journey toward the goal. In a true sense the ideal individual and the perfect society arise together.[11]

The redemption of the world is not to be treated completely *sub specie historiae.* It is an eternal operation. There is a steady advance in our apprehension of the ideal which belongs to the eternal world. Nicolas of Cusa says:

> To be able to know ever more and more without end, this is our likeness to the eternal wisdom. Man always desires to know better what he knows and to love more what he loves; and the whole world is not sufficient for him because it does not satisfy his craving for knowledge.

Our ultimate aim is to live in the knowledge and enjoyment of the absolute values. When this aim is reached, the mortal becomes the immortal and time is taken over into eternity. Temporal life, is treated as contingent, transient, perishable, non-eternal, as its end is to be transfigured. Human life, on this planet, is a brief episode and its eternal value is however preserved in the abode of all eternal values, the Absolute-God.

The actual fabric of the world with its loves and hates, with its jealousies and competitions, with its unasked helpfulness, sustained intellectual effort and intense moral struggle, are no more than existences dancing on the stillness of Pure Being. They are not final and fundamental. They are

[10] April 28th 1819. *Colvin's ed.,* 256.
[11] IVL (1932), 307.

not by any means illusory, an evil dream from which we have to wake up as soon as possible. It is wrong to think that the universe exists for us only to escape from it. Existence, rather, is here to be redeemed. If the Supreme is one and many, if He is Being and Activity, if He is transcendent and immanent, then the Spirit lives in the world, Being is in existence. The aim of the cosmic evolution is to reveal the Spirit.

God and the World. In his book on *God and the Astronomers* (1933) Dr. W. R. Inge refers to my view and points out that, if God is bound up with and immanent in the evolving universe, He must share the fate of the universe. If the second law of thermodynamics is true, that the universe is running down like a clock and a time will come when there will be no life or consciousness, the universe will reach a state of static eventlessness which is another name for extinction. If God is the soul of the universe, He is the soul of a doomed universe. If the world is as necessary to God as God is to the world, a time will come when God will be no more. A god under the sentence of death is no god at all.

This objection is not fatal to the view I have indicated. This world is the accomplishment of a specific possibility from the infinite possibilities whose ideal home is the Absolute. From the primary reality of Absolute-God, the derived reality of the world ensues. This world is creaturely being. It exists because and so long as God wills it to be.

While God is distinct from the world He is not separate from it. The world exists by the sustaining presence and activity of God. Without this presence and activity, it would collapse into nothingness. In this world one possibility of the divine is being accomplished in space and time. There is the operation of the divine in it. From this it does not follow that the world is organic to God. If anything, it is organic to this specific divine possibility which is in process of accomplishment. This possibility is regarded as the soul or the entelechy of the world; we may call it the World-Spirit. The soul of this particular world is a manifestation of the Absolute-God. When this possibility is realised, when the plan of the universe is fulfilled, there is an end to this world. Its disappearance is consistent with its created character.

Kant's Antinomy. The whole question of the status of time was raised by Kant in his Antinomies of Pure Reason. "*Thesis:* The world has a beginning in time and is confined within the limits of space. *Antithesis:* The world has neither beginning in time nor bounds in space but is infinite, as in space so also in time." This antinomy cannot be solved, for, according to Kant, reason finds itself in the power of transcendental appearance. Within the limits of the phenomenal world, the contradiction cannot be overcome. We cannot think that time will come to an end in time or that it will go on endlessly. How can the end of time occur within time?

When the end of the cosmic history is reached, we have passed beyond the limits of history. We have transcended time. It is not a question of an end in time but an end of time.

Brahmaloka or the Kingdom of God. So long as there is the struggle, the process of becoming, the overcoming of non-being by being, we have the time process. But when all individuals have escaped from their alienation, from their slavery to the world, when all externality is overcome, there is the awakening of the Spirit in them all. When the Kingdom of Spirit is established on earth as it is in heaven above, God the antecedent becomes God the consequent. There is a coincidence of the beginning and the end. If it is held that the end will never be accomplished, that there will be perpetual singing and no completion in a song, that it is always a journeying without any journey's end, then the cosmic process will have no meaning at all. "Thy kingdom come" is the meaning of history, and the coming of the kingdom is the triumph of meaning. The truth about the earth is the *brahmaloka,* the transfiguration of the cosmos, the revolutionary change in men's consciousness, a new relationship among them, an assimilation to God. It is the attainment of wholeness, the overcoming of disruption, the surmounting of all the false antinomies, the transcending of time in eternity, which we objectify as *brahmaloka.*

Universal Salvation. The attainment of spiritual freedom by all, universal salvation or *sarvamukti* is not inconsistent with the law of entropy. When we are all liberated, time is transcended, saṁsāra becomes mokṣa or nirvāṇa. According to the Mahāyāna Buddhism, universal redemption is the aim of the Buddha. St. Paul extends his hope of "redemption into the glorious liberty of the children of God" to the "whole creation." This cosmic deliverance, which is the close of the world, cannot be accurately described as a terrestrial future for it is a supramundane present. When everyone achieves his fulfilment, the cosmic purpose is fulfilled. Pure undistorted truth of eternity burns up the world. The end of the process is in continuity with the beginning and when the two coincide, cosmic existence lapses into Absolute Being.

The End of the World. The possibility of the passing away of the present order of things is not only admitted but demanded by the view here set forth. When humanity, still captive in its germ, reaches its full stature of which we can not now imagine the greatness and the majesty, it unites with its source in the past. The World-Spirit, called Brahmā, Hiraṇyagarbha, is admitted to be finite, mortal, though he creates beings who gain immortality.[12] He is said to be the first-born, the first embodied being.[13] "Death is his body." [14] He strives to express his spirit through the body of non-being, the principle of objectivity. He is *tamaś śarīraka paramātmā.*

The meaning of time is beyond the confines of time. Time has meaning because it comes to an end. If it is unending, it is meaningless. Time process can be understood only in the light of the end it aims at; the victory over time, the victory over this disrupted, fallen condition, victory over alienation, estrangement, enslavement by the objective. We conceive the end itself as taking place in historical time, though it is illogical to relate to history in simply historical terms what is beyond history. Though it may not be possible for us to think of the end of time except in terms of time, yet the end is not a term in the time series. It belongs to another order of existence, inasmuch as it marks the end of time itself. It is victory over time. It is life eternal.

Though the present order of things must pass away, there will be other world orders in an endless series; for God is infinite possibility. We do not equate God with this evolutionary process. The dissolution of the world does not in any way affect the Absolute-God; for its knowledge of all possibilities is free from relativity. God is not merely the past, the present, and the future of this world, he is the transcendental principle of this and all possible worlds, whether they are to be realised or not. Even from the strictly scientific point of view the process of gradual degradation of energy must have had a beginning. If the whole universe is running down like a clock, it must have been wound up at the beginning. If it was wound up once, what prevents it from being wound up again, if another possibility requiring this type of structure is to be started?

[12] atha yan martyaḥ sann amṛtān asṛjata. *Bṛhad-āraṇyaka Upaniṣad.* Again, hiraṇyagarbhaṁ paśyata jāyamānam. Behold the World-Spirit, as he is being born. *Śvetāśvatara Upaniṣad* IV, 12.

[13] *Śiva Purāṇa.* V.1.8.22.

[14] *yasya mṛtyuś śarīram. Subāla Upaniṣad.*

Ernest Nagel

Naturalism Reconsidered *

It is surely not the highest reach for a philosopher to be a combatant in the perennial wars between standardized "isms" which fill conventional handbooks of philosophy. Philosophy at its best is a critical commentary upon existence and upon our claims to have knowledge of it; and its mission is to help illuminate what is obscure in experience and its objects, rather than to profess creeds or to repeat the battle-cries of philosophical schools aiming at intellectual hegemony. The conception of philosophy as a struggle between competing systems is especially sterile when the "ism" defended or attacked covers as miscellaneous an assortment of not always congruous views as fly the banner of naturalism. The number of distinguishable doctrines for which the word "naturalism" has been a counter in the history of thought, is notorious. Even among contemporaries who proclaim themselves to be naturalists in philosophy, there are not only important differences in stress and perspective, but also in specific doctrines professed and in intellectual methods used to support commitments made. I am aware, therefore, that in taking naturalism as my subject this evening, I ran the risk of becoming involved in futile polemics—a risk graver by the fact that although the stated title of my address may have aroused different expectations, it is not my intention to recant and to confess past errors. I must explain why, notwithstanding the hazards of my theme, I have elected to discuss it.

The past quarter century has been for philosophy in many parts of the world a period of acute self-questioning, engendered in no small measure by developments in scientific and logical thought, and in part no doubt by fundamental changes in the social order. In any event, there has come about a general loss of confidence in the competence of philosophy to provide

* The Presidential Address to the American Philosophical Association, Eastern Division, 1954. From *Proceedings and Addresses of The American Philosophical Association,* Volume 28. Reprinted by permission of The American Philosophical Association and the author.

by way of a distinctive intellectual method a basic ground-plan of the cosmos, or for that matter to contribute to knowledge of any primary subject-matter except by becoming a specialized positive science and subjecting itself to the discipline of empirical inquiry. Although the abysses of human ignorance are undeniably profound, it has also become apparent that ignorance, like actual knowledge, is of many special and heterogeneous things; and we have come to think, like the fox and unlike the hedgehog of whom Mr. Isaiah Berlin has recently reminded us, that there are a great many things which are already known or remain to be discovered, but that there is no one "big" thing which, if known, would make everything else coherent and unlock the mystery of creation. In consequence, many of us have ceased to emulate the great system-builders in the history of philosophy. In partial imitation of the strategy of modern science, and in the hope of achieving responsibly held conclusions about matters concerning which we could acquire genuine competence, we have tended to become specialists in our professional activities. We have come to direct our best energies to the resolution of limited problems and puzzles that emerge in the analysis of scientific and ordinary discourse, in the evaluation of claims to knowledge, in the interpretation and validation of ethical and esthetic judgments, and in the assessment of types of human experience. I hope I shall not be regarded as offensive in stating my impression that the majority of the best minds among us have turned away from the conception of the philosopher as the spectator of all time and existence, and have concentrated on restricted but manageable questions, with almost deliberate unconcern for the bearing of their often minute investigations upon an inclusive view of nature and man.

Some of us, I know, are distressed by the widespread scepticism of the traditional claims for a *philosophia perennis,* and have dismissed as utterly trivial most if not all the products of various current forms of analytical philosophy. I do not share this distress, nor do I think the dismissal is uniformly perspicacious and warranted. For in my judgment, the scepticism which many deplore is well-founded. Even though a fair-sized portion of recent analytical literature seems inconsequential also to me, analytical philosophy in our own day is the continuation of a major philosophic tradition, and can count substantial feats of clarification among its assets. Concentration on limited and determinate problems has yielded valuable fruits, not least in the form of an increased and refreshing sensitivity to the demands of responsible discourse.

On the other hand, philosophers like other men conduct their lives within the framework of certain comprehensive if not always explicit assumptions about the world they inhabit. These assumptions color evaluations of major ideals and proposed policies. I also suspect that the directions taken by analyses of specific intellectual problems are frequently if subtly controlled by the expressed or tacit beliefs philosophers hold concerning the over-all nature of things, by their views on human destiny, and by their conceptions of the scope of human reason. But conversely, resolutions of special problems made plausible by recent philosophical analysis, as well as by the findings of various positive sciences, seem to me to support certain broad generalizations about the cosmos and to disconfirm others. It is clearly desirable that such basic intellectual commitments, which are at once the matrix and the outcome of inquiries into specific problems, be made as explicit as possible. A philosopher who is a reflective man by profession, certainly owes it to himself to articulate, if only occasionally, what sort of world he thinks he inhabits, and to make clear to himself where approximately lies the center of his convictions.

The discharge of the important obligation which is mine this evening, seems to me an appropriate occasion for stating as simply and as succinctly as I can the substance of those intellectual commitments I like to call "naturalism." The label itself is of no importance, but I use it partly because of its historical associations, and partly because it is a reminder that the doctrines for which it is a name are neither new nor untried. With Santayana, I prefer not to accept in philosophic debate what I do not believe when I am not arguing; and naturalism as I construe it merely formulates what centuries of human experience have repeatedly confirmed. At any rate, naturalism seems to me a sound generalized account of the world encountered in practice and in critical reflection, and a just perspective upon the human scene. I wish to state briefly and hence with little supporting argument what I take to be its major tenets, and to defend it against some recent criticisms.

Claims to knowledge cannot ultimately be divorced from an evaluation of the intellectual methods used to support those claims. It is nevertheless unfortunate that in recent years naturalists in philosophy have so frequently permitted their allegiance to a dependable method of inquiry to obscure their substantive views on things in general. For it is the inclusive intellectual image of nature and man which naturalism supplies that sets it off from other comprehensive philosophies. In my conception of it, at any rate, naturalism embraces a generalized account of the cosmic scheme and of man's place in it, as well as a logic of inquiry.

I hasten to add, however, that naturalism does not offer a theory of nature in the sense that Newtonian mechanics, for example, provides a theory of motion. Naturalism does not, like the latter, specify a set of substantive principles with the help of which the detailed course of concrete happenings can be explained or understood. Moreover, the principles affirmed by naturalism are not proposed as competitors or underpinnings for any of the special theories which the positive sciences assert. Nor, finally, does naturalism offer its general view of nature and man as the product of some special philosophical mode of knowing. The account of things proposed by naturalism is a distillation from knowledge acquired in the usual way in daily encounters with the world or in specialized scientific inquiry. Naturalism articulates features of the world which, because they have become so obvious, are rarely mentioned in discussions of special subject-matter, but which distinguish our actual world from other conceivable worlds. The major affirmations of naturalism are accordingly meager in content; but the principles affirmed are nevertheless effective guides in responsible criticism and evaluation.

Two theses seem to me central to naturalism as I conceive it. The first is the existential and causal primacy of organized matter in the executive order of nature. This is the assumption that the occurrence of events, qualities and processes, and the characteristic behaviors of various individuals, are contingent on the organization of spatio-temporally located bodies, whose internal structures and external relations determine and limit the appearance and disappearance of everything that happens. That this is so, is one of the best-tested conclusions of experience. We are frequently ignorant of the special conditions under which things come into being or pass away; but we have also found repeatedly that when we look closely, we eventually ascertain at least the approximate and gross conditions under which events occur, and we discover that those conditions invariably consist of some more or less complex organization of material substances. Naturalism does not maintain that only what is material exists, since many things noted in experience, for example, modes of action, relations of meaning, dreams, joys, plans, aspirations, are not as such material bodies or organizations of material bodies. What naturalism does assert as a truth about nature is that though *forms* of behavior or *functions* of material systems are indefeasibly parts of nature, forms and functions are not themselves agents in their own realization or in the realization of anything else. In the conception of nature's processes which naturalism affirms, there is no place for the operation of disembodied forces, no place for an immaterial spirit directing the course of events, no place for the survival of personality after the corruption of the body which exhibits it.

The second major contention of naturalism is that the manifest plurality and variety of things, of their qualities and their functions, are an irreducible feature of the cosmos, not a deceptive appearance cloaking some more homogeneous "ultimate reality" or transempirical substance, and that the sequential orders in which events occur or the manifold relations of dependence in which things exist are *contingent* connections, not the embodiments of a fixed and unified pattern of logically necessary links. The existential primacy of organized matter does not make illusory either the relatively permanent or the comparatively transient characters and forms which special configurations of bodies may possess. In particular, although the continued existence of the human scene is precarious and is dependent on a balance of forces that doubtless will not endure indefinitely, and even though its distinctive traits are not pervasive throughout space, it is nonetheless as much a part of the "ultimate" furniture of the world, and is as genuine a sample of what "really" exists, as are atoms and stars. There undoubtedly occur integrated systems of bodies, such as biological organisms, which have the capacity because of their material organization to maintain themselves and the direction of their characteristic activities. But there is no positive evidence, and much negative evidence, for the supposition that all existential structures are teleological systems in this sense, or for the view that whatever occurs is a phase in a unitary, teleologically organized, and all-inclusive process or system. Modern physical cosmology does indeed supply some evidence for definite patterns of evolutionary development of stars, galactic systems and even of the entire physical universe; and it is quite possible that the stage of cosmic evolution reached at any given time causally limits the types of things which can occur during that period. On the other hand, the patterns of change investigated in physical cosmogony are not patterns that are exhaustive of everything that happens; and nothing in these current physical speculations requires the conclusion that changes in one star or galaxy are related by inherent necessity to every action of biological organisms in some remote planet. Even admittedly teleological systems contain parts and processes which are causally irrelevant to some of the activities maintained by those systems; and the causal dependencies known to hold between the parts of any system, teleological or not, have never been successfully established as forms of logically necessary relations. In brief, if naturalism is true, irreducible variety and logical contingency are fundamental traits of the world we actually inhabit. The orders and connections of things are all accessible to rational inquiry; but these orders and connections are not all derivable by deductive methods from any set of premises that deductive reason can certify.

It is in this framework of general ideas that naturalism envisages the career and destiny of man. Naturalism views the emergence and the continuance of human society as dependent on physical and physiological conditions that have not always obtained, and that will not permanently endure. But it does not in consequence regard man and his works as intrusions into nature, any more than it construes as intrusions the presence of heavenly bodies or of terrestrial protozoa. The stars are no more foreign to the cosmos than are men, even if the conditions for the existence of both stars and men are realized only occasionally or only in a few regions. Indeed, the conception of human life as a war with nature, as a struggle with an implacable foe that has doomed man to extinction, is but an inverted theology, with a malicious Devil in the seat of Omnipotence. It is a conception that is immodest as well as anthropomorphic in the importance it imputes to man in the scheme of things.

On the other hand, the affirmation that nature is man's "home" as much as it is the "home" of anything else, and the denial that cosmic forces are *intent* on destroying the human scene, do not warrant the interpretation that every sector of nature is explicable in terms of traits known to characterize only human individuals and human actions. Man undoubtedly possesses characteristics which are shared by everything that exists; but he also manifests traits and capacities that appear to be distinctive of him. Is anything gained by confusion when all forms of dependence between things, whether animate or inanimate, and all types of behaviors they display, are subsumed under distinctions that have an identifiable content only in reference to the human psyche? Measured by the illumination they bring, there is nothing to differentiate the thesis that human traits are nothing but the properties of bodies which can be formulated exclusively in the language of current physical theory, from the view that every change and every mode of operation, in whatever sector of the cosmos it may be encountered, is simply an illustration of some category pertinent to the description of human behavior.

Indeed, even some professed naturalists sometimes appear to promote the confusion when they make a fetish of continuity. Naturalists usually stress the emergence of novel forms in physical and biological evolution, thereby emphasizing the fact that human traits are not identical with the traits from which they emerge. Nevertheless, some distinguished contemporary naturalists also insist, occasionally with overtones of anxiety, that there is a "continuity" between the typically human on the one hand, and the physical and biological on the other. But is man's foothold in the scheme of things really made more secure by showing that his distinctive traits are in some sense "continuous" with features pervasive in nature, and would man's place in nature be less secure if such continuity did not obtain? The actual evidence for a continuity of development is conclusive in some instances of human traits, however it may be in others. But I sometimes suspect that the cardinal importance philosophers assign to the alleged universality of such continuity is a lingering survival of that ancient conception, according to which things are intelligible only when seen as teleological systems producing definite ends, so that nature itself is properly understood only when construed as the habitat of human society. In any event, a naturalism that is not provincial in its outlook will not accept the intellectual incorporation of man into nature at the price of reading into all the processes of the cosmos the passions, the strivings, the defeats and the glories of human life, and then exhibiting man as the most adequate, because most representative, expression of nature's inherent constitution. No, a mature naturalism seeks to understand what man is, not in terms of a discovered or postulated continuity between what is distinctive of him and what is pervasive in all things. Without denying that even the most distinctive human traits are dependent on things which are non-human, a mature naturalism attempts to assess man's nature in the light of *his* actions and achievements, *his* aspirations and capacities, *his* limitations and tragic failures, and *his* splendid works of ingenuity and imagination.

Human nature and history, in short, are *human* nature and history, not the history and nature of anything else, however much knowledge of other things contributes to a just appraisal of what man is. In particular, the adequacy of proposed ideals for human life must be judged, not in terms of their causes and origins, but in reference to how the pursuit and possible realization of ideals contribute to the organization and release of *human* energies. Men are animated by many springs of action, no one of which is intrinsically good or evil; and a moral ideal is the imagined satisfaction of some complex of impulses, desires, and needs. When ideals are handled responsibly, they therefore function as hypotheses for achieving a balanced exercise of human powers. Moral ideals are not self-certifying, any more than are the theories of the physical sciences; and evidence drawn from experienced satisfactions is required to validate them, however difficult may be the process of sifting and weighing the available data. Moral problems arise from a conflict of specific impulses and interests. They cannot, however, be effectively resolved by invoking standards derived from the study of non-human nature, or of what is allegedly beyond nature. If moral problems can be resolved at all, they can be resolved only in the light of specific human capacities, historical circumstance and acquired skills, and the opportunities (revealed by an imagination disciplined by knowledge) for altering the physical and social environment and for redirecting habitual behaviors. Moreover, since human virtues are in part the products of the society in which human powers are matured, a naturalistic moral theory is at the same time a critique of civilization, that is, a critique of the institutions that channel human energies, so as to exhibit the possibilites and limitations of various forms and arrangements of society for bringing enduring satisfactions to individual human careers.

These are the central tenets of what I take to be philosophical naturalism. They are tenets which are supported by compelling empirical evidence, rather than dicta based on dogmatic preference. In my view of it, naturalism does not dismiss every other different conception of the scheme of things as logically impossible; and it does not rule out all alternatives to itself on a priori grounds. It is possible, I think, to conceive without logical inconsistency a world in which disembodied forces are dynamic agents, or in which whatever happens is a manifestation of an unfolding logical pattern. In such possible worlds it would be an error to be a naturalist. But philosophy is not identical with pure mathematics, and its ultimate concern is with the actual world, even though philosophy must take cognizance of the fact that the actual world contains creatures who can envisage possible worlds and who employ different logical procedures for deciding which hypothetical world is the actual one. It is partly for this reason that contemporary naturalists devote so much attention to methods of evaluating evidence. When naturalists give their allegiance to the method of intelligence commonly designated as the method of modern empirical science, they do so because that method appears to be the most assured way of achieving reliable knowledge.

As judged by that method, the evidence in my opinion is at present conclusive for the truth of naturalism, and it is tempting to suppose that no one familiar with the evidence can fail to acknowledge that philosophy. Indeed, some commentators there are who assert that all philosophies are at bottom only expressions in different idioms of the same conceptions about the nature of things, so that the strife of philosophic systems is mainly a conflict over essentially linguistic matters. Yet many thinkers for whom I have a profound respect explicitly reject naturalism, and their espousal of contrary views seems to me incompatible with the irenic claim that we really are in agreement on fundamentals.

Although I do not have the time this evening to consider systematically the criticisms currently made of naturalism, I do wish to examine briefly two repeatedly voiced objections which, if valid, would in my opinion seriously jeopardize the integrity and adequacy of naturalism as a philosophy. Stated summarily, the first objection is that in relying exclusively on the logico-empirical method of modern science for establishing cognitive claims, naturalists are in effect stacking the cards in their own favor, since thereby all alternative philosophies are antecedently disqualified. It is maintained, for example, that naturalism rejects any hypothesis about trans-empirical causes or time-transcending spiritual substances as factors in the order of things, not because such hypotheses are actually shown to be false, but simply because the logic of proof adopted dismisses as irrelevant any evidence which might establish them.

This criticism does not seem to me to have merit: the logico-empirical method of evaluating cognitive claims to which naturalists subscribe does not eliminate by fiat any hypothesis about existence for which evidence can be procured, that is, evidence that in the last resort can be obtained through sensory or introspective observation. Thus, anyone who asserts a hypothesis postulating a trans-empirical ground for all existence, presumably seeks to understand in terms of that ground the actual occurrences in nature, and to account thereby for what actually happens as distinct from what is merely imagined to happen. There must therefore be some connection between the postulated character of the hypothetical trans-empirical ground, and the empirically observable traits in the world around us; for otherwise the hypothesis is otiose, and not relevant to the spatio-temporal processes of nature. This does not mean, as some critics of naturalism suppose the latter to maintain, that the hypothetical trans-empirical ground must be characterized exclusively in terms of the observable properties of the world, any more than that the sub-microscopic particles and processes which current physical theory postulates must be logical constructions out of the observable traits of macroscopic objects. But it does mean that unless the hypothesis implies, even if only by a circuitous route, some statements about empirical data, it is not adequate to the task for which it is proposed. If naturalists reject hypotheses about trans-empirical substances, they do not do so arbitrarily. They reject such hypotheses either because their relevance to the going concerns of nature is not established, or because, though their relevance is not in question, the actual evidence does not support them.

Nor does naturalism dismiss as unimportant and without consideration experiences such as of the holy, of divine illumination, or of mystical ecstacy, experiences which are of the greatest moment in the lives of many men, and which are often taken to signify the presence and operation of some purely spiritual reality. Such experiences have dimensions of meaning for those who have undergone them, that are admittedly not on par with the import of more common experiences like those of physical hunger, general well-being, or feelings of remorse and guilt. Yet such experiences are nonetheless events among other events; and though they may be evidence for something, their sheer occurrence does not certify *what* they are evidence for, any more than the sheer occurrence of dreams, hopes, and delusions authenticates the actual existence of their ostensible objects. In particular, whether the experience labelled as an experience of divine illumination is evidence for the existence of a divinity, is a question to be settled by inquiry, not by dogmatic affirmations or denials. When naturalists refuse to acknowledge, merely on the strength of such experiences, the operation or presence of a divine power, they do so not because their commitment to a logical method prevents them from treating it seriously, but because independent inquiry fails to confirm it. Knowledge is knowledge, and cannot without confusion be identified with intuitive insight or with the vivid immediacy of profoundly moving experiences. Claims to knowledge must be capable of being tested; and the testing must be conducted by eventual reference to such evidence as counts in the responsible conduct of everyday affairs as well as of systematic inquiry in the sciences. Naturalists are therefore not engaged in question-begging when, through the use of the logic of scientific intelligence, they judge non-naturalistic accounts of the order of things to be unfounded.

There is, however, a further objection to naturalism, to the effect that in committing itself to the logic of scientific proof, it is quite analogous to religious belief in resting on unsupported and indemonstrable faith. For that logic allegedly involves assumptions like the uniformity of nature or similar principles which transcend experience, cannot be justified empirically, and yet provide the premises that constitute the ultimate warrant for the conclusions of empirical inquiry. But if naturalism is thus based on unprovable articles of faith, on what cogent grounds can it reject a different conception of the true order of governance of events which rests on a different faith?

I cannot here deal adequately with the complex issues raised by this objection. Its point is not satisfactorily turned by claiming, as some have done, that instead of being articles of faith, the alleged indemonstrable postulates of scientific method are simply rules of the scientific game which *define* what in that game is to be understood by the words "knowledge" and "evidence." As I see it, however, the objection has force only for those whose ideal of reason is demonstration, and who therefore refuse to dignify anything as genuine knowledge unless it is demonstrable from self-luminous and self-evident premises. But if, as I also think, that ideal is not universally appropriate, and if, furthermore, a *wholesale* justification for knowledge and its methods is an unreasonable demand and a misplaced effort, the objection appears as quite pointless. The warrant for a proposition about some specific inter-relations of events does not derive from a faith in the uniformity of nature or in other principles with a cosmic scope. The warrant derives exclusively from the specific evidence available for that proposition, and from the contingent historical fact that the special ways employed in obtaining and appraising the evidence have been generally effective in yielding reliable knowledge. Subsequent inquiry may show that we were mistaken in accepting a proposition on the evidence available earlier; and further inquiry may also reveal that a given inductive policy, despite a record of successful past performance, requires correction if not total rejection. Fortunately, however, we are not always mistaken in accepting various propositions or in employing certain inductive policies, even though we are unable to demonstrate that we shall never fall into error. Accordingly, though many of our hopes for the stability of beliefs in the face of fresh experience may turn out to be baseless, and though no guarantees can be given that our most assured claims to knowledge may not eventually need revision, in adopting scientific method as the instrument for evaluating claims to knowledge, naturalists are not subscribing to an indemonstrable faith.

The bitter years of cataclysmic wars and social upheavals through which our generation has been passing have also witnessed a general decline of earlier hopes in the possibilities of modern science for achieving a liberal and humane civilization. Indeed, as is well known, many men have become convinced that the progress and spread of science, and the consequent secularization of society, are the prime sources of our present ills; and a not inconsiderable number of thinkers have made widely popular various revived forms of older religious and irrationalistic philosophies as guides to human salvation. Moreover, since naturalists have not abandoned their firm adherence to the method of scientific intelligence, naturalism has been repeatedly charged with insensitivity toward spiritual values, with a shallow optimism toward science as an instrument for ennobling the human estate, and with a philistine blindness toward the ineradicable miseries of human existence. I want to conclude with a few brief comments on these allegations.

It is almost painful to have to make a point of the elementary fact that whatever may happen to be the range of special interests and sensibilities of individual naturalists, there is no incompatibility, whether logical or psychological, between maintaining that warranted knowledge is secured only through the use of a definite logical method, and recognizing that the world can be experienced in many other ways than by knowing it. It is a matter of record that outstanding exponents of naturalism, in our own time as well as in the past, have exhibited an unequaled and tender sensitivity to the esthetic and moral dimensions of human experience; and they have been not only movingly eloquent celebrants of the role of moral idealism and of intellectual and esthetic contemplation in human life, but also vigorous defenders of the distinctive character of these values against facile attempts to reduce them to something else.

It seems to me singularly inept, moveover, to indict naturalism as a philosophy without a sense for the tragic aspects of life. For unlike many world-views, naturalism offers no cosmic consolation for the unmerited defeats and undeserved sufferings which all men experience in one form or another. It has never sought to conceal its view of human destiny as an episode between two oblivions. To be sure, naturalism is not a philosophy of despair. For one facet in its radical pluralism is the truth that a human good is nonetheless a good, despite its transitory existence. There doubtless are foolish optimists among those professing naturalism, though naturalism has no monopoly in this respect, and it is from other quarters that one usually receives glad tidings of a universal nostrum. But in any event, neither the pluralism so central to naturalism, nor its cultivation of scientific reason, is compatible with any dogmatic assumption to the effect that men can be liberated from *all* the sorrows and evils to which they are now heirs, through the eventual advances of science and the institution of appropriate physical and social innovations. Indeed, why suppose that a philosophy which is wedded to the use of the sober logic of scientific intelligence, should thereby be committed to the dogma that there are no irremediable evils? On the contrary, human reason is potent only against evils that are *remediable.* At the same time, since it is impossible to decide responsibly, *antecedent* to inquiry, *which* of the many human ills can be mitigated if not eradicated by extending the operations of scientific reason into human affairs, naturalism is not a philosophy of *general* renunciation, even though it recognizes that it is the better part of wisdom to be equably resigned to what, in the light of available evidence, cannot be avoided. Human reason is not an omnipotent instrument for the achievement of human goods; but it is the only instrument we do possess, and it is not a contemptible one. Although naturalism is acutely sensitive to the actual limitations of rational effort, those limitations do not warrant a romantic philosophy of general despair, and they do not blind naturalism to the possibilities implicit in the exercise of disciplined reason for realizing human excellence.

Relations and Modes of Being

Moritz Schlick

Causality in Everyday Life and in Recent Science *

There is an old rule, formulated long ago in scholastic philosophy, that warns us against confusing the "post hoc" and the "propter hoc." This means that from the fact that an event E happened after another event C we must not infer that E happened "because of" C. In other words, the rule maintains that the meaning of the proposition "E follows C" is entirely different from the meaning of the proposition "E is the effect of the cause C." But what *is* the difference between the two meanings? This question, it seems to me, is the philosophical problem of Causality.

I call it philosophical, because it is a question of meaning only, not of truth. It deals with the signification of the word "propter" or "because of"; we have to know what these words signify in order to understand the mere meaning of the principle of causality; the question whether this principle (if we can discover any meaning in it) is true or false would be a scientific problem, i.e., it could be decided only by observation and experience.

Our rule seems to presuppose that we are already acquainted with the signification of the words *post* and *propter,* for if we were not, there would be no possibility of ever applying the rule to any particular case. At best it would yield us an information of an entirely negative nature: it would tell us that the causal relation is *not* merely the relation of temporal succession, but something more; yet it would not give the slightest hint as to the positive essence of the causal relation.

Now there is no doubt that we do apply the rule continually and that it is a perfectly good and sound rule which people ought to follow even much more frequently than they do. If we take a certain medicine and get well after it, it would be very rash to assert that the medicine was the

* From "Causality in Everyday Life and in Recent Science," Section I, by Moritz Schlick, in *University of California Publications in Philosophy,* 15, 1932. Reprinted by permission of University of California Press.

cause of our getting well. Or if we try to discover the causes of the depression, we know we are looking for much more than merely for events which *preceded* the depression. It is evident, therefore, that we actually are in possession of some kind of criterion which enables us to distinguish between events that merely follow each other and events that cause each other; for we do make this distinction every day, and we make it with a sufficient accuracy to have nearly all our behavior guided by it.

We simply have to observe how this distinction is actually made in order to find out the meaning of the concept of causality as it is used in our daily experience. This simple proceeding will surely not be difficult, and yet it is the general method—and I am convinced the only method—of philosophy: it discovers the meaning of propositions by finding out just how they are verified, i.e., how their truth or falsity is tested.

This is what I propose to do with propositions in which the concept of causality is used. I shall certainly not propose any "theory of causality"; I believe there can be no such thing. There are no theories and hypotheses in philosophy; hypotheses are the material out of which the sciences are constructed, and I believe that philosophy is something different from the sciences.

How, then, do we verify the statement that the taking of some medicine was not only the antecedent but also the *cause* of the recovery of the patient?

At a first glance there seem to be two different ways of such a verification (remember, we do not ask how it *should* be done, but how it is really done in practice):

1. We try the medicine many times and perhaps on many different patients. If we find that in every single case a person suffering from a particular complaint is cured, we shall say: the recovery after the use of the medicine was not a mere *chance,* but was *caused* by it. In other words: if the event E *always* occurs after the event C has occurred before, if C never occurs without being followed by E, then we do not hesitate to call C the cause and E the effect. It is important to notice that we do this whether we are able to "explain" the cure or not; there are cases in which we just know that a medicine is good without knowing how it works.

This is a fact; and I should like to express it, as it has often been expressed by thinkers of the positivist school, by saying that the difference between a mere temporal sequence and a causal sequence is the regularity, the uniformity of the latter. If C is *regularly* followed by E, then C is the cause of E; if E only "happens" to follow C now and then, the sequence is called a mere chance. And since (as we just saw) the observation of the regularity was, in this case, the *only* thing that was done, it was necessarily the *only* reason for speaking of cause and effect, it was the *sufficient* reason. The word cause, as used in everyday life, implies *nothing but* regularity of sequence, because *nothing else* is used to verify the propositions in which it occurs.

I am sure the reader must feel very much disappointed to have me repeat these old "positivistic" statements which have been discussed and, some believe, refuted so many times. I appeal to his patience and hope he will presently see the import of these remarks for the higher aspects of the problem of causality as they are presented by recent science.

Metaphysicians will, of course, find fault with our representation of the facts. Although they will admit, I think, that in the above example the verification consisted entirely in the observation of uniformity and nothing else, they will probably maintain that even the most unprejudiced observer never thinks that the regularity of sequence constitutes the whole of causality, but regards it only as a sign or as the consequence of something else, of some "real connection" or some peculiar "intimacy" between the cause and effect, or by whatever name he may call the unobservable "tie" which he believes to be present in causation.

I do not deny that this may be so, but I answer: we are not concerned with what any observer thinks or says; our investigation of meaning is concerned only with what he *does* and can show us. Speaking, thinking, believing implies interpretation; we must not discuss interpretations or the results of philosophical analysis, we have to do with verification only, which is always an act or an activity. With regard to meaning we have to be pragmatists, whatever we may be with regard to the conception of truth. If the existence of that mysterious "tie" is verified *only* by the observation of regular sequence, then this regularity will be all the meaning the word "tie" actually has, and no thinking, believing, or speaking can add anything to it.

Perhaps the best known objection against the identification of causality and regularity is the remark that nothing is more regular than the succession of day and night, and yet we do not call the one the cause of the other. But this is simply accounted for by the fact that "day" and "night" are really not names for "events" at all in the sense in which this word is used in science. And as soon as we analyze day and night into the series of natural events for which these names stand, we find that the sequence of those events must be regarded as a very good example of "causal connection."

The real difficulties involved in the notion of uniformity are of a different nature and much more serious. We said that E was called the effect of a cause C, if in many cases it was observed to follow C each time without exception. Should we not ask: *how many* times? A physician who has tried a medicine in six cases and has seen the patient get better six times may feel pretty confident that his remedy was the cause of the recovery of his patients (provided, of course, that in his former experience they did not get well without the medicine), but undoubtedly it is possible that in all future cases the remedy will fail to have the desired result; and then we shall say: those first six times were nothing but a chance, the word "chance" meaning simply the negation of causality. If instead of six times the experiment were repeated successfully a hundred times, surely everybody would believe in the beneficial effect of the medicine; nevertheless it must be admitted that the future may bring exceptions and destroy the regularity. A hundred will be considered better than six, but evidently *no* number will be considered absolutely satisfactory; for if in one single case only C were not followed by E, one would feel no longer justified to call C the cause of E, and for all we know such a crucial case might always occur in the future.

So this is the state of affairs: the proposition "C is the cause of E" seemed to mean nothing but "C is always followed by E"; but this latter proposition can unfortunately never be verified on account of the unfortunate "always" it contains. Verification would be possible only if a finite number is substituted for "always," but no finite number is satisfactory, because it does not exclude the possibility of exceptions.

This difficulty has been pointed out about as many times as the problem of induction has been discussed, and the conclusion has usually been that causality cannot be explained as meaning simply uniformity, but that it must mean something else. Perhaps so. But we must insist: it *can* mean something else only if there is a way of verifying causal judgments different from the one we have described. What shall we do if no such way is discovered?

We can do nothing but stick to the facts with absolute frankness. Since the meaning of a proposition lies entirely in its verification, it will have meaning only *in so far* as it is verified. And if the verification is never considered complete and final, if we never declare a certain C to be the cause of a certain E without reserving the right of revocation (and this, it is important to notice, not on account of any incorrect observation or similar "mistake"), then we shall have to admit that we simply have no clear concept of causality. Where there is no definite verification, there can be no definite meaning. The function of the world "cause" will be vague. A sentence containing this word may serve a very good purpose in the practice of everyday life as well as of science, but it will have no theoretical meaning.

There is a very curious way in which the difficulty hidden in the word "always" is sometimes apparently overcome. It consists in saying: if it cannot be verified that E *always* follows C, it can also never be falsified, for the cases in which it does not seem to be the case can be explained as mere appearances, and so our belief in the causal relation between C and E can never be proved to be false. A physician, for instance, who has had complete success with a cure in ninety-nine cases but finds it to fail in the hundredth case, will by no means give up his belief that his treatment has been the "cause" of the ninety-nine recoveries, but will explain that in the negative case there must have been a circumstance which intervened and prevented the effect. And we shall very likely accept this explanation as very natural, just as we would not blame a medicine for not making a patient well, if five minutes after taking it he were killed by an automobile accident. Theoretically, and in a very crude symbolism, we might say that in the negative case the cause is not any more C at all, but $C + C'$, where C' is the intervening circumstance, and $C + C'$ does *not* have the effect E, which C alone would have had. This statement must, of course, be capable of being verified by really observing C'; if we were to admit unobservable C's we could consider *any* event to be the cause of any other event by merely assuming the existence of convenient C's, and then surely our judgments about causal relations would lose all meaning. There are certain philosophers, those who advocate the doctrine of "conventionalism," who believe that this is really the nature of all our causal judgments; in their opinion all these judgments—which would include all laws of nature—have no real meaning, they do not say anything about the world, but only indicate the way in which we select, or even arbitrarily invent, events in order to make them fit into a preconceived scheme, which we have decided to use as our most convenient means of describing nature. Among famous scientists the astronomer A. S. Eddington may be mentioned as holding similar views.

We must note here that the interpretation of negative cases by means of disturbing influences—intervening C's—does *not* offer any criterion of causality other than uniformity of sequence; on the contrary, it saves causality only by substituting a hidden regularity for an apparent irregularity.

The regularity may at first be hidden, but it must be discoverable, if we are not to fall into the snares of conventionalism; that is, we must be able to find a C′ such that C and C′ together will always be followed by an E′ which is different from E. And if there should be cases in which C + C′ is not followed by E′, we have to find a new event C″, and so on. Evidently it would be a great advantage and would help to elucidate special cases of causality, if there were a way of making sure that no further C's could possibly intervene. There would be no hope of doing this, if *any* event in the world could eventually play the rôle of the C′ for which we are looking. But if these events were restricted in a certain way so that it would be possible to examine *all* of them, then we would know that no other disturbing element could come into question, and verification would become more satisfactory.

Now it has usually been assumed by science that the possible causes were indeed very definitely restricted. In looking for the cause of a given event E it was thought that we could exclude all events happening *long before* E, and all events happening *at a great distance* from E (events occurring *after* E had, of course, been already ruled out by pre-scientific thinking). Assuming these conditions in their most rigorous and consistent form one arrived at the idea that no event could be regarded as the proper cause of E unless it occurred in the immediate spatial and temporal vicinity of E. So the causal relation between two events C and E was thought to imply their contiguity in space and time. Action-at-a-distance (temporal as well as spatial distance) was considered impossible. If this were so, one would have to look for the causes of any event only in its immediate neighborhood, there would indeed be no time and no room for any other event to interfere. It is irrelevant that this view was supported by *a priori* arguments such as "an event can act only at the place where it occurs, and nowhere else"; nevertheless such arguments show that one believed one could *understand* the causal relation better if there was contiguity; if cause and effect were separated from each other, their relation appeared to be more mysterious. This brings us to the consideration of the second way in which the existence of a causal relation seems to be established (the first one being observation of uniformity of sequence).

2. Supposing there were a case in which we believed we really and completely "understood" the working of a certain treatment or medicine in the human body: in such a case we should not have to wait for any repetition of the sequence treatment-recovery in order to assert a causal relation between these two events; we could assert it even before it occurred a single time, because our "understanding" of this particular causation would imply our conviction that the first event would entail the second one, or, as it is

often put, C would *necessarily* be followed by E. If a surgeon amputates a man's leg, he will know beforehand that the man will be one-legged afterwards. Nobody thinks that we must wait for a long series of experiences in order to know that amputation results in the loss of a limb. We feel we "understand" the whole process and therefore know its result without having experienced it

So there seems to be a second way of verifying a causal judgment independent of observation of regularity: it consists in simply pointing to the "understanding" of the particular causal relation. And those who believe in this second way will immediately add that it is the only real way, the only legitimate method, and that our first criterion—uniformity of occurrence—with nothing but an untrustworthy symptom, which might be good enough for an empiristic scientist, but could never satisfy the philosopher.

But let us examine what exactly is meant by "understanding" as the word is used here.

It is usually supposed to be a matter of "pure reason." Now, the only sense I can find for this term is the purely logical, which would mean the same as the purely deductive, the merely analytical. And there is indeed a purely logical element in the case we have just been examining. That amputation of a leg causes a man to be one-legged is an identical inference; it is, like all logical inferences, a mere tautology. But it is easy to see, unfortunately, that this has nothing to do with causation. The causal connection is hidden in the word "amputation." We usually believe we understand this connection, because we think we comprehend the process, say, of a saw cutting through a bone: the hard particles of the steel are in immediate contact with the soft particles of the bone, and the latter somehow must give way to the former. Here again we have contiguity in space and time, which appears to flatter our imagination, but apart from that we have again nothing but a sequence of events which we have often observed to happen in a similar way and which we therefore expect to happen again. For aught we know we might some day come across a bone that would resist any saw and that no human power would be able to cut in two.

So we see that, at least in our example, we were led to think we understood or comprehended the causal nexus: partly by a misinterpretation of the way in which logical inference entered into our thought, and partly by analyzing the causal process into a spatial and temporal continuity of events. This means that our second criterion is really only a hidden application of the first one; it is not different, and consequently not any better.

The examination of any other example leads to the same result. What, for instance, is the difference between a case in which we *understand* that a certain medicine must have a certain effect, and another case in which we just know by experience that it does have that effect? It is evidently this: in the second case we observe only two events, the application of the drug and, after a reasonable lapse of time, the recovery of the patient; in the first case we know how the gap between cause and effect is filled by an unbroken chain of events which are contiguous in space and time. The drug, e.g., is injected into the veins, we know it comes into immediate contact with the blood particles, we know that these will then undergo a certain chemical change, they will travel through the body, they will come into contact with a certain organ, this organ will be changed in a particular way, and so on. In this way we infer that in the end the patient *must* be healed, *if* all the other events follow each other in the way we have assumed. And how do we know that they do follow each other so? All we know is that in former experiences in the laboratory this has always been the regular course of things.

From all this we must draw the negative conclusion that it is impossible —at least in so far as the judgments of everyday life and of qualitative science are concerned—to find any meaning for the word causation, except that it implies regularity of sequence. And this is rather vague, because there is no rule as to how many instances have to be observed in order to justify our speaking of regularity.

But the two chief things we can learn from the foregoing considerations seem to me to be these:

1. The "understanding" of a causal relation is not a process of logical reasoning; what is called causal necessity is absolutely different from logical necessity (which is nothing but identity). But at the same time we see why former philosophers so frequently made the mistake of confusing the two and believing that the effect could be logically inferred from the cause. The only serious philosopher of our present time who still believes that there must be some kind of identity of cause and effect and therefore believes the relation between them to be in some way rational or logical, is (so far as I know) E. Meyerson. He tries to prove this historically by analyzing the statements of famous philosophers and scientists; but the psychological explanation of his view lies in the fact that he started as a chemist, who is used to thinking in terms of identical substances, whereas the physicist, who goes more deeply into the explanation of nature, has to think in terms of events.

2. We learn that the causal relation between two separate events is actually explained or understood when we can conceive the two as being connected by a chain of intermediate events. If some of these are still separated, we have to look for new events between them, and so on, until all the gaps are filled out and the chain has become perfectly continuous in space and time. But evidently *we can go no further,* and it would be nonsense to expect more of us. If we look for the causal link that links two events together, we cannot find anything but another event (or perhaps several). Whatever can be observed and shown in the causal chain will be the links, but it would be nonsense to look for the linkage.

This shows that we are perfectly right when we think of cause and effect as *connected* by a causal chain, but that we are perfectly wrong when we think that this chain could consist of anything but events, that it could be a kind of mysterious tie called "causality." The conception of such a "tie," which is really not a concept but a mere word, is due to a faulty process of thinking that is very common in the history of philosophy: the continuation of a thought beyond its logical limit; we transcend the region in which a word makes sense and necessarily find ourselves in the region of nonsense. After the scientist has successfully filled up all the gaps in his causal chains by continually interpolating new events, the philosopher wants to go on with this pleasant game after all the gaps are filled. So he invents a kind of glue and assures us that in reality it is only his glue that holds events together at all. But we can never find the glue; there is no room for it, as the world is already completely filled by events which leave no chinks between them. Even in our times there are some philosophers who say that we directly experience causation, e.g., in the act of volition, or even in the feeling of muscular effort. But whatever such feelings of willing or of effort may be, they are certainly events in the world; they can be glued to other events, but they cannot be the glue.

All this has of course been seen very clearly by Hume when he said that it was impossible to discover any "impression" for the idea of causal nexus. Only we can express this even more strongly by saying that we are already committing a kind of nonsense when we try to *look* for such an impression. At this point we find complete agreement between Hume and Kant. Kant applauded Hume for seeing that when we speak of causation we cannot possibly mean a sort of tie which connects the events or establishes a kind of intimacy between them, and he conceived causality as something entirely different, namely as a Principle of Order. He believed that the human mind imposed a certain order on the events of its experience, and that causality was one of the principles according to which this was done. And according to him, the human mind did this because it could not help doing it; the Principle was simply part of its metaphysical nature.

Although we must of course reject the latter part of Kant's view, we can most heartily consent to his opinion that if causality is anything at all it can be nothing but a Principle of Order.

A. C. Ewing

A Defence of Causality

What positive account can we now give of the nature of causation? What characteristics can we ascribe to it? In the first place, though we have rejected the regularity view as a complete account of causation, we may accept it gratefully as a partial account, and affirm that causality involves among other things uniform sequence. How this is best defined it is not necessary to discuss here. But what of the four other points mentioned earlier as involved in the "common-sense view"? To show that the regularity view is insufficient is not necessarily to show that there is a relation in the real world which has all the four features in question. To repeat what I have said earlier, I described them as follows:—"(1) The effect is held to be continuous with, dependent on something in the cause so that the two do not merely happen in regular succession, but are intrinsically connected with each other. (2) The cause is held to explain the effect; we commonly assume that there is a logical or quasi-logical connexion between the two such that the cause is at least part of the reason for the effect.[1] (3) The cause is held actively to produce or determine the effect in a sense in which the effect cannot be said to determine the cause. (4) Causality involves necessity."

All my arguments against the regularity view were arguments in favour of causal connexion in the first of these senses, which I may therefore regard as established, but it is not possible for me really to think the first sense without also involving the second or something very like the second. I cannot conceive both that the content of cause and effect are intrinsically connected in such a way that the effect is determined by the cause, and yet that the one could be logically quite independent of

* From *Proceedings of The Aristotelian Society,* New Series, Vol. XXXIII, 1933, pp. 119–128. Reprinted by permission of The Aristotelian Society and the author.

[1] The first and the second senses are only provisionally distinguished. I cannot really think the one without the other, and have only distinguished them because some people seem to hold the first without the second.

the other, that the cause could be itself logically coherent if isolated from the effects with which it was intrinsically connected or *vice versa.*

This view has, however, often been stated in a radically wrong way. It is often said that the effect must be contained in the cause or that there must be identity between cause and effect. These statements, taken strictly, are preposterous. The effect cannot be contained in the cause, for otherwise all causation would be simultaneous, and it cannot be identical with the cause in the proper sense of the word, for otherwise it would not be a different event. Both views would do away with change and so with causation itself. Even if it were true that the effect consists merely of a redistribution in space of the same entities as are present in the cause and that causation does not involve a change in their qualities, a conception which played an enormous part in the development of the mechanistic view of the universe, the second distribution would still not be, properly speaking, either contained in or identical with the first. There is something present that was not present before, namely, a new arrangement of the same things, and "contained in" becomes only a metaphor. If there is a logical connexion between cause and effect, it must still be a synthetic and not an analytic connexion. If we assume all logical connexion to be merely analytic, Hume's argument certainly holds against the view that causality has any kinship with such a connexion.

That causality is analogous to a logical connexion is confirmed by the fact that we can argue from the cause to the effect, which, as I have contended, seems to imply that in some manner and sense the one logically involves the other. We do not see any logical connexion, we do not understand why they should be connected, but I cannot possibly be entitled to argue from A to B unless I assume a connexion by which A really implies B, though I cannot see how it does so.

This view is flagrantly inconsistent with certain widely held theories of inference. If logical relations can only hold between propositions and not between facts in the real world, or if all inferences are merely "analytic," or if inference and logic have merely to do with symbols and not with the realities to which the symbols refer, then it will be impossible to suppose that a logical connexion between cause and effect could ever be perceived by any mind, even by Omniscience itself. I feel bound on general grounds other than any connected with causation to reject these views as untenable. I reject them because they are incompatible with our ever obtaining, as we clearly do obtain, new knowledge by inference about reality. The connexion between cause and effect is indeed synthetic, but so, I hold, is the logical relation of entailment, at least in some cases.

"To entail" does not mean "to include." At the same time rationalistic philosophers are going too far if they simply identify cause with logical ground. The relation between cause and effect is in one respect analogous to but is certainly not identical with the relation subsisting between logical or mathematical propositions in virtue of which one or more propositions entail another. The relations in the two cases are too different and the terms too different to be classed together by us. The difference was grossly slurred over by most pre-Kantian thinkers, but I doubt whether the modern reaction against this tendency has not gone as far wrong in the opposite direction. In that case the world possesses more of the characteristics of a logical system than is now usually admitted. If I had been writing three hundred or, for that matter, thirty years ago, I should, if I had been wise enough (which, in fact, I doubtless should not), have insisted rather on the difference between causality and non-causal logical entailment; but this is remembered far too well nowadays to need stressing, what is fogotten is their similarity.

The principal difficulty which has led to the abandonment of the older view of causation is that we seem unable in any case to see an *a priori* connexion between a cause and its effect or *vice versa.* No causal law which we can formulate is either logically self-evident or, as far as we can see, deducible *a priori* from any self-evident propositions. This does not prove, of course, that there is no *a priori* connexion. An Egyptian thinker of three thousand years ago would have no doubt denied any *a priori* connexion between the different properties of triangles on the ground that he could see none. Inability to detect the presence of an *a priori* connexion cannot prove its absence. Obviously the properties of concrete events are far more complex than the properties of triangles; and even the advocates of the coherence theory do not and need not maintain that particular causal laws are logically necessary when taken by themselves. Their necessity on that view lies only in their relation to the whole system, which we cannot possibly be expected to understand, so that if there is an *a priori* connexion there are very good reasons to explain why we cannot see it. That there might be a very large number of *a priori* connexions of which we are not aware a realist should be the last person to deny. To maintain, as Hume does, that if we can see no connexion between two events therefore they are quite separate and unconnected is sheer dogmatism, though it comes from one who is reputed the most sceptical of philosophers.

Even though we cannot see such a connexion, the assumption that there is such has been implicit from the earliest ages in our demand for causes and in our inductions. To ask for a cause was primarily to ask for a reason or explanation, and the usual reason why men have assumed the past to be a valid guide to the future in induction is because they assumed that there was a relation between cause and effect such that the former inherently involved the latter and that the latter [2] was *impossible,* and not merely did not occur in fact, without the other. If men had seriously held from the beginning the views of causation which most realist philosophers hold to-day, half the inspiration of the scientific search for causes would have been missing and induction would never have been trusted at all. It is the opposite view, the type of view I am defending, which has led science to look for causes and to suppose that its findings had universal validity, in so far as they were correct at all, and that they could be used in arguments from the observed to the unobserved. Hence, despite the fact that they could not see such an intelligible logical connexion between facts in the physical world, thinkers in the past have generally held that there was such a connexion.

Further, it seems to me that in the psychological, though not in the physical sphere, we may have faint glimmerings of such *a priori* insight. It seems to me that we can see and to some extent really understand why an insult should give rise to anger, why love should lead to grief if the object of one's love die or prove thoroughly unworthy, why a success should give pleasure. It does seem more reasonable on *other than inductive* [3] grounds to suppose that if A loves B that will tend to make him sorry when B dies than to suppose that it will make him intensely glad, or that to be told he is a fool will be unpleasant rather than pleasant, when he thinks that the remark is really meant. It may, of course, happen that by the time B dies A will have gone mad and actually rejoice in the occurrence, or that owing to some violent quarrel the love will have changed to hate. It is, again, possible that A may school himself actually to rejoice in being abused as a part of his moral training or as an opportunity for the exercise of patience, but what we perceive if we perceive anything is not that love [4] *must* lead to grief or that an insult *must* give rise to anger, but that

[2] It is another question whether they were right in distinguishing between cause and effect in this fashion.

[3] I mean by induction here non-intuitive or, as Mr. Johnson calls it, problematic induction.

[4] It may be objected that there only appears to be a connexion of the kind in question because we do not call a sentiment love unless it involves a tendency to feel grief at the loss of its object, or call a remark an insult unless it is liable to arouse a tendency to anger. But this cannot be the explanation, for the characteristics of tending to arouse grief at the loss of its object and tending to arouse anger are certainly not the only characteristics of love and of insults respectively. It is therefore not a merely verbal judgment that these characteristics tend to accompany the other characteristics of love and insults. If it were,

there is a causal tendency for it to do so which will operate unless prevented by other circumstances, but which *may* be counteracted. If A loves B, there is a tendency at least for him to feel grief at B's death. Nor do I suppose that men perceived this general principle to be true in advance of experience; as with all general principles, we first apprehend it in particular instances in our experience, and then by abstraction reach the general principle. I do not hold that such a principle is self-evident in the sense in which a logical principle may be so, but I should insist that we must admit different degrees of self-evidence. In this case our insight is lacking in certainty and clearness, but is present for all that. We may be in a position in regard to some of the general laws of psychology analogous to that in which an unintelligent schoolboy who is just beginning to comprehend the proofs of the most elementary theorems stands in regard to geometry. He does not yet fully grasp the points involved, his notions are obscure and confused, but yet he is in a higher position than if he had a total and absolute lack of insight. Our power of insight is not marked enough to help us much in reaching conclusions as to laws, which have therefore to be based on problematic induction, but in some cases we seem to be able to see a certain intelligibility, if not necessity, in the law discovered that we do not see in any causal laws of the physical sciences. But anybody who denies the insight for which I am contending will have to hold that it is just as reasonable to think of love as causing intense joy at the death of the person loved, except that this does not in fact happen. My case is even clearer when put negatively. Can anybody maintain that, apart from empirical evidence as to its consequences, love is intrinsically no less likely to cause joy under these circumstances than to cause sorrow? Anybody who denies such insight altogether should at least explain why it is that the connexion between love and grief at the death of the person loved, success and joy, insults and anger, seems natural and instrinsically suitable in a way in which the even more frequently experienced connexion between the eyes and vision, fire and heat, a prick and pain, a tree and leaves does not.

If it be true that we can have even glimmerings of an *a priori* connexion in the case of the mind, the fact that we do not have them in the case of matter need not trouble us, for we have no knowledge of the real nature of matter, only of some of its relational properties,[5] and therefore

we could not say that A loved B till he had lost or thought he had lost B and felt grief in consequence. There is a real causal connexion between the different manifestations of love which occur at different times, and not merely a verbal one.

[5] The "primary qualities," which are the only ones generally recognized as causally effective, are all relational.

it would be strange indeed if we could see an *a priori* connexion there. But in the case of mind we do possess knowledge of its real nature through our immediate experiences.

As regards the third characteristic usually ascribed to causality, "*activity,*" I cannot at present arrive at any precise conclusions. It *seems* obvious that the cause determines the effect in a sense quite different from any in which the effect can determine the cause, but I know neither of any way of proving that it does so nor of any satisfactory analysis of the asymmetrical relation in question, if there be one. But the reason *may* be that the principle is self evident and the relation indefinable.[6]

The fourth characteristic, necessity, is sometimes associated with the third and sometimes with the second. The effect is considered necessary both in the sense that it is conceived as if the cause in some manner compelled it by exerting an active force, and in the sense that it is supposed to follow with something like logical necessity from the cause. Necessity in the former sense we must leave with "activity" in the limbo of unsolved problems; necessity in the latter sense follows inevitably from the view of causation I have maintained, provided, that is, we are speaking of the whole cause. The effect does not merely in fact follow, but must follow the cause. The cause being what it is, the effect could not be otherwise without contradicting the nature of the cause.

But the proviso I have added constitutes an exception more important than the rule, because we are in practice very rarely, if ever, in a position to speak of the whole cause. It certainly is not true that the effect follows with strict necessity on an important part of the cause, and what we usually mean when we speak of "cause" is not the whole cause but an important part of the cause. From the occurrence of any part of the cause it does, however, follow necessarily that (in the absence of certain knowledge of its non-occurrence) the effect is more probable relatively to all given data than it would have been without this additional datum.[7]

I have not assumed that causation is universal,[8] though personally I believe it to be so, and have in a published book argued in favour of this view.[9] For even if it is not universal it is obvious that, if we are to retain even the ordinary scientific view of the universe, it does play at least a

[6] The adoption of an "activity" view need not involve animism. It may be held that the relation present in physical causation is analogous to but not identical with the relation between will and a willed change. What seems to me to be required is that cause and effect should be connected by some asymmetrical relation other than temporal succession.

[7] I agree with Mr. Keynes in holding probability to be an objective relation.

[8] *i.e.,* that every change is completely determined in character by causes.

[9] *Kant's Treatment of Causality,* ch. IV. For an attempt to reconcile this with human freedom, v. *id.,* pp. 215–22.

part in determining every event we know in the physical realm, and that any mind in which causality played no part would be unthinkable to us, for it would be a mind that never acted from any motive whatever. Consequently, if I be right in my contentions as to the nature of causality, we cannot in any case refuse to the universe as far as known by us the title of a real system, though it would, like many other systems, not completely determine all its members unless causality be completely universal.

But we need not assume that all causality is of the same type as the mechanical causality which has been so prominent in the physical sciences but according to many is now breaking down even there, nor is it a necessary consequence of what I have said that the set of events known as the cause must be the whole logical ground of the effect, the whole reason for its occurrence. That must be found rather in the system as a whole. But, whatever the ground is held to be, whether it be found in the whole or in a timeless reality of which physical events are mere appearances, *part* of the ground must lie in the physical cause, for what is to be explained is the sequence of E on C and the special nature of C and E must be relevant to this. Even if we were to adopt Berkeley's view and to regard every physical event as due to the will of God operating without the mediation of any other event or object, yet we should be bound to suppose that there was something in the apparent cause which made God think it suitable that it should be followed by the apparent effect, for otherwise the act of God in connecting the two would be unmotived and irrational, so we should even then have to suppose a connexion between cause and effect in theory deducible *a priori* from their intrinsic character.

Causality I look upon as the application to events of the principle of system, which is a cardinal assumption of thought, whether this principle be conceived as a pragmatic postulate verified by success, or as a necessity of logic, or as a perhaps somewhat dim and confused but nevertheless genuine intuition of the nature of the real world.

R. B. Braithwaite

Teleological Explanation *

We must now turn to a type of explanation . . . which has given rise to a great deal of discussion among philosophers and philosophically minded biologists, because it has been thought to raise peculiar scientific and philosophical difficulties. This type of explanation is that in which the 'Why?' question about a particular event or activity is answered by specifying a goal or end towards the attainment of which the event or activity is a means. Such explanations will be called "teleological explanations." If I am asked why I am staying in Cambridge all through August, I should reply "In order to finish writing my book"; to reply thus would be to give a teleological explanation. If I am asked why my cat paws at the door on a particular occasion, I might well reply "In order that I should open the door for it"—another teleological explanation. If an ornithologist is asked why a cuckoo lays its egg in the nest of another bird, and replies "So that the other bird may hatch out and nurture its young", or if a physiologist is asked why the heart beats, and replies "To circulate the blood round the body" or (in more detail) "To convey oxygen from the lungs to the tissues and carbon dioxide from the tissues to the lungs" or (in terms of an ultimate biological end) "In order that the body may continue to live", he will be giving in each case a teleological explanation of the action in terms of the goal or end of the action. The explanation consists in stating a goal to be attained: it describes the action as one directed towards a certain goal—as a 'goal-directed activity' (to use E. S. Russell's convenient phrase [1]), the word "directed" being used (as it will here be used) to imply a direction but not to imply a director.

If we take an explanation (as we are doing) to be any answer to a

* From *Scientific Explanation* by R. B. Braithwaite. Cambridge: The Syndics of the Cambridge University Press, 1953, pp. 322–336. Reprinted by permission of Cambridge University Press. This chapter was originally presented as a paper in the *Proceedings of The Aristotelian Society,* 1946/47.

[1] *The Directiveness of Organic Activities* (Cambridge, 1945).

'Why?' question which in any way answers the question, and thereby gives some degree of intellectual satisfaction to the questioner, there can be no doubt that teleological answers of the sort of which I have given examples are genuine explanations. The fact that they all may give rise to further questions does not imply that they are not perfectly proper answers to the questions asked. My answer as to why I am staying in Cambridge all through August would almost certainly not lead to a further question, unless my friend wished to start a philosophical discussion as to the correct analysis of the motives of rational action. My answer as to why my cat paws the door might lead to the further question as to why the cat (to use common-sense languange) 'wants to be let out', to which another teleological answer would be appropriate, or to the question as to how the cat has learnt to paw the door to show that he wants to be let out, which would lead to a description, which might or might not be in teleological terms, of the processes of learning in cats. But all these would be regarded as further and different questions; the first simple teleological answer would be taken as what the questioner was asking for, and if it did not give him adequate intellectual satisfaction, he would expect not to repeat the question but to ask another.

But, having insisted that teleological explanations are perfectly good first-stage explanations, we have to admit that they have one feature which distinguishes them from causal explanations, and that this feature has proved very puzzling to philosophers, whether concerned with philosophical psychology or with the philosophy of biology. In a causal explanation the explicandum is explained in terms of a cause which either precedes or is simultaneous with it: in a teleological explanation the explicandum is explained as being causally related either to a particular goal in the future or to a biological end which is as much future as present or past. It is the reference in teleological explanations to states of affairs in the future, and often in the comparatively distant future, which has been a philosophical problem ever since Aristotle introduced the notion of 'final cause'; the controversy as to the legitimacy of explanations in terms of final causes rages continually among philosophers of biology and, to a less extent, among working biologists.

Now there is one type of teleological explanation in which the reference to the future presents no difficulty, namely, explanations of an intentional human action in terms of a goal to the attainment of which the action is a means. For my teleological answer to the question as to why I am staying in Cambridge all through August—that I am doing so in order to finish writing my book—would be regarded by my questioner as equivalent to an answer that I am doing so because I intend to finish writing my book, my staying in Cambridge being a means to fulfil that intention; and this answer would have been an explanation of the causal sort with my intention as cause preceding my stay in Cambridge as effect.[2] Teleological explanations of intentional goal-directed activities are always understood as reducible to causal explanations with intentions as causes; to use the Aristotelian terms, the idea of the 'final cause' functions as 'efficient cause'; the goal-directed behaviour is explained as goal-intended behaviour.

This is not to say that there is no philosophical difficulty about intentional action; there is the problem—fundamental for philosophical psychology—as to the correct analysis of the intention to act in a certain way. But this is different from our problem as to how a future reference can occur in an explanation, unless indeed an extreme behaviouristic analysis is adopted, according to which there is no conscious element in an intention, and goal-intended behaviour is simply what we call goal-directed behaviour in the higher animals. But for this extreme behaviourism psychology reduces to biology, and intentional action falls under biological goal-directed activity and the type of teleological explanation we meet in the sciences concerned with life in general and not especially with mind.

The difficulty about the future reference occurs then in all teleological explanations which are not reducible to explanations in terms of a conscious intention to attain the goal. Here one cannot obviously reduce the teleological answer, which explains a present event by means of a future event, to a non-teleological answer in terms of a present or past cause. It is teleological explanations which cannot obviously be so reduced which present the philosophical problem; and the rest of this chapter will be devoted to this type of teleological explanations and to the problems raised by them.

CURRENT ATTEMPTS TO ELIMINATE FINAL CAUSES

There are two ways of solving this problem which are fashionable to-day. Both are attempts to reduce all teleological explanations to causal explanations, and thus to eliminate the special puzzle presented by future reference; but the attempts are made in opposite directions.

[2] Jonathan Cohen has pointed out (*Proceedings of The Aristotelian Society,* n.s., vol. 51 (1950–1), pp. 262ff.) that such an explanation would differ from an ordinary causal explanation in that it is more difficult to specify the total cause of which the intention is only a part than it is to specify the total cause in an ordinary causal explanation. But this difference is only one of degree (as Cohen seems prepared to admit; loc. cit. p. 268 n.); and, however partial the intention may be as a factor in a total cause, it will not be later in time than the action which it is put forward to explain.

The first way is to emphasize the similarity between teleological explanations of the type with which we are now concerned and the teleological explanations of intentional actions in which the future reference can be explained away, and to argue by analogy that in all cases the teleological explanation is reducible to one in which an intention, or something analogous to an intention, in the agent is the 'efficient cause', so that goal-directed activity is always a sort of goal-intended activity. My cat's behaviour in pawing at the closed door, it may be said, is sufficiently similar to a man's behaviour in knocking at a locked door for it to be reasonable to infer that the cat, like the man, is acting as it does because of a conscious intention, or at least a conscious desire, to be let through the door. Similarly a neurotic's goal-directed behaviour may be explained by his having an unconscious intention or desire; a bird's nest-building by its having an instinct to do so. When the goal-directed activity to be explained is that of a part of a whole organism, as in my example of the heart's beating, the analogue to the intention—the drive or conatus or nisus or urge—is usually posited not in the separate organ but in the organism as a whole—an urge towards self-preservation, for example. Sometimes the analogy is pressed so far that a purposiveness similar to that of voluntary action is assumed in all teleological behaviour. William McDougall, for instance, after explaining that by 'purposiveness' in human movements he means not only that "they are made for the sake of attaining their natural end" (i.e. that they are teleological in my sense), but that "this end is more or less clearly anticipated or foreseen", goes on to speak of a "scale of degrees of purposiveness", at the lower end of which there is a "vague anticipation of the goal" which may also be ascribed to an animal's goal-directed behaviour.[3]

Other writers (e.g. E.S. Russell) would reject as unduly anthropomorphic the attribution of purposiveness to such activities, and would describe the efficient cause as a conatus or drive. But all writers who deal with the problem of teleological explanation in the first way agree in postulating something in the organism which is present whenever goal-directed behaviour is taking place and which is to explain it in the ordinary causal way, and agree in supposing that this something cannot be analysed purely in physico-chemical terms.

The biological orthodoxy of to-day, however, would say that the postulation of this 'something', not explicable in physico-chemical terms, to account for teleological behaviour was an assumption which was either methodologically vicious (if the 'something' was supposed to have no

[3] W. McDougall, *An Outline of Psychology* (London, 1923), pp. 47f.

properties other than that of being the cause of the goal-directed behaviour) or metaphysical and non-empirical (if it was supposed to have additional properties such as McDougall's purposiveness). And orthodox biologists would go on to say that satisfactory explanations had been given of many goal-directed activities in physico-chemical terms, and that as the new sciences of biochemistry and biophysics advance, there is less and less reason to suppose that there will be any teleological action (or at any rate any teleological action in which consciousness is not involved) that will not be explicable by means of the concepts and laws of chemistry and physics alone.

This attitude is equivalent to an attempt to solve the problem of teleological explanations in a second way, by reducing them to physico-chemical explanations of the ordinary causal sort. It is admitted that biochemistry and biophysics at the moment cannot effect this reduction in the great majority of cases, but it is expected that some day they will be able to. Teleological explanations must be accepted as irreducible to causal explanations at present, but not as in principle irreducible. Thus the philosophical problem presented by the reference to the future in such explanations is a temporary problem only, to be solved by the progress of science. A teleological explanation is to be regarded as a very poor sort of explanation indeed, to be discarded as soon as the real, physico-chemical causes have been discovered.

It seems to me that the orthodox biologists are right in rejecting the postulation of a conatus or drive which is non-physical and *sui generis* in order to explain the goal-directed behaviour which they meet in their biological studies, but wrong in minimizing the intellectual satisfaction to be derived from teleological explanations. I believe that we can go on the orthodox assumption that every biological event is physico-chemically determined, and yet find an important place in biology for such explanations. So what I propose to do is to try to give an account of the nature of teleological explanations which will resolve the philosophical difficulty about the apparent determination of the present by the future without either contravening the usual determination principles of science or reducing all biological laws to those of chemistry and physics.[4]

[4] Analyses of teleological explanations which have more or less resemblance to my analysis have been given by E. Rignano, *Mind,* n.s., vol. 40 (1931), p. 337; A. Rosenblueth, N. Wiener and J. Bigelow, *Philosophy of Science,* vol. 10 (1943), p. 24 ("Teleological behavior becomes synonymous with behavior controlled by negative feed-back"); L. von Bertalanffy, *British Journal for the Philosophy of Science,* vol. 1 (1950), p. 157. The field of study called by Wiener "cybernetics" is largely concerned with 'teleological mechanisms'.

TELEOLOGICAL CAUSAL CHAINS

If we make the ordinary determination assumptions of physical science, the apparent determination of the explicandum by a future event in a teleological explanation is not direct, but works by means of a causal chain of events lying between the explicandum and the goal. Even in intentional action the intention does not directly produce the goal: it starts a chain of action whose final stage is attainment of the goal. In non-intentional goal-directed action the goal-directedness consists simply in the fact that the causal chain in the organism goes in the direction of the goal, unless one wishes to suppose that there is always an extra 'something'—conatus or drive—involved in goal-directedness, an assumption which I do not wish to make. Thus the notion of causal chain is fundamental. Of course this notion is equally fundamental in the non-teleological explanations provided by the physical sciences, where the explaining cause is frequently given not as a preceding event continuous with the explicandum but as a preceding event connected with the explicandum by a causal chain. Let us approach our problem, therefore, by asking what (if any) is the peculiarity of the causal chains, which are involved in teleological explanations.

Bertrand Russell, in his behaviouristic account of desire, approached our problem in the same way as I am doing by asserting that the peculiarity of teleological causal chains of actions is that they form 'behaviour-cycles'. But the only criterion he gave to enable us to pick out the behaviour-cycles from other repeated series of events in the life of an animal was that the final stage in a behaviour-cycle is "normally a condition of temporary quiescence".[5] He illustrated this by an animal falling asleep after it has eaten. But temporary quiescence is quite inadequate to serve as the *differentia* for which we are seeking. After a bomb has exploded, or a volcano ceased to erupt, a state of temporary quiescence is attained. Here no teleology is concerned in the causal chains. It seems impossible to find any characteristic of the final state by itself of a teleological causal chain which is general enough to cover all the goals of goal-directed actions and yet specific enough to differentiate such actions from other repeated cycles of behaviour. It is necessary, I think, to look at the whole causal chain and not merely at its final state.

It seems to me that a distinguishing criterion can be found in one of the characteristics which biologists have emphasized in their descriptions of goal-directed behaviour, namely persistence towards the goal under varying conditions. To quote E. S. Russell: "Coming to a definite end or

[5] *The Analysis of Mind,* p. 65.

terminus is not *per se* distinctive of directive activity, for inorganic processes also move towards a natural terminus. . . . What *is* distinctive is the active persistence of directive activity towards its goal, the use of alternative means towards the same end, the achievement of results in the face of difficulties".[6] Examples of the 'plasticity' of goal-directed behaviour will spring to every mind. To give one example only, Lashley's rats who had learnt to obtain their food by running his maze were still able to traverse the maze without false turns in order to obtain food after their powers of motor coordination had been seriously reduced by cerebellar operations, so that they could no longer run but could only crawl or lunge.[7] Plasticity is not in general a property of one teleological causal chain alone: it is a property of the organism with respect to a certain goal, namely that the organism can attain the same goal under different circumstances by alternative forms of activity making use frequently of different causal chains. Let us try to elucidate the logical and epistemological significance of this plasticity, in order to see whether it will serve our purpose of preserving the importance of teleological explanations without introducing extra-physical causation.

Consider a chain of events in a system b. The system may be a physical system of more or less complexity (a pilotless plane or an electron) or it may be an organic system (a complete organism or a relatively isolable part of a complete organism, e.g. the kidneys). Make the ordinary determination assumption that every event in the system is nomically determined by the whole previous state of the system together with the causally relevant factors in the system's environment or field (which will be called the "field-conditions"). Then the causal chain c of events in b throughout a period of time is nomically determined by the initial state e of the system together with the totality of field-conditions which affect the system with respect to the events in question during the period. Call this set of field-conditions f. Then, for a given system b with initial state e, c is a one-valued function of f; i.e. for given b and e, the causal chain c is uniquely determined by f—the set of field-conditions.

Now consider the property which a causal chain in a system may possess of ending in an event of type Γ without containing any other event of this type. Call this property the Γ-goal-attaining property, and the class of all causal chains having this property the Γ-goal-attaining class γ. Every causal chain which is a member of γ contains one and only one event of type Γ, and contains this as its final event.

Define the variancy ϕ with respect to a given system b with given

[6] *The Directiveness of Organic Activities*, p. 144.
[7] K. S. Lashley, *Brain Mechanisms and Intelligence* (Chicago, 1929).

initial state *e,* and to a given type of goal Γ, as the class of those sets of field-conditions which are such that every causal chain in *b* starting with *e* and determined by one of these sets of Γ-goal-attaining. To express this more shortly with the symbols already used, the variancy ϕ is defined as the class of those *f*'s which uniquely determine those *c*'s which are members of γ. According to this definition, to say that a causal chain *c* in a system *b* starting from a state *e* ends (without having previously passed through) a state of type Γ is logically equivalent to saying that the set of field-conditions is a member of ϕ. The variancy is thus (to repeat the definition in a looser form) the range of circumstances under which the system attains the goal.

The variancy ϕ defined in relation to *b, e* and Γ may have no members, in which case there is no nomically possible chain in *b* starting from *e* and attaining a goal of type Γ. Or ϕ may have one member, in which case there is exactly one such chain which is nomically possible. Here the system starting from *e* has no plasticity; there is only one set of field-conditions which, together with *e,* is nomically sufficient for the attainment of a goal of type Γ.

The case in which we are interested, in which the system has plasticity, occurs when the variancy ϕ has more than one member, so that the occurrence of any one of alternative sets of field-conditions is, together with *e,* sufficient for the attainment of a goal of type Γ. It is important to notice that the variancy may have many members and yet there be only one nomically possible chain: it is because the size of the variancy may be greater than the number of possible causal chains that the notion of the variancy has been introduced. For it may be the case that there are various sets of field-conditions each of which, together with *e,* determines exactly the same causal chain. This might happen if the ultimate causal laws concerned are such that each of the events in the chain might be determined by two or more alternative field-conditions. But it more frequently happens when the events in the chain are taken as being events which attribute properties to the system as a whole, and when, although alternative field-conditions determine different part-events in the system or in parts of the system, these part-events are causally so connected that the whole event determined by them remains unchanged. For example, if the causal chain of events with which we are concerned is the chain of body temperatures throughout a period of time of one of the higher animals, a change in the relevant environmental conditions (e.g. external temperature and available sources of food) will produce changes in the activities of the animal (both changes in its total behaviour, e.g. its feeding and migration habits, and changes in its parts, e.g. its sweat glands), yet these changes will be such as to compensate for the changed environmental conditions so that the animal's body temperature does not vary. Another example would be the path of a pilotless plane, in which the machine is fitted with 'feed-back' devices so designed that the plane will maintain a straight course at the correct height to the desired goal irrespective of the weather conditions it may encounter.

But usually when the variancy has more than one member, there is more than one nomically possible chain in the system in question which attains the required goal. An animal can move to get its food in many ways, a great variety of physiological processes can be called into play to repair damaged tissue, a bird can adapt its nest-building to the kind of material available. Nevertheless the essential feature, as I see it, about plasticity of behaviour is that the goal can be attained under a variety of circumstances, not that it can be attained by a variety of means. So it is the size of the variancy rather than the number of possible causal chains that is significant in analysing teleological explanation.

Let us now take the standpoint of epistemological or inductive logic and consider what are the types of situation in which we reasonably infer that there will be a goal-attaining chain of events in a system. To predict that, starting from an initial state e of a system b, there will be a causal chain which will attain a goal of type Γ is, by the definition of variancy, equivalent to predicting that the set of field-conditions which will occur will be a member of the variancy ϕ. So the reasonableness of the prediction depends upon the reasonableness of believing that ϕ is large enough to contain every set of field-conditions that is at all likely to occur.[8] Call the class of these sets of field-conditions ψ. For simplicity's sake I shall for the moment assume that we know that any set of field-conditions that will occur will be contained in ψ; that is, that the system will not in fact encounter a very unlikely environment (e.g. the next Ice Age starting suddenly to-morrow). Then the reasonableness of the prediction that the system will attain the goal depends upon the reasonableness of believing that ψ is included in ϕ.

Now there are two ways in which we may have derived our knowledge of the variancy ϕ. We may have deduced ϕ from knowledge of the relevant causal laws, or we may have inferred it inductively from knowledge of the sets of field-conditions under which similar causal chains had attained their goals in the past. In the first case, that in which the members of ϕ

[8] The phrase "at all likely to occur" can be interpreted in different ways; but their difference does not affect the argument.

have been obtained by deduction, there are two interesting subcases in which we take positive steps to secure that ψ—the class of the sets of field-conditions at all likely to occur—is included in the variancy ϕ. The first subcase is that in which ϕ is small, but we deliberately arrange that ψ shall be smaller still. This happens when scientific demonstrations are performed for students in a laboratory, when elaborate precautions are taken (e.g. the experiment is done in a vacuum or distilled water is used) in order to eliminate unwanted relevant causal factors (air-currents or chemical impurities) and thus to secure that every set of conditions that may occur will fall within the known variancy ϕ so that the demonstration will be a success. The second subcase is that in which ψ is large, but we deliberately arrange that ϕ shall be larger still. This happens when a machine is deliberately designed to work under a large variety of conditions. This object may be achieved by using suitable materials: a motor-car is built to stand up to a lot of rough and careless treatment. Or it may be achieved by incorporating in the machine special self-regulating devices to ensure that the machine adjusts its method of working according to the conditions it encounters, as in the pilotless plane.

When our knowledge of the relevant variancy has been obtained by deduction from previous knowledge of the causal laws concerned, a teleological explanation of an event in terms of its goal-directedness is felt to be almost valueless.[9] For in this case, that the causal chain which will occur will lead to the goal—the 'teleology' of the system—has been calculated from its 'mechanism'. To give a teleological answer to the 'Why?' question would require forming (and suppressing) an ordinary causal answer, which would (if expressed) have given intellectual satisfaction to the questioner, in order to deduce from it a teleological answer. This would be an unprofitable, and indeed disingenuous, way of answering his question.

The situation is entirely different when our knowledge or reasonable belief about the variancy ϕ has not been derived from knowledge of the causal laws concerned. In this case our knowledge as to what sets of conditions make up the variancy has been obtained either directly by induction from previous experience of goal-attaining behaviour that was similar to the behaviour with which we are concerned, or indirectly by deduction

[9] In the case of a machine or of a laboratory demonstration a teleological explanation can of course be given of the action of a man in starting and controlling the machine or demonstration. Derivatively we can apply such a teleological explanation (as a 'transferred epithet') to the working of the machine itself. But these explanations are all in terms of intentions as efficient causes, and so do not raise the special problem with which we are here concerned.

from general teleological propositions which have themselves been established by induction from past experience. Neither of these ways makes use of laws about the mechanisms of the causal chains. The variancy ϕ is inferred—inductively inferred—from knowledge of classes similar to ψ; that is, from past observation of the conditions under which similar teleological behaviour has taken place. For example, my knowledge of the conditions under which a swallow will migrate is derived from knowledge about past migrations of swallows and of other migrants, fortified perhaps by general teleological propositions which I accept about the external conditions for self-preservation or the survival of the species, themselves derived inductively from past experience.

It is when our knowledge of the relevant variancy has been obtained independently of any knowledge of the causal laws concerned that a teleological explanation is valuable. For in this case we are unable, through ignorance of the causal laws, to infer the future behaviour of the system from our knowledge of the causal laws; but we are able to make such an inference from knowledge of how similar systems have behaved in the past.

It should be noted that in all cases of teleological explanation of a present event by a future event, whether reducible or irreducible, inductive inferences occur at two stages of the argument. One stage is in the inference of the variancy, whether this itself is obtained inductively, or whether it is obtained deductively from causal laws or teleological generalizations which have themselves been established inductively. The other inductive stage in the argument is the inference that the set of relevant conditions that will in fact occur in the future will fall within the variancy. Every teleological answer, however reasonable, may be mistaken in each of these two ways.

But in general irreducible teleological explanations are no less worthy of credence than ordinary causal explanations. A teleological explanation of a particular event is intellectually valuable if it cannot be deduced from known causal laws: other things being equal, it is the more valuable the wider the variancy of the conditions, and hence the greater the plasticity of the behaviour concerned. It is because we are acquainted with systems—organisms and parts of organisms—which exhibit great plasticity that we make use of teleological explanations. Such an explanation may be regarded as merely another way of stating the fact of the plasticity of the goal-directed behaviour. But to state this fact is to bring the explicandum under a general category; moreover it enables us to make reliable predictions as to how the system will behave in the future. It seems ridiculous to deny the title of explanation to a statement which performs both of the functions characteristic of scientific explanations—of enabling us to appreciate connexions and to predict the future.

The analysis which has here been given of teleological explanation of non-intentional goal-directed activities supposes that the goal to which the activity is directed is later in time than the action (this indeed creates the philosophical problem) and makes great use of the notion of causal chain. It has been objected that this analysis will not cover the case of explanations of biological facts which are given in terms, not of a future goal, but of a biological end which is as much present as future; but that this case, as well as that in which the explanation is in terms of a future goal, will be covered by the more general notion of *functional explanation* in which the explanation is in terms of another part of a whole of which the explicandum is a part.[10] But the questions which seem to call for a more general functional explanation rather than for a causal-chain teleological explanation turn out on examination to be ambiguous questions. If a physiologist is asked why the heart beats, he may take this question as a request for an explanation of a particular fact, the beating of a particular heart on a particular occasion, in which case the explanation "In order to circulate the blood round the body" will also refer to the movement of the blood in a particular body on a particular occasion. But, on this interpretation, the particular movement of blood outside the heart due to a particular beating of the heart is an event whose beginning is later in time than the beginning of the event which is the heart's beating: the latter event is connected with the former event by a causal chain of events, and is a teleological explanation of it in terms of a future goal. But the physiologist may more naturally take the question, not to be a question about one particular heart on one particular occasion, but to be a question about all beatings of all hearts (or of all human hearts, or of all mammalian hearts, or etc.), in which case the question is a request for a teleological generalization of which the particular teleological explanation of the beating of one particular heart on one particular occasion would be an instance. In both cases, however, the explanation would be in terms of goal-directed activities with future goals. The peculiarity of a biological end is that it is a permanent goal; at all

[10] Jonathan Cohen, *Proceedings of The Aristotelian Society,* n.s., vol. 51 (1950–1), pp. 270, 292. Cohen holds that "a functional explanation asserts the explanandum to be [a] necessary condition (logically, causally or in any other generally recognised way) of the explanans and thereby also of the persistence under varying circumstances of a whole of which both explanans and the explanandum are parts" (loc. cit. p. 292). But the beating of my heart is not a *necessary* condition for the circulation of my blood: it is only because my anatomy includes a heart but no other mechanism for circulating my blood that it is causally necessary that the heart should *beat* in order that the blood should circulate.

times during the life of the organism there are activities of the organism to be explained in terms of the biological end. My heart's beating at one moment is responsible for the circulation of my blood a short time afterwards; and my heart will have to *continue* beating for my blood to *continue* circulating. The teleological generalization of which the particular teleological explanation of the beating of my heart on a particular occasion is an instance will have instances at every moment of my life, unlike teleological laws concerning goals upon the attainment of which the animal sinks into a 'temporary quiescence'.[11]

[11] The term "functional explanation" may sometimes also be used to cover a mere description of the *modus operandi* of an organ like the heart. This would correspond to J. H. Woodger's third sense of 'function' (*Biological Principles* (London, 1929), p. 327).

Arthur O. Lovejoy

The Meanings of "Emergence" and Its Modes *

There is an old and persistent tendency in the human mind to conceive of the causal relation as rationally explanatory, and, therefore, to assimilate it, vaguely or explicitly, to the logical relations of inclusion, implication, or equivalence. That "there cannot be more in the effect than there is in the cause" is one of the propositions that men have been readiest to accept as axiomatic; a cause, it has been supposed, does not "account for" its effect, unless the effect is a thing which the eye of reason could somehow discern *in* the cause, upon a sufficiently thorough analysis. This antipathy to the notion of an absolute epigenesis has left its mark deep and wide upon the history of thought; it appears, indeed, at the very outset of Western speculation in the struggles of the physiologers with the supposed difficulty of admitting qualitative change. Two of the later episodes in the history of what may be named the preformationist assumption about causality may pertinently be remembered here.

The first is the doctrine of the most mediaeval European metaphysics that all the "perfections," or positive attributes, of the creatures must be possessed by the First Cause—even though it was found necessary to assert with equal emphasis that that Cause and its creatures have no attributes in common. In this theological form the preformationist principle implied an addition to the empirically known sum of reality; it left undiminished the abundance and diversity of nature and did not exclude quantitative and qualitative change from the natural order, but placed behind these a supersensible cause in which all this abundance and diversity were declared to be in some fashion antecedently or eternally contained. Since this way of construing the assumption meant no simplification of the universe for our understanding, it was not serviceable to natural science. But in the seventeenth century there began to develop a conception which,

* From *Proceedings of the Sixth International Congress of Philosophy,* 1926, pp. 20–33. Reprinted by permission of the author.

while it fulfilled the same assumption, did so in a significantly different way—the conception, namely, of natural events as combinations or rearrangements of relatively simple, pre-existent entities, of which the total number or quantity remains invariant, and of each of which the qualities and laws of action remain the same through all the combinations into which it may enter. By this mechanistic conception of causation there is nothing *substantive* in the consequent which was not in the antecedent, and the supposed paradox of epigenesis is thus avoided. But in this second form the preformationist assumption implied a program of reduction or simplification; it was in its essence a scheme for abating the difference of things. For if complexes contain nothing (except their patterns) not already in their simple components, *rerum cognoscere causas* means learning to see in the complex nothing but its beggarly elements—the meager qualities and limited repertoire of the simple, merely multiplied a certain number of times. Scientific explanation becomes equivalent to mathematical analysis; and if the method is universalized, all philosophy, in Hobbes's phrase, becomes "nothing but addition and subtraction." But many complex things have properties not convincingly describable as multiples of the properties of the simple things through the combination of which they arise; and thus the notion of observed causal processes as rearrangements of the unchanging, while formally denying that there is "more" in the effect than there is in the cause, nevertheless seemed to imply that there is less in the cause than is apprehended in the effect. The mechanistic conception escaped this paradox only through its conjunction with another feature of most seventeenth-century and subsequent philosophy; its plausibility at the outset and ever since has been wholly dependent upon its association with some form of psycho-physical dualism. By means of this all that considerable part of the data of experience, together with the phenomenon of experiencing itself, which seemed plainly irreconcilable with the principle of quantitative and qualitative constancy could conveniently be assigned to the side of the "merely subjective." The eventual triumphs of that principle in modern science were made possible through the restriction of its literal application to the physical order, after that order had first been carefully purged of the classes of facts most recalcitrant to such application.

I have recalled these historical commonplaces because they lead up to the first of a series of distinctions which I wish to propose. The phrasing of the question laid down for our discussion implies, and most judicious readers of recent English and American philosophy, I suspect, feel, that the now modish terms "emergence" and "emergent evolution" stand in some need of clarification. In current use their meanings are various and usually vague; and though it may be recognized that they point towards some real and important philosophical issues, the precise nature of those issues, their relations to one another, and the logical procedure suitable for dealing with them have not yet, perhaps, been formulated quite so clearly and methodically as could be wished. It is, therefore, towards such preliminary definition, discrimination, and correlation of problems that I shall chiefly attempt to contribute. While some opinions on certain of the issues themselves will be expressed, it must be with the brevity that is indistinguishable from dogmatism; and the primary purpose of this paper is merely to offer some prolegomena to any future discussion of "emergence."

What is needed, however, is not an extreme narrowing of the signification of the general term. In this case, as often in philosophical terminology, it is better to leave to the generic term a meaning so broad as to appear vague, and to approach precise definitions and clear-cut issues by progressively distinguished species within the genus. "Emergence," then (or "epigenesis," which would be a much more appropriate word), may be taken loosely to signify any augmentative or transmutative event, any process in which there appear effects that, in some one or more of several ways yet to be specified, fail to conform to the maxim that "there cannot be in the consequent anything more than, or different in nature from, that which was in the antecedent." And the first distinction which it is essential to make, in reducing this vague general notion to something more definite and discussable, is between what I shall call the theses of the possibility of general and the actuality of specific emergence, theses antithetic respectively to the first and second sorts of preformationism.[1] To affirm the possibility of general emergence is to reject the preformationist assumption formally and absolutely, and therefore to deny the validity of any argument from it to the existence of a metempirical cause or causes which somehow pre-contain "all that is in the effects." But to many this assumption apparently still has the force of an axiom, and the argument in question, therefore, figures conspicuously in some recent discussions of our theme. Thus Taylor repeats the scholastic maxim: "The principle *e nihilo nihil fit,"* he writes, "is fundamental to all explanation"; and it is therefore "true that no cause can contribute to its effect what it has not to give. The full and ultimate cause of every effect in a process of evolution will have to be found not simply in the special character of its recognized antecedents but in the

[1] The adjectives "general" and "specific" are not free from ambiguity; the former here means "predicable of the whole, but not necessarily of every part," the latter, "predicable of some part or parts, but not necessarily of the whole."

character of the eternal which is at the back of all development. And this must contain"—though "in a more eminent manner"—"all that it bestows, though it may contain much more." [2] Boodin has recently built a highly original superstructure upon the same ancient foundation; for the main argument of his interesting volume on *Cosmic Evolution* appears to be, in brief, that philosophy must "explain" the seeming emergence of novelty in the course of evolution, that "causality from behind cannot account for more than there is in the antecedents," and that therefore the higher forms of being which are progressively attained in terrestrial history must have pre-existed in, and been communicated through ready-made "energy-patterns" from, some other part of the universe,—the "evolution of new levels" being "obviously" impossible, since it would be tantamount to "something coming from nothing." [3]

The issue here is not only the most fundamental one in our topic but one of the crucial issues in all philosophy. If we really know that an absolute or general emergence is impossible we know something very curious and important about the universe. But the proof of its impossibility usually offered I find unconvincing for numerous reasons, of which a few may be briefly indicated. The universal cause or set of causes in which all that is in the (temporal) effects is declared to be pre-contained must be one of three things: a temporal *prius,* or an eternal which contains the temporal effects as its parts, or an eternal extraneous to those effects. If taken in the first of these senses, the assumption of which the argument rests cannot, of course, mean that the effects themselves are in the cause; it can only mean either (a) that the effects collectively do not *differ* either qualitatively or quantitatively from the *prius*—that is to say, that they are either mere repetitions of it, or else that they differ only in some relational property which is regarded as unimportant, such as the arrangement or distribution of the qualities and components present in the cause; or (b) that they are never of higher metaphysical rank or excellence than the cause. This latter is what the supposed axiom seems often to reduce to; the "lower" we are told, can come from the "higher," but not the "higher" from the "lower"; the stream of being cannot rise higher than its source. But—though this will seem to some a hard saying—neither of these forms of the preformationist assumption appears to be justified by anything better than a prejudice—an idol of the tribe, at best. The supposed axiom lacks self-evidence, and though there are some, there are no cogent, reasons for postulating it. Concerning the qualitative and quantitative relations of two

[2] A. E. Taylor, *Evolution in the Light of Modern Knowledge* (1925), p. 460.
[3] J. E. Boodin *op. cit.,* (1925), pp. 44, 67, 82, 96–98, 101 and *passim.*

existents of different dates we have no *a priori* knowledge. It is entirely conceivable that temporal reality as a whole is not only augmented, but attains higher levels, within any finite time which we may choose to consider; and there are some to whom this evidently seems the more satisfying thing to postulate. Certainly, if consistently carried out, metaphysical preformationism has less edifying and cheering implications than are sometimes attributed to it. If the sum of being and the sum of realized value are constant—and unless they are either constant or diminishing the pretended axiom is false, and there *is* at times an absolute emergence—then the whole movement and travail of the creation is but a barren shuffling-about of the same pieces; an increase or ascent in one region must be simultaneously compensated by an equivalent decrease or decline elsewhere; the more the universe changes, the more it is the same thing. If, however, the "Cause" is conceived as a supratemporal totality which contains the temporal effects, the impossibility of general emergence undeniably follows; an "eternal" cannot grow or improve. But such a conception implies the true inclusion of a real succession in a *totum simul;* and no ingenuity has ever succeeded in showing this to be other than a self-contradiction. This aside, since the temporal world is still admitted to be in some sense real, the whole of *that* world may in that same sense conceivably differ at different moments in the number of its elements or in their value. Finally, if the Cause by which "all that is in the effects" is said to be possessed is conceived as an eternal that does *not* contain those effects within its being—which I take to be the orthodox scholastic view—the same difficulties present themselves as in the first case, together with some additional ones. The notion of an existent which at once is alien to all succession or change, and yet is the efficient cause of a series of temporal changes, is, to say the least, elusive; and the supposition that that cause must "possess" all that is in the temporal effects seems not only gratuitous—the same venerable prejudice as before—but also self-contradictory. None of their *distinctive* qualities can be predicable of it, except in a sense so eminent as to be no sense at all. And even if the qualities were the same, their "communication" to the effects would mean the emergence of additional existence *instances* of those qualities, unless they were at the same time lost by the Cause. And in any case, there is nothing in this last form of the argument which would preclude emergence in the world in which alone, by hypothesis, change occurs at all.

There is, then, no valid *a priori* argument against the possibility of general (which, of course, does not necessarily mean perpetual) emergence to be drawn from the notion of causality. The subject is one on which we have no means of arriving at objective conclusions, unless it be through more or less probable inferences from experience. It may be suggested that reasons for regarding general emergence as impossible (or meaningless) are to be found in the experimental data upon which the special theory of relativity is based. An examination of the sufficiency of those data as grounds for such a conclusion cannot be attempted in the time at my disposal.

The thesis of specific emergence means denial of the second form of preformationism; it is the assertion on empirical grounds of the occurrence, among the phenomena investigable by science, of events which are not mere rearrangements of pre-existent natural entities in accordance with laws identical for all arrangements of those entities. It is to be observed that the reality of specific emergence is usually asserted by those who declare general or absolute emergence to be inconceivable. This combination of views is, at least on the face of it, logically possible, since the denial of qualitative and quantitative constancy in certain empirically observable changes does not of itself forbid the supposition of an ulterior general cause of whose relation to the entire series of changes the supposed axiom about causality would hold good; and the combination is natural, because there is a radical incompatibility of temper between the two types of preformationism. On the other hand, if such a compensatory general cause is excluded, any instance of specific emergence, however slight, would obviously imply also general emergence, an augmentation of the total sum of things. The opposition in certain scientific quarters to current doctrines of specific emergence seems to be due in no small part to the same feeling as is expressed in the scholastic principle—the feeling that there would be something queer and illogical about a universe in which substantive increments popped into existence. The chief significance of our problem is, then, that it raises definitely the question of the tenability of this historic assumption, common to and potent in both traditional theology and mechanistic science in spite of their mutual antipathy.

Agreeing in what they deny, doctrines of specific emergence may differ in two respects in what they affirm: in their accounts, namely, of the occasions of emergence, and of the types of actual emergents. In the first regard we must first of all distinguish between indeterminist and determinist theories. The former declare that there are instances of emergence which are reducible to no causal law; no fixed occasions can be formulated upon which they invariably occur. The hypothesis of "undetermined evolution" to which Professor Driesch has referred is, I take it, a theory of this sort; but it is undesirable to define this as the only or the "strict" sense of "emergent evolution." The determinist kind of theory declares that whenever certain specific occasions appear a specific variety of emergent uniformly arises. The general nature of these occasions may be variously conceived. One abstractly possible sort would consist merely in intervals in the proper time of one or another physical system; but the most widely current hypothesis on the matter—the so-called theory of creative synthesis—finds the chief, if not the only, occasions of emergence to consist in the formation of special integrations of matter and (or) energy. The question what, in fact, these occasions are, must, of course, depend upon the character of the emergents which can be shown really to arise. Before raising this question of fact it is useful to consider what types of emergent there conceivably *may* be—what, in other words, are the ways in which it is possible to think of a consequent as differing positively, otherwise than in the rearrangement of the same elements, from its causally necessary antecedent. In distinguishing these modes of possible emergence I shall—in order to gain brevity by combining two definitions—put the enumeration in the form of a statement of the meaning of "emergent evolution," that term in general here signifying the occurrence as a feature of the evolutionary process of *any* of the modes of emergence. An "emergent evolution" may, then, be said to have taken place if, upon comparison of the present phase (called Ph.N), of earth-history (say that since the appearance of *homo sapiens*) with any prior phase (called Ph.A), there can be shown to be present in Ph.N any one or more of the five following features lacking in Ph.A. (1) Instances of some general type of change admittedly common to both phases (e.g., relative motion of particles), of which instances the manner of conditions of occurrence could not be described in terms of, nor predicted from, the laws which would have been sufficient for the description and (given the requisite determination of the variables) the prediction of all changes of that type occurring in Ph.A. Of this evolutionary emergence of laws one, though not the only conceivable, occasion would be the production, in accordance with one set of laws, of new local integrations of matter, the motions of which, and therefore of their component particles, would thereupon conform to vector, i.e., directional, laws emergent in the sense defined. This first mode differs from the others in that it implies no quantitative variability of the prime or irreducible *existents* (other than relations) in the system under consideration. (2) New qualities and, especially, classes of qualities (e.g., the so-called secondary qualities) attachable as adjectives to entities already present, though without those accidents, in Ph.A. (3) Particular entities *not* possessing all the essential attributes characteristic of those found in Ph.A, and having distinctive types of attributes (not merely configurational) of their own. (4) Some type or types of event or process irreducibly different in kind from any occurring Ph.A. (5) A greater quantity, or number of instances, not explicable by transfer from outside the system, of any one or more types of prime entity common to both phases.

In the enumeration of types of possible emergence included in this definition, the most significant point is the contrast between the first, which may be called functional, and the remaining four, which may be called existential, emergence. Several writers have recently declared that any attempt to prove the reality of the first mode is subject (for familiar reasons, inherent in the notion of a "law," which need not be recalled here) to an intrinsic logical limitation. Our inability, they remark, at any given time to discover, or even conceive of the general nature of, any single law or set of joint laws from which all the motions of matter in its differing integrations would be deducible, is not conclusive proof that no such law is formulable; "within the physical realm it always remains logically possible," Broad has said, "that the appearance of emergent laws is due to our imperfect knowledge of microscopic structure or to mathematical incompetence." This *non possumus* does not seem to me to be itself conclusively established; but as there is no time to give reasons, I shall not here challenge it. Even supposing it true, it would not follow that the emergence of laws can be said to be improbable. Such emergence would, to be sure, imply the impossibility of a complete unification of science; and there is for this reason, we are often told, a decisive methodological presumption against it. But here we must distinguish between heuristic rules and propositions of fact. It is the business of the scientific investigator to look for identities of law in seemingly diverse phenomena, and to find as many of them as he can; it is not the business of the philosopher to assume *a priori* that nature must to an indefinite degree lend itself to the gratification of this ambition. Though rigorous and conclusive proof of the first mode of emergence be impossible, the hypothesis of its occurrence seems to me to be patently the more probable in the present state of our knowledge. But with these cursory dogmatizings I leave to others the question of functional emergence, in order to consider somewhat less summarily that of existential emergence.

Concerning this the first thing to remark is that an attempt to prove it is not subject to the same general logical disability said to inhere in any argument for emergent laws. An existential emergent would be a quality, or a thing or event possessing distinctive non-configurational qualities, which was found in the subsequent and not in the prior phase of some causal process; and its presence in the one case and absence in the other would be facts determinable either by observation or by inference from observed data. Where observation of both phases is possible the proof of existential emergence can be direct and virtually complete, as in the case of the qualitative changes (whether they be "objective" or "subjective") incident to chemical synthesis, which have long been recognized, under a different terminology, as examples of such emergence. This simplest instance—which, however, is not quite so simple logically as it looks—obvious and commonplace though it is, has a crucial importance which some writers on the subject do not appear to realize; for it alone suffices to show that there can be no general and decisive theoretical presumption against *other* hypotheses of existential emergence, that nature is assuredly no affair of mere rearrangements. In less simple but philosophically more consequential and controversial cases, the argument for existential emergence may involve somewhat complex and difficult reasonings, and therefore attain a less high degree of probability; but even in these cases, to which I shall shortly return, the difficulty is of a kind different from, and less fundamental than, that said to infect all reasonings concerning emergence of laws.

With the distinction between functional and existential emergents in mind we are also in a position to deal with the commonest general or antecedent objection brought against theories of specific emergence. The objection was raised, in differing terms, by several participants in the recent discussion of the subject by the English philosophical societies. To characterize an effect as "emergent," it is urged, is to give up the attempt to "explain" it; and since science cannot give up this attempt, the characterization can have, at best, no more than a provisional validity, as a way of admitting that certain things have not as yet been completely "explained." Now, what sort of explanation is it that these critics desiderate in theories of emergence? "Causal explanation" in the empirical sense—the assumption that every event follows upon some other *nach einer Regel,* the "determinism of the experimentalist"—is, as we have seen, entirely compatible with the belief in emergence. The sort of explanation which specific emergence, or emergent evolution, would exclude, is simply that demanded by the second form of preformationism—the conception of an event as *neither* (a) manifesting any law, or mode of uniform behavior *nor* (b) containing any existent, not found in the antecedent phase of the sequence to which it belongs. To maintain then, that everything is "explicable," in the sense incongruous with emergence, is to raise a definite, though by no means simple, question of fact; it is to imply, for example, that, barring mere summations or rearrangements, there is to be found in the present phase of terrestrial history no existence whatever—no quality, type of entity, or kind of process—which could not already have been discerned by a scientific angel observing the cold-gaseous-nebula stage of the development of our solar system. This proposition cannot be said to have a high degree of *prima facie* plausibility; and its truth cannot be assumed *a priori* merely because it is one of the two conceivable ways of satisfying the demand for a special type of so-called "explanation" which is not practically indispensable to science.

Wholesale attempts to rule out, *ab initio,* all specific hypotheses of existential emergence by *a priori* assumptions of this sort being excluded, both assertors and deniers of any such hypotheses must address themselves to the analysis of definite empirical data. The assertor must (if the question be that of emergent evolution) point out some type of observable entity, event, or quality—call it E—existent in Ph.N which does not appear to be adequately describable in the same terms as would describe any entity, event, etc., which we can with probability suppose to have existed in Ph.A. The denier must attempt to show that everything in E *is* describable in the same terms as some class of entities, events, or qualities in Ph.A; to this end he may employ either of two methods, which may be termed the reductive and the retrotensive; i.e., he may either (1) seek by analysis to reduce E to the same descriptive terms as are sufficient for certain events, etc., admittedly found in Ph.A; or (2) admitting that E has the characters attributed to it by the assertor of emergence, he may maintain that these characters were already present in the earlier phase—in other words, must be supposed to be present in all phases—of the process.

The general logical nature of the problem being thus formulated, we may consider a particular hypothesis of existential emergence, which I hold to be true. It is nowise original, being substantially the same as the theory of which Broad has given the name of "emergent materialism"—though that designation seems to me a veritable *lucus a non lucendo.* According to this hypothesis, both the third and fourth modes of emergence—i.e., emergence of new types of entities and of new kinds of event or process—have appeared in evolution, in the form, but only in the form, of what may be called "trans-physical" emergence. By this I mean the production, as effects of the formation of certain complex and late-evolved integrations of living matter, when acted upon by certain forms of radiant energy, of psychical events and psychical objects. An example of a psychical event is an act of awareness. By psychical objects I mean individual entities empirically existent, having extension and certain other of the properties commonly called psychical, but differing from true physical objects in that they do not conform to the laws of physics, have individually only an ephemeral existence, have collectively no quantitative or numerical constancy, have no direct dynamical relations with one another, and are grouped into "private" sets, i.e., each is accessible only to an act of awareness of an individual organism. Examples of such entities are sensa and images, both delusive and veridical. In other words the "generative theory of sensa," recently defended by a number of writers, is a part of the hypothesis of existential emergent evolution I am presenting. The initial cases of trans-physical emergence were followed by a further evolution of the same type, conditioned upon the formation of new and still more complex integrations of matter and (or) energy, and the process thus far apparently culminates in the cognitive and affective functions of the human organism.

To the plain man, and to some men of science, these theses will, I dare say, seem rather obvious, and not much in need of defence. But in philosophy they manifestly raise numerous highly controversial issues. The existential emergence they assert is attacked chiefly from two sides, and by the two methods already defined; the reductive method is at present represented by behaviorism,[4] the retrotensive mainly by pan-psychism, or the mind-stuff theory. The behavioristic argument I shall not here examine; the view that both the act and the content of awareness, when I apprehend an object distant in space or time, are adequately describable as present changes of the relative position of molecules under my skin, really seems to me to be itself adequately describable by Broad's epithet, "silly." There is, however, an important contemporary doctrine which would apply the reductive method to the immediate objects of awareness, but not to the act of awareness; the former, it declares, are simply parts of the physical world, and, if emergent at all, are at any rate not trans-physical emergents. This contention is assuredly deserving of serious discussion; but the reasons for rejecting it are too complex to be presented here. The attempts of pan-psychists to escape from the admission of trans-physical emergence seem plainly to be due, in part, to the influence of an attenuated, vestigial form of the ancient pseudo-axiom mentioned at the outset; while it is not necessarily maintained by them that specific emergence is impossible in principle or nonexistent in fact. They apparently feel that a causal antecedent cannot be so *very* different in nature from its effect as a physical event is from a mental one. Thus the author of a recent admirably lucid

[4] A behaviorist might without inconsistency admit functional while denying existential emergence.

defence of the mind-stuff theory remarks that "discontinuity in evolution would be a baffling and unintelligible phenomenon," and declared that the mind-stuff theory alone "gives us a universe without such unintelligible breaches." "If a mind is simply a brain regarded from the outside, . . . the gradual evolution of a brain *is* the gradual evolution of a mind"; thus "there is no need to postulate any discontinuity in evolution to account for the appearance upon the scene of minds, of consciousness, of qualities." Yet the same writer tells us that "the units" of mind-stuff "which make up our mental states" and also our brains "are not *aware* of anything—neither of anything else nor of themselves. They just *exist;* . . . the fact of their constituting a group of units that function together, or the fact of their being in such and such a position in space and time, is a fact about them, not an aspect of their psychic being." Nor do they possess any of (at least) the secondary qualities. It is only when, "as a product of organic evolution," brains are formed, that "awareness," and therewith qualities, make their appearance.[5] This, however, is to strain at an emergent gnat and swallow an emergent camel. The cognition of external objects and their relations, which is somehow achieved through the brain, is not the sum of the atomic, non-cognitive sentiencies supposed to inhere in its component particles; and it is therefore no more "accounted for" by the assumed sentiency of those particles than it is by their motion. It is as blankly different and discontinuous a new fact as anything could be. So little, at best, can be accomplished by the retrotensive method that it is not surprising to find in some recent pan-psychism a tendency to invoke the aid of the reductive, i.e., to describe the *higher* mental functions in somewhat vaguely behavioristic terms. But behaviorism does not, by becoming vaguer, become more convincing.

Another attempt to employ the retrotensive method for avoiding the admission of trans-physical emergence is to be seen in the parallelistic form of emergent evolutionism, the view that psycho-physical "duality of nature does not *arise* in the course of evolutionary advance, it is there *ab initio,*" but that emergence occurs (in just what modes is not very clear) in the psychical as well as the physical sense, though in each independently. Such a view, however, appears to involve the general doctrine, at once confused and incredible, that physical events can have no causal relation to mental ones—which implies that sensations are not due to physical stimuli, and that if a man, after receiving a blow on the head, loses his memory, the blow is wholly irrelevant to the amnesia, which is causally explicable, if at all, solely by the thoughts he was thinking before he was hit. This

[5] Drake, *Mind and Its Place in Nature* (1926), pp. 97–100, 241–243.

doctrine does not appear to me to lie within the bounds of serious discussion. The retrotensive method, therefore, not only gratuitously extends to the whole of nature a concomitance for which there is probable evidence only in a special class of cases; it also either falls short of its objective or else implies impossible consequences.

We have, therefore, abundant reason to believe that in the history of our planet there have occurred genuine new births of time, a sheer increase and diversification and enrichment of the sum of things here. And no reason, except an arbitrary pseudo-axiom, can be given for assuming that this has been merely a cosmical game of beggar-my-neighbor. On the other hand, we have no empirical reasons for asserting—and serious reasons for doubting—that a similar process is the general rule throughout the physical universe, or that the higher emergents occur at all frequently in space and time. Yet, even though no knowledge which we possess concerning evolution justifies that generalized or cosmic meliorism which now so widely does duty for a religion, there nevertheless lies before our terrestrial race in its own little corner of the world a future which, if dim with uncertainties and beset with perils, is not necessarily devoid of possibilities immeasurably transcending all that the past has brought forth. There perhaps yet remain to mankind, we are told, some thousand million years; if it be so, before this long day ends it is possible that, besides all that man's laboring reason may achieve, there may yet emerge out of the latent generative potencies of matter, as there quite certainly have emerged before our strange planetary history, new and richer forms of being, such as no prescience of ours could foresee and no contrivance of ours create.

A. N. Whitehead

Nature Lifeless *

Philosophy is the product of wonder. The effort after the general characterization of the world around us is the romance of human thought. The correct statement seems so easy, so obvious, and yet it is always eluding us. We inherit the traditional doctrine: we can detect the oversights, the superstitions, the rash generalizations of the past ages. We know so well what we mean and yet we remain so curiously uncertain about the formulation of any detail of our knowledge. This word 'detail' lies at the heart of the whole difficulty. You cannot talk vaguely about Nature in general. We must fix upon details within nature and discuss their essences and their types of inter-connection. The world around is complex, composed of details. We have to settle upon the primary types of detail in terms of which we endeavour to express our understanding of Nature. We have to analyse and to abstract, and to understand the natural status of our abstractions. At first sight there are sharp-cut classes within which we can sort the various types of things and characters of things which we find in Nature. Every age manages to find modes of classification which seem fundamental starting points for the researches of the special sciences. Each succeeding age discovers that the primary classifications of its predecessors will not work. In this way a doubt is thrown upon all formulations of Laws of Nature which assume these classifications as firm starting points. A problem arises. Philosophy is the search for the solution.

Our first step must be to define the term 'Nature' as here used. 'Nature', in these chapters, means the world as interpreted by reliance on clear and distinct sensory experiences, visual, auditory, and tactile. Obviously, such an interpretation is of the highest importance for human understanding. These final chapters are concerned with the question,—How far does it take us?

* From *Modes of Thought* by A. N. Whitehead, pp. 173–201. Copyright 1938 by The Macmillan Company. Reprinted by permission of The Macmillan Company and Cambridge University Press.

For example, we can conceive nature as composed of permanent things, namely bits of matter, moving about in space which otherwise is empty. This way of thinking about nature has an obvious consonance with common-sense observation. There are chairs, tables, bits of rock, oceans, animal bodies, vegetable bodies, planets, and suns. The enduring self-identity of a house, of a farm, of an animal body, is a presupposition of social intercourse. It is assumed in legal theory. It lies at the base of all literature. A bit of matter is thus conceived as a passive fact, an individual reality which is the same at an instant, or throughout a second, an hour, or a year. Such a material, individual reality supports its various qualifications such as shape, locomotion, colour, or smell, etc. The occurrences of nature consist in the changes in these qualifications, and more particularly in the changes of motion. The connection between such bits of matter consists purely of spatial relations. Thus the importance of motion arises from its change of the sole mode of interconnection of material things. Mankind then proceeds to discuss these spatial relations and discovers Geometry. The geometrical character of space is conceived as the one way in which Nature imposes determinate relations upon all bits of matter which are the sole occupants of space. In itself, Space is conceived as unchanging from Eternity to Eternity, and as homogeneous from infinity to infinity. Thus we compose a straightforward characterization of Nature, which is consonant to common sense, and can be verified at each moment of our existence. We sit for hours in the same chair, in the same house, with the same animal body. The dimensions of the room are defined by its spatial relations. There are colours, sounds, scents, partly abiding and partly changing. Also the major facts of change are defined by locomotion of the animal bodies and of the inorganic furniture. Within this general concept of Nature, there have somehow to be interwoven the further concepts of Life and Mind.

I have been endeavouring to sketch the general commonsense notion of the Universe, which about the beginning of the sixteenth century, say in the year 1500 A.D., was in process of formation among the more progressive thinkers of the European population. It was partly an inheritance from Greek thought and from mediaeval thought. Partly it was based on the deliverance of direct observation, at any moment verified in the world around us. It was the presupposed support supplying the terms in which the answers to all further questions were found. Among these further questions, the most fundamental and the most obvious are those concerning the laws of locomotion, the meaning of life, the meaning of mentality, and the inter-relations of matter, life, and mentality. When we examine the procedures of the great men in the sixteenth and seventeenth centuries, we find them presupposing this general commonsense notion of the Universe, and endeavouring to answer all questions in the terms it supplies.

I suggest that there can be no doubt, but that this general notion expresses large, all-pervading truths about the world around us. The only question is as to how fundamental these truths may be. In other words, we have to ask what large features of the Universe cannot be expressed in these terms. We have also to ask whether we cannot find some other set of notions which will explain the importance of this commonsense notion, and will also explain its relations to those other features ignored by the commonsense notion.

When we survey the subsequent course of scientific thought throughout the seventeenth century up to the present day, two curious facts emerge. In the first place, the development of natural science has gradually discarded every single feature of the original commonsense notion. Nothing whatever remains of it, considered as expressing the primary features in terms of which the Universe is to be interpreted. The obvious commonsense notion has been entirely destroyed, so far as concerns its function as the basis for all interpretation. One by one, every item has been de-throned.

There is a second characteristic of subsequent thought which is equally prominent. This commonsense notion still reigns supreme in the work-a-day life of mankind. It dominates the market-place, the playgrounds, the Law Courts, and in fact the whole sociological intercourse of mankind. It is supreme in literature and is assumed in all the humanistic sciences. Thus the science of nature stands opposed to the presuppositions of humanism. Where some conciliation is attempted, it often assumes some sort of mysticism. But in general there is no conciliation.

Indeed, even when we confine attention to natural science, no special science ever is grounded upon the conciliation of presuppositions belonging to all the various sciences of nature. Each science confines itself to a fragment of the evidence and weaves its theories in terms of notions suggested by that fragment. Such a procedure is necessary by reason of the limitations of human ability. But its dangers should always be kept in mind. For example, the increasing departmentalization of Universities during the last hundred years, however necessary for administrative purposes, tends to trivialize the mentality of the teaching profession. The result of this effective survival of two ways of thought is a patchwork procedure.

Presuppositions from the two points of view are interwoven sporadically. Every special science has to assume results from other sciences. For example, biology presupposes physics. It will usually be the case that these loans from one specialism to another really belong to the state of science thirty or forty years earlier. The presuppositions of the physics of my boyhood are today powerful influences in the mentality of physiologists. Indeed we do not need even to bring in the physiologists. The presuppositions of yesterday's physics remain in the minds of physicists, although their explicit doctrines taken in detail deny them.

In order to understand this sporadic interweaving of old and new in modern thought, I will recur to the main principles of the old commonsense doctrine, which even today is the common doctrine of ordinary life because in some sense it is true. There are bits of matter, enduring self-identically in space which is otherwise empty. Each bit of matter occupies a definite limited region. Each such particle of matter has its own private qualifications, such as its shape, its motion, its mass, its colour, its scent. Some of these qualifications change, others are persistent. The essential relationship between bits of matter is purely spatial. Space itself is eternally unchanging, always including in itself this capacity for the relationship of bits of matter. Geometry is the science which investigates this spatial capacity for imposing relationship upon matter. Locomotion of matter involves change in spatial relationship. It involves nothing more than that. Matter involves nothing more than spatiality, and the passive support of qualifications. It can be qualified, and it must be qualified. But qualification is a bare fact, which is just itself. This is the grand doctrine of Nature as a self-sufficient, meaningless complex of facts. It is the doctrine of the autonomy of physical science. It is the doctrine which in these lectures I am denying.

The state of modern thought is that every single item in this general doctrine is denied, but that the general conclusions from the doctrine as a whole are tenaciously retained. The result is a complete muddle in scientific thought, in philosophic cosmology, and in epistemology. But any doctrine which does not implicitly presuppose this point of view is assailed as unintelligible.

The first item to be abandoned with the set of qualifications which we distinguish in sense-perception, namely colour, sound, scent, and analogous qualifications. The transmission theories for light and sound, introduced the doctrine of secondary qualities. The colour and the sound were no longer in nature. They are the mental reactions of the percipient to internal bodily locomotions. Thus nature is left with bits of matter, qualified by mass, spatial relations, and the change of such relations.

This loss of the secondary qualities was a severe restriction to Nature. For its value to the precipient was reduced to its function as a mere agent of excitement. Also the derived mental excitement was not primarily concerned with factors in nature. The colours and the sounds were secondary factors supplied by the mental reaction. But the curious fact remained that these secondary factors are perceived as related by the spatiality which is the grand substratum of nature. Hume was, I think, the first philosopher who explicitly pointed out this curious hybrid character of our perceptions, according to the current doctrine of the perception of secondary qualities. Though of course this hybrid characteristic was tacitly presupposed by Locke when he conceived colour as a *secondary* quality of the things in Nature. I believe that any cosmological doctrine which is faithful to the facts has to admit this artificial character of sense-perception. Namely, when we perceive the red rose we are associating our enjoyment of red derived from one source with our enjoyment of a spatial region derived from another source. The conclusion that I draw is that sense-perception for all its practical importance is very superficial in its disclosure of the nature of things. This conclusion is supported by the character of delusiveness—that is, of illusion—which persistently clings to sense-perception. For example, our perception of stars which years ago may have vanished, our perceptions of images in mirrors or by refraction, our double vision, our visions under the influence of drugs. My quarrel with modern Epistemology concerns its exclusive stress upon sense-perception for the provision of data respecting Nature. Sense-perception does not provide the data in terms of which we interpret it.

This conclusion that pure sense-perception does not provide the data for its own interpretation was the great discovery embodied in Hume's philosophy. This discovery is the reason why Hume's Treatise will remain as the irrefutable basis for all subsequent philosophic thought.

Another item in the commonsense doctrine concerns empty space and locomotion. In the first place, the transmission of light and sound shows that space apparently empty is the theatre of activities which we do not directly perceive. This conclusion was explained by the supposition of types of subtle matter, namely the ether, which we cannot directly perceive. In the second place, this conclusion, and the obvious behaviour of gross ordinary matter, show us that the motions of matter are in some way conditioned by the spatial relations of material bodies to each other. It was here that Newton supplied the great synthesis upon which science was based for more than two centuries. Newton's laws of motion provided a skeleton framework within which more particular laws for the interconnection of bodily motions could be inserted. He also supplied one example of such a particular law in his great law of gravitation, which depended upon mutual distances.

Newton's methodology for physics was an overwhelming success. But the forces which he introduced left Nature still without meaning or value. In the essence of a material body—in its mass, motion, and shape—there was no reason for the law of gravitation. Even if the particular forces could be conceived as the accidents of a cosmic epoch, there was no reason in the Newtonian concepts of mass and motion why material bodies should be connected by any stress between them. Yet the notion of stresses, as essential connections between bodies, was a fundamental factor in the Newtonian concept of nature. What Newton left for empirical investigation was the determination of the particular stresses now existing. In this determination he made a magnificent beginning by isolating the stresses indicated by his law of gravitation. But he left no hint, why in the nature of things there should be any stresses at all. The arbitrary motions of the bodies were thus explained by the arbitrary stresses between material bodies, conjoined with their spatiality, their mass, and their initial states of motion. By introducing stresses—in particular the law of gravitation—instead of the welter of detailed transformations of motion, he greatly increased the systematic aspect of nature. But he left all the factors of the system—more paricularly, mass and stress—in the position of detached facts devoid of any reason for their compresence. He thus illustrated a great philosophic truth, that a dead nature can give no reasons. All ultimate reasons are in terms of aim at value. A dead nature aims at nothing. It is the essence of life that it exists for its own sake, as the intrinsic reaping of value.

Thus for Newtonians, Nature yielded no reasons: it could yield no reasons. Combining Newton and Hume we obtain a barren concept, namely a field of perception devoid of any data for its own interpretation, and a system of interpretation, devoid of any reason for the concurrence of its factors. It is this situation that modern philosophy from Kant onwards has in its various ways sought to render intelligible. My own belief is that this situation is a *reductio ad absurdum,* and should not be accepted as the basis for philosophic speculation. Kant was the first philosopher who in this way combined Newton and Hume. He accepted them both, and his three Critiques were his endeavour to render intelligible this Hume-Newton situation. But the Hume-Newton situation is the primary presupposition for all modern philosophic thought. Any endeavour to go behind it is, in philosophic discussion, almost angrily rejected as unintelligible.

My aim in these lectures is briefly to point out how both Newton's contribution and Hume's contribution are, each in their way, gravely defective. They are right as far as they go. But they omit those aspects of the Universe as experienced, and of our modes of experiencing, which jointly lead to the more penetrating ways of understanding. In the recent situations at Washington, D.C., the Hume-Newton modes of thought can only discern a complex transition of sensa, and an entangled locomotion of molecules, while the deepest intuition of the whole world discerns the President of the United States inaugurating a new chapter in the history of mankind. In such ways the Hume-Newton interpretation omits our intuitive modes of understanding.

I now pass on to the influence of modern science in discrediting the remaining items of the primary commonsense notion with which science in the sixteenth century started its career. But in the present-day reconstruction of physics fragments of the Newtonian concepts are stubbornly retained. The result is to reduce modern physics to a sort of mystic chant over an unintelligible Universe. This chant has the exact merits of the old magic ceremonies which flourished in ancient Mesopotamia and later in Europe. One of the earliest fragments of writing which has survived is a report from a Babylonian astrologer to the King, stating the favourable days to turn cattle into the fields, as deduced by his observations of the stars. This mystic relation of observation, theory, and practice, is exactly the present position of science in modern life, according to the prevalent scientific philosophy.

The notion of empty space, the mere vehicle of spatial interconnections, has been eliminated from recent science. The whole spatial universe is a field of force, or in other words, a field of incessant activity. The mathematical formulae of physics express the mathematical relations realized in this activity.

The unexpected result has been the elimination of bits of matter, as the self-identical supports for physical properties. At first, throughout the nineteenth century, the notion of matter was extended. The empty space was conceived as filled with ether. This ether was nothing else than the ordinary matter of the original common-sense notion. It had the properties of a jelly, with its continuity, its cohesion, its flexibility, and its inertia. The ordinary matter of common-sense then merely represented certain exceptional entanglements in the ether—that is to say, knots in the ether. These entanglements, which are relatively infrequent throughout space, impose stresses and strains throughout the whole of the jelly-like ether. Also the agitations of ordinary matter are transmitted through the ether as agitations of the stresses and strains. In this way an immense unification was effected of the various doctrines of light, heat, electricity, and energy, which now coalesced into the one science of the ether. The theory was gradually elaborated throughout the nineteenth century by a brilliant group of physicists and mathematicians, French, German, Dutch, Scandinavian, British, Italian, American. The details of their work, and the relative contributions of various individuals are not to the point here.

The final result is that the activities of the ether are very different from any of the modes of activity which the common-sense analysis ascribes to ordinary matter. If the doctrine of either be correct, then our ordinary notions of matter are derived from observations of certain average results which cloak the real nature of the activities of ether. The more recent revolution which has culminated in the physics of the present day has only carried one step further this trend of nineteenth century science. Its moral is the extreme superficiality of the broad generalizations which mankind acquires on the basis of sense-perception. The continuous effort to understand the world has carried us far away from all those obvious ideas. Matter has been identified with energy, and energy is sheer activity; the passive substratum composed of self-identical enduring bits of matter has been abandoned, so far as concerns any fundamental description. Obviously this notion expressed an important derivative fact. But it has ceased to be the presupposed basis of theory. The modern point of view is expressed in terms of energy, activity, and the vibratory differentiations of space-time. Any local agitation shakes the whole universe. The distant effects are minute, but they are there. The concept of matter presupposed simple location. Each bit of matter was self-contained, localized in a region with a passive, static network of spatial relations, entwined in a uniform relational system from infinity to infinity and from eternity to eternity. But in the modern concept the group of agitations which we term matter is fused into its environment. There is no possibility of a detached, self-contained local existence. The environment enters into the nature of each thing. Some elements in the nature of a complete set of agitations may remain stable as those agitations are propelled through a changing environment. But such stability is only the case in a general, average way. This average fact is the reason why we find the same chair, the same rock, and the same planet, enduring for days, or for centuries, or for millions of years. In this average fact then time-factor takes the aspect of endurance, and change is a detail. The fundamental fact, according to the physics of the present day, is that the environment with its peculiarities seeps into the group-agitation which we term matter, and the group-agitations extend their character to the environment. In truth, the notion of the self-contained particle of matter, self-sufficient within its local habitation, is an abstraction. Now an abstraction is nothing else than the omission of part of the truth. The abstraction is well-founded when the conclusions drawn from it are not vitiated by the omitted truth.

This general deduction from the modern doctrine of physics vitiates many conclusions drawn from the applications of physics to other sciences, such as physiology, or even such as physics itself. For example, when geneticists conceive genes as the determinants of heredity. The analogy of the old concept of matter sometimes leads them to ignore the influence of the particular animal body in which they are functioning. They presuppose that a pellet of matter remains in all respects self-identical whatever be its changes of environment. So far as modern physics is concerned, any characteristics may, or may not, effect changes in the genes, changes which are as important in certain respects, though not in others. Thus no *a priori* argument as to the inheritance of characters can be drawn from the mere doctrine of genes. In fact recently physiologists have found that genes are modified in some respects by their environment. The presuppositions of the old common-sense view survive, even when the view itself has been abandoned as a fundamental description.

This survival of fragments of older doctrines is also exemplified in the modern use of the term space-time. The notion of space with its geometry is strictly coördinated to the notion of material bodies with simple location in space. A bit of matter is then conceived as self-sufficient with the simple location of the region which it occupies. It is just there, in that region where it is; and it can be described without reference to the goings on in any other region of space. The empty space is the substratum for the passive geometrical relationships between material bodies. These relationships are bare, static facts and carry no consequences which are essentially necessary. For example, Newton's law of gravitation expresses the changes of locomotion which are associated with the spatial relations of material bodies with each other. But this law of gravitation does not result from the Newtonian notion of mass combined with the notion of the occupancy of space, together with the Euclidean geometry. None of these notions either singly or in combination give the slightest warrant for the Law of Gravitation. Neither Archimedes, nor Galileo, by puzzling over these notions could have derived any suggestion for the gravitational law. According to the doctrine, space was the substratum for the great all-pervading passive relationship of the natural world. It conditioned all the active relationships, but it did not necessitate them.

The new view is entirely different. The fundamental concepts are activity and process. Nature is divisible and thus extensive. But any division, including some activities and excluding others, also severs the patterns of process which extend beyond all boundaries. The mathematical formulae indicate a logical completeness about such patterns, a completeness which boundaries destroy. For example, half a wave tells only half the story. The notion of self-sufficient isolation is not exemplified in modern physics. There are no essentially self-contained activities within limited regions. These passive geometrical relationships between substrata passively occupying regions have passed out of the picture. Nature is a theatre for the inter-relations of activities. All things change, the activities and their inter-relations. To this new concept, the notion of space with its passive, systematic, geometric relationship is entirely inappropriate. The fashionable notion that the new physics has reduced all physical laws to the statement of geometrical relations is quite ridiculous. It has done the opposite. In the place of the Aristotelian notion of the procession of forms, it has substituted the notion of the forms of process. It has thus swept away space and matter, and has substituted the study of the internal relations within a complex state of activity. This complex state is in one sense a unity. There is the whole universe of physical action extending to the remotest star-cluster. In another sense it is divisible into parts. We can trace inter-relations within a selected group of activities, and ignore all other activities. By such an abstraction, we shall fail to explain those internal activities which are affected by changes in the external system which has been ignored. Also, in any fundamental sense, we shall fail to understand the retained activities. For these activities will depend upon a comparatively unchanging systematic environment.

In all discussions of nature we must remember the differences of scale, and in particular the differences of time-span. We are apt to take modes of observable functioning of the human body as setting an absolute scale. It is extremely rash to extend conclusions derived from observation far beyond the scale of magnitude to which observation was confined. For example, to exhibit apparent absence of change within a second of time tells nothing as to the change within a thousand years. Also no apparent change within a thousand years tells anything as to a million years; and no apparent change within a million years tells anything about a million million years. We can extend this progression indefinitely. There is no absolute standard of magnitude. Any term in this progression is large compared to its predecessor and is small compared to its successor.

Again, all special sciences presuppose certain fundamental types of things. Here I am using the word 'thing' in its most general sense, which can include activities, colours and other sensa, and values. In this sense, 'thing' is whatever we can talk about. A science is concerned with a limited set of various types of things. There is thus in the first place this variety of types. In the second place, there is the determination as to what types are exhibited in any indicated situation. For example, there is the singular proposition,—This is green; and the more general proposition,—All those things are green. This type of enquiry is what the traditional Aristotelian Logic takes care of. Undoubtedly such enquiries are essential in the initial stage of any science. But every science strives to get beyond it. Unfortunately, owing to the way in which for over two thousand years philosophic thought has been dominated by its background of Aristotelian Logic, all attempts to combine the set of special sciences into a philosophic cosmology, giving some understanding of the Universe—all these attempts are vitiated by an unconscious relapse into these Aristotelian forms as the sole mode of expression. The disease of philosophy is its itch to express itself in the forms, 'Some S is P', or 'All S is P'.

Returning to the special sciences, the third step is the endeavour to obtain quantitative decisions. In this stage, the typical questions are, 'How much P is involved in S?' and 'How many S's are P?' In other words, number, quantity, and measurement, have been introduced. A simple-minded handling of these quantitative notions can be just as misleading as undue trust in the Aristotelian forms for propositions.

The fourth stage in the development of the science is the introduction of the notion of pattern. Apart from attention to this concept of pattern, our understanding of Nature is crude in the extreme. For example, given an aggregate of carbon atoms and oxygen atoms, and given that the number of oxygen atoms and the number of carbon atoms are known, the properties of the mixture are unknown until the question of pattern is settled. How much free oxygen is there,—How much free carbon,—How much carbon monoxide,—How much carbon dioxide? The answers to some of these questions, with the total quantities of oxygen and of carbon presupposed, will determine the answer to the rest. But even allowing for this mutual determination, there will be an enormous number of alternative patterns for a mixture of any reasonable amount of carbon and oxygen. And even when the purely chemical pattern is settled, and when the region containing the mixture is given, there are an indefinite number of regional patterns for the distribution of the chemical substances within the containing region. Thus beyond all questions of quantity, there lie questions of pattern, which are essential for the understanding of nature. Apart from a presupposed pattern, quantity determines nothing. Indeed quantity itself is nothing other than analogy of functions within analogous patterns.

Also this example, involving mere chemical mixture, and chemical combination, and the seclusion of different substances in different subregion of the container, shows us that notion of pattern involves the concept of different modes of togetherness. This is obviously a fundamental concept which we ought to have thought of as soon as we started with the notion of various types of fundamental things. The danger of all these fundamental notions is that we are apt to assume them unconsciously. When we ask ourselves any question we will usually find that we are assuming certain types of entities involved, that we are assuming certain modes of togetherness of these entities, and that we are even assuming certain widely spread generalities of pattern. Our attention is concerned with details of pattern, and measurement, and proportionate magnitude. Thus the laws of nature are merely all-pervading patterns of behaviour, of which the shift and discontinuance lie beyond our ken. Again, the topic of every science is an abstraction from the full concrete happenings of nature. But every abstraction neglects the influx of the factors omitted into the factors retained. Thus a single pattern discerned by vision limited to the abstractions within a special science differentiates itself into a subordinate factor in an indefinite number of wider patterns when we consider its possibilities of relatedness to the omitted universe. Even within the circle of the special science we may find diversities of functioning not to be explained in terms of that science. But these diversities can be explained when we consider the variety of wider relationships of the pattern in question.

Today the attitude among many leaders in natural science is a vehement denial of the considerations which have here been put forward. Their attitude seems to me to be a touching example of baseless faith. This judgment is strengthened when we reflect that their position of the autonomy of the natural sciences has its origin in a concept of the world of nature, now discarded.

Finally, we are left with a fundamental question as yet undiscussed. What are those primary types of things in terms of which the process of the Universe is to be understood? Suppose we agree that Nature discloses to the scientific scrutiny merely activities and process. What does this mean? These activities fade into each other. They arise and then pass away. What is being enacted? What is effected? It cannot be that these are merely the formulae of the multiplication table—in the words of a great philosopher, merely a bloodless dance of categories. Nature is full-blooded. Real facts are happening. Physical Nature, as studied in Science, is to be looked upon as a complex of the more stable interrelations between the real facts of the real universe.

This lecture has been confined to Nature under an abstraction in which all reference to life was suppressed. The effect of this abstraction has been that Dynamics, Physics, and Chemistry were the sciences which guided our gradual transition from the full commonsense notions of the sixteenth century to the concept of nature suggested by the speculative physics of the present day.

This change of view, occupying four centuries, may be characterized as the transition from Space and Matter as the fundamental notions to Process conceived as a complex of activity with internal relations between its various factors. The older point of view enables us to abstract from change and to conceive of the full reality of nature *at an instant,* in abstraction from any temporal duration and characterized as to its inter-relations solely by the instantaneous distribution of matter in space. According to the Newtonian view, what had thus been omitted was the change of distribution at neighbouring instants. But such change was, on this view, plainly irrelevant to the essential reality of the material universe at the instant considered. Locomotion, and change of relative distribution, was accidental and not essential.

Equally accidental was endurance. Nature at an instant is, in this view, equally real whether or no there be no nature at any other instant, or indeed whether or no there be any other instant. Descartes, who with Galileo and Newton, cooperated in the construction of the final Newtonian view, accepted this conclusion. For he explained endurance as perpetual re-creation at each instant. Thus the matter of fact was, for him, to be seen in the instant and not in the endurance. For him, endurance was a mere succession of instantaneous facts. There were other sides to Descartes' cosmology which might have led him to a greater emphasis on motion. For example, his doctrines of extension and vortices. But in fact, by anticipation, he drew the conclusion which fitted the Newtonian concepts.

There is a fatal contradiction inherent in the Newtonian cosmology. Only one mode of the occupancy of space is allowed for—namely, this bit of matter occupying this region at this durationless instant. This occupation of space is the final real fact, without reference to any other instant, or to any other piece of matter, or to any other region of space. Now assuming this Newtonian doctrine, we ask—What becomes of velocity, at an instant? Again we ask—What becomes of momentum at an instant? These notions are essential for Newtonian physics, and yet they are without any meaning for it. Velocity and momentum require the concept that the state of things at other times and other places enter into the essential character of the material occupancy of space at any selected instant. But the Newtonian concept allows for no such modification of the relation of occupancy. Thus the cosmological scheme is inherently inconsistent. The mathematical subtleties of the differential calculus afford no help for the removal of this difficulty. We can indeed phrase the point at issue in mathematical terms. The Newtonian notion of occupancy corresponds to the value of a function at a selected point. But the Newtonian physics requires solely the limit of the function at that point. And the Newtonian cosmology gives no hint why the bare fact which is the value should be replaced by the reference to other times and places which is the limit.

For the modern view process, activity, and change are the matter of fact. At an instant there is nothing. Each instant is only a way of grouping matters of fact. Thus since there are no instants, conceived as simple primary entities, there is no nature at an instant. Thus all the interrelations of matters of fact must involve transition in their essence. All realization involves implication in the creative advance.

The discussion in this lecture is only the prolegomenon for the attempt to answer the fundamental question,—How do we add content to the notion of bare activity? Activity for what, producing what, Activity involving what?

The next lecture will introduce the concept of Life, and will thus enable us to conceive of Nature more concretely, without abstraction.

Henri Bergson

Life and Consciousness *

. . . The evolution of life, from its earliest origins up to man, presents to us the image of a current of consciousness flowing against matter, determined to force for itself a subterranean passage, making tentative attempts to the right and to the left, pushing more or less ahead, for the most part encountering rock and breaking itself against it, and yet, in one direction at least, succeeding in piercing its way through and emerging into the light. That direction is the line of evolution which ends in man.

Now why did mind engage in such an enterprise? What interest could it have had in boring the tunnel? To answer this inquiry, we should have again to follow several new lines of facts and see them converge on one single point. But this would require us to go into details concerning psychical life, concerning the psycho-physiological relation, concerning the moral ideal and social progress. Let us rather go at once to the conclusion. Here are matter and consciousness confronting one another. Matter is primarily what brings division and precision. A thought, taken by itself, is a reciprocal implication of elements of which we cannot say that they are one or many. Thought is a continuity, and in all continuity there is confusion. For a thought to become distinct, there must be dispersion in words. Our only way of taking count of what we have in mind is to set down on a sheet of paper, side by side, terms which in our thinking interpenetrate. Just in this way does matter distinguish, separate, resolve into individualities, and finally into personalities, tendencies before confused in the original impulse of life. On the other hand, matter calls forth effort and makes it possible. Thought which is only thought, the work of art which is only conceived, the poem which is no more than a dream, as yet cost nothing in toil; it is the material realization of the poem in words, of the artistic conception in statue or picture, which demands effort. The effort is toil-

* From *Mind-Energy* by Henri Bergson, pp. 21–28. Copyright 1920 by Henry Holt and Co. Reprinted by permission of Presses Universitaires de France on behalf of Mlle. J. A. Bergson.

some, but it is also precious, more precious even than the work which it produces, because, thanks to it, one has drawn out from the self more than it had already, we are raised above ourselves. This effort was impossible without matter. By the resistance matter offers and by the docility with which we endow it, it is at one and the same time obstacle, instrument and stimulus. It experiences our force, keeps the imprint of it, calls for its intensification.

Philosophers who have speculated on the meaning of life and on the destiny of man have failed to take sufficient notice of an indication which nature itself has given us. Nature warns us by a clear sign that our destination is attained. That sign is joy. I mean joy, not pleasure. Pleasure is only a contrivance devised by nature to obtain for the creative the preservation of its life, it does not indicate the direction in which life is thrusting. But joy always announces that life has succeeded, gained ground, conquered. All great joy has a triumphant note. Now, if we take this indication into account and follow this new line of facts, we find that wherever there is joy, there is creation; the richer the creation, the deeper the joy. The mother beholding her child is joyous, because she is conscious of having created it, physically and morally. The merchant developing his business, the manufacturer seeing his industry prosper, are joyous,—is it because money is gained and notoriety acquired? No doubt, riches and social position count for much, but it is pleasures rather than joy that they bring; true joy, here, is the feeling of having started an enterprise which goes, of having brought something to life. Take exceptional joys,—the joy of the artist who has realized his thought, the joy of the thinker who has made a discovery or invention. You may hear it said that these men work for glory and get their highest joy from the admiration they win. Profound error! We cling to praise and honours in the exact degree in which we are not sure of having succeeded. There is a touch of modesty in vanity. It is to reassure ourselves that we seek approbation; and just as we wrap the prematurely born child in cotton wool, so we gather round our work the warm admiration of mankind in case there should be insufficient vitality. But he who is sure, absolutely sure, of having produced a work which will endure and live, cares no more for praise and feels above glory, because he is a creator, because he knows it, because the joy he feels is the joy of a god. If, then, in every domain the triumph of life is creation, must we not suppose that human life has its goal in a creation which, unlike that of the artist and philosopher, can be pursued always by all men—creation of self by self, the growing of personality by an effort which draws much from little, something from nothing, and adds unceasingly to whatever wealth the world contains?

Regarded from without, nature appears an immense inflorescence of unforeseeable novelty. The force which animates it seems to create lovingly, for nothing, for the mere pleasure of it, the endless variety of vegetable and animal species. On each it confers the absolute value of a great work of art. It seems as much attached to the first comer as to man himself. But the form of a living being, once designed, is thenceforward indefinitely repeated, and the acts of this living being, once performed, tend to imitate themselves and recommence automatically. Automatism and repetition, which prevail everywhere except in man, should warn us that living forms are only halts: this work of marking time is not the forward movement of life. The artist's standpoint is therefore important, but not final. Richness and originality of forms do indeed indicate an expansion of life, but in this expansion, where beauty means power, life also shows a stop of its impulse, a momentary powerlessness to push further, like the boy who rounds off in a graceful curve the end of the slide.

The standpoint of the moralist is higher. In man alone, especially among the best of mankind, the vital movement pursues its way without hindrance, thrusting through that work of art, the human body, which it has created on its way, the creative current of the moral life. Man, called on at every moment to lean on the totality of his past in order to bring his weight to bear more effectively on the future, is the great success of life. But it is the moral man who is a creator in the highest degree,—the man whose action, itself intense, is also capable of intensifying the action of other men, and, itself generous, can kindle fires on the hearths of generosity. The man of moral grandeur, particularly those whose inventive and simple heroism has opened new paths to virtue, are revealers of metaphysical truth. Although they are the culminating point of evolution, yet they are nearest the source and they enable us to perceive the impulsion which comes from the deep. It is in studying these great lives, in striving to experience sympathetically what they experience, that we may penetrate by an act of intuition to the life principle itself. To pierce the mystery of the deep, it is sometimes necessary to regard the heights. It is earth's hidden fire which appears at the summit of the volcano.

Of the two great routes that the vital impulse has found open before it, along the series of the arthropods and the series of the vertebrates, instinct and intelligence, at first wrapped up confusedly within one another, have in their development taken divergent directions. At the culminating point of the first evolution are the hymenoptera, at the culminating point of the second, man. In each, in spite of the radical difference in the forms attained and the growing separation of the paths followed, it is to social life that evolution leads, as though the need of it was felt from the beginning, or rather as though there were some original and essential aspiration of life which could find full satisfaction only in society. Society, which is the community of individual energies, benefits from the efforts of all its members and renders effort easier to all. It can only subsist by subordinating the individual, it can only progress by leaving the individual free: contradictory requirements, which have to be reconciled. With insects, the first condition alone is fulfilled. The societies of ants and bees are admirably disciplined and united, but fixed in an invariable routine. If the individual is forgotten in the society, the society on its part also has forgotten its destination. Individual and society, both in a state of somnambulism, go round and round in the same circle, instead of moving straight forward to a greater social efficiency and a completer individual freedom. Human societies, alone, have kept full in view both the ends to be attained. Struggling among themselves and at war with one another, they are seeking clearly, by friction and shock, to round off the angles, to wear out antagonisms, to eliminate contradictions, to bring about that individual wills should insert themselves in the social will without losing their individual form, and that different and diverse societies should enter in their turn into a wider and more inclusive society and yet not lose their originality or their independence. The spectacle is both disquieting and reassuring, for we cannot contemplate it without saying that, here too, across innumerable obstacles, life is working both by individualization and integration to obtain the greatest quantity, the richest variety, the highest qualities, of invention and effort.

To conclude, then, the aspirations of our moral nature are not in the least contradicted by positive science. On this, as on many other points, I quite agree with the opinion expressed by Sir Oliver Lodge in many of his works, and especially in his admirable book on *Life and Matter*. How could there be disharmony between our intuitions and our science, how especially could our science make us renounce our intuitions, if these intuitions are something like instinct,—an instinct conscious, refined, spiritualized,—and if instinct is still nearer life than intellect and science? Intuition and intellect do not oppose each other, save where intuition refuses to become more precise by coming into touch with facts scientifically studied, and where intellect, instead of confining itself to science proper (that is, to what can be inferred from facts or proved by reasoning), combines with this an unconscious and inconsistent metaphysic which in vain lays claim to scientific pretensions.

If we now take into account that the mental activity of man overflows his cerebral activity, that his brain is a storehouse of motor habits but not of memories, that the other functions of thought are even more independent of the brain than memory is, that preservation and even intensification of personality are not only possible but even probable after the disintegration of the body, shall we not suspect that, in its passage through the matter which it finds here, consciousness is tempering itself like steel and preparing itself for a more efficient action, for an intenser life? That life, as I imagine it, is still a life of striving, a need of invention, a creative evolution: to it each of us might come by the play of natural forces alone, taking our place on the moral plane to which in this life the quality and quantity of our effort had already virtually raised us, as the balloon set free takes the position in the air which its density assigns it. I admit that this is no more than a hypothesis. We were just now in the region of the probable, this is the region of the simply possible. Let us confess our ignorance, but let us not resign ouselves to the belief that we can never know. If there be a beyond for conscious beings, I cannot see why we should not be able to discover the means to explore it. Nothing which concerns man is likely to conceal itself deliberately from the eyes of man. Sometimes, moreover, the information we imagine to be far off, even infinitely distant, is at our side, waiting only till it pleases us to notice it. Recollect what has happened in regard to another beyond, that of ultra-planetary space. Auguste Comte declared the chemical composition of the heavenly bodies to be forever unknowable by us. A few years later the spectroscope was invented, and to-day we know, better than if we had gone there, what the stars are made of.

By C. A. Mace

Some Implications of Analytical Behaviourism *

In philosophical discussion it is well to avoid, if we can, the use of technical expressions, but for the purposes of the present occasion, one or two special terms may save much circumlocution. The chief of these is "analytical behaviourism."

Behaviourism in general is an attempt to deal with what to the scientist in general is a troublesome class of facts—those commonly described as "the facts of mental life." Common to all its forms, behaviourism offers an alternative to the widespread doctrine that the world contains two sorts of stuff—the stuff of which material things are made and the stuff of mind. According to this widespread doctrine, these two sorts of stuff are irreducibly different and are equal in status. Behaviourism, in all its forms, accords a superior scientific status to the facts of matter, and offers a systematic account of facts of mind in terms of the behaviour of material things. There are, however, several ways in which this may be done; and we may distinguish three sorts of behaviourism: the metaphysical, the methodological and the analytical.

By the metaphysical behaviourists I mean those who admit that the two contrasted sorts of stuff are at least conceivable, but deny, however, that mind as so conceived is realized in fact. They deny, or appear to deny, that minds or consciousness exist. The methodological behaviourists concede rather more. They appear to admit not only that mind or consciousness is conceivable as irreducibly different from matter, but also that this conception is realized in fact. They take their stand on a principle of scientific method. A mind, or a state of consciousness, they say, may be a fact of interest and importance to a poet or, for that matter, to anyone who has one, but this interest is "merely emotional or aesthetic." "Mind" and "consciousness" are not amenable to systematic treatment by scientific method.

* From *Proceedings of The Aristotelian Society,* Volume XLIX (1948–49), pp. 1–16. Reprinted by permission of The Aristotelian Society and the author.

More radical, and of greater philosophical interest, is the variety of behaviourism which I am calling "analytic." To the analytical behaviourist the existence of mind or consciousness defined as irreducibly distinct from matter and its behaviour is not even conceivable in any positive terms. It enjoys, so to speak, the status of a prime number which is greater than 19 and less than 23. Statements about mind or consciousness just turn out to be, on analysis, statements about the behaviour of material things. Statements about "perceiving" turn out to be statements about "differential responses," statements about "liking" and "desiring" turn out to be statements about "abient" and "adient" responses, and so on for every kind of "experience" or "psychical phenomenon." This is the sort of doctrine, not metaphysical or methodological behaviourism, which I wish to discuss.

First, however, a word or two about "analysis."

This, again, is a technical or semi-technical term, and I must confess that I do not quite know how to define it. I can at best give some account of the way in which I wish to use it.

Analysis is a sort of elucidation. When we analyse an expression we state more fully and in more detail what was previously said in a briefer way. In so doing, we draw attention to the components of what we analyse, to the relations between these components and often to their relations to other things. Connections with other things are often of greater interest and importance than the relations between the "components" of the thing. Thus, if the analysis of "*x* is an uncle" is "*x* is the brother of a father or mother," the elucidation draws attention to the fact that at least two or three persons are implicated in what might first appear to be a statement involving only one. Of course, this is a very trivial case and it might plausibly be suggested that no one could intelligently use the term "uncle" without full appreciation of all that is involved in this analysis. Such an analysis seems to tell us nothing that we did not know before, and it excludes no very possible error or misunderstanding. But in other cases an analysis of the same kind seems to be more informative and to offer information which might even be disputed. Thus, in a discussion of "perceiving" and "believing," we might be challenged to elucidate the meanings of these terms, and with this in view we might proceed as follows: "Perceiving" entails a percipient, a subject that perceives; and it entails an object, that which is perceived. Likewise with "believing." Believing entails someone who is believing and something which is believed. Moreover, you cannot believe an object as you perceive a tree; when you believe, you believe *that* something is the case. In fact, what happens when a belief occurs can always be stated more fully in the form: S believes that P is Q or that A has *r* to B.

This is only a first step in an analysis, but it is from this only a very small step further to highly controversial statements, e.g., that belief entails the existence of a "psychological subject," of "objectives" or "propositions" of "multiple relations" connecting a subject, terms and relations in a peculiar unity.

Certainly, too, a proposed analysis goes beyond the trivial in the case in which it is suggested that the analysis of a psychological proposition can be given in a statement about "behaviour"; e.g., that the analysis of "A likes B" is of the form "A is disposed to seek B's company, to perform acts conducive to B's welfare, and to exhibit distress when harm befalls B." The analysis is apt to evoke the protest that something has been left out or that something has been put in. But any other analysis is equally controversial, and any other analysis—to be an analysis at all—will introduce a reference to components or connections which were not plainly present in the original statement. In fact, it is the exception rather than the rule for an analysis to exhibit the simplicity and self-evidence of the proposed analysis of "*x* is an uncle." Whether in using the term "analysis" in the way I have tried to illustrate I am indulging in technicality I find difficult to decide; but this brief explanation is intended to offer some reassurance that in using it as I do, I have—to the best of my belief—no rabbits up my sleeve.

So to analytical behaviourism. It is, of course, difficult to present and defend any sort of behaviourism whatever without committing oneself to nonsense, but I am myself fairly well satisfied that behaviourism of the analytic type carefully stated, and stated with certain reservations, is a defensible position. I do not propose here to defend it, but rather to consider what, if true, would be its implications not only for psychology, but also for other semi-philosophical sciences. Something, however, must be said about the reservations.

A reasonable behaviourism of the analytic type is, I believe, defensible subject to the following conditions: First, the concept of behaviour must be extended to cover not only bodily acts, but also bodily states, bodily dispositions, bodily "states of readiness" to behave or to act in various ways. The point of this reservation may be seen from the objection which Broad rightly points out to one sort of behaviouristic analysis of perception. It is clear that when I perceive in a single glance many of the contents of a room, there is no evidence that I am behaving (in any ordinary sense of the word) in regard to all the objects I perceive. It may, however, be said with some plausibility that in perceiving any object, I am in a "state of readiness" to behave in a way in which I should not be ready to behave if I did not perceive it. And this "adjustment" might be said to constitute the perception.[1] This extension of the word "behaviour" enables the behaviourist to deal with many psychological facts which otherwise might nonplus him.

Second, we must restrict the behaviouristic analysis to the analysis of so-called "mental acts" as distinct from the so-called "objects" or "contents" of those acts. So many behaviouristic arguments have come to grief in the attempt to deal with "mental images." To avoid the obvious absurdity of a behaviouristic analysis of what is imagined, the behaviourist is apt to take refuge in the scarcely less absurd endeavour to deny the fact of imagining itself. There is, however, another behaviouristic solution along entirely different lines. It may plausibly be argued that images do not exist not because we do not picture things to ourselves or dream, but because we do not need an *existent* picture to picture with. The dreamer exists and he dreams, but the dream does not "exist." The argument turns not on the nature of the dream, but upon the nature of dreaming and on the meaning of the word "exist."

This argument goes for "sense data" or "sensa" as well; and in any case not even the toughest behaviourist who knows what he is saying would attempt to give a behaviourist analysis of the "sensum." His analysis can properly apply to the "act" of sensing.

Third, the behaviouristic thesis must be stated in a manner consistent with the recognition of the fact that we can observe objects, acts and dispositions through more than one sense. Even physicists and chemists not only look, they also listen and smell in making their observations. In general, however, they seem to have adopted the convention that their final results must be presented in visual terms—so far, that is to say, as they have to be presented in sensory terms at all.

This convention is less convenient in psychology where observations are made through each of the modalities of sense, and of these the somatic and proprioceptive senses are especially informative. The emotions of other persons can be observed only through their overt behaviour; one's own emotions are best observed through the felt inclinations and dispositions to behaviour presented in the main through the internal senses.[2]

[1] The suggestion that what we perceive we are disposed to react to is one that would admit of empirical test by a reaction-time technique. And if we could establish that wherever we may be said to perceive something there is some verifiable *disposition* to react, it might prove a convenient convention to define perception by reference to this fact.

[2] We introspect a belief or an emotion by attending to the sensed disposition to say or do certain things—just as we introspect a cold by attending to the sensed disposition to snuffle or sneeze.

Briefly stated, then, the sort of behaviourism which appears to me to be defensible is one that could be developed along the following lines:

The world in which we live and of which we are the human population is entirely a world of material things which are in the main the sort of things that they appear to be. These things may appear, of course, to be other than they really are. Lines appear to converge when they are really parallel. Distant mountains appear to be blue when they are really green. We sometimes persuade ourselves that we love our neighbours when, in fact, we dislike them. In general, we know how to correct mistaken beliefs and misleading appearances—through the study of the laws of perspective, through psycho-analysis, and through the theory of perception. Among the most fundamental of procedures is that of submitting the deliverance of one sense to the test of conformity with the deliverance of the others.

Psychology is essentially a biological science. It differs from other biological sciences through the use of the method of introspection. Introspection is a special case of the method of making use of the data of more than one sense. I observe that someone other than myself sees a thing, likes the look of it, and wishes to possess it, in the main by visually observing an extremely complex pattern of behaviour. I observe that I myself see it, that I like the look of it, and I desire to possess it by observing my own dispositions and inclinations. I observe these latter things by directing my attention to the felt tensions set up by these dispositions.

I am not here concerned with the details of the psychologist's programme, but only with the basic concepts which this programme requires. What I have described as "analytical behaviourism" is the thesis that the concepts of psychology are related to the concepts of biology in this way: psychology is concerned with dispositions to behaviour (as presented through the proprioceptive and organic senses); biology (including physiology) is concerned with the structure of the organism and the actual behaviour (as presented in the main to the exteroceptors) through which these dispositions are expressed. The distinction arises from the fact that the biologist observes only animals and men other than himself, whereas the psychologist can, in addition, be his own guinea-pig. Further, I am not at the moment, concerned to defend this position, but only to consider its implications, if defensible it be.

The implications which I propose to consider fall broadly under three heads: (i) implications for the general theory of mind; (ii) implications for social philosophy and the social sciences; and very briefly (iii) implications for the evaluative sciences and other cognate interests in life.

(i) In general, analytical behaviourism leaves the main theses of the classical psychologists unaffected in respect of factual content. Among the "classical psychologists" I include those who based their findings on "the method of introspection," and who on this basis distinguished the mental act both from the psychological "Subject" who performs it and from the "object" or "content" upon which this act is directed.

Most behaviourists appear to hold themselves under the obligation to deny the reality or importance of any of these distinctions; but analytical behaviourism, which in essentials is more radical than any other form, leaves all this body of doctrine precisely as it stood before—except, of course, in respect of analysis.

This is what on general grounds might have reasonably been presumed. An analysis does not decide an issue of fact. One analysis may be inconsistent with another, it cannot show that a proposition is true or false, except, of course, when the proposition is itself one concerning an analysis.

The denial by some behaviourists of the distinction between external observation and introspection is not only a denial of a fact, it is also an internal inconsistency in the behaviourist position. If, for example, "X is perceiving a tree" becomes on analysis "X is reacting differentially to the presence of a tree," then "X is perceiving that he perceives a tree," becomes on analysis "X is reacting differentially to his differential reaction to the tree." So too, if "X is perceiving a tree" becomes on analysis "X is disposed to react differentially to a tree" then "X is perceiving that he perceives a tree" becomes on analysis "X is disposed to react differentially to his disposition to react differentially to a tree." In other words, the analytic behaviourist does not deny the fact of introspection; he gives a behaviouristic analysis of the introspective act. This applies with equal force to the distinctions which have been drawn in regard to the facts observed by the introspective act. By a curious irony, the inclination of behaviourists to deny the existence of the psychological Subject and its acts has left them only with the one component in the situation of which a behaviouristic account cannot with any plausibility be given.

Starting from the simple and obvious fact that what I see and like I often want to possess we plainly can distinguish the seeing, liking and wanting both from that which sees, likes and wants, and from what is seen, liked and wanted; and it is difficult to understand why anyone should doubt the reality and importance of these distinctions. The difficulty for the behaviourist arises from the fact that that which sees, likes and wants cannot be quite immediately identified with the body as observed and described by an outside observer or an ordinary anatomist and from the fact that seeing, liking and wanting cannot be exhaustively described in terms of externally observable behaviour. But this difficulty disappears with the recognition that the subject, his acts and dispositions, can be presented by what Stout rather obscurely described as "internal perception." The "double-aspect" character of "mental phenomena" is perhaps their most interesting feature; and it is misleading either to describe the externally observed aspect as merely "the expression" of what is observed by introspection or to describe the latter as merely "epiphenomenal" to the former. It is (roughly) as if we described thunder as the "expression" of lightning or lightning as "epiphenomenal" to thunder, or both as epiphenomenal to a certain kind of electrical disturbance.

So far, I have been in the main concerned with the negative aspect of the implications of analytical behaviour for general psychology. It eliminates neither the statements nor the problems regarding the psychological subject and his acts. In fact, one might almost say that so far as it eliminates problems at all, it eliminates all the problems except those pertaining to the subject, his acts and his dispositions. And this leads us to the positive aspect of these implications. In part these are obvious. Within the framework of analytical behaviourism psychological statements are "material-object statements," not statements about sense-data, experiences or sense contents, and the psychologist is throughout concerned only with things that exist in the elementary sense in which existence entails being in a certain place at a certain time, and with things that happen at certain places at certain times.

Of course, the psychologist like the physicist may have philosophical interests. Both may be interested in defining with precision the nature of the steps by which they pass from their raw observational data to the scientific facts with which they are concerned. Suppose, for example that a physicist and a psychologist with the help of a professional philosopher are considering the situation in the Garden of Eden when Eve saw an apple and liked the look of it. The physicist would be especially interested in the part of the story which tells how you pass from what the philosopher might describe as a round red "sense datum" to a statement about a red Worcester Pearmain. The psychologist would be interested in the part of the story which tells how you or Eve might pass from certain other "sense-data" to statements about seeing an apple and liking the look of it. So far the two sorts of transition are of a similar kind. Suppose, however, that they had selected the example of Eve seeing a ghost, or an angel with a flaming sword. The physicist would then be disappointed in his expectations. The statements about the "sense-data" do not lead to a statement about any physical object which corresponds to the appearance of the angel in the way in which the real apple corresponds with the appearance of an apple. The psychologist is more fortunate. All the "sense data" involved lead to some or other statements about Eve, her acts and her dispositions, and all these statements will be "scientific" statements about a real person in a real world.

If all this could be sustained, the "technical advantages" to psychology would be immense. By the "technical advantages" I mean, of course, all those that contribute to affording it a well-defined place in the unified system of the sciences as a whole.

(ii) Among the "technical advantages" of behaviourism not the least are those that accrue to the social sciences. Roughly speaking, psychology stands to the social sciences as physics stands to the other "natural" sciences; and simplicity, precision and verifiability of psychological concepts contribute to simplicity, precision and verifiability in the concepts employed in the study of societies.

The possibility of a psychology of society (as distinct from the mere applications of individual psychology to social problems) would seem to rest upon two not unplausible propositions:

1. That the social group is a natural entity—as good a natural entity as the individual person—and that a group has properties which may be ascertained independently of the knowledge of corresponding properties of the individuals of which it is composed.

2. That some of these properties are of a psychological nature.

The two parts of the first proposition are little more than alternative ways of saying the same thing. To say that the Great Bear constellation is a natural entity is a way of saying that there are properties, such, for example, as the properties of dimension and shape which the Great Bear may be known to have independently of any knowledge of the corresponding properties of its component stars.

In regard to the relations which hold between the properties of complex wholes and the corresponding properties of the component parts, Herbert Spencer adduces an instructive example. Out of bricks with square angles, he observes, a bricklayer can build, even without mortar, a high rectilinear wall of some stability. A dockyard labourer piling spherical cannon balls can only build forms such as that of the pyramid or the wedge. Spencer draws the general conclusion that the character of an aggregate is determined by the character of the units.

But the general fact can be better stated in another way. There are many relations to be determined between the characters of wholes and the characters of parts. Sometimes the character of a whole is clearly determined by the character of the parts. Sometimes, a change in the character of the whole appears to determine changes in the character of the parts. What in the present context is more important is that the characters in question are in fact independently and empirically ascertained, and causal relations only subsequently defined. This is especially important in the case of the psychological properties of groups. The apparently irrepressible tendencies of social philosophers perpetually to revive the doctrine of the "group mind" has some basis in reason and fact. It has a basis in the convenience that attaches to the use of psychological terms for the description of observed properties and actions of groups. Groups make decisions and these decisions express in varying degree the presence or absence of intelligence and foresight.

The problem is to attach a meaning—a verifiable meaning—to such statements, and one that makes clear both the similarities and the differences between the attribution of a mental characteristic to an individual and the attribution of this characteristic to a group. This is all but impossible to do within the framework of philosophical dualism, but becomes simple almost to the point of triviality within the framework of the behaviouristic analysis of mind.

Statements about the mental life of a group may be clear, informative and verifiable when the group has a constitution and acts in accordance with formal procedures. By reference to formal and constitutional procedures we can distinguish with comparative ease the acts of the group from the acts of each of the individuals of which the group is composed, and can make significant statements of the form: "The intelligence of the group was greater (or less) than the intelligence of its most (or least) intelligent member." It would not, in fact, be difficult to devise standardized tests of intelligence applicable to groups whereby such distinctions could be expressed in a quantitative form. And what applies to the intelligence of groups applies in principle to its traits of personality or character.

In the same way, significance can be attached to the statement that a group, like an individual, has a conscious and an unconscious mind. But although there are many analogies between the minds of individuals and the minds of groups (as behaviouristically defined), we can never *argue* from these analogies. The corresponding characteristics of the individual and of the group must be independently ascertained, and their relations empirically determined. In some cases a psychological property is more readily determined in the individual, sometimes it is more readily determined in the group. Finding the property in one case may suggest its presence in the other but the suggestion may not always be realized in fact.[3]

It is perhaps within the field of social psychology that some advance may be recorded in the assimilatioin by science of the odd phenomena of psychical research. It is perhaps still reasonably possible to contest the facts alleged regarding telepathy and precognition, or at least to contest the interpretations placed upon the raw data collected in psychical research. But it is not reasonably possible to contest the scientific status of the claims presented.

Hypothesis without fact is empty, but fact without hypothesis is blind. Interpretation is the Achilles heel of psychical research; and its most responsible exponents would be the first to approve the need for exploring new lines of interpretation.

My suggestion is that a behaviouristic psychology is at least as good as any other as a point of departure in any such inquiry. I would, in fact, go rather further. Psychical research has, I think, much to gain by assembling its data within the framework of a naturalistic and positivistic methodology; and it would be good for methodologists with a naturalistic and positivistic bias to test their principles against the alleged facts of psychical research.

The venture would not be entirely devoid of promise. Among the most suggestive of current hypotheses in this field is Whately Carrington's attempt to provide an interpretation of telepathic phenomena by generalizing the law of association. If the hypothesis works at all, there is no reason why it should not work as well if re-expressed in behaviouristic terms. Behaviourism in general has found it easy to assimilate the law of association, and might perhaps with equal ease assimilate the proposed extension of this law. The "collective unconscious" in behaviouristic terms becomes "the group mind," and the group mind becomes in effect a "behaving

[3] The fact that individuals differ in intelligence may lead us to look for intelligence differences in groups and such differences may be found. The fact that individuals differ in sex does not provide a fruitful hypothesis for the study of differences in groups since the group belongs to the sort of organism which reproduces itself by other than sexual means.

The concept of the "unconscious mind" on the other hand has its simpler and most easily verified application in the case of the group. Many of the distinctive concepts of Freud's psychology consist in the application to the individual mind of mechanisms observed in the behaviour of groups, e.g., the concept of the "forum of consciousness," the concepts of the Censor and repression. Freud's psychology in fact might almost be described as a technical development of individual psychology on the analogy afforded by a simple non-technical and commonsense psychology of society.

organism of a higher order." The problems of psychical research in other words become problems of a behaviouristic social psychology.

It is not, however, my purpose here to defend or even to develop any such hypothesis. I have, however, of set purpose concerned myself in this discussion with the more obscure and more suspect concepts of psychology and its allied studies. My intention has been to suggest that it is characteristic of what I have called analytical behaviourism to endeavour to explain not merely to "explain away."

(iii) In all that has gone before I have been concerned with the "technical" advantages of a behaviouristic theory of mind. But, it may be said, technical advantages are bought too dearly if they are bought at the expense of spiritual values. And true enough it is that materialistic philosophies, naturalistic philosophies and positivistic philosophies have shown a certain lack of sympathy with, and perhaps a certain lack of insight into, the spiritual needs of man.

Speaking for myself alone, and speaking only in a temperamental way, I am prepared to admit that the most important truths about the world are those that have been only obscurely spoken by the poets, the prophets and the seers. Yet, if we look at the facts with entirely innocent eyes, uncorrupted by history, it becomes something of a mystery that a regard for spiritual values should be strongly associated with one rather than any other ontological theory, or with any particular suggestion rather than any other as to the *analysis* of a fact.

My suggestion is that, in this connection at least, facts and values are logically independent. If a thing is beautiful, then on any analysis its beauty will remain; and if a mind can be good, then on a behaviouristic analysis as on any other it will continue to be good.

In a less *a priori* vein we might perhaps observe that there appears to be in the affairs of man a certain principle of conservation of values. When a value has somehow come to be attached to a given conception of fact and that conception is shown to be mistaken, the value quickly loses its adhesion and attaches itself elsewhere. It was, as we know, something of a shock when science first suggested that man had an ape-like origin, but the shock was quickly followed by aesthetic and moral adjustment. At first men argued "If we have come from the apes what poor things we are." But on second thoughts, they said, "If the apes produced us, how wonderful are the apes!" So it would be, I think, if we all became behaviourists.

The conception of an immaterial substance has acquired through history intense emotional significance. If then we came to the conclusion that material things are the only things that exist, shock, to those who felt it, would be followed by emotional adjustment. "If matter is all there is," they would say, "What wonderful stuff it is!" And why not, indeed? If material things can be literally beautiful, why should not the behaviour of material things, and dispositions of behaviour, be literally good?

Josiah Royce

The Nature of Community *

THE COMMUNITY AND THE TIME-PROCESS

Now when many contemporary and distinct individual selves so interpret, each his own personal life, that each says of an individual past or of a determinate future event or deed: "That belongs to my life;" "That occurred, or will occur, to me," then these many selves may be defined as hereby constituting, in a perfectly definite and objective, but also in a highly significant, sense, a community. They may be said to constitute a community *with reference* to that particular past or future event, or group of events, which each of them accepts or interprets as belonging to his own personal past or to his own individual future. A community constituted by the fact that each of its members accepts as part of his own individual life and self the same *past* events that each of his fellow-members accepts, may be called a *community of memory*. Such is any group of persons who individually either remember or commemorate the same dead,—each one finding, because of personal affection or of reverence for the dead, that those whom he commemorates form for him a part of his own past existence.

A community constituted by the fact that each of its members accepts, as part of his own individual life and self, the same expected *future* events that each of his fellows accepts, may be called a *community of expectation,* or upon occasion, a *community of hope.*

A community, whether of memory or of hope, exists relatively to the past or future facts to which its several members stand in the common relation just defined. The concept of the community depends upon the interpretation which each individual member gives to his own self,—to his own past,—and to his own future. Every one of us does, for various reasons, extend his interpretation of his own individual self so that from his own

* From *The Problem of Christianity* by Josiah Royce, Volume 2, pp. 49–53, 60–69, 79–95.

point of view, his life includes many faraway temporal happenings. The complex motives of such interpretations need not now be further examined. Enough,—these motives may vary from self to self with all the wealth of life. Yet when these interests of each self lead it to accept any part or item of the same past or the same future which another self accepts as its own,—then pluralism of the selves is perfectly consistent with their forming a community, either of memory or of hope. How rich this community is in meaning, in value, in membership, in significant organization, will depend upon the selves that enter into the community, and upon the ideals in terms of which they define themselves, their past, and their future.

With this definition in mind, we see why long histories are needed in order to define the life of great communities. We also see that, if great new undertakings enter into the lives of many men, a new community of hope, unified by the common relations of its individual members to the same future events, may be, upon occasion, very rapidly constituted, even in the midst of great revolutions.

The concept of the community, as thus analyzed, stands in the closest relation to the whole nature of the time-process, and also involves recognizing to the full both the existence and the significance of individual selves. In what sense the individual selves constitute the community we can in general see, while we are prepared to find that, for the individual selves, it may well prove to be the case that a real community of memory or of hope is necessary in order to secure their significance. Our own definition of a community can be illustrated by countless types of political, religious, and other significant communities which you will readily be able to select for yourselves. Without ignoring our ordinary social pluralism, this definition shows how and why many selves may be viewed as actually brought together in an historical community. Without presupposing any one metaphysical interpretation of experience, or of time, our definition shows where, in our experience and in our interpretation of the time-process, we are to look for a solution of the problem of the community. Without going beyond the facts of human life, of human memory, and of human interpretation of the self and of its past, our definition clears the way for a study of the constitution of the real world of the spirit. . . .

THE BODY AND THE MEMBERS

. . . The *first* condition upon which the existence of a community, in our sense of the word, depends, is the power of an individual self to extend his life, in ideal fashion, so as to regard it as including past and future events which lie far away in time, and which he does not now personally remember. That this power exists, and that man has a self which is thus ideally extensible in time without any definable limit, we all know.

This power itself rests upon the principle that, however a man may come by his idea of himself, the self is no mere datum, but is in its essence a life which is interpreted, and which interprets itself, and which, apart from some sort of ideal interpretation, is a mere flight of ideas, or a meaningless flow of feelings, or a vision that sees nothing, or else a barren abstract conception. How deep the process of interpretation goes in determining the real nature of the self, we shall only later be able to estimate.

There is no doubt that what we usually call our personal memory does indeed give us assurances regarding our own past, so far as memory extends and is trustworthy. But our trust in our memories is itself an interpretation of their data. All of us regard as belonging, even to our recent past life, much that we cannot just now remember. And the future self shrinks and expands with our hopes and our energies. No one can merely, from without, set for us the limits of the life of the self, and say to us: "Thus far and no farther."

In my ideal extensions of the life of the self, I am indeed subject to some sort of control,—to what control we need not here attempt to formulate. I must be able to give myself some sort of reason, personal, or social, or moral, or religious, or metaphysical, for taking on or throwing off the burden, the joy, the grief, the guilt, the hope, the glory of past and of future deeds and experiences; but I must also myself personally share in this task of determining how much of the past and the future shall ideally enter into my life, and shall contribute to the value of that life.

And if I choose to say, "There is a sense in which *all* the tragedy and the attainment of an endless past and future of deeds and of fortunes enter into my own life," I say only what saints and sages of the most various creeds and experiences have found their several reasons for saying. The fact and the importance of such ideal extensions of the self must therefore be recognized. Here is the first basis for every clear idea of what constitutes a community.

The ideal extensions of the self may also include, as is well known, not only past and future events and deeds, but also physical things, whether now existent or not, and many other sorts of objects which are neither events nor deeds. The knight or the samurai regarded his sword as a part of himself. One's treasures and one's home, one's tools, and the things that one's hands have made, frequently come to be interpreted as part of the self. And any object in heaven or earth may be thus ideally appropriated by a given self. The ideal self of the Stoic or of the Mystic may, in various fashions, identify its will, or its very essence, with the whole universe. The Hindoo seer seeks to realize the words: "I am Brahm;" "That art thou."

In case such ideal extensions of the self are consciously bound up with deeds, or with other events, such as belong to the past or future life which the self regards as its own, our definition of the community warrants us in saying that many selves form one community when all are ideally extended so as to include the same object. But unless the ideal extensions of the self thus consciously involve past and future deeds and events that have to do with the objects in question, we shall not use these extensions to help us to define communities.

For our purposes, the community is a being that attempts to accomplish something in time and through the deeds of its members. These deeds belong to the life which each member regards as, in ideal, his own. It is in this way that both the real and the ideal Church are intended by the members to be communities in our sense. An analogous truth holds for such other communities as we shall need to consider. The concept of the community is thus, for our purposes, a practical conception. It involves the idea of deeds done, and ends sought or attained. Hence I shall define it in terms of members who themselves not only live in time, but conceive their own ideally extended personalities in terms of a time-process. In so far as these personalities possess a life that is for each of them his own, while it is, in some of its events, common to them all, they form a community.

Nothing important is lost, for our conception of the community, by this formal restriction, whereby common objects belong to a community only when these objects are bound up with the deeds of the community. For, when the warrior regards his sword as a part of himself, he does so because his sword is the instrument of his will, and because what he does with his sword belongs to his literal or ideal life. Even the mystic accomplishes his identification of the self and the world only through acts of renunciation or of inward triumph. And these acts are the goal of his life. Until he attains to them, they form part of his ideal future self. Whenever he fully accomplishes these crowning acts of identification, the separate self no longer exists. When knights or mystics form a community, in our sense, they therefore do so because they conceive of deeds done, in common, with their swords, or of mystical attainments that all of them win together.

Thus then, while no authoritative limit can be placed upon the ideal extensions of the self in time, those extensions of the self which need be considered for the purposes of our theory of the community are indeed extensions in time, past or future; or at all events involve such extensions in time.

Memory and hope constantly incite us to the extensions of the self which play so large a part in our daily life. Social motives of endlessly diverse sort move us to consider "far and forgot" as if to us it were near, when we view ourselves in the vaster perspectives of time. It is, in fact, the ideally extended self, and not, in general, the momentary self, whose life is worth living, whose sense outlasts our fleeting days, and whose destiny may be worthy of the interest of beings who are above the level of human individuals. The present self, the fleeting individual of to-day, is a mere gesticulation of a self. The genuine person lives in the far-off past and future as well as in the present. It is, then, the ideally extended self that is worthy to belong to a significant community.

The *second* condition upon which the existence of a community depends is the fact that there are in the social world a number of distinct selves capable of social communication, and, in general, engaged in communication.

The distinctness of the selves we have illustrated at length in our previous discussion. We need not here dwell upon the matter further, except to say, expressly, that a community does *not* become one, in the sense of my definition, by virtue of any reduction or melting of these various selves into a single merely present self, or into a mass of passing experience. That mystical phenomena may indeed form part of the life of a community, just as they may also form part of the life of an individual human being, I fully recognize.

About such mystical or quasi-mystical phenomena, occurring in their own community, the Corinthians consulted Paul. And Paul, whose implied theory of the community is one which my own definition closely follows, assured them in his reply that mystical phenomena are not essential to the existence of the community; and that it is on the whole better for the life of such a community as he was addressing, if the individual member, instead of losing himself "in a mystery," kept his own individuality, in order to contribute his own edifying gift to the common life. Wherein this common life consists we have yet further to see in what follows.

The *third* of the conditions for the existence of the community which my definition emphasizes consists in the fact that the ideally extended past and future selves of the members include at least some events which are, for all these selves, identical. This third condition is the one which furnishes both the most exact, the most widely variable, and the most important of the motives which warrant us in calling a community a real unit. The Pauline metaphor of the body and the members finds, in this third condition, its most significant basis,—a basis capable of exact description. . . .

We have still to see, however, the degree to which this consciousness of unity can find expression in an effectively united common life which not only contains common events, but also possesses common deeds and can arouse a common love—a love which passes the love wherewith individuals can love one another.

And here we reach that aspect of the conception of the community which is the most important, and also the most difficult aspect.

A great and essentially dramatic event, such as the imagined resurrection of the bodies of all men,—an event which interests all, and which fixes the attention by its miraculous apparition,—is well adapted to illustrate the union of the one and the many in the process of time. When Paul's genius seized upon this picture,—when, to use the well-known later scholastic phraseology, the spirits of men were thus "individuated by their bodies," even while the event of the resurrection fixed the eye of faith upon one final crisis through which all were to pass "in a moment, in the twinkling of an eye,"—when the Apostle thus instructed the faithful, a great lesson was also taught regarding the means whereby the ideal of a community and the harmonious union of the one and the many can be rendered brilliantly clear to the imagination, and decisively fascinating to the will.

But the lives of communities cannot consist of miraculous crises. A community, like an individual self, must learn to keep the consciousness of its unity through the vicissitudes of an endlessly shifting and often dreary fortune. The monotony of insignificant events, the chaos of lesser conflicts, the friction and the bickerings of the members, the individual failures and the mutual misunderstandings which make the members of a community forget the common past and future,—all these things work against the conscious unity of the life of a community. Memory and hope are alike clouded by multitudes of such passing events. The individual members cannot always recall the sense in which they identify their own lives and selves with what has been, or with what is yet to come.

And—hardest task of all—the members, if they are to conceive clearly of the common life, must somehow learn to bear in mind not merely those grandly simple events which, like great victories, or ancestral feats, or divine interferences, enter into the life of the community from without, and thus make their impression all at once.

No, the true common life of the community consists of deeds which are essentially of the nature of processes of coöperation. That is, the common life consists of deeds which many members perform together, as when the workmen in a factory labor side by side.

Now we all know that coöperation constantly occurs, and is necessary to every form and grade of society. We also know that commerce and industry and art and custom and language consist of vast complexes of coöperations. And in all such cases many men manage in combination to accomplish what no one man, and no multitude of men working separately, could conceivably bring to pass. But what we now need to see is the way in which such coöperations can become part, not only of the life, but of the consciousness of a community.

Every instance of a process of coöperation is an event, or a sequence of events. And our definition of a community requires that, if such coöperative activities are to be regarded as the deeds of a community, there must be individuals, each one of whom says: "That coöperation, in which many distinct individuals take part, and in which I also take part, is, or was, or will be, an event in my life." And many coöperating individuals must agree in saying this of the same process in which they all coöperate.

And all must extend such identifications of the self with these social activities far into the past, or into the future.

But it is notoriously hard—especially in our modern days of the dreary complexity of mechanical labor—for any individual man so to survey, and so to take interest in a vast coöperative activity that he says: "In my own ideally extended past and future that activity, its history, its future, its significance as an event or sequence of events, all have their ideally significant part. That activity, as the coöperation of many in one work, is also my life." To say such things and to think such thoughts grow daily harder for most of the coworkers of a modern social order.

Hence, as is now clear, the existence of a highly organized social life is by no means identical with the existence of what is, in our present and restricted sense, the life of a true community. On the contrary, and for the most obvious reasons, there is a strong mutual opposition between the social tendencies which secure coöperation on a vast scale, and the very conditions which so interest the individual in the common life of his community that it forms part of his own ideally extended life. We met with that opposition between the more or less mechanically coöperative social life,—the life of the social will on the one side, and the life of the true community on the other side,—when we were considering the Pauline doctrine of the law in an earlier lecture. In fact, it is the original sin of any highly developed civilization that it breeds coöperation at the expense of a loss of interest in the community.

The failure to see the reason why this opposition between the tendency to coöperation and the spirit of the community exists; the failure to sound to the depths the original sin of man the social animal, and of the natural social order which he creates;—such failure, I repeat, lies at the basis of countless misinterpretations, both of our modern social problems, and of the nature of a true community, and of the conditions which make possible any wider philosophical generalizations of the idea of the community.

Men do not form a community, in our present restricted sense of that word, merely in so far as the men coöperate. They form a community, in our present limited sense, when they not only coöperate, but accompany this coöperation with that ideal extension of the lives of individuals whereby each coöperating member says: "This activity which we perform together, this work of ours, its past, its future, its sequence, its order, its sense,—all these enter into my life, and are the life of my own self writ large."

Now coöperation results from conditions which a social psychology such as that of Wundt or of Tarde may analyze. Imitation and rivalry, greed and ingenuity, business and pleasure, war and industry, may all combine to make men so coöperate that very large groups of them behave, to an external observer, as if they were units. In the broader sense of the term "community," all social groups that behave as if they were units are regarded as communities. And we ourselves called all such groups communities in our earlier lectures before we came to our new definition.

But we have now been led to a narrower application of the term "community." It is an application to which we have restricted the term simply because of our special purpose in this inquiry. Using this restricted definition of the term "community," we see that groups which coöperate may be very far from constituting communities in our narrower sense. We also see how, in general, a group whose coöperative activities are very highly complex will require a correspondingly long period of time to acquire that sort of tradition and of common expectation which is needed to constitute a community in our sense,—that is, a community conscious of its own life.

Owing to the psychological conditions upon which social coöperation depends, such coöperation can very far outstrip, in the complexity of its processes, the power of any individual man's wit to understand its intricacies. In modern times, when social coöperation both uses and is so largely dominated by the industrial arts, the physical conditions of coöperative social life have combined with the psychological conditions to make any thorough understanding of the coöperative processes upon which we all depend simply hopeless for the individual, except within some narrow range. Experts become well acquainted with aspects of these forms of coöperation which their own callings involve. Less expert workers understand a less range of the coöperative processes in which they take part. Most individuals, in most of their work, have to coöperate as the cogs coöperate in the wheels of a mechanism. They work together; but few or none of them know how they coöperate, or what they must do.

But the true community, in our present restricted sense of the word, depends for its genuine common life upon such coöperative activities that the individuals who participate in these common activities understand enough to be able, first, to direct their own deeds of coöperation; secondly, to observe the deeds of their individual fellow workers, and thirdly to know that, without just this combination, this order, this interaction of the coworking selves, just this deed could not be accomplished by the community. So, for instance, a chorus or an orchestra carries on its coöperative activities. In these cases coöperation is a conscious art. If hereupon these coöperative deeds, thus understood by the individual coworker, are viewed by him as linked, through an extended history with past and future deeds of the community, and if he then identifies his own life with this common life, and if his fellow members agree in this identification, then indeed the community both has a common life, and is aware of the fact. For then the individual coworker not only says: "This past and future fortune of the community belongs to my life;" but also declares: "This past and future deed of coöperation belongs to my life." "This, which none of us could have done alone,—this, which all of us together could not have accomplished unless we were ordered and linked in precisely this way,—this we together accomplished, or shall yet accomplish; and this deed of all of us belongs to my life."

A community thus constituted is essentially a community of those who are artists in some form of coöperation, and whose art constitutes, for each artist, his own ideally extended life. But the life of an artist depends upon his love for his art.

The community is made possible by the fact that each member includes in his own ideally extended life the deeds of coöperation which the members accomplish. When these deeds are hopelessly complex, how shall the individual member be able to regard them as genuinely belonging to his own ideally extended life? He can no longer understand them in any detail. He takes part in them, willingly or unwillingly. He does so because he is social, and because he must. He works in his factory, or has his share, whether greedily or honestly, in the world's commercial activities. And his coöperations may be skilful; and this fact also he may know. But his skill is largely due to external training, not to inner expansion of the ideals of the self. And the more complex the social order grows, the more all this coöperation must tend to appear to the individual as a mere process of nature, and not as his own work,—as a mechanism and not as an ideal extension of himself,—unless indeed love supplies what individual wit can no longer accomplish.

If a social order, however complex it may be, actually wins and keeps the love of its members; so that,—however little they are able to understand the details of their present coöperative activities,—they still—with all their whole hearts and their minds and their souls and their strength—desire, each for himself, that such coöperations should go on; and if each member, looking back to the past, rejoices in the ancestors and the heroes who have made the present life of this social group possible; and if he sees in these deeds of former generations the source and support of his present love; and if each member also looks forward with equal love to the future,—then indeed love furnishes that basis for the consciousness of the community which intelligence, without love, in a highly complex social realm, can no longer furnish. Such love—such loyalty—depends not upon losing sight of the variety of the callings of individuals, but upon seeing in the successful coöperation of all the members precisely that event which the individual member most eagerly loves as his own fulfilment.

When love of the community, nourished by common memories, and common hope, both exists and expresses itself in devoted individual lives, it can constantly tend, despite the complexity of the present social order, to keep the consciousness of the community alive. And when this takes place, the identification of the loyal individual self with the life of the community will tend, both in ideal and in feeling, to identify each self not only with the distant past and future of the community, but with the present activities of the whole social body.

Thus, for instance, when the complexities of business life, and the dreariness of the factory, have, to our minds, deprived our present social coöperations of all or of most of their common significance, the great communal or national festivity, bringing to memory the great events of past and future, not only makes us, for the moment, feel and think as a community with reference to those great past and future events, but in its turn, as a present event, reacts upon next day's ordinary labors. The festivity says to us: "We are one because of our common past and future, because of the national heroes and victories and hopes, and because we love all these common memories and hopes." Our next day's mood, consequent upon the festivity, bids us say: "Since we are thus possessed of this beloved common past and future, let this consciousness lead each of us even to-day to extend his ideal self so as to include the daily work of all his fellows, and to view his fellow members' life as his own."

Thus memory and hope tend to react upon the present self, which finds the brotherhood of present labor more significant, and the ideal identification of the present self with the self of the neighbor easier, because the ideal extension of the self into past and future has preceded.

And so, first, each of us learns to say: "This beloved past and future life, by virtue of the ideal extension, is my own life." Then, finding that our fellows have and love this past and future in common with us, we learn further to say: "In this respect we are all one loving and beloved community." Then we take a further step and say: "Since we are all members of this community, therefore, despite our differences, and our mutual sunderings of inner life, each of us can, and will, ideally extend his present self so as to include the present life and deeds of his fellow."

So it is that, in the ideal church, each member not only looks backwards to the same history of salvation as does his fellow, but is even thereby led to an ideal identification of his present self with that of his fellow member that would not otherwise be possible. Thus, then, common memory and common hope, the central possessions of the community, tend, when enlivened by love, to mould the consciousness of the present, and to link each member to his community by ideal ties which belong to the moment as well as to the stream of past and future life.

N. I. Bukharin

The Theory of Historical Materialism *

The laws of materialistic dialectic are all-embracing, general laws of becoming. As we have seen, a deep and all-embracing historicism is at their basis, that is to say, a historicism which can embrace all forms of movement. This Marxist dialectical method is much wider and more universal than the idealist dialectic of Hegel, the limitation of which does not merely lie in exalting a limited sphere of consciousness into the substance of the universal. The limitation of the Hegelian dialectic also lies in its two most important qualities. Firstly, with Hegel nature has no history. Secondly, history itself settles down with the bourgeois landlord state (here Hegel's system in fact conflicts with his method). Both these limitations, which are of quite exceptional importance, are undoubtedly connected with the idealist character of Hegelian dialectic. Hence, by the way, the unsurpassably wretched poverty of those "thinkers" ("manufacturers of ideology", as Marx called them), who suggest that the difference between the Marxian and Hegelian dialectic is simply a matter of a change of label and that in fact Marx remained a Hegelian to the end of his life. Whereas Marxian dialectic as a doctrine of historical development was the first to conquer the whole sphere of nature comprehended from the point of view of an historical process, and broke those fetters which Hegel put upon the understanding of social development. This remarkable expansion of outlook proceeds entirely from Marx, a thing which bourgeois investigators cannot understand. Even very recently this sort of gap between nature and society played, and still plays to this day, a very important part. The whole conception of the Rickert school proceeds from the historical character of society and the unhistorical character of nature. The whole laborious

* From "Marx's Teaching and its Historical Importance" by N. I. Bukharin, in *Marxism and Modern Thought* by N. I. Bukharin and others, translated by Ralph Fox. London: George Routledge & Sons, Ltd., 1935, pp. 29–46. Reprinted by permission of Routledge & Kegan Paul Ltd.

Note: Footnotes are here omitted.

differentiation between the generalising method of the natural sciences and the individualising method of the social sciences, between nomothetics (or nomology), on the one hand, and ideography on the other, between "natural laws" and "reference to worth" is founded in the last resort on the absolute rupture between society and nature. This is, in essence, a softened and refined theology, converting human society into a supernatural quantity. Whereas society and nature are a unity, but a contradictory unity. Society itself is a product of the historical development of nature, but a product which relatively is in opposition to nature, reacts upon it and even in the process of historical development transforms external nature itself into its product (the so-called cultivated landscape). Therefore Marx said that in fact there is one science, the science of history, which embraces both the history of the inorganic world, and the history of the organic world and the history of society. In the sphere of the natural sciences this meant a decisive break with mechanistic-mathematical rationalism which in Marx is bound up with the criticism of mechanistic materialism.

Natural matter was conceived as being all of the same kind, as only a quantitatively defined quantity, as a combination of qualitatively similar parts. Diversity of quality was from this point of view merely an illusion of a subjective character.

> Matter as such is a pure creation of thought and an abstraction. In bringing under the conception of matter the things examined by us as bodily existing we are distracted from the qualitative differences in them. Therefore matter as such, in distinction from *definitely existing matters* (our emphasis, N.B.), is not something existing sensually . . . It (this point of view, the "one-sided mathematical point of view", N.B.) is even a return to Pythagoras who already regarded number, quantitative definition as the essence of things.

In other words qualityless matter would bring us back to the position of so-called logical realism, in opposition to nominalism. It does not, however, in any way follow from this that "matter has disappeared". It only follows that, objectively and independently of our consciousness, it exists in all the wealth of its qualitatively different and varied forms, with an historical process of transition from one form to another, with specific forms of movement and, consequently, with specific laws for this movement. Even in the limits of inorganic nature mechanical movement and chemical movement are distinct, although they pass into one another. The organic world grows out of the inorganic in the process of historical development, but, once it has arisen, it develops its specific forms of movement. Society arises historically from the biological species, through the herd, but once it has arisen, it develops in turn through its conditioned laws. It passes through different stages of development. It is always historical, that is it exists really only in its historical form, with its own historically defined laws, etc. In this way we here have all the wealth and all the variety of the world which in the historical process of thought, on the basis of the historical process of the development of social practice, is ever more adequately of the development of social practice, is ever more adequately "grasped" by this thought. Every new form of moving matter thus has its own special laws. But this enriched form and these new laws are not cut off by a Chinese wall from those historically preceding them. The latter exist in these in "sublated form". Herein lies the historical succession of processes. On the other hand, variety does not exclude unity. So it is no question of a flat monism of knowledge for which variety has no meaning and to which all cats are grey, nor is it a matter of pluralism for which unity does not exist, but of dialectical and materialist monism, which is adequate to the real unity in variety and variety in unity, with all its forms of contradiction, with its ruptures and catastrophes, with its transition of one form into another, which is adequate to the mighty and general historical process of development.

The historical view of society therefore presupposed the breaking down of the mathematical-atomistic-individualist conception of rationalism. However, here the essence of the matter did not lie at all in the fact (as the Kantians argue) that society must be torn out of (absolutely) its natural historical environment and converted into a substance creating the world out of its spiritual depths and dictating its laws to the cosmos, but in the ascertaining of specific social laws on the basis of an historical view of nature itself. The great limitation of the natural scientific theories before Marx lies in the "eternity" of the laws of nature, i.e. in the supposition that the connections between things and processes are constant. This presupposed the constancy and unchangingness of things. Whereas "the eternal laws of nature are more and more becoming transformed into historical laws. That water is liquid from 0° to 100° is an eternal law of nature, but in order that it may have any force there must be: (1) Water, (2) a given temperature and (3) a normal pressure . . . All our official physics, chemistry, and biology are exclusively goecentric, and calculated for the earth . . ." So here there is no difference in principle between society and nature. The Kantians and idealists generally have to make use of a sophism. They wish, starting from a correct notion of the originality of social development, to draw the conclusion that this originality is principally in the sense of the supernatural character of society. Just as "spirit" is in no way an efflorescence of matter but the real substance of matter, so human society is a special quantity insofar as it is not relatively but absolutely opposed to nature. So the laws of social development, if they exist at all, are supernatural laws having nothing in common with the laws of nature. Their specific character here in fact becomes a supernatural character which serves in its turn as a bridge to God.

So it is obvious how Marx's peculiar terminology is explained. Marx frequently, beginning with the first volume of *Capital,* speaks of the social process as a "natural historical" process, of the laws of social movement as "natural laws like the law of gravity", etc. On the other hand, Marx energetically emphasises the specific nature of social relationships and the corresponding laws ("Nature does not create the owners of money on the one hand and the owners of nothing but their own labour power on the other. This relation is anything but natural-historical" (*ibid.*)). But only stupid minds can deduce from this an "inconsistency" in Marx. For it is clear where his main approach lies. Society is the link in the chain of the general historical development of the world, a link which develops according to law like the development of nature (in this sense the laws of society are natural-historical laws however "critically thinking persons" might wish to jump out into a world of supernatural being). But this law is a special law. It is not a law of either physical, chemical or biological type. It is a specifically social law which must be "theoretically grasped" in precisely this specific character. In the one case (against the idealists) Marx emphasises the connection with nature. In the other (against mechanistic materialism, the "organology" of the biological school of sociologists and positivists of Comte and Spencer and their epigones) he emphasises the specifically social character, the new quality. Even a very slightly thoughtful attitude towards the subject makes the full wealth of the Marxian method absolutely clear in comparison with all other schools and tendencies. The overcoming of the "naturalist" point of view (which does not start from the unity of society and nature, together with their opposition, but from their identity) is far from implying an obligatory (which the bourgeois ideologists reach) transition to the standpoint of idealist metaphysics. The idea of historicism is far from being the private property of the idealist tendencies in thought. Historical "laws of movement" of society can in fact be discovered only by means of materialist dialectic.

So the laws of social development are specific laws. It is therefore, for example, fundamentally incorrect and methodologically impermissible to transfer mechanically laws of a biological order into processes of social development. Society has developed historically out of the animal herd but it is itself no longer a herd. The "way of life" of an animal species, that is the uniformity of vital behaviour of animals of one species, is still not a "mode of production". The natural organs of an animal differ fundamentally from artificial technique which is itself the product of active labour, that is of active adaptation to environment. And so on and so on. The transition from the herd to productive society is, from the point of view of world history, a leap, although this in its turn was a whole immense and lengthy historical period. But, insofar as society has already formed as a new link in the general and universal historical process, it develops its special contradictions and discloses a special form of movement. "It was necessary in this case, therefore, just as in the realm of nature, to set aside these artificial inter-relations by the discovery of the real, a task which finally culminated in the discovery of the universal laws of movement which established themselves as the dominating ones in the history of human society." These "universal laws of movement which established themselves as the dominating ones in the history of human society" were formulated by Marx in his theory of historical materialism, a doctrine of genius the creation of which certainly marks a new epoch in the development of the social sciences. So the general laws of dialectic here found a special, concrete, social form of manifestation. Society was included as a link in the universal chain of history, in full correspondence with objective historical reality.

But it is just in this that the superiority of the bold, fearless, revolutionary and materialist dialectic of Marx showed itself with striking power. We must once again emphasise with all force the originality of Marxist historicism in comparison with the historicism of the "historical school" in all its various manifestations. It is well known how viciously Marx flayed it. In practice taking its direction from the eternalising of the datum, in theory it simply included any "interruption in gradualness," whereas Marx's revolutionary dialectic starts from the inevitable change of social forms, including an historically conditioned contradictoriness of development, the sharpening of inner contradictions, the class struggle, the catastrophic transition of one social form into another by means of revolution, etc.

The strict knowledge of the objective laws of social development is a long way from presupposing in Marx, despite the numerous critics who wage a permanent guerilla warfare of dwarfs against the giant of thought and action, any kind of "destiny" or "fate". With Marx history itself is a long way from hypostasising and is not transformed into a peculiar subject standing above human beings. On the contrary, as long ago as the time of his controversy with Bruno Bauer Marx demolished such a treatment of the problem. "History", he wrote in the *Holy Family,* "is not some kind of special personality which man makes use of to attain his ends. History is simply the activity of man pursuing his ends." Another circumstance should be remarked here. Marx is often transformed into a vulgar apostle of "progress". This also does not correspond to fact. "In spite of the pretensions of 'progress' cases are always to be observed of retrogression and roundabout movement." So in Marx there is not on the one hand a trace of fatalism, nor of Panglossian teleology on the other.

But it does not follow from the fact that "men make history" that human activity is outside the control of any laws. Society is not a sum of isolated and mechanically united individuals. It is a definite whole, divided and contradictory, with a variety in its elements. So objective social laws do not correspond with subjective aim-purposes and they cannot be deduced from individual "motivisations". On the contrary, every individual is already born "socialised" and his activities are determined by the aggregate of his conditions of life. He already finds this environment of his life ready for him, although he also reacts upon it. So for Marx it was important to discover the "laws of movement" of the special form of combination human society, and moreover, of historical society. It is interesting to note that a number of Marx's critics who attack him for his so-called mechanistic approach to society, also reproach him with starting from society and not from the human unit. Whereas it is just from the surpassing of the mechanistic, qualityless, quantitatively mathematical conception of society that there arises the originality of the laws of the specific whole ("Totalität"); of a whole (and not its "parts") specifically social (and not generic, special, biological, physico-chemical).

But Marx does not take this whole, society, as an empty abstraction.

If, for example, we begin our analysis with population, then this will be an abstraction if we leave out classes; classes are an abstraction ("leeres Wort") unless we know their elements, and so on.

> If [says Marx] we start out therefore with population, we do so with a chaotic idea of the whole, and by closer analysis we shall gradually arrive at simpler ideas; thus we shall proceed from the represented concrete to less and less complex abstractions, until we get at the simplest conception. This once attained, we might start on our return journey until we would finally come back to population, but this time not as a chaotic notion of an integral whole, but as a rich aggregate of many conceptions and relations.

The method of this transition, from the chaotic conception of the concrete to the simplest abstract and then back to the enriched concrete aggregate, is Marx's method, a method which cannot be contained within the formal—logical and usual oppositions of induction and deduction, analysis and synthesis, concrete and abstract. So the concept of society with Marx is no longer an empty abstract and extra-historical concept, but a concept which includes the whole divided variety of its concrete historical definitions, which are given in their development, in correspondence with the real course of the real historical process. Here Marx really solves that problem of knowledge which Rickert considered specific for human history, the problem of the "individual" and the "typical". Marx, on the basis of a painstaking study of history, reached a conception of the economic structure of society which is the morphological principle of all the social whole, of "the mode of production", both historically of the "individual" (and at the same time the "typical"), and of the specific stage of historical development. Max Weber had already remarked that the "individual" cannot be understood without "nomological knowledge". But it is impossible to imagine the individual, even of a "minor order", as a Kantian thing in itself, without relation to an "other"; as outside of all connection with others, outside of the social aggregate. Weber is therefore forced to restore the "generalising method" buried by Rickert on the basis of the Rickertian premises which have an absolutely definite social sense, as do all the tendencies of the Kantian "practical reason", and to have recourse to the construction of so-called "ideal types", of a bad, idealistically deformed copy of the Marxian "economic formations" ("economic structures", i.e. "means of production"), whilst, as Tröltsch justly points out, an "intellectual contemplation (Anschauung) of the great sociological complexes and evolutionary relations" predominates in him.

So:

1. With Marx society is a part of nature, but a part in opposition to it, a special and specific part which arises historically (thus here is a unity, but not an identity; the division of the one).

2. It actively influences nature and changes it (mutual interpenetration of opposites).

3. It has its specific laws (social laws) which differ qualitatively from the laws of the inorganic world and the laws of biology (a new quality arising historically) but which are anything but "laws" of a supernatural kind (materialism).

4. Society is taken in the variety of its historic definitions and in the

process of its historical development (the dialectic of the abstract and concrete).

5. There is no teleological "world conception" in Marx ("aims of history", "progress", "united humanity"; "in fact what is meant by the words 'purpose', 'aim', 'germ', 'idea' in previous history is nothing but the abstraction of later history, the abstraction of the active influence exercised by past history on later history").

The most remarkable explanation of the theory of historical materialism, with the exception of the brilliant and monumental introduction to *The Critique of Political Economy,* is undoubtedly the *German Ideology,* particularly that part of it which is devoted to the criticism of Feuerbach.

From the very beginning the authors place the whole problem within the widest limits. "We know one science alone, the science of history. History can be examined from two aspects and divided into the history of nature and the history of man. But it is impossible to separate these two aspects from one another. So long as men exist the history of nature and human history will condition one another." In the last instance the whole further movement also conditions this division of a simple nature into opposing principles. The movement of this opposition, the struggle of society with nature, the growing process of "humanising" nature, the constant penetration of the one opposite into the other, lies at the bottom of the whole movement. This is the law of development of the productive forces of society and the basis of its self-movement. The relation to nature is an active, practical relation, it is labour, the process of production. Social man is above all, not an animal rationale, but homo faber, a tool-making animal. Thus the first premise is the "bodily organisation of individuals and the connection with nature given thereby". The production of the means of life and means of production is the production of material life. But this production is not the mechanical juxtaposition of separate labouring individuals, but production of which the subjects are social individuals in a definite type of social connection. The types of this connection are explained by empirical observation. This is the "productive relations", the main social division (in class society, division in the first place into classes), that basis on which the political, moral, philosophical, religious, etc., "superstructure" grows up. Practice engenders theory, material production gives off spiritual; the latter, with the growth of a manifold division of labour and the fixation of the divided functions in classes (which are distinguished from one another by their relationship to the means of production, in the first place by their position in the process of production and distribution), is relatively split off from its foundation and creates the illusion of sovereign independence in the consciousness of its agents. So there arises the illusion of an "independent" history of religion and morality, of law and philosophy, of science and art, etc. Men, social-historical men "as they are conditioned by the means of production of their material life", "are the producers of their own imaginings, ideas, etc." The latter are thus "the ideological reflections and expressions of this vital process". Which far from excluding, on the contrary, presupposes their active character. Thus society acts on the arena of history in its concrete historical definitiveness. Its productive forces (the unity of means of production and labour power), its economic structure corresponding to the technical production basis and the level of productive forces; its state organisation, its "mode of presentation", comprise a definite morphological unity. So this historical social whole (Totalität) appears as a concrete subject of history with a multitude of its own concrete qualities and corresponding definitions. The task of science is "to represent the whole thing in the aggregate and therefore the reaction of these different aspects on one another". But all this aggregation of influences and connections has its material basis even for the cloudiest sublimations: the material mode of production and consequently, in movement, the process of direct material production of life, active social practice, which gets its expression in social consciousness.

It is not social consciousness which determines social being, but, on the contrary, social being as the foundation determines social consciousness.

But historical society is itself a dialectical unity of opposites. The process of the production of life, that is the process of labour, the process of the growth of productive forces, is its material content, fundamental and direct. The "economic structure of society" is its content form in which the movement of productive forces takes place concretely and historically. The opposition of form and content becomes a contradiction. When this contradiction between productive forces and productive relations breaks up the whole unity, social revolution takes place, society passes from one stage into another. The juridical relations of property (the juridical translation of productive relations), the state superstructure, the old "modes of presentation", all collapse and give place to new forms. The old forms were once "forms of development". They have been dialectically converted into "fetters on development", into their own opposite. This contradiction is "cancelled" in the process of revolution. But the process of revolution is not an automatic process: men make their own history. However, the laws of social development revealed by Marx tell us how great masses of people, divided and united by common conditions of life, behave when these conditions of life change. The contradiction between the mode of production and the development of productive forces is shown and expressed in a number of other contradictions which lay bare the opposition of classes, intensify class polarisation, sharpen class interests, produce an ideological demarcation of classes, force on the formation of the class self-consciousness of the revolutionary class and its allies, and through the revolution of living people, through the struggle of the revolutionary class against the class which fortifies the old productive relations in the concentrated form of its state power, through the destruction of this power and the smashing of its opponents' forces, through the emancipation of productive forces and the organisation of new forms of movement of these forces, society passes into another form of historical being.

So Marx looks at society as an historically concrete society, the historical form of which is a transitional form. The "general laws" of historical development therefore include the laws of the transition of one social form into another and presuppose specifically historical special laws for different social-economic formations.

There lies at the basis of the theory of historical materialism the materialist premise that all the vital wealth of society, the whole content of its complete process of life, is in the long run determined by the level of power over nature, by the degree of real mastery (and thus of real change) of the external world, i.e. by the movement and self-movement of productive forces, by the process of material labour which always takes place in a concrete historical social form, that is to say, which is continuously connected with the economic structure of society. In relation to the material, productive, motive forces and the changing economic structure of society, the natural premises are, as such, a relative constant, although an extremely important constant as being historically the starting-point of development. Moreover, the movement of these natural premises, as premises of social development, is derived from the movement of productive forces. The hidden, so-called "natural resources" do not function socially. They must cease to be "hidden". Only when they are transformed from matter into material, from "things in themselves" into "things for us", entering the stream of artificial material transformation, that is the stream of the material labour process, becoming objects of change, are they changed (both qualitatively and quantitatively), as "elements" of social development. But this quantitative and qualitative change is a consequence of the development of productive forces. It is just the same also with biological "human nature", that is with the other aspect of "the natural premises" for social development. "Corporeal organisation", man of the "race" or "species", is the historical premise of social and historical man, and a relatively constant one. Once again, a change in "human nature" (either a corporeal one or its spiritual correlation) is derived from social development. The law of its development is determined by the law of the development of society as a whole at the basis of which lies the law of the development of productive forces, that is a specifically social law. In this way one-sided "geographical materialism" which deduces all historical development from climatic conditions, the soil, rainfall and water supply, and such factors, is rejected, as also is biological materialism (i.e. positivism) which mechanically transfers biological laws to society and deduces the laws of social development from so-called "human nature" as its biological nature. But the materialist conception of history in the first place strikes a mortal blow at all forms of idealism in the social sciences. Phenomena of social consciousness are derived from the phenomena of social being. The material fact of the process of the development of productive forces (or their decline) in its social-historical form, that is the changes in the productivity of social labour and in human relations in the process of that labour (productive relations), these are the main determinants which in the last resort, either directly or indirectly, immediately or through a number of intermediate links, condition the changes in the whole sphere of superstructures, political, juridical, moral, scientific, æsthetic, philosophical. The morphological unity of society (although contradictory and moreover developing these inner contradictions in different directions) is conditioned precisely by the fact that it has a single material basis. The superficial idealist point of view in the social sciences starts from a different species of the forms of social consciousness, without even posing the problem of the objective determinants of this consciousness. The materialist conception of history, on the other hand, analyses just these material determinants, the movement of which determines the movement of the corresponding thought forms. "According to the different modes of production in different countries in different epochs, a hierarchy of soul, mind and understanding corresponds to the definite economic hierarchy. . . . The psychology of classes corresponds to the hierarchy of social relations and the economic development of classes." The class struggle fills the whole history of class societies, is the vital nerve of the historical process. But this struggle itself, the disposition of class forces, their concrete combination, is conditioned by the development of a definite mode of production. It breaks out, on the other hand, not only in the realm of the struggle of direct material interests, but also in the highest realms of ideas. Even the general forms of thought in an age express and reflect its specific style and its class division, that is, in the long run they express the mode of production together with the level of productive forces.

Marx's doctrine of the movement of social-economic formations is far from being an artificial intellectual system. It generalises an enormous practical and theoretical experience. Of course "economic structures" and their superstructures cannot express all the fullness of the concrete historical stream of full life in all its variety. But, as has already been remarked earlier, while poorer than life, these generalisations are richer than the mosaic offered by banal empiricism which is usually spiced with a dose of "morality". They express the main and decisive relationships, those which determine the routes of historical movement. "Pure capitalism" is, undoubtedly, an abstraction, though in many cases a very useful abstraction. But "impure" capitalism is the reality, both as a combination of "capitalisms" and as "world capitalism" in whose pores the relics of pre-capitalist formations are also contained. Its "pure class structure" is, of course, an abstraction. But the class structure of real capitalism is actually such a structure that the masses are composed of wage workers while the monopolists of the means of production command economy (and the state). The "pure proletariat" is an abstraction. But the living unity of the mass of proletarians of various qualifications with its outer circumference and with a strong, real core, is a reality which is really struggling for its real rule. Therefore the doctrine of the change of historical and economic formations, as a doctrine of the process of "history", adequately expresses the real historical process. The Windelband-Rickert opposition of "history" to "theory" must be put away in the archives. History as a mechanical load of separate facts is not history as a science. The co-ordination of individual facts and their ranking under the teleological and theological command of the Kantian categorical imperative is not a science. "Zweckwissenschaft" à la Stammler, Stolzmann, etc., is not a science. On the other hand, there can be no scientific system which merely gives a bare scheme of abstract character. But the question of the empty abstract character of this or that theory is a concrete question, a question of the factual analysis of that theory, a question of checking it. The opposition of "theory" and "history" is a relic of the outlook which supposed that nature has no history and therefore that its laws are eternal. "Natural" eternal law and the shame-faced system of relations fixed by these "eternal laws" is a basis of "theory". "Theory", according to this view, is a system of "eternal laws" brought into connection and formulated. History, on the other hand, is the outflow of the free creative spirit which creates the new, producing chiefly ever new ethical values. So human history is, as Stammler expresses it, "Gegenstück" with regard to nature, while the sciences of the spirit are "Gegenstück" with regard to the natural sciences. Together with the destruction of the dualism in principle of nature and society, of natural and social laws, there also goes the opposition in principle of theory and history.

So the materialist conception of history is materialist dialectic in its specific and enriched form; it is the dialectic of a social and historical process which reveals its objective of dialectic. Marx was the first to deduce the laws of historical development on the basis of a wealth of material, a great sea of facts, a vast acquaintance with the historical material of various ages and peoples, an unusually rich experience of modern European history and of the practice of the social class struggle of which he was himself a great master in all its spheres. This is a monumental theoretical structure the like of which the world has never seen. Where formerly "chance" ruled, the actions of warriors and kings, Cleopatra's nose or Napoleon's stomach, where man saw an incomprehensible struggle of abstractions and symbols, a bloody carnage for the forms of religion or the sign of cross against crescent, where idealist philosophy gave a substitute for explanation by compelling the "spirit" to embody itself permanently in the real historical process, here for the first time real science assumed its place, destroying the illusory connections of things and processes and putting actual connections in their place. Society, historical society, was scientifically "discovered" as alive and complex, internally contradictory and mobile, connected with nature and actively influencing it, a unity developing its contradictions and passing from one qualitatively defined formation to another, with peculiar specific laws. So the general laws of social and historical development (Engels) already melt into themselves the special laws of the movement of specific social and historic formations expressing the specific forms of moving contradictions. The laws of the development of feudalism, for example, are not the same as the laws of the development of capitalism. The laws of movement of each such formation are original, although they also "act" on the basis of general laws, established by the theory of historical materialism. Nor can it be otherwise, for the productive forces are different (both qualitatively and quantitatively), the economic structures are different, the classes are different, the whole vital unity and all its contradictions are different. Therefore, for example, it would be foolish to look for the law of periodical crises of over-production in natural forms of economy—just as it would be foolish to look for flexible forms of scientific thought in stagnant societies. This is not the consensus of Comte, with its wooden hierarchical categories. Here everything is contradictory, mobile, dialectic, here vital historical life is at play. Marx established an infinite variety of general and partial laws of "the second order" besides the vast and mighty generalisations which form the "core" of the materialist conception of history. His brilliant analysis of the groups within a class, of ideologues and practicians; his analysis of the division of labour and the influence of this division on the whole structure of thought; his analysis of the different forms of superstructure and, in the first place, his teaching on the state, which is in itself a whole revolution in thought and the sharpest weapon in the practical political struggle of the proletariat, and so on, and so on, these are all most important achievements in science. It can be said without any exaggeration that his very footnotes (the theoretical ones, of course) have nourished a whole pleiade of the most important minds in the camp of official science. Take, for example, his remark about the rôle of Protestantism in the genesis of capitalism, which has evoked a whole literature (Sombart, Max Weber, in particular, Tröltsch, etc).

In the theory of historical materialism the teaching on classes and class struggle has particular importance. Classes are the living collectors and agents of the contradictions of each (class, i.e. presupposing class society) mode of production. The movement of these contradictions and their revolutionary solution runs through the class struggle in its triune economic, political and theoretical form. Certainly the dominant ideas are the ideas of the dominant class and the dominant "mode of presentation" (or "Wissensform", as Max Scheler calls it "for originality") is the "mode of presentation" characteristic of it. Thus here are formed within society its living Totalitäten, classes of which one in the course of development becomes the revolutionary class par excellence. Under definite historical conditions it becomes the grave-digger of the old society.

The materialist conception of history, with its doctrine of class struggle and revolution, is an objective scientific theory. It explains, by starting from the most general laws of being and becoming (materialist dialectic or dialectical materialism), the general objective laws of human history. This is not a subjectivist structure. It is not a voluntarist theory with the will as primal and all-determining factor. The will is limited at each given moment by definite conditions. But this theory is in the highest degree active and revolutionary. It has nothing in common with the disgusting fatalistic caricature on Marxism of which social-democracy is the organised apostle. The "objectivism" of this caricature is historical fatalism, which is, in its turn, the weapon of Fascist activism. The Marxist doctrine of the laws of social development is an instrument for the overthrow of capital. It gets its further interpretation in the theory of capitalist development, in which the general laws of social dialectic assume an even more concrete form as the laws of the development and doom of capitalist society and the laws of its inevitable transition into socialism through the revolution of the proletariat and its dictatorship.

Paul Tillich

The Actuality of God *

GOD AS BEING

a) *God as being and finite being.*—The being of God is being-itself. The being of God cannot be understood as the existence of a being alongside others or above others. If God is a being, he is subject to the categories of finitude, especially to space and substance. Even if he is called the "highest being" in the sense of the "most perfect" and the "most powerful" being, this situation is not changed. When applied to God, superlatives become diminutives. They place him on the level of other beings while elevating him above all of them. Many theologians who have used the term "highest being" have known better. Actually they have described the highest as the absolute, as that which is on a level qualitatively different from the level of any being—even the highest being. Whenever infinite or unconditional power and meaning are attributed to the highest being, it has ceased to be a being and has become being-itself. Many confusions in the doctrine of God and many apologetic weaknesses could be avoided if God were understood first of all as being-itself or as the ground of being. The power of being is another way of expressing the same thing in a circumscribing phrase. Ever since the time of Plato it has been known—although it often has been disregarded, especially by the nominalists and their modern followers—that the concept of being as being, or being-itself, points to the power inherent in everything, the power of resisting nonbeing. Therefore, instead of saying that God is first of all being-itself, it is possible to say that he is the power of being in everything and above everything, the infinite power of being. A theology which does not dare to identify God and the power of being as the first step toward a doctrine of God relapses into monarchic monotheism, for if God is not being-itself, he is subordinate to it, just as Zeus is subordinate to fate in Greek religion.

* Reprinted from *Systematic Theology* by Paul Tillich, Volume I, pp. 235–241, by permission of The University of Chicago Press.

The structure of being-itself is his fate, as it is the fate of all other beings. But God is his own fate; he is "by himself"; he possesses "aseity." This can be said of him only if he is the power of being, if he is being-itself.

As being-itself God is beyond the contrast of essential and existential being. We have spoken of the transition of being into existence, which involves the possibility that being will contradict and lose itself. This transition is excluded from being-itself (except in terms of the christological paradox), for being-itself does not participate in nonbeing. In this it stands in contrast to every being. As classical theology has emphasized, God is beyond essence and existence. Logically, being-itself is "before," "prior to," the split which characterizes finite being.

For this reason it is as wrong to speak of God as the universal essence as it is to speak of him as existing. If God is understood as universal essence, as the form of all forms, he is identified with the unity and totality of finite potentialities; but he has ceased to be the power of the ground in all of them, and therefore he has ceased to transcend them. He has poured all his creative power into a system of forms, and he is bound to these forms. This is what pantheism means.

On the other hand, grave difficulties attend the attempt to speak of God as existing. In order to maintain the truth that God is beyond essence and existence while simultaneously arguing for the existence of God, Thomas Aquinas is forced to distinguish between two kinds of divine existence: that which is identical with essence and that which is not. But an existence of God which is not united with its essence is a contradiction in terms. It makes God a being whose existence does not fulfil his essential potentialities; being and not-yet-being are "mixed" in him, as they are in everything finite. God ceases to be God, the ground of being and meaning. What really has happened is that Thomas has had to unite two different traditions: the Augustinian, in which the divine existence is included in his essence, and the Aristotelian, which derives the existence of God from the existence of the world and which then asserts, in a second step, that his existence is identical with his essence. Thus the question of the existence of God can be neither asked nor answered. If asked, it is a question about that which by its very nature is above existence, and therefore the answer—whether negative or affirmative—implicitly denies the nature of God. It is as atheistic to affirm the existence of God as it is to deny it. God is being-itself, not *a* being. On this basis a first step can be taken toward the solution of the problem which usually is discussed as the immanence and the transcendence of God. As the power of being, God transcends every being and also the totality of beings—the world. Being-itself is beyond finitude and infinity; otherwise it would be conditioned by something other than itself, and the real power of being would lie beyond both it and that which conditioned it. Being-itself infinitely transcends every finite being. There is no proportion or gradation between the finite and the infinite. There is an absolute break, an infinite "jump." On the other hand, everything finite participates in being-itself and in its infinity. Otherwise it would not have the power of being. It would be swallowed by nonbeing, or it never would have emerged out of nonbeing. This double relation of all beings to being-itself gives being-itself a double characteristic. In calling it creative, we point to the fact that everything participates in the infinite power of being. In calling it abysmal, we point to the fact that everything participates in the power of being in a finite way, that all beings are infinitely transcended by their creative ground.

Man is bound to the categories of finitude. He uses the two categories of relation—causality and substance—to express the relation of being-itself to finite beings. The "ground" can be interpreted in both ways, as the cause of finite beings and as their substance. The former has been elaborated by Leibniz in the line of the Thomistic tradition, and the latter has been elaborated by Spinoza in the line of the mystical tradition. Both ways are impossible. Spinoza establishes a naturalistic pantheism, in contrast to the idealistic type which identifies God with the universal essence of being, which denies finite freedom and in so doing denies the freedom of God. By necessity God is merged into the finite beings, and their being is his being. Here again it must be emphasized that pantheism does not say that God is everything. It says that God is the substance of everything and that there is no substantial independence and freedom in anything finite.

Therefore, Christianity, which asserts finite freedom in man and spontaniety in the nonhuman realm, has rejected the category of substance in favor of the category of causality in attempting to express the relation of the power of being to the beings who participate in it. Causality seems to make the world dependent on God, and, at the same time, to separate God from the world in the way a cause is separated from its effect. But the category of causality cannot "fill the bill," for cause and effect are not separate; they include each other and form a series which is endless in both directions. What is cause at one point in this series is effect at another point and conversely. God as cause is drawn into this series, which drives even him beyond himself. In order to disengage the divine cause from the series of causes and effects, it is called the first cause, the absolute beginning. What this means is that the category of causality is being denied while it is being used. In other words, causality is being used not as a category but as a symbol. And if this is done and is understood, the difference between substance and causality disappears, for if God is the cause of the entire series of causes and effects, he is the substance underlying the whole process of becoming. But this "underlying" does not have the character of a substance which underlies its accidents and which is completely expressed by them. It is an underlying in which substance and accidents preserve their freedom. In other words, it is substance not as a category but as a symbol. And, if taken symbolically, there is no difference between *prima causa* and *ultima substantia.* Both mean, what can be called in a more directly symbolic term, "the creative and abysmal ground of being." In this term both naturalistic pantheism, based on the category of substance, and rationalistic theism, based on the category of causality, are overcome.

Since God is the ground of being, he is the ground of the structure of being. He is not subject to this structure; the structure is grounded in him. He *is* this structure, and it is impossible to speak about him except in terms of this structure. God must be approached cognitively through the structural elements of being-itself. These elements make him a living God, a God who can be man's concrete concern. They enable us to use symbols which we are certain point to the ground of reality.

b) *God as being and the knowledge of God.*—The statement that God is being-itself is a nonsymbolic statement. It does not point beyond itself. It means what it says directly and properly; if we speak of the actuality of God, we first assert that he is not God if he is not being-itself. Other assertions about God can be made theologically only on this basis. Of course, religious assertions do not require such a foundation for what they say about God; the foundation is implicit in every religious thought concerning God. Theologians must make explicit what is implicit in religious thought and expression; and, in order to do this, they must begin with the most abstract and completely unsymbolic statement which is possible, namely, that God is being-itself or the absolute.

However, after this has been said, nothing else can be said about God as God which is not symbolic. As we already have seen, God as being-itself is the ground of the ontological structure of being without being subject to this structure himself. He *is* the structure; that is, he has the power of determining the structure of everything that has being. Therefore, if anything beyond this bare assertion is said about God, it no longer is a direct and proper statement, no longer a concept. It is indirect, and it points to something beyond itself. In a word, it is symbolic.

The general character of the symbol has been described. Special emphasis must be laid on the insight that symbol and sign are different; that, while the sign bears no necessary relation to that to which it points, the symbol participates in the reality of that for which it stands. The sign can be changed arbitrarily according to the demands of expediency but the symbol grows and dies according to the correlation between that which is symbolized and the persons who receive it as a symbol. Therefore, the religious symbol, the symbol which points to the divine, can be a true symbol only if it participates in the power of the divine to which it points.

There can be no doubt that any concrete assertion about God must be symbolic, for a concrete assertion is one which uses a segment of finite experience in order to say something about him. It transcends the content of this segment, although it also includes it. The segment of finite reality which becomes the vehicle of a concrete assertion about God is affirmed and negated at the same time. It becomes a symbol, for a symbolic expression is one whose proper meaning is negated by that to which it points. And yet it also is affirmed by it, and this affirmation gives the symbolic expression an adequate basis for pointing beyond itself.

The crucial question must now be faced. Can a segment of finite reality become the basis for an assertion about that which is infinite? The answer is that it can, because that which is infinite is being-itself and because everything participates in being-itself. The *analogia entis* is not the property of a questionable natural theology which attempts to gain knowledge of God by drawing conclusions about the infinite from the finite. The *analogia entis* gives us our only justification of speaking at all about God. It is based on the fact that God must be understood as being-itself.

The truth of a religious symbol has nothing to do with the truth of the empirical assertions involved in it, be they physical, psychological, or historical. A religious symbol possesses some truth if it adequately expresses the correlation of revelation in which some person stands. A religious symbol *is* true if it adequately expresses the correlation of some person with final revelation. A religious symbol can die only if the correlation of which it is an adequate expression dies. This occurs whenever the revelatory situation changes and former symbols become obsolete. The history of religion, right up to our own time, is full of dead symbols which have been killed not by a scientific criticism of assumed superstitions but by a religious criticism of religion. The judgment that a religious symbol *is* true is identical with the judgment that the revelation of which it is the adequate expression is true. This double meaning of the truth of a symbol must be kept in mind. A symbol *has* truth: it is adequate to the revelation it expresses. A symbol *is* true: it is the expression of a true revelation.

Theology as such has neither the duty nor the power to confirm or to negate religious symbols. Its task is to interpret them according to theological principles and methods. In the process of interpretation, however, two things may happen: theology may discover contradictions between symbols within the theological circle and theology may speak not only as theology but also as religion. In the first case, theology can point out the religious dangers and the theological errors which follow from the use of certain symbols; in the second case, theology can become prophecy, and in this role it may contribute to a change in the revelatory situation.

Religious symbols are double-edged. They are directed toward the infinite which they symbolize *and* toward the finite through which they symbolize it. They force the infinite down to finitude and the finite up to infinity. They open the divine for the human and the human for the divine. For instance, if God is symbolized as "Father," he is brought down to the human relationship of father and child. But at the same time this human relationship is consecrated into a pattern of the divine-human relationship. If "Father" is employed as a symbol for God, fatherhood is seen in its theonomous, sacramental depth. One cannot arbitrarily "make" a religious symbol out of a segment of secular reality. Not even the collective unconscious, the great symbol-creating source, can do this. If a segment of reality is used as a symbol for God, the realm of reality from which it is taken is, so to speak, elevated into the realm of the holy. It no longer is secular. It is theonomous. If God is called the "king," something is said not only about God but also about the holy character of kinghood. If God's work is called "making whole" or "healing," this not only says something about God but also emphasizes the theonomous character of all healing. If God's self-manifestation is called "the word," this not only symbolizes God's relation to man but also emphasizes the holiness of all words as an expression of the spirit. The list could be continued. Therefore, it is not surprising that in a secular culture both the symbols for God and the theonomous character of the material from which the symbols are taken disappear.

A final word of warning must be added in view of the fact that for many people the very term "symbolic" carries the connotation of nonreal. This is partially the result of confusion between sign and symbol and partially due to the identification of reality with empirical reality, with the entire realm of objective things and events. Both reasons have been undercut explicitly and implicitly in the foregoing chapters. But one reason remains, namely, the fact that some theological movements, such as Protestant Hegelianism and Catholic modernism, have interpreted religious language symbolically in order to dissolve its realistic meaning and to weaken its seriousness, its power, and its spiritual impact. This was not the purpose of the classical essays on the "divine names," in which the symbolic character of all affirmations about God was strongly emphasized and explained in religious terms, nor was it a consequence of these essays. Their intention and their result was to give to God and to all his relations to man more reality and power than a nonsymbolic and therefore easily superstitious interpretation could give them. In this sense symbolic interpretation is proper and necessary; it enhances rather than diminishes the reality and power of religious language, and in so doing it performs an important function.

IV. VALUE

Value

I

Value theory in the twentieth century was born into a rich, varied, and exciting setting. For an unusual proliferation of vital movements had taken place in the century that was fast receding.

Earlier in the nineteenth century, utilitarianism had held the intellectual driver's seat, with John Stuart Mill pulling at the reins as the horses veered to left or right. A forthright, hard-working secular philosophy, dedicated to the spread of happiness by encouraging individual production, self-seeking, or self-development, it had penetrated deeply into economics, law, and politics. The individualistic liberalism with which it was closely interwoven was imbued with the confidence that took the advance of democratic progress to be the natural order of mankind in the future.

Constant rumblings had been heard on its right. There were critiques of its secularism emanating from traditional religious outlooks (although religion also had its utilitarian wing); there were attacks upon its quantitative emphasis, its surrender to the desires of the masses. But more threatening than the earlier tirades of a Carlyle was the flash of fire in the Nietzschean outlook—the "transvaluation of values" that would spurn humanitarian ideals as weakness, and elevate a spontaneous even ruthless will to power.

There had also been thunder on the left. Materialist ethics had taken a foothold on the intellectual stage with the rise of socialist and communist doctrines. Marx and Engels had forged an armory of theoretical weapons for analyzing human striving and its manifold value expressions in terms of material social and historical conditions. Still a lesser strain in the nineteenth century, and in many of its forms linked to traditional humanitarian philosophies, socialism was to become increasingly permeating in the scope of its challenge.

As the nineteenth century drew to an end, Darwinism held the spotlight. Placing man firmly in the animal world, it forced value theory to reckon man's spiritual aims afresh. It obviously supported materialism, but it also led in other directions. Herbert Spencer combined the new biology with his utilitarianism, fashioning a predatory survival-of-the-fittest outlook whose popular vogue far transcended academic rivals. And in America the new biology played a foundation role in the construction of pragmatic philosophies. By the end of the century John Dewey was already maturing his campaign for a philosophical naturalization of the human spirit, which flowered in his twentieth century writings. And Sigmund Freud was pushing on in his discoveries that were to add a psychological dimension to the Darwinian biological and the Marxian historical, and set the stage for penetrating reevaluations of the nature of man.

The threat of the naturalization of the spiritual life had long been sensed in philosophy. It was precisely to meet this that Kant, a century before, had fashioned a critical philosophy which hemmed in science by limiting it to the world of phenomena (not interfering thereby in its own operations), and gave to faith full scope in the domain of practice. But the problem gained new urgency after Darwin. Thus when T. H. Green's influential PROLEGOMENA TO ETHICS appeared in 1883—to synthesize his life's teachings—it warned at the outset that man's ethical experience was about to be reduced to some complicated form of fear reaction; with a fusion of Kantian and Hegelian elements he urged that it be salvaged by recognizing the sense of obligation as the key to conceiving man's spiritual place over and beyond the natural world.

Apart from specifically intellectual movements, the general tenor of nineteenth-century life, continued and intensified in the twentieth, posed genuinely new problems that demanded decision in the century that was now emerging. The accelerating growth in technology and the productive capacities of man, the multiplying populations, the widening horizon in which the whole globe was thrown open for economic organization, predatory conquest, as well as the expansion of knowledge—all these broke up every isolation and scattered all provincialisms, finally bringing man face to face with ultimate decisions. Not only intellectual satisfaction and emotional balance but basic directions of development were now at stake in the selection of values.

II

There is a strange contrast between the theoretical calm of twentieth-century value theory in its dominant expressions and the turbulence of the century itself. Two world wars, the rise and defeat of Nazism, the rise and spread of Communism on the world scene, fill the pages of a half century's history. But value theory rises to passionate heights only in conflicts over the verifiability of value judgments, the problem of ethical relativism, and the emotive theory of value. This is a remarkable phenomenon, and its analysis is not wholly clear. It will have to be left to future intellectual historians of philosophical ideas. In part, it may be the expression of the philosophical virtue of cool and analytic reflection in dealing with basic theoretical problems—an extension of the habit of mind in the sciences, of dealing with fundamental ideas in a reflective deliberate manner. In part, it may be, the relation to the great problems of the age was not stressed because it was taken to be obvious. For example, the intensified theoretical struggle over the arbitrariness or rationality of moral judgments in the '30's and '40's certainly was widely felt as related to the clash of ultimate systems in the setting of World War II; yet even here the connections are rarely traced with explicit application. Perhaps the most favorable interpretation one can offer is that the philosophers of our time are sufficiently conscious of the importance of fundamental ideas to know that they can take practical implications and social applications for granted, and assume the worthwhileness of pursuing the intellectual problems in their own right. They know, for example, that a shift in the analysis of the concept of force was allied to the change from an Aristotelian to a Newtonian physical science, that a shift from natural law to natural rights was part and parcel of the political revolutions of the early modern world, that different social systems are epitomized in different interpretations of the economic concept of value, or the political opposition of liberty and equality. And so, to split an idea and analyze its components may be a mode of releasing intellectual energy as splitting an atom is of releasing physical energy, and the synthesis of ideas has a comparable analogy to thermo-nuclear processes!

III

The distinctive phenomenon in twentieth-century study of the human spirit on the philosophical side is the rise of a unified category of value. It was sensed as new. Writing when the first quarter of the century had passed, John Laird said[1]:

> In the main, therefore, it is possible that the current philosophy of value is essentially new; with the wine of adventure in its veins. Value may prove to

[1] John Laird, The Idea of Value (Cambridge University Press, 1929), p. xix. Quoted by permission of the publisher.

> *be the key that will eventually release all the human sciences from their present position of pathetic if dignified futility. It would be imprudent, however, to cherish this hope without remembering an essential circumstance. In a part, at least, of the older tradition, an "enquiry into moral matters" did not mean an enquiry into virtue and righteousness only, but an enquiry into mores. It was an enquiry into qualities "useful or agreeable to ourselves or to others"—or, in other words, an enquiry into humanism and into the human sciences. . . . It is the recovery rather than the invention of this attitude which should be the pride of the newer theories. What they have recovered, let us hope, they have also improved.*

The new category, however, was also felt to be a response to important needs of the time. Urban is a spokesman for the self-conscious development of the idea. In one of the early value treatises of the twentieth century, he says.[2] "More and more the conviction gains ground that a general theory of value, which shall comprehend in a systematic and scientific way all types of human values, is an absolute necessity." The current division of labor among the special fields, Urban believes, no longer meets the issues with which philosophy must reckon. And in his preface he gives us a brief but insightful picture of the controversies taking shape.[3] Science has been taking over the whole "choir of heaven" as well as the "furniture of earth." Life, art, morals, and religion are disaffected. There is a reaction against intellectualism "which if not widespread is at least profound." Apparently then, although Urban does not say this, the value concept is a closing of the ranks, against a common foe, by the fields that had in a haphazard way hitherto divided the human spirit! Urban, however, rejects any new doctrine of "two-fold truth." He avows himself on the side of knowledge, and expects to bring together the concepts of value and science. He expects that "there will always be new ventures in faith and science alike," and these must in every case be followed by new evaluations in a scientific spirit. Meanwhile, the foundations for the general theory of value are to be firmly laid.

In fact, the movement towards a unification of the various value disciplines was more advanced than perhaps Urban recognized, and its sources were more diverse. Trends within the scientific picture of man seemed as likely to promote it as trends in opposition to science. Already, more than a century before, Bentham had acted as a grandparent of the general value concept by bringing every human activity under the rubric of a single search for pleasure. And the various naturalistic trends, what-

[2] Wilbur Marshall Urban, *Valuation, Its Nature and Laws,* Being an Introduction to the General Theory of Value, (New York, Macmillan, 1909) p. 3.
[3] *Ibid.,* p. vii.

ever explanatory principles they employed, sought in different ways to give an account of man's unified development. Thus, in addition to problems in the theory of ethics and movements in the philosophy of religion, there were powerful influences from the growth of economic theory and psychological theory. And, once the unification was launched, other fields such as art readily found their place, and all the sciences could be invoked in the search for underpinnings. The outcome was unavoidable: twentieth-century value theory could be monopolized by no single philosophical point of view, but became the ground upon which many perspectives explored many phases and offered diverse, often competing, theories of unification.

Of the various special disciplines, certainly ethics was in no position at the end of the nineteenth century, to take the lead in the growing federation. For in spite of the universalist ambitions of the Utilitarian structure, her long-range drift had been towards contraction. Once mistress of the good and ready to legislate in any field—for all decision requires a view of what is good for men—she had been turned more and more into the inwardness of the individual self. The ancients cast ethics in terms of the good life; the moderns, now with the weight of Kant behind them, placed her in charge of the "ought," the individual's inside conformity to duty as he recognized it. This narrowing of the stage had as an outcome the reduction of ethics to a concern with the individual's "moral values," his values of character, leaving broad issues of social and economic policy to other domains.[4] Ethics was thus ready to be pruned to a species under the genus value.

The theory of religion manifested at least two opposing tendencies, both favorable to the growth of value theory. Perhaps the dominant one was that of religious idealism stemming from the Hegelian philosophy, which had a direct impact on the unification of value theory. For Hegel had seen the history of the universe in all its phases, including the physical, as the onward march of spirit. And so religious idealism could thrust aside the dichotomy of the supernatural and the natural and treat all life as the expression of a single spiritual principle whose structure could be traced in any field of phenomena.

The second tendency, which we have indicated already, separated the human spirit sharply from the natural world, looking to the human sense of value as the phenomenon appointed to save man from permanent descent into the natural. Transcendence became its key concept, whether

[4] Compare R. H. Tawney's complaint, in his *Religion and the Rise of Capitalism*, concerning the religious abdication of social judgment in the last few centuries.

it be transcendence of man over himself, of value to man, of God to man. Many of these approaches were strongly influenced by the Kantian philosophy and cast their picture of spirit in moral rather than metaphysical or ontological terms. Many others—increasingly in the twentieth century—looked back to Kierkegaard and developed the existentialist approach with its emphasis on the concrete individual subjective situation.

The two trends in religious theory, although they often felt sharply opposed to one another, had a common impact in their tendency to unify the value field.

Of the other areas mentioned, economics played what at first seems a surprisingly large role. Actually it ought not to surprise us, since economics is one of the areas in which the problems of comparative worth are quickly pressed upon theory. For example, the rise of a world market in which all sorts of qualitatively different things are exchanged through the medium of money raised the problem of the bases of exchange. Here economic theory had long since achieved a kind of generality in its value categories, both in analyzing use or consumption (use value) and exchange (exchange value). The theory of value had been tied to the idea of labor in the economics of Adam Smith, Ricardo, and Marx; but in the later work of Jevons and the Austrian School it was coupled with a hedonistic psychology. Out of this fusion of economic and psychological concepts there came a major source of general value theory in the work of what Eaton calls the Second Austrian School, "hinting at their intimate relations with the first Austrian School of economic theory." [5]

In addition, the model of an economy itself proved fruitful in the extension of value theory. All life could be seen as a congeries of enterprises working themselves out and accommodating themselves to one another. In R. B. Perry's early THE MORAL ECONOMY (1909), this was explicitly applied, and it fashioned many of the ideas that later appeared in his GENERAL THEORY OF VALUE (1926), one of the foundation works in American value theory.

Aesthetics does not seem to have played as large a formative role in general value theory, but it slipped quite smoothly into the growing outlook, finding a ready task in the treatment of "intrinsic value." For unlike economics which is often construed as dealing merely with means, or even morality which is at least sometimes construed as instrumental (whether to salvation or to general happiness) and in any case involves

[5] Howard O. Eaton, *The Austrian Philosophy of Values* (University of Oklahoma Press, 1930), p. 16. Eaton surveys the work of Brentano, Meinong, and Ehrenfels in developing value concepts and problems.

complex strands to be unravelled, art focusses on relatively isolated objects of direct value. And so the province of the immediately valuable, the intrinsically valuable, the directly valuable, the intuited values in experience, came to be seen through the eyes of aesthetic theory. The result was a mutual influence on both the species and the genus. Aesthetics was broadened; it spoke less of beauty and more of aesthetic values in experience, and was led further afield in its analysis of human experience, both creative and appreciative, beyond the usual "arts." And value theory found itself facing the problem of immediate value aesthetically conceived, and its relation to broader contexts. For example, there emerged a constant theoretical tension between the private valuable end and the public instrumental means, which Dewey especially attacked as a reflection of fundamental undesirable dichotomies in the life of modern man with its separation of drab work and grasping enjoyment.

Many other influences and models played a role in the philosophical unification of value theory. Some saw all life unified in biological terms as a constant effort to survive, so that all its qualitative proliferations would exhibit the fundamental animal appetitive structure. Some followed a more complicated psychological theory, seeing the structure of human personality and effort imposed in all fields. Some assumed a unification of all life through the social and historical structuring of men's problems in each succeeding era. Some assumed the unity of value simply because they saw the judgment of value focussed in a single act of human consciousness which could be introspectively explored.

Whatever the motives, the sources, and the weight of influence, the outcome was clear and unmistakeable. With a single magnificent sweep, twentieth-century value theory threw all fields into a single subject-matter, reducing them to species or provinces under a single generic concept, and sought a systematic account of the fundamental idea, with systematic criteria for comparison. It took the unity for granted, and soon it became the most natural thing in the world to see the texts list moral goodness and right and wrong as moral values, beauty as an aesthetic value, usefulness or efficiency as an economic value, the sense of awe and communion with the divine as a religious value, health as a biological value, fellowship as a social value, and so on. Even now, considerable effort is required to see that this is a momentous hypothesis of the unification of disparate and possibly incomparable types of experience, rather than something that stands to reason, or even just a matter of nomenclature.

It is perhaps too early for a systematic critique of value theory in our century. At the present time the concept has acquired considerable circulation in the social sciences, and many of the issues there raised are repeating the battles waged on the philosophical scene in the first half of the century. Much is yet to be learned from a comparison of experiences in philosophy and the sciences. But a few criticisms may be ventured of tendencies which may still be corrected in the studies and development of the concept. Chief of these are: an insufficiently critical attitude to its own foundations and the assumptions of its own questions; a tendency to override the distinctiveness of its provinces and to assume (instead of establish), universal applicability of its concepts and methods; an overreliance on formulations in individualistic introspective terms and on biological rather than psychological, social, and historical materials.

On the other hand, its positive contributions are already clear and firm. Value theory broke down provincialisms and raised broad questions of the identification of the value phenomenon, of verifiability, of relativity, and of the place of value in the total world picture. It pursued these inquiries up many avenues, even some dead-ends, and through many approaches. It opened doors and asked questions which had never been asked in quite that way. And so it matured problems and methods, which in collaboration with the wider range of studies of human life increasingly available, can come to achieve increasingly significant results.

IV

The selections that follow have been chosen primarily to show the growth and broadening of knowledge, the accumulation of results, methods and modes of analysis, and secondarily the variety of schools and approaches.

The first focus of attention is, of course, on the concept of value itself. Is it an intellectual phenomenon, a perceptual or affective quality? Is it a quality at all, or a relational pattern to be found in striving and behavior? Collectively, the selections exhibit the many-sidedness of the value phenomenon through its proposed identifications—its direct qualitative character (Moore, Hartmann, Lewis), its relation to interest (Perry), the appraisal component in the phenomenon itself (Dewey), its systematic component (Bosanquet), its relation to fundamental emotions in man (Scheler), its linguistic-emotive force (Stevenson), and so forth.[6]

Value theory also shares the prevalent twentieth-century concern with methodological questions, and especially with trying to sift what is verifiable and consequently capable of scientific treatment from what is not.

[6] For a historical study of types of analysis of the value concept, see John Laird, *The Idea of Value* (Cambridge University Press, 1929).

Can value fields employ a deductive model, or else an inductive model? Or are they limited to a kind of pluralistic or contextual analysis which Ryle has aptly spoken of as unscheduled logics? Or is the basic method some direct intuition? Or must the concept of validity give way altogether in this domain except as a disguise for emotive expression? The selections present the refinement of methods of many types and in various shades. There is the outright intuitionism of Hartmann, and Moore's introspective analytic self-evidence. Scheler, Hartmann, and Duncker exhibit the phenomenological method. Perry, Lewis, and Dewey are avowedly empirical, but the meaning of empiricism is wide enough to go from the behavioristic to a kind of affective immediacy. Stevenson applies the general category of emotive meaning in a way that makes ethics predominantly practical and rejects concepts of validity. This trend puts the problem of the logic of justification in a central position on the agenda of ethical theory. How it has been developed in the contemporary British analytical school can be seen in the argument of Hare. The attempt to synthesize a variety of approaches in a coherent account of justification is well presented in the treatment of aesthetic judgment by Rice; although whether this kind of synthesis is possible for value generally or for ethics particularly is a distinct question. In general, it will be found that methods overlap, and no sharp or tidy listing can be a substitute for observing the detailed and masterly analysis in many of the longer selections.[7]

The problems of relativism and absolutism have loomed large in twentieth-century value theory. The problems themselves are very old. That values change, that moralities have taken widely different forms, that values are possibly relative to individual or culture, that man is by nature sufficiently plastic so that no one set of values can claim a natural or inherently superior status, are theses that have been debated over and over again in the past. These issues have been intensified in the twentieth century in two respects. One has been the tremendous growth within the psychological and social sciences of study touching on the presuppositions of opposing philosophical positions—for example, the conflicts of behaviorist and gestalt approaches on questions of conditioning versus insight, or anthropological controversy over value invariants. The other has been the extreme philosophical forms that relativism has taken both in the emotive theory, which at first regarded value statements as purely expressive, and in the sociology of knowledge, which issued in claims that

[7] For further critical discussion of many methodological themes, see Ray Lepley, ed., Value: A Cooperative Inquiry, (Columbia University Press, 1949), a symposium in which a dozen philosophers explore a number of questions of value theory specifically raised by Dewey.

our very knowledge of man is itself relativistically value-bound.[8] The problems of absolutism and relativism are directly involved in many of the selections—e.g., in Hartmann's intuitive absolutism, Bosanquet's whole world absolutism, or on the other side, Stevenson's denial of any meaning to "validity" in value judgment. A number of the selections are exclusively devoted to these issues—Spranger's psychological perspectivism yielding a relativism based on types of men, Mannheim's conclusions about the penetration of value into knowledge, and Duncker's use of phenomenological method in a search for value invariants.

Although most of the selections thus throw light on descriptive, analytic, and evaluative issues, and even some on causal context or underlying general philosophy, they have been grouped into three sections on the basis of dominant or substantial relevance to the three questions:

What is value? (Moore, Bosanquet, Perry, Dewey, Scheler)
What methods are available in value fields? (Hartmann, Lewis, Stevenson, Hare, Rice)
Are values relative or absolute? (Spranger, Mannheim, Duncker)

Naturally, space has forced many decisions that philosophical desire would have settled otherwise. Thus, no systematic attempt has been made to illustrate the application of these general concepts and modes of analysis in the special fields of morality, religion, aesthetics, social philosophy, and so forth, nor could the coverage of general positions itself be exhaustive. However, some illustrations of further specific value approaches will be found in the selections of part V, dealing with Vision and Action.

[8] For a treatment of absolutism and relativism in relation to their underlying assumptions and the evidence of the several sciences, see Abraham Edel, *Ethical Judgment: The Use of Science in Ethics* (Free Press, 1955).

What Is Value?

G. E. Moore

Principia Ethica *

THE SUBJECT-MATTER OF ETHICS

6. What, then, is good? How is good to be defined? Now, it may be thought that this is a verbal question. A definition does indeed often mean the expressing of one word's meaning in other words. But this is not the sort of definition I am asking for. Such a definition can never be of ultimate importance in any study except lexicography. If I wanted that kind of definition I should have to consider in the first place how people generally used the word 'good', but my business is not with its proper usage, as established by custom. I should, indeed, be foolish, if I tried to use it for something which it did not usually denote: if, for instance, I were to announce that, whenever I used the word 'good,' I must be understood to be thinking of that object which is usually denoted by the word 'table.' I shall, therefore, use the word in the sense in which I think it is ordinarily used; but at the same time I am not anxious to discuss whether I am right in thinking that it is so used. My business is solely with that object or idea, which I hold, rightly or wrongly, that the word is generally used to stand for. What I want to discover is the nature of that object or idea, and about this I am extremely anxious to arrive at an agreement.

But, if we understand the question in this sense, my answer to it may seem a very disappointing one. If I am asked 'What is good?' my answer is that good is good, and that is the end of the matter. Or if I am asked 'How is good to be defined?' my answer is that it cannot be defined, and that is all I have to say about it. But disappointing as these answers may appear, they are of the very last importance. To readers who are familiar with philosophic terminology, I can express their importance by saying that they amount to this: That propositions about the good are all of them synthetic and never analytic; and that is plainly no trivial mat-

* From *Principia Ethica* by G. E. Moore, pp. 6–10, 14–17, 82–84, 146–150. Cambridge University Press, First edition 1903. Reprinted 1922, 1929. Reprinted by permission of The Syndics of the University Press.

ter. And the same thing may be expressed more popularly, by saying that, if I am right, then nobody can foist upon us such an axiom as that 'Pleasure is the only good' or that 'The good is the desired' on the pretence that this is 'the very meaning of the word.'

7. Let us, then, consider this position. My point is that 'good' is a simple notion, just as 'yellow' is a simple notion; that, just as you cannot, by any manner of means, explain to any one who does not already know it, what yellow is, so you cannot explain what good is. Definitions of the kind that I was asking for, definitions which describe the real nature of the object or notion denoted by a word, and which do not merely tell us what the word is used to mean, are only possible when the object or notion in question is something complex. You can give a definition of a horse, because a horse has many different properties and qualities, all of which you can enumerate. But when you have enumerated them all, when you have reduced a horse to his simplest terms, then you can no longer define those terms. They are simply something which you think of or perceive, and to any one who cannot think of or perceive them, you can never, by any definition, make their nature known. It may perhaps be objected to this that we are able to describe to others objects which they have never seen or thought of. We can, for instance, make a man understand what a chimaera is, although he has never heard of one or seen one. You can tell him that it is an animal with a lioness's head and body, with a goat's head growing from the middle of its back, and with a snake in place of a tail. But here the object which you are describing is a complex object; it is entirely composed of parts, with which we are all perfectly familiar—a snake, a goat, a lioness; and we know, too, the manner in which those parts are to be put together, because we know what is meant by the middle of a lioness's back, and where her tail is wont to grow. And so it is with all objects, not previously known, which we are able to define: they are all complex; all composed of parts, which may themselves, in the first instance, be capable of similar definition, but which must in the end be reducible to simplest parts, which can no longer be defined. But yellow and good, we say, are not complex: they are notions of that simple kind, out of which definitions are composed and with which the power of further defining ceases.

8. When we say, as Webster says, 'The definition of horse is "A hoofed quadruped of the genus Equus,'" we may, in fact, mean three different things. (1) We may mean merely: 'When I say "horse," you are to understand that I am talking about a hoofed quadruped of the genus Equus.' This might be called the arbitrary verbal definition: and I do not

mean that good is indefinable in that sense. (2) We may mean, as Webster ought to mean: 'When most English people say "horse," they mean a hoofed quadruped of the genus Equus.' This may be called the verbal definition proper, and I do not say that good is indefinable in this sense either; for it is certainly possible to discover how people use a word: otherwise, we could never have known that 'good' may be translated by 'gut' in German and by 'bon' in French. But (3) we may, when we define horse, mean something much more important. We may mean that a certain object, which we all of us know, is composed in a certain manner: that it has four legs, a head, a heart, a liver, etc., etc., all of them arranged in definite relations to one another. It is in this sense that I deny good to be definable. I say that it is not composed of any parts, which we can substitute for it in our minds when we are thinking of it. We might think just as clearly and correctly about a horse, if we thought of all its parts and their arrangement instead of thinking of the whole: we could, I say, think how a horse differed from a donkey just as well, just as truly, in this way, as now we do, only not so easily; but there is nothing whatsoever which we could so substitute for good; and that is what I mean, when I say that good is indefinable.

9. But I am afraid I have still not removed the chief difficulty which may prevent acceptance of the proposition that good is indefinable. I do not mean to say that *the* good, that which is good, is thus indefinable; if I did think so, I should not be writing on Ethics, for my main object is to help towards discovering that definition. It is just because I think there will be less risk of error in our search for a definition of 'the good,' that I am now insisting that *good* is indefinable. I must try to explain the difference between these two. I suppose it may be granted that 'good' is an adjective. Well 'the good', 'that which is good,' must therefore be the substantive to which the adjective 'good' will apply: it must be the whole of that to which the adjective will apply, and the adjective must *always* truly apply to it. But if it is that to which the adjective will apply, it must be something different from that adjective itself; and the whole of that something different, whatever it is, will be our definition of *the* good. Now it may be that this something will have other adjectives, beside 'good,' that will apply to it. It may be full of pleasure, for example; it may be intelligent: and if these two adjectives are really part of its definition, then it will certainly be true, that pleasure and intelligence are good. And many people appear to think that, if we say 'Pleasure and intelligence are good,' or if we say 'Only pleasure and intelligence are good,' we are defining 'good.' Well, I cannot deny that propositions of this nature may

sometimes be called definitions; I do not know well enough how the word is generally used to decide upon this point. I only wish it to be understood that that is not what I mean when I say there is no possible definition of good, and that I shall not mean this if I use the word again. I do most fully believe that some true proposition of the form 'Intelligence is good and intelligence alone is good' can be found; if none could be found, our definition of *the* good would be impossible. As it is, I believe *the* good to be definable; and yet I still say that good itself is indefinable.

10. 'Good,' then, if we mean by it that quality which we assert to belong to a thing, when we say that the thing is good, is incapable of any definition, in the most important sense of that word. The most important sense of 'definition' is that in which a definition states what are the parts which invariably compose a certain whole; and in this sense 'good' has no definition because it is simple and has no parts. It is one of those innumerable objects of thought which are themselves incapable of definition, because they are the ultimate terms by reference to which whatever *is* capable of definition must be defined. That there must be an indefinite number of such terms is obvious, on reflection; since we cannot define anything except by an analysis, which, when carried as far as it will go, refers us to something, which is simply different from anything else, and which by that ultimate difference explains the peculiarity of the whole which we are defining: for every whole contains some parts which are common to other wholes also. There is, therefore, no intrinsic difficulty in the contention that 'good' denotes a simple and indefinable quality. There are many other instances of such qualities.

Consider yellow, for example. We may try to define it, by describing its physical equivalent; we may state what kind of light-vibrations must stimulate the normal eye, in order that we may perceive it. But a moment's reflection is sufficient to shew that those light-vibrations are not themselves what we mean by yellow. *They* are not what we perceive. Indeed we should never have been able to discover their existence, unless we had first been struck by the patent difference of quality between the different colours. The most we can be entitled to say of those vibrations is that they are what corresponds in space to the yellow which we actually perceive.

Yet a mistake of this simple kind has commonly been made about 'good.' It may be true that all things which are good are *also* something else, just as it is true that all things which are yellow produce a certain kind of vibration in the light. And it is a fact, that Ethics aims at discovering what are those other properties belonging to all things which are good.

But far too many philosophers have thought that when they named those other properties they were actually defining good; that these properties, in fact, were simply not 'other,' but absolutely and entirely the same with goodness. This view I propose to call the 'naturalistic fallacy' and of it I shall now endeavour to dispose.

. . . There are, in fact, only two serious alternatives to be considered, in order to establish the conclusion that 'good' does denote a simple and indefinable notion. It might possibly denote a complex, as 'horse' does; or it might have no meaning at all. Neither of these possibilities has, however, been clearly conceived and seriously maintained, as such, by those who presume to define good; and both may be dismissed by a simple appeal to facts.

(1) The hypothesis that disagreement about the meaning of good is disagreement with regard to the correct analysis of a given whole, may be most plainly seen to be incorrect by consideration of the fact that, whatever definition be offered, it may be always asked, with significance, of the complex so defined, whether it is itself good. To take, for instance, one of the more plausible, because one of the more complicated, of such proposed definitions, it may easily be thought, at first sight, that to be good may mean to be that which we desire to desire. Thus if we apply this definition to a particular instance and say 'When we think that A is good, we are thinking that A is one of the things which we desire to desire,' our proposition may seem quite plausible. But, if we carry the investigation further, and ask ourselves 'Is it good to desire to desire A?' it is apparent, on a little reflection, that this question is itself as intelligible, as the original question 'Is A good?'—that we are, in fact, now asking for exactly the same information about the desire to desire A, for which we formerly asked with regard to A itself. But it is also apparent that the meaning of this second question cannot be correctly analysed into 'Is the desire to desire A one of the things which we desire to desire?': we have not before our minds anything so complicated as the question 'Do we desire to desire to desire to desire A?' Moreover any one can easily convince himself by inspection that the predicate of this proposition—'good'—is positively different from the notion of 'desiring to desire' which enters into its subject: 'That we should desire to desire A is good' is *not* merely equivalent to 'That A should be good is good.' It may indeed be true that what we desire to desire is always also good; perhaps, even the converse may be true: but it is very doubtful whether this is the case, and the mere fact that we understand very well what is meant by doubting it, shews clearly that we have two different notions before our minds.

(2) And the same consideration is sufficient to dismiss the hypothesis that 'good' has no meaning whatsoever. It is very natural to make the mistake of supposing that what is universally true is of such a nature that its negation would be self-contradictory: the importance which has been assigned to analytic propositions in the history of philosophy shews how easy such a mistake is. And thus it is very easy to conclude that what seems to be a universal ethical principle is in fact an identical proposition; that, if, for example, whatever is called 'good' seems to be pleasant, the proposition 'Pleasure is the good' does not assert a connection between two different notions, but involves only one, that of pleasure, which is easily recognised as a distinct entity. But whoever will attentively consider with himself what is actually before his mind when he asks the question 'Is pleasure (or whatever it may be) after all good?' can easily satisfy himself that he is not merely wondering whether pleasure is pleasant. And if he will try this experiment with each suggested definition in succession, he may become expert enough to recognise that in every case he has before his mind a unique object, with regard to the connection of which with any other object, a distinct question may be asked. Every one does in fact understand the question 'Is this good?' When he thinks of it, his state of mind is different from what it would be, were he asked 'Is this pleasant, or desired, or approved?' It has a distinct meaning for him, even though he may not recognise in what respect it is distinct. Whenever he thinks of 'intrinsic value,' or 'intrinsic worth,' or says that a thing 'ought to exist,' he has before his mind the unique object—the unique property of things—which I mean by 'good.' Everybody is constantly aware of this notion, although he may never become aware at all that it is different from other notions of which he is also aware. But, for correct ethical reasoning, it is extremely important that he should become aware of this fact; and, as soon as the nature of the problem is clearly understood, there should be little difficulty in advancing so far in analysis.

HEDONISM

. . . 'No one,' says Prof. Sidgwick, 'would consider it rational to aim at the production of beauty in external nature, apart from any possible contemplation of it by human beings.' Well, I may say at once, that I, for one, do consider this rational; and let us see if I cannot get any one to agree with me. Consider what this admission really means. It entitles us to put the following case. Let us imagine one world exceedingly beautiful.

Imagine it as beautiful as you can; put into it whatever on this earth you most admire—mountains, rivers, the sea; trees, and sunsets, stars and moon. Imagine these all combined in the most exquisite proportions, so that no one thing jars against another, but each contributes to increase the beauty of the whole. And then imagine the ugliest world you can possibly conceive. Imagine it simply one heap of filth, containing everything that is most disgusting to us, for whatever reason, and the whole, as far as may be, without one redeeming feature. Such a pair of worlds we are entitled to compare: they fall within Prof. Sidgwick's meaning, and the comparison is highly relevant to it. The only thing we are not entitled to imagine is that any human being ever has or ever, by any possibility, *can,* live in either, can ever see and enjoy the beauty of the one or hate the foulness of the other. Well, even so, supposing them quite apart from any possible contemplation by human beings; still, is it irrational to hold that it is better that the beautiful world should exist, than the one which is ugly? Would it not be well, in any case, to do what we could to produce it rather than the other? Certainly I cannot help thinking that it would; and I hope that some may agree with me in this extreme instance. The instance is extreme. It is highly improbable, not to say, impossible, we should ever have such a choice before us. In any actual choice we should have to consider the possible effects of our action upon conscious beings, and among these possible effects there are always some, I think, which ought to be preferred to the existence of mere beauty. But this only means that in our present state, in which but a very small portion of the good is attainable, the pursuit of beauty for its own sake must always be postponed to the pursuit of some greater good, which is equally attainable. But it is enough for my purpose, if it be admitted that, *supposing* no greater good were at all attainable, then beauty must in itself be regarded as a greater good than ugliness; if it be admitted that, in that case, we should not be left without any reason for preferring one course of action to another, we should not be left without any duty whatever, but that it would then be our positive duty to make the world more beautiful, so far as we were able, since nothing better than beauty could then result from our efforts. If this be once admitted, if in any imaginable case you do admit that the existence of a more beautiful thing is better in itself than that of one more ugly, quite apart from its effects on any human feeling, then Prof. Sidgwick's principle has broken down. Then we shall have to include in our ultimate end something beyond the limits of human existence. I admit, of course, that our beautiful world would be better still, if there were human beings in it to contemplate and enjoy its beauty. But that admission makes nothing against my point. If it be once admitted that the beautiful world *in itself* is better than the ugly, then it follows, that however many beings may enjoy it, and however much better their enjoyment may be than it is in itself, yet its mere existence adds *something* to the goodness of the whole: it is not only a means to our end, but also itself a part thereof.

ETHICS IN RELATION TO CONDUCT

88. . . . I propose, first, to deal with the *third* kind of ethical question—the question: What ought we to do?

The answering of this question constitutes the third great division of ethical inquiry; and its nature was briefly explained in Chap. I. (§§15–17). It introduces into Ethics, as was there pointed out, an entirely new question—the question what things are related as *causes* to that which is good in itself; and this question can only be answered by an entirely new method—the method of empirical investigation; by means of which causes are discovered in the other sciences. To ask what kind of actions we ought to perform, or what kind of conduct is right, is to ask what kind of effects such action and conduct will produce. Not a single question in practical Ethics can be answered except by a causal generalisation. All such questions do, indeed, *also* involve an ethical judgment proper—the judgment that certain effects are better, in themselves, than others. But they *do* assert that these better things are effects—are causally connected with the actions in question. Every judgment in practical Ethics may be reduced to the form: This is a cause of that good thing.

89. That this is the case, that the questions, What is right? what is my duty? what ought I to do? belong exclusively to this third branch of ethical enquiry, is the first point to which I wish to call attention. All moral laws, I wish to shew, are merely statements that certain kinds of actions will have good effects. The very opposite of this view has been generally prevalent in Ethics. 'The right' and 'the useful' have been supposed to be at least *capable* of conflicting with one another, and, at all events, to be essentially distinct. It has been characteristic of a certain school of moralists, as of moral common sense, to declare that the end will never justify the means. What I wish to point out is that 'right' does and can mean nothing but 'cause of a good result,' and is thus identical with 'useful'; whence it follows that the end always will justify the means, and that no action which is not justified by its results can be right. That there may be a true proposition, meant to be conveyed by

the assertion 'The end will not justify the means,' I fully admit: but that, in another sense, and a sense far more fundamental for ethical theory, it is utterly false, must first be shewn.

That the assertion 'I am morally bound to perform this action' is identical with the assertion 'This action will produce the greatest possible amount of good in the Universe' has already been briefly shewn in Chap I. (§ 17); but it is important to insist that this fundamental point is demonstrably certain. This may, perhaps, be best made evident in the following way. It is plain that when we assert that a certain action is our absolute duty, we are asserting that the performance of that action at that time is unique in respect of value. But no dutiful action can possibly have unique value in the sense that it is the sole thing of value in the world; since, in that case, *every* such action would be the *sole* good thing, which is a manifest contradition. And for the same reason its value cannot be unique in the sense that it has more intrinsic value than anything else in the world; since *every* act of duty would then be the *best* thing in the world, which is also a contradiction. It can, therefore, be unique only in the sense that the whole world will be better, if it be performed, than if any possible alternative were taken. And the question whether this is so cannot possibly depend solely on the question of its own intrinsic value. For any action will also have effects different from those of any other action; and if any of these have intrinsic value, their value is exactly as relevant to the total goodness of the Universe as that of their cause. It is, in fact, evident that, however valuable an action may be in itself, yet, owing to its existence, the sum of good in the Universe may conceivably be made less than if some other action, less valuable in itself, had been performed. But to say that this is the case is to say that it would have been better that the action should not have been done; and this again is obviously equivalent to the statement that it ought not to have been done—that it was not what duty required. 'Fiat iustitia, ruat caelum' can only be justified on the ground that by the doing of justice the Universe gains more than it loses by the falling of the heavens. It is, of course, possible that this is the case: but, at all events, to assert that justice *is* a duty, in spite of such consequences, is to assert that it is the case.

Our 'duty,' therefore, can only be defined as that action, which will cause more good to exist in the Universe than any possible alternative. And what is 'right' or 'morally permissible' only differs from this, as what will *not* cause *less* good than any possible alternative. When, therefore, Ethics presumes to assert that certain ways of acting are 'duties' it presumes to assert that to act in those ways will always produce the greatest possible sum of good. If we are told that to 'do no murder' is a duty, we are told that the action, whatever it may be, which is called murder, will under no circumstances cause so much good to exist in the Universe as its avoidance.

90. But, if this be recognised, several most important consequences follow, with regard to the relation of Ethics to conduct.

(1) It is plain that no moral law is self-evident, as has commonly been held by the Intuitional school of moralists. The Intuitional view of Ethics consists in the supposition that certain rules, stating that certain actions are always to be done or to be omitted, may be taken as self-evident premisses. I have shewn with regard to judgments of what is *good in itself,* that this is the case; no reason can be given for them. But it is the essence of Intuitionism to suppose that rules of action—statements not of what ought to *be,* but of what we ought to do—are in the same sense intuitively certain. Plausibility has been lent to this view by the fact that we do undoubtedly make immediate judgments that certain actions are obligatory or wrong: we are thus often intuitively certain of our duty, in *a psychological sense.* But, nevertheless, these judgments are not self-evident and cannot be taken as ethical premises since, as has now been shewn, they are capable of being confirmed or refuted by an investigation of causes and effects. It is, indeed, possible that some of our immediate intuitions are true; but since *what* we intuit, *what* conscience tells us, is that certain actions will always produce the greatest sum of good possible under the circumstances, it is plain that reasons can be given, which will shew the deliverances of conscience to be true or false.

91. (2) In order to shew that any action is a duty, it is necessary to know both what are the other conditions, which will, conjointly with it, determine its effects; to know exactly what will be the effects of these conditions; and to know all the events which will be in any way affected by our action throughout an infinite future. We must have all this causal knowledge, and further we must know accurately the degree of value both of the action itself and of all these effects; and must be able to determine how, in conjunction with the other things in the Universe, they will affect its value as an organic whole. And not only this: we must also possess all this knowledge with regard to the effects of every possible alternative; and must then be able to see by comparison that the total value due to the existence of the action in question will be greater than that which would be produced by any of these alternatives. But it

is obvious that our causal knowledge alone is far too incomplete for us ever to assure ourselves of this result. Accordingly it follows that we never have any reason to suppose that an action is our duty: we can never be sure that any action will produce the greatest value possible.

Ethics, therefore, is quite unable to give us a list of duties: but there still remains a humbler task which may be possible for Practical Ethics. Although we cannot hope to discover which, in a given situation, is the best of all possible alternative actions, there may be some possibility of shewing which among the alternatives, *likely to occur to any one,* will produce the greatest sum of good. This second task is certainly all that Ethics can ever have accomplished: and it is certainly all that it has ever collected materials for proving; since no one has ever attempted to exhaust the possible alternative actions in any particular case. Ethical philosophers have in fact confined their attention to a very limited class of actions, which have been selected because they are those which most commonly occur to mankind as possible alternatives. With regard to these they may possibly have shewn that one alternative is better, *i.e.* produces a greater total of value, than others. But it seems desirable to insist, that though they have represented this result as a determination of *duties,* it can never really have been so. For the term duty is certainly so used that, if we are subsequently persuaded that any possible action would have produced more good than the one we adopted, we admit that we failed to do our duty. It will, however, be a useful task if Ethics can determine which among alternatives *likely to occur* will produce the greatest total value. For, though this alternative cannot be proved to be the best possible, yet it may be better than any course of action which we should otherwise adopt.

Bernard Bosanquet

The Teleology of Finite Consciousness—A Sub-Form of Individuality *

2. We are familiar in every-day life with the distinction of "end and means." It embodies a rough discrimination of values, relative to current practice. We care for some things for their own sake, for others because they help us to the former. The former, then, serve to explain the valuation or the acquisition of the latter, and themselves need no defence nor explanation. *Prima facie,* the former come last in time, and the latter, the "means," come before them as conditions precedent of their being attained. "Means" presuppose a degree of impotence. They are *ex hypothesi* not what we want. We take them because, with the resources open to us, we can get what we want, the "end," in no other way. Thus it is the very essence of an "end" to be partial within a whole, though it may be the completion of a part, and to be selected in contrast to something else, and, *prima facie,* to events preceding it in time. Aristotle,[1] indeed, whom in this our argument follows, understands by "end" at once the completion of a positive whole which is developing through a process, and the cessation of the process itself. In modern theory the positive whole tends to drop out. The *prima facie* meaning, based on the current modern usage of "end," has gained the day.

There are indeed facts, in general conformity with Aristotle's view, which might make us pause before treating this temporal and selective character—this essential contrast with a past process and with means—as typical and universal. In many cases of choice it is obvious that consequences have to be discounted on the same footing as means. Our "end,"

* From *The Principle of Individuality and Value* by Bernard Bosanquet, pp. 123–132, 135–138.

[1] Cf. Burnet, Aristotle's *Ethics,* xlvi., with Stout's *Groundwork of Psychology,* p. 21. The modern view makes more of the cessation than of the positive completion. I am referring more especially to the doctrine of vital series.

in the sense of that which we aim at, may come first, or in the middle; and the price to be paid for it, the cost of the means, may extend before and after and all round it. We can seldom, in common life, discharge the whole cost before delivery. Thus, at least the temporal distinction between end and means loses its sharpness. Our view of the end is always qualified by the means, and the means, for computation, include the consequences, or, more largely, the price to be paid. Attainment and conclusion cease to be the same idea; and we become aware that in the whole train of occurrences there is nothing which may not partake of the character of an end[2] or desirable object.

In ordinary life, we continually experience this blending of end and means—the desired object and its price—and when we approach philosophical reflection it is a fact that starts up into importance. We soon come to recognise that what we have called an end, as if it were a goal and a stopping-place, is in reality "not a point, but a line," or even a solid; that it tends to expand itself, irregularly, over the whole process of our activity. When, for example, we are dealing with a total system, whether of life or of nature, how are we to discriminate between end and means? We begin with two natural prejudices, the anthropocentric and the temporal, borrowed from our every-day selective practice, and from our primary association of accomplishment and cessation. But neither will stand a moment's reflection. Why should man be the end? And indeed, is there anything to suggest that he is so? Why again assign pre-eminent value to a

> . . . . . . far off divine event
> To which the whole creation moves?

It is obvious that no such ascription of ultimate value to a particular class of creatures nor to a particular moment in time can be justified as an ultimate conception. It rests on the analogy of the choice of a finite being, compelled, because finite, to exercise selection within the universe. It is an attempt to apply the principle of subordination of means to ends to a system within which we can recognise no necessity, and can conceive no clue, for the distinct being of ends or of means. A finite being selects a possible value, and out of the resources which he can find in his world

[2] So in the modern conation theory, the pleasure and the end are found to fall apart (Stout, *Analytic Psychology,* ii. 273), and the value comes rather to be in the pleasure than in the end = *terminus ad quem;* i.e. the two characters of value and terminus are dissociated—the one is a concomitant of the whole process, the other is only its close. The same is true of the account of the higher desires which Plato employs; the pleasure is not merely in the satiety of the terminus; it is a character of the whole activity.

further selects the instruments by help of which he proposes to make it actual. But we cannot conceive that a perfect reality is divided into ends which have value, and means which a limitation of resources compels to be employed to realise them. Such a conception is drawn from the analogy of a finite contriver.

Thus the principle of Teleology when applied to cosmic theory,[3] loses at once and completely all assistance from the ordinary distinctions of means and ends, and from the presumption of a coincidence between termination and attainment. If it is to retain a meaning, it must abandon the whole analogy of finite contrivance and selection, and must fall back on the characteristics of value which, apart from sequence in time and from selected purposes, attach to the nature of a totality which is perfection. In this transition, the principle of purposiveness, of a nature imperative on every element of a whole, expands into the principle of Individuality, or positive non-contradiction. In working with it, we substitute the idea of perfection or the whole—a logical or metaphysical, non-temporal, and religious idea—for that of *de facto* purpose—a psychological, temporal, and ethical idea. We deal with a substantive criterion of value applicable to every detail of a totality, and equally valid if Time is treated as an appearance. The criterion can deal with purposes, but mere *de facto* purposiveness can neither impeach nor support the criterion. In short, a purpose as such—a *de facto* want or desire—only contributes to intelligibility by serving as a reason for its means. For itself, as a mere purpose, it can never exhibit a justification. Every purpose, no doubt, implies a subjective value, but there is no reason why every true value should be a purpose. In extending the idea of teleology to the universe as a whole we are turning from the question whether this fact or that has the appearance of being contrived for a purpose, to the question whether the totality—contrivance or no contrivance, and without any suggestion of dividing it into part which is means and part which is the end—can be apprehended or conceived as satisfactory, *i.e.* as a supreme value.

The theoretical importance of the transition is this, that the selective conations of finite minds cannot, in face of such a principle, claim a fundamental position as the source of order and value. And this applies to the mind of a finite god, if such a being is to be treated as conceivable. The finite consciousness is to be considered as creative and as possessing initiative in a sense which we shall attempt to explain; but the principles

[3] "Parlar di fine, a proposito dell' universo, è adoperar la parola fine in un significato che non è più quello che le conosciamo."—Varisco, *I Massimi Problemi,* p. 218.

of the universe are thought of as deeper laid than in the choices of finite mind. Minds, as we are aware of them, fall into place rather as an imperfect medium and manifestation of the reality than as an ultimate and sovereign source of it.

3. Along with the idea that the true sense of value in the universe is of a teleological type, we find the idea that the true nature of mental process is conative.[4] And in a certain restricted sense both one and the other doctrine may be sustained, but in the latter case as in the former it is important to note the precise implication.

In the typical conation the important points are the beginning and the close. The beginning is a disturbance, and the close or end is a recovery of equilibrium. As we saw above, in elementary notions of teleology which are drawn in fact from the simplest conative experience, the purpose and the close are one, and the end coincides with both.[5] The recovery of equilibrium means satiety, and this is one with the cessation of the conative process. This is the account of ordinary desire and its satisfaction which Plato on the whole accepted, and it is retained in outline by the modern theory of conation as a "vital series."

But the latent opposition between the two conceptions of the end reveals itself within the pleasure-theory which is continuous from Plato to Aristotle. The "end" for Aristotle's theory was not merely satiety but satisfaction; and satisfactoriness, the power of giving satisfaction, was a positive characteristic, the completeness of a form, and not simply the cessation of a disturbance. It is a twice-told tale how this idea was worked out in the theory of Plato and Aristotle. For our purpose it is enough to repeat that in Aristotle's usage the term "end" is applied to positive maturity as more than the mere cessation of growth which it involves, and to the continuous or perhaps timeless character of the fullest life and fruition, rather than to the completion of any serial process.

Now at bottom fruition is distinct from conation as above described, as Aristotle is at pains to point out in his criticism of anti-Hedonist arguments[6]; and a satisfaction that can be attained and possessed is something other than satiety. Thus the "end" no longer appears as a terminus *ad quem*. It has expanded into something which is either a type of activity independent of and other than conation, or, if it is to be identified with conation, throws a wholly different light, from that by

[4] Cf. Taggart on the full meaning of "Cognition" and "Volition," *Commentary on Hegel's Logic.* sect. 284.

[5] Stout, *Analytic Psychology,* ii. 270; *Groundwork of Psychology,* pp. 21, 25.

[6] *Eth. Nic.* x. iv. I.

which we described it above, upon its nature and the conditions of its value.[7] And so we see in recent pleasure-theory, in spite of the primary doctrine that end and cessation coincide, that the desirable element of a conation, its end in the ethical sense, is taken to lie in its character extending over its process and not in its close or termination.[8] The "End," in the sense of attainment or achievement, expands itself from the idea of a terminus into that of a satisfactory experience which may be taken as including a conative process of a certain type, or as a new independent and perfected self-affirmation following upon the completion of the changes which form the conation. The distinction made familiar by Kant between sensuous desire and aesthetic interest is typical for this difference, which lies at the root of the expansion above referred to as recognised and emphasised by Aritostle in dealing with Plato's theory of pleasure. In sensuous desire and its satisfaction you have a transition followed by satiety; and that is the typical conation with its "end." In aesthetic enjoyment or any other true fruition, you have a response from an object in which the self is at home, and you have not, in principle and in the main, any transition nor any satiety.[9] It may be argued that in the higher fruition as in common desire you have really a conative transition, and that the inexhaustible possibilities of the object are in fact what produce the appearance of an achieved and persistent satisfaction. We may agree that this is an element in the case; but still there seems an unmistakable difference of principle. In the process of a finite mind, no doubt, there will always be succession and transition, but in aesthetic enjoyment, for example, it is not the transition towards an unattained terminus that makes the essence of the activity.[10] The mind's direction in it is outward, not onward; and one moment of it, as Aristotle urges, is self-complete and as good as the next. It borrows nothing from an approach to a future completeness. Such a fruition may be understood, as is perhaps the natural

[7] It is clear that for Aristotle πρᾶξις in the full sense and at the highest value—the quintessence of πρᾶξις—is one with the perfect ἐνέργεια. But this does not mean that the full conception of ἐνέργεια can be reduced to that of every-day πρᾶξις.

[8] See reference, p. 125 above.

[9] No doubt, as Aristotle points out, in the fullest fruition a man is liable to fatigue. But this seems to be in principle an incident of our limited strength, and not a sign of true satiety with reference to the object of interest. It should be explained that the aesthetic interest or desire which makes us, *e.g.* go to look at a picture or wish to buy it, does not undo the peculiarity of aesthetic enjoyment in being directed to the pictured semblance of an object, and not to its actual use or possession.

[10] Aristotle's counter-attack, alleging that self-complete activity or fruition is really the enjoyable part in all conation whatever, even in the painful pleasures, so that conation would not be in any degree the condition of value or pleasure, may be thought to prove too much, and to correct one mistake by another. The view taken in the text avoids this danger (see *Ethics,* vii. 12. 2 and 14. 7).

way of understanding it, to be as it were the protracted terminus of a conation, like eternity coming after time; or may be treated as throwing a light on the true nature and value of conation itself.[11] In either case, it is something different in principle from the conation whose beginning is disturbance and whose end is satiety.

And the importance of this is that the nature of conation itself has led us back to our old conclusion; and we see again that the true "end" or value does not lie in this special relation to a terminus or finite purpose, but in a character of perfection, which may in finite experience be relatively present throughout a process, or as a persistent result of it, or at the beginning of it, or in the middle. I repeat, in the simplest case of conation satiety and satisfaction coincide. But if end is to mean a value, satisfaction must be more than satiety. And the idea of conation must be remodelled to meet this necessity, as the modern pleasure-theory, when it lays stress on positive interest within the conation in contrast to mere escape from tension or disturbance, in some degree recognises.[12]

It seems to be the case that in finite life conation and fruition coincide in different degrees, from a conation which is principally valued as a release from pain to one which is practically indistinguishable from pure positive enjoyment of self-affirmation, in which if there is essentially conation at all, it is wholly latent.[13] Between these two extremes there are all sorts of intermediate cases. But the point for us at present is simply the expansion of the idea of end into a connection with fruition and value, and into throwing off all special connection with the ideas of termination as against a process, and superordination as against means. . . .

5. I will insist on this point again. We have seen, I think, that Teleology is an unlucky term.[14] In the sense of aiming at the unfulfilled it gives an unreal importance to time, and to the part of any whole—it may be a relatively trivial part—which happens to come last in succession. Of the two implications of the term—"end"—completeness and conclusion —the latter, which is an accessory, usurps precedence over the former which is fundamental. But in truth its significance does not depend on what comes first or last, but what there is in the individual real when it is

[11] See above, p. 483 and following note.

[12] Stout, *Analytic Psychology,* ii. 280: "The analogy of a bent spring is not in point." *Groundwork of Psychology,* p. 24. The effect is that pleasures and pains depend on characters of the progress of a conation, not on its completion.

[13] The question is akin to the problem whether feeling involves conation. See Stout, *Groundwork,* pp. 24, 25, and Bradley, *Mind,* n.s. xl. p. 449. There is, of course, a wide gap between the simplest effortless enjoyments and the highest persistent satisfaction (say, aesthetic). But the relation of the two to conation seems analogous.

[14] Cf. McTaggart, *l.c.*

apprehended in its completeness. Action is not truly teleological [15] because in the time-process some deferred element of some subordinate quasi-totality is in it being carried out by means of a finite desire. The "end," in this sense, would not necessarily have teleological [16] value, and if it had it in some degree, would not necessarily be a leading constituent of it. The true question of value would be independent of temporal relations, and would depend on the structure and significance of the whole in course of completion; that is, on its character of individuality, or nearness to the ultimate whole. The great enemy of all sane idealism is the notion that the ideal belongs to the future. The ideal is what we can see in the light of the whole, and the way in which it shapes the future for us is only an incident—and never the most important incident—of our reading of past, present, and future in their unity. Thus when "end" or "purposiveness" or "teleology" merely indicates the fact that some finite consciousness is urged by some pleasurable impulse or by some unfulfilled idea, there is in this, apart from the content of the idea, nothing specially sacred or significant.[17] It is vain to look to the bare fact of conscious purpose or impulse for the essence or significance of teleology. Purpose only means, *prima facie,* that, using consciousness in the very widest sense, some creature consciously wants something. But, omitting all the very serious difficulties connected with criticism of the value of the purpose, does the something lose its value when it is attained? Does everything, then, not merely exhibit its value, real or fancied, in being wanted, but derive its value from being wanted? Are fruition or perfection really the death of value?

Are the ideas of positive fulfilment and satisfaction, of a being which is good in itself, and above the alternations of want and satiety, mere chimeras? If this is so, then there is no Absolute, or, if we appeal to finite experience alone, the character of the Absolute wholly fails to suggest itself in or through the experiences of our lives. But, as I have attempted to show, such a conclusion would be flatly in the face both of fact and of theory. No doubt our wants play a part in the ultimate whole, but it is plain that as given they cannot conceivably be a measure of value. We cannot think of an intuitive intelligence itself as creating

[15] Assuming "teleological" to imply something valuable and desirable, in harmony with the universe as most perfectly experienced.

[16] Refer to previous footnote.

[17] It is all very well to speak, *e.g.* of pleasure as a guide to fulness of life; but facts of natural selection and of anti-Hedonism (I do not mean in philosophical theory but in the temper and deliberate conduct of mankind) show plainly that the *prima facie* case is as strong against its guidance as for it. "If your pleasures are right, you survive" is only the correlative of "If they are wrong you perish."

values out of all relation to a whole with determinate content. It, the supreme experience, whatever name we may give it, must be one with its world and not a creator out of nothing.[18]

Things are not teleological because they are purposed, but are purposed because they are teleological.[19] Thus, when we speak of the ultimate real as an individual or as teleological it is hazardous to say that purpose, in the sense of a craving unfulfilled in time, can play any part in our conception. Teleology which depends on a feature of the time-process is not a teleology which any one but a pragmatist can affirm of ultimate reality; and the lesson thus suggested is only enforced when we come to ask ourselves what is the true test, even for organic evolution, for social progress, or for morals, of the purposiveness of a purpose. Subjective selection is very poor work, except in as far as it becomes more than subjective. Objectiveness of selection, the selection of values which will stand criticism, is the test of true "teleology" or purposiveness.

[18] See Bergson on the "néant" as the chimera of a possible alternative to all positive worlds (*Évolution créatrice,* iv.).

[19] In the sense explained in footnote on previous page.

Ralph Barton Perry

The Definition of Value in Terms of Interest *

One can generally tell a man's special field of investigation by the words he uses carefully and the words he uses carelessly. The physicist now uses the word 'atom' carefully; that is, he is prepared to say what he means by it. The geneticist is careful with such words as 'heredity' and 'environment'; the theologian with the word 'god'; the logician with 'proposition' and 'implication'; the mathematician with the word 'number'; the economist with the words 'price' and 'demand'; the political scientist with the word 'sovereignty.' Everyone except the specialist uses these words carelessly. The philosopher who is engaged in that branch of philosophy now known as "theory of value" is distinguished by the fact that the word which he is most careful about is the word 'value.'

Everyone else uses this word carelessly. There is a usage of common sense, as when it is said that men lose sight of "higher values" when they practice power politics, or lose sight of "values" altogether in the machine age; or when it is said that it is the task of a humanistic education to make students aware of the "values" of life. 'Value' is now a favorite word among the sociologists, psychologists, and psychiatrists. The word is scattered through the text, and even mentioned in the index; but it is used like 'and,' 'but,' and the nouns and adjectives of everyday speech, as though its meaning were so well understood as to require no examination. The theorist of value, on the other hand, is one who asks, of himself and of others, "Precisely what is meant by 'value'?" It is his business to have an answer to that question. In other words, 'value' is his *careful* word.

The question, "What does 'value' mean?" is not the same as the ques-

* Reprinted by permission of the publishers from *Realms of Value* by Ralph Barton Perry. Cambridge, Mass.: Harvard University Press, pp. 1–14.

tion, "What things have value?" Though the two questions are often confused, the difference is evident when attention is called to it. The statement that "a sphere is a body of space bounded by one surface all points of which are equally distance from a point within called its center" is different from the statement that "the earth is (or is not) a sphere." The statement that peace is a condition in which societies abstain from the use of violence in settling their disputes, is different from the statement that the world is (or is not) now at peace. And similarly, a statement, such as is proposed below, of what value is, differs from the statement that peace is valuable.

If the second of each of these pairs of statements is to be definitive and accurate it is clearly advisable to have in mind the first. If, in other words, one is to know whether peace is or is not valuable, it is well to know what 'valuable' is: in other words, to know what it is that is stated about peace when it is stated that it is valuable. But while the question raised by the second statement depends on an answer to the question raised by the first, the two questions are not the same question. And it is the first question with which the present inquiry is primarily concerned. In other words, theory of value ascribes value to things only in the light of what 'value' means.

Some philosophers, unfortunately, put the question concerning value in the form "What *is* meant by 'value'?" or "What *does* one mean by 'value'?" as though that meaning were already determined, and it was only necessary to call attention to it. Those who approach the matter in this way are accustomed to challenge a proposed definition of value by saying, "But this is not what is meant by 'value' " or "This is not what one means by 'value.' " The fact is, however, that there is no such established and universal meaning. Different people mean different things in different contexts. The problem is not to discover a present meaning—there are only too many meanings.

The problem is not solved, however, by simply enumerating these many meanings. This job is already done by the unabridged dictionaries which list, in fine print, all the varieties of meaning which appear in literature and ordinary speech. Theory of value is in search of a preferred meaning. The problem is to define, that is, *give* a meaning to the term, either by selecting from its existing meanings, or by creating a new meaning.

But one must not then leap to the conclusion that this giving of a meaning to the term 'value' is an arbitrary matter, dictated by the caprice, or mere personal convenience, of the author. One can, it is true, make the term mean "anything one likes," but this would not advance knowledge, or be of the slightest importance, or be capable either of proof or of disproof. The man who said "When I say 'value' I mean a purple cow" would not even be listened to, unless by a psychiatrist or a kindergarten teacher. There must, in other words, be a control or set of criteria, by which the definition is justified or rejected.

According to the definition of value here proposed, *a thing—any thing—has value, or is valuable, in the original and generic sense when it is the object of an interest—any interest.* Or, *whatever is object of interest is ipso facto valuable.* Thus the valuableness of peace is the characteristic conferred on peace by the interest which is taken in it, for what it is, or for any of its attributes, effects, or implications.

Value is thus defined in terms of interest, and its meaning thus depends on another definition, namely, a definition of interest. The following is here proposed: interest is *a train of events determined by expectation of its outcome.* Or, *a thing is an object of interest when its being expected induces actions looking to its realization or non-realization.* Thus peace is an object of interest when acts believed to be conducive to peace, or preventive of peace, are performed on that account, or when events are selected or rejected because peace is expected of them.

Both of these definitions require clarification and elaboration; but these summary statements will suffice for the present purpose of indicating the criterion by which the definitions are to be justified. These criteria are three in number, namely, *linguistic, formal,* and *empirical.* When the definition is challenged it must defend itself on three grounds: its use of words; the clarity, definiteness, tenability, and fruitfulness of the concepts which it employs; and its capacity to describe certain facts of life, to which it refers, and by which it is verified. The definition is designed, in other words, to be at one and the same time, a nominal definition, an abstract or *a priori* definition, and a "real" definition.

2

In the first place, then, definition names, or affixes a verbal label; and in thus creating a verbal usage it has to take account of existing verbal usage. The fundamental purpose of naming is "ostensive"; that is to say, it identifies some object (thing, quality, act, relation, region, event) so that it may be subsequently recovered, and referred to in communication with others. It serves the purpose of directing the attention of several minds, or of the same mind at different times, to the same locus in the mind's environment.

Pure naming is conventional, that is, no account need be taken of any antecedent ostensive meaning, but only of brevity, euphony, and duplication. But naming is rarely, if ever, pure. In order that it should be pure the name would have to be new, that is, an arbitrary symbol invented on the spot. Verbal names, however, are usually secondhand; that is, the name has an antecedent usage, which renders its present usage appropriate or inappropriate. Even proper names, such as 'Rose' and 'Violet,' are commonly secondhand names. It is true that their use as proper names may become wholly, or almost wholly, divested of their original meanings; so that it would be absurd to dispute their application to a given person on the ground that she was in fact not rose or violet in color, but white or brown. But there is nevertheless a suggestion of flowerlike fragility which would render it inappropriate to give the name of 'Rose' or 'Violet,' except in an ironic sense, to a heavyweight prize fighter. Place names—of mountains, rivers, cities, and countries—arise from mixed motives. They are not merely labels by which the place is marked on the map for future reference, but like 'Rocky Mountains,' ascribe to it the characteristics already designated by some common name; or, like 'America,' they say something about its history by borrowing the antecedent name of its supposed discoverer.

The words 'value' and 'interest' which are used in the present definition are secondhand names. Although they are here given a sharper meaning, to be consistently maintained, their appropriateness must be judged by their history and suggestiveness. In the light of existing usage do they serve well as pointers to focus the discussion on a certain region of inquiry?

In the present writer's early Harvard days the word 'value' was first beginning to become current in American philosophy, largely through the influence of Hugo Münsterberg, who, in addition to being a psychologist, was also a follower of the neo-Fichtean school of Windelband and Rickert. In fact, since Münsterberg learned to speak English fluently before he learned to pronounce it correctly, his students heard of "walues" before they heard of "values." Münsterberg would be scandalized by the liberties which have been taken with the word since his day. For with Münsterberg and his school, "values" possessed an exalted dignity transcending both nature and sense-perception. They have since become completely secularized, mingling with the affairs of everyday life, and consorting intimately with the vulgar facts of sense-experience. They have even been desecrated by psychologists, in violation of that *Anti-Psychologismus* which was once with German philosophers a sort of Oath of Hippocrates.

Before the word 'value' could acquire that generality of meaning required for a philosophical theory of value, it was necessary to overrule the economists who had become accustomed to claim its exclusive use. But Adam Smith and John Stuart Mill had distinguished "value in use" from "value in exchange," and, in so using the same word twice, had already broadened its meaning to apply to a field of which economic value was only a circumscribed part.

Since the beginning of the present century, the word 'value' has acquired a popular use which has eclipsed its transcendental use by neo-Fichtean philosophers and its technical use by economists. The conscious employment of propaganda has called attention to the diversity of creeds and codes by which different human societies are governed, and these are frequently referred to as different beliefs concerning what has "value," or "supreme value." At the same time the word 'ideology' has acquired vogue as the name for a set of ideas which concern "values" as distinguished from matters of fact. The signal failure of natural science to save mankind from war and its destructive effects is often attributed to the fact that science ignores "values"; and the world looks to religion or liberal education to restore them.

The word 'value' is, then, a good name, because its history suggests that there is something common to duty and piety, price and utility, ideals and codes. At the same time it points toward that aspect of human life for which it is customary to employ the eulogistic-dyslogistic vocabulary. It points to other pointers, and borrows the ostensive meaning of such adjectives as 'good,' 'best,' 'right,' 'ought,' 'worthy,' 'beautiful,' 'sacred,' 'just,' and such nouns as 'happiness,' 'well-being,' and 'civilization.' As a common name for what these words name, it suggests a common meaning, or the attempt to find a common meaning. Of the words which already have such ostensive meaning, and which will therefore serve as guideposts, 'value' best combines specific reference with breadth and flexibility.

The word 'value' has also a grammatical convenience, in that it possesses substantive, adjectival, and verbal variants. We can speak of "values," of "valuable," and of the act of "valuing." This is, however, a dubious advantage, since it has given rise to serious ambiguities. Thus *a* value, in the substantive sense, may mean either *that which* has value, such as gold or justice; or a *kind* of value which it has, such as economic or moral. These distinctions are analogous to those between the determinable 'color,' the determinant 'red,' and the instance, such as 'the rose.'

'Valuable' like 'value' suffers from the defect that it is sometimes taken to refer only to what is "good," "right," etc., and to exclude the opposites, 'bad,' 'wrong,' etc., which clearly belong to the same field of discourse. There is no way of escaping this difficulty except by the awkward expedient of distinguishing the "positively" and "negatively," or "eulogistically" and "dyslogistically," valuable, thus giving a broader meaning to the unmodified adjective when it refers to both.

Most insidious and disastrous of all is the ambiguity attaching to the verb 'to value,' which may mean *making* valuable, or *judging* to be valuable. Similarly, to "value a thing highly" may mean either to care greatly for it, and thus to *give* it great value, as when one loves money; or it may mean to *ascribe* great value to it in some scale of comparative magnitude, as when one judges money to be more precious than sleep. And sometimes 'to value,' or 'to evaluate,' means to assign value to an object for *reasons,* that is, because it possesses certain characteristics, as when one values money for what it will buy. These differences must not be overlooked as a result of economy of speech.

3

The second of the words employed in the proposed definition of value is the word 'interest.' Here, again, the word selected is an old word, already used as a name, but selected because of all the old words it seems the best word to substitute for a class of words—'liking,' 'desiring,' 'willing,' 'loving,' 'hoping,' etc., and their opposites; and to suggest a common ostensive meaning as distinguished from that of another class of words embracing 'sensing,' 'perceiving,' 'thinking,' 'judging,' etc. If the word is to be used in this sense, however, it is necessary to exclude certain senses which are either too broad or too narrow.

In its broader use 'interest' is a synonym of attention; and the adjective 'interesting' is applied to any object or topic which attracts attention or excites curiosity, such as the sudden, novel, surprising, or contrasting. In this sense, a noise breaking into silence, or one's own name unexpectedly pronounced, immediately draws attention to itself and alerts the hearer. No doubt interest in this sense is commonly associated with feeling, desire, etc., but there is a difference nonetheless between sheer attentiveness—the turn of the head, shift of the eye, or focusing of consciousness—and the liking, desiring, etc., by which this may be conditioned, accompanied, or followed. This broader reference being eliminated, the word 'interest' points to attitudes of *for* and *against,* or what are sometimes called "motor-affective" attitudes, as when one says, "I am interested in the outcome," or "all interested parties should be excluded."

But here we encounter a sense of the word that is excessively narrow, its reference, namely, to self-interest or selfishness, which is a special case of interest. We need a use of the word such that the nurse's interest in her patient's recovery or relief from pain is as much an interest as her interest in gainful employment. The latter, or selfish, meaning is reflected in the use of the word 'disinterestedness' to signify interest directed to others. This word involves a flagrant ambiguity. There is a crucial difference between the absence or subordination of self-interest, and that state of apathy in which there is no interest at all. It is unfortunate that the word 'disinterested,' as when we speak of the disinterested judge, is used to mean breadth and inclusiveness of interest. It would be less misleading to say 'all-interested.'

A second excessively narrow use of the word 'interest' is that in which it refers to the collective, and more or less permanent, interest of a social group, as when one speaks of "the interests of labor" or "the interest of the consumer." The expression '*the* interests,' used in a political context, suggests interest that is both selfish and collective or permanent. But if the word is to be used in these restricted senses, then there is need of another and broader use which makes it possible to speak of interests which are generous, or fleeting and individual.

Despite these ambiguities, the word 'interest' is the least misleading name for a certain class of acts or states which have the common characteristic of *being for or against.* The expressions of 'motor-affective attitudes' or 'attitudes of favor and disfavor' serve as its best paraphrases. 'Caring' and 'concern' are also convenient synonyms. The absence of interest is indifference, as when one says, "It makes no difference to me," "I do not care," or "It is of no concern to me." Indifference is to be distinguished from negative interest. Thus one speaks of not caring, or of its making no difference "one way or the other," implying that interest embraces both ways. It is especially significant to note that the words for which 'interest' is substituted come in pairs of opposites, which are not related simply as grammatical positives and negatives.

'Interest,' then, is to be taken as a class name for such names as 'liking'-'disliking,' 'loving'-'hating,' 'hoping'-'fearing,' 'desiring'-'avoiding,' and countless other kindred names. What they all ostensibly mean is what *it* ostensibly means. It invites attention to that to which they in their severalty and community already invite our attention. It will occasionally, for reasons of diction, be convenient to use some one of these more restricted names to stand for the rest. But if the term 'interest' is used with reasonable consistency to stand for them all then these richer words can be used as names for the different species of the genus which will be introduced in the further elaboration of the subject.

4

Definition does not merely name, it also *conceives.* It fixes upon an intelligible meaning. It may put together old meanings, so as to create new meanings. Although the mind may conceive freely—that is, may conceive or not, and may conceive an infinite variety of abstract or ideal objects—when it does conceive, and whatever it conceives, it is subject to certain requirements which are inherent in the nature of conceiving. These may be referred to as the "formal" requirements of a definition. They are the conditions which a theory must satisfy *qua* theory; that is, in advance of being verified. Are the concepts here employed "intelligible?" How are statements about interest as here conceived to be translated into statements about value? Does such a translation result in contradiction, confusion, and sterility? Is it fruitful and illuminating? Does it violate any fundamental logical or epistemological requirement? But at this point it is appropriate to introduce certain objections which, if val[illegible]uld save the trouble of proceeding further.

It has been objected, in the first place, that all or most of the words of the class here represented by the word 'value' (words such as 'good,' 'bad,' etc.) have *no* conceptual meaning, but only a so-called "emotive" meaning.[1] In other words, statements in which such words appear as predicates are not statements at all, but utterances. They have no objectivity, and are neither true nor false; but merely express the attitude of the person who makes them, and his desire to convert others to the same attitude. They are communicative and persuasive, but they are not cognitive and informative. Thus it is held that the word 'good' in the judgment that "Francis of Assisi was good," refers to no Franciscan characteristic, actual or alleged, but merely reflects the fact that the maker of the judgment esteems Saint Francis, and desires that others shall also esteem him.

[1] Cf. C. L. Stevenson, *Ethics and Language,* 1948, *passim.* Much of the ethical controversy which this book has excited would have been avoided if the book had held strictly to its title. It would then have been treated like a book on "physics and language"—interesting, but not physics.

There is no doubt of the fact that words are commonly used with an expressive, commendatory, or disparaging intent. A love poem or a political diatribe is not the same thing as a mathematical theorem or scientific statement. Words such as 'fascist' and 'red' lose their conceptual meaning and degenerate into smear words; "the land of the free and the home of the brave" may serve only to express and arouse a love of country. Most verbal statements, however, have *both* an objective and an emotive meaning. The mixture of meanings appears in the fact that either of two retorts is appropriate. Thus if a man is called a "red" in a community in which this word is offensive, he may either become angry, or affirm his belief in capitalism. Ordinarily he will do both: that is, angrily affirm his belief in capitalism. If a man is called a "reactionary" he is no doubt condemned; but he is also conceived as wedded to the past. He can defend himself either by retaliating upon his accuser with the word 'radical,' or by pointing to his interest in the future.

A word having only an emotive meaning like the word 'fie!' is the extreme opposite of a word having only a conceptual meaning, like the word 'ellipse.' The great body of human discourse, however, lies between these extremes. If verbal usage were to be so amended as to leave only exclamations, exhortations, compliments, and insults, on the one hand, and rigorous scientific concepts, on the other hand, most persons all of the time, and all persons, including scientists, most of the time, would have to remain mute. Statements which employ such terms as 'good' and 'bad' may, and usually do, convey objectively meaningful concepts, either expressly or by implication. Thus when Saint Francis is judged to be good, the fact that he fed the birds, and thus manifested loving-kindness to living things, is taken as *constituting* his goodness. Or, suppose that *A,* addressing himself to *B,* states that Lincoln was a "good" man *in that* he hated war, felt compassion for soldiers, and emancipated the slaves. *A* is not simply expressing his admiration for the kind of man Lincoln was, and his desire that *B* shall feel likewise. He is identifying the concept of good with the concept of humanity, and ascribing it to Lincoln on the objective evidence of Lincoln's behavior.

The fact is that what force the argument has arises not from the absence of objective conceptual meanings, but from their abundance and variety. The argument reduces, then, to this: that there are no *invariable* objective meanings attaching to such terms as 'good' and 'bad' in common usage. Sometimes they mean one thing, sometimes another. Well, what of it? It is the business of theory of value to define such an invariable meaning. It is unlikely that because the word 'matter' has no common objective meaning as currently used it therefore has only a subjective or social meaning. Similarly, there is not the slightest reason why theory of value should be limited to ready-made meanings; should, in other words, be content to be a contemporary history of ideas, instead of undertaking that systematization of concepts which is the essential task of theory of value, of physical and chemical theory, in short, of all theory.

To reject the extravagances of the emotivist theory does not imply that judgments employing value terms are not peculiarly likely to be imbued with emotive meaning; nor does it forbid the supposition that judgments employing these terms may, in certain contexts, be wholly, or almost wholly expressive and persuasive in their intent.

5

It may be objected, secondly, that while the word 'value' does have an objective, conceptual meaning, that meaning is indefinable. According to one variety of this view, value, or some equivalent, such as good or right, is a specific, irreducible, "non-natural" characteristic.[2] Its being "non-natural" means that it is neither physical nor mental, and therefore cannot be empirically observed. It can, however, so it is alleged, be seen by the eye of the mind, and, when so seen, it is seen to be unique and unanalyzable.

Although volumes have been written for and against this contention, it should require no argument whatever. If unanalyzable value is *there* within the range of intellectual vision, it should be possible, after a reasonable amount of effort, to bring it into focus. He who fails to find it cannot but conclude that there is no such thing; especially when the authors of the doctrine do not agree among themselves on what they find.

According to another variety of the view, value is an indefinable empirical quality, or a class of indefinable qualities such as pleasant, enticing, fascinating, awesome, revolting, etc.[3] These qualities are in some way connected with feelings—either they consist in feeling, or are apprehended through feeling—hence they may be designated "affective qualities." Since, like the "secondary qualities" color and sound, they have a *prima facie* objectivity, they are sometimes called "tertiary qualities."

This is not the place to examine the merits of this view, except as

[2] This is the position taken by G. E. Moore, W. D. Ross and others of the so-called "Cambridge" or "Intuitionist" school.

[3] This view is to be found in G. Santayana, *Sense of Beauty,* 1899; and in J. Laird, *Study in Realism,* 1920.

concerns the question of analyzability. As sensation blends with sensation to create a new quality (such as a fused tone or color), so sensation blended with feeling possesses an integral character which is distinguishable from the characters of its constituents. But this can scarcely be cited as evidence against analyzability since it is a statement of precisely what, in the field of sense-perception, analysis is. The problem presented is the problem presented by all analysis. There is a sense in which nothing is analyzable—namely, if it is assumed that analysis must leave things precisely as it finds them. Analysis here as elsewhere destroys beyond recovery the first blush of the immediately presented. But if all this be true, and if it applies to value, it is already too late to speak of value as unanalyzable or indefinable.[4]

The history of human knowledge creates a presumption against indefinables. At the outset of any inquiry its subject matter is, as yet, undefined; nothing is, as yet, said about it; it possesses the character of a questionable vagueness located in a certain indefinitely bounded quarter of the field. When the definition takes place, this pseudo-simplicity of ignorance is superseded by articulate complexity. There is always something which escapes the final knowledge of a given subject matter, namely, the antecedent phases of ignorance. But to allow this to deter us from definition would be a cognitive defeatism. Self, activity, causality, substance, matter, force, heat, have all appeared in the role of indefinables only to prove definable. The history of thought is strewn with abandoned indefinables; and it seems highly probable that the value-indefinable will shortly come to rest among these relics of man's unfinished business.

There is a further meaning of 'indefinability' which can, for present purposes, be eliminated. Logic and mathematics employ so-called indefinables in a sense which is relative to their own systematic procedures. Certain terms are *taken* as indefinable. The choice of the word 'indefinable' in this sense is unfortunate, since it appears to say that the concepts in question *can* not be defined, when it really means only that they *are* not defined. Their selection as indefinables within the system is quite independent of definable meanings which they may or may not have outside the system.

The final proof that a conceptual definition of value is possible is to provide such a definition. The definition here proposed must satisfy two sets of requirements. In the end it will appear that it must be descriptive, that is, must fit a certain select body of facts. But in advance of this

[4] The Author has discussed this question in "Value as Simply Value," *Journal of Philosophy, 28* (1931), pp. 522–6.

empirical test the definition must satisfy certain formal, that is, logical and epistemological, requirements. These requirements have to do with the *framing* of the theory—with its internal structure. It must be "theoretically" acceptable. The concepts which it employs must not only be clear and intelligible, but must lend themselves to judgments which are capable of systematization and elaboration. More specifically, the present definition must be capable of defending itself against charges of circularity, self-contradiction, and sceptical relativism.

6

The charge that the definition is *circular* consists in pointing out that when a thing is affirmed to be good because it is an object of positive interest, it is always possible to raise the question of the goodness of the interest. Thus it is generally agreed that the goodness of drugs is questionable despite the intense craving of the addict; and it is usually concluded that the drug is bad because the craving is bad. It would seem to follow that in order that a thing shall be good it must be the object of a good interest, in which case 'good' is defined in terms of good.

But this objection loses its force altogether when it is recognized that an interest may itself possess value, positive or negative, by the application of the same definition as that which is applied to its object. While the craving does invest its object with positive value, the craving may be invested with negative value from the standpoint of other interests; and this second value may be considered as overruling the positive value owing to its taking the higher ground of health or morals. The appetitive goodness of the drug does not include or imply the hygienic or moral goodness of the appetite. There are two goods, one of which is, in some sense yet to be examined, superior to the other. In other words, the definition does not state that a thing is good only when it is the object of a good interest, but when it is the object of any interest, good or bad. When the interest is good, its object is thereby enhanced, but there is no circularity.

But in escaping circularity does one not fall into *contradiction?* Is it not contradictory to affirm that the same object is both good and bad? The charge of contradiction is lightly made and, as a rule, superficially examined. The important thing is to discover just what propositions would, and what propositions would not, be contradictory. It is sometimes supposed that the expression 'one man's meat is another man's poison' involves a contradiction. But there would be a contradiction only provided the same proposition was both affirmed and denied. Thus it would be contradictory to say that one man's meat was not that man's meat, or that another man's poison was not his poison. Meat to one man and poison to another are not contradictories, but are two different and consistent propositions.

By a kind of grammatical license the term 'contradiction' is sometimes applied to interests. Strictly speaking, interests do not contradict, but *conflict.* Only propositions contradict. But interests are sometimes allowed to borrow the contradictoriness or consistency of their objects when these are stated as propositions. Thus the interests in preserving and in destroying the life of the same individual are said to be contradictory, because the will of one can be expressed by the resolve "he shall live" and the will of the other by the resolve "he shall not live." But to speak of interests themselves as contradictory is confusing and misleading. Two contradictories cannot both be true, but two conflicting forces can coexist.

To assert of the same object that it is good and that it is bad *seems* to be contradictory, because the two assertions are elliptical, that is, because of the omission of the axis of reference. It may seem to be contradictory to assert of the same body that it is "above" and "below" when one fails to specify *what* it is above and below. Similarly, it seems to be contradictory to say of the same thing that it is both good and bad when one omits to specify the interests from which it derives its goodness and badness. The interests being specified, there is no contradiction whatever in asserting that the same object is practically useful and aesthetically ugly, or that the same act is selfishly beneficent and socially injurious.

But is not contradiction escaped only by falling into *relativism?* Well, if one may be permitted a vulgarism, and so what? The word 'relativism' has a bad sound; even the word 'relativity,' despite its association with the latest physics, conveys a suggestion of philosophical untenability. But suppose that one substitute the more colorless word 'relational' and, instead of rejecting it as a fault, boldly affirm it as a merit; since it provides not only for value, but for ambivalence and multi-valence.

Many of the most familiar characteristics of things are relational. There is no disputing the fact that brother and son are relational characteristics. In other words, when one describes a man as a brother or a son, one states his relation to another human being. For any man, there is someone to whom he is related: "God gives us relations." So, according to the theory here proposed, when one describes a thing as good or bad one describes it in terms of its relation, direct or indirect, to a second thing, namely, an interest.

This, be it noted, is not the same as to say that one value is definable only by its relation to another *value,* which may or may not be the case. There is nothing in the relational view which forbids a thing's being conceived as absolutely valuable; that is, valuable regardless of the value of anything else.

There is only one kind of relativism which is epistemologically objectionable, and which is commonly known as "vicious relativism." The viciousness lies in its scepticism. It consists in the doctrine that all statements are elliptical unless they are introduced by the words "it seems to me at this moment." Were this the case I should not even be stating what I am saying now. I should say, "it seems to me that it seems to me that it seems to me," etc. *ad infinitum;* in which case I would never get to *what* seems to me, and I might as well have saved myself the trouble of making any statement at all.

Suffice it to say that the theory of value here proposed is no more relativistic in this vicious sense than any other theory, whether of value or of any other matter. The supposition that a relational theory of value is peculiarly vicious in its relativism rests on a confusion. It is mistakenly supposed that because objects derive their value, positive and negative, from interest it is implied that the interest from which they derive value is the interest of the knower or judge. This would mean that if I am to judge that an object possesses positive value to me *I* must like, desire, will, or love it. When, however, value is defined in terms of interest, then *any* interest will satisfy the definition; and if I observe that anyone else likes, desires, loves or wills a thing, then I am bound by the definition to judge it good. The evidence of its goodness or badness is the observable fact of interest, which is just as objective, and just as open to agreement, as any other fact of life or history.

7

The present definition of value is proposed not only as a nominal and conceptual, but as a "real" or "descriptive," definition.[5] Its justification requires that the names which it employs shall be well selected in the light of verbal usage; and that its concepts shall yield judgments which are free from circularity, contradiction, and sceptical relativism. But these are only preliminary considerations. A descriptive definition, in

[5] Cf. S. C. Pepper, "The Descriptive Definition," *Journal of Philosophy, 43* (1946); A. Kaplan, "Definition and Specification of Meaning," *ibid., 43* (1946); M. Weitz, "Analysis and Real Definition," *Philosophical Studies, 1* (1950).

short, is an hypothesis. Its crucial test is its bringing to light the systematic structure of some realm of fact—some state of affairs *of* which it is true. As will appear more clearly in the sequel, this does not imply any fundamental antithesis between the descriptive and the normative, but rather that norms themselves are also describable.

As here conceived, theory of value refers to a peculiarly pervasive feature of human existence and history, namely, the emergence of interests having objects; in which interests combine, wax, wane, and disappear; in which certain things are qualified to become objects of interests; and in which there are things and events which promote or defeat objects of interest. It does not deal, except for purposes of illustration, with particular historic societies and epochs, but with general types and structures of interest.

But while the field of personal and social events, like that of physical events, is inexhaustible, it is proper to select major events, or certain human enterprises and pursuits that have a claim to special attention because of their universality or importance. Referring to these as "pursuits," "enterprises," or "institutions," one may then test the theory by its providing a systematic description of morality, conscience, politics, law, economy, art, science, education, and religion. When the master concept of such a description is given the name of 'value,' then these major realms of human life are specifically describable as realms of value. In their aggregate these realms constitute what may properly be given the name of 'civilization,' that total human adventure whose rising and declining fortunes give significance to human life upon this planet.

Theory of value so conceived is a bold and far-flung program which cannot be undertaken without a humble awareness of its immense complexity. It requires the philosopher to enter fields in which specialists have already staked their special claims, and where the philosopher finds himself an amateur among professionals. He cannot hope to do their special work better than they do it, but only to incorporate their results and add items and relationships. The philosopher is accustomed to this somewhat shameless role. He does not, however, undertake the task arrogantly or overconfidently. For it is the philosopher who, having undertaken the task, is most acutely aware of its difficulty.

John Dewey

Theory of Valuation *

VALUATION AS LIKING AND DISLIKING

That liking and disliking in their connection with valuation are to be considered in terms of observable and identifiable modes of behavior follows from what is stated in the previous section. As behavioral the adjective 'affective-motor' is applicable, although care must be taken not to permit the "affective" quality to be interpreted in terms of private "feelings" —an interpretation that nullifies the active and observable element expressed in 'motor.' For the "motor" takes place in the public and observable world, and, like anything else taking place there, has observable conditions and consequences. When, then, the word 'liking' is used as a name for a mode of behavior (not as a name for a private and inaccessible feeling), what sort of activities does it stand for? What is its designatum? This inquiry is forwarded by noting that the words 'caring' and 'caring for' are, as modes of behavior, closely connected with 'liking,' and that other substantially equivalent words are 'looking out for or after,' 'cherishing,' 'being devoted to,' 'attending to,' in the sense of 'tending', 'ministering to,' 'fostering'—words that all seem to be variants of what is referred to by 'prizing,' which, as we saw earlier, is one of the two main significations recognized by the dictionary. When these words are taken in the behavioral sense, or as naming activities that take place so as to maintain or procure certain conditions, it is possible to demarcate what is designated by them from things designated by such an ambiguous word as 'enjoy.' For the latter word may point to a condition of *receiving* gratification *from* something already in existence, apart from many affective-motor action exerted as a condition of its production or continued existence. Or it may refer to precisely the latter activity, in which case 'to enjoy' is a synonym for the activity of taking delight in an effort, having a certain overtone

* Reprinted from *Theory of Valuation* (International Encyclopedia of Unified Science, Volume II, Number 4), by John Dewey, pp. 13–26, 31–33. By permission of The University of Chicago Press.

of relishing, which "takes pains," as we say, to perpetuate *the existence of conditions* from which gratification is received. Enjoying in this active sense is marked by energy expended to secure the conditions that are the source of the gratification.

The foregoing remarks serve the purpose of getting theory away from a futile task of trying to assign signification to words in isolation from objects as designata. We are led instead to evocation of specifiable existential situations and to observation of what takes place in them. We are directed to observe whether energy is put forth to call into existence or to maintain in existence certain conditions; in ordinary language, to note whether effort is evoked, whether pains are taken to bring about the existence of certain conditions rather than others, the need for expenditure of energy showing that there exist conditions adverse to what is wanted. The mother who professes to prize her child and to enjoy (in the active sense of the word) the child's companionship but who systematically neglects the child and does not seek out occasions for being with the child is deceiving herself; if she makes, in addition, demonstrative signs of affection—like fondling—only when others are present, she is presumably trying to deceive them also. It is by observations of behavior—which observations (as the last illustration suggests) may need to be extended over a considerable space-time—that the existence and description of valuations have to be determined. Observation of the amount of energy expended and the length of time over which it persists enables qualifying adjectives like 'slight' and 'great' to be warrantably prefixed to a given valuation. The direction the energy is observed to take, as toward and away from, enables grounded discrimination to be made between "positive" and "negative" valuations. If there are "feelings" existing in addition, their existence has nothing to do with any verifiable proposition that can be made about a valuation.

Because valuations in the sense of prizing and caring for occur only when it is necessary to bring something into existence which is lacking, or to conserve in existence something which is menaced by outside conditions, valuation *involves* desiring. The latter is to be distinguished from mere wishing in the sense in which wishes occur in the absence of effort. "If wishes were horses, beggars would ride." There is something lacking, and it would be gratifying if it were present, but there is either no energy expended to bring what is absent into existence or else, under the given conditions, no expenditure of effort would bring it into existence—as when the baby is said to cry for the moon, and when infantile adults indulge in dreams about how nice everything would be if things were only different. The *designata* in the cases to which the names 'desiring' and 'wishing' are respectively applied are basically different. When, accordingly, 'valuation' is defined in terms of desiring, the prerequisite is a treatment of desire in terms of the existential context in which it arises and functions. If 'valuation' is defined in terms of desire as something initial and complete in itself, there is nothing by which to discriminate one desire from another and hence no way in which to measure the worth of different valuations in comparison with one another. Desires are desires, and that is all that can be said. Furthermore, desire is then conceived of as *merely* personal and hence as not capable of being stated in terms of other objects or events. If, for example, it should happen to be noted that effort ensues upon desire and that the effort put forth changes existing conditions, these considerations would then be looked upon as matters wholly external to desire—provided, that is, desire is taken to be original and complete in itself, independent of an observable contextual situation.

When, however, desires are seen to arise only within certain existential contexts (namely, those in which some lack prevents the immediate execution of an active tendency) and when they are seen to function in reference to these contexts in such a way as to make good the existing want, the relation between desire and *valuation* is found to be such as both to make possible, and to require, statement in verifiable propositions. (i) The content and object of desires are seen to depend upon the particular context in which they arise, a matter that in turn depends upon the antecedent state of both personal activity and of surrounding conditions. Desires for food, for example, will hardly be the same if one has eaten five hours or five days previously, nor will they be of the same content in a hovel and a palace or in a nomadic or agricultural group. (ii) Effort, instead of being something that comes after desire, is seen to be of the very essence of the tension involved in desire. For the latter, instead of being merely personal, is an active relation of the organism to the environment (as is obvious in the case of hunger), a factor that makes the difference between genuine desire and mere wish and fantasy. It follows that valuation in its connection with desire is linked to existential situations and that it differs with differences in its existential context. Since its existence depends upon the situation, its adequacy depends upon its adaptation to the needs and demands imposed by the situation. Since the situation is open to observation, and since the consequences of effort-behavior as observed determine the adaptation, the adequacy of a given desire can be stated in propositions. The propositions are capable of empirical test because the connection that exists between a given desire and the conditions with reference to which it functions are ascertained by means of these observations.

The word 'interest' suggests in a forcible way the active connection between personal activity and the conditions that must be taken into account in the theory of valuation. Even in etymology it indicates something in which both a person and surrounding conditions participate in intimate connection with one another. In naming this something that occurs between them it names a transaction. It points to an activity which takes effect through the mediation of external conditions. When we think, for example, of the interest of any particular group, say the bankers' interest, the trade-union interest, or the interest of a political machine, we think not of mere states of mind but of the group as a pressure group having organized channels in which it directs action to obtain and make secure conditions that will produce specified consequences. Similarly in the case of singular persons, when a court recognizes an individual as having an interest in some matter, it recognizes that he has certain claims whose enforcement will affect an existential issue or outcome. Whenever a person has an interest in something, he has a stake in the course of events and in their final issue—a stake which leads him to take action to bring into existence a particular result rather than some other one.

It follows from the facts here adduced that the view which connects valuation (and "values") with desires and interest is but a starting-point. It is indeterminate in its bearing upon the theory of valuation until the nature of interest and desire has been analyzed, and until a method has been established for determining the constituents of desires and interests in their concrete particular occurrence. Practically all the fallacies in the theories that connect valuation with desire result from taking "desire" at large. For example, when it is said (quite correctly) that "values *spring from* the immediate and inexplicable reaction of vital impulse and from the irrational part of our nature," what is actually stated is that vital impulses are a *causal condition* of the existence of desires. When "vital impulse" is given the only interpretation which is empirically verifiable (that of an organic biological tendency), the fact that an "irrational" factor is the causal condition of valuations proves that valuations have their roots *in an existence* which, like any existence *taken in itself,* is *a*-rational. Correctly interpreted, the statement is thus a reminder that organic tendencies are existences which are connected with other existences (the word 'irrational' adds nothing to "*existence*" as such) and hence are observable. But the sentence cited is often interpreted to mean that vital impulses *are* valuations—an interpretation which is incompatible with the view which connects valuations with desires and interests, and which, by parity of logic, would justify the statement that trees are seeds since they "spring from" seeds. Vital impulses are doubtless conditions *sine qua non* for the existence of desires and interests. But the latter include foreseen consequences along with ideas in the form of signs of the measures (involving expenditure of energy) required to bring the ends into existence. When valuation is identified with the activity of desire or interest, its identification with vital impulse is denied. For its identification with the latter would lead to the absurdity of making every organic activity of every kind an act of valuation, since there is none that does not involve some "vital impulse."

The view that "a value is any object of any interest" must also be taken with great caution. On its face it places all interests on exactly the same level. But, when interests are examined in their concrete makeup in relation to their place in some situation, it is plain that everything depends upon the objects involved in them. This in turn depends upon the care with which the needs of existing situations have been looked into and upon the care with which the ability of a proposed act to satisfy or fulfil just those needs has been examined. That all interests stand on the same footing with respect to their function as valuators is contradicted by observation of even the most ordinary of everyday experiences. It may be said that an interest in burglary and its fruits confers value upon certain objects. But the valuations of the burglar and the policeman are not identical, any more than the interest in the fruits of productive work institutes the same values as does the interest of the burglar in the pursuit of his calling—as is evident in the action of a judge when stolen goods are brought before him for disposition. Since interests occur in definite existential contexts and not at large in a void, and since these contexts are situations within the life-activity of a person or group, interests are so linked with one another that the valuation-capacity of any one is a function of the set to which it belongs. The notion that a value is equally any object of any interest can be maintained only upon a view that completely isolates them from one another—a view that is so removed from readily observed facts that its existence can be explained only as a corollary of the introspectionist psychology which holds that desires and interests are but "feelings" instead of modes of behavior.

PROPOSITIONS OF APPRAISAL

Since desires and interests are activities which take place in the world and which have effects in the world, they are observable in themselves and in connection with their observed effects. It might seem then as if, upon any theory that relates valuation with desire and interest, we had now come within sight of our goal—the discovery of valuation-propositions. Propositions *about* valuations have, indeed, been shown to be possible. But they are valuation-propositions only in the sense in which propositions about potatoes are potato-propositions. They are propositions about matters-of-fact. The fact that these occurrences happen to be valuations does not make the propositions valuation-propositions in any distinctive sense. Nevertheless, the fact that such matter-of-fact propositions can be made is of importance. For, unless they exist, it is doubly absurd to suppose that valuation-propositions in a *distinctive* sense can exist. It has also been shown that the subject matter of personal activities forms no theoretical barrier to institution of matter-of-fact propositions, for the behavior of human beings is open to observation. While there are practical obstacles to the establishment of valid general propositions about such behavior (i.e., about the relations of its constituent acts), its conditions and effects may be investigated. Propositions about valuations made in terms of their conditions and consequences delimit the problem as to existence of valuation-propositions in a *distinctive* sense. Are propositions about existent valuations themselves capable of being appraised, and can the appraisal when made enter into the constitution of further valuations? That a mother prizes or holds dear her child, we have seen, may be determined by observation; and the conditions and effects of different kinds of prizing or caring for may, in theory, be compared and contrasted with one another. In case the final outcome is to show that some kinds of acts of prizing are *better* than others, valuation-acts are themselves evaluated, and the evaluation may modify further direct acts of prizing. If this condition is satisfied, then propositions about valuations that actually take place become the subject matter of valuations in a distinctive sense, that is, a sense that marks them off both from propositions of physics and from historical propositions about what human beings have in fact done.

We are brought thus to the problem of the nature of appraisal or evaluation which, as we saw, is one of the two recognized significations or 'valuation.' Take such an elementary appraisal proposition as "This plot of ground is worth $200 a front foot." It is different in form from the proposition, "It has a frontage of 20 feet." The latter sentence states a matter of accomplished fact. The former sentence states a rule for determination of an act to be performed, its reference being to the future and not to something already accomplished or done. If stated in the context in which a tax-assessor operates, it states a regulative condition for levying a tax against the owner; if stated by the owner to a real estate dealer, it sets forth a regulative condition to be observed by the latter in offering the property for sale. The future act or state is not set forth as a prediction of what will happen but as something which *shall* or *should* happen. Thus the proposition may be said to lay down a norm, but "norm" must be understood simply in the sense of a condition *to be* conformed to in definite forms of future action. That rules are all but omnipresent in every mode of human relationship is too obvious to require argument. They are in no way confined to activities to which the name 'moral' is applied. Every recurrent form of activity, in the arts and professions, develops rules as to the best way in which to accomplish the ends in view. Such rules are used as criteria or "norms" for judging the value of proposed modes of behavior. The existence of rules for valuation of modes of behavior in different fields as wise or unwise, economical or extravagant, effective or futile, cannot be denied. The problem concerns not their existence as general propositions (since every rule of action is general) but whether they express only custom, convention, tradition, or are capable of stating relations between things as means and other things as consequences, which relations are themselves grounded in empirically ascertained and tested existential relations such as are usually termed those of cause and effect.

In the case of some crafts, arts, and technologies, there can be no doubt which of these alternatives is correct. The medical art, for example, is approaching a state in which many of the rules laid down for a patient by a physician as to what it is *better* for him to do, not merely in the way of medicaments but of diet and habits of life, are based upon experimentally ascertained principles of chemistry and physics. When engineers say that certain materials subjected to certain technical operations are *required* if a bridge capable of supporting certain loads is to be built over the Hudson River at a certain point, their advice does not represent their personal opinions or whims but is backed by acknowledged physical laws. It is commonly believed that such devices as radios and automobiles have been greatly improved (bettered) since they were first invented, and that the betterment in the relation of means to consequences is due to more adequate scientific knowledge of underlying physical principles. The argument does not demand the belief that the influence of custom and convention is entirely eliminated. It is enough that such cases show that it is possible for rules of appraisal or evaluation to rest upon scientifically warranted physical generalizations and that the ratio of rules of this type to those expressing mere customary habits is on the increase.

In medicine a quack may cite a number of alleged cures as evidential ground for taking the remedies he offers. Only a little examination is needed to show in what definite respects the procedures he recommends differ from those said to be "good" or to be "required" by competent physicians. There is, for example, no analysis of the cases presented as evidence to show that they are actually like the disease for the cure of which the remedy is urged; and there is no analysis to show that the recoveries which are said (rather than proved) to have taken place were in fact due to taking the medicine in question rather than to any one of an indefinite number of other causes. Everything is asserted wholesale with no analytic control of conditions. Furthermore, the first requirement of scientific procedure—namely, full publicity as to materials and processes—is lacking. The sole justification for citing these familiar facts is that their contrast with competent medical practice shows the extent to which the rules of procedure in the latter art have the warrant of tested empirical propositions. Appraisals of courses of action as better and worse, more and less serviceable, are as experimentally justified as are nonvaluative propositions about impersonal subject matter. In advanced engineering technologies propositions that state the *proper* courses of action to be adopted are evidently grounded in generalizations of physical and chemical science; they are often referred to as *applied* science. Nevertheless, propositions which lay down rules for procedures as being fit and good, as distinct from those that are inept and bad, are different in form from the scientific propositions upon which they rest. For they are rules for the use, in and by human activity, of scientific generalizations as means for accomplishing certain desired and intended ends.

Examination of these appraisals discloses that they have to do with things as they sustain to each other the relation of *means to ends or consequences.* Wherever there is an appraisal involving a rule as to better or as to needed action, there is an end to be reached: the appraisal is a valuation of things with respect to their serviceability or needfulness. If we take the examples given earlier, it is evident that real estate is appraised for the purpose of levying taxes or fixing a selling price; that medicinal treatments are appraised with reference to the end of effecting recovery of health; that materials and techniques are valued with respect to the building of bridges, radios, motorcars, etc. If a bird builds its nest by what is called pure "instinct," it does not have to appraise materials and processes with respect to their fitness for an end. But if the result—the nest—is contemplated as an object of desire, then either there is the most arbitrary kind of trial-and-error operations or there is consideration of the fitness and usefulness of materials and processes to bring the desired object into existence.

And this process of weighing obviously involves comparison of different materials and operations as alternative possible means. In every case, except those of sheer "instinct" and complete trial and error, there are involved observation of actual materials and estimate of their potential force in production of a particular result. There is always some observation of the *outcome attained* in comparison and contrast with that intended, such that the comparison throws light upon the actual fitness of the things employed as means. It thus makes possible a better judgment in the future as to their fitness and usefulness. On the basis of such observations certain modes of conduct are adjudged silly, imprudent, or unwise, and other modes of conduct sensible, prudent, or wise, the discrimination being made upon the basis of the validity of the estimates reached about the relation of things as means to the end or consequence actually reached.

The standing objection raised against this view of valuation is that it applies only to things as *means,* while propositions that are genuine valuations apply to things as *ends.* This point will be shortly considered at length. But it may be noted here that ends are appraised in the same evaluations in which things as means are weighed. For example, an end suggests itself. But, when things are weighed as means toward that end, it is found that it will take too much time or too great an expenditure of energy to achieve it, or that, if it were attained, it would bring with it certain accompanying inconveniences and the promise of future troubles. It is then appraised and rejected as a "bad" end.

The conclusions reached may be summarized as follows: (1) There are propositions which are not merely about valuations that have actually occurred (about, i.e., prizings, desires, and interests that have taken place in the past) but which describe and define certain things as good, fit, or proper in a definite existential relation: these propositions, moreover, are *generalizations,* since they form rules for the proper use of materials. (2) The existential relation in question is that of means-ends or means-consequences. (3) These propositions in their generalized form may rest upon scientifically warranted empirical propositions and are themselves capable of being tested by observation of results actually attained as compared with those intended.

The objection brought against the view just set forth is that it fails to distinguish between things that are good and right in and of themselves, immediately, intrinsically, and things that are simply good *for* something else. In other words, the latter are useful for attaining the things which have, so it is said, value in and of themselves, since they are prized for their own sake and not as means to something else. This distinction between two different meanings of 'good' (and 'right') is, it is claimed, so crucial for the whole theory of valuation and values that failure to make the distinction destroys the validity of the conclusions that have been set forth. This objection definitely puts before us for consideration the question of the relations to each other of the categories of *means* and *end*. In terms of the dual meaning of 'valuation' already mentioned, the question of the relation of *prizing* and *appraising* to one another is explicitly raised. For, according to the objection, appraising applies only to *means*, while prizing applies to things that are *ends*, so that a difference must be recognized between valuation in its full pregnant sense and evaluation as a secondary and derived affair.

Let the connection between prizing and valuation be admitted and also the connection between desire (and interest) and prizing. The problem as to the relation between appraisal of things as means and prizing of things as ends then takes the following form: Are desires and interests ('likings,' if one prefers that word), which directly effect an institution of end-values, independent of the appraisal of things as means or are they intimately influenced by this appraisal? If a person, for example, finds after due investigation that an immense amount of effort is required to procure the conditions that are the means required for realization of a desire (including perhaps sacrifice of other end-values that might be obtained by the same expenditure of effort), does that fact react to modify his original desire and hence, by definition, his valuation? A survey of what takes place in any deliberate activity provides an affirmative answer to this question. For what is deliberation except weighing of various alternative desires (and hence end-values) in terms of the conditions that are the means of their execution, and which, as means, determine the consequences actually arrived at? There can be no control of the operation of foreseeing consequences (and hence of forming ends-in-view) save in terms of conditions that operate as the causal conditions of their attainment. The proposition in which any object adopted as an end-in-view is statable (or explicitly stated) is *warranted* in just the degree to which existing conditions have been surveyed and appraised in their capacity as means. The sole alternative to this statement is that no deliberation whatsoever occurs, no ends-in-view are formed, but a person acts directly upon whatever impulse happens to present itself.

Any survey of the experiences in which ends-in-view are formed, and in which earlier impulsive tendencies are shaped through deliberation into a *chosen* desire, reveals that the object finally valued as an end to be reached is determined in its concrete makeup by appraisal of existing conditions as means. . . .

Every person in the degree in which he is capable of learning from experience draws a distinction between what is desired and what is desirable whenever he engages in formation and choice of competing desires and interests. There is nothing far-fetched or "moralistic" in this statement. The contrast referred to is simply that between the object of a desire as it first presents itself (because of the existing mechanism of impulses and habits) and the object of desire which emerges as a revision of the first-appearing impulse, after the latter is critically judged in reference to the conditions which will decide the actual result. The "desirable," or the object which *should* be desired (valued), does not descend out of the a priori blue nor descend as an imperative from a moral Mount Sinai. It presents itself because past experience has shown that hasty action upon uncriticized desire leads to defeat and possibly to catastrophe. The "desirable" as distinct from the "desired" does not then designate something at large or a priori. It points to the difference between the operation and consequences of unexamined impulses and those of desires and interests that are the product of investigation of conditions and consequences. Social conditions and pressures are part of the conditions that affect the execution of desires. Hence they have to be taken into account in framing ends in terms of available means. But the distinction between the "is" in the sense of the object of a casually emerging desire and the "should be" of a desire framed in relation to actual conditions is a distinction which in any case is bound to offer itself as human beings grow in maturity and part with the childish disposition to "indulge" every impulse as it arises.

Desires and interests are, as we have seen, themselves causal conditions of results. As such they are potential means and have to be appraised as such. This statement is but a restatement of points already made. But it is worth making because it forcibly indicates how far away some of the theoretical views of valuation are from practical common-sense attitudes and beliefs. There is an indefinite number of proverbial sayings which in effect set forth the necessity of not treating desires and interests as final in their first appearance but of treating them as means—that is, of appraising them and forming objects or ends-in-view on the ground of what consequences they will tend to produce in practice. "Look before you leap"; "Act in haste, repent at leisure"; "A stitch in time saves nine"; "When angry count ten"; "Do not put your hand to the plow until the cost has been counted"—are but a few of the many maxims. They are summed up in the old saying, "*Respice finem*"—a saying which marks the difference between simply *having* an end-in-view for which *any* desires suffice, and *looking*, examining, to make sure that the consequences that will actually result are such as will be actually prized and valued when they occur. Only the exigencies of a preconceived theory (in all probability one seriously infected by the conclusions of an uncritically accepted "subjectivistic" psychology) will ignore the concrete differences that are made in the content of "likings" and "prizings," and of desires and interests, by evaluating them in their respective causal capacities when they are taken as means.

Max Scheler

Towards a Phenomenology of Love and Hatred *

NEGATIVE CONSIDERATIONS

We may have said enough to dispose of the idea that love and hatred can be derived from fellow-feeling; but it is equally out of the question to derive them from more elementary facts of any kind, or to regard them as a 'complex' of such elements. Any attempt to seek their origin in a complex of feelings and impulses is doomed to failure. Consider, for instance, the complete futility of Spinoza's definition, that love is *'quædam lætitia concomitante causa externa'*. Malebranche was already justified in asking of this whether we therefore love a fruit which we consume and know to be a cause of pleasure? [1] In love (and hatred) between human beings these acts remain wholly independent of changes in the state of feeling, as is shown by the fact that throughout such changes they *remain fixed* upon their objects, as with a steady, unwavering light. Our love for someone does not alter, for all the pain and grief the loved one may cause us, nor our hatred, for all the joy and pleasure the hated one may afford. And throughout all the daily vicissitudes of joy and sorrow among men their ties of love and hatred persist unaltered. One can only say this about it, that a beloved object offers more abundant possibilities of joy as well as sorrow. But the same is also true of our hatreds; the more we hate a person, the more galling his happiness and prosperity, the more gratifying his misery and failure, and the more abundant the possibilities he offers for our sorrow and our joy.

Quite a different set of facts is involved once the love and hate-relationships are regarded as *causes* of emotional states (and not as their effects). It now becomes plain that the *pursuance* of these acts is itself the deepest of all sources of joy and sorrow, bliss and despair. Thus, even when love

* From *The Nature of Sympathy* by Max Scheler, translated by Peter Heath, pp. 147–154, 157–158. Published 1954 by Routledge & Kegan Paul Ltd. Reprinted by permission of Routledge & Kegan Paul Ltd., and Yale University Press.

[1] Cf. N. Malebranche: *Recherche de la Vérité.*

is 'unhappy' in the sense of being unrequited, the act itself is still accompanied by a feeling of great happiness—and equally so when the loved one occasions pain and sorrow. And conversely, even where the distress of a hated person is a source of joy (as in envy, malice, spite, etc.), the *pursuance* of the act of hatred itself is still felt to have a sombre and dismal quality about it.

Even if, abstaining from consideration of love and hatred as emotional states, we merely enquire if they represent a feeling 'of something' in intention, this question must also receive a negative answer. For a thing can certainly be felt to have positive value without therefore arousing love. It is the merit of Franz Brentano to have recognized that love and hatred are by nature acts, and acts of an elementary kind. He actually regards them as prior even to judgment itself. We are the more ready to stress this here because it is our conviction that this one small observation shows how vastly Brentano's insight into these matters transcends the misconceptions now prevailing in psychology, whereby love and hatred are successively assigned to the spheres of feeling, conation and affect, or construed as a medley of ingredients from all three. Yet we cannot follow him in equating them, as he does in *The Origin of the Knowledge of Right and Wrong,*[2] with 'preference' and 'rejection'. The relationship of these acts to love and hate has been fully explained by me in another work.[3] Here I would only emphasize that preference and rejection belong to the sphere of *value-apprehension* (and indeed to the apprehension of grades of value), whereas love and hatred cannot be reckoned as acts of apprehension *at all.* They represent a unique attitude towards objects of value, and it is certainly not just a cognitive function. They may indeed serve as a basis for the apprehension of value (as we shall see), but they are not themselves apprehensions of this kind. Moreover, these attitudes are not directed intentionally towards value, let alone 'higher' value, as when we prefer one value to another; they refer to *objects* inasmuch and insofar as these possess value. It is never values we love, but always something that possesses value.

In Malebranche's admirable discussions of love and hatred[4] they are taken to be feelings, but of a kind in which a value-judgement is presupposed, as to whether the object is worthy to arouse a certain degree of joy. From this point of view he engages in criticism of Spinoza's theory. It is easy to see that this position involves a *mistaken rationalization* of love

[2] *Der Ursprung sittlicher Erkenntnis* [tr. by C. Hague, Constable, 1902].
[3] *Der Formalismus in der Ethik,* p. 63 seq., p. 260 seq.
[4] *Op. cit.*

and hatred.[5] There may be emotional acts which presuppose the passing of a judgement (or rather, an evaluation). Respect, for instance, seems to me to be one of these. It presupposes that initial detachment from the object, which alone makes it possible for a value-*judgement* to precede the onset of the emotional act; and it also requires a specific awareness of the presence of the value by which it is evoked. But this detachment is just what is lacking in love and hatred. They are entirely *primitive* and *immediate* modes of emotional response to the value-content itself; so much so that, phenomenologically speaking, they do not even disclose a process of apprehending value (e.g. feeling, preference, etc.), let alone the making of a value-judgement. In particular, the value in question is not specifically envisaged beforehand, as it is in the case of *respect.* Nothing shows this better than the extraordinary perplexity which can be seen to ensue when people are asked to give 'reasons' for their love or hatred. It is then that one sees how these 'reasons' are invariably looked for after the event, and how the whole inventory of them is never sufficient to account for the nature and intensity of the acts they are alleged to justify. It is also noticeable that though other objects may have value-qualities identical to those alleged as reasons for love or hatred, no such emotions are addressed to them. Love and hatred necessarily fasten upon the individual core in things, the *core of value*—if I may be allowed the expression—which can never be wholly resolved into values susceptible of judgement, or even of distinct apprehension in feeling. On the contrary, our standards for the appreciation of value-attributes are governed by our love or hatred of the things exhibting these values; it is not our appreciation that governs our love or our hate. Indeed, curious as it may appear, we feel it a kind of offence and transgression, a profane intrusion upon love (*and* hatred), that we should apply conceptual categories of valuation to the values of objects we love or hate, or should observe others doing so. When reading a letter from a loved one it is out of the question to judge it by ordinary standards of grammar, æsthetics or style. It seems 'disloyal' to do so. The qualities, the activities and the achievements of the loved one acquire all their value from him or her alone, as the object in which they inhere or the subject who carries them out.

[5] H. Blüher has made the assertion, which reappears in almost all his writings that 'Love is directed to the (whole) man, regardlesss of value'. If his intention was only to repudiate *this* fallacious rationalization, he would be quite right; but not if he means to imply that the act of love itself takes place without reference to value. Baader shows much greater insight in observing that beauty (loveliness) is derived from love and ugliness (the hateful) from hate, while *charis,* or grace(fulness), is identical with *charitas* (graciousness) (*Religiöse Erotik,* p. 15).

From the rationalist point of view this is sufficient reason for regarding love and hatred as 'blind'. But this tells us very little. For the fact that the inner 'spiritual vision' of love and hatred should see something *other* in values, high or low, than that which the 'eye' of reason can discern, is no indication that we are merely getting a worse view here of the *same* thing which the eye of reason would discern more clearly. Love and hatred afford an *evidence of their own,* which is not to be judged by the evidence of reason. Only those to whom this evidence is denied, or who are constitutionally liable to vacillation about it, will be disposed to attribute the fact to a general 'blindness' of functions and acts, rather than to shortcomings in their own individual *exercise* of them.

It has already been emphasized that love and hatred do not represent acts of conation. It is precisely the element of 'uneasiness' in conation which is increasingly expunged from love and hatred, the more definite, pure and lucid they become. Nor do they contain any consciousness of something 'to be realized'. But more of this later.

The most important thing to notice is the way in which love and hatred differ, *as* acts even, from all other acts and from each other; the point being that they do not first *become* what they are by virtue of either their exponents, their objects or their possible effects and results. No other truth has been more grievously flouted by our current habits of thought. It is implied in the foregoing, firstly, that love and hatred are *in no sense relative* to the polar co-ordinates of *'myself'* and *'the other'*. In other words, love and hatred are *not intrinsically social dispositions,* as are the functions of fellow-feeling, for example.[6] Thus, one can 'love or hate oneself', but cannot have fellow-feeling for oneself. For if it is said of someone that he 'pities himself' or that he 'rejoices to find himself so happy today' (statements which undoubtedly designate phenomena of a quite specific kind), a closer analysis invariably discloses the presence of an element of phantasy, in which the person concerned regards himself *'as if he were someone else'* and shares his own feelings in this (fictitious) capacity. Thus I can fancy myself in the position of taking part in my own funeral, etc. But even then the act of fellow-feeling remains, phenomenologically, a social one. No such illusion is necessary in the case of self-love and self-hatred. Hence it is by no means a necessary condition for the occurrence of love and hatred, that the act should be directed on someone else, or that there should be any consciousness of human relationships.

[6] Other examples of intrinsically social acts are those of promising, obeying, commanding, pledging oneself, etc. Cf. the penetrating analysis of 'psycho-social' acts in H. L. Stoltenberg: *Soziopsychologie,* Berlin, 1914.

If acts that are addressed to others, as such, are described as 'altruistic', then love and hatred are in no way intrinsically altruistic acts. For the primary orientation of love is towards values, and towards the objects discernible, through those values, as sustaining them; whence it is essentially a matter of indifference whether the values concerned belong to the self or to others. The basic contrast is therefore between love, whether of self or others, and hatred, of self or others likewise. Conversely, acts addressed to others, as such, are by no means necessarily loving. For envy, malice and spite are so addressed. If by 'altruism' be meant an orientation towards other men, a predominant tendency to aversion from the self and its subjective experience, there is nothing in such a 'social' attitude to connect it, as such, with a 'loving' or 'kindly' one. Moreover, if love for others is based in this way upon an act of aversion, it must equally be founded upon a still more ultimate *hatred*, namely of *oneself*. Self-aversion, the *inability* to endure one's own company (of which the 'clubman' is a typical example), has nothing to do with love.[7]

But if it be no essential part of love that it should address itself to others, there is equally little necessity for it to relate to the *group*. There is such a thing as love for a group, and that in a twofold sense, namely love for the group as a whole, and love for each of its members, as 'belonging to the group'. But this can also co-exist with a quite independent love for the individual himself, considered without reference to a group of any kind, or, it may be, in actual opposition to one. (Love for the uniquely private self.) The group, in all its aspects, is thus only *one* object of love among others. If by a 'social outlook' one is taken to mean a special liability to preoccupation with social matters, this also has nothing whatever to do with *love*. Though it is certainly possible for love, of a kind, to be realized in a 'social outlook'. Thus one may wish to benefit an entire nation, profession, community or race, 'out of love for them' (but never a class, for this is an embodiment of interests and, as such, valueless); but in doing so it should be realized that this involves a total exclusion of love or goodwill towards *individuals*. For it is a commonplace of observation that one may hate a group while loving certain of its members—not because they are members of the group, but in their individual capacity. Hence antisemitism, germanophobia, gallophobia, etc., are quite consistent with love for individuals in any given case.

[7] In my essay 'Das Ressentiment im Aufbau der Moralen' I have exposed the limitless confusions inherent in the positivist equation of love and 'altruism'. Conversely, many of Nietzsche's arguments against love, in the chapter on 'Love of one's neighbour' in *Also sprach Zarathustra* are applicable only to this positivist misrepresentation of love as altruism.

Self-love and self-hatred are therefore no less fundamental than love or hatred of others. Nor is *'egoism'* the same as 'self-love'.[8] For in 'egoism' the given object of love is not my individual self, released from all social ties and thought of as merely a vessel for such supreme categories of value as those which find expression, for instance, in the concept of 'salvation'. Its object is simply myself, as one in competition with others, who thereupon simply 'fails to observe' that others have any value. It is typical of Egoism that it implies a *glance at other people* and their values and goods, and consists in just this *'failure to observe'* the claims engendered by these values (which is already a *positive* act, and not just a failure to perform one). Egoism does not consist in behaving 'as if one were alone in the world'; on the contrary, it is taken for granted that the individual is a member of society. The egoist is a man so taken up with his 'social self' that he loses sight of his individual private self. It is not that he loves this social self; he is merely 'taken up' with it, i.e. *lives* in it. Nor is his concern for his own values, as such (for it is only by chance that he finds them in himself); it is for *all* values, in things or in other people, but only *insofar* as they are, or might come to be *his,* or have something to do with *him.* All of which is the very *opposite* of self-love.

POSITIVE DELINEATION OF THE PHENOMENA [9]

The ultimate essences of love and hatred, as inherent in acts, can only be *exhibited;* they cannot be defined.

In the first place love and hatred cannot be radically distinguished on the grounds that hatred is simply love for the non-existence of a thing. For hatred is really a *positive act,* involving a presentation of *disvalue* no less immediate than the presentation of *positive* value in the act of love. But love is a movement, passing from a lower value to a higher one, in which the higher value of the object or person suddenly flashes upon us; whereas hatred moves in the opposite direction. It can be seen from this that hatred looks to the possible existence of a lower value (itself of negative value, on that account), and to the removal of the very possibility of a higher value (which again has a negative value). Love, on the other hand,

[8] Compare Aristotle's penetrating discussion in the chapter on 'Self-love' in the Nichomachean Ethics. How vastly superior he is, on this point, to all who advocate a 'sociological' explanation for love and hatred!

[9] Karl Jaspers' treatment in the chapter on 'Die enthusiastische Einstellung in die Liebe' of his *Psychologie der Weltanschauungen* (Berlin, 1919), is in agreement on all fundamental points with the analysis presented in this chapter. On the problem itself, cf. Alexander Pfänder: 'Zur Psychologie der Gesinnungen' [*Jahrbuch für Philosophie und phänomenologische Forschung,* Vol. III, Niemeyer, Halle, 1916].

looks to the establishment of higher possibilities of value (which itself has a positive value), and to the maintenance of these, besides seeking to remove the possibility of lower value (which itself has a positive moral value). Hate, therefore, is by no means an utter repudiation of the whole realm of values generally; it involves, rather, a *positive* preoccupation with lower possibilities of value.

This 'higher' or 'lower' quality of values is something inherently given, requiring no such comparison of value as is always involved in 'preference', for example. Preference is not choice, nor is it in any sense a conative act, but an act of emotional cognition.[10] We can prefer Beethoven to Brahms, for instance, without actually choosing anything. Choice always relates to volition—never to objects as such. But preference always assumes the existence of two values A and B, of which one is then preferred to the other. This is not the case in love and hatred. For love is that *movement of intention* whereby, from a given value A in an object, its higher value is visualized. Moreover, it is just this *vision* of a higher value that is of the essence of love. In its ultimate nature, therefore, love, is not just a 'reaction' to a value already felt, such as 'happiness' or 'grief', for example, nor is it a modally determinate function, such as 'enjoyment', nor yet an attitude to a pair of previously given values, such as 'preference'. Though all preference is based on love, inasmuch as it is only in love that the higher value flashes out and can thereafter be preferred.

Those who treat love as a merely consequential 'reaction' to a value already felt, have failed to recognize its nature as a *movement,* of which Plato was already so shrewdly aware.[11] Love does not simply gape approval, so to speak, at a value lying ready to hand for inspection. It does not reach out towards given objects (or real persons) merely on account of the positive values inherent in them, and already 'given' *prior* to the coming of love. For this idea still betrays that gaping at mere *empirical* fact, which is so utterly uncongenial to love. Of course there *is* an awareness, in love, of the positive value of the things loved, for instance, the beauty, the charm and the goodness of a person; but we can also be aware of this without any love at all. Love only occurs when, upon the values already acknowledged as 'real' there supervenes a *movement,* an intention, towards potential values still *'higher'* than those already given and presented. These additional values are *not* yet manifested as positive

[10] Cf. on this *Der Formalismus in der Ethik,* p. 63 seq., p. 260 seq.
[11] In his definition in the Symposium (205), according to which it is 'a cause whereby anything proceeds from that which is not, into that which is' [Shelley's translation].

qualities, being merely envisaged concurrently as potential ingredients of a corporate structural pattern. In so doing, love invariably sets up, as it were, an *'idealized' paradigm of value* for the person actually present, albeit conceiving this at the same time as an embodiment of his 'true' nature and 'real' value, which only awaits confirmation in feeling. To be sure, this 'paradigm' is *implicit* in the values already disclosed empirically in feeling—and only the fact that it is so implicit keeps it free from interpolation, empathic projection, etc., and hence from delusion. But, for all that, it is not empirically 'latent' in them, save as an appointed goal, an objective ideal challenge to a better and more beautiful fulfilment of the whole.

It is essentially as a movement tending to the enhancement of value that love acquires its significance (already explicit in Plato), as a creative force. This is not to say that love first creates these values or itself enhances them. Certainly not. But in all feeling and finding of values, all preference even (in relation, that is, to the spheres of feeling and preference), it is love that within *these* spheres of experience brings utterly new and superior values into existence; as it also does for the whole field of will, choice and action to which preference gives rise. Love, in short, is *creative* of 'existence', relative to these spheres. Hatred, on the other hand, is in the strictest sense *destructive,* since it does in fact destroy the higher values (within these spheres), and has the *additional effect* of blunting and blinding our feeling for such values and power of discriminating them. It is only because of their destruction (within these spheres) by hatred, that they *become* indiscernible.[12] . . .

. . . For in love there is no attempting to fix an objective, no deliberate shaping of purpose, aimed at the higher value and its realization; *love itself, in the course of its own movement,* is what brings about the continuous *emergence* of ever-higher value in the object—just as if it was streaming out from the object of its own accord, without any sort of exertion (even of wishing) on the part of the lover. We may take love to consist in the mere fact that a value already present beforehand comes to light at this point (as though love simply opens our eyes to such higher values, whereas hate closes them); *or* regard it, on the other hand, as a mere 'occasion' of the promotion and deliberate cultivation of these values, by education, for instance; or we may suppose it to create the new values effortlessly, out of itself. But all such attempts to confine this *basic phenomenon* to an either-or are but crude and inadequate charac-

[12] As Jaspers pertinently remarks: 'In love we do not discover values, we discover that everything is more valuable', op. cit.

terizations, serving only to obscure the thing itself. For *love* is not present in any of these cases. It can certainly be said that true love opens our spiritual eyes to ever-higher values in the object loved. It enables them to *see* and does not blind them (as is suggested in a most foolish proverb, which obviously thinks of love in terms of a mere impulse of sensual passion). The blinding element in an empirical infatuation is never the *love,* but the sensual *impulses* which always accompany love and by which it is actually constricted and confined. But this 'wide-awakeness' is no more than a *consequence* of love, occurring in the varying degrees of 'interest', 'attention', 'notice', 'heed' and so on. In love itself there is no such seeking for new values in the object loved. On the contrary, to search around for higher values like this would undoubtedly indicate a prevailing *absence* of love. It would involve both an increased interest in the merits of the object and a lessening of interest in its failings; but this would imply an attitude which is at least heading towards *illusion.* While the genuineness of love is displayed throughout by the fact that we do indeed see the faults of these objects as they stand, but love them all the same. If love were a search of this kind, how would it be if the higher values sought were not forthcoming? Then, at all events, disillusionment would set in, and the search would come to an end. But whatever ended at this point could certainly not be *love* for the object. For this simply does *not* come to an end, because a value sought is not encountered. Hence the fact of being wide-awake to higher values than those actually present does not make love what it is, being at most a consequence thereof, and that without looking for anything in particular. Love opens our eyes to values higher than those which 'interest' would discern, and even the latter is far more than merely 'increased attention', being itself the actual cause of such an increase.

What Methods Are Available in Value Fields?

Nicolai Hartmann

The Ideal Self-Existence of Values *

Values have self-existence. This proposition is simply the positive formulation of what was given above in our criticism of Kantian subjectivism. Values subsist independently of the consciousness of them. Consciousness can grasp or miss them, but cannot make them or spontaneously decree them. This does not hold true of the material. By his co-operation a subject can very well—within certain limits—produce the material (for example, he can set up a relation of confidence): but he cannot thereby prevent such a material from being of value—or the contrary. Such a material simply "is" so, without any co-operation, and even if it is believed not to be so. Hence, concerning the characteristics which values have, the proposition holds good that they have self-existence. . . .

The moral judgment of values, which declares that a breach of trust is revolting or that malicious joy in another's misfortune is reprehensible, does not refer to the sensation as revolting or reprehensible. The judgment is rather itself this sensation, or its expression. What it means is something else, an objective revoltingness and reprehensibleness, which is independent of the sensation. It means something objective, something existing in itself. But, of course, a self-existence that is of an ideal nature.

In harmony with this is the conviction, which accompanies every genuine judgment of values, that everyone else must judge in the same way and have the same impression. And here also the universality and necessity, which betray themselves in such a conviction, are not a psychological factum. For, actually, other persons occasionally feel and judge otherwise. And the one judging knows, or may very well know, of the deviation of the judgment of others from his own.

* From *Ethics* by Nicolai Hartmann, translated by Stanton Coit. London: George Allen & Unwin Ltd., and New York: The Macmillan Company, 1932, Volume I, pp. 218, 225–229. Reprinted by permission of The Macmillan Company and George Allen & Unwin Ltd.

But it is here just as it is with mathematical insight. Not everyone is capable of it; not everyone has the eye, the ethical maturity, the spiritual elevation, for seeing the situation as it is. Nevertheless, the universality, necessity and objectivity of the valuational judgment hold good in idea. For this universality does not at all mean that everyone is capable of the insight in question. It only means that whoever is capable of it—that is, whoever has attained the adequate mentality—must necessarily feel and judge thus and not otherwise. This is a quite commonplace truth. Not everyone, for instance, has sense and understanding for the moral value of a noble-minded act matured in quiet meditation, or of consideration for others practised in a fine way; but everyone who has the understanding for them must judge them as something of value and must respect the personality of the doer.

In this sense—the only one under consideration—moral judgment and the primal moral feeling which underlies it are universal, necessary and objective. In this sense also the value expressing itself in the judgment is independent of the subject who judges. It has as genuine an ideal self-existence as any mathematical law.

The principle that values have an ideal self-existence has a striking significance for ethics. It affirms more than the mere apriority of valuational discernment and the absoluteness of discerned values. It affirms that there is a realm of values subsisting for itself, a genuine κόσμος νοητός which exists beyond reality just as much as beyond consciousness—an ethical ideal sphere, not manufactured, invented or dreamed, but actually existing and capable of being grasped in the phenomenon of the feeling for values—a sphere which perdures side by side with the ethical real and the ethical actual sphere, just as the logical ideal realm exists side by side with the ontological real and the gnoseological positive realm.[1]

VALUATIONAL DELUSION AND BLINDNESS

The doctrine of apriority and that of self-existence are not identical. To see the truth of the former is relatively easy; it was sufficient to understand that standards of value are the presupposition of moral phenomena. But prejudices, arbitrary assumptions, presentations, emotional attitudes can also be a priori. Now values announce themselves primarily as enlistments of emotion. They are therefore exposed to doubt as to their ob-

[1] In both departments, by the "actual" sphere is understood the phenomenal realm of transcendent acts; therefore, in the department of theory, the realm of cognitive acts; in the department of ethics, the acts of conduct, disposition and will. Cf. the passage on the ideal sphere in *Metaphysik der Erkenntnis*, second edition, Chapter XXVII (*c*).

jectivity so much the more, because feelings are less objective than discernments.

The concept of self-existence first raises them above all such doubts. But it itself is rooted in the fact that it is as little possible to summon up arbitrarily a sense of value as it is to construct a mathematical truth arbitrarily. In both cases there is an objectively beheld existent, which presents itself and which the feeling, the intuition, the thought only follows but cannot dominate. We can experience as valuable only what in itself is so. We may of course also be incapable of such an experiencing: but if we are in general capable of it, we can experience the value only as it is in itself, but not as it is not. The sense of value is not less objective than mathematical insight. Its object is only more veiled through the emotional character of the act; it must be especially raised above the act, if we want to become aware of it. But even this later making of it known to ourselves can change nothing in the structure of the object (the value).

The opposite question here forces itself to the front, whether the evidence of the primary discernment of value is not also subject to delusion. And it is natural to believe that, if there is valuational delusion, the self-existence of values becomes again doubtful and gives way to a certain relativity.

That is a great mistake. On the contrary, where there are delusion and error, these consist of non-agreement with the fact. The fact, as something fixed and independent of the truth or error of the knowledge —that is, the fact as something existing in itself—is precisely the presupposition of delusion; otherwise delusion would not be delusion. But the "fact" is in this case the value itself. Accordingly, if anything is proof for the self-existence of values, it is exactly the phenomenon of delusion.

If values were only things posited by the subject, if they consisted of nothing except the act of valuing—that is, of the evaluating sense as such— then every chance enlistment of feeling would be as justifiable as every other. Valuational delusion would then be altogether impossible.

But there are many authenticated delusions as to values, even falsifications which rest upon perversions of the sense of values, as in the manifestations of resentment.[2] These manifestations, as well as their exposure through normal moral feelings, would be an impossibility—that is, they would not be falsifications, if the genuine values which were lack-

[2] As in Nietzsche; cf. also Scheler, *Ueber Ressentiment und Moralisches Werturteil,* 1909. Nietzsche is a case in proof. In his statement that there is such a thing as falsification of values, he actually gives the lie to the relativism of values which he proclaims.

ing did not have a self-existence independent of them. It is possible to be mistaken and to be set right only where the object is a fixed one and has its own definite character which is not changed by being understood or misunderstood.

The ordinary kind of delusion as to values is of course purely negative, the incapacity to discriminate, valuational blindness. But this is not delusion proper, but only a defect of the sense of value concerning a definite point. It stands on all fours with the theoretical incapacity of the mathematically untrained and untalented person. There are such things as education and lack of education of the sense of values, talent and lack of talent for the discernment of them. There is such a thing as individual maturity of the power of discrimination in the individual man, and there is a historical maturity in mankind. Whether the latter always means progress must remain undecided; possibly it brings with it a narrowness of the consciousness of values, so that there is always lost on the one side what is gained on the other. Perhaps there is also an enlargement of the field of valuational vision. But the fact is that we always survey only a limited section of the realm of values, while we remain blind to the other sections. That is the reason why the historical shifting of our gaze, with its circle of light, on the plane of self-existent values—which is reflected in the multiplicity and transiency of moral systems—is so very instructive for philosophical investigation. And at the same time the reason lies here why this shifting and this variability do not constitute a "transvaluation of values," but a revaluation and re-orientation of human life. Values do not change, but our insight into them changes. The insight however changes, because the values themselves and their ideal order do not change with the movements of the mental eye, and because they are objective and self-existent.

Clarence Irving Lewis

The Immediately Valuable *

1. The conception outlined in the preceding chapter implies that there is one single kind of desideratum which is the ultimate concern in all valuations; since it takes all valuings to be either direct apprehensions of value-quality in the empirically presented, or predictions of such findings as possible, or judgments of a thing in question as capable of conducing to such realization of value-quality in experience. Prizings and disprizings of the presently given content of experience, are formulatable in expressive statements, the reference of which terminates in the immediate and phenomenal. With respect to these, the subject whose experience is in question can make no mistake, unless a verbal one in the manner of expressing what he finds. By the same token, such value-apprehensions of the given are not judgments and are not items of knowledge, though expression of them is true or false (since false report is possible). Valuations other than those which thus refer to a quality of the presently given, are value-judgments; and are either of the terminating sort which predict some value-quality as findable under certain conditions, or they are ascriptions to some actuality, or to some conceived entity, or to some *kind* of entity, of a potentiality for contributing a value-quality to experience. Thus the conception is that the only thing intrinsically valuable—valuable for its own sake—is a goodness immediately found or findable and unmistakable when disclosed: all values of any other sort, including all values attributable to objects, are extrinsic, and valued for the sake of their possible contribution to such realizations of the immediately good.

In its major intent, this conception is one which has often enough been put forward. Hedonism in general represents one expression of this type of view; since pleasure is a kind of good which is immediate, and concerning which finding or not finding is conclusive. This is presumably

* From *An Analysis of Knowledge and Valuation* by C. I. Lewis, pp. 397–403. Copyright 1946 by The Open Court Publishing Company. Reprinted by permission of the publishers.

what Mill intended to point out in asserting that the sole evidence of desirability in a thing, is its being actually desired. But the fundamental thesis in point is by no means limited to those who are willing to identify immediate goodness in general with pleasure. All those who would define value in a way which brings it home in the end to a quality directly disclosed or disclosable in experience, and a quality which *when* disclosed is unmistakable, represent the same generic type of conception which is here put forward.

What we would particularly point out, however, is the importance, for any view of this type, of remarking the distinction between value-determination as addressed to that which by being immediate is unmistakable, and evaluation addressed to existents and the objective properties of them, with respect to which there is always possibility of error. Because when it is objects or situations or states of affairs that are in question, it is possible to desire what is *not* in its real nature desirable; to have an interest which is mistaken; to believe that a thing will conduce to satisfaction when in fact it will lead to pain. And it is only by attention to this distinction between what is valuable in the sense of directly *prized*, and what is valuable by contributing to realization of this intrinsically valuable quality—what is valuable in the sense in which value is to be judged or *appraised*—that a view of the type in question can distinguish itself from others with which it will not wish to be confused.[1]

2. Every such view might be called a naturalistic or humanistic conception of values; since it holds that the natural bent of the natural man stands in no need of correction in order validly to be the touchstone of *intrinsic* value. It repudiates the conception that with respect to intrinsic values we are natively incompetent, or born in sin, and can discern them justly only by some insight thaumaturgically acquired, or through some intimation of a proper vocation of man which runs athwart his natural bent. But in repudiating such redemptionist norms of the intrinsically valuable, such a naturalistic view does not wish to fall into the arms of a Protagorean relativism. It does not intend to put evaluations which the fool makes in his folly on a par with those of the sage in his wisdom. Rather it would recognize that while the natural man does not need any change of heart or any more than natural insight in order to make just evaluations, still he does stand in need of all that can be learned from the experience of life in this natural world. Nor does such a naturalistic

[1] These terms 'prized' and 'appraised' are, of course, borrowed from Dewey (see *Theory of Valuation;* Internat. Encycl. of Unified Science, vol. II, no. 4) though they are not here used in exactly the sense Dewey gives to them.

view wish to be confused with that neopositivism which, in the realm of values, is cynical or nihilistic, and denies all truth or falsity to valuations, classing them as expressions of feeling or emotion merely, and hence as having no criterion of determinable truth or falsity. In repudiating transcendental norms which would impose themselves as imperatives which must overrule our natural desires, it still does not mean to repudiate the normative significance for action which is implicit in all valuation, and is the reason for our interest in making correct judgments of value as against those which, upon trial, would prove to be mistaken. It intends to recognize a truth or falsity of valuations which is independent of our supposition or our wish, and which, like truth in general, has its imperative significance for belief and for sensibly taken action.

However, we shall not find any middle ground between transcendentalism on the one hand and Protagorean relativism on the other, unless we find a sense in which valuations—or *some* valuations—are judgments; are determinably true or false by reference to the natural consequences of acting in accordance with them; unless some value-predications are assertions which are confirmable but are not beyond the possibility of error when made; unless some things of which value is predicated have this predicated character in a manner not determined by immediate liking or desire or interest, but determined independently of what one may think or feel about them. And similarly, we can find no middle ground between the admission of norms in the sense of transcendental imperatives,[2] having extra-natural sanction, and that cynical repudiation of normative significances of every kind, unless we recognize that some value-statements affirm a kind of truth which experience may confirm, and which stands in need of such corroboration.

In order to be distinguished from transcendentalism, from Protagorean subjectivism, and from nihilism, all three, it is essential for a naturalistic conception of values to hold that some valuations have the significance of empirical cognition. But also it is essential for a naturalistic view to maintain that the quality or character by reference to which, ultimately, all things are to be judged valuable or disvaluable, is a quality unmistakably identifiable in the direct apprehension of it when disclosed in experience. It must hold that such immediately apprehensible value-quality or value-character constitutes the criterion by reference to which, eventually, those value-predications which are subject to possible error and need

[2] The reference here is not to that ethical imperative which demands respect for others, but to an imperative which should find no adequate sanction by relation to the actual interests of anybody.

confirmation are to be attested. Thus such a naturalistic view can hardly attain to clarity and cogency unless the distinction be remarked between value-predications which are merely expressive statements of a value-quality immediately discovered, and those which attribute to some existent the objective property of conducing to such realization of the immediately valuable.

It is amongst predications of objective value to things—evaluations which are judgments and have the sense of appraisal—that the most important and difficult problems of valuation are encountered. Nevertheless it is plain that the nature of value as immediate and prized, constitutes an anterior problem, with which it is appropriate to begin.

3. With respect to value as immediate, there are two kinds of questions. There is first the question of identifying it or locating it, and of expressing it appropriately; of determining what sort of entity it is. And second there are questions concerning the precise import of any statement of the general form "X has value," where 'value' is to be taken in this sense of value immediately found.

The problem of characterizing the immediately good is a baffling one; an irritating one even; because, in the first place, everybody knows what it is; and if anyone should not, we could hardly tell him. We here arrive at a point where we realize that between words and what they signify there is a gap; and more words will not build a bridge across it. So we are likely to say that such a quality as immediate goodness is ineffable; or that it is a simple quality, like the redness of a red rose, and being unanalyzable, is indefinable. It has no parts or distinct ingredients, by reference to which and their relations we can convey what is intended. And it stands in no invariant context and has no stable correlations, by reference to which we might locate it map-wise through its external relationships.

And second, men so speak of the intrinsically good which experience may disclose as sometimes to arouse suspicion that they are not talking about the same thing. For some say that it is pleasure, but others that the life aimed at pleasure is "as little dogs biting one another, and as little children laughing and then straightway weeping." And some say that activity that befits a man represents this character of the intrinsically good; but some say the serenity of withdrawal, and some, a blessedness which the natural man cannot know. And some say that it lies in the satisfaction of interests; but some that it is found in Nirvana where all interests fade away.

But if those who thus differ about the intrinsically good were not all the while intending the same thing, then there would be no controversy; and instead of confronting here a final question about the most important thing in life, we should only be wandering in a maze of verbal confusions. If we have no patience to penetrate through such veils of language to what is meant, then we might remind ourselves of what Plato said about misologists, attributing it to the father of western ethics in his last and most serious talk to his friends.[3] There is no acceptable alternative: we must make attempt upon this troublesome problem.

4. Immediate or directly findable value is not so much one quality as a dimensionlike mode which is pervasive of all experience. There is not one goodness and one badness to be found in living but uncountably many variants of good and bad, each like every other most notably in being a basis for choosing and preferring. Value or disvalue is not like the pitch of middle C or the seen color of median red or the felt hardness of steel. It is not one specific quale of experience but a gamut of such; more like color in general or pitch or hardness in general. It is like seen bigness or apparent littleness of things. Or more closely; immediate value is related to the quality-complexes of presentations exhibiting it, as seen bigness would be related to visual patterns exhibiting size if the world were so constituted that from description of the *other* aspects of any such pattern we could conclude, with fair safety, as to its apparent bigness. It seems hardly accurate to speak of value-disvalue as a dimension of experience: a dimension should be a respect in which things can vary independently of other and similarly dimensional characteristics. Whereas if the content of experience can sometimes vary with respect to value while remaining invariant in other respects, at least this is untypical: more nearly we could say; "Describe the given content adequately in *other* respects than value, and we can make shift to evaluate it from that description."

Also value-disvalue fails to be strictly a dimension of presentation by as much as there can be doubt that the value characterizing our presented content can always be compared with that of any other and decisively found greater or less or equal. On this point values disclosed are like seen bignesses, in that comparison of two sizes may be a trouble because one is the bigness of a triangle and the other of a circle. One could, of course, cut the Gordian knot by the convention that, since we here deal with what is apparent only, that which is not found of greater value or of less is to be taken as equal. But such a conventional determination of 'equal value' should be suspect: equality so determined might not prove

[3] *Phaedo*, Step. 89.

to be a transitive relation. The locus represented by it in the order of our immediate valuings might be less like a point on a line than like a stretch within which discrimination fails. In fact, we observe here one of those difficulties frequently confronting the descriptive psychologist, and sometimes inducing him to discard the phenomenal altogether, because of the difficulty of 'being scientific' about it: that is, the difficulty of embracing it in categories drawn from mathematics and physics.

There could also be doubt that value-disvalue is a quite universal aspect of presentation: it would appear that the given content of experience is sometimes a matter of indifference. And again, this 'zero' of immediate value is subject to the same kind of doubt as is the 'equality' determined by the absence of preference. This 'zero' might not prove invariant in different comparisons.

However, these failures of immediate values to fall into a decisively one-dimensional array should not be a matter of disappointment if we do not approach the subject with the presumption that accuracy and clarity imply measurement. There are excellent reasons—which will appear later, and are more decisive than those mentioned here—why any 'calculus of values' must be foreign to the facts and quite impossible. And to be pseudo-scientific at the cost of dubiety in the very foundations of construction, would be nowhere more out of place than here. If there is any topic concerning which no one of us is better informed than another, this should be it. There are none who are anaesthetic to good and bad in general, or inattentive to this character of things. Concerning the directly valued and valuable, only such errors are to be expected as are due to failures of reflection; and we should do well if, within reason, we concede the doubtfulness of what is doubted.

Perhaps we shall do best here to avoid terms like 'dimension' having mathematical and physical connotations, and say that value-disvalue is a general *mode* of presentation; that it is subject to degree in the sense that for any specific modality—the value-characteristic of a given content—there will be other such modalities related to it as better or worse. But that it cannot be presumed that any two modalities will be comparable with a decisive result; or that non-preference establishes a relation of 'equivalence' that is transitive. However, it is perhaps worth remarking that there would be poor ground in this for thinking that the value-disvalue mode of experience is more amorphous than other modes or aspects. Rather we here confront a *general* difficulty which besets any attempt to formulate the phenomenal as such. Most neat categorizing of the empirically presented is subject to suspicion of being in some measure the product of ingenious conventions and convenient ignorings of what spills over the edges of the verbal containers. And in particular, the passage from the phenomenal or given to the objective, is quite universally accomplished only by the conventional dictum of indiscernible differences. Without that, no general property of things, as directly experienced, will exhibit the order requisite to precise dimensionality.

We here deal with a mode of the phenomenal as such. And we are the less dependent for accuracy upon any conventions of determination in that what we are concerned with is universally familiar and universally regarded. Value-disvalue is that mode or aspect of the given or the contemplated to which desire and aversion are addressed: and it is that by apprehension of which the inclination to action is normally elicited.

Charles L. Stevenson

Ethics and Language *

WORKING MODELS

Our conclusions about disagreement have prepared the way for a study of the ethical terms, and the characteristic features of ethical methodology. The present chapter will deal with both of these topics, but in a manner that is deliberately oversimplified. In place of a detailed analysis of ethical judgments, it will provide only "working models" for analysis—definitions which approximate to ethical meanings with sufficient accuracy to be of temporary help. Methods of proving or supporting ethical judgments will be considered only to the extent that the working models suggest them. This procedure will serve to introduce the essential features of our study, stress their interdependence, and indicate the points that will later require more careful development.

Let us begin with some remarks about meaning. This much will be directly evident from the preceding chapter: Any definition which seeks to identify the meaning of ethical terms with that of scientific ones, and which does so without further explanation or qualification, is extremely likely to be misleading. It will suggest that the questions of normative ethics, like those of science, give rise to an agreement or disagreement that is exclusively in *belief*. In this way, ignoring disagreement in attitude, it will lead to only a half-picture, at best, of the situations in which the ethical terms are actually used.

This conclusion must not be pressed insensitively, without regard to the ambiguities and flexibilities of language. It may well be that at *some* times *all* of the effective meaning of ethical terms is scientific, and that at *all* times *some* of it is; but there remain multitudes of familiar cases in which the ethical terms are used in a way that is *not exclusively* scientific,

* From *Ethics and Language* by Charles L. Stevenson, pp. 20–23, 27–28, 153–156, 158–160, 210, 218. Copyright 1944 by Yale University Press. Reprinted by permission of the publisher.

and we must recognize a meaning which suits them to their additional function.

What is the nature of this extrascientific meaning? Let us proceed by analogy, comparing ethical sentences with others that are less perplexing but have a similar use.

Interesting analogues can be found in ordinary imperatives. Is there not a ready passage from "You ought to defend your country" to "Defend your country"? Or more prosaically, is not the expression, "You oughtn't to cry," as said to children, roughly interchangeable with "Stop crying"? There are many differences, unquestionably; but there are likewise these similarities: Both imperative and ethical sentences are used more for encouraging, altering, or redirecting people's aims and conduct than for simply describing them. Both differ in this respect from the sentences of science. And in arguments that involve disagreement in attitude, it is obvious that imperatives, like ethical judgments, have an important place. The example about the restaurant, for instance, by which the conception of disagreement in attitude was first introduced, might begin with the use of imperatives exclusively:

> A: Meet me at the Glenwood for dinner at 7.00.
> B: Don't let's go to a restaurant with music. Meet me at the Ambassador instead.
> A: But do make it the Glenwood . . . etc.

So the argument might begin, disagreement in attitude being indicated either by the ordinary second person form of the imperative, or by the first person plural form that begins with "Let's."

On account of this similar function of imperative and ethical sentences, it will be useful to consider some definitions that *in part* identify them. These definitions will not be adequate to the subtleties of common usage; they will be markedly inaccurate. But they will preserve in rough form much that is essential to ethical analysis, and on that account will be instructive approximations. It is they which will constitute the "working models" that have previously been mentioned.

There are many ways in which working models can be devised, but those which follow are perhaps the most serviceable:

(1) "This is wrong" means *I disapprove of this; do so as well.*
(2) "He ought to do this" means *I disapprove of his leaving this undone; do so as well.*
(3) "This is good" means *I approve of this; do so as well.*

It will be noted that the definiens in each case has two parts: first a declarative statement, "I approve" or "I disapprove," which describes the attitudes of the speaker, and secondly an imperative statement, "do so as well," which is addressed to changing or intensifying the attitudes of the hearer. These components, acting together, readily provide for agreement or disagreement in attitude. The following examples will illustrate how this is so:

A: This is good.
B: I fully agree. It is indeed good.

Freely translated in accordance with model (3) above, this becomes,

A: I approve of this; do so as well.
B: I fully concur in approving of it; (continue to) do so as well.

Here the declarative parts of the remarks, testifying to convergent attitudes, are sufficient to imply the agreement. But if taken alone, they hint too much at a bare description of attitudes. They do not evidence the *contagion* of warmly expressed approval—the interaction of attitudes that makes each man's favorable evaluation strengthen and invigorate the other's. This latter effect is highly characteristic of an articulate ethical agreement; and the imperatives in our translated version of the example do something (though in a most imperfect way) to make it evident.

Let us consider an example of disagreement:

A: This is good.
B: No, it is bad.

Translated in accordance with the working models, this becomes,

A: I approve of this; do so as well.
B: No, I disapprove of it; do so as well.

The declarative parts of the remarks show that the men have opposed attitudes, one approving and the other disapproving. The imperative parts show that each man is suggesting that the other redirect his attitudes. Since "disagreement in attitude" has been defined with exclusive reference to an opposition of attitudes and efforts to redirect them or call them into question, it will be clear that a place for this sort of disagreement is retained (though again only in an imperfect way) by the working models that have been suggested.

But if the models are to help us more than they hinder us, they must be used with extreme caution. Although they give a needed emphasis to agreement and disagreement in attitude, they give no emphasis to agreement and disagreement in belief. Hence the *dual* source of ethical problems is not made evident. If traditional theory too often lost sight of attitudes in its concern with beliefs, we must not make the opposite error of losing sight of beliefs in our concern with attitudes. The latter error, which would give ethics the appearance of being cut off from reasoned argument and inquiry, would be even more serious than the former.

. . . The possibility that ethical judgments may have a *different sort* of proof has not been considered. Or rather, since "proof" may be a misleading term, let us put it this way: It has yet to be considered whether there is some "substitute for a proof" in ethics, some support or reasoned argument which, although different from a proof in science, will be equally serviceable in removing the hesitations that usually prompt people to ask for a proof.

If there is some such analogue to proof, it must unquestionably be considered in the present study of methodology. Otherwise the study will be open to a gross misunderstanding. It may lead people to suppose that the meagerness of proof *in the strict sense* deprives ethics of a "rational foundation" or "intersubjective validity" that is sorely needed; whereas all that is needed may in fact be provided for by the analogue mentioned.

To develop this point, let us return to imperatives, which have presented a methodological perplexity. Although imperatives cannot be "proved," are there not reasons or arguments which may at least "support" them?

The question is by no means difficult. An imperative may be met by the question "Why?" and this "Why?" asks for a *reason*. For instance: If told to close the door, one may ask "Why?" and receive some such reason as "It is too drafty," or "The noise is distracting." Or again, if a person is told to work harder, he may ask "Why?" and receive some such reply as "If you don't you will become an unhappy sort of dilettante." These reasons cannot be called "proofs" in any but a dangerously extended sense, nor are they demonstratively or inductively related to an imperative; but they manifestly do *support* an imperative. They "back it up," or "establish it," or "base it on concrete references to fact." And they are analogous to proofs in that they may remove the doubts or hesitations that prevent the imperative from being accepted.

The *way* in which the reasons support the imperative is simply this: The imperative is used to alter the hearer's attitudes or actions. In asking "Why?" the hearer indicates his hesitancy to comply. He will not do it "just because he is told to." The supporting reason then describes the situation which the imperative seeks to alter, or the new situation which the imperative seeks to bring about; and if these facts disclose that the new situation will satisfy a preponderance of the hearer's desires, he will hesitate to obey no longer. More generally, reasons support imperatives by altering such beliefs as may in turn alter an unwillingness to obey.

But do these remarks require elaboration? A moment's consideration will show that they do not; for they coincide with the remarks about agreement that have been made in Chapter I. We saw there that since attitudes tend to alter with altered beliefs, agreement in attitude may often be obtained by securing agreement in belief. Here we need only apply this general principle to a special type of case. The connection becomes apparent when the above paragraph is stated in different terminology:

An imperative is used to secure the satisfaction of the speaker's desire. The question "Why?" expressing the hearer's hesitation to comply, indicates an actual or incipient counterdesire. There is accordingly a disagreement in attitude. The reason, supporting the imperative, locates a possible source of disagreement in belief; and if the latter is settled, then, since beliefs and attitudes stand in intimate causal relationship, the disagreement in attitude may be caused to vanish in a way that makes the imperative willingly obeyed.

The "substitute proofs" or "supporting reasons" that we have been seeking can thus be recognized as familiar acquaintances under a new name: they are the expressions of belief that so often play an important, if indirect, role in situations that involve disagreement in attitude. Nor are these supporting reasons peculiar to imperatives. They may be used wherever disagreement in attitude occurs, whether it is indicated by laudatory or derogatory words, rhetorical questions, metaphors, animated inflections of voice, and so on.

With regard to the judgment that here particularly concerns us—"This is good" as schematically analyzed by definition (3),—the relevance of the supporting reasons will be obvious. Although the imperative component of the definiens, "Approve as well," is inadequate to the subtleties of ethics, it is doubly marked for use in disagreement in attitude; the very fact that it is an imperative at all so marks it, and it is marked again by its direct mention of the hearer's approval. Since reasons may support any statement that leads to agreement or disagreement in attitude, they clearly may support this one. . . .

VALIDITY

. . . One of the peculiarities of ethical arguments lies in the inference from a factual reason to an ethical conclusion. . . . Now in a valid ethical argument, must *this* step, no less than the steps in confirming the reasons, be valid? Or does the term "valid" here introduce an irrelevant consideration? That is: if "R" and "E" stand respectively for a set of reasons and an ethical conclusion, related neither deductively nor inductively, then is it of interest to ask whether an inference from E to R is valid?

Clearly, the inference will be neither *demonstratively* nor *inductively* valid, by hypothesis. By these standards of validity, it will always be *invalid*. But this is a triviality. When an inference does not purport to comply with the usual rules, any insistence on its failure to do so is gratuitous. We have marked out the step between R and E as different from any found in logic or science, and cannot expect it to be valid in the same way.

The only interesting issue is of another sort. Granted that demonstrative and inductive validity are irrelevant to this step, is there not some *other kind* of validity, peculiar to normative arguments, that deserves equal emphasis? Perhaps the usual rules for demonstrative and inductive inference need to be *supplemented* by special rules for inferences from R to E—rules which are enough like the others to be said, generically, to mark off *valid* inferences, but which are enough unlike the others to mark off a distinct *kind* of validity.

The term "validity" is not free from vagueness, and so can be defined in several alternative senses without "unnatural" distortions of language. One might, accordingly, devise some broad definition of the term in which certain inferences from R to E could be called "valid." It seems wholly impracticable and injudicious, however, to sanction such a sense. The grounds for saying this will be elaborated later in the chapter, but in brief they are as follows:

No matter how else we may define "valid," we shall very likely want to retain a sense which is intimately related to "true." The precise way in which the terms are to be related, and the precise meaning of them both, may occasion no little perplexity; but we shall in any case want to say that a "valid" method is more conducive to establishing truths, or probable truths, than any "invalid" one. Should anyone deny this, we should usually insist that he must be using either "valid" or "true" in some other sense than the perhaps poorly defined but still roughly intelligible one that we prefer. But if "valid" is to be applied to the step from R to E, then—as we shall see in a moment—the word could not have its accustomed connection with "true." Such a sense, which would almost certainly persist *in addition* to the truth-related sense or senses, might foster a misleading ambiguity, and keep people from making the requisite distinctions between reasons in ethics and reasons in logic or science. In the interest of clarity, then, it will be expedient to deny the word any application to the ethical cases in question.

But why will "valid," applied to an inference from R to E, be deprived of its connection with "true"? The answer must not depend on the contention that ethical judgments "cannot sensibly be called either 'true' or 'false.' " This is not so, even for the first pattern of analysis; for although the emotive meaning of an ethical judgment has nothing to do with truth or falsity (subject to a qualification to be made in Section 5), its descriptive meaning, which refers to the speaker's attitudes, may be true or false in the ordinary way. The point is rather that, for the step in argument we are considering, the reasons *do not establish or call into question* the truth of an ethical judgment's (descriptive) meaning. This can be made clearer by example: Suppose that A declares X to be good, and B declares it to be bad. And suppose that A supports his contention by pointing out the consequences of X. . . . A is not thereby calling into question the truth of B's ethical judgment; for B has said (according to the first pattern, and ignoring emotive meaning) only that he disapproves of X. So far from denying this, A may be presumed to believe it; and he is certainly free to do so, since between A's own judgment—which descriptively means that he, A, approves of X—and B's judgment—which descriptively means that he, B, disapproves of X—there is no logical contradiction. The opposition is in attitude, not in belief. What A is trying to do is not to question the truth of what B has said about his attitudes, but rather, as we have repeatedly seen, to *redirect* B's attitudes. Acknowledging that B began with the attitudes to which his initial judgment testified, A is pointing out the consequences of X in order to make B have different attitudes to X later on. This in no way questions the truth of B's initial judgment; [1] nor does it prove the truth of A's initial judgment, which was descriptive only of A's attitudes.

[1] For the first-pattern sense here in question, the ethical term of B's judgment refers only to his attitudes *at the time of speaking*. . . . His initial judgment is more strictly speaking his initial *utterance* of "X is bad"—that which began the argument. . . .

In general, when E is supported or opposed by R, R neither proves nor disproves the truth of the descriptive meaning of E. So unless "valid" is to have a misleadingly extended sense, the question, "Does R permit a valid inference to E?" is devoid of interest. One may, if he likes, say that such an inference is always "invalid" by the rules of formal logic or induction; but as we have seen, this is not to point out some inadvertency —some failure to observe rules that the inference might have been expected to follow. If anyone sought to make it follow these rules, he would deprive it of its distinctive function.

These remarks will require careful qualification, but in a general way they can be seen to proceed naturally from the foregoing chapters. The notion of validity retains its accustomed application to any aspect of an ethical argument that is concerned wholly with establishing *beliefs.* Illogicalities do not become logical, and lies do not become true, simply because they occur in a broader ethical context. But wherever these matters are in question an ethical argument is factual, its methodology falling within the widely studied fields of logic and scientific method. For the steps which go beyond these, and use beliefs in their turn to alter *attitudes,* questions about validity, in any helpful sense of the term, are irrelevant. In sum, wherever ethical methodology must be *distinguished* from logic and scientific method, validity presents no problem at all.

2

A dismissal of validity, even in this partial way, risks opening the way to certain misunderstandings in the course of guarding against others. The validity of a method stands out as the most conspicuous ground for choosing it; hence when certain methods, or aspects of them, are denied any connection with validity, one may feel that no ground for choice between them remains. Or if such a ground is recognized it may seem to involve only a crude, forensic success. So long as one's opponent is impressed (a hasty critic may suppose), one method is as good as another; for the whole purport of ethics is to sway attitudes. Where Plato and Kant sought eternal principles of reason, are there merely the empty rules of rhetoric? After this one is likely to envisage disillusionment and chaos, and the many other disturbing "implications" which objective theorists so habitually attribute to their opponents.

. . . any decision about what methods are to be used, if it cannot be made with reference to validity, is itself a normative ethical matter. This becomes quite obvious when the question is phrased in ordinary ethical terminology. To ask "What method shall I choose?" is in effect to ask "What method *ought* I choose?" Any argument about the question will involve disagreement in attitude; and the considerations which one adduces as "grounds" for choosing one method or another are simply the "reasons" . . . by which an ethical judgment—here a judgment about the way *another one is to be supported*—is itself supported.

To evaluate or recommend an ethical method (whenever validity can have no bearing on the case [2]) is to moralize about the ways of moralists. Ethical judgments may be made about innumerable actions, and the procedure of supporting a judgment, being itself an action, is open to judgment in its turn. When a man makes a judgment, E^1, which is about X, we may make a judgment, E^2, which is about his way of supporting E^1. Our way of supporting E^2 will then be open to the judgment E^3, and so on.

There is nothing vicious about this series of judgments. It would be vicious only if we had to begin at "the other end" of it, the series by its very nature having no "other end." In point of fact, we usually and quite feasibly begin right at "this" end. We do not withhold all expression of approval until having first decided whether we approve of approving of approving . . . of this kind of expression of approval. We simply *find* ourselves approving, and using certain methods to defend what we approve; and we call our procedure into question only when there is a practical likelihood of conflict or disagreement.

It is a consequence of these views, of course, that the use of an ethical method, whether it is selected out of habit or more self-consciously, will always be open to *possible* criticism. The goodness or badness of certain methods may be a topic of much argument; and the disagreement in attitude that it involves may at times, apart from a heuristic assumption to the contrary, be irreconcilable. Disagreement about the value of methods is like any other ethical disagreement. It can be reconciled by rational methods only if the disagreement in attitude is rooted in disagreement in

[2] There may be normative questions about methods even when the methods raise the ordinary considerations of validity. Thus it may be asked whether a scientist, in the interest of popularizing certain of his conclusions, is morally justified in defending them by superficially plausible methods which he himself knows to be invalid. But this, being obvious, is not of great concern to us. For the scientist, validity still remains as a possible ground for choice; whereas for the moralist, so far as he goes beyond purely logical and scientific inferences, it does not.

Some may wish to contend that "validity" *itself,* even in the conventional sense that applies to logic and science, is a *normative* term; but the writer suspects that any such contention would involve a misleading use of either the term "validity" or the term "normative." A logician who points out an inference as valid is not exhorting anyone to use it; he is simply saying that if anyone does make such an inference, using true premises, his conclusion, being contained in the premises, must also be true.

belief, and if the disagreement in belief is itself practically reconcilable. It can be resolved by persuasive methods only if the persuasion which people decide to use will be sufficiently moving. To say this is simply to specify the factors which could cause or fail to cause an agreement on ethical methods to come about; it is to view controversy about ethical methods with ethical *neutrality,* studying (though in a very general way) under what circumstances, hypothetical or actual, people will come to approve of the same methods, but without in any way taking steps to actualize or change these circumstances, and thus without explicitly trying to alter what ethical methods people may agree to accept. It is just this detachment which the greater part of the present volume, as a working limitation of its subject matter, wishes to preserve. However—and here it is necessary to emphasize, with application to the special case of making judgments about methods, the more general remarks that concluded Chapter IV—this must in no way be permitted to suggest that the reader, having for purposes of analysis been led to suspend any participation in normative controversy, must avoid any such participation forever afterward. A judgment about ethical methods, as distinct from a description of them, may be of great social importance; nor is it predestined to dogmatism or ineffectuality.

Should anyone feel, for instance, that persuasive methods are too frequently used by moralists, there is nothing in the present analysis to prevent him from making urgent ethical judgments to that effect. He will do well, of course, to support his own judgment largely by rational methods—for persuasion to end persuasion, like war to end war, is a disconcerting matter, even though in strictness of logic it is not a contradiction; but in any case there are many methods at his disposal. If he should feel that his ethical judgment, even of this sort, would still be a blind, egotistical effort to impose his preferences on others, contrary to his ideals, the answer is very simple. His effort will be blind and egotistical only if he makes it so, and his protestation of ideals to the contrary is itself evidence that he will not. An effort is usually called "blind" when it proceeds without knowledge of the factual situation, particularly the more remote consequences, with which it deals; and it is usually called "egotistical" when it is an expression of vanity. Hence if a person, in his efforts to make one method more widely used than another, does so in the light of much knowledge, and if his motives in propagating his attitudes are uncolored by vanity, his efforts will be neither blind nor egotistical in any usual sense. And should his efforts, if successful, lead people to be satisfied and thankful for his influence, they at any rate will not say that he has "imposed" his preferences on them, nor will they reproach him with any other abusive term.

But although an effort to judge ethical methods may be of unquestionable importance, the present work does not propose to join in the undertaking, save in passing. The methods of ethics must for the present be seen, all praise or condemnation of them being withheld. . . .

PERSUASIVE DEFINITIONS

. . . Definitions are usually studied as a propaedeutic to science, logic, or mathematics, with emphasis on the way they clarify common notions or make convenient abbreviations. One is likely to think, then, that definitions have the same function in ethics, and that the selection of any defined sense, from the many that the second pattern recognizes, will be guided by purely descriptive interests. In point of fact, this is rarely the case; description is usually a secondary consideration. Ethical definitions involve a wedding of descriptive and emotive meaning, and accordingly have a frequent use in redirecting and intensifying attitudes. To choose a definition is to plead a cause, so long as the word defined is strongly emotive. For the first pattern, attitudes are altered by ethical judgments; for the second, they are altered not only by judgments but by definitions. Thus the disagreements evinced by contrary *predications* of the ethical terms may also be evinced by contrary contentions about their *meaning*. Disagreement in attitude may be debated over the dictionary. It is this characteristic of second-pattern definitions that brings back all the considerations that the first pattern has introduced.

Any further steps in analysis must accordingly be prefaced by a study of the "persuasive definitions," as they will be called, which the second pattern so habitually involves. Since these definitions are not ethically neutral, and since analysis must strive to be so, the present work will not defend any one of them to the exclusion of others; but it will be possible to study typical instances of them in a way that indicates their nature and function.

. . . If "good" is *defined* as conducive to the preponderance of happiness over unhappiness for society as a whole, the effect of the definition is, among other things, to support democratic ideals. It urges us to consider the happiness of *each* man, equally and without exception, allowing nothing else the laudatory force of the ethical term. The fact that so many of us are partially willing to respond to this persuasion, and to employ it, must not blind us from seeing that it is persuasion. There will be others, with different ideals, who will insist on defining "good" with reference to the happiness of some privileged racial or social group. Their ideals clash with ours, if we are utilitarians; and we shall be unlikely to make them abandon their persuasive definition unless we support our own by the many considerations that determine changes in attitude.

R. M. Hare

Decisions of Principle *

. . . It is sometimes said by writers on morals that we have to justify an act by reference to its effects, and that we tell which effects are to be sought, which avoided, by reference to some principle. Such a theory is that of the utilitarians, who bid us look at the effects, and examine these in the light of the principle of utility, to see which effects would maximize pleasure. Sometimes, on the other hand, it is said (as by Mr. Toulmin) [1] that an act is justified directly by reference to the principles which it observes, and these principles in their turn by reference to the effects of always observing them. Sometimes it is said that we should observe principles and ignore the effects—though for the reasons given above 'effects' cannot be here intended in the sense in which I have been using it. What is wrong with these theories is not what they say, but their assumption that they are telling us the only way to justify actions, or decide what actions to do. We do, indeed, justify and decide on actions in all these ways; for example, sometimes, if asked why we did A, we say, 'Because it was a case falling under principle P', and if asked to justify P in turn, we go into the effects of observing it and of not observing it. But sometimes, when asked the same question 'Why did you do A?' we say 'Because if I hadn't, E would have happened', and if asked what was wrong about E happening, we appeal to some principle.

The truth is that, if asked to justify as completely as possible any decision, we have to bring in both effects—to give content to the decision—and principles, and the effects in general of observing those principles, and so on, until we have satisfied our inquirer. Thus a complete justification of a decision would consist of a complete account of its effects, together with a complete account of the principles which it observed, and the effects of observing those principles—for, of course, it is the

* From *The Language of Morals* by R. M. Hare, pp. 68–78. Copyright 1952 by Oxford University Press. Reprinted by permission of the publisher.

[1] *Reason in Ethics,* pp. 144 ff.

effects (what obeying them in fact consists in) which give content to the principles too. Thus, if pressed to justify a decision completely, we have to give a complete specification of the way of life of which it is a part. This complete specification it is impossible in practice to give; the nearest attempts are those given by the great religions, especially those which can point to historical persons who carried out the way of life in practice. Suppose, however, that we can give it. If the inquirer still goes on asking 'But why *should* I live like that?' then there is no further answer to give him, because we have already, *ex hypothesi,* said everything that could be included in this further answer. We can only ask him to make up his own mind which way he ought to live; for in the end everything rests upon such a decision of principle. He has to decide whether to accept that way of life or not; if he accepts it, then we can proceed to justify the decisions that are based upon it; if he does not accept it, then let him accept some other, and try to live by it. The sting is in the last clause. To describe such ultimate decisions as arbitrary, because *ex hypothesi* everything which could be used to justify them has already been included in the decision, would be like saying that a complete description of the universe was utterly unfounded, because no further fact could be called upon in corroboration of it. This is not how we use the words 'arbitrary' and 'unfounded'. Far from being arbitrary, such a decision would be the most well-founded of decisions, because it would be based upon a consideration of everything upon which it could possibly be founded.

It will be noticed how, in talking of decisions of principle, I have inevitably started talking value-language. Thus we decide that the principle *should* be modified, or that it is *better* to steer than to signal. This illustrates the very close relevance of what I have been saying in the first part of this book to the problems of the second part; for to make a value-judgement is to make a decision of principle. To ask whether I ought to do A in these circumstances is (to borrow Kantian language with a small though important modification) to ask whether or not I will that doing A in such circumstances should become a universal law.[2] It may seem a far cry from Kant to Professor Stevenson; but the same question could be put in other words by asking 'What attitude shall I adopt and recommend towards doing A in such circumstances?'; for 'attitude', if it means anything, means a principle of action. Unfortunately Stevenson, unlike Kant, devotes very little space to the examination of this first-person question; had he paid due attention to it, and avoided the dangers of the

[2] Cf. *Groundwork of the Metaphysic of Morals,* tr. H. J. Paton, p. 88.

word 'persuasive', he might have reached a position not unlike that of Kant.

4. 5. As Kant points out in the important passage on the Autonomy of the Will, to which I referred earlier, we have to make our own de-decisions of principle.[3] Other people cannot make them for us unless we have first decided to take their advice or obey their orders. There is an interesting analogy here with the position of the scientist, who also has to rely on his own observations. It might be said that there is a difference here between decisions and observations, to the detriment of the former, in that an observation, once made, is public property, whereas decisions have to made by the agent himself on each occasion. But the difference is only apparent. A scientist would not have become a scientist unless he had convinced himself that the observations of other scientists were in general reliable. He did this by making some observations of his own. When we learnt elementary chemistry at school, we had some theoretical periods and some practical. In the theoretical periods we studied books; in the practical periods we made experiments, and found, if we were lucky, that the results tallied with what the books said. This showed us that what the books said was not all nonsense; so that even if, by reason of disturbing factors ignored by us, our experiments came out wrong, we were inclined to trust the books and acknowledge that we had made a mistake. We were confirmed in this assumption by the fact that we often discovered later what the mistake had been. If our observations, however carefully we did them, were always at variance with the text-books, we should not be tempted to make science our profession. Thus the confidence of the scientist in other people's observations is ultimately based, among other things, on his own observations and his own judgements about what is reliable. He has in the end to rely on himself.

The case of the moral agent is not dissimilar. When in our early days we are given our elementary moral instruction, there are some things that we are told, and some things that we do. If, when we did as we are told, the total effects of our so doing, when they happened, were always such as we would not have chosen, had we known, then we should seek better advice, or, if prevented from so doing, either work out our own salvation or become moral defectives. If we are in general given what we subsequently come to see to have been good advice, we decide in general to follow the advice and adopt the principles of those who have given us this good advice in the past. This is what happens to any child who is well brought up. Just as the scientist does not try to rewrite all that is

[3] *Op. cit.*, pp. 108 ff.

in the textbooks, but takes that for granted and sticks to his own particular researches, so this fortunate child will take over bodily the principles of his elders and adapt them in detail, by his own decisions, to suit his own circumstances from time to time. This is how in a well-ordered society morality remains stable, and at the same time gets adapted to changing circumstances.

4. 6. There are, however, many ways in which this happy state of affairs can deteriorate. Let us consider a process that seems to occur quite often in history; it occurred in Greece during the fifth and fourth centuries, and it has occurred in our own time. Suppose that the people of a certain generation—I will call it the first generation—have got very settled principles, inherited from their fathers. Suppose that they have become so settled as to be second nature, so that generally speaking people act on the principles without thinking, and their power of making considered decisions of principle becomes atrophied. They act always by the book, and come to no harm, because the state of the world in their time remains much the same as that for which the principles were thought out. But their sons, the second generation, as they grow up, find that conditions have changed (e.g. through a protracted war or an industrial revolution), and that the principles in which they have been brought up are no longer adequate. Since, in their education, much stress has been laid on observing principles, and very little on making the decisions on which these principles are ultimately based, their morality has no roots, and becomes completely unstable. Books on 'The Whole Duty of Man' are no longer written or read. Often, when they do what it says in such books, they subsequently find cause to regret their decisions; and there are too many cases of this kind for any confidence in the old principles, as a body, to remain. No doubt there are among these old principles certain very general ones, which will remain acceptable unless human nature and the state of the world undergo a most fundamental change; but the second generation, not having been brought up to make decisions of principle, but to do what it says in the book, will not, most of them, be able to make those crucial decisions which would determine which principles to keep, which to modify, and which to abandon. Some people, the Polemarchuses of the second generation, will have been so steeped in the old principles that they just follow them come what may; and these will on the whole be more fortunate than the others, for it is better to have some principles, even if they sometimes lead to decisions which we regret, than to be morally adrift. The bulk of the second generation, and still more perhaps of the third, will not know which of the principles

to keep and which to reject; and so they will come more and more to live from day to day—not a bad thing, because it trains their powers of decision, but it is an unpleasant and dangerous state to be in. A few among them, the rebels, will shout from the housetops that some or all of the old moral principles are worthless; some of these rebels will advocate new principles of their own; some will have nothing to offer. Though they increase the confusion, these rebels perform the useful function of making people decide between their rival principles; and if they not only advocate new principles, but sincerely try to live by them, they are conducting a moral experiment which may be of the utmost value to man (in which case they go down in history as great moral teachers), or may, on the other hand, prove disastrous both to them and to their disciples.

It may take several generations for this disease to play itself out. Morality regains its vigour when ordinary people have learnt afresh to decide for themselves what principles to live by, and more especially what principles to teach their children. Since the world, though subject to vast material changes, changes only very slowly in matters that are fundamental from the moral point of view, the principles which win the acceptance of the mass of people are not likely to differ enormously from those which their fathers came to distrust. The moral principles of Aristotle resemble those of Aeschylus more than they differ from them, and we ourselves shall perhaps come back to something recognizably like the morality of our grandfathers. But there will be some changes; some of the principles advocated by the rebels will have been adopted. That is how morality progresses—or retrogresses. The process is, as we shall see, reflected by very subtle changes in the uses of value-words; the impossibility of translating Aristotle's catalogue of virtues into modern English may serve as an example, and the disappearance without trace of the word 'righteous' may serve as another.

4. 7. The question 'How shall I bring up my children?' which we have mentioned, is one to the logic of which, since ancient times, few philosophers have given much attention. A child's moral upbringing has an effect upon him which will remain largely untouched by anything that happens to him thereafter. If he has had a stable upbringing, whether on good principles or on bad ones, it will be extremely difficult for him to abandon those principles in later life—difficult but not impossible. They will have for him the force of an objective moral law; and his behaviour will seem to give much evidence in support of intuitionist ethical theories, provided that it is not compared with the behaviour to those

who stick just as firmly to quite different principles. But nevertheless, unless our education has been so thorough as to transform us into automata, we can come to doubt or even reject these principles; that is what makes human beings, whose moral systems change, different from ants, whose moral system does not. Therefore, even if for me the question 'What shall I do in such and such a situation?' is almost invariably answered without ambiguity by the moral intuition which my upbringing has given me, I may, if I ask myself 'How shall I bring up my children?' pause before giving an answer. It is here that the most fundamental moral decisions of all arise; and it is here, if only moral philosophers would pay attention to them, that the most characteristic uses of moral words are to be found. Shall I bring up my children *exactly* as I was brought up, so that they have the same intuitions about morals as I have? Or have circumstances altered, so that the moral character of the father will not provide a suitable equipment for the children? Perhaps I shall try to bring them up like their father, and shall fail; perhaps their new environment will be too strong for me, and they will come to repudiate my principles. Or I may have become so bewildered by the strange new world that, although I still act from force of habit on the principles that I have learnt, I simply do not know what principles to impart to my children, if, indeed, one in my condition can impart any settled principles at all. On all these questions, I have to make up my mind; only the most hide-bound father will try to bring up his children, without thinking, in exactly the way that he himself was brought up; and even he will usually fail disastrously.

Many of the dark places of ethics become clearer when we consider this dilemma in which parents are liable to find themselves. We have already noticed that, although principles have in the end to rest upon decisions of principle, decision as such cannot be taught; only principles can be taught. It is the powerlessness of the parent to make for his son those many decisions of principle which the son during his future career will make, that gives moral language its characteristic shape. The only instrument which the parent possesses is moral education—the teaching of principles by example and precept, backed up by chastisement and other more up-to-date psychological methods. Shall he use these means, and to what extent? Certain generations of parents have had no doubts about this question. They have used them to the full; and the result has been to turn their children into good intuitionists, able to cling to the rails, but bad at steering round corners. At other times parents—and who shall blame them?—suffer from lack of confidence; they are not sure enough what they themselves think, to be ready to impart to their children a stable way of life. The children of such a generation are likely to grow up opportunists, well able to make individual decisions, but without the settled body of principles which is the most priceless heritage that any generation can leave to its successors. For, though principles are in the end built upon decisions of principle, the building is the work of many generations, and the man who has to start from the beginning is to be pitied; he will not be likely, unless he is a genius, to achieve many conclusions of importance, any more than the average boy, turned loose without instruction upon a desert island, or even in a laboratory, would be likely to make any of the major scientific discoveries.

The dilemma between these two extreme courses in education is plainly a false one. Why it is a false one is apparent, if we recall what was said earlier about the dynamic relation between decisions and principles. It is very like learning to drive. It would be foolish, in teaching someone to drive, to try to inculcate into him such fixed and comprehensive principles that he would never have to make an independent decision. It would be equally foolish to go to the other extreme and leave it to him to find his own way of driving. What we do, if we are sensible, is to give him a solid basis of principles, but at the same time ample opportunity of making the decisions upon which these principles are based, and by which they are modified, improved, adapted to changed circumstances, or even abandoned if they become entirely unsuited to a new environment. To teach only the principles, without giving the opportunity of subjecting them to the learner's own decisions of principle, is like teaching exclusively from the textbooks without entering the laboratory. On the other hand, to abandon one's child or one's driving-pupil to his own self-expression is like putting a boy into a laboratory and saying 'Get on with it'. The boy may enjoy himself or kill himself, but will probably not learn much science.

The moral words, of which we may take 'ought' as an example, reflect in their logical behaviour this double nature of moral instruction—as well they may, for it is in moral instruction that they are most typically used. The sentences in which they appear are normally the expression of decisions of principle—and it is easy to let the decisions get separated, in our discussion of the subject, from the principles. This is the source of the controversy between the 'objectivists', as intuitionists sometimes call themselves, and the 'subjectivists', as they often call their opponents. The former lay stress on the fixed principles that are handed down by the father, the latter on the new decisions which have to be made by the son. The objectivist says 'Of course you know what you ought to do; look at what your conscience tells you, and if in doubt go by the consciences of the vast majority of men'. He is able to say this, because our consciences are the product of the principles which our early training has indelibly planted in us, and in one society these principles do not differ much from one person to another. The subjectivist, on the other hand, says 'But surely, when it comes to the point—when I have listened to what other people say, and given due weight to my own intuitions, the legacy of my upbringing—I have in the end to decide for myself what I ought to do. To deny this is to be a conventionalist; for both common moral notions and my own intuitions are the legacy of tradition, and—apart from the fact that there are so many different traditions in the world—traditions cannot be started without someone doing what I now feel called upon to do, decide. If I refuse to make my own decisions, I am, in merely copying my fathers, showing myself a lesser man than they; for whereas they must have initiated, I shall be merely accepting.' This plea of the subjectivist is quite justified. It is the plea of the adolescent who wants to be adult. To become morally adult is to reconcile these two apparently conflicting positions by learning to make decisions of principle; it is to learn to use 'ought'-sentences in the realization that they can only be verified by reference to a standard or set of principles which we have by our own decision accepted and made our own. This is what our present generation is so painfully trying to do.

Philip Blair Rice

Aesthetic Judgment *

This is the Age of Criticism *par excellence,* and never before, perhaps, has there been a body of criticism so massive and so acute. When the philosopher approaches the question of aesthetic standards, it is only at his peril that he by-passes this body of criticism and goes directly and exclusively to the arts themselves. What has been said in preceding chapters about the crystallization of explicit maxims and principles out of evaluative habits already operating in the community receives striking confirmation here. The working critic, who may be innocent of aesthetic philosophy and even contemptuous of it, nevertheless assumes criteria of what is legitimate in art, and of what makes it good or bad, that may correspond closely with the standards formulated and elaborated by philosophers. To the extent that the critic has a consistent point of view, he is tacitly presupposing an aesthetic theory, whether he acknowledges the fact or not; and if he is inconsistent, the philosopher will have no difficulty in exposing a muddled *mélange* of principles.

The philosopher may discover his aesthetic principles by extracting these unformulated assumptions of critics; or, alternatively, through the interaction between his own direct experience of the beautiful and his philosophical categories drawn primarily from other domains of experience. Usually, today, when we have such a lively and insistent body of criticism that the aesthetician cannot escape it, he must shuttle back and forth between the two procedures.

But there is another side to this relation of give-and-take between aesthetics and criticism. Not only may the aesthetician discover and articulate his principles by making explicit the structural presuppositions of the working critic; the only way, finally, that he can test or "justify" them is by a return to the practice of criticism, either in his own person or, in part, vicariously through the success of professional critics in il-

* From *On the Knowledge of Good and Evil* by Philip Blair Rice, pp. 216–230.

luminating art, whether this be by applying the explicit principles devised by the philosopher or, as more commonly, by submitting the corresponding working assumptions to the fire of critical practice. And this justification is a pragmatic one, or a vindication by involvement: hence the relationship between aesthetician and critic both supports the general account of justification we have sketched in Chapters 9 and 10 and illustrates its inconclusiveness. For there can be no definitive criticism of a great work of art. Hence the dubiety of the critic's conclusions is transmitted to the aesthetic principles when they may be taken to "justify."

This dual relation between philosophy and criticism is exemplified by parallel developments in both fields, which have led to the major cleavages in current controversies within each. The philosophical conflict between cognitivists and noncognitivists, or between those who uphold the possibility of aesthetic principles and those who repudiate it, is paralleled by the central dispute between the so-called New Critics and their adversaries. Although the New Criticism is not a "school" but a loose collection of diverse critics, they are usually grouped together because they share a common tendency. This tendency is to distinguish rather sharply the aesthetic attitude from non-aesthetic attitudes, and to make such a distinction the basis of critical practice. Thus the New Critics hold that the focus of critical attention should be on "the poem itself," or the painting itself, etc., rather than on its ambience—historical, biographical, social, moral or political—however much the critic may have to deviate into these fields in order to elucidate the poem. And secondly, criticism is held as by John Crowe Ransom to be "the attempt to define and enjoy the aesthetic or characteristic values of literature." In practice, the New Critics are distinctively concerned with such elements of literature as imagery, metaphor, structure and the linguistic factors in the immediate aesthetic effect.

The most vigorous movement in opposition to the New Criticism objected to what it considered the divorce between the aesthetic and other kinds of attitudes, stressing the psychological, social and ideational context of literature and the mutual dependency of art and "life." Its concern has been with literature as an expression of morals, manners and motivation, and its capacity in turn to shed light on these.

This cleavage within the critical camp—which goes back of the current scene to Coleridge on the one side and Arnold on the other—is reflected by a similar broad division within philosophical aesthetics which has grown up more or less independently. Roughly on the side of the New Critics are Kant and his descendants who try to delimit the aesthetic attitude or aesthetic experience as sharply as possible from such activities as the scientific, the moral and the practical. Thus Kant offered as his criteria of the aesthetic: disinterestedness, the non-conceptual (whether sub-conceptual or supra-conceptual) character of the experience, "purposiveness without a purpose," subjective necessity or universality. And Santayana, in *The Sense of Beauty* (1896), distinguished the aesthetic from the non-aesthetic by the "objectification" of meanings and values in the response to a work of art or of natural beauty.

Aligned on the other side are such aestheticians as John Dewey and (in his early work) I. A. Richards, who emphasize the continuity between so-called aesthetic and non-aesthetic activities, rather than their distinctness, showing how they draw upon each other and shade into each other.

This dispute over the question whether the aesthetic attitude or experience can be distinguished from other types of experience is not directly a controversy over the criteria of aesthetic valuation but, nevertheless, it is a preliminary issue basic to any attempt to define aesthetic value.

In modern aesthetic theory, the two focal questions have been, "What is the aesthetic attitude?" and "What is aesthetic value?" These correspond to the two polar topics of literary criticism, as stated by T. S. Eliot: "What is poetry?" and "Is this a good poem?" (*The Use of Poetry and the Use of Criticism,* 1933).

If both sets of questions are meaningful and legitimate, then in order to establish a principle of aesthetic value we would first (in some sense of first) have to justify a theory of the nature of the aesthetic experience or the aesthetic attitude, and then base a principle of aesthetic value on this together with our general doctrine of intrinsic and extrinsic goodness. Thus: an aesthetic experience is one characterized by properties A, B, C . . . ; an aesthetically valuable experience is an aesthetic experience (as just defined) which conforms to our criterion of intrinsic goodness. Similarly: an aesthetically valuable object is one that is inherently valuable and capable of leading to aesthetically valuable experiences under specified conditions.

The procedure, however, would not in practice be as simple as this, since our analysis of the nature of aesthetic experience itself would be partly dependent on its capacity to fit in with a definition of intrinsic value. The kind of experiences that we would decide to label as aesthetic would in part depend on the fitness of experiences of this kind to satisfy a criterion of valuableness; just as we cannot define art without some conception of what good art would be. Here as elsewhere in philosophy it is hazardous to assign any one principle an absolute priority over related principles.

Furthermore, when we come to aesthetics we cannot simply assume as established certain principles of extrinsic and intrinsic value, and then apply them automatically to the subject matter. For the justification of these principles themselves depends in part on their applicability to special normative domains such as the aesthetic.

2. AESTHETIC PRINCIPLES

The standard aesthetic theories offer a number of competing candidates for the defining property of the aesthetic. They can be classified with rough adequacy into Imitation, Form, and Expression theories: each type of theory has some plausible claim to adequacy for a certain kind of art, but is inapplicable to other kinds. Moreover, within each of these broad types of theories there is a similar partial but incomplete plausibility for its several versions. Imitation theories differ as to what is imitated: whether it is particular objects, or universals, or universals in particulars, or actions in their historical and social contexts. The divergence among formalistic theories as to what is meant by Form is notorious. Expression theories are similarly at variance as to what expression consists in: whether an overflowing of the artist's personality or an evocation of a feeling or image in a beholder, or a communication of psychological responses to an object.

But this situation does not entail any radical skepticism or vicious relativism with respect to the possibility of bringing some intellectual order into the aesthetic domain. It simply demonstrates that aestheticians and critics have been looking in the wrong place for principles; that they have been seeking defining properties of the aesthetic at too low a level of generality. In accordance with the general analysis we have offered in this book, they have been seeking to treat as Identifying Properties characteristics of art that are fitted only to serve as Conferring Properties.

The point needs no belaboring where "canons" or rules appropriate to a specific Kind or particular Style are in question. The most that can be claimed for a set of such canons is that they express good-making properties within a specific type of art—Perpendicular Gothic or Baroque architecture, Imagist or Metaphysical poetry, Impressionist or Expressionist painting. The so-called aesthetic principles of artists themselves, and of the critics who write manifestoes for a movement, are often little more than rules of technique for obtaining an effect of a sort that constitutes the peculiar strength of a school, or for exploiting a newly recognized possibility of the art. As such they have their uses, and they constantly turn up new material for the aesthetic philosopher to take account of; but the attempt to erect them into principles applicable to all art can lead to nothing but the most cramping dogmatism or, in reaction against this, the most paralyzing relativism.

Such so-called principles as those of Imitation, Form or Expression theories come closer than legislation of "canons" to serving the purpose with which we are concerned, for each of them can be interpreted as an overemphasis on a structural element that is present in all, or nearly all, instances of the broad aesthetic domain. Thus the Imitation theories, in their wide range, call attention to the fact that the work of art can function as a designative sign—whether a sign of a particular object or an "idea" designating an abstracted set of properties and relationships approximated elsewhere in reality; and that this potential designativeness, whether it becomes explicit in aesthetic experience proper or not, lends dynamic thrust to the response to the work. The Form theories emphasize the fact that the internal relationships—of graphic design, of tonal linkage, or rhythmic pattern, etc.—within the total aesthetic object or aesthetic sign are susceptible of a higher degree of satisfying organization than in the objects encountered in ordinary experience, and that this organization is a major source of the resultant effect. The Expression theory, at least in those versions which treat expression as capacity to arouse an affectively toned resonance in a qualified beholder (rather than, say, the overflow of an emotion in the artist), comes somewhat closer to the required degree of generality than Imitation and Form theories. For it incorporates the insights of the other two types of theory by treating the representational and formal elements as the carriers of expression, one or the other being more prominent in different artistic styles—*e.g.*, in narrative poetry or in non-objective painting.

The Expression theory itself, however, can be defended as definitory of the aesthetic only if it relates the expressive element to the formal and representational factors in a total attitude which is distinguishable generically from such attitudes as the cognitive or practical. A definition of the aesthetic attitude by a set of properties A, B, C, . . . would have to be vindicated in a manner analogous, up to a point, with a vindication of a definition of intrinsic goodness, or aesthetic value. It would, that is to say, have to be justified by showing that it corresponded to a basic cleavage in the structure of our attitudes, and would have to enlist and sustain, through a close critical involvement with art, our sense of the importance of such a distinction for our ordering of experience.

Even those recent philosophers who have opposed a sharp separation between the aesthetic and the non-aesthetic nevertheless make a distinction of degree. Thus, for Dewey, the aesthetic experience is more of "*an* experience" than other types of experience (*i.e.,* has more qualitative unity), and it is a richer source of "delightful perception." For Richards, likewise, though the aesthetic experience is composed of the materials and impulses to be found in ordinary experience, it gives them a finer organization, and it does so by keeping the impulses at an "incipient" level.

Just as in recent criticism there is a tendency for the New and the Old Critics to find some common ground by which their two approaches can be combined when the occasion requires, so in recent aesthetic theory some kind of synthesis between the Kantian and the Deweyan approaches seems possible. Although, of course, nothing resembling complete agreement has been reached, it is possible to list certain characteristics of the aesthetic attitude on which there is considerable convergence. The aesthetic attitude is contemplative of the given, together with its charge of immanent meanings, rather than explicitly directed upon objects external to the immediate presentation and signified by them. The aesthetic experience is meaningful, but it consists in an implict grasp of meanings rather than the kind of explicit exhibition of them that characterizes certain aspects of critical, scientific, and other so-called cognitive activities. The aesthetic experience is highly charged with emotional expression, but tries to keep this charge under control so that it is not placed at the center of attention in such a way as to distract us from the pattern of sounds or visual forms which is at or near the focus of our contemplation. The aesthetic experience is intransitive in the sense that its transitions occur within atention to an aesthetic object rather than pointing us toward something outside this object. The aesthetic attitude is "active" in that it involves an arousal of interpretative attitudes and of incipient strivings toward the object; it is "passive" or contemplative in that it keeps these attitudes and strivings in check, so that we submit ourselves to the guidance of the aesthetic object and do not allow the sign-function of the object to turn us away from it so that we engage in activities prompted by it.

If a more precise and detailed statement of the distinguishing characteristics is offered, this can serve as the defining property of the aesthetic experience presupposed by a definition of the aesthetically valuable.

But a statement of such a defining property would have to be somewhat complicated, and much lengthier than we have come to expect a definition to be. If we are to do justice to any type of activity as complicated as the aesthetic, we cannot expect to put its characterization into one small package. The "definition" therefore would in effect amount to an extended summary of an aesthetic theory: the "principle" would turn out to be a rather elaborate network of related principles.

However the aesthetic experience may be defined, such a criterion by itself does not suffice to delimit aesthetic value, for an object may satisfy the criterion for something's being an aesthetic object and yet the criterion may fail for comparative judgments of value, when we ask on what grounds this object is aesthetically better than that. Consequently our definition of aesthetic value must be based on some one of our concepts of value in general, such as intrinsic or inherent value.

Each of the four major theories we have considered would define these—or dub them indefinable—in its own terms. For the intuitionist, of course, there would be a simple, indefinable, unanalyzable, non-natural quality which, when contemplated aesthetically, is the quality of Beauty. Something like an intuitionist theory is presupposed by the more dogmatic literary and art critics of various persuasions. Thus for Clive Bell and the early Roger Fry (who in fact were influenced by G. E. Moore) "significant form" represents such a quality of Beauty. Or, for the more moralistically inclined critics, such as the late neo-humanists, the intuited quality is essentially a moral property rather than a distinctively aesthetic one; thus the ultimate basis of judgment is an ethical one.

For the emotivists, there is no single defining property of intrinsic value, but any property can serve the purpose if, in the particular case, we approve of it without regard to the consequences of the object and try to persuade others to approve of it also. Emotivism in its cruder forms expresses the presuppositions of the impressionistic critic who conducts the soul on an adventure among masterpieces and does not try to analyze the properties which define the beautiful. It also voices the attitude of the solid citizen who says, "I don't know if it's art but I like it."

The Good Reasons approach seems to correspond much more closely than does the emotivist theory to the practice of a good working critic who has no articulated set of principles. The critic is "giving reasons" for an interpretation and judgment of a work of art. These reasons are usually unsystematic: the critic rarely appeals to explicit principles. He proceeds on the assumption that he has a working knowledge of what distinguishes good or relevant reasons from bad or irrelevant ones.

In some sense he has confidence that he "knows" what makes a good or bad work when he encounters and observes it, even though this knowledge is not an explicit deduction from principles. And certainly this is all that we can demand of the critic *qua critic:* that is to say, in so far as he can be distinguished from the philosophical aesthetician. But when critics disagree, or when their judgments are challenged, we inevitably call for the reasons behind the reasons, that is to say, for principles, criteria and definitions; and the critic cannot escape undertaking the philosopher's function.

3. AN AFFECTIVE THEORY OF AESTHETIC VALUE

When the analytical critic, as distinguished from the impressionistic or dogmatic one, does appeal to valuational principles they usually turn out to be of the general type of those proposed by either an affective theory or a conative theory. I. A. Richards, for example, who is almost the only critic in our time who has sought to work out in detail "principles of literary criticism," defined value as the satisfaction of an interest or an appetency. Art gives us a fuller and finer organization of our impulses, even though these remain at an incipient level, than these impulses can achieve in daily life. The experience of art, furthermore, has "carry-over" value: it makes us more vigilant to the complexities of experience, and—to put the matter in Coleridge's language—better able to cope with the "opposite or discordant qualities" that we encounter in daily life, and to bring them into some sort of "balance or reconcilement." The pleasure that we get from art, according to Richards, is a byproduct, and too variable and slippery a thing for the critic to take into account in his judgments. The critic, consequently, must base his valuation of the work upon its fitness to produce an organization of impulses, either within the aesthetic experience itself or through its after-effects in the course of our lives. Richards does not make it quite clear which, or what is to be given priority when the two conflict.

The tendency of most working critics who make a distinction in principle between the aesthetic and the non-aesthetic is, however, to favor the affective theory rather than the conative theory. Even the sober Wordsworth, who would not be thought of as a hedonist in his general attitude toward life, writes in the Preface to *Lyrical Ballads:*

> The end of poetry is to produce excitement in co-existence with an overbalance of pleasure. . . . The poet writes under one restriction only, namely, the necessity of giving immediate pleasure to a human being possessed of

> that information which may be expected of him; not as a lawyer, a physician, a mariner, an astronomer or a natural philosopher, but as a man.

This view Wordsworth shared with the idealistic Coleridge. It is noteworthy that one of our leading 20th Century critics, T. S. Eliot, who would repudiate emphatically a hedonistic or utilitarian ethics, nevertheless writes that the aim of poetry is to give a kind of refined intellectual enjoyment. He has commented even on his religious poem, *Ash Wednesday,* that its purpose, quoting Byron's remark on *Don Juan,* is to make the reader "a moment merry." In fact, to give poetry a more exalted function than this is, he holds, to follow Arnold in making it a substitute for religion. Eliot does not, however, deny that art can have other values besides the aesthetic. In *The Use of Poetry and the Use of Criticism,* he quotes Horace's dictum that art is both *dulce* and *utile* to show that historically conceived poetry has served both functions—and many others.

I believe that a carefully stated affective theory can take care of both these functions, and also allow for the carry-over value into daily life that Richards assigns to art. Slippery as enjoyment is, it is more accessible to observation than the neural impulses to which Richards ultimately reduces his appetencies. Commitment to an affective theory does not necessarily imply that the critic talks very much directly about the feelings that the work gives to himself or others. Most of his talk has to do exclusively with the elements in the work which are the *sources* of affect. He is concerned with tracing the statement, repetition and variation of themes or symbols, with the fresh employment of language, with the significance of the ideas that are assumed or adumbrated by the poem or novel, and with the writer's capacity to keep these ideas functioning with due unobtrusiveness, with the shimmer of the aesthetic surface and the achievement of contrast along with the maintenance of unity of tone. But the critic must also keep in mind that none of these things is an absolute or necessarily confers intrinsic value. His concern must be with the individual work, and here anything he may say by way of analysis about its elements or structure can be very wide of the mark unless these are traced back to their consummation in feeling. So "ultimately," as Eliot says, all the critic can do is to point to those features of a work which the critic feels to be good.

William Empson says in effect (*Seven Types of Ambiguity,* revised edition, 1947), that there are two kinds of critical dogs: the appreciative dog, who merely relieves himself against the flower of beauty, and the analytical dog, who likes to scratch around the roots to see what makes the flower grow. Although most of his own work has been in the line of analysis, and he holds that this must constitute the bulk of the attention of any critic who is persistently concerned with literature, nevertheless the complete critic would be both kinds of a dog. He must be aware, so in effect Empson suggests, that the ultimate function of the metabolism of the plant is to produce the flower. And the critic cannot ultimately gain our confidence unless he indicates—even if only by a phrase—the kind of total effect on him that the elements he has analyzed add up to, "so straddling a commotion and so broad a calm."

Criticism becomes a sterile and mechanical exercise without this constant reference to fresh response by way of feeling. All this is not to deny the relevance of a conative theory, provided we assign the impulses and strivings their proper role. The feeling response itself arises only out of a rich interplay of incipient impulses, and these impulses take their thrust from the importance that they have in the more fully executed manifestations that they exhibit outside their aesthetic functioning. There is, consequently, a constant need for concern with the so-called truth of art and with the bearing of its insights on our moral economy. But the aesthetic judgment proper can be delimited through a recognition that there is not a simple equation between the truth or moral importance of an impulse outside the contemplative aesthetic act and its reverberation within it. The work of art is arranged to give us these impulses in such a form that they pay immediate dividends, and often their soundness in the long-run context of life must be sacrificed for this; for the artist does not what he wills but what he can, and whatever his alliances with the philosopher, the moralist and the educator, he cannot aim directly at usurping their functions. Art is what morality or philosophy or religion does in its playtime moods, and it must be granted a margin of license and irresponsibility for the sake of its immediate bounties and glories.

An affective theory, however, is not committed to holding that art must be mindless. In fact, it should recognize that the most inexhaustible sources of enjoyment are those that incorporate the activities of mind; and only those works of art which have profound undercurrents of meaning are capable of giving enjoyment on repeated experiences of them.

But the vindication of aesthetic principles is finally, one should repeat, an enterprise to be carried out not by the aesthetician but by the artist, the critic and the loving consumer, with whatever humble collaboration he may obtain from the philosopher.

Are Values Relative or Absolute?

Eduard Spranger

Types of Men *

THE ONESIDED SYSTEMS OF ETHICS

The ethical problem would be greatly simplified if it were possible to emphasize one class of values as the specifically moral one or even to reduce all other values to it as the finally affirmed one. This attempt has actually been made with every class of value, not only in theory but also in ethical practice. There are therefore as many onesided systems of ethics as there are attitudes, so we need only to summarize what we have said about each attitude in regard to its specific ethics.

1. Corresponding to the economic type is the utilitarian system of ethics.[1] It represents an attempt to reduce all values to those of utility: that is, to make everything fundamentally subserve maintainance of life and adaptation to environmental conditions. The apparently discordant moral evaluation in the historically given systems of morals is harmonized, by a theoretic procedure of translation, with the accepted fundamental principles. And to this end classic models are used. Just as the Epicurean

* From *Types of Men* by Eduard Spranger, translated by Paul J. W. Pigors, pp. 257–266, 312–315. Copyright 1928 by Max Niemeyer Verlag. Reprinted by permission of the publisher.

[1] In regard to terminology I mention that I understand by Hedonism the theory which regards the feelings: [i. e. the feelings of pleasant and unpleasant] as the sole criteria of morality, quite regardless of whether pleasure is viewed as the accompaniment of the act or the reflex effect of the result. By Utilitarianism I mean that system of ethics which sees the only motive of purposive behavior in values of utility and thus correlates the moral and the useful. It is secondary whether one refers to one's own use or the benefit of society. (Egoism plus Altruism equals collective utilitarianism). Eudaemonism on the other hand seeks the criterion of morality in the total satisfaction-fulfilling value and meaning which is reflected from the result of activity guided by value to the subject and the formation of his motives. As many levels of Eudaemonism are conceivable as there are levels of human total satisfactions. Energism is a kind of Eudaemonism which finds the moral factor in the act and its value content itself and not necessarily in the actual result. — All these forms of economic ethics confront the ethics of duty; the latter starts from a different point of view but may finally coincide to some extent with the higher forms of Eudaemonism as soon as the thought is added that the ultimate satisfaction of man is found in being and doing what he ought to be and do.

conceived of morality as a kind of balance of happiness, they make here a balance of utility. It has been shown, for instance, that anti-social behavior is injurious to the agent himself just like error and dishonesty. Collective utilitarianism develops if everyone acts in accordance with his own benefit but is also forced to consider the good of others for his own sake. As a rule this is reduced to a biological foundation of impulses and instincts. Conscience is finally represented as an inherited social instinct which contains unconscious purposiveness. Thus there seems to appear a connected, strictly logical system of morals in which, through the whole evolutionary process, utility is always the criterion of genuine evaluation.

And indeed the prevailing system of morals not only condones but demands the striving for one's own good. If anyone neglects his own life, his house, his clothes or his business, society usually blames him. Only in a community of recluses, of beggar monks or of ascetics would the moral judgment be different. Economic egoism may therefore belong among the positive ethical values. There only remains to ask whether it can, alone and to an unlimited extent, be called moral.

The answer must be in the negative. And this because of the simple consideration that utility is not essentially a final but only an intermediary value. The maintenance of life is a *conditio sine qua non* for the actualization of all other values. And consequently economic values are always to a certain degree the most urgent but not the highest.[2] In Plato there is a statement made by Socrates to the effect that doctors cure people without asking whether it is a good thing that they should live. And really it is always a question what is the worth of life, which is preserved by economic means. If life in itself, regardless of how one lives, is an independent value then of course economic values are final. But civilized ethics has progressed beyond this point of view. The man who can in certain circumstances renounce life in order to create a mental value is no longer utilitarian; or better: he is so only to the degree in which he is capable of fulfilling his highest value destiny. The values of utility point then toward an ethical value of its own, and from this only is the ethical character reflected onto the economic region also.

2. Corresponding to the theoretic type is not the ethics of truth (this being instead a branch of the social ethics) but the ethics of general legality. Its essence is the formation of behavior into a closed system,

[2] Gossen's law of final utility which has been evolved out of an isolated economic theory of values, grades within the economic the kinds of needs only in accordance with their urgency.

the achievement of inner consequentiality and consistency of personality. Thus the values of objectivity and of legal order are elevated to the highest determining powers of life. To be moral is to live by maxims.

There is no doubt that consistency of behavior is a genuine ethical value regardless of whether we are dealing with a law identical for all beings (as rational creatures) or whether it is a definite law for individuality in its specific structure (as for instance the law of gravity is identical everywhere on earth but the specific gravity of bodies is different). But few will agree with Kant that this consistency, or autonomous normativity in accordance with general laws, solves the whole problem of morality. The proof of general causality in the theory of cognition does not explain all of physics, nor, similarly, is the ethical value problem solved by a metaphysic of morals which only gives the form of ethics, that is, its logic. The point is rather to say from which value content one should derive the general maxims of behavior. Our position in regard to Kant's ethics is thus a divided one insofar as we believe that he has (1) correctly designated the criterion of morality in the normative experience (in its character of duty); and (2) that he has developed a onesided form of ethics, namely that of consistency of behavior united with the ethics of freedom . . . but that he has not done justice to the entire scope of the ethical value problem because he has confined himself to the theoretic type. Legality, rationality and identity of personality in the will to value are part of ethics but only part.

3. Not very different is the third onesided form of ethics which corresponds to the aesthetic type; the ethics of inner form. Its essence is the binding of individuality and the universality of experience into a totality, an inner whole in which every impulse of life is correctly measured according to its importance for the personality. The striving for inner wealth of experience and harmony, for calokagathy, for the μέτρον ἔχον of Plato and for the golden mean of Aristotle, for the aesthetic balance of form and matter, of reason and sensuality is certainly a genuine ethical principle.[3] But it cannot be carried out without the others, for, if we speak of the proper form and harmony of values the latter must enter into ethical experience. As Shaftesbury has correctly pointed out we must find, for instance, the mean between egoism and altruism. But even between individuality (as a concrete principle of life) and the general validity of ethical maxims, correct balance must be aimed at. According to aesthetic ethics this is entirely a matter of natural taste

[3] For further explanation of this type cf. the introduction to my book *Wilhelm v. Humboldt und die Humanitaetsidee.*

which judges the proportions of subjectivity. But this is only possible if the individuals themselves and their ethical value content are given to the judging taste. Otherwise we have again the dangerous morality of good instincts and of the heart, whose subjectivity has always been the fate of 'Werther', 'Allwill' and their noble successors. Again only a form has been mentioned, and it almost seems that Kant was right when he asserted that the essential characteristic of ethical consciousness is not only normativity but also formalism.

4. Morality is usually thought of as a product of social life which would immediately disappear if men lived in isolation. That one might have duties toward one's self does not seem to occur to the average man, and consequently solipsism is put on a par with complete immorality; though as a matter of fact if all seeming existence were within myself, the responsibility for the whole world would rest on me and so my conscience would have to be much finer. But the ethical attitude of Christianity, love for one's neighbor [4] and morality are regarded as practically equal. To do something for another person is equivalent, according to this point of view to moral action. The morality of neighborly love has lifted itself above all other forms of morality. And in the context of this Christian value system self-denial, self-surrender and love are regarded as the main virtues.

And indeed, to this social type there corresponds the ethics of helpful love and loyalty. And one might formulate its categorical imperative as—live for the other person.

Certainly this embodies a genuine ethical principle. And indeed we have seen that the special emphasis of love in the highest sense is justified by its close connection to the religious. A turning toward the value possibilities of the other soul is based on the sanctity of all life and this belief is genuinely religious. But the principle must be correctly understood and reduced to its meaningful sphere of validity. It has frequently been pointed out that a world where each person always sacrificed himself for someone else would annihilate itself. Love is only a shell in which value should appear. As we have said above, love founds community in value. This cannot, therefore, mean that the lover should sacrifice his own value content.[5] The duty of love, or if anyone objects to this term, the meaningful impulse to love, only goes so far as that the mutual value

[4] I remark in passing that I mean by altruism only the attitude toward another which remains on the level of utility.

[5] The error is rooted partly in the fact that altruism as a rule embodies an element of renunciation, but only because economic goods may only be shared if they are divided.

belief should be furthered by it and the lover himself subjectively and psychically enriched, that is, made purer. Indeed even the renunciation through love of subordinated value contents of existence is not necessarily moral. For, life and culture would be extirpated if everyone destroyed and wasted himself through love. When love ceases to enrich and further the value-meaning of life it is no longer a creative love but the mortifying love of the transcendental mystic who rejects life and civilization. Thus the ethical principle of love and unselfishness is only one factor of morality. It finds its obvious limitation in the healthy self-affirmation and individual developing of power without which both life and civilization would be finally blotted out.

5. Thus the morality of self-denial is opposed by the morality of self-affirmation, self-appreciation and—insofar as the soul should only affirm the highest—self-control. Every morality which enjoys life and civilisation embodies the conviction that life, even in the individual man, is something positive and deserving of help so that one can joyfully develop all one's powers which subserve the realization of value. The highest energy (not in the modern but in the Aristotelian sense) is something moral. Even Aristotle thought of the self-development of man as an evolution from biological to mental make-up. Goethe has further ennobled and spiritualized this natural principle into a purified self-realization. And since then the theory of the struggle for existence has brought it into still closer relations with the natural foundations of life. Nietzsche too built upon such an original biological basis in formulating the superman and the 'will to power'. But his creed of power contains a singular feeling of contrast to the herd morality just as if he had not been quite certain of his inner power and had only freed himself in anger from the early Christian table of values. At heart he too knew that the highest subjective power may also be a generous virtue. He only combatted the love which throws itself away, those who wallow in misery, the mystical hallucination that denial and self-annihilation are the highest virtues, and the popular standards of human values.

The will to power is thus a genuine form of ethics, and corresponds to the onesided type of the political man, in our broader sense of the word. We have, however, already seen that all power begins with inner self-control. This we might call freedom. It signifies then the freedom to do one's duty, moral liberty in the highest sense, which is also subjection to the highest objective law of value and self-determination. The ethics of freedom, of autonomous avowal of one's duty also belong in this context. To be free from the lower impulses of one's own nature is the true morality of self-control, which originates with Plato and the Stoics, reappears in Christianity as mastery of the flesh by the spirit, and reaches its climax in the philosophies of Kant and Fichte.

But the moralities of love and of freedom share the fact that they are really only formal principles, which must get their content, namely the direction to the highest objective value, from somewhere else. For, in love the question is raised: in the spirit of which value should one love man? And in regard to freedom or power the similar question, which is only too often forgotten in political dissension, arises: freedom for what and in what value order?

Let us summarize the foregoing discussion. All previous ethical principles were in themselves dependent and onesided. The principle of utility referred to a higher value which it served. The legality of behavior likewise, as well as inner form, demanded a value-determining content for law and form respectively. Love and freedom were in themselves only socially founded attitudes whose content had to come from outside. Does the last and highest ethical value then only reside in religion?

6. It cannot surprise us that the content of morality may only be grasped by a religious ethics. For, we have said that the essence of religiosity is the relation of all value experiences to the highest value. Consequently, the essence of morality is the determination of behavior by the highest normative value which connects the person with the objective meaning of the world and by the gradation of the other values according to their contribution to the final value (hierarchy of values).

But we proceed at first as in the former onesided forms of ethics. Corresponding to the religious type is the ethics of blessedness in God, being beloved by Him or made in His image (purity). And by God we mean the revealing principle of the highest value, whether it is perceived in the objective world context or immanently in the depths of the soul. This ethics is differentiated in accordance with the variations of the religious type. The highest value may be derived from the highest affirmation of all positive values of life. It ranks the other values according to the proportion of religious content which each contains; in religious terminology, the nearness or distance of each to God. To be religious then is to devote one's life to the highest of these values. But the highest value may also arise in a rejection of all positive values of life, from their being outbid by a wholly inner, specifically religious value. Thus the ethics of world renunciation, of life rejection, of absolute subjectivity, indeed ultimately of complete depreciation of self is formed in graded order. So we might conceive at first two forms of ethics in the religious sphere: the ethics of the highest expansion of life and that of its greatest limitation.[6]

We have already seen however that those extreme religious types are the two ends of a scale within which the manifold forms of the dualistic religious type may be arranged. And corresponding to this latter type is a dualistic ethics, i.e. an ethics of yes and no, of expansion and limitation of life.

And indeed every historically given system of ethics which does not actualize one of the extremes clearly contains both directions. We might simply speak of an ethics of 'Thou Shalt' and one of 'Thou Shalt Not' of which commanding and forbidding are the respective meaning directions. 'Creative morality' and 'restrictive morality' always conflict. Life is the material of both and is everywhere endowed with religious meaning so that the content of morality is everywhere and always religious. The separation of religion and morality is only based on the fact that morality guides the character and behavior of the subject in accordance with the value maximum, while ethical religiosity illuminates with the highest normative value the total of life and world and all active objective (overindividual) contexts.

Man would be a God if he could realize unlimited values in his character and behavior. And if he could realize no values whatsoever he would have no moral destiny at all. In each case he would be beyond good and evil but in a different sense. The ethical point of view only originates in the fact of his finity.[7] Because man is finite he feels the demand to broaden himself. But since he cannot do so infinitely he experiences a second demand, to limit himself in a meaning which is in accordance with some objective value. In the conflict of possible values he should follow that which is objectively higher which also means that value which gives him the really moral value. In the first case therefore ethics commands and expands and in the second—at least temporarily—it forbids and restricts, but finally uplifts and purifies.

Let us elucidate this by some examples. (1) The expansive ethics: a man whose character it is to live intensively in just one kind of values should draw the others also into the circle of his world of self-formation. If he turns only to economic values he is confronted by the expanding demands of the regulation of life, form, love and freedom. Assume however that he is directed to the lives of others, then he ought to form

[6] 'Life' of course always means here mental life, not mere vitality or egoism.

[7] I utilize this concept only as a heuristic construction and not in the metaphysical sense of the 18th century.

himself and give value to his own existence because this is the only way in which love receives true value content. Such an ethics fires Faust: he cannot be satisfied with any value of life because he cannot simultaneously live in the other values also. He would like to be a superman, indeed a God. But his destiny teaches him that the moral fate of man has another side which one might call the tragic one.

(2) The restrictive ethics: a man who tries to live in different value directions simultaneously, finds himself in the conflict which arises from the finity of his being. One cannot at the same time search for one's own highest good and sacrifice oneself through love for another. One cannot strive simultaneously for highest truth and beauty, one cannot both will the greatest power and renounce it. If one value-direction, in these situations of conflict which in reality always exhibit a highly unique and complex character, is distinguished from the other by the characteristic of duty, then this value has an objectively higher rank order. The ethical problem which still remains unsolved is: upon what is based the character of this objective superiority of a value direction (not only the mere subjective fact of its being thus experienced)? We seek the reasons for duty in an objective rank order of values. Is such a one valid always and in all situations? And by what criteria can we philosophically develop this objective order which founds the law of duty? No matter how impressive the mere experience of duty may be, it does not contain the philosophical guarantee of its binding power.

We consider the objective rank order of values for the present only as a methodological idea and so may leave it undecided whether there is a gradation between the individual classes of value or whether only the value complexes which are created by concrete life (i.e. the personal value standards in their totality) can be measured with one another. For, as living beings we never confront solely one species of value. Rather, in accordance with our preliminary theory, in every section of life a factor of every value is somehow contained. Our very personality, regarded as an enduring (mental) structure is a hierarchy of values. And this is even more true of historical individual situations where we reach an ethical conclusion: factors of value are here distributed in a way which no science can calculate in advance.

Nevertheless we speak of different ethical ranks and clearly feel them in people of the past or of our own time. And this estimation seems to be based on some objective standard. It is perhaps possible to disclose at least the prime forms of preference and rejection whose complicated application we practise in everyday life. Before we go back to this source we must remember that the minute we enter the mental world we find a collective table of values. From the first day of conscious behavior, finished value judgments of the environment in regard to character and behavior limit us and influence the formation of our motives. As a given authority they oppose our autonomous decisions, indeed they develop their influence before we have achieved autonomy. It certainly is a case here of objective powers insofar as they exist and act independent of the self; but whether they can be called a pure precipitation of objective values in the critical sense will be seen only when we have glanced at their origin and development. . . .

THE PERSONAL IDEAL

The most decisive limitations come to a moral individual as demands of society in which he wants to and must be a subordinated part. From infancy he is surrounded by commandments which all preach: 'Thou shalt not!' It is a well-known fact that collective morality expresses itself far more often in negative than positive commands, even though not all as much as the decalogue. It is always a case of respecting the limits of other lives, indeed actively willing them as one's own limits. If perfect freedom is granted to every person social life is impossible. This is true not only of the economic sphere with its divisible goods, but also of the formation of one's entire inner life which, beyond its own value must be a value for others. An individuality is complete only when these socially posited values are adopted as its own. For in moral service man becomes richer and not poorer. When the collective consciousness too is ethically alive within him he is filled with a really wide life content. Giving and receiving are so intimately interwoven in human society, especially in a nation, that it is impossible to keep separate the part of every individual. And thus too the limitation demanded by collective morality is a law, even though it does not deserve a pure moral value, which must be fulfilled before it can be abolished. People should greet the liberators of humanity with suspicion if they go to work in any other way, that is without respect; for then there is something in them which is not wholly pure and clean.

When we ask for the exact relation between the broadening and restricting norms we finds ourselves at the confines of what can be scientifically determined. The reality of moral life which has developed historically, always shows some interfusion of values which we shall later call forms of mental synthesis. Social Utilitarianism is one of them even though still a primitive fusion of economic and social values. Plato's ethics combines the theoretic with the aesthetic, and in the moral theory of Shaftesbury we find a unique interrelation of egoism, altruism and aesthetic morality. Kant unites theoretic with political elements in forming his ethics and every national ideal of culture contains a graded synthesis of values which is meaningfully related to the level of culture and the historically developed national character.

Any individual who consciously tries to create his own moral life is confronted by the same problem. He must organize his value life. The fact that everything cannot simultaneously come to the fore with the same strength is intimated even in the rank order which he grants in his choice to the individual claims of value. And our description of the onesided attitudes has shown that certain value directions even exclude each other. We must not try to hide this fact. Ethical antinomies are contained in the structure of life itself and are not brought into it by the fault of man. Rather, the unknown forces of life are those which make him guilty. The dialectic of life's laws repeatedly brings about collisions of personal value determinations from which he never escapes completely unscathed. He is imbued with an ideal of unbroken total life development. But how often does economic necessity conflict with the will to love, the will to truth with the will to assert another genuine value, the aesthetic inner harmony with the realism of existence in the state, economics and society. These contrasts cannot be explained away. They are there and in them the tragedy of life begins, for life is, throughout, tragic.

That we return here also to different basic ways in which these different personal value decisions are carried out is only an application of our theory of attitudes. This process is apparently most peaceful in the aesthetic nature which achieves a form of life. Culture for this reason is often thought of preferably as an aesthetic quality of man, for the aesthetic set can include the greatest fulness of life, though only as a contemplative and imaginative possession. And the manysidedness of aesthetic contact with life always contains some danger of shallowness, of having no center in life and of relativity. A practical human being cannot form himself in this way. He must assume the guilt of a limited attitude toward life or he would lack the capacity for action. 'An active man rejoices in partisanship.' And this limitation not only results from his own nature but also from other people's right to live which he includes in his economic, political or social life. Anyone who takes up everything can no longer create. This truth applies also to the defenders of a universal general culture.

Individual standards, however, cannot be scientifically deduced. Rather they are only contained in the value constellation which one might call the content of individual conscience. This conscience is not wholly unsupported. For the most part it finds ready-made value decisions of historical society and usually adopts them, and beyond, those highest, timeless, moral guiding stars which we have called ideal systems of value. Every one of them is the result of a moral struggle, so there is no great final world-view whether religious, poetical or philosophical which is not tragic. They are all bloody victories over lower life and one feels in them still the pain of the breach over which they heroically triumphed. No hero is without wounds after the battle. Indeed not even among themselves is there peace: the great religions are in continual conflict with one another. And even within our closed cultural sphere the Christian ideal of love, the Greek-humanistic and the ethico-political ideals of duty signify widely separated world-forces which compete with each other for moral supremacy. The question of what guidance to accept is again wholly a matter of individual conscience when a man has arrived at the point where he no longer merely receives his personal ideal world but builds it from within with free responsibility. And he would really be alone unless the ultimate welled up in him and helped him—his God.

Therefore the norm of the personal ideal can only be pronounced in formal imperatives. As soon as the emphasis is laid in the direction of expansion one might speak of a demand for the compossible maximum of life's value.[8] Whatever things are 'compossible', that is, can exist side by side in an individual manner of moral life formation, can only (disregarding the general theory of types of individual attitudes) be fought through and decided in every individual case. The aim of personal perfection which lies in the autonomy of a moral man might be expressed in the demand:

Be whatever you can, but be it wholly!

And if one wants to express the negative aspect too, the factor of demanded limitation, this maxim must be replaced by the following one:

Be the highest that you can and ought to be within the limits of the demands of social ethics and your personal value capacity!

[8] I choose this expression in order to indicate a concealed connection with motives of the Leibnizean philosophy. There even God's choice of values is bound to these limits of value agreement.

Only the value testing voice in one's own breast, which we call conscience, can tell what this highest is concretely, unless it is taken from the ethico-social mind and the ideal value system which is developed above it:

> 'Sofort nun wende dich nach innen,
> Das Zentrum findest du dadrinnen,
> Woran kein Edler zweifeln mag.
> Wirst keine Regel da vermissen;
> Denn das selbstaendige Gewissen
> Ist Sonne deinem Sittentag.'

Karl Mannheim

Ideology and Utopia *

We should like to turn now to the genetic approach. Here we should first point out that the genetic point of view, which is bound up with the psychological approach, has contributed in many ways to a deeper understanding of life in the sense above indicated. The dogmatic exponents of classical logic and philosophy are accustomed to maintain that the genesis of an idea has nothing to say concerning its validity or meaning. They always evoke the hackneyed example to the effect that our knowledge of the life of Pythagoras and of his inner conflicts, etc., is of little value in understanding the Pythagorean proposition. I do not believe, however, that this point holds for all intellectual accomplishments. I believe that from the standpoint of strict interpretation, we are infinitely enriched when we attempt to understand the biblical sentence, "The last shall be first," as the psychic expression of the revolt of oppressed strata. I believe that we shall understand it better if, as Nietzsche and others have indicated in various ways, we consider and become aware of the significance of resentment in the formation of moral judgments. In this case, for example, one could say in the case of Christianity, it was resentment which gave the lower strata courage to emancipate themselves, at least psychically, from the domination of an unjust system of values and to set up their own in opposition to it. We do not intend to raise the question here whether with the aid of this psychological-genetic analysis which deals with the value-generating function of resentment we can decide whether the Christians or the Roman ruling classes were in the right. In any case, through this analysis we are led more deeply into the comprehension of the meaning of the sentence. It is not irrelevant for an understanding of it to know that the phrase was not uttered by anybody

* From *Ideology and Utopia* by Karl Mannheim, pp. 22–27, 35–39, 168–171. Copyright 1936 by Paul, Trench, Trubner & Co., Ltd., London. ("International Library of Psychology, Philosophy, and Scientific Method".) Reprinted by permission of Harcourt, Brace and Company, Inc., and Routledge & Kegan Paul Ltd.

in general and was not addressed to men in general, but rather that it has a real appeal only for those who, like the Christians, are in some manner oppressed and who, at the same time, under the impulse of resentment, wish to free themselves from prevailing injustices. The interconnection between psychic genesis, the motivation which leads to meaning, and the meaning itself is, in the case just cited, different from that which exists in the Pythagorean propositions. The specially concocted examples which logicians adduce may under certain circumstances make one unreceptive to the deepest differences between one meaning and another and may lead to generalizations which obscure relevant relationships.

The psychogenetic approach may then contribute in a great many cases to a deeper understanding of meaning, where we are concerned not with the most abstract and formal interrelationships but rather with meanings, the motivation of which can by sympathetically experienced, or with a complex of meaningful conduct, which can be understood in terms of its motivational structure and experiential context. So, for example, when I know what a man was as a child, what severe conflicts he experienced and in which situations they occurred and how he solved them, I will know more about him than if I merely had a few bare details of his external life-history. I will know the context [1] from which novelty is produced in him and in the light of which every detail of his experience will have to be interpreted. It is the great achievement of the psychogenetic method that it destroyed the earlier mechanical conception which treated norms and cultural values as material things. When confronted with a sacred text, the genetic method has replaced the formally acquiescent obedience to a norm with the living appreciation of the process in which norms and cultural values first arise and with which they must be kept in continual contact in order that they may be ever newly interpreted and mastered. It has shown thereby that the life of a psychic phenomenon is the phenomenon itself. The meaning of history and life is contained in their becoming and in their flux. These insights were first stumbled upon by the Romantics and by Hegel, but since then have had to be rediscovered again and again.

There was, however, from the very beginning a two-fold limit to this concept of psychic genesis as it gradually developed and penetrated into the cultural sciences (such as the history of religions, literary history, art

[1] It should be noted how the genetic point of view emphasizes interdependence in contrast with the mechanistic approach which concerns itself with the atomization of the elements of experience.

history, etc.); and this limit threatened in time to become a definite restriction on the value of this approach.

The most essential limitation of the psychogenetic approach is the important observation that every meaning is to be understood in the light of its genesis and in the original context of life-experience which forms its background. But this observation contains within it the injurious constriction that this approach will be found only in an individualistc application. In most cases the genesis of a meaning has been sought in the individual context of experience rather than in its collective context. Thus, for example, if one had before one some idea (let us take the above-mentioned case of the transformation of a hierarchy of moral values as it is expressed in the sentence: "The last shall be first") and wished to explain it genetically, one would fasten upon the individual biography of the author and attempt to understand the idea exclusively on the basis of the special events and motivations of the author's personal history. Now it is clear that very much can be done with this method, for just as the experiences that truly motivate me have their original source and locus in my own life-history, just so the author's life-history is the locus of his experiences. But it is also clear that while it may be sufficient for the genetic explanation of a quite special individual mode of behaviour to go back to the early period of an individual's history (as would, for instance, be done by psycho-analysis to explain the symptoms of later developments in character from the experiences of early childhood), for a mode of behaviour of social significance, such as the transvaluation of values which transforms the whole system of life of a society in all its ramifications, preoccupation with the purely individual life-history and its analysis is not sufficient. The transvaluation, as indicated in the sentence above, has its roots basically in a group situation in which hundreds and thousands of persons, each in his own way, participate in the overthrow of the existing society. Each of these persons prepares and executes this transvaluation in the sense that he acts in a new way in a whole complex of life-situations which impinge upon him. The genetic method of explanation, if it goes deep enough, cannot in the long run limit itself to the individual life-history, but must piece together so much that finally it touches on the interdependence of the individual life-history and the more inclusive group situation. For the individual life-history is only a component in a series of mutually intertwined life-histories which have their common theme in this upheaval; the particular new motivation of a single individual is a part of a motivational complex in which many persons participate in various ways. It was the merit of the sociological point of view that it set alongside the individual genesis of meaning the genesis from the context of group life.

The two methods of studying cultural phenomena dealt with above, the epistemological and the psychological, had in common an attempt to explain meaning from its genesis in the subject. What is important in this case is not so much whether they were thinking of the concrete individual or of a generalized mind as such, but that in both cases the individual mind was conceived as separate from the group. Thereby they unwittingly brought false assumptions into the fundamental problems of epistemology and psychology which the sociological approach has had to correct. What is most important about the latter is that it puts an end to the fiction of the detachment of the individual from the group, within the matrix of which the individual thinks and experiences.

The fiction of the isolated and self-sufficient individual underlies in various forms the individualistic epistemology and genetic psychology. Epistemology operated with this isolated and selfsufficient individual as if from the very first he possessed in essence all the capacities characteristic of human beings, including that of pure knowledge, and as if he produced his knowledge of the world from within himself alone, through mere juxtaposition with the external world. Similarly in the individualistic developmental psychology, the individual passes of necessity through certain stages of development in the course of which the external physical and social environment have no other function than to release these preformed capacities of the individual. Both of these theories grew out of the soil of an exaggerated theoretical individualism (such as was to be found in the period of the Renaissance and of individualistic liberalism) which could have been produced only in a social situation in which the original connection between individual and group had been lost sight of. Frequently in such social situations the observer loses sight of the role of society in the moulding of the individual to the extent that he derives most of the traits, which are evidently only possible as the result of a common life and the interaction between individuals, from the original nature of the individual or from the germ plasm. (We attack this fiction not from some ultimate philosophical point of view but because it simply draws incorrect data into the picture of the genesis of knowledge and experience.)

In actuality it is far from correct to assume that an individual of more or less fixed absolute capacities confronts the world and in striving for the truth constructs a world-view out of the data of his experience.

Nor can we believe that he then compares his world-view with that of other individuals who have gained theirs in a similarly independent fashion, and in a sort of discussion the true world-view is brought to light and accepted by the others. In contrast to this, it is much more correct to say that knowledge is from the very beginning to co-operative process of group life, in which everyone unfolds his knowledge within the framework of a common fate, a common activity, and the overcoming of common difficulties (in which, however, each has a different share). Accordingly the products of the cognitive process are already, at least in part, differentiated because not every possible aspect of the world comes within the purview of the members of a group, but only those out of which difficulties and problems for the group arise. And even this common world (not shared by any outside groups in the same way) appears differently to the subordinate groups within the larger group. It appears differently because the subordinate groups and strata in a functionally differentiated society have a different experiential approach to the common contents of the objects of their world. In the intellectual mastery of life problems, each is allotted different segments with which each deals quite differently according to his different life-interests. The degree in which the individualistic conception of the problem of knowledge gives a false picture of collective knowing corresponds to what would occur if the technique, mode of work, and productivity of an internally highly specialized factory of 2,000 workers were thought of as if each of the 2,000 workers worked in a separate cubicle, performed the same operations for himself at the same time and turned out each individual product from beginning to end by himself. Actually, of course, the workers do not do the same thing in parallel fashion but rather, through a division of functions, they collectively bring the total product into existence. . . .

In political discussion in modern democracies where ideas were more clearly representative of certain groups, the social and existential determination of thought became more easily visible. In principle it was politics which first discovered the sociological method in the study of intellectual phenomena. Basically it was in political struggles that for the first time men became aware of the unconscious collective motivations which had always guided the direction of thought. Political discussion is, from the very first, more than theoretical argumentation; it is the tearing off of disguises—the unmasking of those unconscious motives which bind the group existence to its cultural aspirations and its theoretical arguments. To the extent, however, that modern politics fought its battles with theoretical weapons, the process of unmasking penetrated to the social roots of theory.

The discovery of the social-situational roots of thought at first, therefore, took the form of unmasking. In addition to the gradual dissolution of the unitary objective world-view, which to the simple man in the street took the form of a plurality of divergent conceptions of the world, and to the intellectuals presented itself as the irreconcilable plurality of thought-styles, there entered into the public mind the tendency to unmask the unconscious situational motivations in group thinking. This final intensification of the intellectual crisis can be characterized by two slogan-like concepts "ideology and utopia" which because of their symbolic significance have been chosen as the title for this book.

The concept "ideology" reflects the one discovery which emerged from political conflict, namely, that ruling groups can in their thinking become so intensively interest-bound to a situation that they are simply no longer able to see certain facts which would undermine their sense of domination. There is implicit in the word "ideology" the insight that in certain situations the collective unconscious of certain groups obscures the real condition of society both to itself and to others and thereby stabilizes it.

The concept of *utopian* thinking reflects the opposite discovery of the political struggle, namely that certain oppressed groups are intellectually so strongly interested in the destruction and transformation of a given condition of society that they unwittingly see only those elements in the situation which tend to negate it. Their thinking is incapable of correctly diagnosing an existing condition of society. They are not at all concerned with what really exists; rather in their thinking they already seek to change the situation that exists. Their thought is never a diagnosis of the situation; it can be used only as a direction for action. In the utopian mentality, the collective unconscious, guided by wishful representation and the will to action, hides certain aspects of reality. It turns its back on everything which would shake its belief or paralyse its desire to change things.

The collective unconscious and the activity impelled by it serve to disguise certain aspects of social reality from two directions. It is possible, furthermore, as we have seen above, to designate specifically the source and direction of the distortion. It is the task of this volume to trace out, in the two directions indicated, the most significant phases in the emergence of this discovery of the role of the unconscious as it appears in the history of ideology and utopia. At this point we are concerned only with delineating that state of mind which followed upon these insights since it is characteristic of the situation from which this book came forth.

At first those parties which possessed the new "intellectual weapons", the unmasking of the unconscious, had a terrific advantage over their adversaries. It was stupefying for the latter when it was demonstrated that their ideas were merely distorted reflections of their situation in life, anticipations of their unconscious interests. The mere fact that it could be convincingly demonstrated to the adversary that motives which had hitherto been hidden from him were at work must have filled him with terror and awakened in the person using the weapon a feeling of marvellous superiority. It was at the same time the dawning of a level of consciousness which mankind had hitherto always hidden from itself with the greatest tenacity. Nor was it by chance that this invasion of the unconscious was dared only by the attacker while the attacked was doubly overwhelmed—first, through the laying bare of the unconscious itself and then, in addition to this, through the fact that the unconscious was laid bare and pushed into prominence in a spirit of enmity. For it is clear that it makes a considerable difference whether the unconscious is dealt with for purposes of aiding and curing or for the purpose of unmasking.

To-day, however, we have reached a stage in which this weapon of the reciprocal unmasking and laying bare of the unconscious sources of intellectual existence has become the property not of one group among many but of all of them. But in the measure that the various groups sought to destroy their adversaries' confidence in their thinking by this most modern intellectual weapon of radical unmasking, they also destroyed, as all positions gradually came to be subjected to analysis, man's confidence in human thought in general. The process of exposing the problematic elements in thought which had been latent since the collapse of the Middle Ages culminated at last in the collapse of confidence in thought in general. There is nothing accidental but rather more of the inevitable in the fact that more and more people took flight into scepticism or irrationalism.

Two powerful currents flow together here and reinforce one another with an overwhelming pressure: one, the disappearance of a unitary intellectual world with fixed values and norms; and, two, the sudden surge of the hitherto hidden unconscious into the bright daylight of consciousness. Man's thought had from time immemorial appeared to him as a segment of his spiritual existence and not simply as a discrete objective fact. Reorientation had in the past frequently meant a change in man himself. In these earlier periods it was mostly a case of slow shifts in values and norms, of a gradual transformation of the frame of reference from which men's actions derived their ultimate orientation. But in modern times it is a much more profoundly disorganizing affair. The resort to the unconscious tended to dig up the soil out of which the varying points of views emerged. The roots from which human thought had hitherto derived its nourishment were exposed. Gradually it becomes clear to all of us that we cannot go on living in the same way once we know about our unconscious motives as we did when we were ignorant of them. What we now experience is more than a new idea, and the questions we raise constitute more than a new problem. What we are concerned with here is the elemental perplexity of our time, which can be epitomized in the symptomatic question "How is it possible for man to continue to think and live in a time when the problems of ideology and utopia are being radically raised and thought through in all their implications?"

It is possible, of course, to escape from this situation in which the plurality of thought-styles has become visible and the existence of collective-unconscious motivations recognized simply by hiding these processes from ourselves. One can take flight into a supra-temporal logic and assert that truth as such is unsullied and has neither a plurality of forms nor any connection with unconscious motivations. But in a world in which the problem is not just an interesting subject for discussion but rather an inner perplexity, someone will soon come forth who will insist against these views that "our problem is not truth as such; it is our thinking as we find it in its rootedness in action in the social situation, in unconscious motivations. Show us how we can advance from our concrete perceptions to your absolute definitions. Do not speak of truth as such but show us the way in which our statements, stemming from our social existence, can be translated into a sphere in which the partisanship, the fragmentariness of human vision, can be transcended, in which the social origin and the dominance of the unconscious in thinking will lead to controlled observations rather than to chaos". The absoluteness of thought is not attained by warranting, through a general principle, that one has it or by proceeding to label some particular limited viewpoint (usually one's own) as supra-partisan and authoritative.

Nor are we aided when we are directed to a few propositions in which the content is so formal and abstract (e.g. in mathematics, geometry, and pure economics) that in fact they seem to be completely detached from the thinking social individual. The battle is not about these propositions but about that greater wealth of factual determinations in which man concretely diagnoses his individual and social situation, in which concrete interdependences in life are perceived and in which happenings external to us are first correctly understood. The battle rages concerning those propositions in which every concept is meaningfully oriented from the first, in which we use words like conflict, breakdown, alienation, insurrection, resentment—words which do not reduce complex situations for the sake of an externalizing, formal description without ever being able to build them up again and which would lose their content if their orientation, their evaluative elements, were dropped out. . . .

We arrive then at the third alternative to which we ourselves are committed. It is the view that, at the point where what is properly political begins, the evaluative element cannot easily be separated out, at least not in the same degree as is possible in formal sociological thinking and other sorts of purely formalizing knowledge. This position will insist that the voluntaristic element has an essential significance for knowledge in the political and historical sphere proper, even though in the course of history we may observe a gradual selection of categories which more and more acquire validity for all parties. Nonetheless, though there is a *consensus ex post* [2] or an increasingly broader stratum of knowledge which is valid for all parties, we should not allow ourselves to be misled by this or to overlook the fact that at every given historical point in time there is a substantial amount of knowledge which is accessible to us only seen in social perspective. But since we do not as yet live in a period free from mundane troubles and beyond history, our problem is not how to deal with a kind of knowledge which shall be "truth in itself", but rather how man deals with his problems of knowing, bound as he is in his knowledge by his position in time and society. If we advocate a comprehensive view of that which is not yet synthesizable into a system, we do this because we regard it as the relative optimum possibility in our present situation, and because in so doing we believe (as is always the case in history) we are taking the necessary steps preparatory to the next synthesis. But having stated this solution to the problem, we should be ready to add at once that the disposition to achieve a synthesis from the most comprehensive and most progressive point of view also has implicit in it a prior judgment, namely, our decision to arrive at a dynamic intellectual mediation. Certainly we would be the last to deny that we have made this value-judgment. Indeed, it is our main thesis that political knowledge, as long as politics conforms to the definition previously made, is impossible without some such decision, and that this decision in favour of dy-

[2] Cf. for further details the paper presented by the author in 1928 at Zurich ("Die Konkurrenz im Gebiete des Geistigen"), in which there is a discussion of the nature and genesis of *ex post* consensual knowledge.

namic intellectual mediation must be seen as an element in the total situation. But it makes a good deal of difference whether this presupposition influences one's point of view unconsciously and naïvely (which will hinder a fundamental enlargement of our perspective), or whether it appears only after everything of which we can become aware and which we already know has entered into our deliberations.

The very quintessence of political knowledge seems to us to lie in the fact that increased knowledge does not eliminate decisions but only forces them farther and farther back. But what we gain through this retreat from decisions is an expansion of our horizon and a greater intellectual mastery of our world. Consequently, we may expect, from the advances in sociological research into ideology, that interrelations of social position, motives, and points of view, which have hitherto been only partially known, will now become more and more transparent. This will enable us, as we have already indicated, to calculate more precisely collective interests and their corresponding modes of thought and to predict approximately the ideological reactions of the different social strata.

The fact that the sociology of knowledge gives us a certain foundation does not free us from the responsibility of arriving at decisions. It does, however, enlarge the field of vision within the limits of which decisions must be made. Those who fear that an increased knowledge of the determining factors which enter into the formation of their decisions will threaten their "freedom" may rest in peace. Actually it is the one who is ignorant of the significant determining factors and who acts under the immediate pressure of determinants unknown to him who is least free and most thoroughly predetermined in his conduct. Whenever we become aware of a determinant which has dominated us, we remove it from the realm of unconscious motivation into that of the controllable, calculable, and objectified. Choice and decision are thereby not eliminated: on the contrary, motives which previously dominated us become subject to our domination; we are more and more thrown back upon our true self and, whereas formerly we were the servants of necessity, we now find it possible to unite consciously with forces with which we are in thorough agreement.

Increasing awareness of previously uncontrolled factors and the tendency to suspend immediate judgments until they are seen in a broader context appears to be the principal trend in the development of political knowledge. This corresponds to the fact, mentioned earlier, that the sphere of the rationalizable and of the rationally controllable (even in our most personal life) is always growing, while the sphere of the irrational becomes correspondingly narrower. We shall not discuss here whether such a development will ultimately lead us to a fully rationalized world in which irrationality and evaluation can no longer exist, or whether it will lead to the cessation of social determination in the sense of freedom through a complete awareness of all the social factors involved. This is a utopian and remote possibility and is therefore not subject to scientific analysis.

However, this much may be safely asserted: politics as politics is possible only as long as the realm of the irrational still exists (where it disappears, "administration" takes its place). Furthermore, it may be stated that the peculiar nature of political knowledge, as contrasted with the "exact" sciences, arises out of the inseparability, in this realm, of knowledge from interest and motivation. In politics the rational element is inherently intertwined with the irrational; and, finally, there is a tendency to eliminate the irrational from the realm of the social, and in close connection therewith, there results a heightened awareness of factors which have hitherto dominated us unconsciously.

In the history of mankind this is reflected in man's original acceptance of social conditions as unalterable destiny in the same way that we shall probably always have to accept such natural and inevitable limitations as birth and death. Together with this outlook there went an ethical principle—the ethics of fatalism, the main tenet of which was submission to higher and inscrutable powers. The first break in this fatalistic outlook occurred in the emergence of the ethics of conscience in which man set his self over against the destiny inherent in the course of social events. He reserved his personal freedom, on the one hand, in the sense of retaining the ability through his own actions to set new causal sequences going in the world (even though he renounced the ability of controlling the consequences of these acts) and, on the other hand, through the belief in the indeterminateness of his own decisions.

Our own time seems to represent a third stage in this development: the world of social relations is no longer inscrutable or in the lap of fate but, on the contrary, some social interrelations are potentially predictable. At this point the ethical principle of responsibility begins to dawn. Its chief imperatives are, first, that action should not only be in accord with the dictates of conscience, but should take into consideration the possible consequences of the action in so far as they are calculable, and, second, which can be added on the basis of our previous discussion, that conscience itself should be subjected to critical self-examination in order to eliminate all the blindly and compulsively operating factors.

Max Weber has furnished the first acceptable formulation of this conception of politics. His ideas and researches reflect the stage in ethics and politicis in which blind fate seems to be at least partially in the course of disappearance in the social process, and the knowledge of everything knowable becomes the obligation of the acting person. It is at this point, if at any, that politics can become a science, since on the one hand the structure of the historical realm, which is to be controlled, has become transparent, and on the other hand out of the new ethics a point of view emerges which regards knowledge not as a passive contemplation but as critical self-examination, and in this sense prepares the road for political action.

Karl Duncker

Ethical Relativity? *

1. THE PROBLEM

What is meant by "ethical relativity"? That morals vary no one will deny. They are undoubtedly different at different times and in different places.

There is a widespread view that the sole invariant of morals is their *sociological* function to secure the preservation and welfare of a social group. This function, however, is external to the *psychological* situation. There may, of course, be cases in which conduciveness to social welfare figures as a motive and thus becomes part of the psychological situation, but these are exceptional rather than typical.

There is according to this thesis of ethical relativity nothing invariable within the psychological content of morality. Any conceivable behaviour may, in appropriate historical or ethnological circumstances, take its turn in fulfilling the function of social expediency.

The thesis of ethical relativism has found its classical formulation in Locke's *Essay Concerning Human Understanding.*[1]

> "He that will carefully peruse the history of mankind and look abroad into the several tribes of men, and with indifferency survey their actions, will be able to satisfy himself, that there is scarce that principle of morality to be named, or rule of virtue to be thought on (those only excepted that are absolutely necessary to hold society together, which commonly too are neglected betwixt distinct societies), which is not, somewhere or other, slighted and condemned by the general fashion of whole societies of men, governed by practical opinions and rules of living quite opposite to others."

Similar opinions have been expressed at intervals ever since, in fact they have become one of the supposed strongholds of *Positivism.* Many

* From "Ethical Relativity? (An Enquiry into the Psychology of Ethics)" by Karl Duncker. *Mind,* Volume XLVIII, No. 189, January 1939, pp. 39–44. Reprinted by permission of *Mind.*

[1] Book I, 3 (No innate practical principles), 10.

anthropologists, like Westermarck, who would question the wholesale validity of the particular instances brought forward by Locke and his followers and attribute apparent ethical differences in part to "cognitive causes," nevertheless consider "ethical relativity" to be an adequate formulation of their views.[2]

To be sure, some philosophers have launched good arguments against Locke's conventionalism in the name of a "moral sense," [3] but I do not think the issue has become quite clear.—As more recent critics I may mention Max Scheler,[4] Max Wertheimer,[5] and H. Spiegelberg.[6]

2. THREE EXAMPLES OF ETHICAL VARIABILITY

Here are some instances of moral variability. In ancient times, and especially throughout the Middle Ages, it was considered immoral or even sinful to practice "usury", *i.e.* to take interest on money lent. With the rise of capitalism the same practice gradually lost its moral stigma and forced its way into respectability. Now economists are not slow in pointing out that circumstances, the enormous increase of commerce and industrial investments, no longer permitted of those old moral fetters. Morals had to yield to altered circumstances. (They always show a considerable inertia, but in the end they are bound to give way.) The case of usury thus presents a fair example of the same act's having at different times a different moral value.

To take another example: decency in dress is admittedly of the utmost variability. There is no degree of concealment between nudity and the swathings of a Moslem woman which is not, somewhere or other, found to represent the fine border-line between the decent and the indecent. Even in our own community standards vary. A bathing dress is taboo in the street. A woman may show herself undressed in the presence of her male physician, but not in that of her male acquaintances. Prof. Sumner would appear to be quite justified in saying that "the *mores* can make everything right".[7] Customs are, of course, in their turn shaped by all sorts of circumstances and necessities.

[2] E. A. Westermarck, *Ethical Relativity,* London, 1932.

[3] *Cf.* Dugald Stewart in his *Philosophy of the active and moral powers of man,* vol. 1 (Coll. Works VI, pp. 237 ff.), 1855.

[4] *Der Formalismus in der Ethik und die materiale Wertethik,* pp. 307 ff.

[5] "Some Problems in the Theory of Ethics" (*Social Research,* vol. 2, pp. 351–367, 1935).

[6] *Antirelativismus,* 1935.

[7] Sumner, *Folkways,* ch. 15.

One more example from the classical store of comparative anthropology: there have been many peoples, all the world over, who indulged in the practice of killing new-born infants or superannuated parents. To our civilised minds this appears to be a rude custom. Here again the particular act has undergone a radical change in moral valuation. We can no doubt link up the difference in custom with different circumstances, such as the hardships of the nomadic life, the domination of the group, the various superstitious beliefs, etc. But our understanding of the causes does not seem to obviate the ethical difference.

For the moment these three examples may suffice to make it clear that the theory of ethical relativism could not possibly be wrong if the only factors to be considered were the act, the sociological function and the circumstances.

3. PSYCHOLOGICAL ANALYSIS OF THE EXAMPLES

Let us, however, subject our examples to a psychological analysis. In the case of "usury" the act in question was "the taking of interest on money lent", which we found to have been repudiated at one time and recommended at another. But do we in both cases deal with the *same* act? Is money always identical with money, or interest with interest? From a genetical point of view the usage of the identical word is well justified. But in early stages of civilisation loans were employed predominantly for consumption, whereas in capitalism loans are employed mainly as capital for profitable production. That makes all the difference. Where the borrower borrows in order to gain, it is only fair to make the lender a partner in the undertaking by paying him some "share in the profit". Interest no longer means an exploitation of necessities or passions. It has changed its typical *"meaning"*.[8] Of course, this is due to changed economical circumstances, to the increase of productive investments, etc. However, these circumstances do not remain external to the act, but enter into the psychological essence of the objects dealt with in the act. They provide what I shall call the *"pattern of situational meanings"*. It is on this pattern of situational meanings that the moral essence of an act, its ethical quality and value, depends.[9] *In our example we have not two*

[8] Even in earlier times interest was sometimes defended as meaning a "compensation for the risk" (*cf.* the *foenus nauticum*).

[9] Note how the sociological understanding is necessary for, but not identical with, the ethical understanding.

different ethical valuations of usury, but two different meanings of money-lending each of which receives its specific valuation.

Before proceeding any further on theoretical lines I will give some additional empirical data, this time concerning infanticide and the killing of the old.

Let me begin by quoting two field accounts, selected from a large collection of similar observations. Peter Kolben, in his *Present State of the Cape of Good Hope,*[10] gives us the following account, "a little meliorated", of Hottentot feelings with regard to exposing superannuated parents to starvation in a solitary hut:

> "If you represent to the Hottentots, as I have done very often, the inhumanity of this custom, they are astonished at the representation, as proceeding, in their opinion, from an inhumanity of our own. The custom, in their way of thinking, is supported by very pious and very filial considerations. 'Is it not a cruelty', they ask you, 'to suffer either man or woman to languish any considerable time under a heavy, motionless old age? Can you see a parent or relative shaking and freezing under a cold, dreary, heavy, useless old age, and not think, in pity of them, of putting an end to their misery by putting, which is the only means, an end to their old days?' "

The next example, taken from Ellis' *Voyage for the discovery of a North-West Passage,* has already played a part in the history of ethical thought. (It was used against Locke by Beattie.)

In some of the nations adjoining Hudson's bay,

> "they have a custom which is very extraordinary; that when their parents grow so old, as to be incapable to support themselves by their labour, they require their children to strangle them, and this is esteemed an act of obedience in the children to perform. The manner of discharging this duty is thus. The grave of the old person being dug he goes into it, and after having conversed, and smoked a pipe, or perhaps drunk a dram or two with his children, the old person signifies he is ready: upon which two of the children put a thong about his neck, one standing on the one side and the other opposite, and pull violently till he is strangled, then cover him with earth and over that erect a kind of rough monument of stones. As for such old persons as have no children, they request this office from their friends though in this last case it is not always complied with".

I think everybody would agree that the mere fact of "killing" is too abstract a topic to allow of any serious ethical consideration. Many people,

[10] p. 319 (London 1731).

however, seem to believe that "killing superannuated parents" is sufficiently concrete. But is it really? "Killing an aged parent" may, according to circumstances, mean sparing him the miseries of a lingering death or an existence which, as a born warrior, he must feel to be exceedingly dull and unworthy; or it may mean protecting him against injuries from enemies or beasts, or causing him to enter the happy land which is not open save to those who die by violence. Such "meanings" clearly give to the act a quality of benevolence rather than of cruelty. But even where it is not performed out of benevolence it may still be in full accordance with the victim's feelings. For he has done the same sort of thing to his elders, he has known his own fate all his life long, and he knows that neither will the next generation be exempted. That is to say, the being killed "means" to him about as natural a thing as death itself means to us. On the other hand, what is done to him may be done for the benefit of the group. He is of no further use, and life may be hard and food scarce to the point of starvation. Surely, then, it is more reasonable to cast off that part of the ballast than to kill young and healthy members. Or, again, the old man may be sacrificed (as a "substitute") in order to appease the gods and avert from the tribe their anger as embodied in some epidemic, famine, flood, etc.

To say that this is a credit to the group spirit at the cost of filial piety is to leave two important features out of account. In the first place the aged parent is not only a victim but a subject apt to appreciate the call of the hour himself. It may be his point of honour to die for the group. Assuredly the victim's own view of the matter is a most essential constituent of what I have called the "pattern of situational meanings". In the second place it is a mistake tacitly to substitute one's own individualistic outlook for that of a primitive group. Where the individual is felt to be a mere "limb of the group body" we should be the less surprised at the body's decision to sacrifice one of its limbs.

This meaning of a man as a "limb" rather than a "person of his own" is extremely important for a genuine *ethical* understanding of many other phenomena. For instance, blood-revenge is not genuinely understood unless one takes into consideration that the victim is felt to be just an organ, the available "vulnerable spot" of the other clan, which, as a collective whole, is felt to be the real offender. Neither is it justifiable to treat of infanticide without enquiring into the meaning of the infant in question: whether it is conceived of as an inanimate thing, a limb of the group, a piece of property belonging to the pater familias, a person of its own, or finally as an immortal soul (which would be doomed to everlasting perdition if it died unbaptised).

4. CONFRONTATION OF FORMULAE

Locke wondered why the principle (note what he calls a principle) 'parents, preserve and cherish young children' had not received any general consent throughout history. Well, if one leaves out "meanings", *i.e.* if one fails to define the situation in psychological terms, how can one expect to meet with general consent? *For ethical valuation is not concerned with acts as abstract events in space-time. The ethical essence of an act depends upon its concrete pattern of situational meanings.* The term "situational meanings" is meant to convey the notion of "relevant features of the actual psychological situation with reference to which the subject behaves". It should be emphasised that personal reactions are not made direct to the "stimuli" (the positivistic-behaviouristic fallacy!), but to the psychological situation which is a joint product of stimuli, beliefs, sentiments, etc.—We have seen that the "same" things and acts, in short the same materials, may have different meanings (Wertheimer). And the reverse is no less true: different materials may have the same meaning. Now, if our moral valuation depends upon meanings it is not fair to connect it with meaningless, with abstract acts. But this, precisely, is what ethical relativism does.

In place of the relativistic formula: morals depend on circumstances according to the function of social expediency—I put forward the following three statements: An act which receives a positive valuation must needs satisfy certain functions of promoting, or at least agreeing with, the social good in the given circumstances. But whether a given act can be positively valued from an *ethical* point of view, depends upon the meanings involved, according to certain basic invariable relationships. And, in their turn, these meanings depend upon the circumstances. (Meanings are, as it were, a reflection of the circumstances within the inner, psychological make-up of the ethical situation. Meanings are not identical with circumstances. The meaning of interest is that it is a share in the profit. The corresponding circumstances are capitalism as a whole. Again, the Christian meaning of a human being is that it is an immortal soul. The responsible circumstances are for the most part still a problem for the sociologist.)

The new formula indicates, besides a sociological invariant, certain invariable relationships between valuations and meanings. They amount to this: given the same situational meanings an act is likely to receive the same ethical valuation. If an act is found to receive different valuations at different times or places, this is generally found to be due to different meanings.

V. VISION AND ACTION

Vision and Action

I

William Pepperell Montague has called our attention to the role of philosophical vision which, in the heat of analysis, we are likely to forget: [1]

> To confine one's attention to the actual is to narrow one's spirit to brutish dimensions. The distinctive glory of the human mind is its power to detach itself, not only from the here and now but from the there and then of existence, and bathe its tired memories in ideal waters. So it is that the great visions of philosophy, even if considered merely as visions, are precious and imperishable possessions of our culture. Even when their content has been proved false to the world of fact they lend to that world depth and richness of meaning, and norms for appraising its values which otherwise could never come. The pride of philosophy is in its disclosure of significant possibility.

The unified consciousness involved in vision is not, however, merely contemplative. It is a kind of energy, brimful and about to overflow, yet very directed. It is a spring wound up about to be released, a lion ready for the pounce, a builder with plans complete about to launch construction. Philosophy in this sense is the potentiality of organized purposeful action on a total scale. The field of action may be as wide as the globe or as narrow as the individual being. The action may be as far-reaching as to reorganize the character of human life or as restricted as the struggle to resign oneself to the play of forces about one. To the ordinary man philosophy has always meant the determination of a way of life. And it is likely that it has meant this to philosophers as well for the greater part of the philosophical tradition. It is true of Plato and not merely of the Stoics and Epicureans. It is taken for granted about mediaeval religious philosophy. But it is too often forgotten that the writers of the great epistemological treatises—a Locke or a Hume—were self-conscious about the preliminary character of these disciplines. To know the limits of human knowledge would tell us why to stop persecuting and to practice tolerance;

[1] *Great Visions of Philosophy* (La Salle, Illinois, Open Court Publishing Co. 1950), p. 16. Quoted by permission of the publisher.

to know the way in which knowledge is acquired would lay the ground for a study of the passions and the direction of morals.

No simple thesis of correlation of intellectual belief and social action is envisaged. It is rather the recognition that the continuities of thought and action pertain to philosophies as well as to daily life, that philosophers have always embodied in their philosophies attitudes in action, that to hold a philosophy in this sense is an act of self-orientation. The twentieth century in its academic philosophy, in the Anglo-American tradition at least, has often tended to ignore this. Impressed by the aloofness of much of its professional activity it forgets that aloofness itself is an attitude with grounds, conditions and consequences peculiar to it, and that if it be desirable in certain ways this too is a matter of philosophical value justification. One can in any case ask what the orientational effect of a philosophy has proved to be, and suspect that such aspects play a role in philosophical creativity as well, even if they may not be clear on the surface. Meanwhile one may take illustrations from cases of clear connection, leaving to future philosophical biography the discovery of more indirect relations. (One has to read J. M. Keynes' TWO MEMOIRS to discover what was the immediate attitudinal impact of so aloof an analytical philosopher as G. E. Moore on intellectual circles of his time.) But on the wider scene, we need only look to the role of philosophy in Europe—from the place of dialectical materialism in Russia to the role of existentialism in Parisian culture—to see its more intimate relation to life attitudes. Nor is this a specialized phenomenon of exceptional conditions or unusual cultures. A glance at a study like Romanell's MAKING OF THE MEXICAN MIND will show the almost practical character of varying shades of philosophy in the history of that country—not merely the striking political role of positivism at one point, but the way in which each new philosophical departure entailed a revision of educational outlook which involved a break, often a revolutionary one, in the path of social development.

II

Traditional differences in philosophical attitude have run the whole gamut from the resignation of Job and the contemplation of Aristotle to the activism of the voluntarist movements and the aestheticism of Walter Pater's injunction "to burn always with this hard gemlike flame". Mystical self-surrender has been a perennial theme, the despair of systematic pessimism an occasional one. The principled virtue of the Stoics has crossed threatening glances with the cynicism of the pursuit of power.

The twentieth century, beset with divergent movements and sharpening conflicts, has witnessed traditional attitudes intensified—even to the point of a negation of philosophy and a philosophy of negation. Optimism and pessimism, a sense of immediacy and urgency or a contemplative sense of eternity are found in a variety of schools, flourishing, as it were, in a diversity of soils. Lives and thoughts, and even chance happenings, are intimately intertwined. Drama—even tragedy—shows no partiality for schools. In Europe and Asia practical men hammer out their philosophical outlooks in jail, or in periods of enforced respite from the pursuit of their aims, whereas men who make a vocation of philosophical thought are often driven to practical tasks or buffeted about by the impact of political events. Thus, Gandhi develops his conception of non-violence in the struggle against discrimination and for national freedom; and Nehru tangles with that concept in the respite given him in prison. Hitler fashions his irrationalism of blood into the semblance of a system in prison. Lenin, who had read endless volumes to write his MATERIALISM AND EMPIRIO-CRITICISM, *and annotated his Hegel to keep himself and his colleagues on a correct dialectical path in the dark days of failure and hiding, breaks off his* STATE AND REVOLUTION *in 1917 with the words "It is more pleasant and useful to go through the 'experience of the revolution' than to write about it."*

*The theoretical philosophers of the age—whether outstanding masters or influential secondary figures, and whether their struggles are in the public arena or in the individual confines of their studies or their spirits—are usually led sooner or later to render explicit their outlook on practice, and even occasionally to embody it in specific action. Early in the century William James, whose intense spiritual struggles to forge an outlook he could live with had made him sensitive to the psychological aspect of the philosopher's endeavor, offers his well-known temperamental classification of philosophical beliefs (*PRAGMATISM*, 1907). The "tender-minded" are rationalistic, intellectualistic, idealistic, optimistic, religious, free willist, monistic, dogmatical; the "tough-minded" are empiricist, sensationalistic, pessimistic, irreligious, fatalistic, pluralistic, sceptical. And James goes on in book after book and lecture after lecture to make the effect on practical outlook one of the bases of decision in philosophical doctrine. Bertrand Russell early challenges the cosmos in his famous essay, "A Free Man's Worship", and while "omnipotent matter rolls on its relentless way" he calls on the free man "to worship at the shrine that his own hands have built" and "to preserve a mind free from the wanton tyranny that rules his outward life." And in his long career he goes on to challenge the state (even* being imprisoned for pacifism in World War I), and, in varied contexts, men's prejudices in religion and morals. Croce finds a strong sense of the human spirit spread in the historical process, and cherishes the liberal outlook even when it seems a dying flame, while he opposes an ascendant fascism in Italian public life. Unamuno, haunted by the contradictoriness of life to the point at which he defines philosophy itself as the science of the tragedy of life, suffers exile from a land in turmoil. Freud, watching the shadows gather over Europe, finds a basis for a pessimism in the very constitution of the human material. Buber, going from the anguish of a retreating and oppressed people in the Germany of the Nazis to the problems of an embattled Israel, keeps a constant eye on the living moment of the spirit. Sartre expresses the sense of aloneness in a cosmos in which every man is the responsible creator of himself; and he fashions himself in the decisive mood of the French resistance to Nazism. Maritain, converted to Catholicism, finds his philosophical vocation clear—"Woe to me if I do not Thomisticize," he says in an autobiographical account—but the path is a hard one as he seeks to fashion a traditional doctrine into a mold to meet the vital problems of the age. Santayana alone, while recognizing with piety the matter whose potency is at the root of all that comes and goes, is able to remain through life the spectator, looking with the eyes of his spirit on the ideals that are momentarily embodied—while war surges to his very gate.

Even in the comparative calm of America where the personal lives of philosophers usually present a quieter picture, the role of philosophy as attitude is often to be found just below the surface. It does not surprise us that a Dewey who conceives of philosophy as a guide to change, as constant criticism of the culture from within in response to its problems, should think of philosophy itself in terms of education, personal growth and transition in social change. And we expect a Niebuhr, whose religious outlook carries with it a religious vocation, to be concerned with the impact of theory on attitude. But even a philosopher who thought in terms of a purely intellectual outlook and stoutly defended it against all forms of practicalism reveals in his autobiography the sense of vocation that guided his work. Morris Raphael Cohen writes: [2]

> But the enthusiasm of Davidson that influenced me most was the dream of an Encyclopedia of Philosophy that should do for the culture of the twentieth century what the Brothers of Sincerity did for the tenth, and Diderot and d'Alembert did for the eighteenth. This dream has dominated my whole intellectual life. All my reading somehow or other gets fitted into that

[2] *A Dreamer's Journey* (The Free Press, 1949), p. 109.

> scheme. And though I was never to realize that youthful ambition, it has given form to all my fragmentary efforts at the statement of a philosophical position adequate to the understanding of the problems of modern civilization.

Moreover, the sharp challenge of logical positivism on the American philosophical scene and the conflicts and passions that it roused, exhibited clearly that not merely doctrines but attitudes to life were the crux of the controversy.

We must bring our roll-call to an end, even though we have sampled but a few. There are, of course, innumerable others—the cynicism of the Machiavellians, the despair of latter-day Schopenhauerians, and a whole multitude of outlooks expressed not only in philosophical writings but in literary materials, critical and historical reflection, and even scientific comments on the wider cosmic scene. It is the task of the intellectual historian to estimate ultimately the causal factors and central events which influenced men's outlooks. In such an estimate of the first half of the century it is likely that fascism will have an important place—even more than communism. For communism on its theoretical side still fell within the western rationalist tradition—a Maritain, for example, could still see it as simply the last and most extreme of the heresies!—but fascism with its irrationality and vaunted brutality broke with even the pretense of the humane. Cross-currents of despair, guilt, bewilderment, are not then surprising in the philosophical mood; for no sensitive spirit failed to feel its impact, to sense the utterness of its challenge.

III

The selections that follow may serve to illustrate the variety of moods that the twentieth century has embraced. They come from various contexts of the writers' work. For there is no advance way of predicting where a thinker's deepest vision in practice will appear. Sometimes it is in a personal recollection of a critical experience. Sometimes it is a summons to others for action. Sometimes it is in surveying the evolution of the cosmos and getting the sense of man's frontier position. Sometimes it is in expressing the sense of effort. Sometimes the outlook is found in a picture of the emotions, sometimes even in the definition of philosophy and its tasks, often in reflections on virtue and duty. Even in such a question the human spirit shows its complex diversity.

Jacques Maritain

Action and Contemplation *

GREEK PHILOSOPHY

The debate between action and contemplation not only concerns each of us personally, but is also of vital importance to human culture and to the destiny of civilization. I hold it to be of special moment to this continent, as I shall try to suggest at the end of this chapter.

We know well enough how emphatic the East is about its calling to the contemplative life and how proud of it; while the West with no less pride,—a pride which is beginning to suffer much,—boasts that it has chosen action. Could this lead us to affirm without more ado that the East is contemplation and the West action? Such an affirmation would be all too simple. Things do not tell their secrets so easily. Occidental activism might be, in its misery and agony, a degenerated and pathetic form of what was once an incomparable sentiment of life and human values. The West, I believe, had once a habit of contemplation in harmony with the deepest postulations of spiritual reality.

In philosophical language the problem of action and contemplation is that of *transitive* (or *productive*) and *immanent* activity (immanent activity in its most typical and purest function).

Transitive activity is that which one being exercises upon another, the so-called patient, in order to act upon it, imparting to it movement or energy. This activity, which is quite visible, is characteristic of the world of bodies; through it all elements of material nature inter-communicate, and through it we act on matter, transforming it. It passes away in Time, and with Time. Not only is it transitory, it is transition. The Greeks were right in saying that in this activity, the action in which the agent

* From *Scholasticism and Politics* by Jacques Maritain. New York: The Macmillan Company, 1940, pp. 170–178, 190–193. Reprinted by permission of The Macmillan Company and Geoffrey Bles Ltd.

and the patient intercommunicate is accomplished in the patient, *actio in passo,* and being common in both, makes the agent (notwithstanding its being as such the nobler of the two) dependent on the patient, in which alone it obtains perfection. The Agent is itself *in actu* and attains its perfection only by acting on another than itself, and in the instant of this action. Transitive action is a mendicant action, which achieves itself in another being, and is essentially in need of another being. On the other hand, while the agent's perfection is also, in fact, that of the patient, the agent as such does not seek the patient's good, but its own (this is a typical characteristic of purely transitive action). Hence its 'egotism'. People who exercise philanthropy as a transitive activity need the poor to help if they want to be helpful, sinners to preach to if they want to be preachers, victims whose wrongs they can redress. They need *patients.*

Immanent activity is of quite a different order. It is the characteristic activity of life and spirit. Here the agent has its own perfection in itself; it elevates itself in being. Immanent action is a self-perfecting quality. The acts of knowing and of loving are not only within the soul, they are for the soul an active superexistence, as it were, superior to the merely physical act of existence. Thus the soul, when it knows, becomes thereby something that it is not, and when it loves, aspires toward what it is not, as to another self. This action, as such, is above time.

It speaks for Aristotle's greatness to have known and taught that immanent (or vital or interiorizing) action is nobler and more elevated than transitive (or non-vital or exteriorizing) action.

In their doctrine of immanent action, the Greeks held that the immanence of the intellectual act is, as such, more perfect than that of the act of will; that is why, according to a thesis which St. Thomas made classical, intelligence is nobler than will, from the sole point of view of the degrees of immanence and immateriality of the powers of the soul.

All this led the Greeks to a two-fold conclusion, which, in its first part, formulated a most valuable truth; and, in its second part, transformed that truth into a great error.

The great truth which the Greeks discovered (and which their philosophers conceptualized in very divers spiritual ways) is the superiority of contemplation, as such, to action. As Aristotle puts it, life according to the intellect is better than a merely human life.

But the error follows. What did that assertion mean to them practically? It meant that mankind lives for the sake of a few intellectuals. There is a category of specialists,—the philosophers,—who lead a superhuman life; then in a lower category, destined to serve them, come those who lead the ordinary human life, the civil or political one; they in turn are served by those who lead a sub-human life, the life of work,—that is, the slaves. The high truth of the superiority of contemplative life was bound up with the contempt of work and the plague of slavery. Even the work of freemen, of the artist or the artisan, was scorned. Plutarch wrote: 'Who, having the choice, would not prefer enjoying the contemplation of Phidias' works, to being Phidias himself?' 'All artisans have a despicable occupation, because there can be nothing noble in a workshop,' said 'the good Cicero.' And farther to the East, the Brahmin's contemplation reposes socially on the untouchables' misery; wisdom, on offence and humiliation.

CHRISTIANITY

Christianity has transfigured everything.

What innovations did Christianity introduce on the subject with which we are dealing? I should say they are fourfold.

First, it teaches us that love is better than intelligence. St. Thomas admits, like Aristotle, that considering the degrees of immanence and immateriality of the powers of the soul in themselves, intelligence is nobler than will, but he adds that considering the *things* we know and love, these things exist in us by knowledge according to the mode of existence and the dignity of our own soul, but by love they attract us to them according to their own mode of existence and their own dignity, and therefore it must be said that to love things that are superior to man is better than to know them. It is better to love God than to know Him; it is also better to love our brethren, in whom the mystery of God's likeness is concealed, than to know them. And the love which is *Caritas* is, not in the moral order only, but in the ontological as well, that which is most excellent and most perfect in the human soul and in the Angel.

Second, Christianity has transfigured the notion of contemplation, and endowed it with a new meaning. Albert the Great sums it up in his admirable treatise *de Adhaerendo Deo:* 'The contemplation of the philosophers', he writes, 'is concerned with the perfection of the contemplator, and hence does not go farther than the intellect, so that their end is intellectual knowledge. But the contemplation of the saints is concerned with the love of the one who is contemplated—of God. And this is why, not content with the intellect, with knowledge as its ultimate end, it attains the heart through love, *transit ad affectum per amorem.*' And love indeed is its own instrument, love's dark fire is its light. *Quia ubi amor, ibi oculus.* This leads to consequences, which we shall presently see, and which make the word 'contemplation' rather unsatisfactory.

Third, Christianity has also transfigured the notion of action and has given it a new meaning. Christian wisdom has seen, better than the wisdom of philosophers, that the action which man exercises on matter or other men, though it is transitive, cannot be reduced to transitive action such as is found in the world of bodies. It is an essentially human activity. It has not only been thought and willed before being exercised,—being born in the heart before being made manifest in the external world; it not only necessarily proceeds from an immanent act, but, moreover, it goes beyond the work it serves, and by an instinct of communication which demands to be perfected in goodness, proceeds to the service of other men. You can give high wages to a workman for work manifestly useless,—for instance, the task, which used to be imposed on convicts, of digging holes and then filling them up,—and this workman will be driven to despair. It is essential to human work that it be useful to men.

As has often been remarked, Christ in assuming for Himself the work and condition of an artisan in a small village, rehabilitated labour, and manifested its natural dignity, a dignity which Antiquity had denied. The *hardship* of work is a consequence of the Fall and of the loss of privileges proper to the state of innocence, but not *work in itself.* Adam in the state of innocence worked—without any pain—and had the mission of cultivating and keeping the Garden.

Man's labour in its first and humblest stage is a co-operation with God the Creator, and Christianity's rehabilitation of labour in the moral order is bound up with revelation, in the dogmatic order, of creation *ex nihilo. Pater meus usque modo operatur, et ego operor.* My Father worketh hitherto and I work too. Here is the foundation of labour ethics, which the modern world is seeking and has not yet found. The work with Antiquity most despised, manual work, imposes the forms of reason on matter, and delivers man from the fatalities of material nature (provided however he does not turn his industry into an idol which enslaves him even more); thus, work has a value of natural redemption; it is like a remote prefiguration of the communications of love. Man is both *homo faber* and *homo sapiens,* and he is *homo faber* before being in truth and actually *homo sapiens* and in order to become the latter.

Fourth, and this is a consequence of the preceding considerations, another innovation which Christianity has introduced, relevant to our subject, is that contemplation (supernatural contemplation, which would be better called *entrance into the very states of God, of God Incarnate*) is not only the business of specialists or of the chosen few. This was an astounding revolution in the spiritual order. Greeks and Jews, masters and slaves, men and women, poor and rich (but the poor, first), souls who have known evil and souls (if there be such) who have not, whatever their condition, race and wounds,—all are called to the feast of divine Love and divine wisdom. That wisdom calls them all, it clamours in the public places and in the roadways. All, without exception, are called to perfection, which is the same as that of the Father who is in heaven; in a manner either close or distant, all are called to the contemplation of the saints, not the contemplation of the philosophers, but to loving and crucified contemplation. All without exception. The universality of such an appeal is one of the essential features of Christianity's *catholicity.*

At the same time and symmetrically, all are bound by the law of work. There are no more privileged by pain and labour. Work is for everyone, as well as the sin of which everyone must be cured. If any will not work, neither shall he eat. It is St. Paul who said this, and the evolution of modern societies shows more clearly every day how universal that assertion is. I know well that some people who have adopted it as a motto, not knowing its author, perhaps, give it a wrong interpretation, believing that there is but one kind of work,—that which creates economic values. They fail to see the admirable analogical variety of the notion of work. According to the social conscience which the Christian leaven has awakened, no one can be dispensed from activities directed to the good of men, be it to clothe or feed their bodies, to teach them or guide them, to bring them to truth and beauty or delights of the spirit, to feed them with the words of God or, like those dedicated to contemplative life, to wear oneself out in praying for them. All those varied activities are fraternal, and communicate analogically in that notion of work which the Christian spirit has renewed.[1]

I have just said that the notion of work is verified in a most refined

[1] I do not think that the word 'work' and concept of work must be reserved only to manual work and to intellectual activities preparing for or regulating the latter. I consider the fact of some things, being *per se,* or by itself, related to the utility of the human community, as the true criterion of work in the ethico-social sense. And lawyers, statesmen, teachers, have an activity no less related to the usefulness of the community than the activity of farmers or miners.

way, even in those dedicated to the contemplative life. It is true that contemplation itself is in fact not work, not a thing of utility. It is a fruit. It is not ordinary leisure; it is a leisure coinciding with the very highest activity of the human substance. Accordng to the profound views of St. Thomas Aquinas, following Aristotle, those who go beyond the socio-temporal life achieve in themselves the suprasocial good to which the social trends as to a transcendent term, and by that very act are free from the law of labour. There remains no more for them but Thee and I, Him whom they love, and themselves.

But in virtue of that generosity which is inherent in immanent activity at its highest degrees, loving contemplation overflows as a protection and a benediction to society. And though not itself a useful service or a work, even in the widest meaning of the word, that which is beyond usefulness superabounds thus in a usefulness, in which the notion of work is still realized at the extreme limit of refinement.

Thus, it will be understood why I have said above that all activities, from manual labour to the gratuitously added utility of contemplative leisure, are fraternal activities, in which the notion of work can be found at very different degrees of analogy.

Christianity has not condemned slavery as a social and juridical form, save in its most extreme modes, which are absolutely incompatible with human dignity. It has done better by annihilating, from within, its functional necessity in human conscience. It has evacuated that necessity from conscience, and is evacuating it progressively from existence (for ancient slavery is not the only form of servitude), and it will require the entire history of mankind to have completely finished with it. For Christian conscience, as I have just pointed out, there do not exist two categories in humanity, *homo faber* whose task is to work, and *homo sapiens* whose task is the contemplation of truth. The same man is both *faber* and *sapiens*, and wisdom calls us all to the freedom of the children of God. . . .

ORIENT AND OCCIDENT

To come back to where we started, to the debate of East and West, we see, if what we have said be true, that activism and pragmatism, the rejection of contemplative values, the dethronement of Wisdom, are the West's greatest woe. It seems as if to-day the West sought a remedy in the frantic exaggeration of this evil. The attempts to create new civilizations which are taking form before our eyes,—where the civil community becomes the soul of a dynamism which is purely activistic, industrial and warlike, and mobilizes for that active end both science and thought,—do not make our prognostications optimistic. The West has here much to learn from the East and from its fidelity to the primacy of contemplative values.

But, at the same time, what I want to point out is that, while denouncing the errors and shortcomings of our unhappy West, the Christian feels for it a piety that is filial, and can plead its cause in the face of the East. For this activism and pragmatism are the catastrophe of a truly great thing which the spirit of separation from God has led astray. I mean the generosity, the propensity to give and communicate, the sense of ontological superabundance springing from Evangelical Love, and of holy contemplation superabounding in activity.

And the impassible contemplation which the East boasts of,—which proceeds from the energies of the soul striving toward liberation by techniques and formulas, by the athletic efforts of ascetics, and of active concentration,—manifests, on its part, in the very order of spiritual things, a pragmatism that is infinitely more subtle, but which no less withdraws from the testimony that God expects from mankind.

Let us remember the great words which St. Thomas wrote about the Incarnation, and which to my mind throw the deepest light upon those problems: 'In the Mystery of Incarnation,' he says, 'the movement of *descent* of divine plenitude into the depths of human nature is more important than the movement of ascent of human nature towards God.' This is a truth that holds good, not only for the Head but for the whole of the Body. It explains to us how supernatural contemplation, proceeding thus from the descent within us of divine plenitude, superabounds within us in love and activity.

We hold that the West will not surmount the crises in which it is engaged, unless it reconquers that vital truth, and understands that external activity must overflow from a superabundance of internal activity, by which man is united to truth and to the source of being. If the East, perhaps because its efforts toward contemplation aspired above all toward philosophical forms of contemplation, has given great importance to natural contemplation and spirituality, even in things that belonged to the secular and temporal order; one might ask if in the West, by a sort of division of labour, spirituality and contemplation,—not philosophical but supernatural contemplation,—has not been too much the exclusive preoccupation of souls consecrated to God and to the things of His Kingdom;

while the rest of mankind was abandoned to the law of immediate, practical success and the will to power. If a new age of Christian civilization should dawn, it is probable that the law of contemplation superabounding in action would overflow in some way into the secular and temporal order. It will thus be an age of the sanctification of the profane.

As I have said at the beginning of this chapter, the debate between action and contemplation is particularly important to this continent. Is it not a universally repeated commonplace that America is the land par excellence of pragmatism and of the great undertakings of human activity? There is truth in this, as in most commonplaces. Whitman celebrates the pioneers in a manner which is certainly characteristic of the American soul. But, in my opinion, there are in America great reserves and possibilities for contemplation. The activism which is manifested here assumes in many cases the aspect of a remedy against despair. I think that this activism itself masks a certain hidden aspiration to contemplation. To my mind, if in American civilization certain elements are causing complaints or criticisms, those elements proceed definitely from a repression of the desire, natural in mankind, for the active repose of the soul breathing what is eternal. In many unhappy creatures, good but wrongly directed, nervous breakdown is the price of such repression. On the other hand, the tendency, natural in this country, to undertake great things, to have confidence, to be moved by large idealistic feelings, may be considered, without great risk of error, as disguising that desire and aspiration of which I spoke.

To wish paradise on earth is stark naïveté. But it is surely better than not to wish any paradise at all. To aspire to paradise is man's grandeur; and how should I aspire to paradise except by beginning to realize paradise here below? The question is to know what paradise is. Paradise consists, as St. Augustine says, in the joy of the Truth. Contemplation is paradise on earth, a crucified paradise.

The cult of action is not specifically American. It is a European idea, an idea of post-Renaissance and post-Reformation Europe. What may mislead us in this matter, so it seems to me, is that the New Continent, with terrible loyalty, has taken some of the Old World's ideas, transplanted in virgin soil, and carried them to their limits. When in America some few come to realize better the value of contemplative activity, its superiority and fecundity, I believe that the possibilities I have spoken of will manifest themselves, at least in a small way, but forcefully enough gradually to modify the general scheme of values. Then this country will give some of its generosity, good will, confidence in the future and courage, to things contemplative, to contemplation overflowing in action. And this is one of the reasons why even if a moment of general catastrophe should befall civilization, I would still not despair of civilization.

Reinhold Niebuhr

The Self's Search for Ultimate Meaning *

The task of penetrating the ultimate mystery prompts many responses, but they could all be placed into three general categories:

(A) The first category embraces all religious responses in which the self seeks to break through a universal rational system in order to assert its significance ultimately. It may seek to do this individually, as in modern romantic and existentialist thought; or it may be so conscious of its finiteness as an individual that it finds no opportunity to assert the ultimate significance of itself in history except by asserting the significance of the collective self. This category, in short, embraces all the idolatrous religions of ancient history, including both primitive polytheism and the imperial religions of Egypt and Babylon, and (in more artificial terms) of Rome. Until a recent day this idolatry, in which the individual self finds the ultimate source of its meaning in the history of the collective self so much more imposing though also so much closer to the flux of nature, was thought to be a phase of history which was overcome by the rise of rigorously monotheistic religions and monistic philosophies. But the recrudescence of religious nationalism and the pseudo-universalistic Messianism of communism have instructed us that this idolatry, this worship of the collective self as if it were ultimate and not finite, is not merely due to the limits of a primitive imagination. It corresponds to a perennial desire in the human heart to eat one's cake and have it, too; to subordinate the finite self to something greater than it but not so great that the self may not participate in the exaltation of the finite value. Naturally this idolatrous religion must have baneful effects, not only because it complicates the problem of group relations by exaggerating the claims of contingent historical forces in competition with each other, but because the unconditioned commitment of the self to the collective self must rob it of its freedom; for the collective

* From *The Self and the Dramas of History* by Reinhold Niebuhr, pp. 62–72. Copyright 1955 by Reinhold Niebuhr. Reprinted by permission of Charles Scribner's Sons and Faber and Faber Limited.

self is, though more imposing and more long-lived than the individual self, also so much more bound to nature and its necessities, so defective in organs of self-transcendence and therefore so much farther removed from the ultimate source of meaning, that the self debases itself by this uncritical devotion.

(B) The second alternative of explicit religious response has been defined by Aldous Huxley as "The Perennial Philosophy." He is right in asserting that it is a fairly universal response, but wrong in concluding that this universality guarantees its validity. This response, generally, defined as "mysticism," stands at the opposite pole of idolatry. It is in fact an heroic effort to transcend all finite values and systems of meaning, including the self as particular existence, and to arrive at universality and "unconditioned" being. The persistence of this mystic tendency in the religions of the world is a telling proof of the ability of the self, in the ultimate reaches of its freedom and self-awareness, to discern some affinity between the mystery within itself and the mystery behind the observable phenomena and to find the key to universality in the joining of these two mysteries. This "perennial philosophy" embraces not only the systems, stemming from the thought of Plotinus, in the Western world but practically all religions of the Orient. It is expressed in the Brahman overtones of Hindu polytheism; in the Sufist tradition of Mohammedanism; in the Taoist tradition of Chinese culture and, most classically, in Buddhism. Here the search for undifferentiated being reaches the height of asserting a type of being as the goal of existence about which one can not be certain whether it is the fullness or the absence of being. It is certainly being bereft of all relationships and meanings.

(C) The third alternative, an explicitly religious answer to the self's search for the ultimate, embraces the two Biblical faiths of Judaism and Christianity. These faiths interpret the self's experience with the ultimate in the final reaches of its self-awareness as a dialogue with God. The idea of a dialogue between the self and God assumes the personality of God, an assumption which both rationalists and mystics find untenable, but to which Biblical faith clings stubbornly. Selfhood or personality is supposedly not attributable to God because the idea of personality is loaded with connotations of finiteness and therefore casts a suspicion of "anthropomorphism" upon Biblical faith. But it is significant that both mystics and rationalists have as much difficulty in ascribing personality to man as to God. This fact suggests that it is not the connotations of finiteness which create the difficulty but rather the fact that personality is characerized by both a basic structure and a freedom beyond structure. The rationalists can comprehend the structure within a system of rational cohesion; and the mystics are able to interpret the freedom as part of a system of undifferentiated potentiality. But neither is able to comprehend the total fact of personality within its system.

The dialogue between the self and God results in the conviction of the self, but not for reason of its finiteness. It is convicted rather of its pretension or "sin"; of claiming too much for its finiteness, and for the virtue and wisdom, which it achieves in its finiteness. The idea of such an encounter therefore permits the Biblical faiths both to affirm the life of the self in history and to challenge its achievements in any particular instance. "Enter not into judgment with thy servant, for in thy sight is no man living justified," declares the Psalmist. Kierkegaard sums up this theme of Biblical religions with the affirmation that "Before God all men are in the wrong." The fact that the self is judged for every inclination which affronts God's "majesty" by pride or lust for power is the religious dimension of sin. The prophets are however equally conscious of the social dimension which is the inclination of the self to take advantage of its fellow men. This "injustice" is never speculatively defined, as in Greek philosophy, but rigorously defined by reactions to injustice in particular situations.

The "severity" of God's judgement is matched by the "goodness" of His mercy. In the dialogue between the individual and God, this validates itself as the indeterminate possibilities of self-realization and fulfillment of the self's potentialities once it has ceased to seek fulfillment of life from the standpoint of itself. The problem of how the mercy of God is related to His justice is a perpetual problem in the Old Testament. The new Biblical faith of Christianity enters into history with the affirmation that the drama of Christ's life is in fact a final revelation, in which this problem is clarified by the assurance that God takes the demand of His justice upon Himself through Christ's suffering love and therefore "God was in Christ reconciling the world unto Himself."

The dying and rising again of Christ is the key to the self's possibilities in history. All of life is given this norm for the realization of selfhood. "I am crucified with Christ," declares St. Paul, "nevertheless I live." This theme is in perfect harmony with the words attributed to Jesus in the Johannine Gospel: "Except a corn of wheat fall into the ground and die, it abideth alone: but if it die, it bringeth forth much fruit." (John 12:24)

Thus the encounter of the self with God is defined in Biblical faith in terms of a norm which has been set by an historical "revelation." And this revelation is an historical event or series of events which are not essentially miraculous (miracles such as the "virgin birth" are afterthoughts) but are events in history which are discerned by faith to have revelatory power into the ultimate mystery. Both Biblical religions are covenant faiths, which organize covenant communities upon the basis of a common commitment of faith in the divine significance of these events. We must postpone until later, then, a consideration of the relation of revelation to the drama of history. In this connection it is necessary to observe that the discernment of ultimate significance of an historic event makes the Biblical religions seem primitive and unsophisticated in the eyes of both rationalists and mystics, who look for the ultimate or "unconditioned" in either the permanent structures of existence or in an undifferentiated ground of being. They may fail to note, however, that the Biblical presupposition is the only one of the three alternatives which asserts a discontinuity between the self and God. This discontinuity makes explicit faith indispensable in the ultimate dialogue; but it also prevents the self either from usurping the place of the divine for itself or from imagining itself merged with the divine. If we test these three alternative solutions for the self's search for the ultimate by the two tests of consistency or coherence with other truth, and by conformity with established facts subject to empirical tests, it will soon become apparent that the religions which tend to the exaltation of finite values and centers of meaning are most easily ruled out, as indeed they have been ruled out in principle for centuries. The collective self may be momentarily imposing; but its mortality is obvious and the perils to the individual self by its pretensions of divinity are very great.

It is however very significant that a religious solution which has been ruled out in principle for centuries should have so much practical force in our day, both in the version of a religious nationalism and in a pseudo-universalistic Messianic creed. These contemporary ventures into idolatry are proof of the difficulty of containing the collective self within any more general scheme of validity than its own interests. They prove that an affirmation of historical meaning as we have it in Western civilization is almost inevitably attended by pretentious efforts to close the system of meaning prematurely with some cherished value of the self at the center of the system.

It is equally significant that modern culture has generated less plausible and dangerous forms of individualistic pretention, in which the freedom and the uniqueness of the individual is asserted in defiance of any systems of consistency or universal meaning. The romantic revolt of the nineteenth century culminated in Nietzsche's effort to achieve the affirmation of unique vitality of the individual and his transcendence over the flux of history, thus seeking to combine classical with Hebraic attitudes toward time and eternity.

It must be apparent that modern existentialism is but another version of this romantic revolt. It has obviously learned from Biblical faith about the unique freedom of the individual and the distinction between the self's reason and personality. It is however unable to make the venture of faith of Biblical religion and therefore ends in the quasi-idolatrous attitude of making the individual his own creator and end. "Thus there is no human nature," declares the French existentialist Sartre, "because there is no God to conceive it. Man simply is. Not that he is simply what he conceives himself to be. But he is what he wills. . . . He is what he wills to be after that leap toward existence." [1]

Heidegger's concern for "authentic being," for the affirmation of the uniquely human freedom against the necessities of nature and the inevitability of death, is distantly related to Nietzsche's defiance of death. It is in the same category of quasi-idolatry. It may not make the self into its own God but it asserts the uniqueness of the self without reference to its relations to the community or to any general value.

If we rule out the idolatrous and quasi-idolatrous, the individualistic and collectivistic forms of these idolatries, as valid answers to the self's quest for ultimate meaning even though we recognize that the popularity of such answers is not confined to past history but is an ever recurring phenomenon, we are left with the two alternatives of the Biblical faith and Mr. Huxley's "perennial philosophy" or the mystic answer to the problem.

The answer of Biblical faith embodies, as we have seen, several presuppositions and affirmations which the modern mind finds particularly difficult, not to say impossible: the personality of God; the definition of the relation between the self and God as a dialogue; and the determination of the form of that dialogue in terms of a previous historic "revelation," which is an event in past history, discerned by faith to give a key to the character and purpose of God and of His relationship to man. It is therefore understandable that when confronted with these two alternatives, sophisticated moderns who have become aware of a depth of selfhood which can not be comprehended within the limits of the self as a biological organism or the self as mind, are inclined to turn to the mystic alternative in preference to the Biblical one. It is even understandable that they should do this at the price of defying the very ethos of their own life-affirming and history-affirming culture and choose an alternative which annuls every partial and particular meaning including the particular self. This is under-

[1] *Existentialism and Humanism,* p. 28.

standable in the sense that it proves how powerful are the compulsions to comprehend reality in a self-consistent scheme and to leave the mystery beyond the system of rational intelligibility unsolved.

Thus Professor Stace uttered a cry of despair some years ago because he became aware that the world which modern science explicated had no place for the human self or for any of the values which the self holds dear. Subsequently he published his considered answer to this problem in his *Time and Eternity.* He had accomplished his escape from the naturalistic prison by embracing the "perennial philosophy" of Mr. Huxley and the oriental mystics. He defined religion as the search for "the impossible, the unattainable and the inconceivable." Professor Stace thus bears testimony to the capacity of the self to reach for the ultimate; but he is sceptical of any venture of faith in an ultimate which would purify and complete the particular meanings of history. He finds it more acceptable to assert the pure mystery of the divine. He is impressed by the fact that the mystic approach arrives at the conclusion that God is both the fullness and the absence of being. Reporting on the account of divinity in the mystic tradition, he records that "God is non-Being, nothingness, emptiness, the void, the abyss . . . God is the great silence, the great darkness . . . yet God is also in the language of the medieval mystics, the supreme reality, the '*ens realissimum.*' " "This supreme God," he declares, "is contrasted by the mystics with the worthlessness of the world . . . the world then is worthless trash. This is seen by all men more dimly or more clearly, but it is seen by the mystics with absolute clarity." [2]

Professor Stace refers frequently to the Hindu desire to achieve unity of the self and God, to realize the assurance that "Brahman and Atman are one." This seems to him to be pure religion in comparison with the religions of the Bible with their appreciation of particular selfhood.

The impulse to annul the meaning of particular selfhood and the significance of the whole drama of existence is expressed even more significantly in the view of the eminent philosopher George Santayana. Despite his essential Platonism, and his consequent faith in a "realm of essences," Santayana makes it clear, in his *Platonism and the Spiritual Life,* that the final goal of religion must be to transcend even these ghostly structures of particular meaning. "At the risk of parting company with Dean Inge, or even with Plato," he declares, "the spiritual life is not a worship of values, whether found in things or hypostasized into supernatural powers. It is the exact opposite. It is the disintoxication from their influence. . . . The great masters of the spiritual life are evidently not the

[2] *Time and Eternity,* p. 126.

Greeks, not even the Alexandrian Greeks, but the Indians and their disciples elsewhere in the East; and those Moslems, Jews and Christians who have surrendered precisely that early unregenerate claim to be enveloped in a protecting world." Santayana makes it quite clear that such a faith annuls all historic possibilities and responsibilities. "Obligations are moral," he writes, "they presuppose physical and social organisms and immanent spontaneous interests. . . . All values fall within the preview of ethics, which is a part of politics. Spirituality is the supreme good for those who are called to it, the few intellectuals who can be satisfied only by the impartial truth and by the self annihilating contemplation of all being." [3]

It is rather revealing that Santayana reserves the mystic *summum bonum* for a few intellectuals. It reveals how aristocratic is the conception; and how closely mysticism is related to rationalism. From Aristotle to Santayana, mysticism is in fact the perennial overtone of rationalism. The drama of history is not comprehended in the categories of meaning supplied by either the rationalists or the mystics. In the one case the categories fail to comprehend the dramatic variety and the complex causal relations of history. In the other case the mystic conception of the fulfillment of meaning obviously results in the annulment of any particular meaning in history.

It will be regarded as futile by all pure "empiricists" to compare the Biblical and the mystic conceptions of the ultimate dimensions of selfhood and to judge between the thesis that the self is in "dialogue with God" and the thesis that the self on that level is in the process of merging with a universal divine consciousness. But if the evidence of introspection is accepted (though it is admittedly inexact) it can not be too difficult to prove that the abstraction of the universal subject from the self as particular object is a futile procedure because the particular self always remains obtrusively in these exercises of introversion. There is furthermore the social evidence that the mystics never succeed in eliminating particular selfhood or in transcending the self as a particular organism. The erotic overtones in the mystic visions of an absolute consciousness is a rather pathetic symbol of the futility of the self's attempt to escape from the "body" and time into an undifferentiated eternity.

In short, we are confronted with evidence that the thesis of Biblical faith, that the self is in dialogue with a God who must be defined as a "person" because He embodies both the structure of being and a transcendent freedom, is more valid than the alternative theses which find much greater favor among the sophisticated. The Biblical thesis requires a more

[3] Pp. 34–40.

explicit act of faith because it leaps a gap of discontinuity between man and God and because it dares to give a specific meaning to the divine, which is relevant to the partial and fragmentary meanings of history. It both fulfills and corrects these meanings, loyalties and values, and therefore has a more valid attitude to the self's historic existence which the various rationalistic systems affirm too simply and the mystic thesis annuls too absolutely. This character of Biblical faith is therefore the crux of the question, why a faith which is more explicit than alternative ones should be more justified by actual experience than these. It gives a key to the seeming mystery of our whole cultural history. That mystery is why an allegedly "dogmatic" faith should be justified by the experiences of the human self more than the allegedly "empirical" approaches to selfhood, which obscure their potent, though implicit, dogmas within their prescriptions for empirical observation.

Miguel De Unamuno

The Practical Problem *

> L'homme est périssable. Il se peut; mais périssons en résistant, et, si le néant nous est reservé, ne faisons pas que ce soit une justice.—SÉNANCOUR: *Obermann,* lettre xc.

Several times in the devious course of these essays I have defined, in spite of my horror of definitions, my own position with regard to the problem that I have been examining; but I know there will always be some dissatisfied reader, educated in some dogmatism or other, who will say: "This man comes to no conclusion, he vacillates—now he seems to affirm one thing and then its contrary—he is full of contradictions—I can't label him. What is he?" Just this—one who affirms contraries, a man of contradiction and strife, as Jeremiah said of himself; one who says one thing with his heart and the contrary with his head, and for whom this conflict is the very stuff of life. And that is as clear as the water that flows from the melted snow upon the mountain tops.

I shall be told that this is an untenable position, that a foundation must be laid upon which to build our action and our works, that it is impossible to live by contradictions, that unity and clarity are essential conditions of life and thought, and that it is necessary to unify thought. And this leaves us as we were before. For it is precisely this inner contradiction that unifies my life and gives it its practical purpose.

Or rather it is the conflict itself, it is this self-same passionate uncertainty, that unifies my action and makes me live and work.

We think in order that we may live, I have said; but perhaps it were more correct to say that we think because we live, and the form of our thought corresponds with that of our life. Once more I must repeat that our ethical and philosophical doctrines in general are usually merely the justification *a posteriori* of our conduct, of our actions. Our doctrines

* From *Tragic Sense of Life* by Miguel De Unamuno, translated by J. E. Crawford Flitch, 1921, Chapter XI, pp. 260–269. Copyright 1954 by Dover Publications, Inc. Reprinted by permission of the estate of J. Crawford Flitch.

are usually the means we seek in order to explain and justify to others and to ourselves our own mode of action. And this, be it observed, not merely for others, but for ourselves. The man who does not really know why he acts as he does and not otherwise, feels the necessity of explaining to himself the motive of his action and so he forges a motive. What we believe to be the motives of our conduct are usually but the pretexts for it. The very same reason which one man may regard as a motive for taking care to prolong his life may be regarded by another man as a motive for shooting himself.

Nevertheless it cannot be denied that reasons, ideas, have an influence upon human actions, and sometimes even determine them, by a process analogous to that of suggestion upon a hypnotized person, and this is so because of the tendency in every idea to resolve itself into action—an idea being simply an inchoate or abortive act. It was this notion that suggested to Fouillée his theory of idea-forces. But ordinarily ideas are forces which we accommodate to other forces, deeper and much less conscious.

But putting all this aside for the present, what I wish to establish is that uncertainty, doubt, perpetual wrestling with the mystery of our final destiny, mental despair, and the lack of any solid and stable dogmatic foundation, may be the basis of an ethic.

He who bases or thinks that he bases his conduct—his inward or his outward conduct, his feeling or his action—upon a dogma or theoretical principle which he deems incontrovertible, runs the risk of becoming a fanatic, and moreover, the moment that this dogma is weakened or shattered, the morality based upon it gives way. If the earth that he thought firm begins to rock, he himself trembles at the earthquake, for we do not all come up to the standard of the ideal Stoic who remains undaunted among the ruins of a world shattered into atoms. Happily the stuff that is underneath a man's ideas will save him. For if a man should tell you that he does not defraud or cuckold his best friend only because he is afraid of hell, you may depend upon it that neither would he do so even if he were to cease to believe in hell, but that he would invent some other excuse instead. And this is all to the honour of the human race.

But he who believes that he is sailing, perhaps without a set course, on an unstable and sinkable raft, must not be dismayed if the raft gives way beneath his feet and threatens to sink. Such a one thinks that he acts, not because he deems his principle of action to be true, but in order to make it true, in order to prove its truth, in order to create his own spiritual world.

My conduct must be the best proof, the moral proof, of my supreme desire; and if I do not end by convincing myself, within the bounds of the ultimate and irremediable uncertainty, of the truth of what I hope for, it is because my conduct is not sufficiently pure. Virtue, therefore, is not based upon dogma, but dogma upon virtue, and it is not faith that creates martyrs but martyrs who create faith. There is no security or repose—so far as security and repose are obtainable in this life, so essentially insecure and unreposeful—save in conduct that is passionately good.

Conduct, practice, is the proof of doctrine, theory. "If any man will do His will—the will of Him that sent me," said Jesus, "he shall know of the doctrine, whether it be of God or whether I speak of myself" (John vii. 17); and there is a well-known saying of Pascal: "Begin by taking holy water and you will end by becoming a believer." And pursuing a similar train of thought, Johann Jakob Moser, the pietist, was of the opinion that no atheist or naturalist had the right to regard the Christian religion as void of truth so long as he had not put it to the proof by keeping its precepts and commandments (Ritschl, *Geschichte des Pietismus,* book vii., 43).

What is our heart's truth, anti-rational though it be? The immortality of the human soul, the truth of the persistence of our consciousness without any termination whatsoever, the truth of the human finality of the Universe. And what is its moral proof? We may formulate it thus: Act so that in your own judgement and in the judgement of others you may merit eternity, act so that you may become irreplaceable, act so that you may not merit death. Or perhaps thus: Act as if you were to die to-morrow, but to die in order to survive and be eternalized. The end of morality is to give personal, human finality to the Universe; to discover the finality that belongs to it—if indeed it has any finality—and to discover it by acting.

More than a century ago, in 1804, in Letter XC of that series that constitutes the immense monody of his *Obermann,* Sénancour wrote the words which I have put at the head of this chapter—and of all the spiritual descendants of the patriarchal Rousseau, Sénancour was the most profound and the most intense; of all the men of heart and feeling that France has produced, not excluding Pascal, he was the most tragic. "Man is perishable. That may be; but let us perish resisting, and if it is nothingness that awaits us, do not let us so act that it shall be a just fate." Change this sentence from its negative to the positive form—"And if it is nothingness that awaits us, let us so act that it shall be an unjust fate"—and you get the firmest basis of action for the man who cannot or will not be a dogmatist.

That which is irreligious and demoniacal, that which incapacitates us for action and leaves us without any ideal defence against our evil tendencies, is the pessimism that Goethe puts into the mouth of Mephistopheles when he makes him say, "All that has achieved existence deserves to be destroyed" (*denn alles was ensteht ist wert dass es zugrunde geht*). This is the pessimism which we men call evil, and not that other pessimism that consists in lamenting what it fears to be true and struggling against this fear—namely, that everything is doomed to annihilation in the end. Metphistopheles asserts that everything that exists deserves to be destroyed, annihilated, but not that everything will be destroyed or annihilated; and we assert that everything that exists deserves to be exalted and eternalized, even though no such fate is in store for it. The moral attitude is the reverse of this.

Yes, everything deserves to be eternalized, absolutely everything, even evil itself, for that which we call evil would lose its evilness in being eternalized, because it would lose its temporal nature. For the essence of evil consists in its temporal nature, in its not applying itself to any ultimate and permanent end.

And it might not be superfluous here to say something about that distinction, more overlaid with confusion than any other, between what we are accustomed to call optimism and pessimism, a confusion not less than that which exists with regard to the distinction between individualism and socialism. Indeed, it is scarcely possible to form a clear idea as to what pessimism really is.

I have just this very day read in the *Nation* (July 6, 1912) an article, entitled "A Dramatic Inferno," that deals with an English translation of the works of Strindberg, and it opens with the following judicious observations: "If there were in the world a sincere and total pessimism, it would of necessity be silent. The despair which finds a voice is a social mood, it is the cry of misery which brother utters to brother when both are stumbling through a valley of shadows which is peopled with—comrades. In its anguish it bears witness to something that is good in life, for it presupposes sympathy. . . . The real gloom, the sincere despair, is dumb and blind; it writes no books, and feels no impulse to burden an intolerable universe with a monument more lasting than brass." Doubtless there is something of sophistry in this criticism, for the man who is really in pain weeps and even cries aloud, even if he is alone and there is nobody to hear him, simply as a means of alleviating his pain, although this perhaps may be a result of social habits. But does not the lion, alone in the desert, roar if he has an aching tooth? But apart from this, it cannot be denied that there is a substance of truth underlying these remarks. The pessimism that protests and defends itself cannot be truly said to be pessimism. And, in truth, still less is it pessimism to hold that nothing ought to perish although all things may be doomed to annihilation, while on the other hand it is pessimism to affirm that all things ought to be annihilated even though nothing may perish.

Pessimism, moreover, may possess different values. There is a eudemonistic or economic pessimism, that which denies happiness; there is an ethical pessimism, that which denies the triumph of moral good; and there is a religious pessimism, that which despairs of the human finality of the Universe, of the eternal salvation of the individual soul.

All men deserve to be saved, but, as I have said in the previous chapter, he above all deserves immortality who desires it passionately and even in the face of reason. An English writer, H. G. Wells, who has taken upon himself the rôle of the prophet (a thing not uncommon in his country), tells us in *Anticipations* that "active and capable men of all forms of religious profession tend in practice to disregard the question of immortality altogether." And this is because the religious professions of these active and capable men to whom Wells refers are usually simply a lie, and their lives are a lie, too, if they seek to base them upon religion. But it may be that at bottom there is not so much truth in what Wells asserts as he and others imagine. These active and capable men live in the midst of a society imbued with Christian principles, surrounded by institutions and social feelings that are the product of Christianity, and faith in the immortality of the soul exists deep down in their own souls like a subterranean river, neither seen nor heard, but watering the roots of their deeds and their motives.

It must be admitted that there exists in truth no more solid foundation for morality than the foundation of the Catholic ethic. The end of man is eternal happiness, which consists in the vision and enjoyment of God *in sæcula sæculorum*. Where it errs, however, is in the choice of the means conducive to this end; for to make the attainment of eternal happiness dependent upon believing or not believing in the Procession of the Holy Ghost from the Father and the Son and not from the Father alone, or in the Divinity of Jesus, or in the theory of the Hypostatic Union, or even in the existence of God, is, as a moment's reflection will show, nothing less than monstrous. A human God—and that is the only kind of God we are able to conceive—would never reject him who was unable to believe in Him with his head, and it is not in his head but in his heart that the wicked man says that there is no God, which is equivalent to saying that he wishes that there may not be a God. If any belief could be bound up with the attainment of eternal happiness it would be the belief in this happiness itself and in the possibility of it.

And what shall we say of that other proposition of the king of pedants, to the effect that we have not come into the world to be happy but to fulfil our duty (*Wir sind nicht auf der Welt, um glücklich zu sein, sondern um unsere Schuldigkeit zu tun*)? If we are in the world *for* something (*um etwas*), whence can this *for* be derived but from the very essence of our own will, which asks for happiness and not duty as the ultimate end? And if it is sought to attribute some other value to this *for,* an objective value, as some Sadducean pedant would say, then it must be recognized that the objective reality, that which would remain even though humanity should disappear, is as indifferent to our duty as to our happiness, is as little concerned with our morality as with our felicity. I am not aware that Jupiter, Uranus, or Sirius would allow their course to be affected by the fact that we are or are not fulfilling our duty any more than by the fact that we are or are not happy.

Such considerations must appear to these pedants to be characterized by a ridiculous vulgarity and a dilettante superficiality. (The intellectual world is divided into two classes—dilettanti on the one hand, and pedants on the other.) What choice, then, have we? The modern man is he who resigns himself to the truth and is content to be ignorant of the synthesis of culture—witness what Windelband says on this head in his study of the fate of Hölderlin (*Praeludien,* i.). Yes, these men of culture are resigned, but there remain a few poor savages like ourselves for whom resignation is impossible. We do not resign ourselves to the idea of having one day to disappear, and the criticism of the great Pedant does not console us.

The quintessence of common sense was expressed by Galileo Galilei when he said: "Some perhaps will say that the bitterest pain is the loss of life, but I say that there are others more bitter; for whosoever is deprived of life is deprived at the same time of the power to lament, not only this, but any other loss whatsoever." Whether Galileo was conscious or not of the humour of this sentence I do not know, but it is a tragic humour.

But, to turn back, I repeat that if the attainment of eternal happiness could be bound up with any particular belief, it would be with the belief in the possibility of its realization. And yet, strictly speaking, not even with this. The reasonable man says in his head, "There is no other life after this," but only the wicked says it in his heart. But since the wicked man is possibly only a man who has been driven to despair, will a human God condemn him because of his despair? His despair alone is misfortune enough.

But in any event let us adopt the Calderónian formula in *La Vida es Sueño:*

> *Que estoy soñando y que quiero*
> *obrar hacer bien, pues no se pierde*
> *el hacer bien aun en sueños* [1]

But are good deeds really not lost? Did Calderón know? And he added:

> *Acudamos a lo eterno*
> *que es la fama vividora*
> *donde ni duermen las dichas*
> *no las grandezas reposan.*[2]

Is it really so? Did Calderón know?

Calderón had faith, robust Catholic faith; but for him who lacks faith, for him who cannot believe in what Don Pedro Calderón de la Barca believed, there always remains the attitude of *Obermann.*

If it is nothingness that awaits us, let us make an injustice of it; let us fight against destiny, even though without hope of victory; let us fight against it quixotically.

And not only do we fight against destiny in longing for what is irrational, but in acting in such a way that we make ourselves irreplaceable, in impressing our seal and mark upon others, in acting upon our neighbours in order to dominate them, in giving ourselves to them in order that we may eternalize ourselves so far as we can.

Our greatest endeavour must be to make ourselves irreplaceable; to make the theoretical fact—if this expression does not involve a contradiction in terms—the fact that each one of us is unique and irreplaceable, that no one else can fill the gap that will be left when we die, a practical truth.

For in fact each man is unique and irreplaceable; there cannot be any other I; each one of us—our soul, that is, not our life—is worth the whole Universe. I say the spirit and not the life, for the ridiculously exaggerated value which those attach to human life who, not really believing in the spirit—that is to say, in their personal immortality—tirade against war and the death penalty, for example, is a value which they attach to it precisely because they do not really believe in the spirit of which life is the servant. For life is of use only in so far as it serves its lord and master,

[1] Act II., Scene 4: "I am dreaming and I wish to act rightly, for good deeds are not lost, though they be wrought in dreams."

[2] Act III., Scene 10: "Let us aim at the eternal, the glory that does not wane, where bliss slumbers not and where greatness does not repose."

spirit, and if the master perishes with the servant, neither the one nor the other is of any great value.

And to act in such a way as to make our annihilation an injustice, in such a way as to make our brothers, our sons, and our brothers' sons, and their sons' sons, feel that we ought not to have died, is something that is within the reach of all.

Martin Buber

I and Thou *

If I face a human being as my *Thou,* and say the primary word *I-Thou* to him, he is not a thing among things, and does not consist of things.

This human being is not *He* or *She,* bounded from every other *He* and *She,* a specific point in space and time within the net of the world; nor is he a nature able to be experienced and described, a loose bundle of named qualities. But with no neighbour, and whole in himself he is *Thou* and fills the heavens. This does not mean that nothing exists except himself. But all else lives in *his* light.

Just as the melody is not made up of notes nor the verse of words nor the statue of lines, but they must be tugged and dragged till their unity has been scattered into these many pieces, so with the man to whom I say *Thou.* I can take out from him the colour of his hair, or of his speech, or of his goodness. I must continually do this. But each time I do it he ceases to be *Thou.*

And just as prayer is not in time but time in prayer, sacrifice not in space but space in sacrifice, and to reverse the relation is to abolish the reality, so with the man to whom I say *Thou.* I do not meet with him at some time and place or other. I can set him in a particular time and place; I must continually do it: but I set only a *He* or a *She,* that is an *It,* no longer my *Thou.*

So long as the heaven of *Thou* is spread out over me the winds of causality cower at my heels, and the whirlpool of fate stays its course.

I do not experience the man to whom I say *Thou.* But I take my stand in relation to him, in the sanctity of the primary word. Only when I step out of it do I experience him once more. In the act of experience *Thou* is far away.

Even if the man to whom I say *Thou* is not aware of it in the midst of

* From *I and Thou* by Martin Buber, translated by Ronald Gregor Smith. Edinburgh: T. & T. Clark, 1937, pp. 8–9, 33–34, 39–46. Reprinted by permission of Charles Scribner's Sons and T. & T. Clark.

his experience, yet relation may exist. For *Thou* is more than *It* realises. No deception penetrates here; here is the cradle of the Real Life. . . .

The world of *It* is set in the context of space and time.

The world of *Thou* is not set in the context of either of these.

The particular *Thou,* after the relational event has run its course, *is bound* to become an *It.*

The particular *It,* by entering the relational event, *may* become a *Thou.*

These are the two basic privileges of the world of *It.* They move man to look on the world of *It* as the world in which he has to live, and in which it is comfortable to live, as the world, indeed, which offers him all manner of incitements and excitements, activity and knowledge. In this chronicle of solid benefits the moments of the *Thou* appear as strange lyric and dramatic episodes, seductive and magical, but tearing us away to dangerous extremes, loosening the well-tried context, leaving more questions than satisfaction behind them, shattering security—in short, uncanny moments we can well dispense with. For since we are bound to leave them and go back into the "world", why not remain in it? Why not call to order what is over against us, and send it packing into the realm of objects? Why, if we find ourselves on occasion with no choice but to say *Thou* to father, wife, or comrade, not say *Thou* and mean *It?* To utter the sound *Thou* with the vocal organs is by no means the same as saying the uncanny primary word; more, it is harmless to whisper with the soul an amorous *Thou,* so long as nothing else in a serious way is meant but *experience* and *make use of.*

It is not possible to live in the bare present. Life would be quite consumed if precautions were not taken to subdue the present speedily and thoroughly. But it is possible to live in the bare past, indeed only in it may a life be organised. We only need to fill each moment with experiencing and using, and it ceases to burn.

And in all the seriousness of truth, hear this: without *It* man cannot live. But he who lives with *It* alone is not a man. . . .

Spirit in its human manifestation is a response of man to his *Thou.* Man speaks with many tongues, tongues of language, of art, of action; but the spirit is one, the response to the *Thou* which appears and addresses him out of the mystery. Spirit is the word. And just as talk in a language may well first take the form of words in the brain of the man, and then sound in his throat, and yet both are merely refractions of the true event, for in actuality speech does not abide in man, but man takes his stand in speech and talks from there; so with every word and every spirit. Spirit is not in the *I,* but between *I* and *Thou.* It is not like the blood that circulates in you, but like the air in which you breathe. Man lives in the spirit, if he is able to respond to his *Thou.* He is able to, if he enters into relation with his whole being. Only in virtue of his power to enter into relation is he able to live in the spirit.

But the destiny of the relational event is here set forth in the most powerful way. The stronger the response the more strongly does it bind up the *Thou* and banish it to be an object. Only silence before the *Thou*—silence of *all* tongues, silent patience in the undivided word that precedes the formed and vocal response—leaves the *Thou* free, and permits man to take his stand with it in the reserve where the spirit is not manifest, but *is.* Every response binds up the *Thou* in the world of *It.* That is the melancholy of man, and his greatness. For that is how knowledge comes about, a work is achieved, and image and symbol made, in the midst of living beings.

But that which has been so changed into *It,* hardened into a thing among things, has had the nature and disposition put into it to change back again and again. This was the meaning in that hour of the spirit when spirit was joined to man and bred the response in him—again and again that which has the status of object must blaze up into presentness and enter the elemental state from which it came, to be looked on and lived in the present by men.

The fulfilment of this nature and disposition is thwarted by the man who has come to terms with the world of *It* that it is to be experienced and used. For now instead of freeing that which is bound up in that world he suppresses it, instead of looking at it he observes it, instead of accepting it as it is, he turns it to his own account.

Take knowledge: being is disclosed to the man who is engaged in knowing, as he looks at what is over against him. He will, indeed, have to grasp as an object that which he has seen with the force of presence, he will have to compare it with objects, establish it in its order among classes of objects, describe and analyse it objectively. Only as *It* can it enter the structure of knowledge. But when he saw it, it was no thing among things, no event among events, but exclusively present. Being did not share itself with him in terms of the law that was afterwards elicited from the appearance, but in terms of its very self. When a man thinks a general thought in this connexion he is merely unravelling the tangled incident; for it was seen in particular form, in what was over against him. Now the incident is included in the *It* of knowledge which is composed of ideas. He who frees it from that, and looks on it again in the present moment, fulfils the nature of the act of knowledge to be real and effective *between* men. But knowledge can also be managed in such a way that it is affirmed that "this, then, is how the matter stands, the thing is called this, made in this way, its place is over there"; that which has become *It* is left as *It,* experienced and used as *It,* appropriated for the undertaking to "find one's bearings" in the world, and then to "conquer" it.

So too in art: form is disclosed to the artist as he looks at what is over against him. He banishes it to be a "structure". This "structure" is not in a world of gods, but in this great world of men. It is certainly "there", even if no human eye seeks it out; but it is asleep. The Chinese poet tells how men did not wish to hear the tune he played on his jade flute; then he played it to the gods, and they inclined their ears; since then men also listened to the tune: thus he went from the gods to those whom the "structure" cannot dispense with. It longs as in a dream for the meeting with man, that for a timeless moment he may lift the ban and clasp the form. Then he comes on his way, and experiences what there is to be experienced: it is made in this way, or this is expressed in it, or its qualities are such and such, and further, it takes this place in the scheme of things.

It is not as though scientific and æsthetic understanding were not necessary; but they are necessary to man that he may do his work with precision and plunge it in the truth of relation, which is above the understanding and gathers it up in itself.

And, thirdly, there is pure effective action without arbitrary self-will. This is higher than the spirit of art, for there the mortal bodily man does not need to mix himself with the more lasting stuff, but himself outlasts it as structure; encircled by the sounding music of his living speech he reaches the starry heaven of the spirit. Here the *Thou* appeared to the man out of deeper mystery, addressed him even out of the darkness, and he responded with his life. Here the word has from time to time become life, and this life is *teaching.* This life may have fulfilled the law or broken it; both are continually necessary, that spirit may not die on earth. This life is presented, then, to those who come later, to teach them not what is and must be, but how life is lived in the spirit, face to face with the *Thou.* That is, it is itself ready on every occasion to become *Thou* for them, and open up the world of *Thou*—no; it is not ready: it continually approaches and touches them. But they, having become disinclined and unfitted for the living dealings that would open the world to them, are fully equipped with information. They have pinned the person down in history, and secured his words in the library. They have codified, in exactly the same way, the fulfilment or the breaking of the law. Nor are they niggards with admiration and even idolatry, amply mixed with psychology, as befits modern man. O lonely Face like a star in the night, o living Finger laid on an unheeding brow, o fainter echoing footstep!

The development of the function of experiencing and using comes about mostly through decrease of man's power to enter into relation.

How does this same man, who made spirit into a means of enjoyment for himself, behave towards the beings that live round about him?

Taking his stand in the shelter of the primary word of separation, which holds off the *I* and the *It* from one another, he has divided his life with his fellow-men into two tidily circled-off provinces, one of institutions and the other of feelings—the province of *It* and the province of *I*.

Institutions are "outside", where all sorts of aims are pursued, where a man works, negotiates, bears influence, undertakes, concurs, organises, conducts business, officiates, preaches. They are the tolerably well-ordered and to some extent harmonious structure, in which, with the manifold help of men's brains and hands, the process of affairs is fulfilled.

Feelings are "within", where life is lived and man recovers from institutions. Here the spectrum of the emotions dances before the interested glance. Here a man's liking and hate and pleasure are indulged, and his pain if it is not too severe. Here he is at home, and stretches himself out in his rocking-chair.

Institutions are a complicated market-place, feelings a boudoir rich in ever-changing interests.

The boundary line, to be sure, is constantly in danger since the wanton feelings break in at times on the most objective institutions; but with united goodwill it may be restored.

Most difficult of all is the reliable drawing of the boundary line in the realms of so-called personal life. In marriage, for instance, the line is occasionally not to be fully drawn in any simple way; but in the end it is possible. In the realms of so-called public life it can be perfectly drawn. Let it be considered, for instance, how faultlessly, in the year of the parties and the groups with their "movements" which aimed at being above parties, the heaven-storming sessions on the one hand, and on the other hand business, creeping along the ground (smoothly like a machine or slovenly and organically), are separated from one another.

But the separated *It* of institutions is an animated clod without soul, and the separated *I* of feelings an uneasily fluttering soul-bird. Neither of them knows man: institutions know only the specimen, feelings only the "object"; neither knows the person, or mutual life. Neither of them knows the present: even the most up-to-date institutions know only the lifeless past that is over and done with, and even the most lasting feelings know only the flitting moment that has not yet come properly into being. Neither of them has access to real life. Institutions yield no public life, and feelings no personal life.

That institutions yield no public life is realised by increasing numbers, realised with increasing distress: this is the starting-point of the seeking need of the age. That feelings yield no personal life is understood only by a few. For the most personal life of all seems to reside in feelings, and if, like the modern man, you have learned to concern yourself wholly with your own feelings, despair at their unreality will not easily instruct you in a better way—for despair is also an interesting feeling.

The men who suffer distress in the realisation that institutions yield no public life have hit upon an expedient: institutions must be loosened, or dissolved, or burst asunder, by the feelings themselves; they must be given new life from the feelings, by the introduction into them of the "freedom of feeling". If the mechanical State, say, links together citizens alien to one another in their very being, without establishing, or promoting, a being together, let the State, these men say, be replaced by the community of love; and this community will arise when people, out of free, abundant feeling, approach and wish to live with one another. But it is not so. The true community does not arise through peoples having feelings for one another (though indeed not without it), but through, first, their taking their stand in living mutual relation with a living Centre, and, second, their being in living mutual relation with one another. The second has its source in the first, but is not given when the first alone is given. Living mutual relation includes feelings, but does not originate with them. The community is built up out of living mutual relation, but the builder is the living effective Centre.

Further, institutions of the so-called personal life cannot be given new life by free feeling (though indeed not without it). Marriage, for instance, will never be given new life except by that out of which true marriage always arises, the revealing by two people of the *Thou* to one another. Out of this a marriage is built up by the *Thou* that is neither of the *I*'s. This is the metaphysical and metapsychical factor of love to which feelings of love are mere accompaniments. He who wishes to give new life to marriage from another source is not essentially different from him who wishes to abolish it. Both clearly show that they no longer know the vital factor. And indeed, if in all the much discussed erotic philosophy of the age we were to leave out of account everything that involves experience in relation to the *I,* that is, every situation in which the one is not present to the other, given present status by it, but merely enjoys itself in the other—what then would be left?

True public and true personal life are two forms of connexion. In that they come into being and endure, feelings (the changing content) and institutions (the constant form) are necessary; but put together they do not create human life: this is done by the third, the central presence of the *Thou,* or rather, more truly stated, by the central *Thou* that has been received in the present.

The primary word *I-It* is not of evil—as matter is not of evil. It is of evil—as matter is, which presumes to have the quality of present being. If a man lets it have the mastery, the continually growing world of *It* overruns him and robs him of the reality of his own *I,* till the incubus over him and the ghost within him whisper to one another the confession of their non-salvation.

Gandhi and Nehru

The Philosophy of Non-Violence

GANDHI: DOCTRINE OF AHIṀSĀ *

Literally speaking, Ahiṁsā means "non-killing." But to me it has a world of meaning, and takes me into realms much higher, infinitely higher. It really means that you may not offend anybody; you may not harbour an uncharitable thought, even in connection with one who may consider himself to be your enemy. To one who follows this doctrine there is no room for an enemy. But there may be people who consider themselves to be his enemies. So it is held that we may not harbour an evil thought even in connection with such persons. If we return blow for blow we depart from the doctrine of Ahiṁsā. But I go farther. If we resent a friend's action, or the so-called enemy's action, we still fall short of this doctrine. But when I say we should not resent, I do not say that we should acquiesce: by the word "resenting" I mean wishing that some harm should be done to the enemy; or that he should be put out of the way, not even by any action of ours, but by the action of somebody else, or, say, by divine agency. If we harbour even this thought we depart from this doctrine of Non-Violence. Those who join the Ashram have literally to accept that meaning.

This does not mean that we practise that doctrine in its entirety. Far from it. It is an ideal which we have to reach, and it is an ideal to be reached even at this very moment, if we are capable of doing so. But it is not a proposition in geometry; it is not even like solving difficult problems in higher mathematics—it is infinitely more difficult. Many of us have burnt the midnight oil in solving those problems. But if you want to follow out this doctrine you will have to do much more than burn the midnight oil. You will have to pass many a sleepless night, and go through

* This and the two following selections are from *Mahatma Gandhi, Essays and Reflections on his Life and Work,* presented to him on his seventieth birthday, October 2, 1939. Edited by S. Radhakrishnan. Second edition. London: George Allen & Unwin, Ltd., 1949, pp. 489–490, 498–502, 502–503. Reprinted by permission of the publisher.

many a mental torture, before you can even be within measurable distance of this goal. It is the goal, and nothing less than that, which you and I have to reach, if we want to understand what a religious life means.

A man who believes in the efficacy of this doctrine finds in the ultimate stage, when he is about to reach the goal, the whole world at his feet. If you express your love—Ahiṁsā—in such a manner that it impresses itself indelibly upon your so-called enemy, he must return that love. Under this rule there is no room for organized assassinations, or for murders openly committed, or for any violence for the sake of your country or even for guarding the honour of precious ones that may be under your charge. After all, that would be a poor defence of their honour. This doctrine tells us that we may guard the honour of those under our charge by delivering our own lives into the hands of the man who would commit the sacrilege. And that requires far greater courage than delivering of blows. If you do not retaliate, but stand your ground between your charge and the opponent, simply receiving the blows without retaliating, what happens? I give you my promise that the whole of his violence will be expended on you, and your friend will be left unscathed. Under this plan of life there is no conception of patriotism which justifies such wars as you witness to-day in Europe.

GANDHI: THE DOCTRINE OF THE SWORD (1920)

In this age of the rule of brute force, it is almost impossible for anyone to believe that anyone else could possibly reject the law of the final supremacy of brute force. And so I receive anonymous letters advising me that I must not interfere with the progress of Non-co-operation, even though popular violence may break out. Others came to me and, assuming that secretly I must be plotting violence, inquire when the happy moment for declaring open violence is to arrive. They assure me that the English will never yield to anything but violence, secret or open. Yet others, I am informed, believe that I am the most rascally person living in India, because I never give out my real intention and that they have not a shadow of a doubt that I believe in violence just as much as most people do.

Such being the hold that the doctrine of the sword has on the majority of mankind, and as success of Non-co-operation depends principally on absence of violence during its pendency and as my views in this matter affect the conduct of a large number of people, I am anxious to state them as clearly as possible.

I do believe that, where there is only a choice between cowardice and violence, I would advise violence. Thus when my eldest son asked me what he should have done, had he been present when I was almost fatally assaulted in 1908, whether he should have run away and seen me killed or whether he should have used his physical force which he could and wanted to use, and defended me, I told him that it was his duty to defend me even by using violence. Hence it was that I took part in the Boer War, the so-called Zulu rebellion and the late war. Hence also do I advocate training in arms for those who believe in the method of violence. I would rather have India resort to arms in order to defend her honour than that she should in a cowardly manner become or remain a helpless witness to her own dishonour.

But I believe that non-violence is infinitely superior to violence, forgiveness is more manly than punishment (ksamā virasya bhūṣaṇam). Forgiveness adorns a soldier. But abstinence is forgiveness only when there is the power to punish; it is meaningless when it pretends to proceed from a helpless creature. A mouse hardly forgives a cat when it allows itself to be torn to pieces by her. I therefore appreciate the sentiment of those who cry out for the condign punishment of General Dyer and his ilk. They would tear him to pieces if they could. But I do not believe India to be helpless. I do not believe myself to be a helpless creature. Only I want to use India's and my strength for a better purpose.

Let me not be misunderstood. Strength does not come from physical capacity. It comes from an indomitable will. An average Zulu is any way more than a match for an average Englishman in bodily capacity. But he flees from an English boy, because he fears the boy's revolver or those who will use it for him. He fears death and is nerveless in spite of his burly figure. We in India may in a moment realize that one hundred thousand Englishmen need not frighten three hundred million human beings. A definite forgiveness would therefore mean a definite recognition of our strength. With enlightened forgiveness must come a mighty wave of strength in us, which would make it impossible for a Dyer or a Frank Johnson to heap affront upon India's devoted head. It matters little to me that for the moment I do not drive my point home. We feel too downtrodden not to be angry and revengeful. But I must refrain from saying that India can gain more by waiving the right of punishment. We have better work to do, a better mission to deliver to the world.

I am not a visionary. I claim to be a practical idealist. The religion of non-violence is not meant merely for the Rashis and saints. It is meant for the common people as well. Non-violence is the law of our species as violence is the law of the brute. The spirit lies dormant in the brute and he knows no law but that of physical might. The dignity of man requires obedience to a higher law—to the strength of the spirit.

I have therefore ventured to place before India the ancient law of self-sacrifice. For Satyāgraha and its offshoots, Non-co-operation and civil resistance are nothing but new names for the law of suffering. The Rashis, who discovered the law of non-violence in the midst of violence, were greater geniuses than Newton. They were themselves greater warriors than Wellington. Having themselves known the use of arms, they realized their uselessness and taught a weary world that its salvation lay not through violence but through non-violence.

Non-violence in its dynamic condition means conscious suffering. It does not mean meek submission to the will of the evil-doer, but it means the pitting of one's whole soul against the will of the tyrant. Working under this law of our being, it is possible for a single individual to defy the whole might of an unjust empire to save his honour, his religion, his soul and lay the foundation for that empire's fall or its regeneration.

And so I am not pleading for India to practise non-violence, because it is weak. I want her to practise non-violence being conscious of her strength and power. No training in arms is required for realization of her strength. We seem to need it, because we seem to think that we are but a lump of flesh. I want India to recognize that she has a soul that cannot perish and that can rise triumphant above every physical weakness and defy the physical combination of a whole world. What is the meaning of Rāma, a mere human being, with his host of monkeys, pitting himself against the insolent strength of ten-headed Rāvan surrounded in supposed safety by the raging waters on all sides of Lanka? Does it not mean the conquest of physical might by spiritual strength? However, being a practical man, I do not wait till India recognizes the practicability of the spiritual life in the political world. India considers herself to be powerless and paralysed before the machine-guns, the tanks and the aeroplanes of the English. And she takes up Non-co-operation out of her weakness. It must still serve the same purpose, namely, bring her delivery from the crushing weight of British injustice, if a sufficient number of people practise it.

I isolate this Non-co-operation from Sinn Feinism, for it is so conceived as to be incapable of being offered side by side with violence. But I invite even the school of violence to give this peaceful Non-co-operation a trial. It will not fail through its inherent weakness. It may fail because of poverty of response. Then will be the time for real danger. The high-souled men, who are unable to suffer national humiliation any longer, will want to vent their wrath. They will take to violence. So far as I know, they must perish without delivering themselves or their country from the wrong. If India takes up the doctrine of the sword, she may gain momentary victory. Then India will cease to be the pride of my heart. I am wedded to India because I owe my all to her. I believe absolutely that she has a mission for the world. She is not to copy Europe blindly. India's acceptance of the doctrine of the sword will be the hour of my trial. I hope I shall not be found wanting. My religion has no geographical limits. If I have a living faith in it, it will transcend my love for India herself. My life is dedicated to the service of India through the religion of non-violence, which I believe to be the root of Hinduism.

GANDHI: THE TRIAL SPEECH (1922)

Before I read this statement, I would like to state that I entirely endorsed the learned Advocate-General's remarks in connection with my humble self. It is the most painful duty with me, but I have to discharge that duty knowing the responsibility that rests upon my shoulders, and I wish to endorse all the blame that the learned Advocate-General has thrown on my shoulders in connection with the Bombay, Madras, and Chauri Chaura occurrences. Thinking over these deeply and sleeping over them, night after night, it is impossible for me to dissociate myself from the diabolical crimes of Chauri Chaura, or the mad outrages of Bombay. He is quite right when he says that, as a man of responsibility, a man having received a fair share of education, having had a fair share of experience of this world, I should have known the consequences of every one of my acts. I know that I was playing with fire. I ran the risk, and if I was set free, I would still do the same. I have felt it this morning that I would have failed in my duty, if I did not say what I said here just now.

I wanted to avoid violence; I want to avoid violence. Non-violence is the first article of my faith. It is also the last article of my creed. But I had to make my choice. I had either to submit to a system which I considered had done an irreparable harm to my country, or incur the risk of the mad fury of my people bursting forth, when they understood the truth from my lips. I know that my people have sometimes gone mad. I am deeply sorry for it, and I am therefore here to submit, not to a light penalty, but to the highest penalty. I do not ask for mercy. I do not plead any extenuating act. I am here, therefore, to invite and cheerfully submit to the highest penalty that can be inflicted upon me for what in law is a deliberate crime, and what appears to me to be the highest duty of a citizen. The only course open to you, the Judge, is, as I am just going to say in my statement, either to resign your post or inflict on me the severest penalty, if you believe that the system and law you are assisting to administer are good for the people. I do not expect that kind of conversion but by the time I have finished with my statement, you will perhaps have a glimpse of what is raging within my breast to run this maddest risk which a sane man can run.

NEHRU: NONVIOLENCE AND THE DOCTRINE OF THE SWORD *

The sudden suspension of our movement after the Chauri Chaura incident was resented, I think, by almost all the prominent Congress leaders—other than Gandhiji, of course. My father (who was in jail at the time) was much upset by it. The younger people were naturally even more agitated. Our mounting hopes tumbled to the ground, and this mental reaction was to be expected. What troubled us even more were the reasons given for this suspension and the consequences that seemed to flow from them. Chauri Chaura may have been and was a deplorable occurrence and wholly opposed to the spirit of the nonviolent movement; but were a remote village and a mob of excited peasants in an out-of-the-way place going to put an end, for some time at least, to our national struggle for freedom? If this was the inevitable consequence of a sporadic act of violence, then surely there was something lacking in the philosophy and technique of a nonviolent struggle. For it seemed to us to be impossible to guarantee against the occurrence of some such untoward incident. Must we train the three hundred and odd millions of India in the theory and practice of nonviolent action before we could go forward? And, even so, how many of us could say that under extreme provocation from the police we would be able to remain perfectly peaceful? But even if we succeeded, what of the numerous *agents provocateurs,* stool pigeons, and the like who crept into our movement and indulged in violence themselves or induced others to do so? If this was the sole condition of its function, then the nonviolent method of resistance would always fail.

We had accepted that method, the Congress had made that method its own, because of a belief in its effectiveness. Gandhiji had placed it

* From *Toward Freedom* by Jawaharlal Nehru, pp. 80–81, 82–83. Copyright 1941 by The John Day Company. Reprinted by permission of the publisher and the author.

before the country not only as the right method but as the most effective one for our purpose. In spite of its negative name it was a dynamic method, the very opposite of a meek submission to a tyrant's will. It was not a coward's refuge from action, but the brave man's defiance of evil and national subjection. But what was the use of the bravest and the strongest if a few odd persons—maybe even our opponents in the guise of friends—had the power to upset or end our movement by their rash behavior?

Gandhiji had pleaded for the adoption of the way of nonviolence, of peaceful nonco-operation, with all the eloquence and persuasive power which he so abundantly possessed. His language had been simple and unadorned, his voice and appearance cool and clear and devoid of all emotion, but behind that outward covering of ice there was the heat of a blazing fire and concentrated passion, and the words he uttered winged their way to the innermost recesses of our minds and hearts, and created a strange ferment there. The way he pointed out was hard and difficult, but it was a brave path, and it seemed to lead to the promised land of freedom. Because of that promise we pledged our faith and marched ahead. . . .

We were moved by these arguments, but for us and for the National Congress as a whole the nonviolent method was not, and could not be, a religion or an unchallengeable creed or dogma. It could only be a policy and a method promising certain results, and by those results it would have to be finally judged. Individuals might make of it a religion or incontrovertible creed. But no political organization, so long as it remained political, could do so.

Chauri Chaura and its consequences made us examine these implications of nonviolence as a method, and we felt that, if Gandhiji's argument for the suspension of civil resistance was correct, our opponents would always have the power to create circumstances which would necessarily result in our abandoning the struggle. Was this the fault of the nonviolent method itself or of Gandhiji's interpretation of it? After all, he was the author and originator of it, and who could be a better judge of what it was and what it was not? And without him where was our movement?

Many years later, just before the 1930 civil disobedience movement began, Gandhiji, much to our satisfaction, made this point clear. He stated that the movement should not be abandoned because of the occurrence of sporadic acts of violence. If the nonviolent method of struggle could not function because of such almost inevitable happenings, then it was obvious that it was not an ideal method for all occasions, and this he was not prepared to admit. For him the method, being the right method, should suit all circumstances and should be able to function, at any rate in a restricted way, even in a hostile atmosphere. Whether this interpretation, which widened the scope of nonviolent action, represented an evolution in his own mind or not I do not know.

Oswald Spengler

The Hour of Decision *

Little as one knows of events in the future—for all that can be got from a comparison with other civilizations is the general form of future facts and their march through the ages—so much is certain: the forces which will sway the future are no other than those of the past. These forces are: the will of the Strong, *healthy* instincts, race, the will to possession and power; while justice, happiness, and peace—those dreams which will always remain dreams—hover ineffectively over them.

Further, in our own civilization since the sixteenth century it has rapidly grown more impossible for most of us to gain a general view of the ever more confusing events and situations of world politics and economics or to grasp (let alone control) the forces and tendencies at work in them. True statesmen become rarer and rarer. Most of the doings (as distinct from the events) in the history of these centuries was indeed the work of semi-experts and amateurs with luck on their side. Still, they could always rely upon the people's instinct to back them. It is only now that this instinct has become so weak, and the voluble criticism of blithe ignorance so strong, as to make it more and more likely that a true statesman, with a real knowledge of things, will not receive this instinctive support—even at the level of grudging tolerance—but will be prevented from doing what has to be done by the opposition of all the "know-betters." Frederick the Great experienced the first of these types of opposition; Bismarck almost fell a victim to the second. Only later generations, and not even they, can appreciate the grandeur and creativeness of such leaders. But we do have to see to it that the present confines itself to ingratitude and incomprehension and does not proceed to counteraction. Germans in particular are great at suspecting, criticizing, and voiding creative action. They have none of that historical experience and force of

* Reprinted from *The Hour of Decision* by Oswald Spengler, pp. 8–15, 18–22, by permission of Alfred A. Knopf, Inc., and George Allen & Unwin Ltd. Copyright 1934 by Alfred A. Knopf, Inc.

tradition which are congenital with English life. A nation of poets and thinkers—in the process of becoming a nation of babblers and persecutors. Every real governor is unpopular among his frightened, cowardly, and uncomprehending contemporaries. And one must be more than an "idealist" to understand even this.

We are still in the *Age of Rationalism,* which began in the eighteenth century and is now rapidly nearing its close.[1] We are all its creatures whether we know and wish it or not. The word is familiar enough, but who knows how much it implies? It is the arrogance of the urban intellect, which, detached from its roots and no longer guided by strong instinct, looks down with contempt on the full-blooded thinking of the past and the wisdom of ancient peasant stock. It is the period in which everyone can read and write and therefore must have his say and always "knows better." This type of mind is obsessed by concepts—the new gods of the Age—and it exercises its wits on the world as it sees it. "It is no good," it says; "we could make it better; here goes, let us set up a program for a better world!" Nothing could be easier for persons of intelligence, and no doubt seems to be felt that this world will then materialize of itself. It is given a label, "Human Progress," and now that it has a name, it *is.* Those who doubt it are narrow reactionaries, heretics, and, what is worse, persons devoid of democratic virtue: away with them! In this wise the fear of reality was overcome by intellectual arrogance, the darkness that comes from ignorance of all things of life, spiritual poverty, lack of reverence, and, finally, world-alien stupidity—for there is nothing stupider than the rootless urban intelligence. In English offices and clubs it used to be called *common sense;* in French salons, *esprit;* in German philosophers' studies, *Pure Reason.* The shallow optimism of the cultural philistine in ceasing to fear the elemental historical facts and beginning to *despise* them. Every "know-better" seeks to absorb them in his scheme (in which experience has no part), to make them conceptually more complete than actually they are, and to subordinate them to himself in his mind because he has not *livingly* experienced them, but only perceived them. This doctrinaire clinging to theory for lack of experience, or rather this lack of ability to *make* experience, finds literary expression in a flood of schemes for political, social, and economic systems and Utopias, and practical expression in that craze for organization which, becoming an aim in itself, produces bureaucracies that either collapse through their own hollowness or destroy the living order. Rationalism is at bottom nothing but criticism, and the critic is the reverse of a creator: he dissects and he reassembles;

[1] Spengler: *The Decline of the West,* II, English translation, pp. 305 et seq.

conception and birth are alien to him. Accordingly his work is artificial and lifeless, and when brought into contact with real life, it *kills.* All these systems and organizations are paper productions; they are methodical and absurd and live *only* on the paper they are written on. The process began in the time of Rousseau and Kant with philosophical ideologies that lost themselves in generalities; passed in the nineteenth century to scientific constructions with scientific, physical, Darwinian methods—sociology, economics, materialistic history-writing—and lost itself in the twentieth in the literary output of problem novels and party programs.

But let there be no mistake: idealism and materialism are equally parts of it. Both are rationalist through and through, in the case of Kant as of Voltaire and Holbach; of Novalis as of Proudhon; of the ideologues of the Wars of Liberation as of Marx; of the materialist conception of history quite as much as the idealistic, whether the meaning and aim of it is "progress," technics, "liberty," the "happiness of the greatest number," or the flowering of art, poetry, and thought. In both cases there is the failure to realize that destiny in history depends on quite other, robuster, forces. Human history is war history. Among the few genuine historians of standing, none was ever popular, and among statesmen Bismarck achieved popularity only when it was of no more use to him.

But Romanticism too, with its lack of a sense for reality, is just as much an expression of rationalist arrogance as are Idealism and Materialism. They are all in fact closely related, and it would be difficult to discover the boundary between these two trends of thought in any political or social Romantic. In every outstanding Materialist a Romantic lies hidden.[2] Though he may scorn the cold, shallow, methodical mind of others, he has himself enough of that sort of mind to do so in the same way and with the same arrogance. Romanticism is no sign of powerful instincts, but, on the contrary, of a weak, self-detesting intellect. They are all infantile, these Romantics; men who remain children too long (or for ever), without the strength to criticize themselves, but with perpetual inhibitions arising from the obscure awareness of their own personal weaknesses; who are impelled by the morbid idea of reforming society, which is to them too masculine, too healthy, too sober. And to reform it, not with knives and revolvers in the Russian fashion—heaven forbid!—but by noble talk and poetic theories. Hapless indeed they are if, lacking creative power, they lack also the artistic talent to persuade at least them-

[2] Haeckel's *Riddle of the Universe,* for instance, is the work of a pure sentimentalist and a weak logician. A faith that is stronger than any proofs is the distinguishing mark of the Romantic.

selves that they possess it. Yet even in their art they are feminine and weak, incapable of setting a great novel or a great tragedy on its legs, still less a pure philosophy of any force. All that appears is spineless lyric, bloodless scenarios, and fragmentary ideas, all of them displaying an innocence of and antagonism to the world which amounts to absurdity. But it was the same with the unfading "Youths" (*Jünglinge*), with their "old German" coats and pipes—Jahn and Arndt, even, included. Stein himself was unable to control his romantic taste for ancient constitutions sufficiently to allow him to turn his extensive practical experience to successful account in diplomacy. Oh, they were heroes, and noble, and ready to be martyrs at any moment; but they talked too much about German nature and too little about railways and customs unions, and thus became only an obstacle in the way of Germany's *real* future. Did they ever so much as hear the name of the great Friedrich List, who committed suicide in 1846 because no one understood and supported his far-sighted and modern political aim, the building of an economic Germany? But they all knew the names of Arminius and Thusnelda.

And these same everlasting "Youths" are with us again today, immature, destitute of the slightest experience or even real desire for experience, but writing and talking away about politics, fired by uniforms and badges, and clinging fantastically to some theory or other. There is a social Romanticism of sentimental Communists, a political Romanticism which regards election-figures and the intoxication of mass-meeting oratory as deeds, and an economic Romanticism which trickles out from behind the gold theories of sick minds that know nothing of the inner forms of modern economics. They can only feel in the mass, where they can deaden the dull sense of their weakness by multiplying themselves. And this they call the overcoming of Individualism.

And like *all* Rationalists and Romantics, they are as sentimental as a street ditty. Even the *Contrat social* and the Rights of Man are products of the Age of Sensibility. Burke, on the contrary, like a true statesman, argued that on his side of the Channel men demanded their due as Englishmen and not as human beings, and he was right. This was practical political thinking, not the rationalistic issue of undisciplined emotions. For this evil sentimentality which lies over all the theoretical currents of the two centuries—Liberalism, Communism, Pacifism,—and all the books, speeches, and revolutions, originates in spiritual indiscipline, in personal weakness, in lack of the training imparted by a stern old tradition. It is "bourgeois" or "plebeian," in so far as these are terms of abuse. It looks at human things, history, and political destiny *from below,* meanly, from the cellar window, the street, the writers' café, the national assembly; not from height and distance. It detests every kind of greatness, everything that towers, rules, is superior; and construction means for it only the pulling-down of all the products of civilization, of the State, of society, to the level of little people, above which its pitiful emotionalism cannot soar to understand. That is all that the prefix "folk" or "people" means today, for the "people" in the mouth of any Rationalist or Romanticist does not mean the well-formed nation, shaped and graded by Destiny in the course of ages, but that portion of the dull *formless* mass which everyone senses as his equal, from the "proletariat" to "humanity."

This domination of the rootless urban intellect is drawing to a close. And there emerges as a final way of understanding things as they are, *Scepticism*—fundamental doubt as to the meaning and value of theoretical reflection, as to its ability to arrive at conclusions by critical and abstract methods or to achieve anything by practical ones; Scepticism in the form of great historical and physiognomic experience, of the incorruptible eye for facts, the real knowledge of men which teaches what they were and are and not what they ought to be; the Scepticism of true historical thought which teaches, amongst other things, that there have been other periods wherein criticism was all-powerful and that these periods have left little impress behind them; and the Scepticism which brings reverence for the facts of world happening, which are and remain inward secrets to be described but never explained, and to be mastered only by men of a strong breed *who are themselves historical facts,* not by sentimental programs and systems. The hard recognition of historical fact which has set in with this century is intolerable to soft, uncontrolled natures. They detest those who establish them, calling them pessimists. Well, but this *strong* pessimism, with which belongs the contempt for mankind of all great factmen who *know* mankind, is quite a different matter from the cowardly pessimism of small and weary souls which fear life and cannot bear to look at reality. The life they hope for, spent in peace and happiness, free from danger and replete with comfort, is boring and senile, apart from the fact that it is only imaginable, not possible. On this rock, the reality of history, every ideology must founder. . . .

For we live in a mighty age. It is the greatest that the Western Civilization has ever known or will know. It corresponds to the Classical Age from Cannae to Actium, to the age illumined by the names of Hannibal, Scipio and Gracchus, Marius, Sulla, and Caesar.[3] The World War was

[3] See *The Decline of the West,* II, English translation, pp. 418 et seq.

but the first flash and crash from the fateful thundercloud which is passing over this century. As then, at the commencement of the *Imperium Romanum,* so today, the *form* of the world is being remoulded from its foundations, regardless of the desires and intentions of "the majority" or of the number of victims demanded by every such decision. But who understands this? Who is facing it? Does one of us consider himself lucky to be there to see it? The age is mighty, but all the more diminutive are the people in it. They can no longer bear tragedy, either on the stage or in real life. They crave happy endings of insipid novels, so miserable and weary are they. But the destiny which pitched them into these decades now takes them by the collar and does with them what has to be done, whether they will or no. The coward's security of 1900 is at an end. Life in danger, the real life of history, comes once more into its own. Everything has begun to slide, and now only that man counts who can take risks, who has the courage to see and accept things as they are. The age is approaching—nay, is already here—which has no more room for soft hearts and weakly ideals. The primeval barbarism which has lain hidden and bound for centuries under the form-rigour of a ripe Culture, is awake again now that the Culture is finished and the Civilization has set in: that warlike, healthy joy in one's own strength which scorns the literature-ridden age of Rationalist thought, that unbroken race-instinct, which desires a different life from one spent under the weight of books and bookish ideals. In the Western European peasantry this spirit still abounds, as also on the American prairies and away in the great plains of northern Asia, where world-conquerors are born.

If this is "Pessimism," then he who feels it to be so must be one who *needs* the pious falsehood or veil of ideals and Utopias to protect and save him from the sight of reality. This, no doubt, is the refuge resorted to by most white men in this century—but will it be so in the next? Their forefathers in the time of the Great Migration and the Crusades were different. They contemned such an attitude as cowardly. It is from this cowardice in the face of life that Buddhism and its offshoots arose in the Indian Culture at the corresponding stage in time. These cults are now becoming fashionable with us. It is possible that a Late religion of the West is in process of formation—whether under the guise of Christianity or not none can tell, but at any rate the religious "revival" which succeeds Rationalism as a world philosophy does hold quite special possibilities of *new* religions emerging. People with tired, cowardly, senile souls seek refuge from the age in something which by reason of its miraculous doctrines and customs is better able to rock them into the sleep of oblivion than the Christian churches. The *credo quia absurdum* is again uppermost. But the profundity of world-suffering—a feeling that is as old as the brooding over the world itself, the moan over the absurdity of history and the cruelty of existence—arises not from things themselves, but from morbid reflection on them. It is the annihilating judgment upon the worth and the strength of men's own souls. A profound view of the world need not necessarily be saturated with tears.

There is a Nordic world-feeling, reaching from England to Japan, which is full of joy just because of the burden of human destiny. One challenges it for the sake of conquering it, and one goes under proudly should it prove stronger than one's own will. This was the attitude depicted in the old, genuine parts of the Mahabharata which tells of the fight between the Kurus and Pandus; in Homer, Pindar, and Aeschylus; in the Germanic sagas and in Shakspere; in certain songs of the Chinese Shu king, and in the world of the Samurai. It is the *tragic* view of life, which is *not* yet dead, but will blossom anew in the future just as it blossomed in the World War. All the very great poets of the Nordic Cultures have been tragedians, and tragedy, from ballad and epic onward, has been the deepest form of this *brave* pessimism. The man who is incapable of experiencing or enduring tragedy can never be a figure of world significance. He cannot *make* history unless he experiences it as it really is—tragic, permeated by destiny, and in consequence meaningless, aimless, and unmoral in the eyes of the worshippers of utility. It marks the parting of the ways between the superior and the subordinate ethos of human existence. The individual's life is of importance to none beside himself: the point is whether he wishes to escape from history or give his life for it. History recks nothing of human logic. Thunder-storms, earthquakes, lava-streams: these are near-relatives of the purposeless, elemental events of world history. Nations may go under, ancient cities of ageing Cultures burn or sink in ruins, but the earth will continue to revolve calmly round the sun, and the stars to run their course.

Man is a beast of prey.[4] I shall say it again and again. All the would-be moralists and social-ethics people who claim or hope to be "beyond all that" are only beasts of prey with their teeth broken, who hate others on account of the attacks which they themselves are wise enough to avoid. Only look at them. They are too weak to read a book on war, but they herd together in the street to see an accident, letting the blood and the screams play on their nerves. And if even that is too much for them, they enjoy it on the film and in the illustrated papers. If I call man a beast of prey, which do

[4] See Spengler: *Man and Technics,* pp. 19 et seq.

I insult: man or beast? For remember, the larger beasts of prey are *noble* creatures, perfect of their kind, and without the hypocrisy of human moral due to weakness.

They shout: "No more war"—but they desire class war. They are indignant when a murderer is executed for a crime of passion, but they feel a secret pleasure in hearing of the murder of a political opponent. What objection have they ever raised to the Bolshevist slaughters? There is no getting away from it: conflict is the original fact of life, is life itself, and not the most pitiful pacifist is able entirely to uproot the pleasure it gives his inmost soul. Theoretically, at least, he would like to fight and destroy all opponents of pacifism.

The further we advance into the Caesarism of the Faustian world, the more clearly will it emerge who is destined ethically to be the subject and who the object of historical events. The dreary train of world-improvers has now come to an end of its amble through these centuries, leaving behind it, as sole monument of its existence, mountains of printed paper. The Caesars will now take its place. High policy, *the art of the possible,* will again enter upon its eternal heritage, free from all systems and theories, itself the judge of the facts by which it rules, and gripping the world between its knees like a good horseman.

Sigmund Freud

Civilization and Its Discontents *

The liberty of the individual is not a benefit of culture. It was greatest before any culture, though indeed it had little value at that time, because the individual was hardly in a position to defend it. Liberty has undergone restrictions through the evolution of civilization, and justice demands that these restrictions shall apply to all. The desire for freedom that makes itself felt in a human community may be a revolt against some existing injustice and so may prove favourable to a further development of civilization and remain compatible with it. But it may also have its origin in the primitive roots of the personality, still unfettered by civilizing influences, and so become a source of antagonism to culture. Thus the cry for freedom is directed either against particular forms or demands of culture or else against culture itself. It does not seem as if man could be brought by any sort of influence to change his nature into that of the ants; he will always, one imagines, defend his claim to individual freedom against the will of the multitude. A great part of the struggles of mankind centres round the single task of finding some expedient (*i.e.* satisfying) solution between these individual claims and those of the civilized community; it is one of the problems of man's fate whether this solution can be arrived at in some particular form of culture or whether the conflict will prove irreconcilable.

We have obtained a clear impression of the general picture presented by culture through adopting the common view as to which aspects of human life are to be called cultural; but it is true that so far we have discovered nothing that is not common knowledge. We have, however, at the same time guarded ourselves against accepting the misconception that civilization is synonymous with becoming perfect, is the path by which man is ordained to reach perfection. But now a certain point of view

* From *Civilization and Its Discontents* by Sigmund Freud, translated by Joan Rivière. London: The Hogarth Press, Ltd., 1930, pp. 60–64, 86–87, 102–103, 143–144. Copyright 1930 by Jonathan Cape & Harrison Smith Inc. Reprinted by permission of the publisher.

presses for consideration; it will lead perhaps in another direction. The evolution of culture seems to us a peculiar kind of process passing over humanity, of which several aspects strike us as familiar. We can describe this process in terms of the modifications it effects on the known human instinctual dispositions, which it is the economic task of our lives to satisfy. Some of these instincts become absorbed, as it were, so that something appears in place of them which in an individual we call a character-trait. The most remarkable example of this process is found in respect of the anal erotism of young human beings. Their primary interest in the excretory function, its organs and products, is changed in the course of their growth into a group of traits that we know well—thriftiness, orderliness and cleanliness—valuable and welcome qualities in themselves, which, however, may be intensified till they visibly dominate the personality and produce what we call the anal character. How this happens we do not know; but there is no doubt about the accuracy of this conclusion. Now, we have seen that order and cleanliness are essentially cultural demands, although the necessity of them for survival is not particularly apparent, any more than their suitability as sources of pleasure. At this point we must be struck for the first time with the similarity between the process of cultural development and that of the libidinal development in an individual. Other instincts have to be induced to change the conditions of their gratification, to find it along other paths, a process which is usually identical with what we know so well as sublimation (of the aim of an instinct), but which can sometimes be differentiated from this. Sublimation of instinct is an especially conspicuous feature of cultural evolution; this it is that makes it possible for the higher mental operations, scientific, artistic, ideological activities, to play such an important part in civilized life. If one were to yield to a first impression, one would be tempted to say that sublimation is a fate which has been forced upon instincts by culture alone. But it is better to reflect over this a while longer. Thirdly and lastly, and this seems most important of all, it is impossible to ignore the extent to which civilization is built up on renunciation of instinctual gratifications, the degree to which the existence of civilization presupposes the non-gratification (suppression, repression or something else?) of powerful instinctual urgencies. This 'cultural privation' dominates the whole field of social relations between human beings; we know already that it is the cause of the antagonism against which all civilization has to fight. It sets hard tasks for our scientific work, too; we have a great deal to explain here. It is not easy to understand how it can become possible to withhold satisfaction from an instinct. Nor is it by any means without risk to do so; if the deprivation is not made good economically, one may be certain of producing serious disorders. . . .

The existence of this tendency to aggression which we can detect in ourselves and rightly presume to be present in others is the factor that disturbs our relations with our neighbours and makes it necessary for culture to institute its high demands. Civilized society is perpetually menaced with disintegration through this primary hostility of men towards one another. Their interests in their common work would not hold them together; the passions of instinct are stronger than reasoned interests. Culture has to call up every possible reinforcement in order to erect barriers against the aggressive instincts of men and hold their manifestations in check by reaction-formations in men's minds. Hence its system of methods by which mankind is to be driven to identifications and aim-inhibited love-relationships; hence the restrictions on sexual life; and hence, too, its ideal command to love one's neighbour as oneself, which is really justified by the fact that nothing is so completely at variance with original human nature as this. With all its striving, this endeavour of culture's has so far not achieved very much. Civilization expects to prevent the worst atrocities of brutal violence by taking upon itself the right to employ violence against criminals, but the law is not able to lay hands on the more discreet and subtle forms in which human aggressions are expressed. The time comes when every one of us has to abandon the illusory anticipations with which in our youth we regarded our fellow-men, and when we realize how much hardship and suffering we have been caused in life through their ill-will. . . .

In all that follows I take up the standpoint that the tendency to aggression is an innate, independent, instinctual disposition in man, and I come back now to the statement that it constitutes the most powerful obstacle to culture. At one point in the course of this discussion the idea took possession of us that culture was a peculiar process passing over human life and we are still under the influence of this idea. We may add to this that the process proves to be in the service of Eros, which aims at binding together single human individuals, then families, then tribes, races, nations, into one great unity, that of humanity. Why this has to be done we do not know; it is simply the work of Eros. These masses of men must be bound to one another libidinally; necessity alone, the advantages of common work, would not hold them together. The natural instinct of aggressiveness in man, the hostility of each one against all and of all against each one, opposes this programme of civilization. The instinct of aggression is the derivative and main representative of the death instinct we have found alongside of Eros, sharing his rule over the earth. And now, it seems to me, the meaning of the evolution of culture is no longer a riddle to us. It must present to us the struggle between Eros and Death, between the instincts of life and the instincts of destruction, as it works itself out in the human species. This struggle is what all life essentially consists of and so the evolution of civilization may be simply described as the struggle of the human species for existence. And it is this battle of the Titans that our nurses and governesses try to compose with their lullaby-song of Heaven! . . .

The fateful question of the human species seems to me to be whether and to what extent the cultural process developed in it will succeed in mastering the derangements of communal life caused by the human instinct of aggression and self-destruction. In this connection, perhaps the phase through which we are at this moment passing deserves special interest. Men have brought their powers of subduing the forces of nature to such a pitch that by using them they could now very easily exterminate one another to the last man. They know this—hence arises a great part of their current unrest, their dejection, their mood of apprehension. And now it may be expected that the other of the two 'heavenly forces', eternal Eros, will put forth his strength so as to maintain himself alongside of his equally immortal adversary.

Bertrand Russell

A Free Man's Worship *

To Dr. Faustus in his study Mephistopheles told the history of the Creation, saying:

"The endless praises of the choirs of angels had begun to grow wearisome; for, after all, did he not deserve their praise? Had he not given them endless joy? Would it not be more amusing to obtain undeserved praise, to be worshipped by beings whom he tortured? He smiled inwardly, and resolved that the great drama should be performed.

"For countless ages the hot nebula whirled aimlessly through space. At length it began to take shape, the central mass threw off planets, the planets cooled, boiling seas and burning mountains heaved and tossed, from black masses of cloud hot sheets of rain deluged the barely solid crust. And now the first germs of life grew in the depths of the ocean, and developed rapidly in the fructifying warmth into vast forest trees, huge ferns springing from the damp mould, sea monsters breeding, fighting, devouring, and passing away. And from the monsters, as the play unfolded itself, Man was born, with the power of thought, the knowledge of good and evil, and the cruel thirst for worship. And Man saw that all is passing in this mad, monstrous world, that all is struggling to snatch, at any cost, a few brief moments of life before Death's inexorable decree. And Man said: 'There is a hidden purpose, could we but fathom it, and the purpose is good; for we must reverence something, and in the visible world there is nothing worthy of reverence.' And Man stood aside from the struggle, resolving that God intended harmony to come out of chaos by human efforts. And when he followed the instincts which God had transmitted to him from his ancestry of beasts of prey, he called it Sin, and asked God to forgive him. But he doubted whether he could be justly forgiven, until he invented a divine Plan by which God's wrath was to

* From *Mysticism and Logic* by Bertrand Russell. New York: W. W. Norton and Co., 1929, pp. 46–58. Reprinted by permission of George Allen & Unwin Ltd.

have been appeased. And seeing the present was bad, he made it yet worse, that thereby the future might be better. And he gave God thanks for the strength that enabled him to forgo even the joys that were possible. And God smiled; and when he saw that man had become perfect in renunciation and worship, he sent another sun through the sky, which crashed into Man's sun; and all returned again to nebula.

" 'Yes,' he murmured, 'it was a good play; I will have it performed again.' "

Such, in outline, but even more purposeless, more devoid of meaning, is the world which Science presents for our belief. Amid such a world, if anywhere, our ideals henceforward must find a home. That Man is the product of causes which had no prevision of the end they were achieving; that his origin, his growth, his hopes and fears, his loves and his beliefs, are but the outcome of accidental collocations of atoms; that no fire, no heroism, no intensity of thought and feeling, can preserve an individual life beyond the grave; that all the labours of the ages, all the devotion, all the inspiration, all the noonday brightness of human genius, are destined to extinction in the vast death of the solar system, and that the whole temple of Man's achievement must inevitably be buried beneath the débris of a universe in ruins—all these things, if not quite beyond dispute, are yet so nearly certain, that no philosophy which rejects them can hope to stand. Only within the scaffolding of these truths, only on the firm foundation of unyielding despair, can the soul's habitation henceforth be safely built.

How, in such an alien and inhuman world, can so powerless a creature as Man preserve his aspiration untarnished? A strange mystery it is that Nature, omnipotent but blind, in the revolutions of her secular hurryings through the absysses of space, has brought forth at last a child, subject still to her power, but gifted with sight, with knowledge of good and evil, with the capacity of judging all the works of his unthinking Mother. In spite of Death, the mark and seal of the parental control, Man is yet free, during his brief years, to examine, to criticise, to know, and in imagination to create. To him alone, in the world with which he is acquainted, this freedom belongs; and in this lies his superiority to the resistless forces that control his outward life.

The savage, like ourselves, feels the oppression of his impotence before the powers of Nature; but having in himself nothing that he respects more than Power, he is willing to prostrate himself before his gods, without inquiring whether they are worthy of his worship. Pathetic and very terrible is the long history of cruelty and torture, of degradation and human sacrifice, endured in the hope of placating the jealous gods: surely, the trembling believer thinks, when what is most precious has been freely given, their lust for blood must be appeased, and more will not be required. The religion of Moloch—as such creeds may generically be called—is in essence the cringing submission of the slave, who dare not, even in his heart, allow the thought that his master deserves no adulation. Since the independence of ideals is not yet acknowledged, Power may be freely worshipped, and receive an unlimited respect, despite its wanton infliction of pain.

But gradually, as morality grows bolder, the claim of the ideal world begins to be felt; and worship, if it is not to cease, must be given to gods of another kind than those created by the savage. Some, though they feel the demands of the ideal, will still consciously reject them, still urging that naked power is worthy of worship. Such is the attitude inculcated in God's answer to Job out of the whirlwind: the divine power and knowledge are paraded, but of the divine goodness there is no hint. Such also is the attitude of those who, in our own day, base their morality upon the struggle for survival, maintaining that the survivors are necessarily the fittest. But others, not content with an answer so repugnant to the moral sense, will adopt the position which we have become accustomed to regard as specially religious, maintaining that, in some hidden manner, the world of fact is really harmonious with the world of ideals. Thus Man creates God, all-powerful and all-good, the mystic unity of what is and what should be.

But the world of fact, after all, is not good; and, in submitting our judgment to it, there is an element of slavishness from which our thoughts must be purged. For in all things it is well to exalt the dignity of Man, by freeing him as far as possible from the tyranny of non-human Power. When we have realised that Power is largely bad, that man, with his knowledge of good and evil, is but a helpless atom in a world which has no such knowledge, the choice is again presented to us: Shall we worship Force, or shall we worship Goodness? Shall our God exist and be evil, or shall he be recognised as the creation of our own conscience?

The answer to this question is very momentous, and affects profoundly our whole morality. The worship of Force, to which Carlyle and Nietzsche and the creed of Militarism have accustomed us, is the result of failure to maintain our own ideals against a hostile universe: it is itself a prostrate submission to evil, a sacrifice of our best to Moloch. If strength indeed is to be respected, let us respect rather the strength of those who refuse that false "recognition of facts" which fails to recognise that facts are often bad. Let us admit that, in the world we know, there are many things that would be better otherwise, and that the ideals to which we do and must adhere are not realised in the realm of matter. Let us preserve our respect for truth, for beauty, for the ideal of perfection which life does not permit us to attain, though none of these things meet with the approval of the unconscious universe. If Power is bad, as it seems to be, let us reject it from our hearts. In this lies Man's true freedom: in determination to worship only the God created by our own love of the good, to respect only the heaven which inspires the insight of our best moments. In action, in desire, we must submit perpetually to the tyranny of outside forces; but in thought, in aspiration, we are free, free from our fellow-men, free from the petty planet on which our bodies impotently crawl, free even, while we live, from the tyranny of death. Let us learn, then, that energy of faith which enables us to live constantly in the vision of the good; and let us descend, in action, into the world of fact, with that vision always before us.

When first the opposition of fact and ideal grows fully visible, a spirit of fiery revolt, of fierce hatred of the gods, seems necessary to the assertion of freedom. To defy with Promethean constancy a hostile universe, to keep its evil always in view, always actively hated, to refuse no pain that the malice of Power can invent, appears to be the duty of all who will not bow before the inevitable. But indignation is still a bondage, for it compels our thoughts to be occupied with an evil world; and in the fierceness of desire from which rebellion springs there is a kind of self-assertion which it is necessary for the wise to overcome. Indignation is a submission of our thought, but not of our desires; the Stoic freedom in which wisdom consists is found in the submission of our desires, but not of our thoughts. From the submission of our desires springs the virtue of resignation; from the freedom of our thoughts springs the whole world of art and philosophy, and the vision of beauty by which, at last, we half reconquer the reluctant world. But the vision of beauty is possible only to unfettered contemplation, to thoughts not weighted by the load of eager wishes; and thus Freedom comes only to those who no longer ask of life that it shall yield them any of those personal goods that are subject to the mutations of Time.

Although the necessity of renunciation is evidence of the existence of evil, yet Christianity, in preaching it, has shown a wisdom exceeding that of the Promethean philosophy of rebellion. It must be admitted that, of the things we desire, some, though they prove impossible, are yet real goods; others, however, as ardently longed for, do not form part of a fully purified ideal. The belief that what must be renounced is bad, though sometimes false, is far less often false than untamed passion supposes; and the creed of religion, by providing a reason for proving that it is never false, has been the means of purifying our hopes by the discovery of many austere truths.

But there is in resignation a further good element: even real goods, when they are unattainable, ought not to be fretfully desired. To every man comes, sooner or later, the great renunciation. For the young, there is nothing unattainable; a good thing desired with the whole force of the passionate will, and yet impossible, is to them not credible. Yet, by death, by illness, by poverty, or by the voice of duty, we must learn, each one of us, that the world was not made for us, and that, however beautiful may be the things we crave, Fate may nevertheless forbid them. It is the part of courage, when misfortune comes, to bear without repining the ruin of our hopes, to turn away our thoughts from vain regrets. This degree of submission to Power is not only just and right: it is the very gate of wisdom.

But passive renunciation is not the whole of wisdom; for not by renunciation alone can we build a temple for the worship of our own ideals. Haunting foreshadowings of the temple appear in the realm of imagination, in music, in architecture, in the untroubled kingdom of reason, and in the golden sunset magic of lyrics, where beauty shines and glows, remote from the touch of sorrow, remote from the fear of change, remote from the failures and disenchantments of the world of fact. In the contemplation of these things the vision of heaven will shape itself in our hearts, giving at once a touchstone to judge the world about us, and an inspiration by which to fashion to our needs whatever is not incapable of serving as a stone in the sacred temple.

Except for those rare spirits that are born without sin, there is a cavern of darkness to be traversed before that temple can be entered. The gate of the cavern is despair, and its floor is paved with the gravestones of abandoned hopes. There Self must die; there the eagerness, the greed of untamed desire must be slain, for only so can the soul be freed from the empire of Fate. But out of the cavern the Gate of Renunciation leads again to the daylight of wisdom, by whose radiance a new insight, a new joy, a new tenderness, shine forth to gladden the pilgrim's heart.

When, without the bitterness of impotent rebellion, we have learnt both to resign ourselves to the outward rule of Fate and to recognise that the non-human world is unworthy of our worship, it becomes possible at last so to transform and refashion the unconscious universe, so to transmute it in the crucible of imagination, that a new image of shining gold replaces the old idol of clay. In all the multiform facts of the world—in the visual shapes of trees and mountains and clouds, in the events of the life of man, even in the very omnipotence of Death—the insight of creative idealism can find the reflection of a beauty which its own thoughts first made. In this way mind asserts its subtle mastery over the thoughtless forces of Nature. The more evil the material with which it deals, the more thwarting to untrained desire, the greater is its achievement in inducing the reluctant rock to yield up its hidden treasures, the prouder its victory, in compelling the opposing forces to swell the pageant of its triumph. Of all the arts, Tragedy is the proudest, the most triumphant; for it builds its shining citadel in the very centre of the enemy's country, on the very summit of his highest mountain; from its impregnable watchtowers, his camps, and arsenals, his columns and forts, are all revealed; within its walls the free life continues, while the legions of Death and Pain and Despair, and all the servile captains of tyrant Fate, afford the burghers of that dauntless city new spectacles of beauty. Happy those sacred ramparts, thrice happy the dwellers on that all-seeing eminence. Honour to those brave warriors who, through countless ages of warfare, have preserved for us the priceless heritage of liberty, and have kept undefiled by sacrilegious invaders the home of the unsubdued.

But the beauty of Tragedy does but make visible a quality which, in more or less obvious shapes, is present always and everywhere in life. In the spectacle of Death, in the endurance of intolerable pain, and in the irrevocableness of a vanished past, there is a sacredness, an over-powering awe, a feeling of the vastness, the depth, the inexhaustible mystery of existence, in which, as by some strange marriage of pain, the sufferer is bound to the world by bonds of sorrow. In these moments of insight, we lose all eagerness of temporary desire, all struggling and striving for petty ends, all care for the little trivial things that, to a superficial view, make up the common life of day by day; we see, surrounding the narrow raft illumined by the flickering light of human comradeship, the dark ocean on whose rolling waves we toss for a brief hour; from the great night without, a chill blast breaks in upon our refuge; all the loneliness of humanity amid hostile forces is concentrated upon the individual soul, which must struggle alone, with what of courage it can command, against the whole weight of a universe that cares nothing for its hopes and fears. Victory, in this struggle with the powers of darkness, is the true baptism into the glorious company of heroes, the true initiation into the overmastering beauty of human existence. From that awful encounter of the soul with the outer world, enunciation, wisdom, and charity are born; and with their birth a new life begins. To take into the inmost shrine of the soul the irresistible forces whose puppets we seem to be—Death and change, the irrevocableness of the past, and the powerlessness of man before the blind hurry of the universe from vanity to vanity—to feel these things and know them is to conquer them.

This is the reason why the Past has such magical power. The beauty of its motionless and silent pictures is like the enchanted purity of late autumn, when the leaves, though one breath would make them fall, still glow against the sky in golden glory. The Past does not change or strive; like Duncan, after life's fitful fever, it sleeps well; what was eager and grasping, what was petty and transitory, has faded away, the things that were beautiful and eternal shine out of it like stars in the night. Its beauty, to a soul not worthy of it, is unendurable; but to a soul which has conquered Fate it is the key of religion.

The life of Man, viewed outwardly, is but a small thing in comparison with the forces of Nature. The slave is doomed to worship Time and Fate and Death, because they are greater than anything he finds in himself, and because all his thoughts are of things which they devour. But, great as they are, to think of them greatly, to feel their passionless splendour, is greater still. And such thought makes us free men; we no longer bow before the inevitable in Oriental subjection, but we absorb it, and make it a part of ourselves. To abandon the struggle for private happiness, to expel all eagerness of temporary desire, to burn with passion for eternal things—this is emancipation, and this is the free man's worship. And this liberation is effected by a contemplation of Fate; for Fate itself is subdued by the mind which leaves nothing to be purged by the purifying fire of Time.

United with his fellow-men by the strongest of all ties, the tie of a common doom, the free man finds that a new vision is with him always, shedding over every daily task the light of love. The life of Man is a long march through the night, surrounded by invisible foes, tortured by weariness and pain, towards a goal that few can hope to reach, and where none may tarry long. One by one, as they march, our comrades vanish from our sight, seized by the silent orders of omnipotent Death. Very brief is the time in which we can help them, in which their happiness or misery is decided. Be it ours to shed sunshine on their path, to lighten their sorrows by the balm of sympathy, to give them the pure joy of a never-tiring affection, to strengthen failing courage, to instil faith in hours of despair. Let us not weigh in grudging scales their merits and demerits, but let us think only of their need—of the sorrows, the difficulties, perhaps the blindnesses, that make the misery of their lives; let us remember that they are fellow-sufferers in the same darkness, actors in the same tragedy with ourselves. And so, when their day is over, when their good and their evil have become eternal by the immortality of the past, be it ours to feel that, where they suffered, where they failed, no deed of ours was the cause; but wherever a spark of the divine fire kindled in their hearts, we were ready with encouragement, with sympathy, with brave words in which high courage glowed.

Brief and powerless is Man's life; on him and all his race the slow, sure doom falls pitiless and dark. Blind to good and evil, reckless of destruction, omnipotent matter rolls on its relentless way; for Man, condemned to-day to lose his dearest, to-morrow himself to pass through the gate of darkness, it remains only to cherish, ere yet the blow falls, the lofty thoughts that ennoble his little day; disdaining the coward terrors of the slave of Fate, to worship at the shrine that his own hands have built; undismayed by the empire of chance, to preserve a mind free from the wanton tyranny that rules his outward life; proudly defiant of the irresistible forces that tolerate, for a moment, his knowledge and his condemnation, to sustain alone, a weary but unyielding Atlas, the world that his own ideals have fashioned despite the trampling march of unconscious power.

George Santayana

Spirituality and Its Corruptions *

. . . Spirituality is nobler than piety, because what would fulfil our being and make it worth having is what alone lends value to that being's source. Nothing can be lower or more wholly instrumental than the substance and cause of all things. The gift of existence would be worthless unless existence was good and supported at least a possible happiness. A man is spiritual when he lives in the presence of the ideal, and whether he eat or drink does so for the sake of a true and ultimate good. He is spiritual when he envisages his goal so frankly that his whole material life becomes a transparent and transitive vehicle, an instrument which scarcely arrests attention but allows the spirit to use it economically and with perfect detachment and freedom.

There is no need that this ideal should be pompously or mystically described. A simple life is its own reward, and continually realises its function. Though a spiritual man may perfectly well go through intricate processes of thought and attend to very complex affairs, his single eye, fixed on a rational purpose, will simplify morally the natural chaos it looks upon, and will remain free. This spiritual mastery is, of course, no slashing and forced synthesis of things into a system of philosophy which, even if it were thinkable, would leave the conceived logical machine without ideality and without responsiveness to actual interests; it is rather an inward aim and fixity in affection that knows what to take and what to leave in a world over which it diffuses something of its own peace. It threads its way through the landscape with so little temptation to distraction that it can salute every irrelevant thing, as Saint Francis did the sun and the moon, with courtesy and a certain affectionate detachment.

Spirituality likes to say, Behold the lilies of the field! For its secret has the same simplicity as their vegetative art; only spirituality has suc-

* From *Reason in Religion* (*The Life of Reason*) by George Santayana, pp. 193–204, 209–213. Copyright 1905 by Charles Scribner's Sons; 1933 by George Santayana. Reprinted by permission of Charles Scribner's Sons and Constable and Company Limited.

ceeded in adding consciousness without confusing instinct. This success, unfortunately so rare in man's life as to seem paradoxical, is its whole achievement. Spirituality ought to have been a matter of course, since conscious existence has inherent value and there is no intrinsic ground why it should smother that value in alien ambitions and servitudes. But spirituality, though so natural and obvious a thing, is subject, like the lilies' beauty, to corruption. I know not what army of microbes evidently invaded from the beginning the soul's physical basis and devoured its tissues, so that sophistication and bad dreams entirely obscured her limpidity.

None the less, spirituality, or life in the ideal, must be regarded as the fundamental and native type of all life; what deviates from it is disease and incipient dissolution, and is itself what might plausibly demand explanation and evoke surprise. The spiritual man should be quite at home in a world made to be used; the firmament is spread over him like a tent for habitation, and sublunary furniture is even more obviously to be taken as a convenience. He cannot, indeed, remove mountains, but neither does he wish to do so. He comes to endow the mountains with a function, and takes them at that, as a painter might take his brushes and canvas. Their beauty, their metals, their pasturage, their defence—this is what he observes in them and celebrates in his addresses to them. The spiritual man, though not ashamed to be a beggar, is cognisant of what wealth can do and of what it cannot. His unworldliness is true knowledge of the world, not so much a gaping and busy acquaintance as a quiet comprehension and estimation which, while it cannot come without intercourse, can very well lay intercourse aside.

If the essence of life be spiritual, early examples of life would seem to be rather the opposite. But man's view of primitive consciousness is humanly biassed and relies too much on partial analogies. We conceive an animal's physical life in the gross, and must then regard the momentary feelings that accompany it as very poor expressions either of its extent or conditions. These feelings are, indeed, so many ephemeral lives, containing no comprehensive view of the animal's fortunes. They accordingly fail to realise our notion of a spiritual human life which would have to be rational and to form some representation of man's total environment and interests. But it hardly follows that animal feelings are not spiritual in their nature and, on their narrow basis, perfectly ideal. The most ideal human passion is love, which is also the most absolute and animal and one of the most ephemeral. Very likely, if we could revert to an innocent and absorbed view of our early sensations, we should find that each was a little spiritual universe like Dante's, with its internal hell, purgatory and heaven. Cut off, as those experiences were, from all vistas and from sympathy with things remote, they would contain a closed circle of interests, a flying glimpse of eternity. So an infant living in his mystical limbo, without trailing in a literal sense any clouds of glory from elsewhere, might well repeat on a diminutive scale the beautific vision, insomuch as the only function of which he was conscious at all might be perfectly fulfilled by him and felt in its ideal import. Sucking and blinking are ridiculous processes, perhaps, but they may bring a thrill and satisfaction no less ideal than do the lark's inexhaustible palpitations. Narrow scope and low representative value are not defects in a consciousness having a narrow physical basis and comparatively simple conditions.

The spirit's foe in man has not been simplicity, but sophistication. His instincts, in becoming many, became confused, and in growing permanent, grew feeble and subject to arrest and deviation. Nature, we may say, threw the brute form back into her cauldron, to smelt its substance again, before pouring it into a rational mould. The docility which instinct, in its feebleness, acquired in the new creature was to be reason's opportunity, but before the larger harmony could be established a sorry chaos was bound to reign in the mind. Every peeping impulse would drop its dark hint and hide its head in confusion, while some pedantic and unjust law would be passed in its absence and without its vote. Secondary activities, which should always be representative, would establish themselves without being really such. Means would be pursued as if they were ends, and ends, under the illusion that they were forces, would be expected to further some activity, itself without justification. So pedantry might be substituted for wisdom, tyranny for government, superstition for morals, rhetoric for art.

This sophistication is what renders the pursuit of reason so perplexing and prolonged a problem. Half-formed adjustments in the brain and in the body politic are represented in consciousness by what are called passions, prejudices, motives, animosities. None of these felt ebullitions in the least understands its own causes, effects, or relations, but is hatched, so to speak, on the wing and flutters along in the direction of its momentary preference until it lapses, it knows not why, or is crossed and overwhelmed by some contrary power. Thus the vital elements, which in their comparative isolation in the lower animals might have yielded simple little dramas, each with its obvious ideal, its achievement, and its quietus, when mixed in the barbarous human will make a boisterous medley. For they are linked enough together to feel a strain, but not knit enough to form a harmony. In this way the unity of apperception seems to light up at first nothing but disunion. The first dawn of that rational principle which involves immortality breaks upon a discovery of death. The consequence is that ideality seems to man something supernatural and almost impossible. He finds himself at his awakening so confused that he puts chaos at the origin of the world. But only order can beget a world or evoke a sensation. Chaos is something secondary, composed of conflicting organisations interfering with one another. It is compounded like a common noise out of jumbled vibrations, each of which has its period and would in itself be musical. The problem is to arrange these sounds, naturally so tuneful, into concerted music. So long as total discord endures human life remains spasmodic and irresolute; it can find no ideal and admit no total representation of nature. Only when the disordered impulses and perceptions settle down into a trained instinct, a steady, vital response and adequate preparation for the world, do clear ideas and successful purposes arise in the mind. The Life of Reason, with all the arts, then begins its career.

The forces at play in this drama are, first, the primary impulses and functions represented by elementary values; second, the thin network of signals and responses by which those functions are woven into a total organ, represented by discursive thought and all secondary mental figments, and, third, the equilibrium and total power of that new organism in action represented by the ideal. Spirituality, which might have resided in the elementary values, sensuous or passionate, before the relational process supervened, can now exist only in the ultimate activity to which these processes are instrumental. Obstacles to spirituality in human life may accordingly take the form of an arrest either at the elementary values—an entanglement in sense and passion—or at the instrumental processes—an entanglement in what in religious parlance is called "the world."

Worldly minds bristle with conventional morality (though in private they may nurse a vice or two to appease wayward nature), and they are rational in everything except first principles. They consider the voluptuary a weak fool, disgraced and disreputable; and if they notice the spiritual man at all—for he is easily ignored—they regard him as a useless and visionary fellow. Civilisation has to work algebraically with symbols for known and unknown quantities which only in the end resume their concrete values, so that the journeymen and vulgar middlemen of the world know only conventional goods. They are lost in instrumentalities and are themselves only instruments in the Life of Reason. Wealth, station, fame, success of some notorious and outward sort, make their standard of happiness. Their chosen virtues are industry, good sense, probity, conventional piety, and whatever else has acknowledged utility and seemliness.

In its strictures of pleasure and reverie this Philistia is perfectly right. Sensuous living (and I do not mean debauchery alone, but the palpitations of any poet without art or any mystic without discipline) is not only inconsequential and shallow, but dangerous to honour and to sincere happiness. When life remains lost in sense or reverts to it entirely, humanity itself is atrophied. And humanity is tormented and spoilt when, as more often happens, a man disbelieving in reason and out of humour with his world, abandons his soul to loose whimseys and passions that play a quarrelsome game there, like so many ill-bred children. Nevertheless, compared with the worldling's mental mechanism and rhetoric, the sensualist's soul is a well of wisdom. He lives naturally on an animal level and attains a kind of good. He has free and concrete pursuits, though they be momentary, and he has sincere satisfactions. He is less often corrupt than primitive, and even when corrupt he finds some justification for his captious existence. He harvests pleasures as he goes which intrinsically, as we have seen, may have the depth and ideality which nature breathes in all her oracles. His experience, for that reason, though disastrous is interesting and has some human pathos; it is easier to make a saint out of a libertine than out of a prig. True, the libertine is pursued, like the animals, by unforeseen tortures, decay, and abandonment, and he is vowed to a total death; but in these respects the worldly man hardly has an advantage. The Babels he piles up may indeed survive his person, but they are themselves vain and without issue, while his brief life has been meantime spent in slavery and his mind cramped with cant and foolish ambitions. The voluptuary is like some roving creature, browsing on nettles and living by chance; the worldling is like a beast of burden, now ill-used and over-worked, now fatted, stalled, and richly caparisoned. Aesop might well have described their relative happiness in a fable about the wild ass and the mule.

Thus, even if the voluptuary is sometimes a poet and the worldling often an honest man, they both lack reason so entirely that reflection revolts equally against the life of both. Vanity, vanity, is their common epitaph. Now, at the soul's christening and initiation into the Life of Reason, the first vow must always be to "renounce the pomps and vanities of this wicked world." A person to whom this means nothing is one to whom, in the end, nothing has meaning. He has not conceived a highest good, no ultimate goal is within his horizon, and it has never occurred to him to ask what he is living for. With all his pompous soberness, the worldly man is fundamentally frivolous; with all his maxims and cant estimations he is radically inane. He conforms to religion without suspecting what religion means, not being in the least open to such an inquiry. He judges art like a parrot, without having ever stopped to evoke an image. He preaches about service and duty without any recognition of natural demands or any standard of betterment. His moral life is one vast anacoluthon in which the final term is left out that might have given sense to the whole, one vast ellipsis in which custom seems to bridge the chasm left between ideas. He denies the values of sense because they tempt to truancies from mechanical activity; the values of reason he necessarily ignores because they lie beyond his scope. He adheres to conventional maxims and material quantitative standards; his production is therefore, as far as he himself is concerned, an essential waste and his activity an essential tedium. If at least, like the sensualist, he enjoyed the process and expressed his fancy in his life, there would be something gained; and this sort of gain, though overlooked in the worldling's maxims, all of which have a categorical tone, is really what often lends his life some propriety and spirit. Business and war and any customary task may come to form, so to speak, an organ whose natural function will be just that operation, and the most abstract and secondary activity, like that of adding figures or reading advertisements, may in this way become the one function proper to some soul. There are Nibelungen dwelling by choice underground and happy pedants in the upper air.

Facts are not wanting for these pillars of society to take solace in, if they wish to defend their philosophy. The time will come, astronomers say, when life will be extinct upon this weary planet. All the delights of sense and imagination will be over. It is these that will have turned out to be vain. But the masses of matter which the worldlings have transformed with their machinery, and carried from one place to another, will remain to bear witness of them. The collocation of atoms will never be what it would have been if their feet had less continually beaten the earth. They may have the proud happiness of knowing that, when nothing that the spirit values endures, the earth may still sometimes, because of them, cast a slightly different shadow across the moon's craters. . . .

. . . Does the Life of Reason differ from that of convention? Is there a spirituality really wiser than common-sense? That there is appears in many directions. Worldliness is arrest and absorption in the instrumentalities of life; but instrumentalities cannot exist without ultimate purposes, and it suffices to lift the eyes to those purposes and to question the will sincerely about its essential preferences, to institute a catalogue of rational goods, by pursuing any one of which we can escape worldliness. Sense itself is one of these goods. The sensualist at least is not worldly, and though his nature be atrophied in all its higher part, there is not lacking, as we have seen, a certain internal and abstract spirituality in his experience. He is a sort of sprightly and incidental mystic, treating his varied succession of little worlds as the mystic does his monotonous universe. Sense, moreover, is capable of many refinements, by which physical existence becomes its own reward. In the disciplined play of fancy which the fine arts afford, the mind's free action justifies itself and becomes intrinsically delightful. Science not only exercises in itself the intellectual powers, but assimilates nature to the mind, so that all things may nourish it. In love and friendship the liberal life extends also to the heart. All these interests, which justify themselves by their intrinsic fruits, make so many rational episodes and patches in conventional life; but it must be confessed in all candour that these are but oases in the desert, and that as the springs of life are irrational, so its most vehement and prevalent interests remain irrational to the end. When the pleasures of sense and art, of knowledge and sympathy, are stretched to the utmost, what part will they cover and justify of our passions, our industry, our governments, our religion?

It was a signal error in those rationalists who attributed their ideal retrospectively to nature that they grotesquely imagined that people were hungry so that they might enjoy eating, or curious in order to delight in discovering the truth, or in love the better to live in conscious harmony. Such a view forgets that all the forces of life work originally and fundamentally *a tergo,* that experience and reason are not the ground of preference but its result. In order to live men will work disproportionately and eat all manner of filth without pleasure; curiosity as often as not leads to illusion, and argument serves to foster hatred of the truth; finally, love is notoriously a great fountain of bitterness and frequently a prelude to crime and death. When we have skimmed from life its incidental successes, when we have harvested the moments in which existence justifies itself, its profound depths remain below in their obscure commotion, depths that breed indeed a rational efflorescence, but which are far from exhausted in producing it, and continually threaten, on the contrary, to engulf it.

The spiritual man, needs, therefore, something more than a cultivated sympathy with the brighter scintillation of things. He needs to refer that scintillation to some essential light, so that in reviewing the motley aspects of experience he may not be reduced to culling superciliously the flowers that please him, but may view in them all only images and varied symbols of some eternal good. Spirituality has never flourished apart from religion, except momentarily, perhaps, in some master-mind, whose original intuitions at once became a religion to his followers. For it is religion that knows how to interpret the casual rationalities in the world and isolate their principle, setting this principle up in the face of nature as nature's standard and model. This ideal synthesis of all that is good, this consciousness that over earth floats its congenial heaven, this vision of perfection which gilds beauty and sanctifies grief, has taken form, for the most part, in such grossly material images, in a mythology so opaque and pseudo-physical, that its ideal and moral essence has been sadly obscured; nevertheless, every religion worthy of the name has put into its gods some element of real goodness, something by which they become representative of those scattered excellences and self-justifying bits of experience in which the Life of Reason consists.

That happy constitution which human life has at its best moments—that, says Aristotle, the divine life has continually. The philosopher thus expressed with absolute clearness the principle which the poets had been clumsily trying to embody from the beginning. Burdened as traditional faiths might be with cosmological and fanciful matter, they still presented in a conspicuous and permanent image that which made all good things good, the ideal and standard of all excellence. By the help of such symbols the spiritual man could steer and steady his judgment; he could say, according to the form religion had taken in his country, that the truly good was what God commanded, or what made man akin to the divine, or what led the soul to heaven. Such expressions, though taken more or less literally by a metaphysical intellect, did not wholly forfeit their practical and moral meaning. God, for a long time, was understood to command what in fact was truly important, the divine was long the truly noble and beautiful, heaven hardly ever ceased to respond to impersonal and ideal aspirations. Under those figures, therefore, the ideals of life could confront life with clearness and authority. The spiritual man, fixing his eyes on them, could live in the presence of ultimate purposes and ideal issues. Before each immediate task, each incidental pleasure, each casual success, he could retain his sweetness and constancy, accepting what good these moments brought and laying it on the altar of what they ought to bring.

John Dewey

Reconstruction in Moral Conceptions *

When the consciousness of science is fully impregnated with the consciousness of human value, the greatest dualism which now weighs humanity down, the split between the material, the mechanical, the scientific and the moral and ideal will be destroyed. Human forces that now waver because of this division will be unified and reinforced. As long as ends are not thought of as individualized according to specific needs and opportunities, the mind will be content with abstractions, and the adequate stimulus to the moral or social use of natural science and historical data will be lacking. But when attention is concentrated upon the diversified concretes, recourse to all intellectual materials needed to clear up the special cases will be imperative. At the same time that morals are made to focus in intelligence, things intellectual are moralized. The vexatious and wasteful conflict between naturalism and humanism is terminated.

These general considerations may be amplified. First: Inquiry, discovery take the same place in morals that they have come to occupy in sciences of nature. Validation, demonstration become experimental, a matter of consequences. Reason, always an honorific term in ethics, becomes actualized in the methods by which the needs and conditions, the obstacles and resources, of situations are scrutinized in detail, and intelligent plans of improvement are worked out. Remote and abstract generalities promote jumping at conclusions, "anticipations of nature." Bad consequences are then deplored as due to natural perversity and untoward fate. But shifting the issue to analysis of a specific situation makes inquiry obligatory and alert observation of consequences imperative. No past decision nor old principle can ever be wholly relied upon to justify a course of action. No amount of pains taken in forming a purpose in a definite case is final; the consequences of its adoption must be carefully noted, and a purpose held only

* From *Reconstruction in Philosophy* by John Dewey, pp. 139–147. Original edition: Copyright 1920 by Henry Holt and Co.; enlarged edition: Copyright 1948 by The Beacon Press. Reprinted by permission of Beacon Press, Inc.

as a working hypothesis until results confirm its rightness. Mistakes are no longer either mere unavoidable accidents to be mourned or moral sins to be expiated and forgiven. They are lessons in wrong methods of using intelligence and instructions as to a better course in the future. They are indications of the need of revision, development, readjustment. Ends grow, standards of judgment are improved. Man is under just as much obligation to develop his most advanced standards and ideals as to use conscientiously those which he already possesses. Moral life is protected from falling into formalism and rigid repetition. It is rendered flexible, vital, growing.

In the second place, every case where moral action is required becomes of equal moral importance and urgency with every other. If the need and deficiencies of a specific situation indicate improvement of health as the end and good, then for that situation health is the ultimate and supreme good. It is no means to something else. It is a final and intrinsic value. The same thing is true of improvement of economic status, of making a living, of attending to business and family demands—all of the things which under the sanction of fixed ends have been rendered of secondary and merely instrumental value, and so relatively base and unimportant. Anything that in a given situation is an end and good at all is of equal worth, rank and dignity with every other good of any other situation, and deserves the same intelligent attention.

We note thirdly the effect in destroying the roots of Phariseeism. We are so accustomed to thinking of this as deliberate hypocrisy that we overlook its intellectual premises. The conception which looks for the end of action within the circumstances of the actual situation will not have the same measure of judgment for all cases. When one factor of the situation is a person of trained mind and large resources, more will be expected than with a person of backward mind and uncultured experience. The absurdity of applying the same standard of moral judgment to savage peoples that is used with civilized will be apparent. No individual or group will be judged by whether they come up to or fall short of some fixed result, but by the direction in which they are moving. The bad man is the man who no matter how good he *has* been is beginning to deteriorate, to grow less good. The good man is the man who no matter how morally unworthy he *has* been is moving to become better. Such a conception makes one severe in judging himself and humane in judging others. It excludes that arrogance which always accompanies judgment based on degree of approximation to fixed ends.

In the fourth place, the process of growth, or improvement and progress, rather than the static outcome and result, becomes the significant thing. Not health as an end fixed once and for all, but the needed improvement in health—a continual process—is the end and good. The end is no longer a terminus or limit to be reached. It is the active process of transforming the existent situation. Not perfection as a final goal, but the ever-enduring process of perfecting, maturing, refining is the aim in living. Honesty, industry, temperance, justice, like health, wealth and learning, are not goods to be possessed as they would be if they expressed fixed ends to be attained. They are directions of change in the quality of experience. Growth itself is the only moral "end."

Although the bearing of this idea upon the problem of evil and the controversy between optimism and pessimism is too vast to be here discussed, it may be worth while to touch upon it superficially. The problem of evil ceases to be a theological and metaphysical one, and is perceived to be the practical problem of reducing, alleviating, as far as may be removing, the evils of life. Philosophy is no longer under obligation to find ingenious methods of proving that evils are only apparent, not real, or to elaborate schemes for explaining them away or, worse yet, for justifying them. It assumes another obligation:—That of contributing in however humble a way to methods that will assist us in discovering the causes of humanity's ills. Pessimism is a paralyzing doctrine. In declaring that the world is evil wholesale, it makes futile all efforts to discover the remediable causes of specific evils and thereby destroys at the root every attempt to make the world better and happier. Wholesale optimism, which has been the consequence of the attempt to explain evil away, is, however, equally an incubus.

After all, the optimism that says that the world is already the best possible of all worlds might be regarded as the most cynical of pessimisms. If this is the best possible, what would a world which was fundamentally bad be like? Meliorism is the belief that the specific conditions which exist at one moment, be they comparatively bad or comparatively good, in any event may be bettered. It encourages intelligence to study the positive means of good and the obstructions to their realization, and to put forth endeavor for the improvement of conditions. It arouses confidence and a reasonable hopefulness as optimism does not. For the latter in declaring that good is already realized in ultimate reality tends to make us gloss over the evils that concretely exist. It becomes too readily the creed of those who live at ease, in comfort, of those who have been successful in obtaining this world's rewards. Too readily optimism makes the men who hold it callous and blind to the sufferings of the less fortunate, or ready to find the cause of troubles of others in their personal viciousness. It thus co-operates with pessimism, in spite of the extreme nominal differences between the two, in benumbing sympathetic insight and intelligent effort in reform. It beckons men away from the world of relativity and change into the calm of the absolute and eternal.

The import of many of these changes in moral attitude focuses in the idea of happiness. Happiness has often been made the object of the moralists' contempt. Yet the most ascetic moralist has usually restored the idea of happiness under some other name, such as bliss. Goodness without happiness, valor and virtue without satisfaction, ends without conscious enjoyment—these things are as intolerable practically as they are self-contradictory in conception. Happiness is not, however, a bare possession; it is not a fixed attainment. Such a happiness is either the unworthy selfishness which moralists have so bitterly condemned, or it is, even if labelled bliss, an insipid tedium, a millennium of ease in relief from all struggle and labor. It could satisfy only the most delicate of mollycoddles. Happiness is found only in success; but success means succeeding, getting forward, moving in advance. It is an active process, not a passive outcome. Accordingly it includes the overcoming of obstacles, the elimination of sources of defect and ill. Esthetic sensitiveness and enjoyment are a large constituent in any worthy happiness. But the esthetic appreciation which is totally separated from renewal of spirit, from recreation of mind and purification of emotion is a weak and sickly thing, destined to speedy death from starvation. That the renewal and re-creation come unconsciously not by set intention but makes them the more genuine.

Upon the whole, utilitarianism has marked the best in the transition from the classic theory of ends and goods to that which is now possible. It had definite merits. It insisted upon getting away from vague generalities, and down to the specific and concrete. It subordinated law to human achievement instead of subordinating humanity to external law. It taught that institutions are made for man and not man for institutions; it actively promoted all issues of reform. It made moral good natural, humane, in touch with the natural goods of life. It opposed unearthly and otherworldly morality. Above all, it acclimatized in human imagination the idea of social welfare as a supreme test. But it was still profoundly affected in fundamental points by old ways of thinking. It never questioned the idea of a fixed, final and supreme end. It only questioned the current notions as to the nature of this end; and then inserted pleasure and the greatest possible aggregate of pleasures in the position of the fixed end.

Such a point of view treats concrete activities and specific interests not as worth while in themselves, or as constituents of happiness, but as mere external means to getting pleasures. The upholders of the old tradition could therefore easily accuse utilitarianism of making not only virtue but art, poetry, religion and the state into mere servile means of attaining sensuous enjoyment. Since pleasure was an outcome, a result valuable on its own account independently of the active processes that achieve it, happiness was a thing to be possessed and held onto. The acquisitive instincts of man were exaggerated at the expense of the creative. Product was of importance not because of the intrinsic worth of invention and reshaping the world, but because its external results feed pleasure. Like every theory that sets up fixed and final aims, in making the end passive and possessive, it made all active operations *mere* tools. Labor was an unavoidable evil to be minimized. Security in possession was the chief thing practically. Material comfort and ease was magnified in contrast with the pains and risk of experimental creation.

These deficiencies, under certain conceivable conditions, might have remained merely theoretical. But the disposition of the times and the interests of those who propagated the utilitarian ideas, endowed them with power for social harm. In spite of the power of the new ideas in attacking old social abuses, there were elements in the teaching which operated or protected to sanction new social abuses. The reforming zeal was shown in criticism of the evils inherited from the class system of feudalism, evils economic, legal and political. But the new economic order of capitalism that was superseding feudalism brought its own social evils with it, and some of these ills utilitarianism tended to cover up or defend. The emphasis upon acquisition and possession of enjoyments took on an untoward color in connection with the contemporary enormous desire for wealth and the enjoyments it makes possible.

If utilitarianism did not actively promote the new economic materialism, it had no means of combating it. Its general spirit of subordinating productive activity to the bare product was indirectly favorable to the cause of an unadorned commercialism. In spite of its interest in a thoroughly social aim, utilitarianism fostered a new class interest, that of the capitalistic property-owning interests, provided only property was obtained through free competition and not by governmental favor. The stress that Bentham put on security tended to consecrate the legal institution of private property provided only certain legal abuses in connection with its acquisition and transfer were abolished. *Beati possidentes*—provided possessions had been obtained in accord with the rules of the competitive game—without, that is, extraneous favors from government. Thus utilitarianism gave intellectual confirmation to all those tendencies which make "business" not a means of social service and an opportunity for personal growth in creative power but a way of accumulating the means of private enjoyment. Utilitarian ethics thus afford a remarkable example of the need of philosophic reconstruction which these lectures have been presenting. Up to a certain point, it reflected the meaning of modern thought and aspirations. But it was still tied down by fundamental ideas of that very order which it thought it had completely left behind: The idea of a fixed and single end lying beyond the diversity of human needs and acts rendered utilitarianism incapable of being an adequate representative of the modern spirit. It has to be reconstructed through emancipation from its inherited elements.

If a few words are added upon the topic of education, it is only for the sake of suggesting that the educative process is all one with the moral process, since the latter is a continuous passage of experience from worse to better. Education has been traditionally thought of as preparation: as learning, acquiring certain things because they will later be useful. The end is remote, and education is getting ready, is a preliminary to something more important to happen later on. Childhood is only a preparation for adult life, and adult life for another life. Always the future, not the present, has been the significant thing in education: Acquisition of knowledge and skill for future use and enjoyment; formation of habits required later in life in business, good citizenship and pursuit of science. Education is thought of also as something needed by some human beings merely because of their dependence upon others. We are born ignorant, unversed, unskilled, immature, and consequently in a state of social dependence. Instruction, training, moral discipline are processes by which the mature, the adult, gradually raise the helpless to the point where they can look out for themselves. The business of childhood is to grow into the independence of adulthood by means of the guidance of those who have already attained it. Thus the process of education as the main business of life ends when the young have arrived at emancipation from social dependence.

These two ideas, generally assumed but rarely explicitly reasoned out, contravene the conception that growing, or the continuous reconstruction of experience, is the only end. If at whatever period we choose to take a person, he is still in process of growth, then education is not, save as a by-product, a preparation for something coming later. Getting from the present the degree and kind of growth there is in it is education.

This is a constant function, independent of age. The best thing that can be said about any special process of education, like that of the formal school period, is that it renders its subject capable of further education: more sensitive to conditions of growth and more able to take advantage of them. Acquisition of skill, possession of knowledge, attainment of culture are not ends: they are marks of growth and means to its continuing.

The contrast usually assumed between the period of education as one of social dependence and of maturity as one of social independence does harm. We repeat over and over that man is a social animal, and then confine the significance of this statement to the sphere in which sociality usually seems least evident, politics. The heart of the sociality of man is in education. The idea of education as preparation and of adulthood as a fixed limit of growth are two sides of the same obnoxious untruth. If the moral business of the adult as well as the young is a growing and developing experience, then the instruction that comes from social dependencies and interdependencies is as important for the adult as for the child. Moral independence for the adult means arrest of growth, isolation means induration. We exaggerate the intellectual dependence of childhood so that children are too much kept in leading strings, and then we exaggerate the independence of adult life from intimacy of contacts and communication with others. When the identity of the moral process with the processes of specific growth is realized, the more conscious and formal education of childhood will be seen to be the most economical and efficient means of social advance and reorganization, and it will also be evident that the test of all the institutions of adult life is their effect in furthering continued education. Government, business, art, religion, all social institutions have a meaning, a purpose. That purpose is to set free and to develop the capacities of human individuals without respect to race, sex, class or economic status. And this is all one with saying that the test of their value is the extent to which they educate every individual into the full stature of his possibility. Democracy has many meanings, but if it has a moral meaning, it is found in resolving that the supreme test of all political institutions and industrial arrangements shall be the contribution they make to the all-around growth of every member of society.

Benedetto Croce

Soliloquy of an Old Philosopher *

Anyone who like myself was born and grew up in the early years of the unity and liberty of Italy must proclaim in every company and against all opponents, that he knows what it is to have lived the greater and best part of his life in a sublime spiritual atmosphere. He 'knows', he does not merely 'feel' it; for these words of his are not mere effusion of a nostalgic sentiment for the past, or even an imaginative picture of it, but an affirmation of the very truth. And as an affirmation, in the strict sense, it claims to be distinguished from that sort of utopia projected into the past, which leads men to think that some golden age ever fleeted the time in 'blissful ignorance', a phrase which is purely nonsensical. At the time of which I speak, as in every other, men lived a human, not a superhuman or heavenly life, a life marred by cares and griefs, sorrows, solitude, despair, sullied by reprehensible deeds. It could not even be called more moral or less moral than the life of earlier or later generations, for morality is an inner energy, whose quality cannot be measured, and whose external manifestations, which alone can be measured, are mere events, and as such neither moral nor immoral. A sophistical trick used to discredit the age of liberalism, and invented by the vulgar for the vulgar, is to air all the dirty linen of this period, the poverty, the blunders, the pride, the scandals, the crimes, of which it may have been guilty, in order to shew that it was politically inferior and contemptible; as if a similar collection of anecdotes could not be made, and a similar picture as fairly painted of any other stage or period of history.

A historical period cannot be truly described or judged by accumulating scandalous stories, but only by pondering and enquiring whether it had a moral ideal governing and illuminating the minds of those mem-

* From *My Philosophy and Other Essays on the Moral and Political Problems of Our Time* by Benedetto Croce, selected by R. Klibansky, translated by E. F. Carritt, pp. 233–240.

bers of human societies who are capable of ideals; capable of loving something above their own happiness or that of others on which it depends, that of sons, wives, friends; capable of something above the 'natural' or 'sensual' love (to use an old phrase of the Churchmen) for the persons or things with which, for all of us, the 'joy of life' and self-preservation is interwoven. There are historical periods in which the power of such moral ideals grows faint, and almost seems to disappear, and these are called ages of barbarism or decadence; while other periods are active and flourishing and signalise advances in civilisation, and the attainment of richer and deeper ideas, with corresponding progress in practical activity.

The period to which my thoughts and memories now recur rejoiced in the calm assurance of a secure, full, and fruitful expansion of energies, and a noble co-operation of man with man. It saw all men as possessed of equal rights, without slavery or despotism, all at liberty to express their thoughts and to further their policies, under the free judgment of public opinion, which, in spite of inevitable oscillations and mistakes, usually in the end supported truth and equity. At this period the development of the human spirit had attained in Italy and Europe a more reflective self-consciousness, coherence, and harmony than had ever before been reached by that dynamic tendency to liberty which gives history its positive progress. It was an exalted ideal of liberty that now shone forth as the rule and guide and ultimate criterion of every effort. Behind this new form could be recognised, illuminated by a new light, the stern ideal of the old Greek and Roman heroes of liberty, but also the more intense and continuous influence of a process, begun or quickened by Christianity, towards a humanity united in love and sorrow and sublime aspirations. The Christian ideal had been brought down from heaven to earth at the Renaissance; it seemed to be denied by the Enlightenment, which celebrated the cult of abstract reason but in fact by this very 'reason' worked towards the same ends, dissipating darkness and promoting liberty, equality, and fraternity. And now, in the time I am speaking of, Christianity reconciled to the long, painful development of which it had been the seed, arose, one might say, refreshed by its contact with philosophy and history. The fact that, nevertheless, the Roman Church grew intolerant of liberation was due to the way in which she came to mould Christian minds into conformity with her political ends; but the close bond between the two was felt, not only by pure liberals, to whose lips religious phrases and metaphors so readily sprang, but also by liberal Catholics, who were the deepest thinkers and most generous spirits of their Church. We still have the proof of this bond today, a proof that liberalism is essentially Christian, when we see that those who hate and abuse it most are either inflamed by the passion for extolling and reviving distant epochs of pre-Christian history, such as paganism, or frankly profess the most crudely materialist, utilitarian, fratricidal conception of human life.

Certainly the ideal of liberty which flourished in the nineteenth century can and must be deepened, defined and widened; and this will be the business of the following periods, whose growth and progress will depend upon new experiences critically sifted and assimilated. But since its essential principle is moral, or rather is the development of morality itself, that principle can never be denied or replaced by any other; nor can we go back on its past history, or abandon the point it has reached; we can only advance further.

It is, of course, possible to 'deny' it by vocal articulations, signifying nothing, and to refute it or claim to refute it, and to cry up as the true ideal its opposite, and to triumph over its supposed death. But since this proclaimed opposite is self-contradictory and morally unacceptable, the idea of liberty remains after all invulnerable, and when the storm has blown over it blossoms freshly and renews its youthful prime.

'When the storm is over'? Is there something in the world which can resist and impede and delay and shatter, for however short a time, the practical influence of this high ideal? Most certainly; and we should not be surprised at it, nor be panic-stricken for the fate of the world, as if it were thereby irrevocably compromised or beyond hope ruined. Nor, on the other hand, is it for the enemies of the ideal to argue that therefore it is essentially invalid and inadequate, and that their substitute has a monopoly of power and permanence. The delays and breakdowns in the advance of liberty are in fact evident in past and present history, the history which goes on within us. But the reason and justification of this fact is not far to seek, and though some through thoughtlessness seem not to see it, or to have forgotten it, a little reflection will bring it to their mind.

The obvious reason is that there can be no life or reality without differences and perpetual opposition or composition of forces, without war and peace, war which brings peace and peace which leads again to war. This is the plain truth, accepted by common sense no less than by profound philosophy, but contested and denied by all Utopians, pessimists and sceptics, ever seeking a good unconditioned by evil, a life whose complement is not death; who, when they are unable to find this good in reality, shudder, or prate about the inscrutable mystery of things. Seen in the dialectical conflicts which are the law of history, man's moral action does not stand alone, an abstraction in a world of abstractions, but, always in relation to that which is at once its material and its instrument, its enemy and its ally, the vital force, whose moving principle is the prime mover. It is this force which continually contributes to the creation not only of the earth with its 'lovely family of beasts and flowers', its volcanoes and earthquakes, but also, by continual conflict, of ever-changing conditions of life. And most directly it operates in that sphere of human life [1] which is called 'the world of affairs', that is the world of business [2] and of practical politics, which is always engendering new patterns of nations and of states.

It is the professed ideal of liberal statesmen, not to extinguish economic and political rivalries, as some airy castle-builders might desire, and thus dry up the very spring of all activity and advance, but so to guide them that they may develop and give room for the necessary changes and re-groupings. Hence the internal policy of liberal states is to maintain with scrupulous firmness a respect for general liberty, and hence also their vigilant precaution that the powers of the government should not exceed its legitimate authority. Hence too the anxiety of the leaders in such states, of the ruling classes, and of all men of goodwill, however they may differ in other opinions and policies, to preserve international peace and to substitute for physical combat diplomacy, compromise and treaties. But all such action, whether internal or external, is itself a kind of warfare, though as we have said, not fought with weapons, or at least with different weapons, and, like other warfare, it has its turns of victory and defeat.

When these defeats occur, liberal constitutions and the love of peace are overcome and destroyed, and for a longer or shorter time, in greater or lesser degrees, give place to their opponent, the savage vital force. Such are the changes which succeed one another on every page of history; and it is unthinkable that this rhythm of victory and defeat should ever cease. The very idea of its cessation, the idea of a liberty completely and finally achieved, settled and immutable, of a liberty without dangers, or with only those fictitious dangers, which can always be escaped or checked, is as self-contradictory and empty as the idea of an end of the world and of universal life and being. But being cannot be annihilated since not-being is within its realm. Serious thinkers will never take the absurd line of preaching and demanding the abolition of war, and the

[1] *Spirito.*
[2] *Economia.*

establishment of perpetual peace and of static material equality. Nor, when they see unleashed the violent wars and revolutions which they have vainly tried to avert by defending peace and liberty to their utmost, will they cherish the equally absurd design of sitting in judgment on these mortal struggles and of arbitrating between parties while passions are still high. Strife knows no law but strife; its only arbiters are the actual results in which it will issue, and what these are to be is no man's secret, for no man knows. It is 'God's secret', as the wise proverb says. And philosophy agrees with common sense in refusing to individuals, each of whom has to fight his own battle in the universal warfare, the right to make himself judge and master in matters too high for him. Each must be content to fulfil his individual duty, in his own situation and state of life, as the voice of conscience bids him. Who, indeed, however sure he felt of rare intellectual and political genius, however sublimely self confident, would accept at God's hand the task of deciding human destiny? Who would presume to decide, by such criterion as he might vainly seek in his own mind, what can only be decided by the outcome?

But it is only in souls apt to despair and to lose their way, only in minds apt to confusion, that the necessary rhythm of history, with its recurring horrors of war and its recurrent back-slidings from peace and liberty, can inspire the thought that liberty can ever vanish even from a world which desires to be governed by a different law. Is liberty then a by-product, which dies and is not born again? Is it not the very *activity* of man, which is by definition free, and which nobody has yet ventured to define as determined? [3] It is within the realm of possibilities that the liberal period of the nineteenth century, which men of my generation have seen, and to which some of them are still loyal, splendid in its achievement, proud of the mutual respect of its citizens, will one day be compared with the great periods of philosophy and art, the Athens of Pericles, the Italy of the Renaissance, the France of Descartes, Corneille and Racine, the Germany of idealism and romance. Such periods open rarely and quickly close, leaving admiration and regret behind them. But though such marvellous seasons of blossoming pass, not for that reason will art and philosophy be banished from the world; arts and philosophical genius will arise again in men as great as those of old, and, what is more the search for truth and the worship of art will never fail to inspire love and longing in the heart of man, and to shine there with all their former splendour. So too liberty has fallen, and will again, on days of opposition, of indifference and of persecution, but none the less it lives in the hearts

[3] *Un essere che serve.*

of its lovers, it lives and operates in the sphere of action, where by right it moves, and which it naturally enlarges. Liberty can settle its account clearly enough with everything that neglects it or opposes it, for whatever 'comes to pass' and comes under its thought and judgment has 'passed' into the conditions of its own activity. The functions of liberty are different in the church triumphant and the church militant, but it can never be condemned to impotence or death, or at least no man has the power to execute the sentence he pronounces.

I have now brought back my argument to its main point of moral duty; I have shown that duty alone can be the end of all our efforts and all our practical activity; I have shown that moral duty is not subservient to the traffic of the world, or to its violent deliriums, to its demands or their satisfaction and appeasement. For the world as Campanella wrote with lyric admiration, is a 'great and perfect animal' which goes its own way and finds its own means from time to time of accomplishing the various stages.

And now I can conclude my argument by pointing out that our duty likewise has its own good and its own means. And one of its first demands is that we should refute the illusion, which these vital forces suffer or create in their activity, when they claim moral worth and the right to fix our standards. No doubt, in political and social struggles, banners are hoisted, slogans are shouted, idols of love and hate are fashioned; and men inspired or maddened by these symbols are ready to fight and die. But all this is quite different from the moral ideals or from the ideal of liberty which comprises them. Factions fight to keep what they have or to gain something for themselves and their own party, where one man's loss is another's gain. But the moral ideal of liberty is a message to universal man as man; it is no incitement to the pursuit of private interests or more or less general goods, it is an educative and redeeming revelation to the heart. Even when, as sometimes happens, the aims of parties are inspired by a moral spirit, that is the moral ideal entering into them and beginning this education, converting them and raising them above themselves. This can be seen in the word 'patriot' which at one time expressed the reverent pride, the loftiest feelings, and the noblest dreams of all who could claim it. Indeed it symbolised their devotion to the cause of humanity, a meaning exactly opposite to that of the word 'nationalist', which came to be substituted for it, as was 'my nation' for 'my country', as though it were a translation, though in fact it was the expression of dominating and predatory natures.

Political ideologies, and slogans bandied against slogans, have no doubt their necessary uses; they call to arms, unite the combatants to attack and defence and intoxicate them with the hope or joy of victory; but they leave empty the heart of man in his simple and essential humanity, which only finds itself at home in union with the universal. It seems as if there were two histories, and two ways of relating history, which run closely parallel but never meet, the political and the moral. But in truth they are two aspects or 'dialectical moments' of the one history, which is the constant creation of life and the perpetual elevation and sublimation of life in its dedication to the universal. A man whose mind is so religiously disposed gladly leaves the care of political history to the politicians and soldiers and economists. He fixes his thoughts on moral history where is unrolled the drama which also goes on in himself, and where throughout the centuries he meets his fathers and brothers, who loved liberty as he does, and like him knew how to work and suffer for her.

J. D. Bernal

Belief and Action *

1. MAN IS THE MEASURE OF ALL THINGS

Both in belief and in action a Marxist is a humanist, he lives by human values achieved through human action. This humanism is not however as in the past based on a mystical feeling of man's affinity with the gods, or on the belief that the whole world has been created and maintained as a stage for man's salvation. We value man more now because we know more. Man's character and man's achievement become greater and not less when viewed objectively and scientifically. The old idea that man was the centre of a universe created for his especial benefit, though wrong as a physical statement, is right in intention; it is equivalent to the present view of human society as the one growing point of universal development. But man is no longer an example of a universal type, an image of his "creator." He is a component—a product and at the same time a producer of a complex, developing and ever more conscious society. The centre of human interest and of human action lies in that society and its development. Because an individual man is a product of society, he needs must incorporate in himself, in behaviour and belief, to the degree in which he is educated, all the traditions and history of that society. This in itself makes him of a different order of existence from any animal. Animals inherit in their bodies the cumulative results of organic evolution. In man this bodily inheritance is only a foundation, his distinctive personality is a social inheritance. "Organisms are born; man is made."

But society is not a fixed order; every man's life adds to it and changes it. Every man is a maker, a poet. "The grass groweth up; in the morning it flourishes and groweth up, in the evening it is cut down and withereth."

* From *The Freedom of Necessity* by J. D. Bernal, pp. 71–85. Copyright 1949 by Routledge & Kegan Paul Ltd. Reprinted by permission of the publishers. The essay was written, the author states, just before D-Day in 1944.

Not so man. No life passes but that something is contributed to the common inheritance. Every human life influences others. The lives of companions and children are consciously or unconsciously, directly or indirectly, changed by it. The pattern of the future society is the product of all such changes.

This makes it both wrong and stupid to treat any man as a machine or part of a machine. The respect for human individuality and human capacity finds its logical basis in the understanding of society and its transformations, given us by Marxism. Respect for the individual man can of course also be reached emotionally and is embedded in the framework of all great religions. Only too often however has the assertion of the uniqueness and sanctity of the individual been used as an excuse to degrade men and to deprive them of education, opportunity and democratic rights. To respect human individuality does not mean such pious acceptance of present conditions of human life. What any man is now is only a small fraction of what he might be if his powers could find direction and scope. Human potential is enormous; we cannot know how great it is—that can only be found out by allowing it to develop itself. The greatest crime in the world is not the denial of food and shelter to the human animal, but depriving man of his inheritance of thought and the possibility of full and constructive expression of it.

Human potential can only be realised in and through society. The balance between society and the individuals composing it is only now coming into human consciousness. Too great an insistence on individuality means an anarchy in which the material conditions necessary for the realisation of full human possibilities cannot be achieved. Too little insistence on it means a tyranny in which the individual is limited to a particular function and in which, by demeaning man, the purpose of the organisation itself is frustrated. The maintenance of the balance between these extremes is the greatest of responsibilities. It is too great to be borne by individuals; it is the responsibility of the people.

2. GOVERNMENT OF THE PEOPLE, BY THE PEOPLE, FOR THE PEOPLE

Belief in the people follows from the understanding of the importance of man in society and of the evolutions of that society. This belief is no more mystical and vague than the equivalent statement of the importance of man. Isolated man is a fiction, man carries society inside himself, therefore there can be no better criterion for understanding, value or action, than in the collective judgment of the people. Ideally, in an equalitarian, communist society, that judgment will be freely expressed. In our present class-divided societies it is more difficult to discover but it is there; it finds expression more in action than in words. The forms of accepted belief may often be traditional, may represent the choice of a dead society; but they are tacitly modified in action in closer accordance with the realities of the moment. The people may err, and err gravely and fundamentally just as the individual man may suffer from lack of judgment or delusion; the miseducation inevitable in a class society, whether or not it is deliberate, may warp judgment for a while but unlike the case of the individual man there are limits to the degree to which the whole of the people can be deceived in the interests of a few. Their experience will in the end be too different from what they have been led to expect and disillusions will lead to a new understanding. Over and over again, and never more than in these last years, the common feelings of justice, fellowship and liberty have reasserted themselves in the breakdown of oppressive systems. A selected élite may come to delude themselves for a while in their superiority to the common herd, but the repressed consciousness of their loss of community and the unfairness of their position always turns them to futility and madness. The fable of Antaeus as Stalin drew it, a giant whose strength came from the earth, is profoundly true. No man or party can separate himself or itself from the people and live. In this sense, democracy has an absolute value; but democracy must be total, covering both the economic and political fields, and also sufficiently widespread so that every member of society can take an active part in it. "Every cook must learn to rule the state."

Democracy is by no means a simple idea. It is today the most abused of words, its different meanings being flung across the conference table in the attack and defence of very different systems of government and as a cloak for interests that have little in common with it. There are real differences such as those between established democracy and democracy of transition. Our British democracy, from long practice, does enable us to secure the people's will without coercion or bloodshed, but clumsily, far too slowly and with a heavy bias on ancient privilege. In countries with a long history of tyranny and feud such democracy is unrealisable. All attempts to reproduce its forms, especially the giving of full freedom to the representatives of wealth and reaction, fatally impede the rapid and drastic decision to rebuild industry and agriculture on which the very lives of the people depend.

3. PLANNED ABUNDANCE

Belief in man and in the people expresses itself concretely in the struggle for better human and social conditions. Individual human capacity can only be realised, collective human activities can only be carried out, if the material and intellectual conditions are suitable. They are not so at present. But now we know enough of what is wrong to set about putting it right. What we have to do is to mobilise the material and human resources of the world in a way in which capitalism has never been able to do. Even in the most populous and already industrialised countries there is everywhere insufficient education, insufficient scope for abilities; above all there is the taint of the profit motive which prevents the majority from even trying to give of their best. The war has shown how this can be altered under the most unfavourable material conditions, once there is a common accepted purpose. The war will be effectively won only when the common purpose is made permanent and is turned from the defence of old civilisation to the achievement of a new and better one.

The most immediate task is the restoration of devastated Europe; the peoples are liberated, they have the will and, in great measure the ability, not only to restore what has been destroyed, but to build something much better in its place. At the moment they lack food, fuel and machinery; we must see to it that they get all these before starvation and disorganisation have seriously weakened their capacity for recovery.

Scarcely less urgent is the situation of the great populations of Asia and the tropics. Some thousand millions there are on the edge of starvation. Most of these are afflicted by preventable diseases, and lack all the mechanical resources which have been developed in the past two hundred years. They have little or no education, are deprived of political rights, and are economically exploited. As things are today, at least 90 per cent of the human race have no chance of developing their potentialities as human beings.

It used to be urged that all this was inevitable; that, on account of climate and race, the natives of Asia and Africa were inherently unadaptable to western civilisation. Now, in the light both of the Soviet Union's experiences in the last thirty years and of many other parts of the world during the war, everybody can see what pernicious nonsense this view was. The undeveloped parts of the world contain a waste of human capacity and a mass of human suffering that call out for instant remedy. And the remedy is clear and simple. It is the organisation of both agricultural and industrial production, planned so as to provide the known needs of the people from known natural resources, by the aid of and soon under the direction of the people of the countries themselves. The more advanced countries will have to provide capital goods and instruction as was done by the Russian Republics in Soviet Central Asia. Within a generation, however, the people themselves should be able to take over and make increasing and independent contributions, both material and cultural, to the world at large.

To realise the existing potential human resources of the whole world is elementary justice, but it is equally important to raise that potential by a steady improvement and rationalisation of the processes of production. Physical and biological sciences, technology and economics, must be welded together in an increasingly conscious way to provide a productive organisation yielding the maximum return with the minimum of monotonous or dangerous labour. We know from the experiences of the Soviet Union that this is a perfectly feasible aim, but to realise it under a capitalist economy, with its tendency to turn more and more to monopoly and restriction, is a difficult but not impossible task. Even the capitalist system, however, can be made or organize production rationally, with due regard to the human factor, in times of war. With the same controls it can be made to do so in peace, pending its reorganization on more rational lines.

The advent of atomic power has removed once and for all any limitation on the material resources at man's disposal. We should have, in a few years' time, means to feed and to supply the whole population of the world at the highest present level of consumption. But this cannot be achieved unless we can dispel the secrecy and suspicion that the atom bomb has brought, and unless we can, on an international scale, put an unprecedented effort into research and development.

It can be done. The single and steady purpose, the unity of the people, the willingness to go all out and put up with every danger and discomfort that marked the peoples at war must not be lost in peace. There are new and real wars to be fought; for health, for knowledge, for the realisation of the human potential—wars against disease and hunger, wars against obscurantism and reaction. These are not metaphors. Such wars can be fought effectively; not, as in the past, solely by devoted individuals, piecemeal, but by bodies of men organised and planned. They will be backed by the material resources with which we fought fascism; the laboratories, the factories, the ships, the bulldozers, the food and drugs and they will canalise in their service the same unity, enthusiasm and devotion.

4. TRANSFORMATION OF VALUES

The continuation of capitalism is conditioned by its economic and political power, but it maintains this very largely through the prevalence of false beliefs. The original ideology of capitalism—material self-seeking and a salvation, other-world religion—was in its time a liberation from the more restrictive ideology of feudal Europe. The advance of science and technology however has revealed it to be as untrue in fact as it has become antisocial in tendency. We do not know the whole truth about the universe and society—the essence of science is that we are always finding out more—but we do know what is nonsense and we should be more courageous in stating it. Much of liberal, capitalist ideology, particularly its economic, political and religious aspects, is demonstrably false. It needs to be transformed so as to bring it into line with our present knowledge of natural and social science and converted into an ideology adequate for a consciously directed human society. Not to do so would be to allow it to degenerate into a mystical, anti-rational fascist ideology.

Ideologies are not transformed so much by argument as by experience and action; however objectively false a religious belief may be, if it provides emotional satisfaction and ethical justification it cannot be destroyed unless people find for themselves something to live for more fully than they could before. Piety, ignorance, economic and political ineffectiveness go together and need to be destroyed together.

Religion in the past has, at its best, represented communal human aspirations based on all that could be known of the world and of man; at its worst, as in Imperial Rome or in the decay of capitalism in our time, it may become an organisation to maintain social tranquillity in an unjust system on the basis of emotional religious experiences and intellectually untenable beliefs. In a society where social injustice no longer rules, religion may well find again its roots in honest human feeling and incorporate the new knowledge of the natural and social sciences. The religion of submission to higher and inscrutable forces, with its implied otherworldliness and acceptance of existing evils, is to be replaced by collective pride and individual achievement in a task which is regarded as a common human effort for human ends. In this, people can retain that deep sense of community and human brotherhood and the duty and enjoyment of mutual help and betterment which is charity.

History and tradition should be powerful allies; when things changed slowly and memories were short, tradition served to preserve things as they were and as it was thought they had always been. Now we are in the midst of the most rapid and world-wide changes that humanity has ever experienced. Tradition can no longer be followed blindly; the material framework in which it operates is everywhere breaking down. Nevertheless, once we understand their nature, history and tradition can become accelerators and not brakes. We are leaving behind a history of dynasties and battles and are coming to see the whole picture of human social development from the first small scattered societies to the conscious, integrated scientific world-society of today as one continuous though dialectical process. A strong people, as the Soviet Union has been showing us, can make its past live—however different from its present—and draw strength and unity from it. We all have our history to help us, nationally in each country, culturally for western Europe or India or China, in common for the whole world. History can at the same time help us to see how changes can be brought about and help us to feel ourselves, in the making of the history of today, as a link between the people who came before us and those who will come after us. Techniques and social forms change, but a common humanity that can be felt as well as known runs through the whole of recorded or discoverable history from the obscure past to the unknown future.

The new phase of world history which we are now entering calls for new men and new virtues; much of what now stands for virtue and morality belongs to the era of capitalist individualism. We are only beginning to realise how far the social vices of capitalism had penetrated the attitudes and moralities, not only of the bourgeoisie, but of the working class itself. Capitalist class society was in itself so fundamentally immoral because it made the status and relations of men dependent on inheriting or making money instead of on their ability to serve the community, and because it actively prevented the expression of fellowship between men and men. This was corruption, however masked by legal forms created in the interests of property-owners seeking to preserve their wealth. The bourgeoisie in some countries has come to tolerate almost any perversion of justice to protect their own position, up to the full horrors of fascism. In the working class there was a double evil; some of the most able, seeking a decent material basis for life, were drawn away into the bourgeoisie; the rest were frightened into a cynical acquiescence by the fear of losing what they had and became so used to accept an unjust inferiority that they could not realise their own power. Because of the class system, the great majority were forced to turn away from things that most concerned them—the possibilities for making a good life for all—to trivial and narrow fears and pleasures.

The immorality of the system was intellectual as well as material and social. Because the system would not stand honest examination, education was warped to prevent any serious study of it. Every child's birthright is the knowledge of the structure and meaning of the society to which he will contribute his life's work. But that knowledge has been deliberately withheld from the education of the people at large and was only permitted to the selected few at the universities in a deliberately distorted form. There is still no provision in schools or universities for the teaching of professed critics of the capitalist system.

When the system itself is basically immoral, it is impossible to build any decent morality which does not attack it. A radical change in morality is in any case required by the new social relations which men are already entering into in an organised and planned society. The relative importance of different virtues is bound to be affected. Old virtues may even appear as vices and new virtues instituted. Many of the basic virtues—truthfulness and good fellowship—are of course as old as humanity and need no changing, but those based on excessive concern with individual rectitude need reorienting in the direction of social responsibility. Altogether new virtues must be added. These are implied in the recognition that a man is not simply the possessor of an immortal soul who will be judged in an after-life on the basis of his following a certain set of rules in this, but is one member of a changing community with a vast task in front of it. His life, mental as well as material, comes from the community and goes on with it. To fulfil it, it needs to be given freely in its service.

Ignorance and innocence are no longer the proofs of sanctity. A man must know and understand the aims of society and the mechanisms of society if he is to be effective in playing his part. This is no question of a blind and obedient carrying out of orders; that is fascism and the "Fuehrer princip." Each one is called upon to understand, to accept and to use his initiative in the furthering of the common aim which he has himself taken part in forming.

The change from individual to collective morality corresponds to the realisation of the relative ineffectiveness of isolated individual action under modern conditions. If in the last century a man was struck by the misery and ignorance of the natives in Central Africa, he went out there as a medical missionary; today he would realise that the health and wealth of the African people is a political and economic problem to be solved by joint action with the African people and the workers and progressives in Britain. We now realise that piecemeal changes not only fail to achieve a general improvement, but actually retard it by diverting effort and by giving a delusive impression that something is being done. Because collective action in the industrial and political field is the only effective action, it is the only virtuous action.

5. TOWARDS A LIVING CULTURE

The building of a world free from disease, ignorance and wearying toil, in which the physical necessities of life have become everyone's birthright, is a practical material aim. It is also a social and spiritual aim. Until we have it the full realisation of human mental and social possibilities cannot be achieved, and unless we are working for it all human effort in the field of art or morals is poisoned at the roots. But the fact that we have a material aim does not mean that these other aspects of life are not considered or are to be neglected in the interim. The pursuit of art or scholarship has often been urged as a justification—or at least an extenuation—of a system that, it is claimed, has made this possible. If we could only attend to the things of the spirit, the apologists for capitalism maintain, we would not find mere material things so distressing. Art and learning, like religion, are held up as things beyond and apart from the economic and social system. History shows this to be palpably false. The arts and humanities of the different epochs grow plainly out of the conditions of those times as Vico had already shown over two hundred years ago.

The forms of art—painting, literature, drama, poetry, music—are all expressions of the impact of society on individual human beings. They achieve the purpose of their makers in so far as they stir and express the feelings and aspirations of the less articulate members of that society. A great work of art may do more; drawing from social roots it may produce a combination of forms or ideas that is absolutely new, but can, once it is established, be taken up and further developed by others. It is in this sense that art is creative. A work of art belongs to its time and is produced in the language of its time, but it may contain such a strong appeal to feelings common to all societies that its message reaches beyond its own time. That is the criterion of great art. The values that the artists express are social values, the relations of men to each other, the relations of men to nature; nature itself has beauty and meaning in so far as it is perceived and worked upon by man. Even the beauty of wild nature was first appreciated only in contrast with that of town and field. The poets absorb unconsciously, but often consciously as well, the social strivings and intellectual achievements of their times and fix them so that they move the feelings as well as the minds of men. If we can help to make a live and positive society which is successfully achieving better material conditions for all, its arts and humanities will look after themselves. It may take time to find the appropriate means of expression. We have only past forms to go on, and past forms will need many modifications before they fit.

Science and scholarship can adapt more quickly. It is, after all, the work of science and education that has brought about both the knowledge of the physical needs of men and the means of satisfying them. The scientist has done this partly directly but even more indirectly by finding the multiple relations that underlie the behaviour of material systems, living and non-living, and using the knowledge of those relations to control them. But the scientist now realises that what has gone before in the history of science are only the first easy steps; steps that could be taken with simple ideas and simple apparatus by men working in isolation or in loose societies. To get to the bottom of real basic problems of physics or biology we now need team-work on a large scale, with far more scientists and full popular appreciation of the meaning and value of science. It is a stupid and wilful misunderstanding to suggest that this will mean the neglect of fundamental science. All those who have worked in applied science realise how absolutely essential it is that fundamental science should be pursued but also how much fundamental science has to gain in the new problems and the new techniques derived from applied science. Human culture is not a sickly plant which can only be kept alive by preserving the artificial conditions in which it is cultivated today, still less by a futile attempt to recreate the conditions of former times. It is a stunted plant which will only grow to its full stature when the latent abilities of all men can be realised in the new society.

Every great age in human history had its characteristic culture, a pattern of thinking and acting which was basically acceptable to the people of that time. The period out of which we are just passing was no exception. The liberal individualistic, almost atomic, philosophy started in the Renaissance and grew to full stature with the French Revolution. It is a philosophy of the "rights of man," of "liberty, equality and fraternity," of private property, free enterprise and free trade. We have known it in such a debased form, so unrelated to the pattern of the needs of the times, that only lip-service is paid to it, and honest but ignorant minds have preferred even the bestialities of fascism to its unreal and useless tenets. Liberal philosophy was not only political—it stretched over the whole field of the intellect; it was the creed of the pure scientist, the scholar, the artist and the genius, each working by himself as he thought fit, but all contributing as surely as the individual trader or the individual manufacturer to that mysterious but perfectly natural process—the greatest good for the greatest number.

That philosophy is now discredited. Whilst recognising the greatness of its achievements, we also recognise that that way of doing things is finished. To try to perpetuate it is to tie down the present to the past. The achievements of liberal philosophy have themselves been incorporated in the new dialectical materialism of Marx and Engels which consciously and often unconsciously is coming to be generally accepted as the basis of thought. It is not the isolation of men but their increasingly conscious co-operation that now needs to be stressed. Dialectical materialism is a philosophy of unity, of interdependence of parts rather than their isolation; it is a philosophy which unites thought and action, analysis and synthesis. It is pre-eminently appropriate to our times, since it is a philosophy of struggle which is thought of as the only way in which new things and processes occur. It is far more a programme of thought and action than it is a system of philosophy in the old sense. In the light of Marxism, many subjects thought to be dull or even closed take on a new significance and acquire new interest. History ceases to be a meaningless chronicle and becomes a field of interplay of economic and social forces which lights our future as well as our past. Biology becomes unified and the phenomena of life are associated on the one hand with their own evolutionary history, and on the other with the present satisfaction of men's needs. Physics, chemistry and even mathematics lose their absolute and unchangeable character and are seen as indissolubly linked with the nature and origin of the universe. Nothing is lost of the invaluable and reliable methods which the exact sciences provide, and much is added to them. Dialectical materialism provides a method of finding out where we are going rather than of verifying the exact spot when we have got there—that remains in the sphere of the natural sciences. The great value of dialectical materialism is in helping to sum up and to comprehend the whole of knowledge in such terms as it can use for successful action here and now. It gives a scale of various developmental levels of the universe which shows us the overriding importance of society and of man, who makes it and is made by it. It is here and now, in the politics and economics of human society, that the decisive events of all time and space are occurring. Man recovers his own importance in the world scheme first conceded by religion, then denied by the materialism that came with the birth of science.

With that new picture comes new responsibility. Men individually must understand and collectively must work together to realise the possibilities that live within them.

6. THE TEST OF ACTION

Belief implies action. The tests of how well we have understood the workings of the universe and of society is how competently we can chart a course of future human development and maintain a conscious control over it. That is the basic difference between our present times and all that went before. What began as an idea in the minds of Marx and Engels under the experiences of the turbulent rise of capitalism, what was tested in action in the Soviet Union by Lenin and Stalin for the past thirty years, has now become a world-wide phenomenon. Man has willy-nilly to control his material and social economy as one organised whole.

That responsibility has already been grasped. The one final attempt to reverse this process and to rob men of their heritage of knowledge and power has been crushed in the war by the united efforts of the people of the Soviet Union and those of Europe and America. The lesson has been a terrible one. The unparalleled suffering and destruction of our time is the penalty that has had to be paid for the hold that reactionary ideas have had in capitalist countries and the inability to break away from them in time. But the lesson has been learned, the war has been won, and the world is about to enter the hard but glorious period of recovery and reconstruction. This time there is no mistaking the people's purpose. Everywhere in Europe, and, most important of all, in Britain, elections have shown that the great majority are determined to control the forces which science and technology have provided and to use them for the common good and not for private profit, for peace and not for war.

That determination in itself is an enormous step forward, but it only marks the beginning of new struggles. By assuming responsibility for control, the popular forces have to meet the enormous physical and organisational problems of repairing the damage of war and bringing order out of the chaos of capitalist production. Everything that can be represented as a mistake will be used by the forces of reaction to weaken the people's faith in themselves and to cause disunion among the popular forces. This will be as true in the international as in the national field. The great alliance of the United Nations which has been achieved through the bitter needs of the war has now become even more important as a guarantee against future wars which might be far worse than that through which we have passed. To maintain that alliance and to guard it against its open enemies and the more subtle disseminators of mutual suspicion will require constant vigilance and continued efforts to reach ever closer understanding. Lack of confidence, confusion, suspicion—all derive from ignorance. The fuller and more comprehensive our knowledge of social forces, the more easily can these be exposed and counteracted. Knowledge is not academic; we have behind us the experience of war organisation in the forces and factories, an experience which has brought us in Britain much closer to the longer and even more dearly won experiences of the Soviet Union. To the degree to which we can see things in the same light can we go foward together in fellowship and hope.

Jean-Paul Sartre

On Freedom

ON FREEDOM AND RESPONSIBILITY*

The essential consequence of our earlier remarks is that man being condemned to be free carries the weight of the whole world on his shoulders; he is responsible for the world and for himself as a way of being. We are taking the word "responsibility" in its ordinary sense as "consciousness (of) being the incontestable author of an event or of an object." In this sense the responsibility of the for-itself is overwhelming since he [1] is the one by whom it happens that *there is* a world; since he is also the one who makes himself be, then whatever may be the situation in which he finds himself, the for-itself must wholly assume this situation with its peculiar coefficient of adversity, even though it be insupportable. He must assume the situation with the proud consciousness of being the author of it, for the very worst disadvantages or the worst threats which can endanger my person have meaning only in and through my project; and it is on the ground of the engagement which I am that they appear. It is therefore senseless to think of complaining since nothing foreign has decided what we feel, what we live, or what we are.

Furthermore this absolute responsibility is not resignation; it is simply the logical requirement of the consequences of our freedom. What happens to me happens through me, and I can neither affect myself with it nor revolt against it nor resign myself to it. Moreover everything which happens to me is mine. By this we must understand first of all that I am always equal to what happens to me *qua* man, for what happens to a man through other men and through himself can be only human. The most terrible situations of war, the worst tortures do not create a nonhuman state of things; there is no nonhuman situation. It is only through fear, flight,

* From *Being and Nothingness* by Jean-Paul Sartre, translated by Hazel E. Barnes, pp. 553–556. Copyright 1956 by the Philosophical Library, Inc., New York. Reprinted by permission of the publishers.

[1] I am shifting to the personal pronoun here since Sartre is describing the for-itself in concrete personal terms rather than as a metaphysical entity. Strictly speaking, of course, this is his position throughout, and the French *"il"* is indifferently "he" or "it." Tr.

and recourse to magical types of conduct that I shall decide on the non-human, but this decision is human, and I shall carry the entire responsibility for it. But in addition the situation is mine because it is the image of my free choice of myself, and everything which it presents to me is *mine* in that this represents me and symbolizes me. Is it not I who decides the coefficient of adversity in things and even their unpredictability by deciding myself?

Thus there are no *accidents* in a life; a community event which suddenly bursts forth and involves me in it does not come from the outside. If I am mobilized in a war, this war is *my* war; it is in my image and I deserve it. I deserve it first because I could always get out of it by suicide or by desertion; these ultimate possibles are those which must always be present for us when there is a question of envisaging a situation. For lack of getting out of it, I have *chosen* it. This can be due to inertia, to cowardice in the face of public opinion, or because I prefer certain other values to the value of the refusal to join in the war (the good opinion of my relatives, the honor of my family, etc). Anyway you look at it, it is a matter of a choice. This choice will be repeated later on again and again without a break until the end of the war. Therefore we must agree with the statement by Jules Romains, "In war there are no innocent victims." [2] If therefore I have preferred war to death or to dishonor, everything takes place as if I bore the entire responsibility for this war. Of course others have declared it, and one might be tempted perhaps to consider me as a simple accomplice. But this notion of complicity has only a juridical sense, and it does not hold here. For it depended on me that for me and by me this war should not exist, and I have decided that it does exist. There was no compulsion here, for the compulsion could have got no hold on a freedom. I did not have any excuse; for as we have said repeatedly, the peculiar character of human-reality is that it is without excuse. Therefore it remains for me only to lay claim to this war.

But in addition the war is mine because by the sole fact that it arises in a situation which I cause to be and that I can discover it there only by engaging myself for or against it, I can no longer distinguish at present the choice which I make of myself from the choice which I make of the war. To live this war is to choose myself through it and to choose it through my choice of myself. There can be no question of considering it as "four years of vacation" or as a "reprieve," as a "recess," the essential part of my responsibilities being elsewhere in my married, family, or

[2] Jules Romains: *Les hommes de bonne volonté, "Prélude à Verdun."*

professional life. In this war which I have chosen I choose myself from day to day, and I make it mine by making myself. If it is going to be four empty years, then it is I who bear the responsibility for this.

Finally, as we pointed out earlier, each person is an absolute choice of self from the standpoint of a world of knowledges and of techniques which this choice both assumes and illumines; each person is an absolute upsurge at an absolute date and is perfectly unthinkable at another date. It is therefore a waste of time to ask what I should have been if this war had not broken out, for I have chosen myself as one of the possible meanings of the epoch which imperceptibly led to war. I am not distinct from this same epoch; I could not be transported to another epoch without contradiction. Thus *I am* this war which restricts and limits and makes comprehensible the period which preceded it. In this sense we may define more precisely the responsibility of the for-itself if to the earlier quoted statement, "There are no innocent victims," we add the words, "We have the war we deserve." Thus, totally free, undistinguishable from the period for which I have chosen to be the meaning, as profoundly responsible for the war as if I had myself declared it, unable to live without integrating it in my situation, engaging myself in it wholly and stamping it with my seal, I must be without remorse or regrets as I am without excuse; for from the instant of my upsurge into being, I carry the weight of the world by myself alone without anything or any person being able to lighten it.

Yet this responsibility is of a very particular type. Someone will say, "I did not ask to be born." This is a naïve way of throwing greater emphasis on our facticity. I am responsible for everything, in fact, except for my very responsibility, for I am not the foundation of my being. Therefore everything takes place as if I were compelled to be responsible. I am *abandoned* in the world, not in the sense that I might remain abandoned and passive in a hostile universe like a board floating on the water, but rather in the sense that I find myself suddenly alone and without help, engaged in a world for which I bear the whole responsibility without being able, whatever I do, to tear myself away from this responsibility for an instant. For I am responsible for my very desire of fleeing responsibilities. To make myself passive in the world, to refuse to act upon things and upon Others is still to choose myself, and suicide is one mode among others of being-in-the-world. Yet I find an absolute responsibility for the fact that my facticity (here the fact of my birth) is directly inapprehensible and even inconceivable, for this fact of my birth never appears as a brute fact but always across a projective reconstruction of my for-itself. I am ashamed of being born or I am astonished at it or I rejoice over it, or in attempting to get rid of my life I affirm that I live and I assume this life as bad. Thus in a certain sense I *choose* being born. This choice itself is integrally affected with facticity since I am not able not to choose, but this facticity in turn will appear only insofar as I surpass it toward my ends. Thus facticity is everywhere but inapprehensible; I never encounter anything except my responsibility. That is why I cannot ask, "Why was I born?" or curse the day of my birth or declare that I did not ask to be born, for these various attitudes toward my birth—i.e., toward the fact that I realize a presence in the world—are absolutely nothing else but ways of assuming this birth in full responsibility and of making it *mine.* Here again I encounter only myself and my projects so that finally my abandonment—i.e., my facticity—consists simply in the fact that I am condemned to be wholly responsible for myself. I am the being which *is* in such a way that in its being its being is in question. And this "is" of my being is as present and inapprehensible.

Under these conditions since every event in the world can be revealed to me only as an *opportunity* (an opportunity made use of, lacked, neglected, etc., or better yet since everything which happens to us can be considered as a *chance,* i.e., can appear to us only as a way of realizing this being which is in question in our being) and since others as transcendences-transcended are themselves only *opportunities* and *chances,* the responsibility of the for-itself extends to the entire world as a peopled-world. It is precisely thus that the for-itself apprehends itself in anguish; that is, as a being which is neither the foundation of its own being nor of the Other's being nor of the in-itselfs which form the world, but a being which is compelled to decide the meaning of being—within it and everywhere outside of it. The one who realizes in anguish his condition as *being* thrown into a responsibility which extends to his very abandonment has no longer either remorse or regret or excuse; he is no longer anything but a freedom which perfectly reveals itself and whose being resides in this very revelation. But as we pointed out at the beginning of this work, most of the time we flee anguish in bad faith.

THE REPUBLIC OF SILENCE *

We were never more free than during the German occupation. We had lost all our rights, beginning with the right to talk. Every day we

* From "The Republic of Silence" by Jean-Paul Sartre. In *The Republic of Silence,* edited by A. J. Liebling, translated by Ramon Guthrie, pp. 498–500. Reprinted by permission of Librairie Gallimard,

were insulted to our faces and had to take it in silence. Under one pretext or another, as workers, Jews, or political prisoners, we were deported EN MASSE. Everywhere, on billboards, in the newspapers, on the screen, we encountered the revolting and insipid picture of ourselves that our oppressors wanted us to accept. And, because of all this, we were free. Because the Nazi venom seeped even into our thoughts, every accurate thought was a conquest. Because an all-powerful police tried to force us to hold our tongues, every word took on the value of a declaration of principles. Because we were hunted down, every one of our gestures had the weight of a solemn commitment. The circumstances, atrocious as they often were, finally made it possible for us to live, without pretense or false shame, the hectic and impossible existence that is known as the lot of man. Exile, captivity, and especially death (which we usually shrink from facing at all in happier times) became for us the habitual objects of our concern. We learned that they were neither inevitable accidents, nor even constant and exterior dangers, but that they must be considered as our lot itself, our destiny, the profound source of our reality as men. At every instant we lived up to the full sense of this commonplace little phrase: "Man is mortal!" And the choice that each of us made of his life and of his being was an authentic choice because it was made face to face with death, because it could always have been expressed in these terms: "Rather death than. . . ." And here I am not speaking of the élite among us who were real Resistants, but of all Frenchmen who, at every hour of the night and day throughout four years, answered NO. But the very cruelty of the enemy drove us to the extremities of this condition by forcing us to ask ourselves questions that one never considers in time of peace. All those among us—and what Frenchman was not at one time or another in this situation—who knew any details concerning the Resistance asked themselves anxiously, "If they torture me, shall I be able to keep silent?" Thus the basic question of liberty itself was posed, and we were brought to the verge of the deepest knowledge that man can have of himself. For the secret of a man is not his Oedipus complex or his inferiority complex: it is the limit of his own liberty, his capacity for resisting torture and death.

To those who were engaged in underground activities, the conditions of their struggle afforded a new kind of experience. They did not fight openly like soldiers. In all circumstances they were alone. They were hunted down in solitude, arrested in solitude. It was completely forlorn and unbefriended that they held out against torture, alone and naked in the presence of torturers, clean-shaven, well-fed, and well-clothed, who laughed at their cringing flesh, and to whom an untroubled conscience and a boundless sense of social strength gave every appearance of being in the right. Alone. Without a friendly hand or a word of encouragement. Yet, in the depth of their solitude, it was the others that they were protecting, all the others, all their comrades in the Resistance. Total responsibility in total solitude—is this not the very definition of our liberty? This being stripped of all, this solitude, this tremendous danger, were the same for all. For the leaders and for their men, for those who conveyed messages without knowing what their content was, as for those who directed the entire Resistance, the punishment was the same—imprisonment, deportation, death. There is no army in the world where there is such equality of risk for the private and for the commander-in-chief. And this is why the Resistance was a true democracy: for the soldier as for the commander, the same danger, the same forsakenness, the same total responsibility, the same absolute liberty within discipline. Thus, in darkness and in blood, a Republic was established, the strongest of Republics. Each of its citizens knew that he owed himself to all and that he could count only on himself alone. Each of them, in complete isolation, fulfilled his responsibility and his role in history. Each of them, standing against the oppressors, undertook to be himself, freely and irrevocably. And by choosing for himself in liberty, he chose the liberty of all. This Republic without institutions, without an army, without police, was something that at each instant every Frenchman had to win and to affirm against Nazism. No one failed in this duty, and now we are on the threshold of another Republic. May this Republic about to be set up in broad daylight preserve the austere virtues of that other Republic of Silence and of Night.

Biographical Notes

Alfred Jules AYER (1910–), University of London. Educated Christ Church, Oxford. His *Language, Truth and Logic* (1936) made him a central spokesman in the spread of logical positivism, especially for its controversial attack on traditional metaphysical problems. His later work has been chiefly in epistemological problems. Among his other writings are: *The Foundations of Empirical Knowledge, The Problem of Knowledge.*

Henri BERGSON (1859–1941). His philosophy, focussing on evolutionary process and interpreting it in terms of a fundamental life force, dominated French philosophy for a considerable part of the twentieth century, and had wide international influence. Among his books are: *Creative Evolution, Time and Free Will, Matter and Memory, Introduction to Metaphysics, The Two Sources of Morality and Religion.*

John Desmond BERNAL (1901–), Professor of Physics, Birkbeck College, London. A versatile scientist with a Marxian philosophical approach, whose interests have extended into the field of the social relations and philosophical bases of science. Among his works are: *The Social Function of Science, Science in History, The Freedom of Necessity.*

Bernard BOSANQUET (1848–1923). One of the most eminent of the British Hegelian idealist school, he exercised great influence in his writing and teaching at Oxford. Among his many books are: *Logic or the Morphology of Thought, The Philosophical Theory of the State, The Principle of Individuality and Value, The Value and Destiny of the Individual, Implication and Linear Inference.*

Richard Bevan BRAITHWAITE (1900–), Cambridge University. Educated King's College, Cambridge. Has contributed chiefly to problems in the theory of science. Among his writings are: *Moral Principles and Inductive Policies, Scientific Explanation.*

Charlie Dunbar BROAD (1887–), Professor Emeritus, Cambridge University. Educated Trinity College, Cambridge. His work has been influential in British and American philosophy for its precise analysis, chiefly in scientific and epistemological theory. Among his books are: *Scientific Thought, The Mind and its Place in Nature, Five Types of Ethical Theory.*

Martin BUBER (1878–), Professor Emeritus, The Hebrew University, Jerusalem. Educated in Austria and Germany, Buber had achieved considerable influence before he left Germany. He is the outstanding representative of the existentialist trend in Jewish religious thought, which he combines with the Hasidic tradition. He has had wide influence in religious philosophy generally, and carried his interpretations into educational and psychological theory as well as social philosophy. Among his works are: *I and Thou, Between Man and Man, Eclipse of God, Images of Good and Evil.*

Nikolai Ivanovich BUKHARIN (1888–1938). A leading Marxian philosopher who played an active part in the Russian Revolution. His major philosophical concern was the philosophy of history and culture. Among his works are: *The ABC of Communism, Culture in Two Worlds, The Economic Theory of the Leisure Class, Historical Materialism.*

Rudolf CARNAP (1891–), University of California at Los Angeles. Ph.D. Jena. A leading member of the Vienna Circle, he has advocated a logical empiricism in general, and made a great many contributions to the formal analysis of logical ideas. Taught at the University of Vienna, German University of Prague, and University of Chicago. Co-editor of the International Encyclopedia of Unified Science. Among his many books are: *Der logische Aufbau der Welt, Logical Syntax of Language, Meaning and Necessity, Logical Foundations of Probability.*

Benedetto CROCE (1886–1952). The leading twentieth-century Italian idealist philosopher, he was also a Senator and Minister of Education. He wrote extensively on aesthetic and historical theory as well as in metaphysics and ethics. Among his works are: *Aesthetic, Philosophy of the Practical, History as the Story of Liberty.*

John DEWEY (1859–1952). Associated chiefly with the University of Chicago and then with Columbia University, Dewey had wide influence, both national and international, in philosophical thought and in educational theory. His instrumental pragmatism stressed both man's place as part of nature and the active role of thought in transforming human life and solving problems. Among his many books are: *Experience and Nature, Democracy and Education, The Quest for Certainty, Reconstruction in Philosophy, Logic: The Theory of Inquiry, Art as Experience, Freedom and Culture.*

Karl DUNCKER (1903–1940). A psychologist employing a Gestalt approach, he also applied his perspective to the analysis of problems of value theory, especially in two influential papers on "Ethical Relativity" (*Mind,* 1939), and "On Pleasure, Emotion and Striving" (*Philosophy and Phenomenological Research,* 1941).

Alfred Cyril EWING (1899–   ), Cambridge University. Educated University College, Oxford. Has written widely on metaphysical and moral problems from an idealist perspective. Among his books are: *Idealism, The Definition of Good, The Fundamental Questions of Philosophy.*

Herbert FEIGL (1902–   ), University of Minnesota. Ph.D. University of Vienna. Early a member of the positivist Vienna Circle, he has been a spokesman for logical empiricism, especially in dealing with problems of the philosophy of science. Has written widely for philosophical journals and symposium volumes. He is Director of the Minnesota Center for the Philosophy of Science and an editor of *Minnesota Studies in the Philosophy of Science.*

Sigmund FREUD (1874–1939). His basic development of psychoanalytic theory had also widespread philosophical ramifications. A general statement of his theory is to be found in his *New Introductory Lectures on Psychoanalysis.* The discovery of unconscious processes and defence mechanisms raised the question of the psychological functions of different forms of thought. His general view of human life and prospects is to be found in such works as *Civilization and its Discontents,* and *The Future of An Illusion.*

Mohandas Karamchand GANDHI (1869–1948). Leading modern exponent of the philosophy of non-violence, he headed the struggle for Indian independence, to which his philosophy gave a characteristic direction. His own account of his development is to be found in *The Story of My Experiments with Truth, An Autobiography.*

Étienne Henry GILSON (1884–   ), Director of the Pontifical Institute of Mediaeval Studies at Toronto. As a teacher at the Sorbonne and elsewhere and in his many scholarly studies of mediaeval philosophy, Gilson has had wide recognition as one of the leading contemporary Catholic philosophers. Among his works are: *Spirit of Mediaeval Philosophy, Le Thomisme, History of Christian Philosophy in the Middle Ages, The Unity of Philosophical Experience.*

Richard Mervyn HARE (1919–   ), Oxford University. Has been concerned especially with the logical structure of moral discourse. His chief work is *The Language of Morals.*

Nicolai HARTMANN (1882–1950). Hartmann, who taught at Marburg and at Berlin, came to hold to an ontological realism as a basis for epistemology. In ethics he applied the phenomenological approach, influenced by the work of Husserl and Scheler. This is best seen in his major three-volume work, *Ethics.*

Martin HEIDEGGER (1889–   ). Taught at Freiburg, Germany. A student of Husserl's, he became the central figure in one wing of contemporary existentialism. His chief work is *Being and Time;* a later essay continuing the development of his thought is *What is Metaphysics?*

Carl Gustav HEMPEL (1905–), Princeton University. Ph.D. University of Berlin. Has written extensively in many philosophical journals on problems of logic and scientific method from the point of view of logical empiricism. His writings also include *Fundamentals of Concept Formation in Empirical Science.*

Edmund HUSSERL (1859–1938). A leading figure in twentieth century German philosophy, he is the recognized founder of phenomenology as a mode of analysis. Among his writings are: *Logische Untersuchungen, Ideas, Experience and Judgment.*

William JAMES (1842–1910). One of the most distinguished American philosophers, he taught at Harvard, developed experimental psychology, and was one of the fathers of pragmatism as a philosophical outlook. Among his philosophical books are: *Pragmatism, Varieties of Religious Experience, The Will to Believe, Essays in Radical Empiricism, A Pluralistic Universe.*

Harold Henry JOACHIM (1868–1938). One of the most influential Oxford philosophers of the first third of the twentieth century. He carried the idealist tradition especially into the fields of logic and theory of knowledge. Among his works are: *Descartes' Rules for the Direction of the Mind, The Nature of Truth, Logical Studies, A Study of the Ethics of Spinoza.*

Clarence Irving LEWIS (1883–), Professor Emeritus, Harvard University. A.B., Ph.D., Harvard. Has made major contributions to the development of logic, and of analysis in epistemology and value theory. His books include: *Survey of Symbolic Logic, Symbolic Logic* (with C.H. Langford), *Mind and the World-Order, An Analysis of Knowledge and Valuation.*

Arthur Oncken LOVEJOY (1873–), Professor Emeritus, Johns Hopkins University. As one of the Critical Realists, he became a leading spokesman for an epistemological dualism; he also played a primary role in developing the history of ideas as a systematic study. Among his major works are: *The Revolt Against Dualism, The Great Chain of Being.*

Cecil Alec MACE (1894–), University of London. Educated Queen's College, Cambridge. Has written on psychological as well as philosophical topics. Among his writings are: *The Psychology of Study, The Principles of Logic.*

Karl MANNHEIM (1893–1947). Taught sociology at Heidelberg, Vienna, and London. His major contributions were in the sociology of knowledge. Among his works are: *Ideology and Utopia, Man and Society, Essays on the Sociology of Knowledge, Essays on the Sociology of Culture.*

Jacques MARITAIN (1882–). A leading exponent of neo-Thomism, Maritain has taught at Paris, Princeton and elsewhere. His writings, which span the fields of religion, metaphysics, ethics, aesthetics, and social and political philosophy, include: *Bergsonian Philosophy and Thomism, The Person and the Common Good, Scholasticism and Politics, The Dream of Descartes, Art and Poetry, Christian Philosophy, Degrees of Knowledge.*

George Edward MOORE (1873–1958), was associated with Cambridge University. A defender of realism and common sense, Moore practised a method of analysis which has grown to central proportions in British philosophy. He was for many years editor of *Mind.* Among his writings are: *Principia Ethica, Ethics, Philosophical Studies, Some Main Problems of Philosophy.*

Charles William MORRIS (1901–), University of Chicago. B.S. Northwestern University; Ph.D. University of Chicago. Co-editor, *International Encyclopedia of Unified Science.* Has worked especially at the application of a scientific empiricism to the theory of mind, signs, and value. Among his books are: *Six Theories of Mind; Signs, Language and Behavior; Varieties of Human Value.*

Ernest NAGEL (1901–), Columbia University. B.S. City College of New York; Ph.D. Columbia. Has dealt especially with the philosophy of science and the impact of a scientific perspective in a philosophical naturalism. His writings include: *Introduction to Logic and Scientific Method* (with M.R. Cohen), *Principles of the Theory of Probability, Sovereign Reason, Logic Without Metaphysics.*

Jawaharlal NEHRU (1899–). An eminent follower of Gandhi in the struggle for India's independence, he became its first Prime Minister. His autobiography, *Toward Freedom,* expresses his philosophical outlook.

Reinhold NIEBUHR (1892–), Union Theological Seminary. B.D. Yale. Niebuhr, who has dealt extensively with theological, general philosophical and ethical and social questions, is perhaps the leading American representative of Protestant Neo-orthodoxy. Among his many books are: *The Nature and Destiny of Man, Moral Man and Immoral Society, An Interpretation of Christian Ethics, The Self and the Dramas of History.*

Charles Sanders PEIRCE (1839–1914). Peirce has been increasingly recognized in the twentieth century as one of the most penetrating thinkers in the development of philosophy in America. He made foundation contributions in mathematical logic and the general theory of signs. His article "How to Make Our Ideas Clear" in the *Popular Science Monthly* (1878) is the acknowledged beginning of pragmatism as a formulated philosophical outlook. Although he lectured for only short periods (at Harvard and Johns Hopkins), he wrote a great deal. Much of this material is published in the several volumes of the *Collected Papers of Charles Sanders Peirce,* edited by Charles Hartshorne and Paul Weiss.

Ralph Barton PERRY (1876–1957). Perry, who taught at Harvard for many years, was one of the Neo-Realists in epistemological theory. His major theoretical contributions were in the philosophy of value, his *General Theory of Value* being one of the classics in the field. In addition, he wrote considerably and continuously on the application of ethical perspectives to political and social questions, concerning himself with particular problems of the day. Among his other books are: *The Moral Economy, The Present Conflict of Ideals, The Thought and Character of William James, Realms of Value.*

Henry Habberley PRICE (1899–), Oxford University. Educated New College, Oxford. Has dealt especially with problems in the theory of perception and thought. Among writings are: *Perception, Truth and Corrigibility; Thinking and Experience.*

Willard Van Orman QUINE (1908–), Harvard University. A.B. Oberlin; Ph.D. Harvard. Has made both technical contributions to symbolic logic, and concerned himself with the impact of logical analysis on basic philosophical ideas. His writings include: *Mathematical Logic, Methods of Logic, From a Logical Point of View.*

Sarvepalli RADHAKRISHNAN (1888–). An internationally eminent Indian philosopher who has attempted to synthesize eastern and western thought in an idealistic perspective, he has also been an outstanding figure in the political life of India. Formerly taught at Oxford; since 1952 has been vice-president of India. Among his works are: *Indian Philosophy, East and West in Religion; Education, Politics and War.*

Philip Blair RICE (1904–1956). Rice, who was educated at Indiana University and at Oxford, and taught at Kenyon College, was the author of many essays dealing especially with questions of value theory and aesthetic theory. He was an editor of the *Kenyon Review.* His *On the Knowledge of Good and Evil* attempted a synthesis in a naturalistic vein of conflicting contemporary interpretations of value.

Josiah ROYCE (1855–1916). Royce, who taught at Harvard, was the most celebrated American exponent of philosophical idealism, producing a rich synthesis of its pluralistic and monistic forms. Among his numerous books are: *The World and the Individual, The Philosophy of Loyalty, The Problem of Christianity.*

Bertrand RUSSELL (1872–). Russell's contributions play a central role in determining the trend of much of contemporary philosophy. His *Principia Mathematica* (with Alfred North Whitehead) inaugurated an era of intensified logical analysis. His varied work in logic, philosophy of science, ethics, politics, history, education, has been characterized by the continuous attempt to apply scientific findings to philosophical problems. Among his very numerous books are: *Principles of Mathematics, The Problems of Philosophy, Mysticism and Logic, Our Knowledge of the External World, The Analysis of Matter, The Analysis of Mind, A History of Western Philosophy, Human Knowledge, Human Society in Ethics and Politics, Education and the Good Life.*

Gilbert RYLE (1900–), Oxford University. Educated Queen's College, Oxford. One of the leading figures among contemporary British philosophers who emphasize the role of analysis of ordinary language as a philosophical aim. Editor of *Mind.* Among his writings are: *The Concept of Mind, Dilemmas.*

George SANTAYANA (1863–1952). Santayana was born in Spain, taught at Harvard as a colleague of James and Royce, and spent the latter part of his life in Italy. His earlier five-volume *Life of Reason,* which sought to reinterpret the life of the spirit on the basis of a materialist metaphysics, has become a classic. He was especially influential in aesthetic theory and in his attempt to give a naturalistic analysis of religion. Among his later books are: *Scepticism and Animal Faith,* and the three volume *Realms of Being.*

Jean-Paul SARTRE (1905–). Sartre is perhaps the most widely known of contemporary existentialists. He represents the atheist wing, stressing man's aloneness and the central unavoidable role of free choice. His conceptions are expressed in literary and dramatic form as well as in psychological and philosophical writings. Among his works are: *Being and Nothingness, Existentialism is a Humanism.*

Max SCHELER (1874–1928). Scheler's work has been influential both in German philosophy and elsewhere in the development of the phenomenological approach, especially in relation to values. His interests carried him also into religious and sociological thought. Among his works are: *The Formalistic Principle in Ethics and the Non-Formal Ethic of Value, The Nature of Sympathy.*

Moritz SCHLICK (1882–1936). Taught at the University of Vienna, and was the founder and one of the most influential members of the Vienna Circle in the development of positivist theory. Among his writings are: *General Theory of Knowledge, Space and Time in Modern Physics, Problems of Ethics, Philosophy of Nature.*

Oswald SPENGLER (1880–1936). German philosopher of history, best known for his *Decline of the West,* which offered a cyclical theory of culture history. Among his other works is *The Hour of Decision.*

Eduard SPRANGER (1882–). Taught at the University of Berlin. He was especially concerned with the basis of the social sciences and the philosophy of history. His best-known work is his *Types of Men.*

Charles Leslie STEVENSON (1908–), University of Michigan. A.B. Yale; B.A. Cambridge; Ph.D., Harvard. Developed the emotive theory into a systematic analysis of ethical language, in his major work *Ethics and Language.*

Peter Frederick STRAWSON (1919–), Oxford University. Has been concerned especially with logical theory. Among his works are: *Introduction to Logical Theory.*

Paul Johannes TILLICH (1896–), Harvard University. Ph.D. Breslau. He has also taught at Frankfort, and at Union Theological Seminary. Tillich, who fuses an existentialist and historical approach, has been very influential in Protestant religious thought. Among his many books are: *The Protestant Era, An Interpretation of History, Systematic Theology, The Courage to Be.*

Miguel de UNAMUNO y Jugo (1864–1936). One of the leading Spanish philosophers of the contemporary world, Unamuno expressed his voluntaristic outlook in literary as well as philosophical form. His elevation of faith over reason is found in his major philosophical work, *The Tragic Sense of Life.*

Friedrich WAISMANN (1896–), Oxford University. Was associated with Schlick in the Vienna Circle, and has worked especially in logic and the philosophy of mathematics. Among his writings is *Introduction to Mathematical Thought.*

Alfred North WHITEHEAD (1861–1947). Was associated with Cambridge University and later with Harvard. After major contributions in mathematical logic, including *Principia Mathematica* (with Bertrand Russell), he went on to work in the philosophy of science and to attempt one of the major philosophical syntheses in the contemporary scene. Among his many books are: *The Principles of Natural Knowledge, The Concept of Nature, Science and the Modern World, Process and Reality, Modes of Thought, Adventures of Ideas.*

Ledger WOOD (1901–), Princeton University. A.B. California; Ph.D. Cornell. Has worked especially in epistemology and the history of modern philosophy. Among his writings are: *The Analysis of Knowledge, A History of Philosophy* (co-author).

Frederick James Eugene WOODBRIDGE (1867–1940). Associated primarily with Columbia University, Woodbridge exercised a profound influence on the contemporary naturalistic school. He was a founder of the *Journal of Philosophy.* Among his works are: *The Realm of Mind, Nature and Mind, The Purpose of History.*